WIPO—中国（上海）知识产权司法保护系列丛书
WIPO—Series on Judicial Protection of Intellectual Property in China (Shanghai)

知识产权案例精选

Selected Intellectual Property Cases
（2015—2016）

上海市高级人民法院知识产权审判庭
同济大学上海国际知识产权学院　编

张　斌　单晓光　主编

Co-edited by Intellectual Property Division of Shanghai High People's Court &
Shanghai International College of Intellectual Property of Tongji University

Chief Editors　Zhang Bin & Shan Xiaoguang

知识产权出版社
全国百佳图书出版单位
—北京—

图书在版编目（CIP）数据

知识产权案例精选.2015-2016／张斌，单晓光主编.—北京：知识产权出版社，2020.3

ISBN 978-7-5130-6774-4

Ⅰ.①知… Ⅱ.①张… ②单… Ⅲ.①知识产权法—案例—汇编—中国 Ⅳ.①D923.405

中国版本图书馆 CIP 数据核字（2020）第 022935 号

责任编辑：彭小华　　　　　　　　　责任校对：王　岩
封面设计：SUN 工作室　韩建文　　　责任印制：刘译文

知识产权案例精选（2015—2016）

上海市高级人民法院知识产权审判庭
同济大学上海国际知识产权学院　编
张　斌　单晓光　主编

出版发行：知识产权出版社 有限责任公司　　网　　址：http：//www.ipph.cn
社　　址：北京市海淀区气象路 50 号院　　　邮　　编：100081
责编电话：010-82000860 转 8115　　　　　　责编邮箱：huapxh@ sina. com
发行电话：010-82000860 转 8101/8102　　　发行传真：010-82000893/82005070/82000270
印　　刷：北京嘉恒彩色印刷有限责任公司　经　　销：各大网上书店、新华书店及相关专业书店
开　　本：720mm×1000mm　1/16　　　　　印　　张：38
版　　次：2020 年 3 月第 1 版　　　　　　　印　　次：2020 年 3 月第 1 次印刷
字　　数：920 千字　　　　　　　　　　　　定　　价：150.00 元
ISBN 978-7-5130-6774-4

序

当前，新一轮科技革命和产业变革正如火如荼展开，知识产权已成为国家发展的战略性资源和国际竞争力的核心内容，是建设创新型国家的重要支撑，也是掌握国家发展主动权的关键要素。2018年4月10日，习近平主席在博鳌亚洲论坛发表主旨演讲，向世界宣布了中国将采取扩大开放的四项重大举措，其中就提出了要加强知识产权保护的明确要求。在中国经济转型升级、改革开放日新月异、国际形势复杂多变的关键时刻，中央高瞻远瞩，准确把握国际、国内发展两个大局，把知识产权保护工作提高到了前所未有的重要位置。

司法保护是知识产权保护中最有效、最权威的手段。2018年2月，中央办公厅、国务院办公厅印发了专门面向知识产权审判领域的纲领性文件《关于加强知识产权审判领域改革创新若干问题的意见》，明确指出人民法院知识产权审判工作，事关创新驱动发展战略实施，事关经济社会文化发展繁荣，事关国内国际两个大局，对于建设知识产权强国和世界科技强国具有重要意义；同时对完善知识产权诉讼制度、加强审判队伍建设、提高审判质效、加大保护力度等做出了全面部署，标志着人民法院知识产权审判体系和审判能力现代化建设正处于难得的历史机遇时期。面对历史机遇，人民法院必须勇于肩负起应有的光荣使命与职责，坚持司法为民、公正司法，坚持深化改革，充分发挥知识产权司法保护主导作用，确保知识产权法律制度全面、有效实施，营造更优的科技创新法治环境和营商法治环境，为知识产权强国和世界科技强国建设提供有力的司法保障。

近年来，上海法院始终注重提升审判工作水平，在知识产权司法保护领域也开展了一系列卓有成效的改革和探索，精心审理了一批在全国甚至国际上具有一定影响力的知识产权案件，并从中确立了一些得到公认和肯定的审判规则。同时，上海法院始终十分重视各类案例的编撰工作，尤其在知识产权审判领域，建立了案例编选和发布机制，如每年编发上海法院知识产权司法保护十大案件，定期出版知识产权精选案例集等，以期通过精品、经典案例的发布，力求在指导知识产权类案司法实践的基础上，发挥对知识产权保护、运用以及激励科技创新的规范、示范、引导功能，对法制普及和宣传有所助益，对化解知识产权矛盾纠纷有所示范。

本书汇编的36件案例是从2015年至2016年上海法院审结的近2万件知识产权案件中精选所得，案件类型覆盖著作权、商标、专利、反不正当竞争等民事案件，以及知识产权刑事、行政案件和涉及知识产权诉讼程序的案件，集中展现了上海法院知识产权审判的专业化水平。例如，上海帕弗洛文化用品有限公司诉上海艺想文化用品有限公司、毕加索国际企业股份有限公司商标使用许可合同纠纷案，涉及商标独占使用重复许可时的合同效力与使用权归属问题，入选"2015年中国法院知识产权司法保护十大案件"；维多利亚的秘密商店品牌管理公司诉上海麦司投资管理有限公司侵害商标权及不正当竞争纠纷案，涉及商品商标指示性使用的认定问题，入选"2015年中国法院知识产权司法保护50件典型案例"；上海晨光文具股份有限公司与得力集团有限公司等侵害外观设计专利权纠纷案，涉及外观设计的客观比对与判断方法，入选"2016年中国法院知识产权司法保护十大案件"；深圳聚网视科技有限公司与北京爱奇艺科技有限公司其他不正当竞争纠纷一案，系全国首例视频聚合不正当竞争案，涉及提供他人视频内容时绕开片前广告是否构成不正当竞争的问题，入选"2016年中国法院知识产权司法保护50件典型案例"，上述四件案例均入选了《最高人民法院公报》案例。再如，上海牟乾广告有限公司诉上海市静安区市场监督管理局、上海商派网络科技有限公司、酷美（上海）信息技术有限公司行政处罚上诉案，系上海市高级人民法院受理的首例知识产权行政案件；上海耀宇文化传媒有限公司与广州斗鱼网络科技有限公司著作权侵权及不正当竞争纠纷案，涉及电竞游戏赛事网络直播行为的不正当竞争认定，入选"2016年中国法院知识产权司法保护50件典型案例"及"2016年度人民法院十大民事行政案件"；勃贝雷有限公司诉陈凯、鲁秋敏侵害商标权纠纷案，涉及权利人未报案的刑事程序是否产生民事诉讼时效中断效力的问题，入选"2015年最高人民法院关于知识产权法院工作情况发布会公布的典型案例"；开德阜国际贸易（上海）有限公司与阔盛管道系统（上海）有限公司、上海欧苏贸易有限公司虚假宣传纠纷案，涉及为说明商品销售商变化而使用他人商标是否构成商标侵权和虚假宣传的认定问题，入选"2015年中国法院知识产权司法保护50件典型案例"及"2015年最高人民法院关于知识产权法院工作情况发布会公布的典型案例"；申请人欧特克公司、奥多比公司与被申请人上海风语筑展览有限公司诉前证据保全案，入选"2015 年最高人民法院关于知识产权法院工作情况发布会公布的典型案例"；浙江淘宝网络有限公司与上海载和网络科技有限公司等申请诉前停止侵害知识产权纠纷案，入选"2015 年中国法院知识产权司法保护 50 件典型案例"。此外，本书继续沿用中英文对照体例，便于更好地向国际社会展示上海法院知识产权司法保护的成果。

需要特别指出的是，2018 年 4 月，上海市高级人民法院与同济大学共同签署《关于加强知识产权法学教育和司法实践的合作框架协议》，积极搭建起法院司法实践与大专院校教学培养有机结合的高端平台，探索建立优势互补、资源共享、相互促进的举措机制，双向培养更多高素质、高要求的应用型、复合型知识产权法律人才，不断提升"院""校"合作的规范化、品牌化、实效化水平，力求在更高层面上实现知识产权法学教育与司法实践的深度融合。而本书的编撰和出版工作即是由上海市高级人民法院和同济大学共同完成，这既是响应双方合作框架协议的具体举措，也突显了"院""校"合作的新成果。同济大学的知识产权法学教育在国内外均享有盛誉，尤其是 2016 年 11 月，在联合国世界知识产权组织（WIPO）、中国国家知识产权局和上海市政府的支持下，同济大学在其原有的知识产权学院基础上，正式成立了"上海国际知识产权学院"。这是联合国世界知识产权组织（WIPO）第七个世界知识产权高端人才培养基地，同时也是国家教育部、知识产权局委托的"一带一路"中国政府知识产权奖学金项目基地，并承担相关国际人才培养项目，充分展示出同济大学良好的知识产权法学教育底蕴。相信随着双方合作的不断深化，定会结出更多、更优的实践研究成果，不断为我国建设知识产权强国和科技强国作出应有的贡献。

是为序。

刘晓云

2019 年 7 月 3 日

Preface

As the new technological and industrial revolution is in full swing, intellectual property rights have become a strategic resource for our national development and a central component of our international competitiveness. They are a crucial support for the development of China as an innovation-driven country, as well as a key factor for taking the initiative in national development. On April 10, 2018, President Xi Jinping gave a keynote speech at the Boao Forum for Asia (BFA) in which he announced the four major movesto be taken by China to further enhance its opening-up campaign. One of them is to strengthen the protection of intellectual property rights. At the critical moment where China is undergoing economic transformation and upgrading and the reform and opening-up campaign progresses by leaps and bounds in a volatile international context, the visionary central government interprets correctly the situation both at home and abroad and gives unprecedented priority to the protection of intellectual property rights.

Judicial protection is the most effective and authoritative instrument in this regard. In February 2018, the General Office of CPC Central Committee and the General Office of the State Council issued a guiding document exclusively for the adjudication of intellectual property cases: *Opinions on Several Issues Concerning Heightening Reform and Innovation in the Field of Intellectual Property Adjudication*. It is clearly stated in the document that the adjudication of intellectual property cases by people's courts is crucial to the implementation of innovation-driven development strategies, the economic, social and cultural development and prosperity, and the situation at home and abroad, and that it is of great significance to the development of China's strength in intellectual property and technology in the world; Meanwhile, the document also contains a full program for improving the intellectual property litigation system, enhancing the development of a talent pool of qualified judges, increasing the effectiveness and efficiency of adjudication, reinforcing the efforts in intellectual property protection, etc. It marks a very precious historic opportunity for the modernization of the intellectual property adjudication system and the judicial capacity of people's courts. The people's courts must rise to the occasion and take on their noble mission and duty in safeguarding an impartial judicial system for the people, enhancing the reform, allowing the judicial system to play its central role in intellectual property protection, ensuring the full and effective enforcement of intellectual property laws and regulations, creating a better legal environment for technological innovation and business, and providing strong judicial for China to be both an intellectual property power and a science and technology power in the world.

The improvement of their adjudicative work has been a focus of Shanghai courts for years. They have launched a series of successful reforms and researches in judicial IP protection and heard a range of IP cases influential in China and even in the world, during which they defined a few widely accepted rules of adjudication. Another focus of their work throughout the years has been the compilation of various cases, especially IP cases. They have released a series of publications of selected cases, including the annually published "Top Ten Cases on Judicial Protection of IP Rights by Shanghai Courts" and the regular issues of selected IP cases. By publishing selected and typical cases, they hope to offer guidelines for judicial practices related to intellectual property protection, based on which they can regulate and guide IP protection and utilization and incentives for technological innovation through the demonstration of a few classic cases. They help educate the public on related laws and regulations and act as examples of how to resolve IP disputes.

This book contains 36 cases selected from the nearly 20,000 IP cases concluded in Shanghai courts in 2015 and 2016, covering several types across multiple fields, including civil cases on copyright, trademark, patent and anti-unfair competition, criminal and administrative IP cases, and other cases involving IP litigation, which makes the book an epitome of how professional Shanghai courts are in adjudication of IP cases. Here are a few examples. The dispute of Shanghai Pafuluo Stationery Co., Ltd. v. Shanghai Yixiang Stationery Co., Ltd. and Picasso International Business Co., Ltd. over the trademark license contract are cases concerning the contractual validity of multiple licenses issued for an exclusive trademark and the ownership of its user license, which is included in the "Ten Major Cases on Judicial Protection of IP Rights in the Courts of China in 2015"; the dispute of Vitoria's Secret Store Brand Management Company v. Shanghai Mice Investment Management Co., Ltd. over the trademark infringement and unfair competition concerns the ascertainment of the indicative use of a trademark, which is included in the "50 Typical Cases on Judicial Protection of IP Rights in the Courts of China in 2015"; the dispute of Shanghai M&G Stationery Inc. v. Deli Group over the infringement of its design patent concerns the objective comparison and judgment of designs, which is included in the "Ten Major Cases on Judicial Protection of IP Rights in the Courts of China in 2016"; and the dispute of Shenzhen Juwangshi Technology Co., Ltd. v. iQIYI over unfair competition, as the first unfair competition case between video platforms, concerns whether it constitutes unfair competition to offer the video content owned by others without showing opening advertisements, which is included in the "50 Typical Cases on Judicial Protection of IP Rights in the Courts of China in 2015." The above four cases are all included in the *Gazette of the Supreme People's Court*. Other examples are: The appeal of Shanghai Mougan Advertising Co., Ltd. against the administrative penalty in its dispute v. Shanghai Jing'an District Market Supervision Administration, Shanghai ShopEx Network Technology Co., Ltd. and Kumei (Shanghai) Information Technology Co., Ltd. is the first administrative IP case accepted by Shanghai High People's Court; the dispute of Shanghai Yaoyu Culture Media Co., Ltd. v. Guangzhou Douyu Network Technology Co., Ltd. over the copyright infringement and unfair competition concerns the ascertainment of whether the live coverage of e-sport events online constitutes unfair competition and it is included in the "50 Typical Cases on Judicial Protection of IP Rights in the Courts of China in 2016" and the "Ten Major Civil and Administrative Cases in People's Courts in 2016"; the dispute of BURBERRY LIMITED v. Chen Kai and Lu Qiumin over the trademark infringement concerns the question of whether a criminal proceeding not reported by right-holder is a valid cause of the discontinuation of the limitation of a civil action and it is included in the "Typical Cases Released by the Supreme People's Court at the Intellectual Property Court Work Progress Press Conference"; the dispute of K. D. F. Distribution (Shanghai) Co., Ltd. v. Aquatherm Pipe System (Shanghai) Co., Ltd. and Shanghai Ousu Trade Co., Ltd.

over false advertising concerns the question of whether the use of others' trademark for the purpose of explaining the change of vendors should be ascertained as constituting infringement of trademark and fraudulent advertising and it is included in the "50 Typical Cases on Judicial Protection of IP Rights in the Courts of China in 2015" and "Typical Cases Released by the Supreme People's Court at the Intellectual Property Court Work Progress Press Conference"; the application for pre-litigation evidence preservation by Autodesk and Adobe against Shanghai Fengyuzhu Exhibition Co. , Ltd. is included in the "Typical Cases Released by the Supreme People's Court at the Intellectual Property Court Work Progress Press Conference"; and the dispute of Zhejiang Taobao Network Co. , Ltd. v. Shanghai Zaihe Network Technology Co. , Ltd. over the pre-trial cessation of intellectual property infringement, which is included in the "50 Typical Cases on Judicial Protection of IP Rights in the Courts of China in 2015. " In addition, the book consists of parallel texts in Chinese and English as before to make it accessible to international readers interested in the achievements of Shanghai's courts in judicial IP protection.

It is worth noting that Shanghai High People's Court and Tongji University signed the *Cooperation Framework Agreement on Strengthening the Legal Education Related to IP Protection and Judicial Practices* in April, 2018, to build a platform combining judicial practices at the courts and training programmes at colleges and universities, develop a system that taps into their complementary advantages, shares resources and contributes to joint progress, launch a two-pronged campaign for training more competent, self-disciplinary and practical professionals in IP laws and regulations with cross-disciplinary knowledge, keep enhancing the development of standardized, branded and effective court-college cooperation projects, and strengthen the thorough coordination between legal education on IP and judicial practices on a higher level. This book is jointly compiled and published by Shanghai High People's Court and Tongji University as a concrete measure within the framework and a new achievement from their cooperation. Tongji University has been a well-acclaimed leader in IP law education both at home and abroad; in November 2016, with the support from WIPO, CNIPA and Shanghai Municipal Government, Shanghai International College of Intellectual Property was formed out of Tongji's former IP faculty. It is the seventh high-caliber and global IP training program of WIPO, as well as a "Belt and Road" Chinese Government IP Scholarship Program Base sponsored by the Chinese Ministry of Education and SIPO for the training of international talents in this field, which makes it a full manifestation of Tongji's heritage in legal education on IP. It is believed that the increasingly enhanced cooperation between the two sides will produce more and better practical results and research findings that may prompt China to become an intellectual property power and a science and technology power in the world.

It is for this reason that this preface is written.

Liu Xiaoyun
July 3, 2019

目　录

一、著作权民事纠纷案件

二、商标权民事纠纷案件

三、专利权民事纠纷案件

四、不正当竞争民事纠纷案件

Ⅰ. Civil Cases on Copyright Infringement

Ⅱ. Civil Disputes Over Trademark Rights

Ⅲ. Civil Disputes over Patent

Ⅳ. Civil Dispute Cases of Unfair Competition

V. Criminal Cases on Intellectual Property

VI. Administrative Cases on Intellectual Property

VII. Cases on Judicial Proceedings of Intellectual Property

一

著作权民事纠纷案件

合理使用在司法实践中的审查认定

——上海美术电影制片厂诉浙江新影年代文化传播有限公司等 著作权侵权纠纷案

【提要】

在审查判断本案是否构成合理使用时，明确了"葫芦娃""黑猫警长"角色形象美术作品使用在涉案电影海报中属于转换性使用。所谓转换性使用，是指对原作品的使用不是单纯地再现原作品本身的文学、艺术价值，而是通过在新作品中的使用使原作品在被使用过程中具有了新的价值、功能或性质，从而改变了其原先的功能或目的。在判断转换性使用是否构成合理使用时，应当综合考察我国著作权法所规定的合理使用构成要件，即在构成转换性使用的前提下，不影响该作品的正常使用，也没有不合理地损害著作权人的合法利益的，构成合理使用。

【案情】

原告（上诉人）：上海美术电影制片厂

被告（被上诉人）：浙江新影年代文化传播有限公司

被告（被上诉人）：华谊兄弟上海影院管理有限公司

案由：著作权侵权纠纷

一审案号：（2014）普民三（知）初字第 258 号

二审案号：（2015）沪知民终字第 730 号

涉案美术作品"葫芦娃"的著作权归属问题，曾有过争议，并引起诉讼。2012 年 3 月上海市第二中级人民法院在（2011）沪二中民五（知）终字第 62 号判决中，就胡进庆、吴云初与上海美术电影制片厂（以下简称美影厂）著作权权属纠纷一案作出过终审判决。上海市第二中级人民法院查明并认定，1985

年年底，美影厂指派其员工胡进庆、吴云初担任美术设计，二人绘制了"葫芦娃"角色造型稿。葫芦七兄弟造型一致，其共同特征是：四方的脸形、粗短的眉毛、明亮的大眼、敦实的身体、头顶葫芦冠、颈戴葫芦叶项圈、身穿坎肩短裤、腰围葫芦叶围裙，葫芦七兄弟的服饰颜色分别为赤、橙、黄、绿、青、蓝、紫。结合"葫芦娃"创作当时的时代背景、历史条件、当时法律法规的规定、单位的规章制度等，法院判决认定"葫芦娃"角色造型美术作品（即本案涉案作品）属于特定历史条件下胡进庆、吴云初创作的职务作品，由美影厂享有除署名权之外的其他著作权。

2014 年 5 月福建省高级人民法院在（2014）闽民终字第 223 号判决书中，就美影厂与福建黑猫警长儿童用品有限公司、福建南华集团侵犯其他著作权纠纷一案作出过终审判决。福建省高级人民法院查明并认定，美影厂于 20 世纪 80 年代拍摄了《黑猫警长》动画片，片中"黑猫警长"角色造型美术作品（涉案作品）的实际创作者为时任美影厂厂长的戴铁郎。"黑猫警长"形象为身着黑色制服，配有红色肩章，头部圆形，戴白色盖黑色鸭舌帽，两色中间有黄色底色蓝色箭头圆形图案，脸部上半部为黑色，黑色覆盖两个翘起的双耳，下半部为特有的白色，眼部外圈金黄内圈黑色，留有笔直的长胡须，白色手套、腰挎一把手枪，背带为白色。法院判决，动画片《黑猫警长》由美影厂享有著作权，在当时计划经济体制下，参与拍摄制作该片的人员均是美影厂工作人员，因此在没有相反证据证明的情况下，美影厂享有"黑猫警长"美术作品（本案涉案作品）的著作权。

电影《80 后的独立宣言》由浙江新影年代文化传播有限公司（以下简称新影年代公司）投资制作，于 2014 年 2 月 21 日正式上映。涉案海报的内容为：上方三分之二的篇幅中突出部分为男女主角人物形象及主演姓名，背景则零散分布着诸多美术形象，包括身着白绿校服的少先队员参加升旗仪式、课堂活动、课余游戏等情景；黑白电视机、落地灯等家电用品；缝纫机、二八式自行车、热水瓶、痰盂等日用品；课桌、铅笔盒等文教用品；铁皮青蛙、陀螺、弹珠等玩具；无花果零食，以及涉案的"葫芦娃""黑猫警长"卡通形象，其中"葫芦娃""黑猫警长"分别居于男女主角的左右两侧。诸多背景图案与男女主角形象相较，比例显著较小，"葫芦娃""黑猫警长"美术形象与其他背景图案大小基本相同。海报下方三分之一的部分为突出的电影名称"80 后的独立宣言"以及制片方、摄制公司和演职人员信息等，并标注有"2014.2.21 温情巨献"字样。

2014 年 3 月 7 日，美影厂申请的保全证据公证显示："华谊兄弟上海影院"微博于 2014 年 2 月 22 日发布有关涉案电影海报的微博，内容为："电影《80

后的独立宣言》讲述了当代80后年轻人在走出校门后，放弃了城市优越的生活环境，放弃了父母为其铺设好的平坦大路，而是选择去到条件相对艰苦的乡下打拼事业、自主创业的故事。影片中，'富一代'父母的教育方式也成了电影中的亮点之一"，微博下方配有涉案电影海报。其后，经 www.baidu.com 网址，搜索"80后的独立宣言 海报"，对相关搜索内容进行链接，网页上显示电影网、新华网、搜狐娱乐、腾讯网、网易娱乐多家媒体网站上配有涉案海报。

经当庭比对，涉案海报中被控侵权形象与美影厂主张权利的"葫芦娃""黑猫警长"角色美术形象特征基本一致，美影厂主张新影年代公司涉嫌擅自修改的部分为：美影厂"黑猫警长"形象肩章上有两条白色横杠，"葫芦娃"形象头顶葫芦上的叶子有两片，项圈上也有两片树叶，而涉案海报"黑猫警长"形象肩章没有两条白色横杠；涉案海报"葫芦娃"形象头顶葫芦上的叶子只有一片，项圈上没有树叶。

《80后的独立宣言》是经国家广电总局电影管理局审查通过并正式公映的电影片，涉案影片中未有涉及"葫芦娃""黑猫警长"的情节或内容。

根据国家电影剧本（梗概）备案、电影片管理相关规定及电影故事片（胶片、数字）送审须知相关规定，电影片送审材料包括相关剧照若干或海报（1~2张）并附光盘，新影年代公司就该影片共制作了两张海报，除涉案海报外，另一张海报内容与"葫芦娃""黑猫警长"无涉。涉案海报系由新影年代公司提供给华谊兄弟上海影院管理有限公司（以下简称华谊兄弟），华谊兄弟为配合电影上映宣传，在其官方微博上使用了本案涉案海报。

原告美影厂诉称：美影厂拥有动画片《葫芦兄弟》中"葫芦娃"角色形象美术作品的著作权，拥有动画片《黑猫警长》中"黑猫警长"角色形象美术作品的著作权。浙江新影年代文化传播有限公司制作的电影《80后的独立宣言》宣传海报上使用了美影厂拥有著作权的"葫芦娃"和"黑猫警长"角色形象美术作品，且有所变动。华谊兄弟上海影院管理有限公司在其新浪官方微博上还发布了该电影的涉案海报。美影厂认为，新影年代公司未经许可，使用"葫芦娃"和"黑猫警长"角色形象美术作品，构成对其修改权、复制权、发行权、信息网络传播权的侵犯；华谊兄弟的行为，构成对其信息网络传播权的侵犯，并与新影年代公司构成共同侵权。故美影厂诉至法院，请求判令：1. 新影年代公司和华谊兄弟在《新闻晨报》或同级别纸质媒体显著位置公开赔礼道歉，消除影响；2. 新影年代公司和华谊兄弟停止侵犯美影厂拥有的"葫芦娃""黑猫警长"角色形象美术作品的著作权；3. 新影年代公司和华谊兄弟连带赔偿美影厂经济损失及维权费用合计531 750元。

被告新影年代公司辩称：现有证据无法证明美影厂对"葫芦娃"和"黑猫

警长"形象美术作品享有著作权；即使其享有著作权，涉案海报主体内容是 80 后男女青年，后面的小图案仅仅是为了点缀主角的年代是 80 后，所以使用了缝纫机、热水瓶、葫芦娃、黑猫警长等图案，是为了说明电影主人公年龄特点；从使用来看，海报中的"葫芦娃""黑猫警长"和原告电影中的形象有所区别，比例上也只是主体画面中很小的一部分，属于合理使用；且影片有两个版本的海报，还有一个卡通版，涉案海报发行量很少，即使构成侵权，图片著作权的判赔金额也是比较低的。

被告华谊兄弟辩称：现有证据无法证明原告美影厂对"黑猫警长"形象美术作品享有著作权；即使原告享有著作权，对于被告华谊兄弟来说，为配合电影公映使用海报作宣传是合理的使用行为，影片是合法公映的影片，涉案海报也是官方海报，并经审查，是制片方提供给发行机构的，其使用海报有合法来源，没有过错；况且，涉案美术作品是 80 后的时代标识，具有社会公益性，在海报中的使用不醒目、比例不大，对原告的利益没有损害；即使构成侵权，图片著作权的判赔金额也是比较低的。

【审判】

上海市普陀区人民法院经审理认为："葫芦娃""黑猫警长"角色形象美术作品属于已经发表的作品；新影年代公司引用他人作品是为了说明某一问题，即涉案电影主角的年龄特征；从被引用作品占整个作品的比例来看，被引用作品作为背景使用，占海报面积较小，且涉案作品的形象并未突出显示，属于适度引用；被控侵权海报的使用也未对美影厂作品的正常使用造成影响，故应当认定新影年代公司在电影海报中对"葫芦娃""黑猫警长"美术作品的使用属于著作权法所规定的合理使用。

综上，上海市普陀区人民法院判决驳回美影厂的诉讼请求。

一审判决后，原告美影厂不服，提起上诉。

上海知识产权法院经审理后认为，根据我国著作权法规定，为介绍、评论某一作品或者说明某一问题，在作品中适当引用他人已经发表的作品，构成合理使用。其中，为说明某一问题，是指对作品的引用是为了说明其他问题，并不是为了纯粹展示被引用作品本身的艺术价值，而被引用作品在新作品中的被引用致使其原有的艺术价值和功能发生了转换；而该被引用作品在新作品中亦不是以必需为前提，即使在新作品中引用作品不是必需的，也会构成合理使用。

本案中，"葫芦娃""黑猫警长"是 20 世纪 80 年代家喻户晓的少儿动画形象，对于经历八十年代少年儿童期的人们可谓深入人心，因此，"葫芦娃""黑猫警长"动画形象自然亦是八十年代少年儿童的部分成长记忆。涉案电影海报中不仅引用了"葫芦娃""黑猫警长"美术作品,还引用了诸多八十年代少年儿童经历的具有代表性的人、景、物,如:黑白电视机、落地灯、缝纫机、二八式自行车、热水瓶、痰盂、课桌、铅笔盒、铁皮青蛙、陀螺、弹珠、无花果及着白绿校服的少先队员升旗仪式、课堂活动、课余游戏等时代元素,涵盖了八十年代少年儿童日用品、文教用品、玩具、零食以及生活学习场景等多个方面,整个电影海报内容呈现给受众的是关于八十年代少年儿童日常生活经历的信息。因此,电影海报中引用"葫芦娃""黑猫警长"美术作品不再是单纯地再现"葫芦娃""黑猫警长"美术作品的艺术美感和功能,而是反映一代共同经历八十年代少年儿童期,曾经经历"葫芦娃""黑猫警长"动画片盛播的时代年龄特征,亦符合电影主角的年龄特征。因此,"葫芦娃""黑猫警长"美术作品被引用在电影海报中具有了新的价值、意义和功能,其原有的艺术价值功能发生了转换,而且转换性程度较高,属于我国著作权法规定的为了说明某一问题的情形。

因此,涉案电影海报为说明八十年代少年儿童的年代特征这一特殊情况,适当引用当时具有代表性的少儿动画形象"葫芦娃""黑猫警长"之美术作品,与其他具有当年年代特征的元素一起作为电影海报背景图案,构成合理使用。故上海知识产权法院判决驳回上诉,维持原判。

【评析】

本案系著作权侵权纠纷案件,判断被控侵权行为是否构成合理使用是本案的关键所在,因而涉及合理使用判断标准及司法实践中需要考虑的相关因素。

合理使用,是指在法律规定的条件下,不必征得著作权人的许可,又不必向其支付报酬,基于正当目的而使用他人著作权作品的合法行为。我国《著作权法》第二十二条详细列举了十二种构成合理使用的行为,该些情形下,可以不经著作权人许可,不向其支付报酬,但应当指明作者姓名、作品名称,并且不得侵犯著作权人依照著作权法享有的其他权利。《著作权法实施条例》第二十一条规定,依照著作权法有关规定,使用可以不经著作权人许可的已经发表的作品的,不得影响该作品的正常使用,也不得不合理地损害著作权人的合法利益。因此审查判断是否构成合理使用,应当综合考虑法律规定的各项要件。比如,《著作权法》第二十二条列举的第二种合理使用情形规定"为介绍、评论某一作品或者说明某一问题"是针对使用目的和性质这一要件的审查,其要求对原作品注入新的内容或含义,产生不同于原作品本身的审美或艺术表达。

考虑该要件时，应关注对原作品的使用是否构成转换性使用，因为对原作品进行转换性使用且转换的程度越高，就越有可能构成合理使用。《著作权法》及实施条例均要求引用的原作品是已经发表的作品，这是对原作品性质这项要件的考查。同时《著作权法》第二十二条规定的"适当引用"及实施条例第二十一条规定的"不得影响该作品的正常使用，也不得不合理地损害著作权人的合法利益"相关规定则是对引用的数量和内容、引用后果即对原作品市场或价值是否产生影响等相关要素的考虑。

考察使用的目的和性质要素时可关注在使用过程中是否对原作品内容进行了转换，如果使原作品产生新的信息、新的美学、新的认识和理解，就属于典型的合理使用行为。本案中，"葫芦娃""黑猫警长"形象与黑白电视机、落地灯等图片共同形成海报的背景构图，无论是契合海报主题还是说明电影主角的年龄身份特征，作品均已被注入了新的内容、含义和信息，呈现了完全不同的审美和艺术表达。换言之，涉案"葫芦娃""黑猫警长"美术作品被引用在电影海报中具有了新的价值、意义和功能，其原有的艺术价值功能发生了转换，而且转换性程度较高。本案电影海报中引用"葫芦娃""黑猫警长"美术作品不再是单纯地再现"葫芦娃""黑猫警长"美术作品的艺术美感和功能，而是反映一代共同经历八十年代少年儿童期，曾经经历"葫芦娃""黑猫警长"动画片盛播的时代年龄特征，亦符合电影主角的年龄特征。

对原作品性质进行审查时，如果原作品属于已经发表的作品，则对原作品的引用更容易构成合理使用。本案涉案作品"葫芦娃"和"黑猫警长"是动画片中的角色造型美术作品，动画片已于20世纪80年代播出，因此涉案作品均属于已经发表的作品。

考虑引用是否适度时，应结合包括"为介绍、评论某一作品或者说明某一问题"这一"使用的目的和性质"在内的相关因素，判断新作品是否对原作品进行转换性使用，而不是简单的替代，从而进一步判断引用行为是否构成合理使用。某些情形下，引用他人整个作品也可能构成合理使用。本案中，虽然涉案"葫芦娃"和"黑猫警长"两个角色造型美术作品在电影海报中整体呈现，但其与其他二十余个表明"80后"时代特征的元素均作为背景使用，从被引用作品占整个作品的比例来看，被引用作品只是属于辅助、配角、从属的地位。从海报的外观来看，涉案海报突出的是电影男女主角，约占整个海报的二分之一。涉案作品占海报面积较小，且与其他背景图案比例协调，"葫芦娃""黑猫警长"的形象并未突出显示。海报并非为了展示"葫芦娃"或"黑猫警长"原有的艺术魅力和审美价值，更多的是反映"80后"曾经经历"葫芦娃""黑猫警长"动画片盛播的时代年龄特征。况且，动画形象被引用不太可能作部分形象的引用，电影海报对两涉案作品进行了完整引用，也是引用之需，在本案中该项因素需结合其他因素来进行综合认定。

引用后果因素主要考虑的是对原作品潜在市场的影响，避免被控侵权作品以合理使用的名义取代原作品，新作品的出现不能造成原作品在市场上被取代或弃用。本案中，涉案电影于2014年2月21日上映，公开上映时间为一至两周，电影内容中并没有出现任何有关"葫芦娃""黑猫警长"的内容，除了海报中的使用外，电影宣传文案中也未涉及"葫芦娃""黑猫警长"内容。因此，新影年代公司在海报中为辅助说明电影主角年龄特征使用"葫芦娃"和"黑猫警长"，与美影厂自身作品的正常使用没有冲突，在市场上未形成竞争关系，不会造成原作品在市场上被取代或弃用的情形。

实践中，综合考虑全面审查合理使用的各项要件，并以引用原作品行为是否构成转换性使用作为重要审查内容，有助于把握合理使用的实质内涵，厘清控侵权行为是否构成合理使用的判断标准。

（撰稿人：陆凤玉　朱永华）

深度链接行为是否构成信息网络传播权侵权

——上海幻电信息科技有限公司与北京奇艺世纪科技有限公司侵害作品信息网络传播权纠纷上诉案

【提要】

当前司法实践中，关于深度链接行为的信息网络传播权侵权判定，存在着不同的审查判断标准，主要包括：1. 服务器标准；2. 用户感知标准；3. 实质替代标准。本案一审法院采用实质替代标准，二审未认同此观点，认为依据知识产权权利法定原则，在判定信息网络传播权侵权与否时应当审查判断被诉行为是否属于信息网络传播权所控制的行为。本案二审判决根据我国《信息网络传播权保护条例》及相关司法解释的分析理解，认为构成信息网络传播权侵权需具备以下条件：1. 未经权利人许可；2. 被诉人将作品置于信息网络中；3. 公众能够在个人选定的时间和地点获得该作品。

【案情】

原告（上诉人）： 北京奇艺世纪科技有限公司

被告（上诉人）： 上海幻电信息科技有限公司

案由： 侵害作品信息网络传播权纠纷

一审案号：（2014）浦民三（知）初字第 1137 号

二审案号：（2015）沪知民终字第 213 号

北京奇艺世纪科技有限公司（以下简称奇艺公司）经独家授权获得包括《快乐大本营》在内的综艺节目之节目视频内容的信息网络传播权，授权性质包括了独家信息网络传播权及维权权利，授权使用领域仅限于互联网领域（PC 电脑终端使用权）、移动无线领域（IPAD、手机等移动无线终端使用权），授权区域为中国大陆地区；授权期限为 2014 年 1 月 1 日起至 2014 年 12 月 31 日止湖南卫视每周六晚 20 时 15 分播出的《快乐大本营》节目，2 年的使用期限，即 2014 年 1 月 1 日至 2015 年 12 月 31 日止；在上述授权期内，领权方有权以自己名义进行维权（包括且不限于发函、投诉、诉讼等）。

上海幻电信息科技有限公司（以下简称幻电公司）系"哔哩哔哩"（www. bilibili.com）网站的经营者。注册用户可以将新浪、优酷、腾讯网上的视频投稿到幻电公司网站，供他人观看和评论。具体过程为：用户将该视频所在播放页面的网络地址复制或填写到幻电公司网站的投稿页面，并填写标题、标签等信息，幻电公司网站内部软件根据该地址提取视频在其所在网站的代码。用户亦可直接提供代码。随后，幻电公司网站根据该代码向视频所在网站服务器发送请求，并根据视频所在网站服务器的回复，提取视频文件数据在幻电公司网站的播放器中进行播放。通过 Live HTTP headers 插件查看幻电公司网站所播放的投稿视频的访问地址，显示为视频源地址，而非幻电公司地址。

根据幻电公司网站管理系统记录显示，本案被控侵权的视频来自乐视网。视频链接由幻电公司网站用户"情怀酱"提供，其于 2014 年 7 月 20 日上传该链接，幻电公司于 2014 年 10 月 28 日在网站删除该链接。奇艺公司确认，就涉案作品，其未与乐视网存在合作关系。

一审法院审理后，判令幻电公司赔偿奇艺公司经济损失 3000 元及合理费用 2500 元。奇艺公司、幻电公司均不服一审判决，提起上诉。

奇艺公司上诉请求撤销原审判决，依法改判幻电公司向奇艺公司赔偿经济损失 10 万元。其主要上诉理由是：1. 幻电公司虽未直接上传涉案节目，但其对链接服务实施了人工干预，是作品提供行为，其在涉案节目首播后数小时内即提供在线播放，其侵权行为性质恶劣，主观恶意明显；2. 奇艺公司获得授权花费巨额资金，每期《快乐大本营》的使用费均在几十万元以上，故一审判赔金额与合理的许可费用差距巨大。奇艺公司为制止侵权实际支出公证费、律师费等。一审判赔经济损失 3000 元及合理费用 2500 元明显过低。

幻电公司针对奇艺公司的上诉答辩称：一审判赔金额过高。幻电公司的涉案网站是知名的分享网站，从中未得任何收益，亦无插入广告；综艺节目每周都有新的节目，过一周就没有人看了，且奇艺公司诉称的许可使用费支出无证据证明。

幻电公司上诉请求二审发回重审或依法改判驳回奇艺公司的一审诉讼请求。其主要上诉理由为：1. 被控侵权视频的链接地址由网络用户上传，上诉人并未对用户投稿进行人工干预和人工选择，提供的仅仅是网络链接服务，并未提供侵权作品，没有直接实施侵权行为，不构成直接侵权；2. 原审判决认为幻电公司的行为势必造成权利人利益的损失系主观臆断，没有充分的事实依据，赔偿金额过高。

奇艺公司针对幻电公司的上诉答辩称：幻电公司实施深度链接行为，不是链接服务商，构成直接侵权。

【审判】

上海市浦东新区人民法院经审理认为：网络用户通过幻电公司网站可以不经由被链网站的界面直接观看涉案视频，被链网站存储该视频的服务器在此阶段已形同幻电公司所控制的远程服务器，且为幻电公司免费使用，幻电公司网站已经在实质上替代了被链网站向公众传播作品，使公众具有了可以在个人选定的时间或地点获得涉案作品的可能性，故应当认定幻电公司构成作品提供行为，侵害了奇艺公司的信息网络传播权。综上，上海市浦东新区人民法院依据《中华人民共和国著作权法》第十条第一款第（十二）项、第四十八条第（一）项、第四十九条，《最高人民法院关于审理著作权民事纠纷案件适用法律若干问题的解释》第二十五条第一款、第二款、第二十六条之规定，判决：幻电公司赔偿奇艺公司经济损失 3000 元以及因制止侵权所支出的合理费用 2500 元。

一审判决后，奇艺公司、幻电公司均不服，提起上诉。

上海知识产权法院经审理后认为，涉案节目实际上来源于乐视网且其传播受控于乐视网，幻电公司通过技术手段为涉案节目的传播提供搜索、链接服务，并未将作品置于网络中，不构成作品提供行为，不属于直接侵权行为。幻电公司对于所搜索、链接的涉案节目未进行网页跳转以指引用户在被链网站上观看，亦未向用户提示涉案节目源自其他网站，故幻电公司应负较高注意义务，应当负有对视频文件授权情况的注意义务。根据涉案节目的知名度、上传时间等信息，其主观上应当知道涉案节目具有较大侵权可能性，客观上帮助了涉案节目侵权后果的扩大，故其行为乃侵犯了奇艺公司的信息网络传播权，构成帮助侵权，应承担赔偿责任，故一审判决并无不当。因此，判决驳回上诉，维持原判。

【评析】

本案系侵害作品信息网络传播权纠纷案件，我国"信息网络传播权"的规定直接来源于《世界知识产权组织版权条约》（WCT）第 8 条，是指以有线或者无线方式向公众提供作品、表演或者录音录像制品，使公众可以在其个人选定的时间和地点获得作品、表演或者录音录像制品的权利。网络用户、网络服务提供者未经许可，通过信息网络提供权利人享有信息网络传播权的作品，构成侵害信息网络传播权。我国著作权法将信息网络传播行为特征限定于"提供行为"，但并未涉及何种行为属于"提供行为"。《最高人民法院关于审理侵害信息网络传播权民事纠纷案件适用法律若干问题的规定》对提供行为作了列举加概括式的规定，明确"提供行为"是将作品置于信息网络之中的内容提供行为，并对应直接侵权责任。

一、目前司法实践中对不跳转深度链接的侵权判定标准

本案中，奇艺公司、幻电公司对于一审已经查明的涉案节目未存储在幻电公司服务器上即幻电公司未直接上传涉案节目到其服务器，涉案节目系由幻电公司链接自乐视网之事实均无异议。由此可见，本案中幻电公司就涉案节目为用户设置了指向第三方网站的深度链接，为涉案节目的传播提供了搜索、链接服务，系网络服务提供者。

当前司法实践中，关于深度链接行为的信息网络传播权侵权判定，存在着不同的审查判断标准，主要包括：1. 服务器标准。这是一种客观标准，如果信息内容存储在设链网站的服务器之上，那设链网站的行为就是信息网络传播行为，在行为人没有得到权利人许可的情况下，超出法定的合理使用范围，即构成信息网络传播权直接侵权；如果设链网站没有存储信息内容，只是采用了不跳转深度链接技术向公众提供搜索链接服务，那么设链网站的行为就是网络服务提供行为，不构成直接侵犯信息网络传播权。在一些案件中，设链网站网络服务提供商的行为不构成直接侵害信息网络传播权，但若其在客观上对于被链网站上作品的传播起到了帮助作用，有可能承担间接侵权责任。在这种情况下，则需要进一步审查判断设链网站是否构成间接侵权，以及如果构成间接侵权是否应当承担赔偿责任。2. 用户感知标准。这是一种以用户感知的信息来源作为依据的主观判断标准，即只要网络服务商提供的网络技术行为的外在表现形式使用户感觉是该网站在提供信息或者使用户认为可以直接从该网站上得到作品内容，行为人的行为就构成作品的提供行为。适用此种标准，网络服务提供者设置不跳转深度链接的行为使一般公众直观感觉其获取的信息来自设链网站，而无法判断其获取的信息资源实质上来源于被链网站，设链网站虽然没有在服务器上存储信息内容，但却使服务对象感觉他们提供的是内容服务而不是技术服务，因此，构成信息网络传播权直接侵权。3. 实质替代标准。根据该标准，设置不跳转深度链接的行为，从结果来看，用户通过设链网站可以不经由被链网站的界面直接获取信息内容，被链网站存储该信息的服务器在此阶段相当于设链网站所控制的远程服务器，设链网站已经在实质上替代了被链网站向公众传播作品。且设链网站免费使用被链网站网盘宽带资源，使其用户具有了在个人选定的时间或地点获得作品的可能性，在一定程度上获取了本应属于被链网站的传播利益。虽然设链网站没有在其服务器上存储信息内容，但其在自己网站上播放未经授权的信息内容，对被链网站有实质性替代之后果。因此认定设链网站实施了提供作品的行为，侵害了权利人的信息网络传播权。本案一审法院即采用了此种标准，认为网络用户通过幻电公司网站可以不经由被链网站的界面直接观看涉案视频，被链网站存储该视频的服务器在此阶段已形同幻电公司所控制的远程服务器，且为幻电公司免费使用，幻电公司网站已经在实质上替代了被链网站向公众二、传播作品，使公众具有了可以在个人选定的时间或地点获得涉案作品的可能性，故认定幻电公司构成作品提供行为，侵害了奇艺公司的信息网络传播权。

二、本案二审判决采用服务器标准的原因分析

根据知识产权权利法定原则，在判定信息网络传播权侵权与否时应当审查判断被诉行为是否属于信息网络传播权所控制的行为。现有法律规定信息网络传播权所控制的行为应具备向公众提供作品即将作品置于信息网络中之特征，并未规定用户感知标准，在此采用用户感知标准缺乏法律依据。此外，虽然一审法院采用实质替代标准，认定幻电公司网站已经在实质上替代了被链网站向公众传播作品，其对链接服务实施了人工干预，构成作品提供行为。但二审法院认为，虽然幻电公司网站未将公众指引到被链网站观看涉案节目，但这不能改变涉案节目来源于乐视网的事实，幻电公司对涉案节目的传播受控于乐视网是否存在涉案节目，乐视网上存在涉案节目是幻电公司得以链接的前提，幻电公司的链接行为不能认定为其实质替代了乐视网实施将作品置于信息网络中从而构成作品提供行为，在此情况下，实质替代标准实际上突破了现行的关于信息网络传播权的相关规定。因此，本案遵循现行法律规定采用服务器标准，认为构成信息网络传播权侵权需具备以下条件：1. 未经权利人许可；2. 被诉人将作品置于信息网络中；3. 公众能够在个人选定的时间和地点获得该作品。此外，《最高人民法院关于审理侵害信息网络传播权民事纠纷案件适用法律若干问题的规定》第五条规定，网络服务提供者以提供网页快照、缩略图等方式实质替代其他网络服务提供者向公众提供相关作品的，人民法院应当认定其构成提供行为。在此需要厘清的是，搜索链接服务提供者提供的缩略图、网页快照，是通过复制缓存在搜索链接服务商的服务器中，即使被链网站将相关内容删除，也不影响缩略图、网页快照的存在，网络用户仍然能够看到缩略图、网页快照。因此，本案例的评析与最高人民法院上述规定的提供缩略图、网页快照等网络

行为还是存在区别的。

本案中，幻电公司通过技术手段为涉案节目的传播提供搜索、链接服务，并不存在将作品置于网络中的行为，未直接提供作品，因此幻电公司的链接行为不构成作品提供行为，亦不构成直接侵权。但是，本案中的涉案节目《快乐大本营》系存在年限较长的国内知名综艺节目，上传时间是2014年7月20日，从幻电公司涉案网站上的节目名称"快乐大本营20140719小时代之男神"即应当知道是在首播次日上传的，幻电公司主观上应当知道该节目具有较大侵权可能性，客观上对于未经授权的涉案节目未采取任何预防或者避免侵权发生的措施，从而帮助了涉案节目侵权后果的扩大。因此，幻电公司的行为侵犯了奇艺公司的信息网络传播权，构成侵权。

（撰稿人：陆凤玉　刘乐）

网络服务提供者以及
网络内容提供者的审查认定

——周维海与上海伊游信息科技有限公司、
上海创正信息技术有限公司著作权侵权纠纷案

【提要】

网络服务提供者以及网络内容提供者的审查认定应当对网站的经营业务、网站内容编排、网站宣传信息、自我介绍信息以及盈利模式等综合审查判断，网站使用被控侵权作品系用于网站主营业务，而非仅向公众传播作品，应认定为网络内容提供者。

【案情】

上诉人（原审被告）： 上海伊游信息科技有限公司

被上诉人（原审原告）： 周维海

原审被告： 上海创正信息技术有限公司

案由： 著作权侵权纠纷

一审案号：（2014）普民三（知）初字第 427 号

二审案号：（2015）沪知民终字第 287 号

周维海提交了涉案 37 幅江苏盐城相关旅游景点摄影作品的胶卷底片及数码电子文档，"周为海_新浪博客"（周为海系周维海的笔名）的盐城旅游景点栏下亦发布有该些照片。该 37 幅照片分别为：《净慧寺》《盐都袁氏宅》《盐城新四军纪念馆》《大纵湖旅游景区》《胡乔木故居》《卢秉枢故居》《施耐庵纪念馆 1》《施耐庵纪念馆 2》《董孝贤祠 1》《董孝贤祠 2》《董永墓》《古庆丰桥 1》《古庆丰桥 2》《盐城永宁寺 – 钟楼》《盐城永宁寺 – 茗山老和尚灵位》《盐城永宁寺 – 天王殿》《盐城永宁寺 – 大悲殿》《盐城永宁寺 – 念佛堂》《盐城永宁寺－藏经楼》《盐城紫云山》《范公堤遗址1》《范公堤遗址2》《范公堤遗址3》《范公堤遗址4》《草堰范公堤》《海春轩塔》《枯枝牡丹园1》《枯枝牡丹园2》《盐城陆公祠1》《盐城陆公祠2》《盐城陆公祠3》《大丰麋鹿保护区》《乔冠华故居1》《乔冠华故居2》《三仓烈士陵园－粟裕纪念堂》《息心寺－玉佛楼》《息心寺－万佛塔》。

上海伊游信息科技有限公司（以下简称伊游公司）经营的耳游网系一家旅游资讯网站，为旅游者、旅行社提供语音导游、景点信息等服务，包括国内景点、国外景点、景点分类、旅游线路等栏目。伊游公司的经营范围主要包括：信息技术、网络技术、计算机技术的技术开发、技术转让、技术咨询、技术服务，旅游咨询（不得从事旅行社业务）等。2014年3月18日，登录耳游网上的"景点搜索盐城"，进入相对应的"耳游网盐城景点图文介绍"，在该页面通过点击相应景点，在所进入的页面上可以找到37幅涉案照片。经比对，耳游网上的三十七幅照片、周为海新浪博客上的三十七幅照片与周维海主张的三十七幅涉案作品一致。周维海遂以伊游公司侵犯其著作权为由提起侵权诉讼。

周维海诉称：原告独立创作了《净慧寺》等37幅摄影作品，并将上述作品发表在个人博客上。2014年3月，原告发现两被告未经许可，擅自将上述摄影作品使用在其共同经营的耳游网上（网址为：www.earsgo.com），未署作者姓名，亦未支付报酬。原告认为，两被告的行为已侵犯了原告的著作权，故诉至法院，要求判令：1. 两被告停止侵权；2. 两被告在其主办的耳游网首页刊登声明，就侵权一事向原告公开赔礼道歉、消除影响，时间不得少于一年；3. 两被告赔偿原告经济损失人民币（以下币种相同）110 000元；4. 两被告赔偿原告因诉讼支出的合理费用3200元。审理中，原告提出，鉴于庭后被告已将涉案作品从耳游网上删除，故放弃主张第一项诉讼请求。

被告伊游公司辩称：不同意原告的诉讼请求。1. 对原告享有涉案作品的著作权有异议，原告提供胶卷底片可以翻拍，数码照片可以随处拷贝，博客上发表的涉案作品亦不能证明原告对涉案作品享有著作权。2. 伊游公司系提供信息存储空间的网络服务提供者，原告主张的涉案作品系耳游网会员上传，根据相关法律规定，如权利人认为其服务所涉及的作品侵犯了自己的著作权，应事先告知并出示相关证据，而原告起诉前未与其联系，没有履行事先告知义务，亦未出示相关证据。3. 根据相关法律规定，伊游公司符合网络服务提供者的免责条款。

被告创正公司辩称：1. 不认可原告享有涉案作品的著作权，理由同伊游公司。2. 创正公司没有接到过原告的任何通知。3. 创正公司只是代伊游公司做ICP备案，并不是耳游网的主办单位，没有参与网站的建设、经营。之前创正公司曾为伊游公司提供服务器租用服务，后服务器所有权已变更归伊游公司所有，现仅向伊游公司提供电信托管服务。

【审判】

上海市普陀区人民法院一审认为，摄影作品的著作权属于作者享有。本案中，根据原告提供的涉案作品胶卷底片、数码电子文档、公证书等一系列证据，可以认定涉案作品的作者系原告，其对涉案作品所享有的著作权受我国法律保护。被告伊游公司未经许可，在其经营的耳游网上使用原告的三十七幅涉案作品，未给原告署名，亦未支付报酬，其行为已构成对原告著作权的侵犯，依法应当承担停止侵权、消除影响、赔礼道歉、赔偿损失等相应的民事责任。原告主张被告创正公司亦系耳游网的共同经营者，证据不足，不予采纳。关于伊游公司辩称其系信息存储空间的网络服务提供者，符合网络服务提供者的免责条款的意见：本案中，被告伊游公司所经营的耳游网系一家专业旅游网络营销平台，为旅游者、旅行社提供各类与旅游相关的信息服务，伊游公司虽提供了耳游网后台操作的相关网页截图，但上述证据不足以证明耳游网系提供单纯的信息存储空间服务，故伊游公司未经原告许可，在其经营的耳游网上使用涉案作品的行为构成侵权。即使退一步说，假设伊游公司辩称其系信息存储空间的网络服务提供者的主张成立，根据我国相关法律规定，网络服务提供者为服务对象提供信息存储空间，供服务对象通过信息网络向公众提供作品、表演、录音录像制品，并具备下列条件的，不承担赔偿责任：（一）明确标示该信息存储空间是为服务对象所提供，并公开网络服务提供者的名称、联系人、网络地址；（二）未改变服务对象所提供的作品、表演、录音录像制品；（三）不知道也没有合理的理由应当知道服务对象提供的作品、表演、录音录像制品侵权；（四）未从服务对象提供作品、表演、录音录像制品中直接获得经济利益；（五）在接到权利人的通知书后，根据本条例规定删除权利人认为侵权的作品、表演、录音录像制品。本案中，根据查明的事实，耳游网会员并非实名制注册，用户仅需提供一个真实有效的电子信箱即可注册成功，伊游公司无法提供其主张上传涉案作品会员的真实姓名、身份信息、有效的联系方式；耳游网并非公益性网站，其使用的耳游币可以通过货币兑换取得，网站内提供"广告服务"，部分会员服务系收费服务；伊游公司在接到原告的起诉状和相关证据材料之后，并未立即删除涉案作品，亦未提供相关证据证明其已经将上述材料转送给其主张的上传涉案作品的会员，故即使假设伊游公司系信息存储空间的网络服务提供者的主张成立，其亦不符合免责条款。

综上所述，上海市普陀区人民法院依照《中华人民共和国著作权法》第三条第（五）项、第九条第（一）项、第十条第一款第（二）项、第（十二）项、第二款、第四十七条第（七）项、第四十八条第（一）项、第四十九条，《信息网络传播权保护条例》第十四条、第十五条、第二十二条及《最高人民法院关于审理著作权民事纠纷案件适用法律若干问题的解释》第七条之规定，判决如下：被告伊游公司在"耳游网"（网址为 www.earsgo.com）首页位置连续一个月刊登致歉声明并赔偿周维海经济损失37 000元、合理开支3000元。

判决后，伊游公司不服，提起上诉。

上海知识产权法院二审另查明，耳游网网站网页左上部均显示"全球景点语音导游第一网"字样，在网站"关于我们"栏目中记载：上诉人是一家专业从事旅游电子商务的高新科技创业企业，主要提供全球旅游景点的汉语与英语的语音导游服务。"耳游网"采用先进的信息网络、语音、集成技术率先创立了实时网络语音导游服务，为广大游客提供方便、轻松的语音导游。"产品介绍"栏目记载有：耳游网会员卡、耳游网景点接口服务、耳游网景点语音导览系统。二审法院认为，首先，根据耳游网网站"关于我们""产品介绍"等栏目内容以及其网页名称宣传语等，能够证明伊游公司经营的耳游网是提供景点语音导游等项目的旅游服务网站。其次，涉案图片均出现在相应景点介绍页面的上部，下部是景点的文字介绍，可见该些图片是作为景点介绍的一部分，用于介绍、展示相应景点。伊游公司采用该些图片亦是用于耳游网介绍、展示相应景点，并非仅提供网络空间给网络用户浏览、下载。据此，其经营的耳游网提供的并非著作权法意义上的信息存储空间，其会员上传景点照片是供耳游网介绍、展示景点之用，而非仅仅向公众提供传播作品。遂判决驳回上诉，维持原判。

【评析】

一、关于网络内容提供者和网络服务提供者及其侵权认定

根据我国著作权法规定，信息网络传播权是指以有线或者无线方式向公众提供作品，使公众可以在个人选定的时间和地点获得作品的权利；网络用户、网络服务提供者未经许可，通过信息网络提供权利人享有信息网络传播权的作品、表演、录音录像制品、除法律、行政法规另有规定外，人民法院应当认定其构成侵害信息网络传播权行为；通过上传到网络服务器、设置共享文件、利用文件分享软件等方式，将作品、表演、录音录像制品置于信息网络中，使公

众能够在个人选定的时间和地点以下载、浏览或者其他方式获得的，人民法院应当认定其实施了前款规定的提供行为；网络服务提供者能够证明其仅提供自动接入、自动传输、信息存储空间、搜索、链接、文件分享等网络服务，主张其不构成共同侵行为的，人民法院应予支持。网络服务提供者能够证明其仅提供网络服务，且无过错的，人民法院不应认定为构成侵权。网络服务提供者是否具有过错是认定其是否构成侵权的要件。而网络服务提供者的过错包括对于网络用户信息网络传播权行为的明知或者应知。具体到信息存储空间服务提供者，可以根据网络用户侵权的具体事实是否明显，是否对作品进行编辑、推荐、收取经济利益，是否采取合理措施等综合案件具体情况，认定其应知网络用户侵害信息网络传播权。因此，在信息网络传播权纠纷案件中，首先应当审理调查被诉侵权人是网络内容提供者还是网络服务提供者，也就是被诉侵权行为是网络内容提供行为还是网络服务提供行为，被诉侵权人提供的是网络内容还是网络服务。

二、信息存储空间服务提供者的审查认定

信息存储空间的网络服务提供者是指以自己的服务器为网络用户提供存储空间，允许其上传信息，以供其他网络用户浏览或下载的网络服务提供商，例如 BBS 服务、FTP 服务、个人主页、MSN 空间和个人博客空间等，以实现网络用户信息分享的目的和需求。在审判实践中，信息存储空间服务提供者的审查认定应对网站的经营业务、网站内容编排、网站宣传信息、自我介绍信息、盈利模式、涉诉作品的传播方式等综合审查判断。信息存储空间服务网站一般以提供信息存储空间服务为主要经营内容，其主要是提供信息分享的网络平台，而非提供信息内容，亦不经营其他业务。

三、将网络用户上传的图片用于主营业务宣传的网站经营者不应认定为信息存储空间服务提供者

本案经审查，首先，耳游网网站网页名称宣传语"全球景点语音导游第一网"；"关于我们"栏记载伊游公司是一家专业从事旅游电子商务的高新科技创业企业，主要提供全球旅游景点的汉语与英语的语音导游服务，"耳游网"采用先进的信息网络、语音、集成技术率先创立了实时网络语音导游服务，为广大游客提供方便、轻松的语音导游；"产品介绍"栏目记载耳游网会员卡、耳游网景点接口服务、耳游网景点语音导览系统。这些信息内容能够证明伊游公司经营的耳游网是提供景点语音导游等项目的旅游服务网站，网站上相关景点语音导游的耳游币价格对此亦予以印证。其次，涉案图片均出现在相应景点介

绍页面的上部，下部是景点的文字介绍，可见，该些图片是作为景点介绍的一部分，用于介绍、展示相应景点。即使如伊游公司所述，该些图片系由耳游网会员上传，伊游公司采用这些图片亦是用于耳游网介绍、展示相应景点，并非仅提供网络空间给网络用户浏览、下载。因此，伊游公司经营的耳游网提供的并非著作权法意义上的信息存储空间，其会员上传景点照片是供耳游网介绍、展示景点之用，而非仅仅向公众提供传播作品用于信息分享。因此，伊游公司未经权利人许可，使用传播涉案图片，侵犯了周维海的著作权。

（撰稿人：陆凤玉 杨青青）

实用艺术品的著作权保护

——蓝盒国际有限公司与多美滋婴幼儿食品有限公司等
侵害作品复制权、发行权纠纷案

【提要】

原告蓝盒国际有限公司诉多美滋婴幼儿食品有限公司等四被告侵害作品复制权、发行权纠纷案涉及的产品兼有实用艺术品的美感与实用功能的物理分离和观念分离的问题，判决对此作了仔细的分析阐述。本案不失为一个准确认定实用艺术品并界定其保护范围的典型案例。共同诉讼中的不同被告是否构成共同侵害著作权，应从行为人的主观过错及具体行为诸方面进行考察，法院根据四被告的不同行为分别判令其承担了不同的责任。

【案情】

原告（被上诉人）： 蓝盒国际有限公司

被告： 多美滋婴幼儿食品有限公司（以下简称第一被告或多美滋公司）

被告： 上海乐巢家居用品有限公司（以下简称第二被告或乐巢公司）

被告： 上海爱士图经贸发展有限公司（以下简称第三被告或爱士图公司）

被告（上诉人）： 浙江克虏伯机械有限公司（以下简称第四被告或克虏伯公司）

案由： 侵害作品复制权、发行权纠纷

一审案号：（2014）浦民三（知）初字第 67 号

二审案号：（2015）沪一中民五（知）终字第 30 号

原告系香港公司，2010 年年初，原告打算开发一款价格为 25 美元左右集滑板车、收纳箱、拉杆箱三种功能为一体的中高档骑乘式玩具车，并指派其雇员马汉森进行设计。设计过程中，出于安全考虑，取消了滑板车功能；在动物

形象方面，考虑过老虎、小猴、小猫等动物形象，最后定型为小熊。至2011年1月已完成设计和样品制作，取名为"小熊游乐行李车"。该行李车由一个小熊脸部图案的面板和一个四轮箱体（同时也是车体）两部分组成。面板系熊脸图案，两个眼睛大而圆，左侧脸颊有一个螺旋花纹（表示酒窝），嘴巴歪向右侧脸颊，头顶有两只半圆形耳朵。拉开熊脸面板、放平箱体时，四个轮子着地可作骑乘之用；拉起的面板便可作为龙头，正好方便骑乘的小孩双手把扶住熊耳。合上面板、提起箱体、拉出拉杆，可作滑轮行李箱使用。2011年1月7日，原告与案外人蓝盒东莞公司达成合作协议，约定由蓝盒东莞公司按照原告设计图纸自行或委托第三方生产、销售产品。之后，蓝盒东莞公司授权另一案外人魔石公司为国内"BLUE - BOX"品牌唯一合作商。2011年12月8日，在"2011年香港玩具业杰出成就奖典礼、香港玩具协会银禧誌庆暨执行委员会就职典礼"晚宴上派发的宣传册封面上，"小男孩乘坐游乐行李车"的图片由原告提供，图片上的行李车与涉案产品相同。2012年3—4月，魔石公司参加了北京玩具展，涉案产品是该公司参展商品之一。

2012年8月10日，案外人胡科迪（第四被告员工）向国家知识产权局申请外观设计专利，外观设计名称为玩具拉杆箱，同年12月获得专利证书，证书所附该玩具拉杆箱的视图显示与本案原告的"小熊游乐行李车"外观一致。2012年10月31日，第四被告法定代表人方家定向国家知识产权局申请实用新型专利，实用新型名称为玩具拉杆箱，2013年4月获得专利证书，证书所附说明书及附图显示与本案原告的"小熊游乐行李车"的使用方法和结构一致。

2013年9月，原告将涉案产品向国家版权局申请作品登记，作者马汉森，著作权人为原告。该登记中的版权归属证明载明："该作品属于职务创作，其著作权归单位（公司）所有"，并有马汉森及原告法定代表人的签名和原告的盖章。

2013年1月23日，原告的委托代理人庄婧在广东省深圳公证处公证员的见证下赴深圳市南山区华侨城沃尔玛商场，以普通消费者身份花费740元购买了四罐多美滋奶粉并获赠一辆涉案的"儿童助步车"。经当庭比对，该"儿童助步车"与原告主张保护的"小熊游乐行李车"除配色不同外，在外形结构、用途、小熊形象等方面都几乎完全相同。赠品包装盒上标注的供应商为第二被告，制造商为第四被告。2013年1月29日，庄婧又在公证员见证下，对第二被告网站www.lovhome.com上的"多美滋1000日抵抗力计划"及其下一页面中的"小熊行李车的操作方法视频"等内容及播放过程，进行点击和录像。

2013年9月26日，原告委托代理人倪晔在上海市东方公证处公证员见证下对案外人魔石公司员工姜湘雯电脑中的相关电子邮件进行保存提取。邮件的主要内容为：2012 年 4 月 5 日至 11 日，姜湘雯与案外人辽宁某公司员工孙艳曾就 3 万件"小熊游乐行李车"进行过洽谈，单价为 98 元。姜湘雯所发送的产品信息中，该商品市场零售价为 349 元。同日及 2013 年 11 月 4 日，倪晔又在公证员见证下，对姜湘雯的邮箱内容和腾讯 QQ 聊天记录内容进行了保存提取，公证处分别制作了两份公证书。内容主要是：姜湘雯，账号 1653502643，QQ 名为"im Maggie（magic stone）"或"魔石（上海）Maggie"，于 2012 年 3 月 28 日、7 月 11 日、8 月 24 日与"FRANK‐爱士图"（周敏林 Frank 上海乐巢家居用品有限公司 上海爱士图经贸发展有限公司地址：上海市徐汇区虹梅路 2007 号 1 号楼 8F 电话：021‐60406051 传真：021‐60406021 QQ：1710209702 邮箱：frank@ lovhome. com）的聊天记录。分别是：姜湘雯向"FRANK‐爱士图"成功发送文件"魔石产品介绍. ppt"；姜湘雯向"FRANK‐爱士图"成功发送文件"样品单‐爱士图 120711. xls"；"FRANK‐爱士图"回传签收单显示"今收到魔石（上海）贸易有限公司的样品如下：……小熊游乐行李车……数量 2，借样公司：上海爱士图经贸发展有限公司（及公司电子公章），样品签收人：FRANK ZHOU"等内容。

2014 年 2 月 28 日，原告的委托代理人倪晔向法院申请调查令，向上海市社会保险事业管理中心调取了周敏林的《单位职工参加城镇基本养老保险情况》，调查结果显示"2011 年 7 月至今，上海爱士图经贸发展有限公司为周敏林交纳社会保险，其中 2012 年 6 月离职，2012 年 7 月返回。"另，原告提供的周敏林名片上的信息，与前述公证书中显示的"周敏林""Frank"的信息相同，并同时标注了第二、第三被告的信息。

原告诉称，其于 2010 年 2 月指派雇员设计了"小熊游乐行李车"的玩具，次年推向市场。该玩具是实用艺术品，著作权由原告享有。2012 年，原告在上海的代理商案外人魔石（上海）贸易有限公司（以下简称魔石公司）参加了北京玩具展，该玩具是参展商品之一。2013 年 1 月，原告发现第一被告为其销售的多美滋奶粉提供赠品"儿童助步车"，该车整体设计及视觉效果与原告的"小熊游乐行李车"几乎完全相同，尤其是最显著部分的面板设计。该"儿童助步车"的包装还显示，第二被告为供应商，第四被告为制造商。原告又发现第二被告与第三被告为关联公司，第三被告曾让其员工周敏林向魔石公司索取"小熊游乐行李车"产品介绍并于 2012 年 7 月 13 日取得样品两件。原告认为，其"小熊游乐行李车"是著作权法保护的立体艺术作品，原告对其整体享有著作权。第二被告通过第三被告获得样品后委托第四被告复制，并提供给第一被告发行，四被告共同侵犯了原告的著作权，故请求判令：四被告立即停止侵权、连带赔偿原告经济损失人民币（以下未标注币种的均为人民币）50 万元及因调查、制止侵权行为所花费的合理费用15万元。

【审判】

上海市浦东新区人民法院经审理认为：美术作品是我国著作权法保护的对象，本案涉案产品既有具观赏性的动物图案，又有可供骑乘、储物、拖行的实用功能。且作为图案的美感部分具有独创性并达到了相当的高度，并能与实用功能在不同的使用方式下，分别从物理上和观念上分离，符合实用艺术品的特征。我国著作权法对实用艺术品作为美术作品保护，但保护的范围仅限于实用艺术品中具有艺术美感、构成美术作品的部分，著作权法不保护实用功能。因此，本案中，涉案产品作为一个实用艺术品，我国著作权法对其保护的范围应是其中熊脸面板即熊脸图案部分，而不是整个"小熊游乐行李车"。

涉案产品的熊脸图案，是马汉森为完成原告交给的工作任务所创作的职务作品，马汉森与原告签署的版权归属证明明确了涉案作品的著作权归原告所有，故涉案作品的著作权属于原告。原告系香港法人，涉案作品也在香港创作完成，但原告享有著作权的作品所附着的产品通过合作商的推广，已在大陆市场公开，即作品已在我国大陆地区公开发行，故原告有权依据《中华人民共和国著作权法》主张保护。

本案涉及的权利作品是原告主张的"小熊游乐行李车"上的熊脸图案，涉及的侵权作品是被告一方的"儿童助步车"上的熊脸图案。经比对，两者几乎完全相同。结合原告在先完成设计、创作涉案产品的事实，可以认定后者是对前者的复制。涉案侵权产品由第四被告生产后销售给第二被告，再由第二被告销售给第一被告，第一被告又通过附赠方式发送到消费者手中。故第四被告未经原告许可复制、发行了原告作品，直接侵害了原告的著作权，应承担停止侵权、赔偿的民事责任。鉴于第二、第三被告及其与周敏林的关系，第二被告应当知道周敏林获取的原告产品及相关信息，但仍然批量购进侵权产品并销售给第一被告，故第二被告对其发行行为主观上有过错，应承担相应的民事责任。原告主张第二被告与第四被告共谋侵权，但未提供证据，因不能排除第四被告从其他途径获取原告产品信息的可能，故不采纳原告要求第二被告就本案承担连带赔偿责任的主张。由于第二被告的侵害发行权行为以第四被告的复制、发行行为为基础，故第四被告对此有过错，应就此与第二被告承担连带责任。第三被告虽有获取原告产品的行为，但其让第二被告获知原告产品信息的行为尚不构成著作权侵权，故不支持原告要求其承担民事责任的诉请。第一被告购买侵权产品用作赠品，侵害了原告的发行权，应承担停止侵权的民事责任，但该产品有明确具体的生产者，尚难以认定第一被告具有明知或应知其为侵权商品的主观过错，故第一被告关于其附赠品有合法来源的抗辩成立，原告要求第一被告就本案承担连带赔偿责任的诉讼请求，法院不予支持。

综上所述，上海市浦东新区人民法院判决：第一、第二被告立即停止侵害原告对"小熊游乐行李车"之"熊脸图案"作品享有的发行权；第四被告立即停止侵害原告对"小熊游乐行李车"之"熊脸图案"作品享有的复制权、发行权；第二被告赔偿原告经济损失 5 万元、合理开支 1.5 万元，第四被告对此承担连带责任；第四被告赔偿原告经济损失 20 万元、合理开支 6 万元；驳回原告其余诉讼请求。

一审判决后，第四被告不服，提起上诉。

上海市第一中级人民法院经审理认为，原审判决认定事实清楚，适用法律正确，程序合法，所作判决并无不当。上诉人的上诉理由缺乏事实和法律依据，应予驳回。依照《中华人民共和国民事诉讼法》第 170 条第 1 款第（1）项的规定，判决：驳回上诉，维持原判。

【评析】

本案涉及实用艺术品的认定及保护范围，以及本案四被告是否构成共同侵权及其各自责任问题。因此，本案的主要争议焦点：一是原告主张对涉案产品的著作权保护是否成立，若原告该主张成立，法律保护的范围有多大；二是若原告主张作品权利的诉请成立，其对四被告主张的侵权责任诉请能否获得支持。

一、关于涉案产品是否受我国著作权法保护及其保护范围

本案涉及实用艺术品的保护问题。我国《著作权法》并未明确规定是否对实用艺术品予以著作权保护。但我国加入的国际条约《伯尔尼公约》允许成员国以著作权法保护实用艺术品。我国在《实施国际著作权条约的规定》中，也明确要求对外国实用艺术品进行保护。在我国的著作权法行政执法和司法实践中，也适用著作权法予以保护。只是对其的保护是有限度的，限度之一体现于实用艺术品的保护条件，也即实用艺术品的认定条件；限度之二体现于对实用艺术品的保护范围。这主要是为了更符合著作权法的基本原理，并且严格体现不同法律制度的功能界限。

关于实用艺术品的认定条件，一般认为应当符合以下几个条件：一是实用艺术品中的实用功能与艺术美感能相互独立；二是独立的艺术设计具有独创性；三是艺术设计达到了一定的艺术高度。本案涉案产品既有具观赏性的动物图案，

又有可供骑乘、储物、拖行的实用功能，且图案的独创性和艺术美感达到一定的高度，符合实用艺术品的特征。一是涉案产品的实用功能和艺术美感能够相互独立。涉案产品由滑轮游乐车车身（同时也是滑轮行李箱箱体）与熊脸面板（同时也是游乐车龙头）两部分组成，从整体上说，它是个具有实用功能的玩具，但它的熊脸图案的面板又有较强的艺术美感。作为滑轮行李箱时，其具有实用功能的箱体与具有艺术美感部分的熊脸面板，从物理上可以区分并相互独立。熊脸面板拉起后，滑轮行李箱变成了可供幼童骑乘的滑轮游乐车，相应地，熊脸面板就成了游乐车的龙头，即具备了游乐车龙头的功能。此时，龙头和车身（即行李箱箱体部分）从物理上仍可分离，但龙头部分本身，既有熊脸图案，又有龙头实用功能，两者是融为一体的。从物理上难以分离，但可以从观念上分离。因为龙头设计成其他动物形象或其他图案、甚至没有图案，都不会影响龙头的实用功能。二是能够独立存在的艺术美感部分的设计具有独创性，并且美感达到了一定的艺术高度。涉案产品上的熊脸面板，是个立体塑胶材质的小熊头部图案，是对小熊形象的卡通化、艺术化表达。熊脸图案中灵动的眼珠、一边脸上的酒窝及歪向另一边的嘴巴等的设计，使得小熊显得俏皮活泼，易获儿童喜爱。不仅体现了创作者的独创性，而且达到了较高的艺术水准，整个熊脸图案已经构成一件美术作品。

关于实用艺术品受著作权法保护的范围。基于著作权法不保护实用功能的基本原理，著作权法对实用艺术品的保护范围是有限度的。我国著作权法对实用艺术品作为美术作品保护，但保护的范围仅限于实用艺术品中具有艺术美感、构成美术作品的部分。因此，本案中，涉案产品作为一个实用艺术品，我国著作权法对其保护的范围应是其中熊脸面板即熊脸图案部分，而不是整个"小熊游乐行李车"。

设置实用艺术品的认定条件、限定著作权法对其的保护范围，是为了更好地体现著作权法的功能，并厘清与外观设计专利制度的界限。本案的判决对实用艺术品的认定条件和著作权法对实用艺术品的保护范围做了详细的分析和准确的界定，较好地把握了著作权法的制度功能。

二、四被告的行为定性及责任承担

原告主张，第三被告骗取原告产品后，由第二被告提供给第四被告复制、发行，第二被告购买后再将侵权产品发行给第一被告，第一被告再通过附赠方式发行。故四被告是共同侵权，应承担共同侵权的连带责任。法院经审理对四被告的行为进行了分别定性和定责。

根据法院查明的事实，涉案侵权产品由第四被告生产后销售给第二被告，再由第二被告销售给第一被告，第一被告又通过附赠方式发送到消费者手中。侵权商品的走向是清楚的，但四被告的行为定性及责任并不那么容易确定。尤其是原告要求法院认定四被告具有侵权的共同故意并判令四被告承担连带责任的诉请，对法院来说认定和支持的难度更大。原因在于：一是共同故意的主观心理状态认定难度本来就大。二是侵犯无形财产的知识产权侵权行为和侵犯有形财产的侵权行为具有不同的特点。有形财产的权利载体具有唯一性，因此对行为人的主观过错和具体行为的参与度容易认定；而知识产权这类无形财产的权利载体呈现多重性，权利人接触权利载体并不当然与侵权行为有关，法律也规定了一定情形下的免责。因此，在知识产权侵权判定中，行为人的过错及行为参与度认定难度较大。

本案中，第四被告的行为比较明确，其责任也容易认定。因其是侵权商品的源头，还应对商品的后续流通承担责任。故法院不仅判决其承担自己侵害复制权、发行权的民事责任，还对第二被告的侵害发行权行为承担连带责任。第一被告作为侵权商品的发行者，必须首先承担停止侵权的责任，至于是否承担其他责任，则应根据案件中查明的事实作出判断。本案第一被告通过第二被告采购商品的情况，尚不足以认定其明知或应知该商品为侵权商品，故适用免责条款不承担赔偿责任。

较难认定的是第二被告和第三被告的行为与责任。原告的证据虽足以证明第二、第三被告是具有紧密关联关系的公司，周敏林获取原告样品的行为及其与第二、第三被告的关系也已查清，但还不能就此认定第二被告与第三被告、第二被告与第四被告有共同的侵权故意。根据现有证据，因本案中发现的侵权行为晚于原告产品在国内市场公开的时间，不排除第四被告从其他途径接触并获取原告产品相关信息的可能，难以认定第二被告直接提供了样品给第四被告。但法院足以把周敏林作为一个接触点，认定第二被告通过此接触点获取了原告产品及相关信息，以此为据认定第二被告从第四被告处购买侵权商品时负有更为谨慎的审查注意义务，其未履行该义务却批量购进侵权产品并销售，故需承担侵权责任。而第三被告虽有获取原告产品的行为，但仅凭第二被告通过其获知原告产品信息，尚不能认定第三被告的行为构成著作权侵权，故原告主张其应就本案承担民事责任的观点，也缺乏事实依据。

（撰稿人：陈惠珍）

判定美术作品间是否构成
实质性相似的基本方法

——艾影（上海）商贸有限公司诉上海丫丫信息科技有限公司等
侵害作品复制权、改编权纠纷案

【提要】

认定被控侵权作品是否剽窃权利人的美术作品过程中，判定作品间是否构成实质性相似是司法实践中的难点。为解决该问题，本案中提出了以下三个步骤：一、如原告主张被控侵权作品剽窃了其作品中的局部，则该局部越是原告作品的精华部分，越是独创性程度高的部分，那么被判定侵权的可能性越大。二、以抽象－过滤－对比测试法为主要的检验方法，在适当考察原、被告作品的基础上，首先确定两者在线条、形状、明暗与色彩等要素的相同或相似之处，然后剔除其中属于思想的部分，再审查剩余要素中是否存在属于公有领域的范围，最后仅仅根据过滤后受保护的相同或相似部分，来综合判断两者是否构成实质性相似。三、再通过整体比较法，将两者整体进行比对，判断两者是否构成实质性相似。

【案情】

原告：艾影（上海）商贸有限公司（以下简称艾影公司）

被告：上海丫丫信息科技有限公司（以下简称丫丫公司）

被告：上海壹佰米网络科技有限公司（以下简称壹佰米公司）

案由：侵害作品复制权、改编权纠纷案

一审案号：（2014）浦民三（知）初字第 1097 号

二审案号：（2015）沪知民终字第 614 号

上海市浦东新区人民法院经审理查明：《哆啦 A 梦》漫画于 1969 年 12 月 1

日在日本首次出版，其中的"哆啦 A 梦"卡通形象为一只猫型机器人，造型特征为头大且圆，身体相对较小，两只眼睛呈圆形挨在一起长在头和脸的分界线，鼻子也呈圆形紧挨在眼睛下，嘴巴很大几乎横跨整个脸，左右各有三根猫须，脖子上有项圈，还有一个铃铛，肚子上有一个大口袋，手为圆形，脚为椭圆形，身后有个球形的尾巴（详见附图 1）。"哆啦 A 梦"卡通形象在全球具有一定知名度，同时在"哆啦 A 梦"中文动画片及出版物中还会使用"哆啦 A 梦"的美术体图形，该图形的笔画为蓝色，笔画较为粗圆，在四个字底部均有一个红色椭圆，"啦"字上方的一点以"哆啦 A 梦"卡通形象中的黄色铃铛替代，"梦"字中的一撇一捺以两只微笑眨眼的眼睛替代，整个字体外有黑色描边（详见附图 2）。原告艾影公司经"哆啦 A 梦"卡通形象著作权人授权，取得了在中国大陆地区以原告名义就"哆啦 A 梦"卡通形象进行及拓展商品授权业务，并在发生侵权行为需要时采取法律等行动的权利。

两被告共同经营"叮咚小区"应用软件，其在宣传推广该软件时使用了"叮咚小区"应用软件图形及文字图形。该应用软件图形为正方形，但四个角为圆边，该图形由四部分组成，上方以上弧线区分隔出红色部分，下方为蓝色部分，在蓝色部分中有一个白色半圆，在红色与蓝色部分间有一个黄色平面门铃，门铃上有蓝色描边（详见附图 3）；"叮咚小区"的文字图形字体较粗圆并为蓝色，还带有蓝色描边，在"咚"与"小"两字间的上方有一个与"叮咚小区"应用软件图形中一致的黄色门铃（详见附图 4）。

被告壹佰米公司与上海创想力营销策划有限公司于 2014 年签订了《叮咚小区品牌建设服务合同》，约定壹佰米公司委托该公司对"叮咚小区项目"进行品牌诉求、品牌广告语及品牌相关设计等工作。被告丫丫公司在"叮咚小区"微信公众号文章中称"3 月 21 日，'叮咚小区'正式上线。与此同时，其蓝白色调的 LOGO 覆盖了上海的各大轨交站点。这样的标识很容易让大家联想到万能的机器猫'小叮当'。而'叮咚小区'也恰如机器猫的百宝袋，将水电煤抄表、收费、号码百事通、宠物配对、论坛交流、周边商户优惠、二手市场买卖、拼车、家政等服务全部囊括在内。"

原告诉称，两被告共同开发、经营的"叮咚小区"应用软件在广告宣传中擅自使用了"哆啦 A 梦"形象的诸多要素特征，两被告行为侵犯了原告对"哆啦 A 梦"卡通形象以及"哆啦 A 梦"文字图形所享有的复制权及改编权。故诉请法院判令两被告：1. 立即停止使用"哆啦 A 梦"形象要素特征；2. 在《法制日报》上发表声明，澄清事实，消除影响；3. 赔偿原告经济损失人民币 200 万元及合理支出 5 万元。

审理中，原告明确，其主张权利的作品为：1."哆啦 A 梦"卡通形象的身体躯干部分，包括了红色项圈（狭长形）、黄色铃铛（两个小半圆，上小下大，中间双线隔开，下半圆有一黑线表示铃铛倾斜 180 度），白色腹部（大半圆）、口袋（半圆）以及蓝色身体等独创性要素（即附图 1 中的躯干部分）；2."哆啦 A 梦"文字图形（即附图 2），该文字图形字体偏胖，部分字的部首、笔画变形为椭圆圆，四个字的最后一笔变形为四个椭圆圆并在一条线上，"啦"字的右上方有一个倾斜 135 度的黄色小铃铛，"梦"字中间有一双呈现笑容的眼睛，文字整体以蓝色为基调色，并进行了白色描边，给人以憨态可掬、引人发笑的感觉，符合了"哆啦 A 梦"卡通形象的性格特征。原告指控两被告的"叮咚小区"应用软件图形（即附图 3）及"叮咚小区"文字图形（即附图 4）分别与原告主张的上述两作品构成实质性相似，因此构成侵权。

被告丫丫公司辩称：涉案的"叮咚小区"应用软件并非由其运营，因此其与本案无关，故请求驳回原告诉请。

被告壹佰米公司辩称：著作权侵权认定应以保护作品的独创性为原则，而"哆啦 A 梦"卡通形象的独创性体现在其整体形象，尤其是头、身子、胡须等要素，这些要素构成了该作品的独创性，而不是原告所主张的项圈、铃铛、口袋等要素；同时，色彩、视角、形状以及审美习惯所支配的艺术法则等是不受著作权保护的，对该些部分，原告无权主张权利；本案中被告的"叮咚小区"应用软件图形在构图、细节的具体表达上具有独创性，与原告的"哆啦 A 梦"卡通形象中的"猫"的形象完全不同；"叮咚小区"的文字图形系由被告独立创作，与"哆啦 A 梦"的文字图形不构成实质性相似，因此，原告所主张的著作权侵权行为不成立；故请求驳回原告全部诉请。

【审判】

上海市浦东新区人民法院经审理认为：原告经权利人授权，可就所涉"哆啦 A 梦"卡通形象著作权侵权行为提起诉讼。但在本案中，没有充分证据证明原告已取得"哆啦 A 梦"文字图形的相关著作权权利，并可向两被告就该文字图形主张著作权侵权。

就"叮咚小区"应用软件图形与"哆啦 A 梦"卡通形象的躯干部分是否构成实质性相似的问题，法院认为，原告主张权利的"哆啦 A 梦"卡通形象的躯干部分独创性较低，就其与"叮咚小区"应用软件图形已经剔除了思想以及公有领域部分的相同及相似之处判断分析，尚不足以构成实质性相似。同时，原、被告作品间存在着较多的不同之处与较大的视觉差异，如对原告作品予以保护，将妨碍他人在法律保护范围内的创作自由。

就两被告所使用的"叮咚小区"文字图形与"哆啦A梦"文字图形是否构成实质性相似的问题，法院认为，两被告所使用的"叮咚小区"文字图形与"哆啦A梦"文字图形的相同及相似之处均属美术作品创作的公有领域范围，不具有独创性，且两者间还存在较大的视觉差异，因此两者不构成实质性相似。

综上所述，原告不能举证证明其取得了"哆啦A梦"文字图形美术作品的相关著作权权利以及维权权利，两被告所经营的"叮咚小区"应用软件图形以及使用的"叮咚小区"文字图形与原告主张权利的"哆啦A梦"卡通造型的躯干部分以及"哆啦A梦"文字图形亦不构成实质性相似，因此两被告行为不构成对上述作品复制权的侵害。同时，两被告的作品也非基于原告作品所创作产生的新作品，因此也未侵害原告对作品享有的改编权。基于两被告行为不构成著作权侵权，故对原告的全部诉讼请求，应予驳回。法院遂根据《中华人民共和国著作权法》第十条第一款第（五）项、第（十四）项、第十一条之规定，判决：驳回原告全部诉讼请求。法院判决后，原告艾影公司提起上诉，后于二审中撤诉。

【评析】

对美术作品间涉嫌剽窃的认定，一般遵循"接触"＋"实质性相似"的标准。对"接触"的认定而言，原告只需要证明其作品完成于被控侵权作品之前，且被告存在接触原告作品的可能性即可，在实践中较易为法官判断认定。但对作品间是否构成"实质性相似"的认定，实践中存在诸多检测方法，因认定过程受限于法官个体对作品表达认知的差异，检测方法、判断尺度的不同，且并无客观标准依据，故始终是司法实践中的难点，较易产生争议。

在长期的司法实践中，就作品间构成实质性相似的比对，主要采取了两种检测方法，第一种方法是抽象－过滤－对比测试法，即对作品进行抽象与剥离，形成不同的抽象层次，将构成思想的普遍性模式剔除，仅就剩下的受保护因素进行比对。第二种方法是整体比较法，即不作任何筛选的将两个作品进行比较，基于整体的印象与感觉判断两者是否构成实质性相似。对上述两种方法加以分析，可以发现前者比对方法更为抽象、严格，可能会导致不利于版权保护的效果。后者则基于整体感官及印象，可能将部分属于思想的要素抑或公有领域的内容带入比对，因此会导致扩张版权保护的倾向。因此，两者各有依据，又各有利弊，如何合理使用这两种检测方法，力求在版权保护与推动新的创作之间达到平衡，值得探讨、研究。

本案中，原告主张两被告使用的"叮咚小区"应用软件图形与"哆啦A梦"卡通形象的躯干部分，以及"叮咚小区"文字图形与"哆啦A梦"文字图形均构成实质性相似，由此得出两被告构成著作权侵权的结论。"哆啦A梦"的卡通形象在"叮咚小区"应用软件推广之前即早已发表，且全球知名，因此两被告存在接触"哆啦A梦"卡通形象的可能性当无争议。因此对两者进行比对，判定是否构成实质性相似就是本案审理的主要争议焦点。法院在对上述作品进行比对时，按如下步骤进行了判定：

一、如果需要认定被控侵权作品剽窃了原告主张权利作品中的局部，则该局部越是原告作品的精华部分，独创性程度越高，那么被判定侵权的可能性越大

与其他类似案件比较，本案的特点在于原告主张被告作品与其"哆啦A梦"卡通形象的躯干部分构成实质性相似，而并非与"哆啦A梦"整体的卡通形象构成实质性相似。因此法院分析认定，对"哆啦A梦"卡通形象而言，其表现的是憨态可掬又机智过人的"哆啦A梦"的猫型机器人造型，而蓝、白色构成的圆脸、圆眼睛、红鼻子、左右各三条猫须以及没有耳朵的猫脸造型无疑是该美术作品中最具有独创性的部分，集中体现了作者所要表达的该猫型机器人憨态可掬、机智过人的特质。而较之猫脸造型部分，"哆啦A梦"躯干部分的独创性不高，其红色项圈、白色口袋、黄色铃铛以及蓝色身体的要素均较为常见，线条亦不复杂。单独将"哆啦A梦"的躯干部分剔出展示，无法完整表达出作者对该猫型机器人所要追求的艺术形象和审美效果。因此，"哆啦A梦"卡通造型的躯干部分作为美术作品的一部分，其独创性水平较低。因此如需认定被告作品构成侵权，则需课以更高的实质性相似标准。

二、以抽象–过滤–对比测试法为主要的检验方法

比较"哆啦A梦"卡通形象的躯干部分与两被告的"叮咚小区"应用软件图形的相同与相似之处，两者在颜色上均选取了红、蓝、黄、白共四种颜色，因这四种颜色的组合易给人带来美观、可爱、平和等视觉感受，故这四种颜色的选择、组合在美术作品中尤其是卡通形象创作中大量存在，如柯南、超人、唐老鸭等卡通形象中即包含了上述颜色的全部组合或大部分组合。因此对原告而言，该选择要素并不具有创造性，不能为其垄断。在构图上，"哆啦A梦"卡通形象的躯干部分表现为在脖颈位置上戴了一个项圈，项圈上系了一个铃铛，铃铛下方为圆形腹部及半圆形口袋，其他为身体部分，整体上是一个卡通化的人的身体躯干造型。"叮咚小区"应用软件图形则采用了目前应用软件图形普遍所使用的正方形，且四个角为圆角。分析两者相同或相似的要素，"哆啦A梦"卡通形象躯干部分下方存在一个半圆形口袋，"叮咚小区"应用软件图形下方亦存在一个半圆，但半圆形口袋或者半圆形本身并不具有独创性，以半圆形这种极为简单的艺术形式来表达口袋应当属于公有领域范围，不能为原告所独占。"哆啦A梦"卡通造型躯干部分的红色项圈与"叮咚小区"应用软件图形红色的上半部分存在相似，但这种选择极为简单且平常，不具有独创性，不能为原告所垄断。"哆啦A梦"卡通造型躯干部分的蓝色身体与"叮咚小区"应用软件图形的蓝色背景相似，但以蓝色为背景亦是美术作品中惯常使用的方法，不具有独创性。

三、以整体比较法为次要检测方法

法院认定，在整体视觉效果上，两者还存在较多的不同之处：(1)在色彩的选取上，"哆啦A梦"卡通形象的躯干部分腹部及腹部上的口袋部分均为白色，而"叮咚小区"应用软件图形下部仅有白色半圆，白色半圆的背景为蓝色。同时"哆啦A梦"卡通形象的躯干部分有黑色描边，而"叮咚小区"应用软件图形色块间均没有黑色描边，两者的视觉效果不同；(2)在构图上，在两者的上半部分，"哆啦A梦"卡通形象躯干部分为狭长形项圈，且在项圈上有圆形铃铛，"叮咚小区"应用软件上半部分则以上弧线划出，且比"哆啦A梦"形象中的项圈更宽，在上弧线中间有一个圆形门铃，该门铃亦与"哆啦A梦"中的铃铛形状完全不同。同时，"哆啦A梦"卡通形象的躯干部分中存在圆形腹部部分，"叮咚小区"应用软件图形中则不存在相应的部分。因此，两者就构图部分存在大量不同，造成了两者视觉差异明显；(3)就两者所使用的线条而言，"哆啦A梦"卡通形象的躯干部分线条相对柔和、圆润，体现了"哆啦A梦"憨态可掬的特质。"叮咚小区"应用软件图形中的线条则多以规范的直线、圆形等呈现，体现的是该应用软件所要表达的简洁明了的意思，因此两者在线条的使用上亦存在显著不同；(4)最为重要的是，就两者的整体视觉效果而言，也存在着较大的差异。"哆啦A梦"卡通形象的躯干部分多出了白色圆形腹部部分，而该部分在整个画面中占了较大的比例，再加上圆且偏胖的身体，形成了一个微胖可爱的猫型机器人身体的整体视觉效果，而"叮咚小区"应用软件图形则是一个普通的带圆角正方形，两者明显不同。两者居中的黄色圆形部分，一个是有立体效果的铃铛，另一个则是平面效果的门铃，在视觉效果上显著不同，而该部分是两者各自最为体现作品独创性的部分。这些不同要素最终造成的整体视觉效果差异是，"哆啦A梦"卡通形象的躯干部分给观者的感受是在表达一个带着项圈、挂有铃铛并有口袋的憨态可掬的猫型机器人身体，而"叮咚小区"应用软件图形则给观者带来有着笑脸、门铃，寓意着在小区愉悦、方便生活的感受，但不会令人产生这是一个猫型机器人身体的视觉效果。

由此法院得出最后结论，原告主张权利的"哆啦A梦"卡通形象的躯干部分独创性较低，就其与"叮咚小区"应用软件图形已经剔除了思想以及公有领域部分的相同及相似之处判断分析，尚不足以构成实质性相似。同时，原、被告作品间存在着较多的不同之处与较大的视觉差异，如对原告作品予以保护，将妨碍他人在法律保护范围内的创作自由。

四、当作品较为简单时，可以整体比较法为主要检测方法

相对前述两作品，"哆啦A梦"文字图形与"叮咚小区"文字图形内容相对简单，因此主要以整体比较法检测判定两者是否构成实质性相似。法院认为，比对"叮咚小区"文字图形与"哆啦A梦"文字图形，两者间相同及相似之处在于均使用了蓝、黄两色、字体粗圆且有描边。在文字图形中使用蓝、黄色，粗圆的字体以及对字体加以描边，意图表现的是憨厚、可爱以及平和、宁静的视觉效果，这些元素都是文字图形创作中通常所使用的方法，不具有独创性，属于公有领域的范围，所有人都可以自由使用。同时两者间还存在以下较大的不同之处："哆啦A梦"文字图形的四个字下部均有红色椭圆、"梦"字里包含了一对微笑并在眨眼的眼睛，而"叮咚小区"文字图形中并不存在上述要素；"叮咚小区"文字图形在"咚"字与"小"字间的上方居中位置有一个黄色平面造型门铃，"哆啦A梦"文字图形的"啦"字上方有一个黄色立体造型铃铛等。因此，两者在细节以及整体上的视觉差异亦较大，故不构成实质性相似。

综上所述，就本案的实际案情，法院在对原、被告作品的实质性相似比对时，首先区分了原告主张作品的局部是否是原告作品的精华部分及其独创性程度的高低，其次以抽象-过滤-对比测试法为主要的检验方法，以整体比较法为次要的检验方法，克服两种检验方法的各自局限性，力求做到在版权保护与推动创作间取得平衡，最后得出两者不构成实质性相似的结论，取得了良好的审判效果。虽对作品间构成实质性相似因个案案情的不同，不能一概以上述方法作检验，但本案的审理无疑为该类案件的审理提供了一定的思路。

（撰稿人：杨捷）

附图1

附图2

附图3

附图4

涉嫌侵权作品的有限保护与限制

——殷文君与上海徐汇区思源教育培训中心侵害作品署名权、复制权、获得报酬权纠纷案

【提要】

作者未经在先权利人同意，批量引用在先创作作品进行再创作，由此产生的"作品"会导致著作权与在先权利之间的交叉或冲突，但著作权法并未剥夺对此类"侵权演绎作品"的保护资格。如果"侵权演绎作品"与已被生效判决认定为侵权作品相比，除去涉嫌侵权部分内容外，具有一定的独创性，构成著作权法意义上的作品，仍应当予以保护，但在计算赔偿额时应有所差别。

【案情】

原告（被上诉人）： 殷文君

被告（上诉人）： 上海徐汇区思源教育培训中心

案由： 侵害作品署名权、复制权、获得报酬权纠纷

一审案号：（2013）徐民三（知）初字第 936 号

二审案号：（2015）沪一中民五（知）终字第 14 号

2011 年 8 月 23 日，原告殷文君与中国福利会出版社签订图书出版合同，约定出版作品为《拼拼玩玩快乐识字》，出版字数 8000 字。

2011 年 9 月，《拼拼玩玩快乐识字》教材由中国福利会出版社第一次出版，编著为殷文君，字数为 10 千字，定价为 80 元（共五册），该教材前三册为《拼玩识字》，第四册为《汉语拼音》，第五册为《硬笔书法》。

上海徐汇区启航进修学校于 2001 年 8 月 13 日经上海市徐汇区民政局批准成立登记，于 2009 年 8 月 3 日经上海市徐汇区民政局及上海市徐汇区社会团体管理局批准更名为上海市徐汇区思源培训中心（以下简称思源培训中心），开

办资金 60 万元，业务范围为中等非学历教育。被告思源培训中心用于经营少儿教育的网站为 www.siyuanchild.com，其经营有徐汇校区、龙柏校区、大华校区、浦东八佰伴校区、南方校区 5 个校区，上述校区均开设拼玩识字、汉语拼音及硬笔书法课程。

原告殷文君系闻广学校的创办人之一，其于 2013 年 4 月委托闻广学校的同事李晴川及徐玲分别前往被告龙柏校区及南方校区报名拼玩识字、汉语拼音及硬笔书法课程，并缴纳了相应费用，获得了被控侵权识字教材、汉语拼音教材及硬笔书法教材。

2009 年 5 月 14 日，案外人陈淑红、宇永权起诉闻广学校，主张闻广学校使用的拼拼玩玩快乐识字教材（以下简称闻广教材）抄袭其编著的《拼玩识字》。同年 11 月 6 日，上海市浦东新区人民法院认定，案外人陈淑红、宇永权的课本 8673 字，闻广教材 4197 字，闻广教材使用案外人课本 4004 字，比例为 95.4%，构成侵权，并作出（2009）浦民三（知）初字第 153 号民事判决书，上海市第一中级人民法院于 2010 年 1 月 12 日维持该判决，业已生效。

原告主张权利的《拼玩识字》与闻广教材均系为教导幼儿识字所编写的教材，其主要内容均是为每个汉字编写一句特定的儿歌进行解读，二者的差异为课程分配及识字顺序并不相同。原告《拼玩识字》共有 80 个小时的课程，含有针对 521 个汉字所编写的 521 句儿歌，其中 265 个汉字在闻广教材中亦有出现。该 265 个汉字对应的 265 句儿歌中共有 18 句儿歌的内容完全一致，原告确认其中的 12 句儿歌其不享有著作权，对应汉字为"尖、晶、多、李、庄、奈、宵、选、叽、他、转、剃"，其余 6 句儿歌其主张为原创，对应汉字为"舌、乒、乓、兵、右、凡"。二者教材在其余 247 句儿歌的表达上存在一定差异，主要分为以下几种类型，一是表达基本相同，但个别词语有增添或替换；二是表达相似，但部分使用词语不相同；三是主要含义及表达均不相同。其中第一种、第二种类型的儿歌共有 208 句，第三种类型的儿歌共有 39 句。

被控侵权识字教材亦为教导幼儿识字所编写的教材，与原告主张权利的《拼玩识字》教材相比较，二者在课程分配及识字顺序上并不相同。从主要内容来看，被控侵权教材共有 31 页，涉及儿歌 276 句，其中第 9 页内容与第 11 页重复。审理中，原告主张被控侵权教材中有 127 句儿歌构成侵权。在该 127 句儿歌中，有 5 句儿歌系重复出现，有 117 句儿歌内容与原告教材完全相同，有 10 句儿歌内容与原告教材相似。结合前述原告教材与闻广教材的比对内容来看，这 10 句儿歌中，汉字"仇"在闻广教材中并无涉及，其余汉字除"果"外，对应儿歌均属于原告教材与闻广教材表达相同或相似的类型。在 117 句内容完全相同的儿歌中，有 7 句系原告认可其不享有著作权的部分，有 61 句儿歌对应汉字未在闻广教材中出现，另有 49 句儿歌对应的汉字在闻广教材中有涉及，结合前述原告教材与闻广教材的比对内容来看，其中有 43 句儿歌属于原告教材与闻广教材表达相同或相似的类型，有 6 句儿歌属于原告教材与闻广教材表达不相同的类型。

原告主张权利的《汉语拼音》与被控侵权汉语拼音教材的比对，两份教材均系为教导幼儿学习汉语拼音所编写的教材，在主要内容上，二者均是围绕韵母、声母、鼻音等音节进行编写，在教材页面布局、课程分配及选字内容上，二者基本相同。原告《汉语拼音》教材共有 36 页，涉及词语约 500 个左右，被控侵权汉语拼音教材共有 34 页，涉及词语与原告教材大致相同，仅有 32 处不同。

原告主张权利的《硬笔书法》与被控侵权硬笔书法教材的比对，两份教材均系为练字设计的练习本，在页面布局上，二者均采用遍布方格，第一竖排及部分横排印刷练习汉字的方式进行排列，在排列顺序上，二者均通过对横、竖、点、撇等基本笔画到结构字形的扩展选择文字展开练习。原告《硬笔书法》共 20 页，涉及笔画及汉字 146 个，并附有前页"硬笔书法练习册——初级班"，主要为对写字姿势及执笔方法的介绍。被控侵权硬笔书法教材共 19 页，涉及笔画及汉字 136 个，无前页。原告《硬笔书法》选用方格为"米字格"，被控侵权硬笔书法教材选用方格为"田字格"，二者所选用的字体亦不相同。在汉字的选择及编排上，被控侵权教材共有 30 个笔画或汉字的选择与原告教材不一致，占被控侵权教材选字总数的 22.06%，有 12 个笔画或汉字的顺序与原告教材排列不一致，占被控侵权教材选字总数的 8.82%。

原告殷文君诉称，原告编著有《拼拼玩玩快乐识字》教材一套（共 5 册），由中国福利会出版社于 2011 年 9 月出版，其中前 3 册为《拼拼玩玩快乐识字》，后 2 册分别为《拼拼玩玩快乐识字 汉语拼音》及《拼拼玩玩快乐识字 硬笔书法练习本》。被告思源培训中心未经原告许可，擅自将原告上述作品用作思源培训中心的教材，主要表现为，将原告《拼玩识字》精华部分改编为其识字教材，将原告《汉语拼音》仅作细微改动改编为其汉语拼音教材，将原告《硬笔书法》翻印为其硬笔书法教材。被告在其经营的上海 5 家校区内使用上述教材，获得了巨大利润，侵害了原告就《拼拼玩玩快乐识字》教材享有的署名权、复制权及获得报酬权，故诉至法院，要求判令：1. 被告立即停止侵权；2. 被告在《解放日报》《文汇报》《新民晚报》、被告网站 www.siyuanchild.com 以及被告徐汇校区、龙柏校区、大华校区、南方校区、浦东八佰伴校区的公告栏上刊登声明，向原告赔礼道歉、消除影响；3. 被告赔偿原告经济损失人民币 100 000 元（以下币种均为人民币）；4. 被告赔偿原告合理开支 13 779 元（包含律师费 5000

元、报名费 8319 元，复印费 360 元，交通费 100 元）。

被告思源培训中心辩称，第一，涉案教材不能构成作品，原告亦不享有涉案教材的著作权。涉案教材主要为汉字拼写、拼音等内容，系教学中惯常采用的方式方法，已进入公知领域，并无独创性，原告不能就此主张著作权。原告是闻广学校的教师，涉案教材系职务作品，即使有著作权也应当属于闻广学校。另外，涉案教材来源于闻广学校的教材，而该教材已被生效判决认定侵权。因此，涉案教材不构成作品，原告就涉案教材并不享有著作权。第二，被告具备自行编写教材的师资力量，并未使用被控侵权教材，原告提供的证据亦无法证明被控侵权教材系从被告处获得。第三，即使被告存在原告主张的侵权行为，因涉案教材出版已久、出版册数不多等，也未对原告造成实际损失，原告主张的经济损失金额没有依据。综上，请求驳回原告全部的诉讼请求。

【审判】

上海市徐汇区人民法院经审理后认为：从汉字的选择、编排来看，《拼玩识字》形成的具有差异性的特殊组合，具备了一定的独创性；从主要内容及对汉字注释的儿歌来看，作者从汉字的字形、读音或含义等方面进行的释义，《拼玩识字》亦体现出作者独创性的内容，是作者智力成果的凝聚。根据原告教材与闻广教材的比对结果，《拼玩识字》教材中占比为 56.62% 的儿歌具备了独创性，能够认定《拼玩识字》构成了新作品，至于该教材是否侵害他人著作权，非本案审理范畴，法院不作评价，亦不影响原告向侵害其著作权的当事人主张权利。《汉语拼音》《硬笔书法》，通过对拼音音节进行注解及词组、笔画结构、执笔方法等进行编排、归纳，具有一定的独创性。因此，《拼拼玩玩快乐识字》教材通过作者的选择、编注而形成，体现了作者的思想，具有一定独创性的表达，并能以有形形式复制，属于我国著作权法律规定的作品，应当受到保护。该教材出版时标明的作者为原告殷文君，在被告未能提出相反证据的情况下，法院认定原告殷文君是《拼拼玩玩快乐识字》教材的作者，对上述作品享有著作权。被告无证据证明其在日常教学活动中使用自行编纂的教材，一并考量原告获得被控侵权教材的过程有相应证人证言及票据予以佐证，并且原告获得的被控识字教材与被告持有的原件一致，可以认定被控侵权教材系从被告处取得，被告在日常经营活动中使用了被控侵权教材。在原告主张被告侵权的 127 句儿歌中，有 62 句儿歌未在闻广教材中出现，7 句儿歌与闻广教材表达不同，而上述儿歌在被控侵权教材中的表达均与原告教材构成相同或近似，因此被控侵权教材中共有 69 句儿歌侵害了原告的著作权。对于原告主张侵权的其余 58 句儿歌，因原告对该部分内容缺乏独创性，与其构成实质性相似的闻广教材相应内容已被生效判决认定侵权，原告不能就此主张权利，因此被控侵权教材中有 25% 的内容与原告享有著作权的儿歌相同或近似，已经超出了巧合的程度，故法院认定，被控侵权识字教材中的该部分内容侵害了原告对《拼玩识字》享有的著作权。其次，关于被控侵权的汉语拼音教材及硬笔书法教材，被控侵权教材在内容布置上均与原告教材构成实质性相似，故法院认定被告使用的汉语拼音及硬笔书法教材均侵害了原告享有的著作权。被告思源培训中心未经原告许可复制原告作品内容，用于日常经营活动，且未标注作者名称，侵害了原告享有的署名权、复制权以及许可他人以上述方式使用作品并获得报酬的权利，应当停止侵权。考虑到被告侵权行为的影响范围以其教学活动所涵盖范围为限，故刊登声明的范围限于被告网站 www.siyuanchild.com 即可。对于原告要求消除影响的诉讼请求，因原告并未提交证据证明其个人声誉及社会评价因侵权行为遭受了损害，故法院对该项诉请不予支持。

综上，上海市徐汇区人民法院依照《中华人民共和国著作权法》第十条第一款第（二）项、第（五）项、第二款、第十一条第四款、第四十七条第（五）项、第（七）项、第四十八条第（一）项、第四十九条、《中华人民共和国著作权法实施条例》第二条、《中华人民共和国侵权责任法》第十五条第一款第（一）项、第（六）项、第（七）项、第二款、《最高人民法院关于审理著作权民事纠纷案件适用法律若干问题的解释》第二十五条第一款、第二款、第二十六条的规定，判决：一、被告上海徐汇区思源教育培训中心于本判决生效之日起立即停止侵害原告殷文君对《拼拼玩玩快乐识字》教材享有的著作权；二、被告上海徐汇区思源教育培训中心于本判决生效之日起连续 72 小时在 www.siyuanchild.com 网站首页上刊登声明，向原告殷文君赔礼道歉（声明的内容须经法院审核，如不履行，法院将在相关媒体上公布本判决的主要内容，费用由被告上海徐汇区思源教育培训中心负担）；三、被告上海徐汇区思源教育培训中心于本判决生效之日起十日内赔偿原告殷文君经济损失及合理开支合计人民币30 000元；四、驳回原告殷文君的其余诉讼请求。

一审判决后，被告思源教育培训中心不服，提起上诉。

上海市第一中级人民法院受理后，因上诉人逾期未缴纳上诉费用，裁定按上诉人自动撤回上诉处理，一审判决现已生效。

【评析】

本案我们所要讨论的保护侵权作品并不是针对在先著作权人权利受到侵害

的情形，而是针对第三人使用侵权作品时，该侵权作品是否能够受到著作权法保护及在何种程度上受到著作权法的保护。

一、具有独创性的"侵权作品"，亦构成作品

根据《中华人民共和国著作权法实施条例》规定，著作权法所称作品是指文学、艺术和科学领域内具有独创性并能以某种有形形式复制的智力成果。该条款对于我国著作权法保护的对象作出了规定，能够受到著作权法保护的必须是作品。因此，我们首先需要判断的是，作者主张保护的侵权作品是否能够构成著作权法意义上的作品。

侵权作品应当是指作品的创作或使用侵犯了他人在先权利的作品，包括但不限于通过侵害他人在先知识产权等手段所创作的作品。此类作品分两种情形，一种是完全剽窃或抄袭他人作品而形成的侵权作品，其缺乏作者本身的独创性，不能够构成我国著作权法意义上的作品，即将被侵犯的作品从侵权作品中抽除，其本身就不能成为作品，当然不能受到著作权法保护。另一种是非完全剽窃或抄袭他人作品，而是在他人作品基础之上进行了创作，其使用他人在先作品已超出了合理引用的范围，但除去该引用部分，侵权作品亦有其作者独立创作的部分，甚至亦可能单独构成作品，对于该种侵权作品，应当认定存在着作者一定的独创性行为，可以构成著作权法上的作品。

一般来说，知识产权法保护的是智力劳动成果，上述侵权作品一方面侵犯了他人的在先著作权利，另一方面该侵权作品中也存在作者的独创性的劳动。本案中，原告主张保护的《拼玩识字》是以汉字选择、编排及联想记忆的解读方式形成的幼儿识字教材，由每个汉字的儿歌按一定顺序排列组合而成，其中的连贯性并不强，按照汉字字形或个人记忆、解读方式的不同，均可能产生不同的汉字选择或组合方式，并且为每个汉字所编写的一句儿歌本身亦包含作者的独创性内容，在原告主张权利作品与在先作品比对认定后，有 56.62% 的儿歌具备了独创性，说明其主张保护作品的一半以上内容均具有独创性，属于侵权作品的第二种情形。如将该部分内容进行编排，能够形成与在先作品完全不一致的新作品，因此，不能仅因作者主张保护作品中含有部分侵权内容，就完全否定该作品。

二、属于作品的"侵权作品"的保护程度

作者自己能否以及以何种方式对作品进行利用，与其获得著作权并无关系，而是取决于法律是否有禁止性规定。给予侵权作品以著作权法保护，并不意味着该侵权作品的作者可以随意利用该侵权作品，因为这必然侵犯他人的著作权，

而仅意味着他人不能随意使用该作品，否则会构成对演绎者的侵权。

从鼓励创作角度看，这种侵权作品存在着作者的独创性行为，在有第三人侵害到该侵权作品相关著作权利时，应当予以保护，故本案被告在经营中使用的识字教材有 25% 内容与原告享有独创性的内容相同或近似的情况下，亦侵害了原告就侵权作品享有的相应著作权利。

从社会公益角度看，此类侵权作品与一般独立创作的作品毕竟有所不同，其所包含的作者的独创性程度较低，且毕竟有为谋取某种利益而批量使用他人在先作品的行为，对其的保护理应有所限制。对于此种情况下的第三人侵权，在计算赔偿额时，不能与完全独立创作的作品等量齐观，判决赔偿损失的金额应当酌情予以减少。

（撰稿人：袁杨）

侵害作品改编权的界限以及
相关宣传行为性质的认定

——完美世界（北京）软件有限公司与上海野火网络科技有限公司等
侵害作品改编权纠纷、虚假宣传纠纷、其他不正当竞争纠纷案

【提要】

改编权是改变作品，创作出具有独创性的新作品的权利。改变作品，一般是指在不改变作品内容的前提下，将作品由一种类型改变成另一种类型。游戏作品是否构成对文字作品的改编，关键在于游戏所展现的人物、人物关系、故事情节发展与文字作品是否构成实质性相似。在构成改编权侵权的情况下，由于游戏作品中确实包含有相关文字作品的元素，故利用相关文字作品的内容对外宣传，并不构成虚假宣传，但仍可能构成不正当竞争。

【案情】

原告（上诉人）： 完美世界（北京）软件有限公司
被告（被上诉人）： 上海野火网络科技有限公司
被告（被上诉人）： 福建博瑞网络科技有限公司
被告（被上诉人）： 广州爱九游信息技术有限公司
被告（被上诉人）： 福建游龙网络科技有限公司
案由： 侵害作品改编权纠纷、虚假宣传纠纷、其他不正当竞争纠纷
一审案号：（2015）杨民三（知）初字第 55 号
二审案号：（2016）沪 73 民终 39 号

2010 年 12 月，广州出版社与花城出版社共同出版发行了《射雕英雄传》《神雕侠侣》《倚天屠龙记》《笑傲江湖》四部作品的第 2 版纸质版书籍，在上述书籍的封面、扉页等位置标注有作者署名为"金庸"，作品为"金庸著"。在

上述书籍的勒口位置印有对金庸的简介，内容为"本名查良镛……"

2002年1月1日，查良镛将《金庸作品集》（包括《射雕英雄传》《神雕侠侣》《倚天屠龙记》《笑傲江湖》在内的十二部作品）在中国境内除以图书形式出版发行本作品简体字中文版本以外的其他专有使用权授予明河社出版有限公司，合同自2002年1月1日在香港签订时生效，至双方达成书面解除协议时止。

2013年4月8日，明河社出版有限公司出具许可书，载明查良镛有权将作品《射雕英雄传》《神雕侠侣》《倚天屠龙记》《笑傲江湖》的移动终端游戏软件改编权，以及改编后游戏软件的商业开发权（包括但不限于游戏软件的开发、制作、发行、宣传、运营、信息网络传播等，以及基于游戏软件的衍生产品的开发、制作、销售等），独家授权完美世界（北京）软件有限公司（以下简称完美世界公司）。

2013年4月30日，查良镛与原告完美世界公司就涉案四部作品分别签订《移动终端游戏软件改编授权合约》，约定改编权授予方查良镛将上述作品的移动终端游戏软件改编权授权给原告，原告有权开发移动终端游戏软件并在世界各地区以各种语言（日本除外）制作、宣传和运营该"改编软件"。原告取得中国大陆地区的独家改编权利的期限均为3年。

2014年5月16日，原告的委托代理人王平来到北京市方圆公证处，申请对查看《六大门派》游戏界面的过程进行保全证据公证：进入"http：//www.6damenpai.com/"，进入"六大门派官网"首页页面，下载安装安卓版的"六大门派"游戏，进行演示操作；在中国版权保护中心网站中进行查询，显示名为"六大门派OL软件"的计算机软件的著作权人为"上海野火网络科技有限公司"，登记日期为2014年5月5日；在"多游网"中有名为"手机游戏《六大门派》封测感恩 武侠造梦也疯狂""无限潜力《六大门派》贸易体系解析"的新闻，新闻显示"由上海野火发行的首款追溯级即时制武侠手游《六大门派》自5月8日开测以来受到众多玩家的追捧……近千用户再次急速涌入游戏二服……游戏开测仅仅4天，已知消耗的元宝数已超过二十多亿，相当于2亿多的人民币啊……"。上海野火网络科技有限公司（以下简称野火公司）当庭承认，涉案游戏由其单独运营，www.6damenpai.com是其网站。

2014年12月16日，上海市华诚律师事务所委托代理人余梦菲来到上海市东方公证处，通过公证处电脑上网进行如下操作：点击进入"http：//www.6damenpai.com/"网站的"新闻中心"网页，在该网页中点击发布于2014年11月1日的"90年我们都记得《六大门派》里的谁"，内容为"飞雪连天射白鹿，笑书神侠倚碧鸳……《倚天》几个版本中，马景涛版是最早被我们熟知和接受的一版⋯⋯说起'哥哥'，那么83版《射雕》中黄日华所饰演的靖哥哥，则是我们童年中的最经典之一⋯⋯"；在"新闻中心"网页点击发布于2014年10月27日的"怀旧90年代《六大门派》我的印象"，内容为"⋯⋯古风武侠《六大门派》传承经典，为玩家还原一个真实的江湖，你可以像无忌那样练就绝世神功，也可以像郭大侠那样保卫襄阳，甚至可以师承东方祸乱江湖⋯⋯加入《六大门派》，激荡人心的江湖之旅现在起航"；在"新闻中心"网页点击发布于2014年7月23日的"武侠大乱斗《六大门派》集侠体系"，内容为"相信凡是看过经典武侠小说的玩家，都会有着自己心目中喜欢的英雄人物或是讨厌的人物，比如说浪荡不羁、重情重义的令狐兄，或是亦正亦邪、一曲荡魂的黄大夫，抑或是刚烈狠毒、令人不齿的灭绝老尼，又或是不择手段、有点傻笨的金轮喇嘛，而在《六大门派》中，玩家可以肆意选择挑战这些名动江湖的英雄好汉⋯⋯"；在"《六大门派》封测期间游戏资料库"页面点击"门派介绍"，显示其对少林寺的介绍为"有着'天下武学出少林'的美誉，是武林中的泰山北斗，镇派绝学易筋经"，对武当派的介绍为"武当派为一代宗师张三丰所创，与少林并称武林中的泰山北斗，其下弟子以侠义著称，更有武当七侠享誉江湖，镇派绝学太极拳、太极剑"，对峨嵋派的介绍为"由大侠郭靖之女郭襄所创，镇派绝学九阴九阳功"；在网站首页点击"加关注"链接，显示该游戏微博账号为"六大门派OL"，粉丝人数为61 590人，微博数量为176，微博认证为"上海野火网络科技有限公司"，简介为"手游《六大门派》"。

　　原告对安卓版"六大门派"游戏的界面、游戏过程、充值信息等进行保全证据公证：1. 登录"www. 6damenpai. com"下载安装名为"六大门派"的应用程序，在使用该程序中进行充值，交易信息显示收款信息为"上海野火网络科技有限公司"；2. 登录"www. miitbeian. gov. cn"，查询显示网站"196手游"的主办单位名称为"福建游龙网络科技有限公司"（以下简称游龙公司），在该网站下载涉案游戏并充值，交易信息显示收款信息为"福建游龙网络科技有限公司"；3. 下载安装"91助手"，进入"91助手"搜索安装"六大门派"应用程序，在充值后，交易信息显示收款信息为"福建博瑞网络科技有限公司"（以下简称博瑞公司）；4. 下载安装"九游"软件，进入"九游"搜索安装"六大门派"应用程序，在充值后，交易信息显示收款信息为"广州爱九游信息技术有限公司"（以下简称爱九游公司）。原告同时查看了涉案游戏在各平台的下载量。

　　经比对，原告主张的四部作品与《六大门派》游戏在内容、人物、人物关系、情节发展等方面的相似程度各有不同：

1. 根据原告提供的公证游戏过程，《六大门派》游戏情节与《笑傲江湖》文字作品前七章基本一致，《笑傲江湖》第七章之后的内容在原告提交的公证的游戏过程中未有体现。

涉案游戏中出现了以下文字作品的主要人物：华山派有君子剑岳不群、宁中则、大师兄令狐冲、二师兄劳德诺、小师妹岳灵珊等；恒山派有定逸师太、仪琳等；嵩山派有左冷禅、费彬等；青城派有余沧海、罗人杰、余人彦等；曲阳、曲非烟、不戒和尚等、林平之等。涉及的武功主要有华山剑法、太岳三清峰、夺命连剑、独孤九剑、紫霞神功。

2. 《倚天屠龙记》中与本案相关的人物和事件

《倚天屠龙记》中重要的线索屠龙刀第一次出现于海沙派与海东青的争夺中。而灭绝师太与明教结仇的原因在于灭绝师太的师兄孤鸿子与明教光明左使杨逍比武，为了确保胜算向灭绝师太借倚天剑，剑未出鞘就被杨逍夺去，杨逍将倚天剑掷地而去，孤鸿子被气死。

涉案游戏中出现了以下《倚天屠龙记》文字作品的主要人物：峨嵋派弟子周芷若、张三丰及其七个弟子、宋远桥之子宋青书、灭绝师太、明教光明左使杨逍等。涉及的武功有武当剑法、武当心法，峨嵋派的武功有峨嵋剑法、飘雪穿云掌、峨嵋心法、截手九式、灭剑剑法、绝剑剑法。

3. 《射雕英雄传》和《神雕侠侣》与本案相关的人物和事件

从原告公证的游戏过程来看，襄阳战场游戏场景中以列表方式出现的芙儿、大武、小武、耶律兄、郭大侠、蓉儿等人名。

另查明，2014年5月5日，野火公司经国家版权局审核，就名称为"六大门派OL手机网络游戏软件【简称：六大门派OL软件】V1.0"的软件取得了计算机软件著作权登记证书，开发完成日期为2014年4月11日。

原告完美世界公司诉称：原告取得了《射雕英雄传》《神雕侠侣》《倚天屠龙记》《笑傲江湖》四部作品在中国大陆地区的移动终端游戏软件之独家改编权，并有权以自己的名义，在授权期限内，采取任何合法手段追究任何第三方的侵权行为及不正当竞争行为的责任。2014年5月，原告发现被告野火公司在未经合法授权的情况下，自行开发了一款名为《六大门派》的手机游戏进行封测，该游戏大量使用了上述作品中的独创性表现元素。此外，野火公司还在其官方网站对《六大门派》的宣传中大量使用了与金庸作品有关的元素。其余三被告也参与了《六大门派》手机游戏的实际运营，并从中获利。综上所述，请求判令：1. 四被告立即停止侵犯金庸著作权的行为；2. 四被告立即停止违反诚实信用原则的不正当竞争行为以及虚假宣传的不正当竞争行为；3. 被告一刊登声明，消除不利影响；4. 四被告共同赔偿原告包括合理费用在内的经济损失共计10 200 000元。

被告野火公司辩称：1. 野火公司独立创作完成了涉案游戏，并于2014年4月11日取得了该游戏的著作权登记证书，野火公司将其享有完整著作权的游戏置于其服务器上运营，并没有实施原告所诉称的侵害著作权的行为；2. 野火公司没有侵害涉案四部金庸作品的改编权，原告诉称的改编行为应当是指在文字作品的基础上对原作品的故事情节和脉络进行游戏方面的改动，但涉案游戏中不存在明确的故事情节；3. 野火公司从未对外宣传涉案游戏是改编自金庸作品，且原告没有证据证明涉案游戏挤占了其市场份额，野火公司没有实施改编和虚假宣传的不正当竞争行为；4. 涉案游戏是野火公司运营的，其余几个被告没有运营游戏；5. 原告与金庸签订的《著作权许可使用合同》约定付款后生效，原告不能证明其已经支付了许可使用费从而享有涉案四部作品的游戏改编权。

被告博瑞公司辩称：1. 涉案游戏并非博瑞公司开发，博瑞公司也没有参与该游戏的运营，没有实施著作权侵权及虚假宣传行为；2. 作为平台商，博瑞公司无法判断涉案游戏是否侵犯他人著作权，野火公司将涉案游戏上传至博瑞公司运营的平台时提供了该游戏的著作权登记证书，博瑞公司只能根据该证书进行核实，没有证据能证明博瑞公司知道或者应当知道涉案游戏是侵权作品；3. 原告在起诉前没有向博瑞公司发出过任何有关侵权的提醒或者其他函件，博瑞公司不存在主观的故意或者过失。

被告爱九游公司辩称：1. 爱九游公司不是游戏的运营方，没有实施任何侵害著作权的行为或者不正当竞争行为；2. 在涉案游戏被上传至爱九游公司运营的平台时，爱九游公司要求野火公司提供了相应的著作权证书，已尽合理审查义务，且涉案游戏的名字是《六大门派》，而非以金庸的小说名称命名，爱九游公司不存在明知或者应知涉案游戏涉嫌侵权的可能；3. 爱九游公司的九游平台为涉案游戏提供了两项技术服务：一是提供一个账号系统；二是为游戏提供充值通道。充值通道是代收费，收益最终由野火公司享有；4. 在涉案游戏运营中，爱九游公司没有收到来自原告的任何权利或者侵权方面的通知。

被告游龙公司书面答辩称：1. 金庸对《六大门派》游戏中相关门派名称以及相关历史人物名称不享有著作权，中国武侠门派及相关人物是真实存在的，并非金庸所创；2. 野火公司已经取得该游戏软件的著作权，游龙公司无法判断游戏软件是否会侵犯第三人的合法权益，只能依赖于野火公司提供的计算机软件著作权登记证书进行判断，已经尽到了合理的审查义务，不存在任何主观过错；3. 游龙公司仅为玩家提供充值的通道，并未获利，不应承担侵权责任。

【审判】

上海市杨浦区人民法院经审理认为：查良镛是《射雕英雄传》《神雕侠侣》《倚天屠龙记》《笑傲江湖》文字作品的作者，享有四部文字作品的著作权。原告经授权，取得了涉案四部作品在中国大陆地区的移动终端游戏软件改编权以及改编后游戏软件的商业开发权独家授权，并有权在授权期限内对任何第三方擅自使用该等作品的侵权或不正当竞争行为追究责任。

从人物、故事情节、细节等因素来看，被告野火公司未经许可擅自将《笑傲江湖》改编成游戏侵害了原告完美世界公司享有的独家游戏改编权及运营改编后的游戏的权益。从原告公证书展现的《六大门派》游戏内容来看，对于《倚天屠龙记》文字作品相关元素的使用主要体现为武当派张三丰、宋远桥等人物名字和人物之间的关系相同，以及灭绝师太的师兄孤鸿子被杨逍气死的事件相同。但是从构成改编最重要的故事情节及脉络发展来看，现有的《六大门派》游戏公证内容没有体现出与《倚天屠龙记》文字作品相同的故事情节。而对于《射雕英雄传》和《神雕侠侣》，公证的《六大门派》游戏内容中仅在襄阳战场游戏场景中以列表方式出现的丐帮诸长老、芙儿、大武、小武、耶律兄、郭大侠、蓉儿等人名，亦未出现与《射雕英雄传》和《神雕侠侣》文字作品相同的故事情节。因此，现有证据不能证明《六大门派》游戏构成对《倚天屠龙记》《射雕英雄传》和《神雕侠侣》的改编。

《六大门派》游戏确实使用了涉案四部文字作品的相关要素，因此被告野火公司对外以涉案四部文字作品的元素进行宣传不构成虚假宣传。但是被告野火公司在《六大门派》游戏中整体上将四部小说予以糅合，同时在游戏的对外宣传中使用金庸小说元素，对完美世界公司开发运营相关游戏产生不利影响，抢夺属于原告的玩家群体，构成不正当竞争。

被告博瑞公司运营的"91助手"软件平台、被告爱九游公司运营的"九游"软件平台、被告游龙公司的www.19196.com网站均系提供软件上传、存储、下载的平台，其难以对所有上传的软件逐一进行实质性审查，且被告野火公司开发的《六大门派》游戏已取得计算机软件著作权登记证，现有证据不能证明被告博瑞公司、爱九游公司、游龙公司有帮助被告野火公司实施侵权行为的故意，该三被告已尽合理注意义务，不应承担赔偿责任。

综上，上海市杨浦区人民法院依照《中华人民共和国反不正当竞争法》第二条、第二十条，《中华人民共和国著作权法》第十条第一款第（十四）项、第二款、第四十八条第（一）项、第四十九条，《中华人民共和国民事诉讼法》

第一百四十四条之规定，判决：一、被告上海野火网络科技有限公司就其实施的侵权行为在其网站首页上端连续 72 小时刊登声明，消除影响；二、被告上海野火网络科技有限公司于本判决生效之日起十日内赔偿原告完美世界（北京）软件有限公司经济损失及合理费用合计500 000元；三、驳回原告完美世界（北京）软件有限公司的其他诉讼请求。

一审判决后，原告提出上诉后撤回上诉，一审判决已经生效。

【评析】

在保留原作品基本表达的情况下，通过改编原作品创作新作品，这是著作权法意义上的改编。故判断是否构成改编，关键在于两者所展现的人物、人物关系、故事情节发展是否构成实质性相似，在司法实践中并没有形成一个普遍的标准。在构成改编权侵权的情况下，被告的行为是否构成不正当竞争，亦需要法官针对不同案件情况具体分析。本案的审理关键在于认定四被告是否实施了侵犯原告享有的独占游戏改编权的行为、是否实施了不正当竞争行为，法院在审理中遵循以下审判思路：

一、侵害作品改编权界限的认定

著作权法并不保护抽象的思想，其保护的是以文字、音乐、美术等有形的方式对思想的具体表达。对于《射雕英雄传》《神雕侠侣》《倚天屠龙记》《笑傲江湖》四部作品而言，其是从一个总的主题思想，衍生出具体的故事情节，最后以具体的文字所表达出来，这是一个从思想到表达、从抽象到具体的渐变过程。改编权指改变作品，创作出具有独创性的新作品的权利。所谓改变作品，一般是指在不改变作品内容的前提下，将作品由一种类型改变成另一种类型。本案中，涉案《六大门派》游戏是否构成对上述四部作品的改编权侵权，关键在于认定其所使用的元素是原文字作品的思想还是表达，即游戏所展现的人物、人物关系、故事情节发展与文字作品是否构成实质性相似。

首先，从人物角度来看。（2014）京方圆内经证字第 11748 号公证书中，《六大门派》游戏中华山派的人物有师父君子剑（岳不群）、师娘宁女侠（宁中则），华山弟子：大师兄令狐冲、二师兄劳德诺、梁发、施戴子、高根明、陆大有、陶钧、英白罗、舒奇、小师妹岳灵珊，剑宗成不忧。与《笑傲江湖》文字作品中的人物名字完全相同。在原告完美世界公司发出侵权函后，从（2014）沪东证经字第 20218 号公证书公证的过程来看，被告野火公司将游戏中的人物名称略做改动，但也仅为同音字替换，如成不忧改为程不忧，或名字前后顺序的调换，如劳德诺改为劳诺德、施戴子改为戴施子等，同时该公证书显示游戏中出现的人物还包括曲阳、曲菲菲，嵩山派左冷禅、费冰，恒山派定逸大师、仪林，衡山派莫掌门、刘正枫、项大年，青城派于人炎、余人壕、罗仁杰，福威镖局林总镖头、少主小林子，采花贼伯光。上述人物名称除同音字替换外，与《笑傲江湖》文字作品中的人物名称在呼叫上基本相同，同时人物之间的相互关系，如师徒关系、师兄关系、对手关系、好友关系也与《笑傲江湖》文字作品一致。

其次，从故事情节发展来看。如前文所述，原告完美世界公司公证的《六大门派》游戏的情节主要包括福威镖局少主小林子因打抱不平杀死青城派于人炎、青城派为夺辟邪剑谱灭福威镖局、令狐少侠从采花贼伯光手下救走恒山派仪林、衡山派刘正枫（风）金盆洗手、嵩山派指责刘正枫与魔教曲阳勾结血洗刘门、刘正枫被曲阳救走、嵩山派费冰杀曲阳孙女曲菲菲、莫掌门杀死费冰，上述情节与《笑傲江湖》文字作品前七章的情节发展基本相同。

最后，从细节设计来看。《六大门派》游戏中福威镖局少主小林子杀死于人炎的原因是于人炎调戏萨老头的孙女、青城派拿从福威镖局掠得的财物送给刘正枫作为贺礼、令狐少侠为救仪林设计与伯光坐斗、令狐少侠为刺激仪林先行离开谎称自己见了尼姑就倒霉，上述的细节设计也与《笑傲江湖》文字作品相同。

因此，从现有证据来看，《六大门派》游戏构成对《笑傲江湖》文字作品前七章的改编。因原告完美世界公司经授权享有对《笑傲江湖》在中国大陆地区的独家游戏改编权及公开发表和运营改编软件的权利，因此被告野火公司的行为构成对原告完美世界公司上述权利的侵害。

对于原告完美世界公司指控的《六大门派》游戏构成对《倚天屠龙记》《射雕英雄传》和《神雕侠侣》的改编。本院认为，从原告公证书展现的《六大门派》游戏内容来看，对于《倚天屠龙记》文字作品相关元素的使用主要体现为武当派张三丰、宋远桥、俞莲舟、殷梨亭、莫声谷、宋青书，峨嵋派灭绝老尼、丁敏君、纪晓芙、周芷若，明教杨道，少林派觉远的人物名字和人物之间的关系相同，以及灭绝师太的师兄孤鸿子被杨道气死的事件相同。但是从构成改编最重要的故事情节及脉络发展来看，现有的《六大门派》游戏公证内容没有体现出与《倚天屠龙记》文字作品的相同的故事情节。而对于《射雕英雄传》和《神雕侠侣》，公证的《六大门派》游戏内容中仅在襄阳战场游戏场景中以列表方式出现丐帮诸长老、芙儿、大武、小武、耶律兄、郭大侠、蓉儿等人名，亦未出现与《射雕英雄传》和《神雕侠侣》文字作品相同的故事情节。因此，现有证据不能证明《六大门派》游戏构成对《倚天屠龙记》《射雕英雄传》和《神雕侠侣》的改编。

二、对相关宣传行为性质的认定

被告野火公司在《六大门派》游戏中对《笑傲江湖》《倚天屠龙记》《射雕英雄传》和《神雕侠侣》四部文字作品相关要素的使用，构成对原告完美世界公司的不正当竞争。

首先，虚假宣传是指经营者利用广告或者其他方法，对商品的质量、制作成分、性能、用途、生产者、有效期限、产地等作引人误解的虚假宣传。如前所述，《六大门派》游戏确实使用了涉案四部文字作品的相关要素，因此被告野火公司对外以涉案四部文字作品的元素进行宣传不构成虚假宣传。

其次，原告完美世界公司从查良镛处获得的授权包括以作品名称、故事、人物、武功、地名为蓝本，参考改作为专供移动终端用户使用的游戏软件，以及公开发表和运营"改编软件"的权利。同时被授权对于使用涉案四部文字作品的侵权和不正当竞争行为有权追究侵权责任。因此，尽管《六大门派》游戏不构成对《倚天屠龙记》《射雕英雄传》和《神雕侠侣》三部文字作品的改编，但是被告野火公司在《六大门派》游戏中整体上将四部小说予以糅合，将经典元素、桥段、人物使用于《六大门派》游戏中，同时在游戏的对外宣传中提及"马景涛所饰演的无忌绝对是我们童年中不能被替代的永久经典回忆"、"那么83版《射雕》中黄日华所饰演的靖哥哥，则是我们童年中的最经典之一"、"那个丰神如玉，爱憎分明的男子也不会被超越，这就是观众对于古天乐版《神雕》的评价"、"古风武侠《六大门派》传承经典，为玩家还原一个真实的江湖，你可以像无忌那样练就绝世神功，也可以像郭大侠那样保卫襄阳，甚至可以师承东方祸乱江湖……加入《六大门派》，激荡人心的江湖之旅现在起航"、"浪荡不羁、重情重义的令狐兄，或是亦正亦邪、一曲荡魂的黄大夫，抑或是刚烈狠毒、令人不齿的灭绝老尼，又或是不择手段、有点傻笨的金轮喇嘛，而在《六大门派》中，玩家可以肆意选择挑战这些名动江湖的英雄好汉"。上述宣传结合游戏内容会吸引《笑傲江湖》《倚天屠龙记》《射雕英雄传》《神雕侠侣》文字作品的爱好者成为《六大门派》游戏的玩家，抢占市场，抢夺属于原告完美世界公司的玩家群体，对完美世界公司开发运营相关游戏产生不利影响，扰乱市场正常的经济秩序，因此被告野火公司的行为构成对原告完美世界公司的不正当竞争。

三、本案中网络服务提供者的责任认定

被告博瑞公司运营的"91助手"软件平台、被告爱九游公司运营的"九

游"软件平台、被告游龙公司的 www.19196.com 网站均系提供软件上传、存储、下载的平台，三被告均属于网络服务提供者。判断网络服务提供者是否构成侵权，关键在于其是否为他人实施的侵权行为提供了帮助，使他人直接实施侵权行为得以发生、侵权结果得以扩大或延伸。判断过错的标准是"应当达到的注意程度"，即有无达到其所应当达到的注意程度，对可能产生的不良后果是否知道或者有合理理由知道，就该标准而言，对于不同的网络服务提供者，对于不同的案件情况，会有所区分。

就本案而言，从客观上来看，开放软件平台上上传的软件数量是海量的，被告博瑞公司、爱九游公司、游龙公司难以对所有上传的软件逐一进行实质性审查。而从形式上来看，被告野火公司开发的《六大门派》游戏已取得计算机软件著作权登记证，并在上传游戏客户端时提供给被告博瑞公司、爱九游公司、游龙公司，游戏名称以及被告野火公司在三个平台上所写的游戏介绍中均不能看出与何作品有关联。再者，原告完美世界公司在发现《六大门派》游戏涉嫌侵权后，并未向被告博瑞公司、爱九游公司、游龙公司发出通知删除游戏的函。因此现有证据不能证明被告博瑞公司、爱九游公司、游龙公司有帮助被告野火公司实施侵权行为的故意。由于被告博瑞公司、爱九游公司、游龙公司主观上没有过错，故不应当承担赔偿责任，本案中的赔偿责任由被告野火公司承担。

（撰稿人：黄洋　沈敬杰）

私人影院观影模式的侵权认定与著作权保护

——北京爱奇艺科技有限公司与上海万幕商务咨询有限公司
侵害作品信息网络传播权纠纷案

【提要】

私人影院作为顺应市场发展的观影新模式，为消费者提供了私密性和个性化选择，但同时这一新业态模式也面临诸多法律问题。本案被告的经营模式是在获得涉案影片后，将视频文件置于服务器中，当用户在私人影院包房内使用预设系统点播某一影片时，该影片通过被告经营场所架设的局域网予以传播，被告的上述行为侵犯了著作权法所保护的作品信息网络传播权而非放映权。本案系全国首例将私人影院观影模式认定为侵权的案例，对类案审理具有一定的借鉴意义。

【案情】

原告： 北京爱奇艺科技有限公司

被告： 上海万幕商务咨询有限公司

案由： 侵害作品信息网络传播权纠纷

一审案号：（2016）沪 0110 民初第 4902 号

一、涉案影片的权属情况和授权情况

（一）关于涉案影片《杀破狼2》

2015 年 5 月 22 日，国家新闻出版广电总局电影局对影片《杀破狼2》出具电审故字〔2015〕第 159 号电影片公映许可证，片名《杀破狼2》（英文片名 SPL2：A Time For Consequences）。影片的出品单位是银都机构有限公司、太阳娱乐文化有限公司（中国香港）、博纳影业集团有限公司、睦谷富投资集团有

限公司（中国香港）。

2015 年 6 月 12 日，银都机构有限公司、博纳影业集团有限公司、睦谷富投资集团有限公司（中国香港）以著作权证明书的形式，确认涉案影片《杀破狼 2》的唯一版权持有人为太阳娱乐文化有限公司（中国香港），授权内容为所有版权权利、转授权权利和维权权利，其中信息网络传播权的授权期限为 2015 年 8 月 28 日至 2065 年 8 月 27 日。

2015 年 8 月 18 日，太阳娱乐文化有限公司（中国香港）以董事会决议的方式确认董事会决议附件所附的著作权证明书内容。著作权证明书内容为，2015 年 6 月 12 日太阳娱乐文化有限公司（中国香港）将其对涉案影片《杀破狼 2》在中华人民共和国境内（不包括香港、澳门、台湾地区）专有独占性享有的所有版权权利、转授权权利和维权权利授予星光联盟影业无锡有限公司，其中信息网络传播权的授权期限从 2015 年 8 月 28 日起至 2065 年 8 月 27 日止。

2015 年 1 月 20 日，星光联盟影业无锡有限公司出具授权书，将其在中国大陆地区（香港、澳门、台湾地区除外）享有的涉案影片《杀破狼 2》的独家信息网络传播权授予北京奇艺世纪科技有限公司，授权期限为网络上线起七年，上线时间为 2015 年 6 月 18 日。

2015 年 1 月 20 日，北京奇艺世纪科技有限公司出具授权书，将其在中国大陆地区（香港、澳门、台湾地区除外）享有的涉案影片《杀破狼 2》的独家信息网络传播权授予本案原告，授权期限与授权方享有权利期限一致。

（二）关于涉案影片《十万个冷笑话》

2014 年 12 月 9 日，国家新闻出版广电总局电影局对影片《十万个冷笑话》出具电审动字〔2014〕第 037 号电影片公映许可证，片名《十万个冷笑话》（英文片名 One hundred thousand bad jokes）。影片的出品单位是上海炫动传播股份有限公司、万达影视传媒有限公司、北京四月星空网络科技有限公司。

2015 年 1 月 20 日，上海炫动传播股份有限公司出具授权书，将其在中国大陆地区（香港、澳门、台湾地区除外）享有的涉案影片《十万个冷笑话》的独家信息网络传播权、转授权及维权的权利授予北京奇艺世纪科技有限公司，授权期限为 2015 年 2 月 1 日至 2065 年 1 月 31 日。

2015 年 1 月 20 日，北京奇艺世纪科技有限公司出具授权书，将其在中国大陆地区（香港、澳门、台湾地区除外）享有的涉案影片《十万个冷笑话》的独家信息网络传播权、转授权及维权的权利授予本案原告，授权期限为 2015 年 2 月 1 日至 2065 年 1 月 31 日。

2015 年 1 月 27 日，万达影视传媒有限公司出具版权证明书，声明其为涉案影片《十万个冷笑话》著作权人之一，授权上海炫动传播股份有限公司可独家全权行使或授权第三人行使涉案影片《十万个冷笑话》的独家信息网络传播权，授权期限从获颁影片公映许可证之日起至版权保护期终止之日为止。

2015 年 1 月 27 日，北京四月星空网络科技有限公司出具版权证明书，声明其为涉案影片《十万个冷笑话》著作权人之一，授权上海炫动传播股份有限公司可独家全权行使或授权第三人行使涉案影片《十万个冷笑话》的独家信息网络传播权，授权期限从获颁影片公映许可证之日起至版权保护期终止之日为止。

二、被告经营场所播放涉案影片的情况

2015 年 10 月 28 日，经原告申请，上海市长宁区公证处的公证员蒋旻峥、公证人员梁永捷及原告代理人王会忠来到上海市沪闵路北侧，古方路、莲花路之间的莲花国际广场内"万幕电影"，公证人员对该影院现场进行拍照。公证人员进入该影院的包房内，打开包房中计算机终端，在终端的播放系统中搜索关键字"杀破狼2"，点击播放并对播放过程进行摄像，得到视频文件两段。公证人员还在现场获得名片一张、宣传单一张、收据一张（充值 600 元）。

2016 年 2 月 25 日，经上海市协力律师事务所申请，上海市东方公证处公证员张志明、公证人员徐立明及委托代理人钱震来到上海市沪闵路 7866 号莲花国际广场 3F"万幕电影"商户，三人一起进入 V4 和 V7 房间后，公证人员使用公证处提供的数码相机对上述房间内的相关播放设备进行拍照。委托代理人钱震使用上述包房内计算机终端设备对涉案影片进行搜索、播放，公证人员将过程进行拍摄，得到相应视频文件。具体搜索、播放步骤如下：1."万幕私人影院"工作人员将房间内计算机终端开机后，投影屏幕显示播放界面；2. 播放界面包括"热力首页""最新影片""怀旧经典""电影分类"等栏目，逐次点开并最终进入"电影分类"栏目；3. 点击"大陆"选项，点击字母 SPL，出现《杀破狼》《杀破狼 2》两部影片；4. 点击《杀破狼 2》进入"剧情介绍"页面，随后点击"剧情介绍"页面中"马上播放"按钮播放影片，播放过程中，拖动播放进度至片中、片尾该片可完整播放，并可清晰显示影片片头的公映许可证号及出品人信息；5. 在影片播放过程中单击鼠标右键弹出一个对话框，该对话框中包含"属性"等栏目，点击对话框中"属性"栏目，显示"播放信息"窗口，该窗口包括"播放信息""文件信息""系统信息"等栏目，逐次点开各栏目，从"文件信息"栏目可以看出影片位于局域网络中的存储地址为：192.168.0.249/G/Saat Po Long2－杀破狼 2 之杀无赦－2015/Saat. Po. Long2. 2015. 1080p. WEB－DL. X264. AAC－XJCTV. mkv；6. 在影片《杀

破狼 2》播放页面中再次点击鼠标右键弹出与步骤 5 相同的对话框，点击该对话框中"打开文件夹"栏目进入"我的电脑"页面，该页面直接显示影片在局域网中的片源存储位置；7. 点击"我的电脑"页面左下侧网络 192. 168. 0. 249，显示网络共享盘 d、e、f、g、users 并选择 g 盘，在 g 盘中可以找到《杀破狼 2》在局域网中的片源并进行播放；8. 重复上述操作步骤播放涉案影片《十万个冷笑话》，并确认该涉案影片也储存在网络地址 192. 168. 0. 249 的服务器终端内。公证人员还在现场获得名片一张、宣传资料一份、上海市地方税务局通用机打发票一张（充值 1000 元）。该公证处于 2016 年 3 月 15 日出具了（2016）沪东证经字第 2647 号公证书，公证员将视频文件刻录成光盘，拍摄的现场照片予以打印，名片、宣传资料、发票等予以复印。上述材料均以附件形式附于该公证书。

被告自述在其经营的万幕私人影院中，每个包厢内设有计算机终端，消费者开机后通过操作计算机终端中预装的播放界面，搜索并播放影片。包厢中计算机终端的硬盘无法存储影片，被告将涉案影片存储在网络地址 192. 168. 0. 249 的服务器终端硬盘内，消费者使用统一的播放界面选择、点播影片，通过店内架设的局域网读取服务器终端的影片并进行播放。

三、被告经营情况及收费标准

被告注册成立于 2013 年 7 月 18 日，注册资本为 200 000 元，经营范围主要包括商务咨询、企业形象策划、电脑图文设计制作等。

被告处设有包厢 20 余间，消费以小时为单位计费，根据包厢的大小，每小时消费标价为 98 元至 398 元不等。在工作日的上午十点至下午四点时段内，有五折的时段折扣优惠，工作日的下午四点后及节假日没有时段折扣优惠。并根据会员的充值金额，在上述价格的基础上再有四折到七折的折扣优惠。

原告北京爱奇艺科技有限公司诉称：原告是中国大型网络视频平台"爱奇艺（iQIYI. COM）"的合法经营者，为采购版权许可支出高额成本。原告经授权享有《杀破狼 2》《十万个冷笑话》等影视作品在中国大陆地区的独家信息网络传播权。被告万幕公司在其经营的"万幕私人影院"中，设有多个豪华包房，在未获得涉案作品信息网络传播权许可的情况下，擅自通过自建的局域网利用计算机终端向消费者提供有偿的视频点播服务。原告认为被告将涉案作品置于其局域网中，使公众能够在个人选定的时间和地点播放涉案影片，侵害了原告享有的涉案作品的信息网络传播权。原告作为独占性被许可人，有权以自己的名义提起诉讼。据上，请求判令被告赔偿原告经济损失及维权支出合理费用计 500 000 元。

被告上海万幕商务咨询有限公司辩称：不同意原告诉请。第一，消费者可以在包厢内利用计算机终端直接登录原告视频网站观看涉案两部影片，有可能是消费者在线观看后，涉案影片被自动缓存在被告的服务器终端中，因此没有证据证明被告实施了侵权行为；第二，即便法院认定被告的行为侵权，原告主张的赔偿金额过高，消费者到店消费并非单纯的买票看电影，被告也提供了一定的空间服务。被告万幕公司未提供证据证明其主张。

【审判】

上海市杨浦区人民法院经审理认为：根据著作权法的相关规定，电影作品的著作权由制片者享有；如无相反证明，在作品上署名的公民、法人或者其他组织为作者。涉案影片《杀破狼2》《十万个冷笑话》均摄制在一定介质上，由一系列有伴音或者无伴音的画面组成，并且借助适当装置放映或者以其他方式进行传播，属于受著作权法保护的电影作品。原告就影片《杀破狼2》《十万个冷笑话》提供了影片公映许可证、出品人的授权文件等证据证明其获得了著作权人的授权，享有独占的信息网络传播权，有权以自己的名义对授权范围内、授权期限内的侵权行为提起诉讼。

本案中，被告的"万幕私人影院"包厢内计算机终端安装有统一的播放界面，虽然每个包厢的计算机终端没有存储涉案影片，但顾客在播放界面自行选择影片后，通过被告自行架设的局域网网络便可链接至服务器终端。被告未经许可将涉案影片存储在服务器终端中，使用户能在自行选定的时间内，通过网络对上述涉案影片进行播放，该行为侵害了原告享有的信息网络传播权。

关于被告辩称涉案影片系消费者通过互联网从原告网站上观看的正版视频而被自动缓存下来的抗辩意见。本院认为，根据公证记录过程，涉案影片确实存储在被告的服务器终端上，且通过被告自己的"热力首页"点播界面进行操作，在被告的影片库中可以搜索到涉案影片并进行播放，而如果是消费者播放后的缓存，则不可能存在上述将涉案影片编辑入影片库的行为，因此对被告的抗辩意见，上海市杨浦区人民法院不予采信。

综上，上海市杨浦区人民法院依照《中华人民共和国侵权责任法》第十五条第一款第（六）项、第三十六条第一款，《中华人民共和国著作权法》第十条第一款第（十二）项、第四十八条第（一）项、第四十九条，《最高人民法院关于审理著作权民事纠纷案件适用法律若干问题的解释》第二十五条第一款、第二款、第二十六条，《最高人民法院关于审理侵害信息网络传播权民事纠纷案件适用法律若干问题的规定》第三条之规定，判决：被告上海万幕商务咨询有限公司于本判决生效之日起十日内赔偿原告北京爱奇艺科技有限公司30 000元（含合理费用12 000元）。

一审判决后，双方当事人均未提起上诉。

【评析】

本案系因私人影院播放他人影片而引发的著作权侵权纠纷，为全市首例私人影院被诉侵权案件。法院最终认定被告的行为侵犯了原告作品的信息网络传播权而非放映权或其他权利。本案的处理结果和裁判思路对于今后类似案件的处理具有一定的指导意义。

一、被告的行为侵犯了原告作品的何种著作权

根据法院在被告经营场所的现场勘验查明，被告的经营模式是在获得涉案影片后，将视频文件置于服务器中，当用户在私人影院包房内使用预设系统点播某一影片时，是通过被告经营场所架设的局域网予以传播的。法院最终判决被告的这一行为和经营模式侵犯了原告作品的信息网络传播权。信息网络传播权旨在赋予著作权人能够阻止他人未经许可，将作品置于信息网络中使作品处于公众可自由获得状态的权利。判断某一行为是否构成信息网络传播，应当符合以下条件：

1. 行为人将作品以"上传到网络服务器、设置共享文件或者利用文件分享软件等方式"置于信息网络中；

2. 该作品所在网络必须对公众开放，公众能够"下载、浏览或者其他方式获得"该作品；

3. 公众能够在"个人选定的时间和地点"按照前述方式获取作品。

从私人影院观影模式来看，被告有"以有线或者无线方式向公众提供作品，使公众可以在其自行选定的时间和地点获得作品的权利。"符合信息网络传播权的规定。用户可以自主决定获取作品的时间和地点，而不是被动地接受作品的传播或播放，这里着眼"交互式"的点播行为，是为了与通过无线（有线）电台等单向传播的网络区别开来，后者是通过作品的广播权予以保护。而强调私人影院播放影片是借助信息网络的传输再播放的模式，而非单纯通过放映机、幻灯机等技术设备的播放，是为了区别于作品的放映权。

二、"信息网络"的范围：局域网的问题

本案中，被告将视频文件置于服务器设备中，当用户在私人影院包房内使

用预设系统点播某一影片时，是通过被告经营场所架设的局域网予以传播的，而局域网是否属于信息网络？信息网络传播权的定义并没有明确规定"信息网络"的具体含义和范围，但根据《最高人民法院关于审理侵害信息网络传播权民事纠纷案件适用法律若干问题》第二条对此定义进行了明确的补充——"本规定所称信息网络，包括以计算机、电视机、固定电话机、移动电话机等电子设备为终端的计算机互联网、广播电视网、固定通信网、移动通信网等信息网络，以及向公众开放的局域网络"。显然，信息网络的定义范围远远超过了我们日常意义上计算机网络的范围。即能够供公众远程自主的（或者说是交互式的）获取所需信息的网络系统，都是著作权法意义上的信息网络。本案中，被告采用"主机存储影视作品＋包房点播系统操作＋局域网传送"的模式，其播放作品的模式是基于被告架设的局域网的基础之上。法院认为，严格要求传播作品"信息网络"是广域网还是局域网并无意义。根据法律规定，设立信息网络传播权的规定在于强调"交互式点播"的作品传播方式而非传播范围。被告的消费者是"不特定的用户"，局域网仅仅是因为被告的经营模式限定了总人数，但公众依然可以随时接触到作品。

三、如何理解"个人选定的时间和地点"

本案中，被告的经营时间是每天的上午 10 点至下午 10 点，消费者也需要支付一定的对价才能在被告的经营场所内，使用被告的点播系统欣赏影视作品。有观点认为，像这样仅能在有限的时间和限定的地域范围内提供作品，是否不属于"使公众可以在其自行选定的时间和地点获得作品"，其实这是对信息网络传播权的误读。我国《著作权法》的"信息网络传播权"来源于 WCT 第 8 条的规定，世界知识产权组织对该条文的解读指出："交互式的按需传播行为是该条规定的范围。实现这一目标的方法是确认相关的传播行为包括使公众中的成员能够从不同的地点和在不同的时间获得作品"，由此可以看出，该规定其实质是强调向公众进行交互式传播，而非要求空间维度上任何一个地点和时间维度上任何一个瞬间。因此在传播者限定的时间和地域范围内，只要公众可以通过网络自行选择时间和地点去"点播"，这一传播就是"交互式传播"，仍然是"信息网络传播权"所规制的范围。因此本案中，虽然必须在每天有限的经营时间内进入被告的经营场所才能播放涉案影片，但依然是对作品信息网络传播权的侵犯。

（撰稿人：居义良）

二

商标权民事纠纷案件

商标独占使用重复许可时的
合同效力与使用权归属

——上海帕弗洛文化用品有限公司诉上海艺想文化用品有限公司、
毕加索国际企业股份有限公司商标使用许可合同纠纷案

【提要】

商标权人先后与他人签订两个独占许可使用合同，且许可期间存在重叠，在后许可合同相对人明知存在在先许可合同的，在后许可合同并不因此无效，但在后许可合同相对人不属于善意第三人，其不能依据在后许可合同获得商标的许可使用权。

【案情】

原告（上诉人）：上海帕弗洛文化用品有限公司

被告（上诉人）：上海艺想文化用品有限公司

被告（被上诉人）：毕加索国际企业股份有限公司

案由：因商标使用许可合同纠纷

一审案号：（2012）沪一中民五（知）初字第 250 号

二审案号：（2014）沪高民三（知）终字第 117 号

毕加索国际企业股份有限公司（以下简称毕加索公司）于 2003 年 5 月 21 日获核准注册涉案商标。2003 年 7 月 9 日，毕加索公司出具《授权证明书》，证明 2003 年 7 月 9 日至 2008 年 12 月 31 日授权上海帕弗洛文化用品有限公司（以下简称帕弗洛公司）在中国大陆地区使用系争商标。2008 年 9 月 8 日，毕加索公司再次出具《授权证明书》，授予帕弗洛公司中国大陆地区在书写工具类别上商业使用涉案商标，权利内容：中国大陆地区独家制造与销售，授权期限自 2008 年 9 月 10 日起至 2013 年 12 月 31 日止。2009 年 3 月 12

日，商标局向毕加索公司发出商标使用合同备案通知书，告知毕加索公司于2008年6月30日报送的许可帕弗洛公司使用涉案商标的使用许可合同备案申请已被核准。2010年2月11日，毕加索公司与帕弗洛公司签订《授权契约书》，约定在原契约基础上延展十年，自2014年1月1日起至2023年12月31日止。

2012年1月1日，毕加索公司与帕弗洛公司签订商标使用许可合同备案提前终止协议，但约定双方关于该商标的其他约定不受影响。2012年3月13日，商标局发布2012年第10期商标公告，提前终止许可合同备案，提前终止日期为2012年1月1日。

2012年2月16日，毕加索公司与上海艺想文化用品有限公司（以下简称艺想公司）在上海签订《商标使用许可合同书》。该合同约定：第二条、独占使用；第五条、许可期限2012年1月15日至2017年8月31日；特别说明：甲方应在签订此合同一年内完成许可合同备案；除因商标局审查程序、期限冗长之外，若因甲方未积极撤销与帕弗洛公司在国家商标局之备案合同或者其他原因未在国家商标局办妥备案的，则乙方有权终止本合同。同日，毕加索公司出具授权书称艺想公司是中国大陆地区唯一独家授权。

帕弗洛公司诉称，第2001022号商标（以下称涉案商标）的商标权人毕加索公司于2008年9月授权其在中国大陆地区独家使用该商标，期限为2008年9月至2013年12月。2010年2月，毕加索公司与帕弗洛公司约定商标使用许可期限在原基础上延展十年。2012年2月，毕加索公司与艺想公司签订《商标使用许可合同书》，约定艺想公司2012年1月至2017年8月期间独占使用该商标，并授权艺想公司进行全国维权打假行动，致使帕弗洛公司产品遭到工商机关查处。毕加索公司与艺想公司擅自签订《商标使用许可合同书》，并向工商机关投诉帕弗洛公司侵权、向法院提起商标侵权诉讼，此行为系"恶意串通，损害第三人合法利益"及"违反法律、行政法规的强制性规定"，请求法院判令系争合同无效、两被告赔偿帕弗洛公司经济损失100万元。

被告艺想公司辩称：1. 帕弗洛公司没有获得毕加索公司关于涉案商标的独占许可使用权。帕弗洛公司在商标局备案的独占使用许可合同系伪造，因此商标局备案所记载的许可方式也不能证实帕弗洛公司享有涉案商标的独占许可使用权。授权证明书中没有关于授权性质的具体约定，故帕弗洛公司获得的仅是涉案商标独家使用权，而非法律规定的独占许可使用权；2. 根据商标局的公告，涉案商标权利人毕加索公司与帕弗洛公司之间的商标授权使用关系已于2012年1月1日提前终止。艺想公司于2012年2月16日获得涉案商标的独占许可实施权，没有侵犯帕弗洛公司的任何权利，艺想公司主观上也不存在与毕加索公司恶意串通的状态；3. 艺想公司在取得涉案商标的独占许可使用权后，帕弗洛公司仍在大量生产使用涉案注册商标的产品，艺想公司为此在全国范围内向工商行政管理部门提出投诉，并提起侵权诉讼，是维护其独占许可使用权的正当行为，该维权行为不是因具有主观恶意而造成的帕弗洛公司损失；4. 毕加索公司与帕弗洛公司及案外人上海大者实业有限公司恶意串通，在本案诉讼期间将涉案商标转让给大者公司，侵犯了艺想公司在合同中约定的优先购买权、独占使用权。

毕加索公司书面答辩称：毕加索公司未对商标使用许可合同进行备案。毕加索公司在与艺想公司签约时，已将涉案商标授权情况告知艺想公司，包括帕弗洛公司仿冒毕加索公司负责人林达光签名以获取商标许可合同备案的情况，艺想公司对该商标前期授权尚未终止非常清楚，仅要求毕加索公司尽快撤销帕弗洛公司在商标局的商标备案合同，同时约定任何一方不得私自与帕弗洛公司和解。因此，其在授权给艺想公司使用涉案商标时，已经履行了相关告知义务，由此给帕弗洛公司带来的任何损失，均应由艺想公司承担。

【审判】

上海市第一中级人民法院对帕弗洛公司主张的关于涉案商标的授权过程之事实予以采信，认为帕弗洛公司获得涉案商标使用权的合同关系真实有效，帕弗洛公司在2008年9月10日至2013年12月31日期间享有涉案商标的独占许可使用权。艺想公司签订系争合同的目的并非出于损害帕弗洛公司的合法权益，也没有实施不正当竞争的主观恶意。艺想公司在与毕加索公司进行合同磋商时得知帕弗洛公司享有独占许可使用权的事实，但已经要求毕加索公司撤销其与帕弗洛公司的独占实施许可合同备案，故不能仅因艺想公司明知帕弗洛公司享有独占许可使用权的事实就认定其具有损害帕弗洛公司利益的主观恶意。艺想公司在与毕加索公司签订了独占实施使用合同并支付了相应独占实施许可费用后，作为涉案商标的独占许可使用权人向工商行政部门提出投诉并非恶意损害帕弗洛公司合法利益的行为。毕加索公司、艺想公司投诉书内容相似亦不能证实两者具有合意损害帕弗洛公司利益的行为事实。合同的订立违反了法律和行政法规的强制性规定时才排除合同当事人的意思自治。帕弗洛公司所主张的《最高人民法院关于审理商标民事纠纷案件适用法律若干问题的解释》第三条的内容是对我国商标法所规定的三种商标使用许可方式的定义，显然并不属于强制性法律规范。因此，系争合同的订立并未违反法律、行政法规的强制性规定，帕弗洛公司据此主张系争合同无效，亦缺乏事实和法律依据。帕弗洛公司要求确认系争合同以及相应授权书无效的诉讼请求，一审法院不予支持。帕弗洛公司在该合同无效的基础上所主张的相应赔偿，一审法院亦不支持。

综上，上海市第一中级人民法院判决驳回帕弗洛公司的全部诉讼请求。

一审判决后，帕弗洛公司、艺想公司均不服，提起上诉。

上海市高级人民法院经审理后认为，一审判决认定事实清楚、适用法律正确，判决驳回上诉，维持原判。

【评析】

在实际的商标运营中，商标权人为一己之利，存在对外重复独占许可的可能，知识产权权利变动规则不如物权变动之清晰可辨，导致被许可人之间产生激烈的利益冲突。本案案情较为复杂，二审法院在一审的基础上，对商标备案的法律意义、恶意串通导致合同无效的条件、负担行为处分行为区分理论在商标法上的运用等，均作出一定的探索，对何者享有独占许可使用权作出了明确回答，为争议双方在全国各地法院的商标侵权诉讼之根本解决奠定了基础，有助于进一步明晰商标许可交易的法律规则，有利于维护公平诚信的商标使用秩序。

一、恶意串通导致合同无效的认定条件

根据《合同法》第五十二条规定，恶意串通损害第三人合法利益的合同无效。恶意串通，是以损害他人利益为目的而相互通谋、相互勾结作出的意思表示，原告不仅要证明被告主观上具有加害的故意，还要证明客观上具有勾结、串通的行为。恶意串通导致合同无效，是中国合同法特别的制度，为其他国家合同法所罕见。合同的核心要义在于允诺、交易和执行，合同是人无法具体感知的一种抽象法律关系，而非其书面或口头的形式。合同的内核是合同方之间的交易，而合同是安排各方未来行为的一项工具。在司法实践中，法院越来越倾向于较少运用合同无效制度，其主因在就于合同是市场交易的工具，认定合同无效的直接后果便是导致交易链条断裂，导致市场运转遭遇工具性的障碍，对于发展市场经济殊为不利。《合同法》第五十二条所规定的恶意串通，通常表现为利用合同形式转移财产、逃避债务以及与相对人之代理人串通损害相对人利益等。合同法无效制度的精髓在于规定违反法律、行政法规强制性规定的合同无效，其行为本身即具违法性，因此法律规定此类合同归于无效。

要认定本案中艺想公司与毕加索公司签订在后的独占许可合同时是否存

在恶意串通，也要从主观要件和客观要件两方面来判断。从主观恶意的认定看，艺想公司与帕弗洛公司生产销售类似书写工具产品，在同一市场展开竞争，且毕加索公司在向法院提交的书面答辩意见中称已将其与帕弗洛公司的商标使用许可情况告知艺想公司；艺想公司与毕加索公司在商标局 2012 年 3 月 13 日公告终止备案之前的 2012 年 2 月 16 日即签订系争商标使用许可合同，虽然商标使用许可合同备案于 2012 年 1 月 1 日终止，但并无证据表明帕弗洛公司与毕加索公司的商标独占使用许可合同关系已经解除，不能仅依据备案之终止而推定商标使用许可合同之解除；艺想公司亦表示其知悉帕弗洛公司与毕加索公司之间的涉案商标使用许可关系。据此，可以认定艺想公司在与毕加索公司签订系争商标使用许可合同时知晓帕弗洛公司与毕加索公司之间存在涉案商标独占使用许可关系，因此艺想公司并不属于在后被授权之善意第三人。然而，艺想公司不属于善意第三人，仅意味着其对毕加索公司与帕弗洛公司之间的涉案商标独占使用许可关系是知情的，并不一定意味着其与毕加索公司间存在恶意串通并损害第三人利益之行为。艺想公司与毕加索公司签订使用许可合同的目的在于使用涉案商标，虽然艺想公司和毕加索公司在签订系争合同时，并未以毕加索公司和帕弗洛公司解除其双方在先的商标独占使用许可合同为合同生效前提之做法存在不妥，导致先后两个商标独占使用许可合同的许可期间存在重叠，但综合艺想公司在其系争合同中要求毕加索公司积极撤销与帕弗洛公司的备案合同等条款，本案中尚无充分证据证明艺想公司有加害帕弗洛公司的主观恶意。

从客观行为的认定看，原告还要证明被告双方存在串通行为。所谓串通，本身即带有一定的否定性评价，意味着双方本着共同损害他人的故意而进行合谋。当然，串通行为在多数时候应该可以从行为外观上推定，但其前提应是合同双方的恶意。本案并无双方串通的直接证据。艺想公司、毕加索公司的投诉、举报行为，系基于其自认为艺想公司已获得涉案商标的独占许可使用权，且相应行政机关并未作出帕弗洛公司违法的决定，难言属于双方恶意串通之行为。系争合同专门设置的限制合同双方与第三方和解的条款，符合艺想公司维护其合同利益的目的，系市场竞争中的常见手段，同样难以认定系恶意串通行为。虽然艺想公司试图影响毕加索公司与帕弗洛公司之间的涉案商标独占使用许可关系的动机是明显的，但鉴于艺想公司与帕弗洛公司系同业竞争者，其采用与涉案商标权利人毕加索公司签订独占使用许可合同、要求毕加索公司不得在同类产品上向第三方授权使用涉案商标的方式展开市场竞争，该竞争方式本身并不具有违法性。本案表明，尽管商标权人对外同时签订多个商标独占使用许可合同的行为有违诚信，但恶意串通导致无效的认定标准较高，在后合同本身并非无效。

二、重复独占许可下商标使用权的归属

本案中艺想公司与毕加索公司之间的商标使用许可合同已成立并生效，但合同已生效并不等于合同已被实际履行，合同中约定的内容是否已被合同双方依约履行，应以双方的实际履行行为为准。艺想公司、毕加索公司均知悉帕弗洛公司与毕加索公司就涉案商标存在的独占使用许可关系，艺想公司相对于帕弗洛公司与毕加索公司之间的商标独占使用许可合同关系而言不属于善意第三人。毕加索公司与帕弗洛公司之间就涉案商标存在独占使用许可合同关系，且该独占使用许可合同正常履行，虽然毕加索公司与帕弗洛公司之间的涉案商标使用许可合同备案于 2012 年 1 月 1 日终止，但在无证据表明帕弗洛公司与毕加索公司的商标独占使用许可合同已被解除的情况下，应认定该独占使用许可合同关系依然存续。《最高人民法院关于审理商标民事纠纷案件适用法律若干问题的解释》第 19 条规定，商标许可使用合同未经备案的，不得对抗善意第三人。对此条款如作反对解释，则可认为商标许可使用合同即使未经备案，仍可对抗非善意的第三人。本案即是此种情形。由于艺想公司不属于善意第三人，因此帕弗洛公司依据其与毕加索公司间的商标使用许可合同取得的涉案商标独占许可使用权，可以对抗艺想公司与毕加索公司之间的商标使用许可合同关系。虽然毕加索公司与艺想公司之间的商标使用许可合同已成立并生效，但由于帕弗洛公司就涉案商标取得的独占许可使用权一直存续，毕加索公司已不能对涉案商标的使用权进行处分。鉴于毕加索公司实际上并未履行其与艺想公司签订的商标使用许可合同之义务，艺想公司也就不能据此系争合同获得涉案商标的使用权。换言之，艺想公司与毕加索公司签订的系争合同，并不能剥夺帕弗洛公司对涉案商标享有的独占许可使用权。由此，帕弗洛公司依据在先的独占使用许可合同已经形成的商标使用的状态，应认定未被在后的商标独占使用许可合同关系打破。

三、商标使用权处分理论

本案二审判决实际将民法上负担行为、处分行为相区分的理论运用到商标权利的变动上。传统民法上所谓负担行为，是指不发生对标的物的处分、只为当事人设定一定义务的行为，仅产生当事人的请求权；所谓的处分行为，是指直接行使支配权的行为，其法律效果是使权利发生部分或整体的被限制或被消灭。处分行为使相对人取得权利，其生效要件为行为人具有处分权，而负担行为的效力在于使行为人承担给付义务。处分行为包括物权行为和准物权行为，

准物权行为是指以债权或无体财产权作为标的之处分行为。本案中毕加索公司通过分别与帕弗洛公司、艺想公司签订商标独占许可使用合同，给自己设定了两项债法上的给付义务。不同于物权之一物一权主义，多项债权或债务是可以并行不悖的，因为债的制度的主要功能在于提供社会交易工具，债权的类型化，某种意义上是一种虚拟，而不同于有体物上物权之实在性。基于两项并存的债权债务关系，毕加索公司在本案中负有向帕弗洛公司、艺想公司分别为给付的合同义务，但这只是合同法上的应为义务，并不意味着已经完成实际给付。何谓实际给付？须依赖于毕加索公司的处分行为。本案中在先的独占许可使用合同，已得到双方的履行，帕弗洛公司获得涉案商标的独占使用权，毕加索公司获得相应许可费，且该履行行为直到毕加索公司与艺想公司签约时，未受到任何干扰。值得注意的是，毕加索公司处分的涉案商标的独占使用权，相当于处分了涉案商标的完整的、所有的使用权，毕加索公司虽然仍是涉案商标的所有权人，但其对商标使用权已经失去处分的权利，除非其通过解除与帕弗洛公司之间的合同以实现处分权的回归。毕加索公司与艺想公司签订的在后许可合同，无论其属于独占许可或是其他方式的许可，均属于无权处分合同。合同并不仅因无权处分而无效。至于在后许可合同有效但难以履行的问题，首先，该合同并非履行不能，如毕加索公司解除在先合同，则在后合同仍可履行；其次，虽合同有效但难以履行，但双方之间的权利义务纠纷可通过违约之诉解决。总而言之，将民法负担行为、处分行为区分理论运用到商标使用许可交易上，可以有效解决现实的法律问题。

四、其他衡量因素

本案终审判决还考虑了肯定商标使用价值以及商标使用秩序的理念。本案中毕加索公司作为商标权人，其并不自行使用涉案商标，或者说对外许可使用为其仅有的商标使用方式，实际的商标使用者为帕弗洛公司。实质意义上的商标权，并非产生于注册。商标权作为一项财产权利，来自商标的实际使用，以及由此而产生的商誉，无论是英美法系还是大陆法系，都没有把商标注册当作获得财产权利的一个途径。商标权产生于、积累于实际使用中，没有实际使用，则商标仅为一符号或标记，便失去予以商标权保护的合法性基础。本案中帕弗洛公司多年经许可使用涉案商标，无疑已建立起一定的市场声誉，消费者已建立起涉案商标与帕弗洛公司之间的特定联系，这是商标权的实质内容，至少积累的商誉除归属于商标权人之外，独占被许可人也应当"利益均沾"，方符合客观实情和实质正义，这或许可视作允许独占被许可人以自己名义单独提起侵权之诉的一种"反射利益"。在其背后，更是一种商标使用的秩序，若未经法定程序或至少是相关方合意即打乱此种秩序，其最终受损者还包括处于信息弱势的相关消费者。本案"始作俑者"毕加索公司的双重授权行为若得以合法化，则无疑有悖公平诚信原则、扰乱商标使用秩序并最终有损相关消费者利益。考虑及此，本案保护在先的被许可方，成为必然的价值取向。

（撰稿人：徐卓斌）

商品商标指示性使用的认定

——维多利亚的秘密商店品牌管理公司诉上海麦司投资管理有限公司侵害商标权及不正当竞争纠纷案

【提要】

合法取得销售商品权利的经营者，可以在商品销售中对商标权人的商品商标进行指示性使用，但应当限于指示商品来源，如超出了指示商品来源所必需的范围，则会对相关的服务商标专用权构成侵害。商标使用行为可能导致相关公众误认为销售服务系商标权人提供或者与商标权人存在商标许可等关联关系的，应认定已经超出指示所销售商品来源所必要的范围而具备了指示、识别服务来源的功能。

【案情】

原告（被上诉人）：维多利亚的秘密商店品牌管理公司

被告（上诉人）：上海麦司投资管理有限公司

案由：侵害商标权及不正当竞争纠纷

一审案号：（2014）沪一中民五（知）初字第 33 号

二审案号：（2014）沪高民三（知）终字第 104 号

原告系涉案四个注册商标的专用权人。2013 年 12 月 20 日，原告向上海市东方公证处申请证据保全，在位于上海市肇嘉浜路 1111 号的美罗城四楼门口有"VICTORIA'S SECRET"字样标牌的商铺内购得两件物品，所获两份宣传资料分别系产品宣传手册和加盟销售手册，均突出使用了"VICTORIA'S SECRET"及"维多利亚的秘密"标志，其中产品宣传手册系对维多利亚的秘密品牌的介绍以及产品的介绍，同时载明加拿大联合麦斯于 1999 年成立于加拿大温哥华，中国总部系被告，末页载明"VICTORIA'S SECRET"品牌运营总公司系加拿大

联合麦斯－上海麦斯投资管理有限公司，并标明了电话、传真、网址、地址等
联系信息；加盟销售手册介绍了"VICTORIA'S SECRET"品牌销售制度，包括
装修风格、规格、标准由被告统一控管、经营理念、企业识别、管理服务、管
理制度的四个一致化等，并列明了大区销售商、省级销售商、省会销售商、市
级销售商、单店加盟商等不同级别销售商年度进货额、品牌使用费、权益保证
金等方面的要求，其中品牌使用费为 6 万元到 50 万元，截至 2013 年 12 月，维
多利亚的秘密商店中国大陆地区共计 21 家，末页载明的联系信息同产品宣传手
册。公证过程还显示，该四楼店铺大门招牌、店内墙面、货柜、收银台、员工
胸牌等处均突出使用了"VICTORIA'S SECRET"标志，销售的产品上也均使用
了"VICTORIA'S SECRET"和"维多利亚的秘密"标志。该大厦地下一层正在
举办内衣时装展览，背景大屏幕也突出使用了"VICTORIA'S SECRET"标志。
2014 年 1 月 16 日，原告又经公证至上述美罗城四楼店铺取得 VIP 会员卡一张，
该会员卡上突出使用"VICTORIA'S SECRET"标志。

中国女装网上有关于维多利亚的秘密的品牌专栏，页面上部突出使用了
"VICTORIA'S SECRET"和"维多利亚的秘密"，具体内容涉及全国招商加盟宣
传，以及被告系中国维多利亚的秘密总行销公司，上海、北京、广州、深圳、
重庆、天津总代理商，维秘中国总部，美罗城店为维多利亚的秘密上海直营店、
旗舰店、形象店等，联系电话、公司网址、联系地址信息均同加盟销售手册。
中国服装品牌网、中国品牌内衣网上亦有众多有关维多利亚的秘密的品牌专栏，
其中品牌标志突出使用了"VICTORIA'S SECRET"标志。扫描加盟销售手册末
页二维码，进入"维多利亚的秘密"的微信账号，账号名中突出使用了
"VICTORIA'S SECRET"标志，相关微信信息中亦有众多有关维多利亚的秘密
的招商加盟信息，被告系该品牌运营总公司等。

2014 年 1 月 16 日，原告向广东省广州市白云公证处申请证据保全，使用
公证处电话拨通 4000008115，咨询维多利亚的秘密加盟事宜，自称是被告员工
的魏云霄接电告知加盟要求，并通过邮件形式发送具体的品牌资料（邮件信息
显示魏云霄系被告品牌市场部总监，传真、招商热线、网址、地址信息均同加
盟销售手册），详细介绍维多利亚的秘密品牌信息及加盟信息，其中亦涉及对
"VICTORIA'S SECRET"和"维多利亚的秘密"的突出使用，以及被告系该品
牌的中国品牌运营商、北上广深渝津大区销售商，在中国开设品牌旗舰店、特
许销售店等。

一审法院另查明，原告是案外人 Intimate Brands Holding, LLC 的全资子公
司，Intimate Brands Holding, LLC 是案外人 Intimate Brands, Inc. 的全资子公司，
Intimate Brands, Inc. 是 LBI 公司的全资子公司。另，LBI 公司旗下还有一家全

资子公司维多利亚的秘密商店有限公司（Victoria's Secret Stores，LLC）（以下简称 VSSLLC 公司）。原告负责 LBI 公司旗下所有"VICTORIA'S SECRET"（维多利亚的秘密）商标的注册、使用、管理和保护，是上述商标的所有权人，LBI 公司和其他全资子公司经原告许可使用"VICTORIA'S SECRET"（维多利亚的秘密）商标。

VSSLLC 公司与 American Fashion Brands，LLC（以下简称 AFB 公司）签订有一份《库存出售协议》，该协议从 2007 年 1 月 1 日起生效，授权 AFB 公司在包括中国在内的多个地区出售某些标记为缺货的库存。该协议第 5.4 条系知识产权的规定，"买方不得并应确保其购买人与关联方和客户不会利用或经销以任何方式带有卖方或其任何关联方的任何名称、商标、商品名、图标或其他知识产权的货物为其做广告，而且买方与任何这类人都无权使用任何产品样本、产品样本图片、副本、互联网或其他媒体或卖方或其任何关联方的知识产权作为其标牌、专用信纸、商业书信、标签或任何其他形式广告的组成部分……"

上海锦天服饰有限公司（以下称锦天公司）2007 年 9 月从 LBI 公司购进了价值约 510 万美元的维多利亚的秘密品牌内衣商品。

2007 年 9 月 10 日，LBI 公司品牌保护总监 Dean Brocious 出具的确认函称"LBI 公司，很高兴确认 AFB 公司被选中来协助清理维多利亚的秘密专卖店当前质量一流的多余库存。LBI 公司将根据与 AFB 公司之间的《库存出售协议》的条款和条件，向 AFB 公司继续提供选定的多余库存产品。AFB 公司的合作伙伴和买家们必须遵守相同的规则和规定……"；2007 年 10 月 6 日，AFB 公司首席执行官 Mohamed A. Barry 出具授权书称"……AFB 公司授权上海锦天服饰有限公司在中华人民共和国境内独家销售维多利亚的秘密产品，并受到 AFB 公司的大力支持，且如 2007 年 9 月 10 日的 LBI 公司的信函所述，获得 LBI 公司的批准。"

锦天公司与被告于 2011 年 11 月签订《战略合作框架协议》，约定"甲方（锦天公司）就自美国 LBI 所购进并经美国 AFB 授权的维多利亚的秘密正品的销售问题，将货品销售、授权经销权利全部托管乙方（被告），乙方享有甲方就美国 AFB 授权所享有的一切权利，甲方除维持现有销售商外自己不再发展销售商……"2012 年 1 月 1 日，锦天公司出具独家经销分销授权书，授权被告为维多利亚的秘密（VICTORIA'S SECRET）系列产品北京市、上海市、广州市、深圳市、天津市、重庆市独家终端零售唯一分销商，暨中国境内商品销售商，同时具有再授权中国各地省市级单店分销商经销权利资格，授权期限自 2012 年 1 月 1 日起至 2022 年 12 月 31 日止。

2013 年 4 月 23 日，在原告诉锦天公司侵害商标权及不正当竞争纠纷一案中，上海市第二中级人民法院作出一审判决，认定锦天公司仅是从原告母公司

LBI 公司处购进了库存产品在国内销售，没有证据证明是美国顶级内衣维多利亚秘密唯一指定总经销商，却自称是美国顶级内衣维多利亚秘密唯一指定总经销商，构成虚假宣传的不正当竞争行为。

原告维多利亚公司诉称：原告"VICTORIA'S SECRET"（中文名：维多利亚的秘密）品牌创立于 20 世纪 70 年代，在本案中主张保护的是在中国注册的"VICTORIA'S SECRET"（第 35 类和第 25 类）、"维多利亚的秘密"（第 35 类和第 25 类）四个商标。原告发现，被告未经许可，擅自在其经营的店铺招牌、员工胸牌、VIP 卡、时装展览等处使用原告的"VICTORIA'S SECRET"商标，在大量的宣传和推广活动中使用原告的"VICTORIA'S SECRET"和"维多利亚的秘密"商标，同时对外宣称其店铺为"VICTORIA'S SECRET"或"维多利亚的秘密"的直营店、专卖店、旗舰店，宣称被告为"VICTORIA'S SECRET"或"维多利亚的秘密"的品牌运营总公司、中国区品牌运营商、中国的总行销公司、北上广深渝津大区总经销、品牌公关行销运营商、维秘中国总部等，开展特许加盟销售活动，构成商标侵权和不正当竞争。故诉至法院，请求判令：被告立即停止商标侵权和不正当竞争行为并赔偿原告经济损失及合理费用共计人民币（以下币种同）510 万元。

被告麦司公司辩称：1. 其销售的维多利亚商品来源于原告母公司有限品牌公司（Limited Brands, Inc.）（以下简称 LBI 公司），被告对原告商标的使用系在商品销售过程中的合理使用，不构成商标侵权和不正当竞争；2. 被告从未实施过原告诉请所主张的虚假宣传行为，也不存在虚假宣传物品；3. 原告涉案商标从未在中国进行过商业使用，故其主张损害赔偿的诉请应予驳回。故请求驳回诉讼请求。

【审判】

上海市第一中级人民法院认为，被告不仅在店铺大门招牌、店内墙面、货柜等处使用了"VICTORIA'S SECRET"标识，还在收银台、员工胸牌、VIP 卡、时装展览等处使用了"VICTORIA'S SECRET"标识，已经超出了指示所销售商品所必需使用的范围；被告在使用上述标识的同时，并没有附加其他标识用以区分服务来源，相反，被告还积极对外宣称美罗城店为维多利亚的秘密上海直营店，被告系维多利亚的秘密中国总部、北上广深渝津大区总经销、中国区品牌运营商等，这使得被告这种超出指示所销售商品所必要范围的标识使用行为具备了表示服务来源的功能，足以使相关公众误认为销售服务系商标权人（原告）提供或者与商标权人（原告）存在商标许可等关联关系。因此，被告对

"VICTORIA'S SECRET" 标识的使用，已经构成了对原告 "VICTORIA'S SECRET" 服务商标（第 35 类）的侵犯，对被告辩称其系对商标的合理使用的主张不予采纳。由于被告在提供服务过程中并没有使用 "维多利亚的秘密" 中文标识，且原告 "维多利亚的秘密"（第 35 类）服务商标并未在中国境内进行过商业性使用，难以认定被告使用的 "VICTORIA'S SECRET" 标识与原告 "维多利亚的秘密"（第 35 类）服务商标构成近似，故被告并不构成对原告 "维多利亚的秘密"（第 35 类）服务商标的侵害。

被告在中国女装网、中国服装品牌网、中国品牌内衣网、微信等网络上发布的信息主要涉及维多利亚的秘密的品牌介绍、产品介绍、门店信息、招商加盟信息，并未涉及产品的网上销售。结合整体网页内容，被告在此广告宣传过程中对 "VICTORIA'S SECRET" 和 "维多利亚的秘密" 标识的使用，向相关公众传达的信息系被告是维多利亚的秘密的品牌经营者，开展该品牌的招商加盟业务，该种使用方式系对服务商标的使用，与 "VICTORIA'S SECRET"（第 35 类）和 "维多利亚的秘密"（第 35 类）商标核定使用的服务类别相同，属于在同一种服务上使用与其注册商标相同的商标，构成商标侵权。

综上，上海市第一中级人民法院判决：麦司公司应于判决生效之日起停止侵犯维多利亚公司享有的核准注册在第 35 类服务上的第 9120211 号 "VICTORIA'S SECRET"、第 4481217 号 "维多利亚的秘密" 注册商标专用权；麦司公司应于判决生效之日起十日内赔偿维多利亚公司经济损失及制止侵权的合理费用共计500 000元。

一审判决后，麦司公司不服，提起上诉。

上海市高级人民法院经审理后认为，麦司公司的上诉请求无事实和法律依据，应予驳回，判决驳回上诉，维持原判。

【评析】

本案涉及的国际知名品牌 "维多利亚的秘密"，具有较大社会影响。被告虽未获得商标授权，但并无证据表明其销售的商品属于假冒商品，故被告可对系争商标进行何种程度的使用成为本案的争议焦点和审理难点。本案裁判正确区分了商标的指示性使用和非指示性使用，清晰界定了商品商标指示性使用与服务商标使用的司法认定标准，即合法取得销售商品权利的经营者，可以在商品销售中对权利人的商品商标进行指示性使用，但应当限于指示商品来源，如超出了指示商品来源所必需的范围，则会对相关的服务商标专用权构成侵害。商标使用行为可能导致相关公众误认为销售服务系商标权人提供或者与商标权人存在商标许可等关联关系的，应认定已经超出指示所销售商品来源所必要的范围，具备了指示、识别服务来源的功能。该案审理对于类似案件具有较好的借鉴意义，也有助于引导、规范市场经营者在商品流通环节的商标使用行为。

一、关于麦司公司是否已经获得维多利亚公司涉案商品商标和服务商标的使用授权

根据《库存出售协议》，库存产品购买者不得自称为卖方的特许或委托代理商或关联方；根据 LBI 公司出具的确认函，锦天公司可以在中国境内销售库存产品，但须遵守《库存出售协议》相关条款。虽然锦天公司与麦司公司签订了《战略合作框架协议》，且锦天公司授权麦司公司为独家终端零售唯一分销商，但仅表明麦司公司有权在中国境内独家销售所购进的标注涉案商标的库存产品。从库存出售的交易链条可以看出，整个交易过程并不涉及涉案商标的授权使用。无论麦司公司是否知晓《库存出售协议》，其作为库存产品的购买者，其依法仅获得该批产品的所有权，即享有对该批产品进行占有、使用、收益、处分的权利。物权的移转并不意味着麦司公司自动获得涉案商标的使用许可，其仅可在销售该批产品所必需的最低限度内，对涉案商标进行指示性使用。本案中，维多利亚公司并未主张麦司公司因进行目录销售和因特网销售而构成侵权，因此即使麦司公司未进行目录销售和因特网销售，也不能将此作为本案中麦司公司不侵权的抗辩理由。维多利亚公司作为涉案商标的权利人，未向 AFB 公司、锦天公司以及麦司公司授权使用其涉案商标 "VICTORIA'S SECRET"、"维多利亚的秘密"。AFB 公司亦未获得维多利亚公司关于涉案商标的使用授权，更无权向他人授权使用涉案商标，其授权书所称的 "独家销售"，不能理解为涉案商品商标和服务商标的使用授权。因此，麦司公司关于其已获得涉案商标使用授权的上诉意见，没有事实基础和法律依据。

二、关于麦司公司是否侵害了维多利亚公司的涉案服务商标专用权

本案中，麦司公司所销售的商品并非假冒 "VICTORIA'S SECRET" "维多利亚的秘密" 商标的商品，维多利亚公司亦未主张麦司公司所售商品为侵权产品，双方争议在于如何评价麦司公司在销售过程中使用 "VICTORIA'S SECRET" "维多利亚的秘密" 标识的行为。值得注意的是，维多利亚公司在第 35 类服务上享有 "VICTORIA'S SECRET" "维多利亚的秘密" 的注册商标专用权，这表明在此类服务上，他人未经许可不得使用 "VICTORIA'S SECRET" "维多利亚的秘密" 注册商标。同时，由于麦司公司所销售的并非假冒商品，因此其也应具有将 "VICTORIA'S SECRET" "维多利亚的秘密" 商品商标在销

售活动中指示商品来源、以便消费者识别商品来源的权利，对此商标权人应当予以容忍。但是，麦司公司在指示性使用涉案商品商标过程中，应当限于指示商品来源，如超出了指示商品来源所必需的范围，则有可能侵害相关的服务商标专用权。如果对销售过程中商品商标的指示性使用不加以限制，则可能危及相关服务商标的存在价值。根据本案查明的事实，麦司公司在店铺大门招牌、店内墙面、货柜以及收银台、员工胸牌、VIP 卡、时装展览等处使用了"VICTORIA'S SECRET"标识，且对外宣称美罗城店为维多利亚的秘密上海直营店、其系维多利亚的秘密中国总部、北上广深渝津大区总经销、中国区品牌运营商等，这可能导致相关公众误认为销售服务系商标权人提供或者与商标权人存在商标许可等关联关系，因此已经超出指示所销售商品来源所必要的范围，具备了指示、识别服务来源的功能，构成对"VICTORIA'S SECRET"服务商标专用权的侵害。麦司公司在网络广告宣传过程中使用"VICTORIA'S SECRET""维多利亚的秘密"标识，目的是利用涉案商标开展产品销售相关的招商加盟业务，系在与涉案服务商标同类的服务上使用与涉案服务商标相同的商标，原审法院认定其构成侵权，并无不当。综上，法院对涉案商品商标和服务商标所进行的区分认定，并进而认定麦司公司侵害了维多利亚公司涉案服务商标专用权，并无不当。

三、关于赔偿数额的确定

根据法律规定，不正当竞争案件中的赔偿数额，按照权利人因被侵权所受到的实际损失确定，实际损失难以确定的可以按照侵权人因侵权所获得的利益确定，权利人的损失或者侵权人获得的利益难以确定的，由法院根据侵权行为的情节进行法定赔偿，且侵权人应当承担被侵害的经营者因调查该经营者侵害其合法权益的不正当竞争行为所支付的合理费用。本案中，维多利亚公司的实际损失、麦司公司的侵权获利均无法查清，应由法院根据侵权行为的情节以法定赔偿方法确定赔偿数额。综合考虑麦司公司在锦天公司被判侵权后仍继续进行虚假宣传、主观过错较大，麦司公司称所收取每家加盟店的品牌使用费达 6 至 50 万元，维多利亚公司的本案维权开支超出 20 万元等因素，原审法院依法酌情确定的包含合理费用在内的 50 万元赔偿数额，并无不妥；麦司公司所开设加盟店的数量，仅为确定损害赔偿数额的参考因素之一，并非原判确定赔偿数额的唯一依据。因此，麦司公司关于原审认定事实错误、赔偿数额畸高的上诉意见，法院不予采信。

（撰稿人：徐卓斌）

企业字号与商标冲突中停止侵权及有
惩罚性功能之法定赔偿的适用问题

——大润发投资有限公司与康成投资（中国）有限公司
侵犯商标权及不正当竞争纠纷案

【提要】

本案是一起典型的故意攀附他人商誉，将他人商标申请为企业名称中字号的侵害商标权和不正当竞争纠纷案件，人民法院在本案中着重考量了责令停止使用企业名称民事责任的承担问题，并探索了具有惩罚性功能的法定赔偿之适用问题。

【案情】

上诉人（原审被告）： 大润发投资有限公司（以下简称大润发公司）

被上诉人（原审原告）： 康成投资（中国）有限公司（以下简称康成公司）

案由： 侵害商标权及不正当竞争纠纷

一审案号： （2016）沪民终 409 号

二审案号： （2015）沪知民初字第 731 号

2013 年 11 月，康成公司受让取得"大润发"商标，核定服务项目第 35 类货物展出、推销（替他人）等，并在大陆地区开设 318 家大型"大润发"超市，多年来在外资连锁企业中名列前茅。2015 年 1 月，"大润发"商标被上海市工商行政管理局评为上海市著名商标，类别第 35 类，认定商品或服务：推销（替他人）。

2014 年 10 月，大润发公司成立，经营范围日用百货等销售，并成立沥林等分公司，正筹备多处特许加盟店。2015 年 8 月，其与案外人签订《大润发特许协议》，许可后者使用大润发公司的店铺字号、服务标识等。在大润发公司

网页上存在"大润发企业"字样，显示商场图片的正上方存在被控侵权标识一
"大润发"。公司简介称：目前在江西省十余城市内开设分店，总营业面
积达四十多万平方米。此外，在沥林等分店收据、购物袋上显示有"大润发投
资有限公司"等字样或者突出使用了被控侵权标识二"大润发"或被控侵权标识
一"大润发"。大润发公司曾因宣称时突出使用"大润发"字样，被赣
州市工商行政管理局和广州开发区市场监督管理局处以罚款。

2015 年康成公司以大润发公司侵害注册商标专用权和不正当竞争为由，要
求法院判令其停止侵权并支付 500 万元的惩罚性赔偿。

【审判】

上海知识产权法院一审认为，大润发公司与康成公司均从事与"大润发"
商标核定使用类别相同的服务业务；大润发公司突出使用的两被控侵权标识和
企业名称均与"大润发"商标有基本相同的文字，容易使相关公众产生误认。
其次，综合"大润发"商标的使用时间、康成公司的经营规模、市场排名等因
素，认定"大润发"商标在大润发公司注册成立时已成为行业内具有较高知名
度的商标。作为同业竞争者，大润发公司明知"大润发"商标已注册使用的情
况下，仍使用与"大润发"商标相同的字号，主观上攀附"大润发"商标知名
度的意图十分明显。因此，大润发公司的行为侵害了康成公司的商标权并构成
不正当竞争，应当立即停止侵害。关于消除影响，考虑到侵权行为的侵权范围
较大，故判令大润发公司在报纸上刊登声明消除影响。至于赔偿损失，由于本
案证据不能直接推定侵权人获利，也无法计算商标许可使用费，故应适用法定
赔偿。对于惩罚性赔偿的诉请，大润发公司的行为虽符合《商标法》第六十三
条第一款"恶意侵犯商标权，情节严重"的规定，但由于确定惩罚性赔偿数额
的基础不存在，亦无法适用惩罚性赔偿。但一审法院认为《商标法》确立填补
损失和惩罚侵权双重目标的损害赔偿制度，作为计算损害赔偿兜底方式的法定
赔偿制度，同样应兼具补偿和惩罚的双重功能。故在确定法定赔偿数额时，可
将大润发公司的主观恶意作为考量因素之一。因此，综合考虑商标知名度及对
康成公司的贡献情况、大润发公司的主观恶意、侵权情节和侵权后果等因素后，
确定大润发公司赔偿康成公司包括合理费用在内的经济损失 300 万元。一审判
决后，大润发公司不服，提起上诉。

上海市高级人民法院二审认为，除一审判决相关理由外，关于停止侵权责
任，鉴于字号是其企业名称中的核心部分，与"大润发"注册商标在文字上完

全相同，而"大润发"商标享有较高的知名度和良好声誉，因此，即便在经营中使用企业名称全称，客观上仍无法避免使相关公众产生该公司与康成公司之间存在关联关系的误认。倘若允许此种行为的延续，显然会破坏诚实信用及公平有序的商业道德准则。因此，只有责令大润发公司停止在其企业字号上对"大润发"文字的使用行为，才能彻底消除相关公众对两家企业存在关联关系的误认。至于消除影响，涉案侵权行为规模和范围较大，同时又涉及普通公众的日常生活，侵权结果较为严重，且使用"大润发"字号的侵权行为客观上攀附了"大润发"商标良好的商誉，需以消除影响之民事责任承担方式弥补该商标商誉受到的损害。此外，大润发公司的侵权行为使得相关公众对其与康成公司之间的关系产生误认，客观上亦存在消除误认及不良影响之必要。关于侵权损害赔偿数额，二审法院认为一审判决综合考虑了商标权利情况以及侵权情节等因素，尤其衡量了侵权人的主观恶意情况及侵权后果这一重要因素，再结合合理费用酌情确定 300 万元的法定赔偿最高金额，于法有据。综上，驳回上诉，维持原判。

【评析】

本案涉及问题较多，但归结起来本案审理的重点在于在企业名称与注册商标相冲突案件中，人民法院如何适用停止企业名称使用的民事责任以及具有惩罚性功能的法定赔偿。

一、停止侵权责任在企业名称使用中的把握

一般而言，对注册商标与企业名称冲突纠纷，人民法院遵循诚实信用、维护公平竞争和保护在先权利等原则，区分不同情形依法处理，即根据当事人的诉讼请求、案件具体情况以及适用责任方式后的效果，确定当事人是承担停止使用还是规范使用企业名称的民事责任，① 不能因突出使用企业名称中的字号就以侵犯商标专用权为由一律判决停止或变更企业名称。

具体来说，人民法院在实践中会根据企业名称与商标的注册顺序、注册行为的合法性、历史因素和使用现状，按当事人诉请区分处理。第一种情况，当企业名称的注册使用行为本身违法，即不正当地将他人具有较高知名度的在先

---

① 《最高人民法院关于审理注册商标、企业名称与在先权利冲突的民事纠纷案件若干问题的规定》第四条规定："被诉企业名称侵犯注册商标专用权或者构成不正当竞争的，人民法院可以根据原告的诉讼请求和案件具体情况，确定被告承担停止使用、规范使用等民事责任。"

注册商标作为字号注册登记为企业名称，无论突出使用或规范使用均难以避免产生市场混淆的，可以按照不正当竞争行为处理，并根据当事人的请求判决停止使用或者变更企业名称。第二种情况，若被诉企业名称注册时该企业并无恶意，系因历史原因导致企业名称注册在先，该市场主体突出使用字号已具有一定知名度、并形成与注册商标可以区分的标识效果，不会导致相关公众混淆的，不构成侵害商标权，此时出于保护注册商标、维护公平竞争市场秩序的考虑，法院允许其在特定范围内使用特定方式突出使用该字号，即对企业名称的使用方式和范围作出限制，便足以制止被告的侵权行为。① 第三种情况，倘若该市场主体不规范使用其在后注册的企业名称，但创设字号系出于历史因素，该注册行为本身不违法，由于在相同或者类似商品上突出使用与他人注册商标相同或相近的字号，易使相关公众产生误认，给他人注册商标权造成损害，按侵犯商标专用权行为处理，故可根据案情和诉请规范使用企业名称或停止突出使用行为。②

综上，根据上述规则确定被诉侵权行为性质后，对于企业名称是否适用停止侵权之民事责任需要结合行为的性质和特点，衡量采用具体的停止侵权民事责任方式后能否达到合目的性、必要性和均衡性。也就是适用后能否实现停止侵害的目的；如若有多种能够有效实现停止侵害目的的手段可以适用，应选择会对被诉侵权人的合法利益造成不利影响较小的手段。③

在"大润发"案中，法院认定双方系同业竞争者，大润发公司亦自认在其创设企业名称时明知"大润发"商标，故大润发公司明显具有攀附他人商誉的主观故意。其在经营中全面使用与"大润发"商标相同的企业字号，又极其容易造成相关消费者的混淆和误认，构成不正当竞争行为。由此，鉴于"大润发"字号是大润发公司登记企业名称中的核心部分，与"大润发"注册商标在文字上完全相同之被诉侵权行为特点；并结合"大润发"商标享有的知名度和良好声誉，即便在经营中使用其企业名称全称，仍无法避免使相关消费者产生该公司与康成公司之间存在关联关系的误认之客观效果；在考虑到如果允许此种注册及使用行为的延续，显然会破坏诚实信用及公平有序的商业道德准则的

① （2016）最高法民申 1405 号，浙江大光明眼镜有限公司诉合肥市大光明眼镜有限责任公司侵害商标权纠纷案，该案判决未认定商标侵权，但为保护注册商标、维护公平竞争市场秩序，要求合肥市大光明眼镜有限责任公司今后使用"大光明"字号时附加地域标识，从而对商品来源有所区分。

② 《最高人民法院知识产权审判案例指导（第三辑）》，中国法制出版社 2011 年 5 月第一版，第 254～255 页。

③ 《最高人民法院知识产权审判案例指导（第六辑）》，中国法制出版社 2014 年 7 月第一版，第 263～264 页。

适用之必要性；综上，法院认为只有责令大润发公司停止在其企业名称中的字号上使用"大润发"文字，才能彻底消除相关公众对两家企业存在关联关系的误认。

二、如何理解法定赔偿兼具补偿与惩罚的双重功能

2013年修订的《商标法》正式规定了惩罚性赔偿制度，但实践中适用商标侵权惩罚性赔偿案例较少。本案商标权利人要求侵权人承担500万元惩罚性赔偿，法院结合具体案情阐述了对于惩罚性赔偿在商标侵权案件中适用的前提条件以及适用具有惩罚性功能法定赔偿的具体考量。

1. 适用惩罚性赔偿的前提条件

《商标法》第六十三条第二款规定，"对恶意侵犯商标专用权，情节严重的，可以在按照上述方法确定数额的一倍以上三倍以下确定赔偿数额"，规定了适用惩罚性赔偿的前提条件。其一，存在"恶意"主观要件，较补偿性赔偿（包括权利人损失、侵权人获利、许可费倍数）惩罚性赔偿更强调对侵权行为的惩罚和遏制。因此，惩罚性赔偿责任的主观要件较补偿性赔偿责任更为严格，即"恶意"不仅要求行为人主观上为故意且有不良的主观目的。例如大润发公司就具有明显攀附他人商标的恶意，多次受到行政处罚后仍实施其侵权行为，并不断扩大其侵权范围意图获取更多不法获利。其二，造成"情节严重"的客观结果，法律虽对此没有具体规定，但可根据商标侵权案件的客观情况，包括侵权行为的时间、次数、规模、范围和方式，以及商标权人利益的损失和侵权人的获利以及对于社会产生的负面影响来具体判断。例如大润发公司侵犯康成公司商标权所涉的业务领域与百姓日常生活息息相关，极有可能影响到社会公众的食品安全，故应认定造成情节严重的后果。

2. 如何适用具有惩罚性功能的法定赔偿

除前述两个适用前提条件外，惩罚性赔偿还有一个适用基础，即我国《商标法》第六十三条规定中的"可以在按照上述方法确定数额⋯⋯"即只有在确切计算出权利人损失、侵权人获利或商标许可使用费倍数的损害赔偿具体数额之基础上，才能得出惩罚性赔偿的具体数额，才可适用惩罚性赔偿。大润发案就属于凭借现有证据无法计算出上述三种补偿性赔偿的具体数额，从而导致惩罚性赔偿适用的前提基础不存在的情形。然而该案中，大润发公司的恶意侵害商标权和不正当竞争行为明显符合前述适用惩罚性赔偿的两个前提条件，其侵权行为后果严重且具有明显主观恶意，因此仅采用补偿性赔偿方式填平康成公司因侵权所受到的相应损失显然并不能起到惩罚并遏制此类侵权行为再次发生的作用。

对于上述应适用惩罚性赔偿却无适用基础的情形，本案审理法院另辟蹊径，探索通过法定赔偿来实现与惩罚性赔偿相同的惩罚和遏制功能之途径。以往观点认为《商标法》规定的法定赔偿，其实质是法院在无法查明实际损害赔偿额的情况下，根据案件事实酌定的一个赔偿额，但酌定仍是以"填平原则"为准则。对此，本案审理法院却认为，法定赔偿的功能并不仅局限于补偿权利人损失，同时也兼顾了惩罚性功能。首先，法院在确定法定赔偿侵权赔偿金时已实际结合了侵权人的主观状态和侵权方式等因素，这些因素也是惩罚性赔偿确定时必须考量的，因此法院适用法定赔偿和惩罚性赔偿时均会考量侵权人的主观恶意程度。其次，由于实践中举证困难，法院适用法定赔偿确定商标侵权判赔金额的比例较高，试想若在适用法定赔偿案件中一律不考虑对恶意侵权人进行惩罚，势必使商标惩罚性赔偿制度形同虚设。最后，《商标法》的修订即是为了加大保护商标权的力度，力求既准确反映被侵害商标权的相应市场价值，又适当考虑侵权行为人的主观状态，因此法定赔偿可实现以补偿为主、以惩罚为辅的双重效果，也是适应新修订《商标法》的发展需求。综上，法院在适用法定赔偿时考量恶意侵权人的主观状态以及是否存在重复侵权、假冒商标等严重情节，并在确定赔偿数额时酌情选取适当高于市场价值的损害赔偿数额，这样使得法定赔偿既有补偿权利人损失的作用又带有惩罚恶意侵权人的作用，同样也符合新修订《商标法》进一步加大损害赔偿力度，意图遏制商标侵权发生之立法目的。

此外，需进一步厘清的是根据《商标法》第六十三条规定，在适用惩罚性赔偿数额的计算时不能以法定赔偿作为基础数额，即具体计算惩罚性赔偿时只能酌情考虑对三种补偿性赔偿金的倍数，这是因为在已是酌情确定法定赔偿之基础上再酌情确定惩罚性倍数将会使惩罚性损失赔偿金出现过大偏差，故不能将惩罚性赔偿与法定赔偿并用。

综上所述，人民法院依照法律规定，强化了在恶意商标侵权和不正当竞争案件中对于权利人合法利益的保护，通过责令侵权人完全停止使用其企业名称以及在适用具有惩罚性功能的法定赔偿的具体考量，有助于给权利人提供充分的司法救济，使侵权人付出足够的侵权代价，营造出严格保护知识产权、坚决制止侵权人的侵权行为法律氛围。

（撰稿人：曹闻佳）

"全面模仿、立体侵权"的商标侵权案件

——宝马股份公司诉上海创佳服饰有限公司、德马集团（国际）控股有限公司、周乐琴侵害商标权及不正当竞争纠纷案

【提要】

1. 当被控侵权商标标识中存在多个相近的侵权商标标识，且其中某个被控侵权商标标识系权利商标驰名前已经注册的，并不能当然免除在权利商标驰名之后注册的被控侵权商标标识的民事责任，而应当根据下述三个条件判断之后注册的被控侵权商标标识是否属于对驰名商标的复制、模仿，应否停止使用：（1）被控侵权人是否具有明显的侵权主观恶意；（2）之后注册的被控侵权商标标识的实际使用情况是否存在对之前注册的商标标识的商誉传承；（3）之后注册的被控侵权标识是否与权利商标相同或近似，足以误导公众并可能致使权利人的利益受到损害。2. 针对被控侵权商标标识的注册、使用等行为由不同主体分别实施的情况，应当根据不同主体之间是否具有共同的主观恶意，是否具有明显的意思联络，判断其应否共同承担侵权民事责任。3. 在针对驰名商标保护的案件中，应当严格遵循驰名商标保护个案认定、因需认定、事实认定等基本制度，针对不同行为、不同标识，分门别类地予以保护或不保护，驰名商标保护或一般商标保护。

【案情】

原告：宝马股份公司（以下简称宝马公司）

被告：上海创佳服饰有限公司（以下简称创佳公司）

被告：德马集团（国际）控股有限公司（以下简称德马公司）

被告：周乐琴

案由：侵害商标权及不正当竞争纠纷

案号：（2015）沪知民初字第 58 号

宝马公司系世界知名的汽车制造商，在第 12 类"机动车辆"等商品上注册有"![商标]"、"寶馬"、"BMW"商标，在第 18 类"皮革及人造皮革"，第 25 类的服装、鞋、帽等商品上，注册有"![商标]""![商标]""BMW"商标。

2008 年 7 月，被告周乐琴使用"宝马"和"BMW"作为字号成立原名为"德国宝马集团（国际）控股有限公司［GERMAN BMW GROUP（INTL）HOLDING LIMITED］"的被告德马公司。嗣后，被告德马公司转让获得第 25 类"![BMN]""![商标]"商标，注册获得第 25 类"BMN"商标。被告周乐琴转让获得第 25 类"![商标]"商标，注册获得第 25 类"![商标]"商标、第 18 类"![商标]"商标，被告德马公司、周乐琴通过将上述商标授权被告创佳公司使用的方式与被告创佳公司自 2009 年共同设立了 BMN 品牌加盟体系。之后，被告德马公司、创佳公司在经营 BMN 品牌加盟体系的过程中，将"![商标]""![商标]"商标着色或使用"![商标]"商标，与"BMN"商标、"BMN"标识，以及德国宝马集团（国际）控股有限公司［GERMAN BMW GROUP（INTL）HOLDING LIMITED］企业名称、德国宝马集团、德国宝马、宝马等文字相组合，并广泛使用于品牌加盟手册、经营场所装潢、广告宣传等 BMN 品牌加盟体系中，以及生产、销售的服装、鞋、包等商品上，并在全国多个省市发展加盟体系并销售至今。

宝马公司诉称：2008 年开始，被告德马公司、被告周乐琴、被告创佳公司共同合谋，通过分工合作的方式设立、经营了 BMN 品牌加盟体系，使用原告宝马公司驰名商标"宝马""BMW"作为字号注册了被告德马公司；模仿原告宝马公司"![商标]""BMW"驰名商标，注册并使用"![商标]""BMN"等商标；使用与原告宝马公司"BMW"（第 18 类）、"![商标]""![商标]"（第 18 类、第 25 类）等商标近似的侵权标识以及德国宝马集团（国际）控股有限公司、德马集团（国际）控股有限公司、德国宝马、德国宝马集团等文字，构成对原告的商标侵权及不正当竞争。请求判令：1. 被告创佳公司、被告德马公司、被告周乐琴立即停止对原告涉案注册商标专用权的侵害；2. 被告德马公司立即停止使用"德马集团（国际）控股有限公司"以及"德国宝马集团（国际）控股有限公司"的企业名称；3. 被告创佳公司、被告德马公司、被告周乐琴连带赔偿宝马公司经济损失人民币 300 万元（包括律师费及合理支出）；4. 被告创佳公司、被告德马公司、被告周乐琴在《中国工商报》以显著位置刊登声明，消除因侵权造成的不良影响。

【审判】

上海知识产权法院认为：（一）鉴于，本案中需对被告德马公司转让获得第 25 类 " $\textit{BMN}$ " " ⊕ " 商标，注册获得第 25 类 " $\textbf{BMN}$ " 商标。被告周乐琴转让获得第 25 类 " ⊗ " 商标，注册获得第 25 类 " ⊗ " 商标、第 18 类 " ⊗ " 商标，是否属于对原告驰名商标 " ⊕ " "BMW" "寶馬" 的复制、模仿，故有认定商标为驰名商标的必要。且原告宝马公司在本案中所提供的证据亦足以证明其 " ⊕ " "BMW" "寶馬" 注册商标至少在 2007 年就已属驰名商标，并持续至今。

（二）被告创佳公司、德马公司、周乐琴明知 " ⊕ " "BMW" "寶馬" 商标属于原告的驰名商标，仍恶意共谋，共同建立 BMN 品牌加盟体系并通过生产、销售被控侵权商品、授权 BMN 品牌授权经销商、广告宣传等商业活动使用侵权标识，实施了如下涉案商标侵权及不正当竞争行为：1. 以 "BMW" "宝马" 作为字号注册成立被告德马公司，并在 BMN 品牌加盟体系的经营中使用德国宝马集团（国际）控股有限公司 [GERMAN BMW GROUP（INTL）HOLDING LIMITED] 并授权 BMN 品牌授权销售商使用的行为构成不正当竞争。2. 在第 25 类、第 18 类商品上使用德国宝马、德国宝马集团并授权 BMN 品牌授权经销商使用，构成对原告 "寶馬" 驰名商标的侵害。3. 在第 25 类商品上注册、使用并授权 BMN 品牌授权经销商使用 " ⊗ " 注册商标，属于模仿原告 " ⊕ " 驰名商标，误导公众，并致使原告的利益可能受到损害的商标侵权行为。4. 鉴于没有证据证明 " $\textit{BMN}$ " 注册商标曾被实际使用，故对 " $\textbf{BMN}$ " 注册商标的注册使用亦不存在对 " $\textit{BMN}$ " 注册商标的商誉传承。因此，被告在第 25 类商品上注册、使用并授权经销商使用 " $\textbf{BMN}$ " 注册商标及 " $\textbf{BMN}$ " 标识，属于模仿原告 "BMW" 驰名商标，误导公众，并致使原告的利益可能受到损害的商标侵权行为。5. 在第 18 类、第 25 类商品上使用 " ⊞ " 标识、" ⊕ " 阴阳纹标识、" ⊗ " 阴阳纹标识、" ⊗ " 标识，侵犯了原告 " ⊕ " " ⊕ " 注册商标（第 18 类、第 25 类）专用权。6. 在第 18 类商品上使用"🔲"、**BMN**、**BMN**标识，侵犯了原告"⊕""◉"
"BMW"注册商标（第18类）专用权。

（三）原告宝马公司下列侵权主张在本案中并不成立。1. 鉴于"⊕"
"⊗"商标标识与原告"◉"驰名商标标识不相近似，也不会造成相关公众的
混淆和误认，故对"⊕""⊗"商标标识的注册使用，不构成对原告"◉"
驰名商标的侵权。2. 鉴于德马公司、德马集团（国际）控股有限公司与原告
"寶馬"商标并不构成相同或近似，不会造成相关公众的混淆和误认，故对德
马公司、德马集团（国际）控股有限公司的使用不构成对原告的不正当竞争和
商标侵权。3. 鉴于没有证据证明"*BMN*"注册商标在本案中被使用，故
原告对被告德马公司注册"*BMN*"商标行为的异议，应由相关行政管理
部门依法予以处理。

综上，上海知识产权法院判决：一、被告创佳公司、德马公司、周乐琴立
即停止对原告宝马公司享有的"◉""寶馬""BMW""◉""⊙"注册商
标专用权的侵害；二、被告德马公司立即停止使用"德国宝马集团（国际）控
股有限公司"的不正当竞争行为；三、被告创佳公司、德马公司、周乐琴在
《中国工商报》刊登声明，消除因侵权行为对原告宝马公司造成的影响；
四、被告创佳公司、德马公司、周乐琴共同赔偿原告宝马公司包括合理费用在
内的经济损失人民币300万元；五、驳回原告宝马公司的其余诉讼请求。一审
判决后，各方当事人均未提起上诉。

【评析】

本案是一起极为新颖和典型的"建立体系、全面模仿、立体侵权"的商标
侵权及不正当竞争纠纷案件。本案中涉及对权利商标驰名之前已注册商标延伸
注册获得的商标，其注册、使用是否受驰名商标的规制；在商标侵权案件中针
对不同主体实施有关联的不同行为，如何认定共同侵权；如何在对驰名商标保
护的案件中正确区分侵权行为、侵权标识等诸多法律问题。本案亦具有如下明
显特征：1. 建立特许经营加盟体系，以合法形式掩盖非法目的。在该类侵权案
件中，被控侵权人往往通过转让、注册商标、注册企业字号等方式，建立特许
经营加盟体系，显示其标识使用的"合法性"，试图掩盖其侵权行为的本质和
目的。2. 全面模仿，侵权行为多样化。在该类商标侵权案件中，被控侵权人通

过全面模仿权利人标识的方法混淆视听，在具体经营过程中不仅涉及针对权利人所有主要商标实施的——对应侵权行为，还涉及字号侵权的不正当竞争行为，甚至是其他侵权行为。3. 不同主体分工合作，共同实施从注册到使用的立体侵权行为。被控侵权人通过分工合作，转让、注册商标、字号，全面模仿权利标识，通过特许经营体系复制侵权等手段，从不同纬度立体地、全方位地实施侵权行为，侵权影响范围大损害严重。

（撰稿人：何渊）

注册商标与企业名称权利冲突的司法判定

——上海国福龙凤食品有限公司与宁波龙凤食品有限公司、
上海亿阳食品有限公司侵害商标权及不正当竞争纠纷

【提要】

在后使用的企业名称与在先注册的商标发生权利冲突时，应考虑在先注册商标知名度、企业名称的使用方式、使用人的主观恶意等因素。企业名称因突出使用而侵犯在先注册商标专用权的，依法按照商标侵权行为处理。企业名称未突出使用，但其使用足以产生市场混淆，依法按照反不正当竞争行为处理。

法官可以通过释明证明责任、适时公开心证的方式，推动当事人积极举证以查明当事人损失或获利情况。对于仿冒纠纷，应综合考量涉案标识对侵权人营利的贡献度等因素，在严格保护的同时注重比例协调，合理确定赔偿金额。

【案情】

原告：上海国福龙凤食品有限公司

被告：宁波龙凤食品有限公司

被告：上海亿阳食品有限公司

生效案号：（2016）沪 0115 民初 11825 号

原告上海国福龙凤食品有限公司（以下简称国福龙凤公司）于 1992 年 8 月 20 日成立，于 1996 年在第 30 类汤圆等商品上注册了第 887059 号"龍鳳"商标，经续展注册，该商标在有效期内。国福龙凤公司自 1994 年起，先后在北京、广州、杭州等地设立分公司，其中宁波分公司于 1997 年设立。国福龙凤公司的关联公司浙江龙凤食品有限公司于 2003 年 6 月 12 日成立。2000 年至 2016 年期间，国福龙凤公司通过平面、电子媒体进行了大量的广告宣传。国福龙凤公司及其关联企业曾获得许多荣誉，包括"中国名牌产品""上海市著名商标"

"上海名牌产品"等。

被告宁波龙凤食品有限公司（以下简称宁波龙凤公司）于1999年2月1日成立，原企业名称为"慈溪市世伟食品有限公司"，于2006年更名为"宁波新汇园食品有限公司"，于2012年更名为宁波龙凤食品有限公司。宁波龙凤公司于2014年10月21日在第30类的汤圆等商品上注册了第12695038号"NBo LongFeng"图文商标。宁波龙凤公司提供的2013年至2015年期间用于报税的账簿显示：（一）2013年营业利润为 -484 944.30元，不含税总销售收入9 170 477.85元，其中销售自产产品的收入为518 237.92元；（二）2014年营业利润为 -115 750.16元，不含税总销售收入8 696 017.96元，其中销售自产产品的收入为433 834.78元；（三）2015年营业利润为 -25 757.77元，不含税总销售收入9 458 788.69元，其中销售自产产品的收入为506 171.76元。宁波龙凤公司承认，上述账簿与企业的实际收支情况有出入，企业存在部分收支未入账的情况。

宁波龙凤公司在公司网站及部分商品包装上标注"宁波龙凤食品有限公司"时，以较大的字号标注"宁波龙凤"字样，而以小得多的字号标注"食品有限公司"字样，且"宁波龙凤"颜色更加醒目。宁波龙凤公司的部分商品名称中有"龙凤"字样，如"龙凤香糯小圆子""龙凤云汤圆""龙凤金汤圆"等。被告上海亿阳食品有限公司（以下简称上海亿阳公司）同时销售原、被告的速冻食品。

国福龙凤公司自2014年开始使用金色为底色的包装袋。包装袋正面左右两侧分别印有龙和凤凰的图案。正面左侧有一纵向的长方形红色装饰条，该装饰条上标注了白色的"龍鳳 LONGFONG"图文标识。正面上方印有商品名称。正面中间有汤圆馅料原材料的图片及一个汤勺，汤勺中有一个已开口可以看到馅料的汤圆。宁波龙凤公司金汤圆系列商品的包装袋以金色为底色。包装袋正面左侧有一纵向的长方形红色装饰条，有一凤凰环绕着装饰条，装饰条上标注了白色的"NBo LongFeng 宁波龙凤"图文标识，在"宁波龙凤"下方以小得多的黑色文字标注"食品有限公司"字样。正面右上方有带下划线的商品名称"金汤圆"。正面中间有一个饰有龙纹的碗、一个汤勺及汤圆馅料原材料的图片，碗中装满汤圆，汤勺中有一个已开口可以看到馅料的汤圆。

原告国福龙凤公司诉称：原告在汤圆等商品上注册了"龍鳳"商标，经过使用，该商标已具有很高的知名度。宁波龙凤公司亦生产销售速冻食品，其以"龙凤"作为企业字号，构成不正当竞争，其在公司网站及商品包装袋上突出使用"宁波龙凤"字号及使用含有"龙凤"字样的商品名称，侵犯了原告的注册商标专用权。原告使用在汤圆金色包装袋上的文字、图案及组合属于知名商品特有包装、装潢。被告宁波龙凤公司在金汤圆系列商品上使用与原告知名商品特有包装、装潢近似的包装、装潢，构成不正当竞争。被告上海亿阳公司是宁波龙凤公司的销售商之一，其主观上存在过错，应与宁波龙凤公司承担部分连带责任。请求法院判令：1. 两被告停止侵犯原告商标权行为；2. 两被告停止侵犯原告知名商品特有包装的不正当竞争行为；3. 被告宁波龙凤公司停止使用其企业名称的不正当竞争行为，变更其企业名称，变更后不得含有"龙凤"或近似字样；4. 被告宁波龙凤公司赔偿原告经济损失及合理费用 300 万元，被告上海亿阳公司对其中的 30 万元承担连带责任。

被告宁波龙凤公司辩称：宁波龙凤公司的企业名称经依法登记，其使用企业名称简称不构成侵权。宁波龙凤公司商品的包装、装潢与原告不同，消费者不会误认。宁波龙凤公司自产商品的销售收入仅占其营业收入的一小部分，公司的营业收入主要来源于代销案外人品牌食品的销售收入。

被告上海亿阳公司辩称：其实际销售了 129 箱涉案商品，销售金额仅 1 万多元。商品来源合法，其与宁波龙凤公司之间无共同侵权的合意，不应当承担赔偿责任。

【审判】

上海市浦东新区人民法院经审理认为，本案涉及侵害商标权纠纷及不正当竞争纠纷。关于侵害商标权纠纷，原告注册并使用在汤圆等商品上的"龍鳳"商标具有较高的知名度，被告宁波龙凤公司在公司网站及商品包装袋上标注企业名称时，突出使用"宁波龙凤"字样，容易导致相关公众的混淆，侵害了原告的注册商标专用权。被告宁波龙凤公司在汤圆等商品上使用含有"龙凤"字样的商品名称，误导公众，亦侵害了原告的注册商标专用权。

关于不正当竞争纠纷。被告宁波龙凤公司于 2012 年开始使用龙凤字号，在此之前，原告的字号和商标已具有较高的知名度，被告使用龙凤字号，主观上有攀附故意，客观上易使相关公众对商品来源产生混淆，其行为违反了诚实信用原则及公认的商业道德，构成不正当竞争。关于擅自使用知名商品特有包装、装潢纠纷，原、被告的汤圆包装袋虽然使用了相似的金黄色，也使用了一些相同的元素，但两者也存在较大差异，以相关公众的一般注意力为标准，不会将被告的商品与原告的商品混淆，不构成不正当竞争。

被告宁波龙凤公司的行为构成侵害商标权及不正当竞争，应承担停止侵权、赔偿损失的民事责任。上海亿阳公司知道被告宁波龙凤公司生产的涉案商品是侵权商品却仍予以销售，主观上具有过错，构成帮助侵权，应当承担相应的赔偿责任。

上海市浦东新区人民法院判决：宁波龙凤公司停止侵权、变更企业名称，变更后的企业名称中不得含有"龙凤"字样；上海亿阳公司停止销售宁波龙凤公司生产的侵权商品；宁波龙凤公司赔偿国福龙凤公司经济损失 100 万元及为制止侵权行为所支出的合理费用136 880元，被告上海亿阳公司对其中的 3 万元承担连带赔偿责任。

一审判决后，双方当事人均未上诉，判决已生效，被告主动履行了判决确定的企业更名和支付赔偿款的义务。

【评析】

一、注册商标与企业名称权利冲突的解决路径

根据《最高人民法院关于审理商标民事纠纷案件适用法律若干问题的解释》（法释〔2002〕32 号）第一条第（一）项的规定，将与他人注册商标相同或者相近似的文字作为企业的字号在相同或者类似商品上突出使用，容易使相关公众产生误认的，属于给他人的注册商标专用权造成其他损害的行为。《最高人民法院关于当前经济形势下知识产权审判服务大局若干问题的意见》（法发〔2009〕23 号）进一步明确了处理原则：按照诚实信用、维护公平竞争和保护在先权利等原则，依法审理该类权利冲突案件。企业名称因突出使用而侵犯在先注册商标专用权的，依法按照商标侵权行为处理；企业名称未突出使用但其使用足以产生市场混淆、违反公平竞争的，依法按照不正当竞争处理。因使用企业名称而构成侵犯商标权的，可以根据案件具体情况判令停止使用，或者对该企业名称的使用方式、使用范围作出限制。因企业名称不正当使用他人具有较高知名度的注册商标，不论是否突出使用均难以避免产生市场混淆的，应当根据当事人的请求判决停止使用或者变更该企业名称。

（一）突出使用企业字号构成商标侵权的认定规则

所谓突出使用是指将企业名称中的字号突出出来，使其具有相对独立的标识意义，强化了字号对于标识商品来源的作用。通常情况下，突出使用字号是将字号在字体、大小、颜色方面的醒目使用。本案中，被告宁波龙凤公司在其网站、商品包装袋上标注"宁波龙凤食品有限公司"这一企业名称时，以较大的字号标注"宁波龙凤"字样，而以小得多的字号标注"食品有限公司"字样，且"宁波龙凤"字样的颜色也比"食品有限公司"更加醒目。"宁波龙

凤"字体、字号、颜色均迥异于其后的"食品有限公司"。在"宁波龙凤"四字中,"宁波"为地名,"龙凤"系该标识中具备识别性的主要部分。因此,被告宁波龙凤公司对"龙凤"的使用构成突出使用。

本案中,原告注册并使用在第30类汤圆等商品上的"龍鳳"商标具有较高的知名度,被告宁波龙凤公司在汤圆等速冻食品上突出使用与原告注册商标近似的"宁波龙凤"标识,易使相关公众对商品的来源产生误认或者认为其来源与原告注册商标的商品有特定的联系。

（二）使用企业名称构成不正当竞争的考量因素

2013年修订的《商标法》第五十八条规定,将他人注册商标、未注册的驰名商标作为企业名称中的字号使用,误导公众,构成不正当竞争行为的,依照《反不正当竞争法》处理。判断对企业名称的使用是否构成不正当竞争,既要审查被告是否有不正当竞争的主观故意,也要审查客观上是否可能误导相关公众。关于被告是否有实施不正当竞争的主观故意,原告通常难以收集直接证据,法院可以通过在先商标的知名度、被告注册该企业名称有无正当理由、使用企业名称的方式、有无其他仿冒行为等间接证据,认定被告是否具有实施不正当竞争的故意。关于是否具有造成混淆可能,主要考虑在先商标的显著性、知名度、在后注册的企业名称是否因经过使用已经具有识别性等因素。

本案中,经过原告的长期使用和宣传,原告的字号及商标具有较高的知名度和商业价值,能给原告带来竞争优势。原告为此所付出的商业努力应该获得尊重,其正当的竞争利益亦应当依法受到保护。在被告使用"龙凤"字号之前,原告的龙凤品牌已经具有较高的知名度,被告以"龙凤"作为企业字号,主观上具有搭便车的故意,客观上容易导致相关公众的混淆,其行为违反了诚实信用原则及公认的商业道德,构成不正当竞争。

二、擅自使用知名商品特有包装、装潢的审理思路

知名商品特有的名称、包装、装潢之所以受《反不正当竞争法》保护,是因为它们具有识别商品来源的作用,成为区别商品来源的标识,如果不加以保护,既不利于维护使用人正当竞争取得的市场成果,也不利于防止市场混淆和保护消费者利益。《反不正当竞争法》所保护的知名商品特有名称、包装、装潢,实际上就是未注册商标。在处理擅自使用知名商品特有包装、装潢纠纷时,要注意区分仿冒和合理借鉴。意大利费列罗公司诉蒙特莎（张家港）食品有限公司、天津经济技术开发区正元行销有限公司不正当竞争纠纷案（指导案例47号）的裁判理由中指出:对商品包装、装潢的设计,不同经营者之间可以相互学习、借鉴，并在此基础上进行创新设计，形成有明显区别各自商品的包装、装潢。这种做法是市场经营和竞争的必然要求。但是，对他人具有识别商品来源意义的特有包装、装潢，则不能作足以引起市场混淆、误认的全面模仿，否则就会构成不正当的市场竞争。

本案中，原、被告的汤圆包装袋虽然使用了相似的金黄色，也使用了一些相同的元素，如汤勺、汤圆、馅料等，但两者整体存在较大差异。宁波龙凤公司金汤圆包装上的文字、图案中，会导致混淆的主要要素为突出标注的"宁波龙凤"字样，而该行为属于侵害原告注册商标权的行为。若不考虑金汤圆包装袋上突出标注的"宁波龙凤"字样，单就商品的包装、装潢而言，以相关公众的一般注意力为标准，不会将被告的商品与原告的商品混淆，故被告宁波龙凤公司不构成不正当竞争。

三、权利冲突纠纷民事责任的确定

（一）停止使用或者规范使用的选择

根据《最高人民法院关于审理注册商标、企业名称与在先权利冲突的民事纠纷案件若干问题的规定》第四条的规定，被诉企业名称侵犯注册商标专用权或者构成不正当竞争的，人民法院可以根据原告的诉讼请求和案件具体情况，确定被告承担停止使用、规范使用等民事责任。在（2010）民提字第15号王将饺子（大连）餐饮有限公司与李惠廷侵犯注册商标专用权案中，最高人民法院认为，如果不正当地将他人具有较高知名度的在先注册商标作为字号注册登记为企业名称，注册使用企业名称本身即是违法，不论是否突出使用均难以避免产生市场混淆的，可以根据当事人的请求判决停止使用或者变更该企业名称；如果企业名称的注册使用并不违法，只是因突出使用其中的字号而侵犯注册商标专用权的，判决被告规范使用企业名称、停止突出使用行为即足以制止被告的侵权行为，因此这种情况下不宜判决停止使用或者变更企业名称。规范使用企业名称与停止使用或变更企业名称是两种不同的责任承担方式，不能因突出使用企业名称中的字号从而侵犯商标专用权就一律判决停止使用或变更企业名称。

在本案中，被告宁波龙凤公司注册使用该企业名称本身即是违法，不论是否突出使用均难以避免产生市场混淆，故被告不仅应停止突出使用"宁波龙凤"，还应当变更企业名称，即停止使用以"龙凤"为字号的企业名称。

（二）赔偿数额的确定

因无法查明原告损失或者被告获利的具体金额，大部分知识产权侵权案件由法院酌定赔偿金额，法官常常面临可裁量的幅度过大的难题，在酌定赔偿金额时容易过低或者过高。近年来，法院在司法政策中强调要加大赔偿力度，但法院在确定判赔金额的时候尤需谨慎。一方面，高额的判赔金额会加大对知识产权人的保护力度，也会加大预防和遏制侵权行为的力度，减少侵权的发生，有利于刺激创新和投资。另一方面，如果将知识产权之外由于侵权人自身的经营努力带来的利润也赔偿给权利人，也会引发过度赔偿的问题①。

为尽量准确确定赔偿金额，法官可以通过释明证明责任、适时公开心证的方式，推动当事人积极举证。在本案中，原告先是举证了从工商局调取的被告的年度报告。根据被告的年度报告，其每年的营业收入近千万元，原告主张根据被告的营业收入确定赔偿金额。此后，被告举证了其企业用于报税的账本，证明公司的营业收入主要来源于代销案外人品牌冷冻食品的销售收入，涉案自产产品的年销售收入只有几十万元。而原告仔细审核了被告的账本，发现被告存在销售收入不入账的情况，即不能完全依据被告的账本确定侵权收入，被告实际的侵权收入大于账本载明的收入，不能完全以账本为依据确定被告的侵权获利金额。最终，法院综合考虑涉案商标知名度、被告侵权行为的性质、被告销售侵权商品的收入、涉案标识对被告营利的贡献度等因素确定了100万元这一较高的赔偿金额。

（撰稿人：邵勋　袁田）

---

① 刘晓："天价索赔满天飞，但想要最终获得高额赔偿你需要做好以下几点"，载《中国知识产权报》2016年7月7日。

商标侵权判定的适用前提及
赔偿数额认定规则

——恒源祥（集团）有限公司与彪马（上海）商贸有限公司等
侵害商标权纠纷案

【提要】

中国古代象形文字作为图形商标获准注册后，他人在同类商品上使用该标识的行为是否属于商标性质的使用、是否构成正当使用，应当根据原、被告的使用情况，结合商标知名度予以判断。按照被告的侵权获利来确定赔偿数额时，一是可以根据被告侵权商品的销售利润认定获利金额，二是按照比例原则，综合考量各因素后予以确定。

【案情】

原告（上诉人）：恒源祥（集团）有限公司（以下简称恒源祥公司）

被告（被上诉人）：彪马（上海）商贸有限公司（以下简称彪马公司）

被告（被上诉人）：佛山市新光针织有限公司（以下简称新光公司）

案由：侵害商标权纠纷

一审案号：（2015）黄浦民三（知）初字第 34 号

二审案号：（2016）沪 73 民终 263 号

原告系第 7823965 号♀商标（以下简称涉案商标）的商标专用权人，核定使用商品为第 25 类夹克（服装）、鞋、针织服装等，注册期限自 2014 年 3 月至 2024 年 3 月 13 日止。2015 年 1 月至 3 月，原告分别在上海、沈阳等店铺以及被告彪马公司开设的天猫官方旗舰店中公证购买了羊年系列跑步鞋及卫衣商品，在运动鞋的鞋舌以及卫衣的后下摆处均印有 "PUMA" 和♀的组合标识，在运动鞋鞋跟外侧处印有♀标识，同时，在天猫 PUMA 官方店中的商品展示及

宣传中使用了 ⛎ 标识。被告新光公司为卫衣的委托生产商。经比对，两被告在商品上使用的 ⛎ 标识与原告涉案商标所包含的构成元素完全相同，仅在长宽比例上略有不同。中华书局出版的 1985 年 7 月第 1 版《金文编》第 615 页、1992 年台北市维新书局股份有限公司出版的《金石字典》"羊部"的象形文字图案 ⛎ 与原告涉案商标所包含的构成元素完全相同，仅在长宽比例上略有不同。

2013 年 8 月 19 日北京市高级人民法院作出的（2012）高行终字第 559 号判决书，认定恒源祥公司拥有的"恒源祥"商标在争议商标申请日之前已经达到驰名程度，恒源祥公司在"服装"商品上未注册的羊头图形商标就与其"恒源祥"商标一起使用，经过长期使用和宣传，该羊头图形商标已为本行业及相关公众所普遍知晓，达到了驰名的程度，可以认定为驰名商标。

经原告申请，法院对被告彪马公司自 2014 年 11 月至 2015 年 5 月涉案商品的进货、销售凭证及相关发票进行了证据保全。涉案的六款商品，被告彪马公司的采购总数量为 38 771 件，总采购金额为 366 万余元，销售总数量为 35 170 件，销售总金额为 964 万余元，其中从被告新光公司的采购金额为 170 余万元，销售金额为 379 万余元。

原告恒源祥公司诉称，涉案商标经过长期使用和宣传，已为本行业及相关公众所普遍知晓，达到了驰名的程度，两被告在同种商品上使用与其注册商标相同的商标，被告彪马公司还销售侵权商品，已侵犯其商标专用权，并造成关联关系的混淆和反向混淆，故诉至法院，请求判令：1. 两被告立即停止生产、销售侵犯原告涉案商标专用权商品的行为；2. 被告彪马公司赔偿原告经济损失人民币（以下均为人民币）1200 万元，被告新光公司在其生产的商品造成的损失范围内与被告彪马公司承担连带赔偿责任，计 471 万余元；3. 两被告连带赔偿原告为制止侵权支出的合理费用 12 万余元；4. 被告彪马公司于判决生效之日起 30 日内在《解放日报》以及 PUMA 天猫官方店铺首页上刊登声明（不少于七天），消除影响。

被告彪马公司辩称，两被告在涉案商品上使用的 ⛎ 标识并不是作为商标使用，是金文 ⛎ 字的一种表现方式，为了指示、说明、描述该服装和运动鞋是中国农历羊年的新年款，属正当使用，这种使用方式并不会构成对于涉案商标的侵权，也不会造成消费者的误认和混淆。即使构成侵权，其获利也仅为 5 万余元，原告要求 1200 万元的损失赔偿无任何事实及法律依据。

被告新光公司辩称，其是被告彪马公司的指定生产商，根据该公司的订单和产品设计生产指定的产品，主观上不存在侵犯原告商标权的故意或企图，在涉案产品上使用▉标识不是作为商标使用，而是用来表示中国生肖羊年，这种使用不会造成消费者混淆，并不构成商标侵权，且生产的产品数量有限，不应承担高达 470 余万元的侵权赔偿责任。

【审判】

上海市黄浦区人民法院经审理认为，原告系第 7823965 号▉商标的专用权人，该商标经过原告长期使用和宣传，已为本行业及相关公众所普遍知晓，具有较高的知名度，应当受到法律保护。两被告对于▉标识的使用方式已超出了说明或者客观描述商品特点的界限，客观上起到了区分商品来源的作用，属于商标意义上的使用。经比对，两被告使用的▉标识与原告的涉案商标仅在长宽比例上略有不同，以相关公众的一般注意力为标准，两者在视觉上基本无差别，可以认定为相同标识。两被告生产的卫衣、运动鞋与原告注册商标核定使用的商品一致。两被告在涉案服装、运动鞋上使用▉标识，被告彪马公司在其天猫官方店的商品广告宣传中使用▉标识的行为，均系未经商标注册人的许可，在同一种商品上使用与其注册商标相同的商标。被告彪马公司的销售行为属于销售侵犯原告注册商标专用权商品的行为。被告彪马公司作为大型的专业运动服装生产销售企业，在进行商品设计时，应当且有能力尽到商标审核的注意义务，被告新光公司接受被告彪马公司的委托，在生产时对于具有较高知名度的原告商标的权属及授权情况未能尽到合理的注意义务，依法均不能予以免责，上述行为均构成对于原告注册商标专用权的侵害，依法应当承担停止侵害、消除影响、赔偿损失的民事责任。

综上，上海市黄浦区人民法院依照《中华人民共和国商标法》第四十八条，第五十七条第（一）项，第（三）项、第六十三条第一款、第三款，《中华人民共和国侵权责任法》第八条，第十五条第一款第（一）项、第（六）项、第（八）项，《最高人民法院关于审理商标民事纠纷案件适用法律若干问题的解释》第十六条第一款、第二款、第十七条的规定，判决：1. 被告彪马公司、新光公司立即停止侵犯原告对第 7823965 号"▉"商标享有的注册商标专用权；2. 被告彪马公司在《解放日报》、彪马天猫官方店铺首页上刊登声明，消除影响；3. 被告彪马公司赔偿原告经济损失 290 万元；被告新光公司对该款项中的 80 万元承担连带赔偿责任；4. 两被告连带赔偿原告合理开支 12 万余元。

一审判决后，原告提起上诉，但未在规定期限内缴纳上诉费，二审法院按上诉人自动撤回上诉处理。双方均按照一审判决执行。

【评析】

本案是一起将中国古代象形文字作为标识使用所引发的商标侵权纠纷，这种使用是否属于正当使用，以及与商标权冲突时侵权界限的划定，在实践中颇有争议。此外，对于两被告侵权获利如何认定，确定赔偿金额时是否应当适用比例原则，本案的判决给出了自己的答案。

一、商标意义上的使用是侵权判定的基础和前提

商标使用是实现商标功能并彰显商标价值的根本途径，我国新修订的《商标法》第 48 条对"商标的使用"做了明确界定，简而言之，商标使用应当包含两个要件：一是商标必须在商业活动中使用；二是通过使用能使相关公众识别商品或服务的来源。意即商标使用是以商业活动中的使用为基本前提，商标根植于商业活动之中，商标使用也不应游离于商业环境之外。同时，这种使用必须发挥了商标的识别功能，在辉瑞公司立体商标侵权案中，最高人民法院认为，对于不能起到标识来源和生产者作用的使用，不能认定为商标意义上的使用，他人此种方式的使用不构成使用相同或近似商标，不属于侵犯注册商标专用权的行为。因此，商标意义上的使用应是指能识别商品或服务来源的使用。本案中，两被告对于 标识的使用显然均属于商业性使用；使用方式上，在运动鞋和卫衣均无生产者相关信息的基础上，无论是 标识在商品上的突出显示位置、标识的大小、组合使用的方式，以及在网络销售平台上进行广告宣传的展示方法、位置等，均与被告彪马公司自身商标的使用方式相互对应，显然已超出了说明或者客观描述商品而使用的界限，客观上也起到了区分商品来源的作用，同时，基于行业内存在的共同联名合作商品的商业惯例，也会使得相关公众产生原告与两被告之间存在商业合作的误认，因此，无论两被告的主观认识如何，这种将 标识使用在商品上的行为已经具有商标的意义，属于商标性质的使用。

二、商标法上正当使用的准确判定

两被告使用古代象形文字的标识是否属于为了描述、说明商品其他特点而构成正当使用，我们认为， 是中国古代金文"羊"字的一种表达方式，从文字角度看，其虽可归入公有领域，但是历经数千年的文字演变，对于现代公众

而言，该🐏已经并非人们日常使用的文字字体，转而具有一种图形的概念，也正是由于原告🐏标识所具有的图形特征，使得原告的商标注册申请得以核准。即便原告的🐏标识相同于公有领域的金文🐏字，但是，经过原告长期使用和广告宣传，已为本行业及相关公众所普遍知晓，具有较高的知名度，🐏标识已经具有一定的显著性，产生了第二含义，起到了区分商品来源的商标标识作用。被告彪马公司作为知名的专业运动服装生产企业，在进行商品设计时，应当且有能力尽到商标审核的注意义务，况且对于新年"羊"字的表述，并非仅仅只有🐏这一种表达方式，两被告完全可以避让与原告涉案商标相同的设计，因此，被告的正当使用抗辩不能成立。

三、确定被告侵权获利时销售利润与营业利润之选择

在本案审理过程中，为防止侵权证据灭失或以后难以取得，原告提出了多项证据保全请求。经审查后，本院对于被告彪马公司就涉案商品的财务账册及原始凭证进行了证据保全，并委托相关机构的注册会计师共同参与。最终，在各方的共同努力下，被告提供了涉案商品的原始进出货凭证、库存记录，证据保全的成功实施，不仅固定了涉嫌侵权产品的生产、销售状况等证据，也有利于更准确地查明被告的侵权获利。根据保全的证据，可以计算得出被告彪马公司就涉案商品的销售利润（销售价格－进货价格）为近600万元。对此，原告主张被告彪马公司就涉案商品的销售利润为其侵权获利，而被告彪马公司则认为其获利应以销售总金额为基准，按照6%的公司营业利润率来计算其获利。法院认为，一是涉案商品系侵犯原告商标权的产品，被告在涉案商品上使用原告商标的行为本身具有违法性，如果在计算被告获利时将该部分产品的运营成本予以扣减，则无异于将涉案商品等同于正常生产经营行为予以对待，而忽略了被告行为本身的违法性，违背了民事审判公平正义的基本原则，低廉的违法成本也不利于引导市场主体规范诚信经营，尊重和保护知识产权；二是公司的营业利润率需要考量的范围非常广泛，包括公司的人力成本、日常运营开销、广告费用、商标授权费用等，而就服装行业的惯例及商业模式而言，相当大的一部分成本来源于其库存压力，包括商品的仓储、物流以及降价促销导致的实际收益减少等。而在本案中，证据保全的会计资料显示，涉案商品的实际销售数量已经超过90%，并不会产生库存滞销所带来的其他成本费用；三是对于涉案侵权商品而言，公司的日常运营成本、人力成本、广告费用等，并非因为本案的侵权商品而直接产生，不能因此而予以扣减；综上，在计算被告的侵权获利时，并不应当扣除涉案侵权商品的运营成本，而应将销售利润作为被告的侵

权获利予以直接认定。

四、比例原则在确定赔偿金额时的具体运用

比例原则，是许多国家行政法上一项重要的基本原则，它由适当性原则、必要性原则以及均衡性原则三个子原则构成，是指行政主体实施行政行为时应兼顾行政目标的实现和保护相对人的利益，如果行政目标的实现可能对相对人的权益造成不利影响，则这种不利影响应当限制在尽可能小的范围和限度之内，二者有适当的比例。2016 年 7 月最高人民法院明确提出了"司法主导、严格保护、分类施策、比例协调"四项知识产权司法保护政策，其中比例协调是指知识产权的保护范围和保护强度与其创新和贡献程度相协调，侵权人的侵权代价与其主观恶性和行为危害性相适应，从而实现权利人权益与他人合法权益及社会公共利益、国家利益的均衡发展。可以说，知识产权审判是探索和实践比例原则的先行者。本案中，考虑到相关消费者在选择购买涉案服装、运动鞋时，除了会关注原告商标所具有的较高知名度外，还会受被告彪马公司具有较高声誉的 PUMA 商标及其商品所蕴含较高品质的影响等因素，因此，被告彪马公司的这部分销售利润并非全部来自于侵害原告的商标，赔偿数额的确定尚需充分考虑被告使用 ⚎ 标识在整个商品中所占比例，即 ⚎ 标识对于商品利润所作的贡献。因此，本案作出了上述判决。

（撰稿人：金民珍 胡嘉祺 戚继敏）

自然人姓名商标权化后的商标侵权认定

——葛军、陶人葛公司与敬华拍卖公司
侵害商标权及不正当竞争纠纷案

【提要】

当自然人选择将自己的姓名注册为商标时，基于姓名的人身符号属性，商标权人欲阻却相同姓名的他人使用时需有所隐忍，即他人合理使用姓名，不会构成侵权，但前提是该种使用必须具正当性，若会造成相关公众的混淆误认，则仍负有谨慎避让义务，否则将构成商标侵权。

【案情】

原告：葛军

原告：上海陶人葛陶艺有限公司

被告：上海敬华艺术品拍卖有限公司

案由：侵害商标权及不正当竞争纠纷

一审案号：（2015）普民三（知）初字第298号

原告葛军在中国陶瓷艺术界具有较高影响力，系江苏省工艺美术大师、江苏省陶瓷艺术大师、中国陶瓷设计艺术大师、中国陶瓷文化研究所紫砂文化研究中心主任。同时，其注册了"葛军""申壶坊"等注册商标，并将所有注册商标独家许可给原告陶人葛公司使用。后，原告收到被告敬华公司寄来的"紫砂壶、陈茶专场"拍卖宣传手册，并在 www.arton.net 和 www.jinghuapaimai.com 网站上宣传其拟拍卖的紫砂壶。原告发现拍卖的紫砂壶中有九把壶的出处标示为"申壶葛军"并使用原告葛军的上述社会名誉简介，致使社会产生错误理解，属虚假宣传。原告遂电话联系被告，要求停止拍卖壶底标有"申壶葛军"字样的紫砂壶。但被告对此未予理睬，并继续进行了拍卖。原告认为，被告在明知所拍卖

的紫砂壶侵犯原告商标权并构成不正当竞争的前提下，仍继续进行了拍卖。被告的拍卖行为不仅导致原告商誉减损，而且还导致了原告葛军社会声誉的降低，并影响到原告所设计、制作的紫砂壶的商业价值。故请求判令：被告停止销售侵犯原告注册商标权的紫砂壶；停止虚假宣传不正当竞争行为；赔偿经济损失及合理费用；公开赔礼道歉、消除影响。

被告敬华公司辩称，被控侵权的标识"申壶葛军"和原告的注册商标"申壶坊""葛军"不相同不近似，不会构成混淆，因此不构成商标侵权，且"申壶葛军"另有其人。拍卖宣传册并非被告制作，作为拍卖行系受委托销售商品，商品来源由委托人担保，其已尽到合理审慎义务；对拍卖行而言，不具备识别拍品来源的能力。被告即使构成侵权，在拍卖现场也已撤回了相关信息，原告亦没有证明其损失及名誉受损，造成的影响轻微。故对原告的所有诉请均不予以认可。

【审判】

普陀区人民法院认为，原告葛军注册"葛军"商标，实质是将其姓名作为商业标识使用，从而实现姓名权商品化的一种方式，其本人在相关领域的知名度亦可一定程度辐射至商标。被告抗辩称其拍卖过程中，使用"申壶葛军"属于对商品制作人的说明，并非"使用商标"，即"申壶葛军"四字指向制壶人，其主张"申壶葛军 +（某某刻）+ 壶款式名称"的标注信息是指壶的制作人（或称烧制人）为申壶葛军，某某是指壶身纹饰的刻印人，印章款"申壶葛军"也是指向制作人。法院认为，被告的上述认知虽具有一定合理性，但是考虑到紫砂壶这一特殊商品在实用性和艺术性上的统一性，商业标识和著作权人署名均可表明该商品的出处来源，特别是在两者趋同的情形下，从发挥区分来源功能的角度分析，并无将两者严格剥离加以识别的需要，实际上也无法实现。"申壶葛军"已具有商业标识利益，实质发挥了区分商品来源的功能。故被控商标侵权行为即"申壶葛军"的使用，属于商标法意义上的商标使用。

本案中，将"申壶葛军"与原告的"申壶坊"和"葛军"商标进行比较，可见系"申壶坊"中的"申壶"两字与"葛军"两字的组合。首先，"申壶坊"虽系图文商标，但从其黑白相间类似印章的图样设计来看，其文字部分"申壶坊"系该商标的核心要素。从中文词组"定语 + 主语"或者说"修饰指向词 + 名词"的构词习惯来看，"申壶坊"的偏正语义中"申壶"更具识别度。"葛军"系文字商标，其核心要素显而易见。其次，根据原告的举证，原告葛军在紫砂业内享有较高的知名度。得以进入拍卖领域的紫砂壶，其售价一般较高，艺术收藏价值较之实用价值更加凸显，故关于相关市场的界定一般而言，相对于普通公众更为精准，了解"葛军"与"申壶坊"两商标具有关联的可能性会有所增加，"申壶葛军"与"申壶坊""葛军"造成相关公众混淆误认的可能性亦增加。被控侵权标识"申壶葛军"（包括印章形式）使用在与原告两个注册商标同种的商品上，且构成混淆性近似，构成商标侵权。最后，拍卖宣传册上关于"申壶葛军"的简介内容，与原告葛军就其荣誉及社会身份的相关举证一致，上述表述易引人误解相关商品来源于原告，同时构成虚假宣传的不正当竞争行为。

另外，针对被告提出的其系受委托销售商品，已经尽到合理审慎义务，无需承担赔偿责任的意见，法院认为，销售主体在拥有合法来源且不知所售商品为侵权商品的情况下才可以免除赔偿责任。本案中，鉴于原告在业内具有较高知名度，被告作为专业的艺术品拍卖机构显然应负更高的注意义务。被告未就涉案紫砂壶向公众做过权利瑕疵担保声明，在接到权利人通知后，未采取相关审慎方式予以应对，可见被告对于涉案商品可能涉嫌侵权应当知晓，故未采纳被告的上述意见。

综上，上海市普陀区人民法院依照《中华人民共和国侵权责任法》第十五条第一款第（一）项、第（六）项和第（八）项、第二款；《中华人民共和国商标法》第三条第一款、第五十七条第三项、第六十三条第三款；《中华人民共和国反不正当竞争法》第二条、第九条、第二十条；《最高人民法院关于审理商标民事纠纷案件适用法律若干问题的解释》第三条第（二）项、第四条第二款、第九条第二款、第十条、第十六条第一款、第二款、第十七条、第二十一条第一款；《最高人民法院关于审理不正当竞争民事案件应用法律若干问题的解释》第八条第一款第（三）项、第三款、第十七条的规定，判决：敬华公司停止侵犯商标权及不正当竞争行为，消除影响，赔偿经济损失及合理费用人民币30 000元。

一审判决后，原、被告均未上诉，判决生效。

【评析】

本案主要争议系自然人姓名商标权化后的商标侵权认定，具有一定典型性。

一、正当使用姓名与商标性使用的界限

姓名是通过语言文字信息区分人类个体的特定符号，而商标则是主要借助文字、字母、图形等可视性要素识别产品或服务来源的标识，两者在符号学上

的共性使得姓名存在作为商标使用的可能性。当自然人姓名作为商标进行注册并使用时，姓名和商标就在某种意义上产生了重合，当然也不可避免地引发一定的冲突。此时自然人的姓名不再仅仅是人格意义上的识别符号，也发挥着区分来源、承载商誉的功能。不过基于自然人姓名可能出现重名或相似的特点，确有必要区分商业活动中正当使用姓名与商标性使用的界限。面对以正当使用姓名为由而不构成商标性使用的抗辩意见时，对"使用商标"行为的判定应以能否起到识别功能为依据，即如果能够起到指示来源的作用，则构成商标性使用；反之则不属于商标性使用。

结合本案的情况，即使如被告所称，其理解的"申壶葛军"系指向制作人，但紫砂壶作为兼具实用性及艺术性特征的商品，其商品属性与美术作品属性统一于一体，表明其出处来源的方式既可以是商标类标识，也可以是著作权人的署名，特别是在两者趋同的情形下，从发挥区分来源功能的角度分析，并无将两者严格剥离加以识别的需要，实际上也无法实现。"申壶葛军"的使用已具有商业标识利益，实质发挥了区分商品来源的功能，属于商标法意义上的商标使用。

二、姓名商标的侵权认定

自然人姓名商标权化后，其侵权认定规则应遵照商标法本身的意旨，即坚持混淆可能性标准，在商标侵权认定的一般规则框架下进行综合考虑。根据相关法律规定，商标近似是指被控侵权的标识与原告的注册商标相比较，其文字的字形、读音、含义或者图形的构图及颜色，或者其各要素组合后的整体结构相似，或者其立体形状、颜色组合近似，易使相关公众对商品的来源产生误认或者认为其来源于原告注册商标的商品有特定的联系。同时，根据系争商标涉及的具体情况，认定商标近似除通常需要考虑其构成要素的近似程度外，还需要综合考虑其他因素，如已注册姓名商标与被诉标识在商业标志意义上显著性的强弱、姓名商标知名度的高低、相关市场和相关公众的细分和界定、使用意图的判断、被诉侵权标识在商业活动中的使用情况以及其他相关市场实际等因素。

本案中，在认定"申壶葛军"系由原告的"申壶坊"和"葛军"商标核心识别要素组成且使用在与原告两个注册商标同种商品的前提下，充分考虑原告在业内的知名度及紫砂壶市场的精准细分，判断被控侵权标识"申壶葛军"造成相关公众混淆误认的可能性较高，且构成混淆性近似。

三、拍卖公司免除赔偿责任情形的判断

拍卖公司受客户委托，对相关物品进行拍卖，但不同公司在拍品来源、拍卖方式、利润获取等方面都各有不同，故对于拍卖公司拍卖行为的性质，必须予以充分考虑。以本案被告为例，其盈利模式并非直接赚取商品差价，而是赚取佣金，因此并不是直接销售方，但其为直接销售方提供交易平台，仍属广义上的销售范畴，为帮助销售。

作为销售主体，拍卖公司可以以涉案拍品有合法来源、不明知侵权存在且已尽到合理注意义务为由，提出不应承担赔偿责任的意见。在判断符合免除销售主体赔偿责任的情形时，必须同时具备两个条件：一是不知道所销售的是侵权商品；二是能够证明所销售的侵权商品具有合法来源。即便存在委托协议，涉案拍品亦有合法来源，但鉴于拍卖公司的专业性以及权利主体的知名度，拍卖公司的注意义务理应相应提高。本案中，未见拍卖公司就涉案拍品向公众做过权利瑕疵担保声明，在得到权利人通知后，亦未采取进一步信息核实、价格区间比较、商标检索等审慎方式加以应对；而对于专业拍卖机构而言，针对当代艺术品采取上述应对方式快捷、高效、经济，并非苛责。可见，被告拍卖公司对于涉案商品可能涉嫌侵权是应当知晓的，故不符合因具有合法来源而免除赔偿责任的条件。

（撰稿人：张佳璐、林抒蔚）

确认不侵害商标权纠纷原告主体资格的审查以及描述性使用的认定

——哥伦比亚运动服装公司与上海兴诺康纶纤维科技股份有限公司
确认不侵害商标权纠纷案

【提要】

确认不侵害商标权诉讼主体资格的审查难点是利害关系人的认定。被控侵权商品同时附有争议标识和自有注册商标，并标注实际生产者的，由于商标的首要功能是区分商品来源，注册商标权利人是否是实际生产者不影响商品来源的认定，该注册商标权利人可基于商品受到侵权警告，双方对商品来源存在争议而以利害关系人身份提起诉讼。描述性正当使用的应有之义是使用本意旨在"描述"，且使用效果尚属"正当"，故应满足两个要件：1. 使用的主观目的上，由于标识内涵与商品特性相符，使用者仅为描述商品而善意使用；2. 使用的客观效果上，争议标识并未起到识别来源的作用，不属于商标意义上的使用。

【案情】

原告（被上诉人）：哥伦比亚运动服装公司（以下简称哥伦比亚公司）。

被告（上诉人）：上海兴诺康纶纤维科技股份有限公司（以下简称兴诺公司）。

案由：确认不侵害商标权纠纷

一审案号：（2013）徐民三（知）初字第 653 号

二审案号：（2014）沪一中民五（知）终字第 88 号

原告哥伦比亚公司在第 25 类（服装、鞋、帽类）上注册了第 1236702 号"◆"菱形图像商标，第 5288005 号"◆Columbia Sportswear Company"和第 5288009 号"Columbia"商标。原告在其中国官网宣称："Columbia 设计了别出心裁而深受欢迎的产品，包括其著名的衬里更换系统，……Columbia 第一件三合一夹克专为狩猎活动而设计，配有防水外层和隔热内衬，可以组合穿或者单穿……"

2005 年至 2012 年间，《品牌》《中国服饰》等媒体杂志对原告及其产品进行了正面的宣传报道。其中，2009 年第 4 期《中外企业文化》在报道中称"1982 年，Columbia 率先提出 Interchange System 三合一新概念，开发了外套的内里可以拆卸的新颖设计，不但获得业界的认同，同时也在市场上引起巨大反响，现在许多户外品牌都采用了这一实用设计理念……"

被告于 2000 年 7 月 26 日成立，经营范围有：从事纺织纤维科技，针纺织品、针纺织原料（除棉花），服装服饰的销售，服装服饰等。被告于 2011 年 2 月 7 日获准在第 25 类上注册第 8022378 号"Base Layer"商标，注册有效期至 2021 年 2 月 6 日止。

太古资源公司是原告在中国地区的总代理商。2012 年 11 月 23 日，被告因发现太古资源公司经销的两款纺织品外包装上使用"Baselayer"标识，委托律师向太古资源公司发函，认为侵犯其注册商标专用权，要求停止侵权、销毁侵权标识。同年 12 月 6 日，原告委托律师回函，表示太古资源公司经销的带有"Baselayer"文字的产品为其生产，其对于"Baselayer"文字的使用是对产品通用名称及描述性阐释的正当使用。同年 12 月 14 日，被告委托律师向原告复函，表示不接受原告关于"Baselayer"构成侵权商品通用名称的观点。同年 12 月 19 日、2013 年 1 月 17 日，被告因发现两家原告授权经营店铺销售上述两款纺织品，又委托律师分别向两家店铺的业主上海港汇房地产开发有限公司和上海第一八佰伴有限公司发函，声称销售上述纺织品也属于侵犯其注册商标专用权的行为，要求停止侵权。

本案涉嫌侵权的是两款商品。外包装是呈长方体的塑料盒，正面中间使用了"Baselayer"文字，在该文字的相邻处，还对应地使用了法文"Premiere couche"（中文翻译为"基础层"），正面上方标明了"❖""Columbia"商标，背面下方贴有合格证标签，合格证上标注的品名分别为休闲上衣和休闲裤，合格证上均标注："商标：❖Columbia Sportswear Company，厂名：远东服装（苏州）有限公司，经销商：太古资源（上海）商贸有限公司"，盒盖上有凹凸的"❖"商标，盒底上也标明了"❖""Columbia"商标，"Baselayer"字体大于其他文字及商标。两款商品本身，上衣左前胸部位、裤腰带及下方部位，以及两款商品的领标或裤标、洗标、吊牌上，标有"❖""Columbia"商标，或"❖Columbia Sportswear Company"商标，均没有使用"Baselayer"文字。

原告提交的证明"Baselayer"在户外运动服装领域是通用名称的证据显示：在维基百科搜索引擎网站搜索"Baselayer"，搜索结果自动跳转到对

"Layered clothing"（多层服装）词条的释义，其中介绍多层服装一般至少三层，即内层、中间层和壳层，内层（Inner layer）也被称为基础层（base layer），并提到"内层保持皮肤干爽、使你有舒适感"；

在 ARC'TERYX（始祖鸟）、THE NORTH FACE（北面）、HENRI LLOYD、OZARK（奥索卡）、DECATHLON（迪卡侬）等全球部分户外运动服装品牌的官网搜索"Baselayer"或"Base layer"，检索结果均为户外运动内层服装；在上海迪卡侬商场购买的男士上衣和背心在外包装使用了"Baselayer"文字；

《户外探险》《设计》《申江服务导报》《京华时报》等期刊及报纸，以及搜狐网、南方体育网、户外资料网上刊登涉及"base layer"的相关文章和报道均显示"base layer"指代户外服装的基础层。

原告哥伦比亚公司诉称：被告屡次向原告的经销商、代理商及相关经营者发送律师函，坚称原告在其生产的两款户外运动内层服装上使用的"Baselayer"标识侵犯其注册商标专用权，要求停止侵权。原告认为，其在产品包装上使用"Baselayer"仅是对商品类型进行说明及描述，以便于消费者正确区分；同时涉案服装已在显著位置醒目地标注字号和注册商标，并只在原告专卖店销售，不会导致混淆。鉴于被告屡次发函，在合理期限内又不向法院起诉，已严重损害原告的良好市场声誉，使原告产品在中国市场的合法经销面临极大困境和不稳定性，故起诉要求确认原告在户外运动内层服装上使用"Baselayer"标识不侵犯被告所拥有的第8022378号"Base Layer"注册商标专用权。

被告兴诺公司辩称：1. 原告并非被告发出侵权警告所涉及之商品的生产商和经销商，原告与本案没有直接利害关系，主体资格不适格；2. 被告获准注册的"Base Layer"商标在核定使用商品上具有显著性，既非商品通用名称，也没有直接表示商品的功能、用途；3. 涉案商品外包装上，"Baselayer"明显大于原告注册商标，构成突出使用，故不属于合理使用。综上，请求中止本案审理，或驳回原告的诉讼请求。

【审判】

上海市徐汇区人民法院经审理认为，本案存在两个争议焦点：一、原告是否有权提起本案确认不侵权之诉；二、原告在其产品的外包装上标注"Baselayer"是否侵犯被告的注册商标专用权。

关于焦点一，本案中，收到商标侵权警告的分别为原告的中国地区总代理商和授权经营店铺所在商场的管理者，且涉嫌侵权商品上均有原告的注册商标。原告及时、亲自向被告回函，明确表示产品所附"Baselayer"文字是正当使用。

被告向原告复函表示不接受其观点，并且被告在本案诉讼前也认可原告与涉嫌侵权商品有利害关系。因被告在合理期限内未提起诉讼，使原告授权在中国市场经销的相关产品是否构成侵权处于不确定状态，原告作为直接利害关系人，有权提出本案确认不侵权之诉。

关于焦点二，由于涉案商品所附"Baselayer"标识与被告"Base Layer"注册商标没有实质区别，所属类别亦与被告核定使用的类别相同，故争议的实质是对是否属于正当使用的争议。判断是否属于描述性正当使用，应当从"baselayer"在户外运动服装领域所具有的含义、原告使用目的、方式以及后果等方面综合考量。首先，综合在案证据可以认定"baselayer"具有表示户外运动服装基础层的含义，原告使用"Baselayer"文字旨在描述性地表明商品特点。其次，纵观原告使用"Baselayer"文字的方式考量其使用效果。原告仅在商品的外包装上使用，在"Baselayer"文字的相同位置还对应使用了中文含义相同的法文，并且在产品外包装上全方位、显著地标明其自有的"❖""Columbia"或"◆Columbia Sportswear Company"等高知名度注册商标，因此实际发挥区分商品来源作用的标识是原告的高知名度商标。"Baselayer"文字标识尽管字体偏大，只是为了向相关公众更清楚地表明商品的功能和用途，并未作为商标使用，也不会造成相关公众对商品来源的混淆和误认。

综上，上海市徐汇区人民法院依照《中华人民共和国商标法实施条例》（2002年）第四十九条〔现《中华人民共和国商标法》（2013年）第五十九条第一款〕，判决：确认原告哥伦比亚运动服装公司在户外运动内层服装的外包装上使用"Baselayer"标识不侵犯被告上海兴诺康纶纤维科技股份有限公司享有的第8022378号"Base Layer"注册商标专用权。

一审判决后，被告上海兴诺康纶纤维科技股份有限公司不服，提起上诉。

上海市第一中级人民法院经审理后认为，一审判决认定事实基本清楚，适用法律正确，所作裁判结论并无不当，故判决驳回上诉、维持原判。

【评析】

本案属于确认不侵害商标权之诉，此类诉讼系知识产权领域特有。判决厘清了原告主体资格的审查标准和商标元素描述性使用的认定方法，为类似案件裁判作出了积极的探索，颇具典型意义。

一、确认不侵害商标权纠纷的原告主体资格认定

在商标法领域，审查此类诉讼主体资格的法律依据阙如。根据《中华人民

共和国民事诉讼法》（以下简称《民事诉讼法》）第一百一十九条，原告是与案件有直接利害关系的公民、法人和其他组织。同时，参照《最高人民法院关于审理侵犯专利权纠纷案件应用法律若干问题的解释》第十八条的规定，司法实践对确认不侵权纠纷的起诉条件已达成的基本共识是：权利人发出侵权警告而又未在合理期限内提起诉讼，使被警告人或者利害关系人的相关行为是否构成侵权处于不确定状态。其中，利害关系人的认定是审查的难点。我们认为，应当严格按照民事诉讼法规定的"直接利害关系"审查原告主体资格，市场主体之间抽象意义上的利害相关不等于直接利害关系。这是因为，各个市场主体基于行业竞争关系、产业上下游利益关联等因素，彼此的抽象利害关系是普遍存在的。如果双方缺乏基于具体的知识产权法律关系形成的直接、明确、特定化的联系，则难以认定双方具有直接利害关系。否则，利害关系人的范围过宽，不仅会导致确认不侵权之诉被滥用，让市场主体遭受不可预测的诉讼风险，也会架空民事诉讼法的明文规定。

就本案而言，涉案商品同时附有两类标识：争议标识"Baselayer"和哥伦比亚运动服装公司（以下简称哥伦比亚公司）的自有注册商标。权利人就涉案商品提出商标侵权警告，但哥伦比亚公司并非涉案商品的实际生产者或销售者，其与权利人发出商标侵权警告却怠于起诉之间是否存在利害关系？是何种利害关系？

判决首先从双方诉前函件往来所反映的争议入手。哥伦比亚公司在其销售商收到侵权警告后，及时亲自回函给权利人表示其仅为正当使用，权利人对此复函，表示不接受关于正当使用的意见，被告在本案诉讼前也认可原告与涉案商品有利害关系。换言之，诉前的函件往来和行为已经佐证双方存在商标法意义上的争议。

为进一步明确是何种特定的、直接的利害关系，判决进而回归商标法原理，从商标区分商品来源这一首要功能展开分析。判决指出，涉案商品上有注册商标，而该注册商标的专用权人是哥伦比亚公司，可以认定该商品来源于哥伦比亚公司。至于该公司是否是涉案商品的实际生产者并不影响商品来源的认定。因此，哥伦比亚公司与本案有直接利害关系，有权提起本案诉讼。这一论断背后的深层逻辑是，商标法律制度的首要目标是保障商标的识别功能，确保消费者可以通过商标识别商品来源。本案商标权利人发出侵权警告，认为涉案产品上的"Baselayer"文字标识有让消费者误认来源之虞，而哥伦比亚公司作为涉案商品上的注册商标所指示之来源，已经与权利人直接陷入商标法意义上的争论：究竟谁是涉案产品的来源。因此，哥伦比亚公司与案件有直接利害关系。本案对利害关系人的界定宽严适度，符合民事诉讼法规定的直接利害关系的要求。

二、商标描述性使用的认定

商标的首要功能在于区别商品来源，侵犯注册商标专用权的标识首先应当是商标意义上使用的标识，具有商标功能。所以，要判断涉案商品上使用"Baselayer"是否构成商标侵权，应当先审查"Baselayer"是商标意义上的使用，还是原告所主张的描述性正当使用。

描述性正当使用是用他人商标中的文字或图形等要素对商品进行描述的行为，其应有之义是使用本意旨在"描述"，且使用效果尚属"正当"。在使用的主观目的上，由于标识中的文字或图形等要素与商品特性相符，使用者仅为描述商品而善意使用；在使用客观效果上，争议标识并未起到识别来源作用，不是商标意义上的使用。

（一）使用的主观目的：文字含义与商品特性相符，为描述商品善意使用

判断使用行为是否出于描述产品特性的目的，应从标识文字的含义与涉案产品的特性的客观联系入手。文字内涵与产品特性相符，是论证"描述性"的前提和基础。

"Baselayer"由两个英文单词"base""layer"组成，中文含义是"基础层"。判决分析了"baselayer"在户外运动服装领域所具有的含义和涉案商品特性之间的对应关系。综合在案证据，包括媒体对户外服装"三层着装法"的报道、维基百科"base layer"词条释义、在全球部分户外运动服装品牌官网对"Base layer"的搜索结果，以及迪卡侬商场商品实物对"Base Layer"的标注，可以认定"baselayer"在中国户外运动服装领域具有表示服装基础层的含义。因此，"Baselayer"的应有之义与涉案商品的特性相符，是对户外服装"基础层"特性的忠实描述，可推断使用者是出于描述产品的目的善意地使用。

（二）使用的客观效果：并未起到识别来源作用，不是商标意义上的使用

实践中，文字或图形等要素的使用情况十分复杂，具体使用方式的细微差别可能导致完全不同的效果。应当分析涉案使用行为呈现给相关公众的整体观感与效果，不具有识别来源作用的，方属于正当、合理的使用。

原告使用"Baselayer"文字的具体方式如下：1. 仅用于商品的外包装，而非商品本身；2. 在该文字的相同位置还对应使用了同样表示"基础层"含义的法文；3. 在外包装的正面上方、盒盖、盒底及背面合格证上全方位显著地标明"◆""Columbia"或"◆ Columbia Sportswear Company"高知名度商标；4. "Baselayer"字体大于其

他文字及商标。

上述使用方式呈现的一个具有类型化意义的问题：涉案商品同时附有争议标识和自有注册商标，争议标识大于自有注册商标的，是否一定属于突出性的商标意义上的使用？这个问题不能一概而论，关键看带给消费者的印象。在以往的"傍名牌"类商标侵权案件中，常有商家在使用自有注册商标的同时，将知名度更高的争议标识突出放大使用，而将自有注册商标淡化使用。在相关受众的观感上，此种突出放大的争议标识实际上发挥着商标的作用。本案中，判决仔细对比"Baselayer"文字和"Columbia"系列商标识别功能的强弱，结合其使用方式，分析何者对消费者发挥了识别作用。

一方面，"Baselayer"文字标识本身识别功能弱。"Baselayer"包含"base"和"layer"两个单词，该文字并非被告臆造。被告公司身处纺织服饰领域，其亦承认是基于文字的"基础层"的含义申请注册了商标，商标的固有显著性弱。同时，被告并未提交其将标有"Base Layer"注册商标的产品投入市场的证据，可见被告尚未在"Baselayer"文字上建立第二含义，其注册商标没有通过使用获得显著性。因此，"Baselayer"文字难以指引消费者区分商品来源。

另一方面，"Columbia"高知名度系列商标识别功能强。原告的"Columbia"品牌是全球著名的户外服装品牌，在中国户外运动服装领域也具有相当高的知名度和美誉度。

两种标识的识别性一弱一强，再纵观争议标识的使用方式，原告仅将"Baselayer"文字用于商品的外包装，该文字旁边使用了同样表示"基础层"含义的法文，并且还全方位、显著地标明原告自有商标，当相关公众看到涉案商品时，只会从其四周全方位标注的高知名度"Columbia"系列商标联想到这是原告的商品，而不会从"Baselayer"文字联想到被告。"Baselayer"文字虽然字体偏大，但只是为了更清楚地向相关公众表明所标示的商品为户外运动服装的基础层。原告的这一使用方式显然不是淡化自有商标突出他人标识，而是通过全方位标注高知名度自有商标对消费者作了较强的视觉提示，与以往"傍名牌"类商标侵权行为完全不同。因此，实际发挥识别来源作用的并非"Baselayer"文字，而是原告的自有商标。"Baselayer"文字即使字体偏大，也并非突出性的商标意义上的使用。

综合以上对使用目的、使用效果的分析，行为人旨在描述产品特性而善意使用争议标识，且在最终呈现给消费者的观感上并未发挥指示商品来源的作用，所以涉案使用行为善意且未超出合理范围，构成描述性正当使用。

本案确认不侵害商标权纠纷涉及原告主体资格的审查和描述性使用的认定，

审理难度较大。判决准确把握该诉讼制度的主旨和商标法的立法目的，为类似案件审理明确了裁判规则。同时，本案也是知名企业通过确认不侵权之诉主动维权的正面典型。哥伦比亚公司作为全球运动服装领域最为著名的企业之一，在竞争对手不当行使知识产权致其企业信誉有损害之虞的情况下，主动出击制止了损害，对企业诉讼维权具有重要的现实意义。

（撰稿人：李晓平　张敏）

地理标志证明商标的正当使用
与侵权使用的界限认定

——杭州市西湖区龙井茶产业协会与上海雨前春茶叶有限公司
侵害商标权纠纷

【提要】

证明商标是我国商标法明确保护的商标之一，其作用在于让相关公众可以通过商标来辨别特定商品或服务的来源，侵犯证明商标的行为使得相关公众无法通过商标来辨识商品或服务的特殊品质，从而给商标的商誉以及商品或服务的声誉造成不良影响。本案中，法院从被告的行为是侵权行为还是对地理标志证明商标的正当使用进行考量，对在司法实践中审理相关案件具有一定的借鉴意义。

【案情】

原告：杭州市西湖区龙井茶产业协会

被告：上海雨前春茶叶有限公司

案由：侵害商标权纠纷

一审案号：（2014）杨民三（知）初字第 422 号

2011 年 7 月，杭州市人民政府批复"为加强西湖龙井茶的保护和发展工作，同意由杭州市西湖区龙井茶产业协会作为主体，负责'西湖龙井'地理标志证明商标的注册和后续监管等工作……"2011 年 6 月 28 日，原告经商标局核准注册了第 9129815 号"西湖龙井"地理标志证明商标，核定使用商品为第 30 类：茶叶，注册有效期至 2021 年 6 月 27 日止。2012 年 5 月，浙江省工商行政管理局向原告颁发了驰名商标证书，证书载明"西湖龙井被国家工商行政管理总局认定为驰名商标"。

《杭州市西湖龙井茶基地保护条例》第二条规定："本条例所称的西湖龙井茶基地，是指杭州市西湖区东起虎跑、茅家埠，西至杨府庙、龙门坎、何家村，南起社井、浮山，北至老东岳、金鱼井的范围内，由市人民政府划定予以保护的茶地。"原告制定的《"西湖龙井"地理标志证明商标使用管理规则》第五条要求"使用'西湖龙井'地理标志证明商标的商品的生产地域范围为杭州市政府划定的西湖龙井茶保护基地……"第六条对使用"西湖龙井"商标的商品的品质进行了规定，第七条为对使用"西湖龙井"商标的商品的采摘、加工工艺的要求。

2014 年 7 月 30 日，上海市徐汇公证处公证员姚卫宇、公证处工作人员卢文及上海市华诚律师事务所委托的宋利君来到位于上海市内江路 472 号的店铺，宋利君以普通消费者的身份购买了一礼盒茶叶，并从该店铺现场取得印有"胡香兰 上海雨前春茶叶有限公司"字样的名片一张和盖有"上海雨前春茶叶有限公司"图章的发票联一张。

经当庭比对，被控侵权商品为礼盒装茶叶，礼盒外有纸质包装袋，礼盒内有四个大小相同的金属茶叶罐，纸袋、礼盒和茶叶罐上均印有竖列的"西湖龍井"字样，购买时取得的名片背面印有"虎牌西湖龙井 杭州市西湖区国家礼品基地 黄山谢裕大茶叶股份有限公司 漕溪 黄山毛峰 苏州吴郡碧螺春茶叶有限公司 吴郡茗茶 云南普洱思茅兴洋茶叶有限公司 兴洋茗茶　上海特约经销商"字样。

被告成立于 2007 年 1 月 18 日，注册资本500 000元，经营范围为预包装食品（不含熟食卤味、冷冻冷藏）批发兼零售；日用百货、工艺美术品、汽摩配件、建材、装潢材料、酒（限零售）、五金交电的销售，室内外装潢。庭审中，被告陈述其销售中低端散装茶，包括龙井、炒青、云雾等，主要品种是绿茶，其本案中销售的是散装"虎"牌龙井，但并没有"虎"牌专用包装，涉案商品是被告自己包装的。

原告杭州市西湖区龙井茶产业协会诉称，"西湖龙井"茶被誉为我国名茶之冠，历史悠久。在杭州市政府的大力支持下，2011 年 2 月 18 日，原告向国家商标局申请注册了"西湖龙井"地理标志证明商标，2011 年 6 月 28 日获得核准注册，注册号为第 9129815 号，商品类别为第 30 类，核定使用商品为"茶叶"。该商标专门证明"西湖龙井"产品的原产地和特定品质，具有较高的商誉，于 2012 年 4 月 27 日被国家商标局认定为中国驰名商标。2014 年 7 月 30 日，原告在被告经营的位于上海市杨浦区内江路 472 号店铺购买了茶叶若干，取得了被告提供的名片和发票。被告销售的茶叶包装上和取得的名片上都显著地使用了"西湖龙井"标识。2014 年 9 月 16 日，原告向被告发送了律师函，要求被告立即停止侵权并就赔偿等事宜与原告联系，但被告置之不理。被告未经许可在其生产、销售的茶叶上擅自使用原告的地理标志证明商标，侵犯了原告的注册商标专用权，请求判令：1. 被告停止侵犯原告"西湖龙井"注册商标专用权的行为；2. 被告赔偿原告经济损失100 000元人民币（包括为制止侵权行为而支出的合理费用，以下币种相同）；3. 被告在《解放日报》《新民晚报》上刊登声明，消除侵权影响。

被告上海雨前春茶叶有限公司辩称，被告以零售茶叶为主，店内备有包装袋及为数不多的各式茶盒以便于顾客保存茶叶和方便携带，且是免费提供的，涉案的包装盒系被告几年前购进的样品，本案是顾客刻意看中标有西湖龙井茶叶的茶盒，并执意要求用其包装，是故意诱导被告用这个包装的。被告销售的散装茶叶不是礼盒茶叶，公证员公证时没有出具身份证件，公证过程违法。

【审判】

上海市杨浦区人民法院经审理认为：原告作为"西湖龙井"商标的商标权人，在自然人、法人或其他组织的产品符合产地、工艺、品质的要求，而请求使用该证明商标的，应当允许，但对于不符合产地、工艺、品质要求的商品上标注该商标的，原告有权禁止，并依法追究其侵权责任。

被告将印有"西湖龍井"字样的包装袋、礼盒和茶叶罐使用于其销售的茶叶，"西湖龍井"四个字显著位于包装的正中位置，属于商标性使用。与涉案商标相比，两者区别仅在于简繁体、字体和横竖排列，足以使相关公众误认为被告商品是来源于特定产地并具有特定品质的商品。被控侵权商品本身或外包装上并无任何"虎"牌字样，被告也不能提供证据证明其产品来源于"西湖龙井"的指定生产区域以及产品符合"西湖龙井"的品质要求，因此其在涉案商品上突出标注"西湖龍井"的行为不属于正当使用范围，是侵犯涉案注册商标专用权的行为。此外，被告在其名片上印制"虎牌西湖龙井"，误导相关公众其销售的茶叶的来源，该字样与原告涉案商标构成近似，亦是侵犯涉案注册商标专用权的行为。

被告在其商品上及广告宣传中使用与涉案商标相近似的商标，且不能提供证据证明其商品符合涉案证明商标所要求的商品产地、品质要求，侵犯了涉案注册商标专用权，应当承担停止侵权、赔偿损失等民事责任。

据此，依照《中华人民共和国商标法》第三条第一款、第三款、第十六条第二款、第四十八条、第五十七条第（二）项、第六十三条第一款、第三款，《中华人民共和国商标法实施条例》第四条第二款，《最高人民法院关于审理商标民事纠纷案件适用法律若干问题的解释》第九条第二款、第十条、第十六条第一款、第二款、第十七条第一款、第二十一条第一款之规定，判决：一、被告上海雨前春茶叶有限公司于本判决生效之日起立即停止侵犯原告杭州市西湖区龙井茶产业协会第9129815号"西湖龙井"注册商标专用权的行为；二、被告上海雨前春茶叶有限公司于本判决生效之日起十日内赔偿原告杭州市西湖区龙井茶产业协会经济损失30 000元（包含合理费用1720元）；三、驳回原告杭州市西湖区龙井茶产业协会的其他诉讼请求。

一审判决后，双方当事人均未提出上诉，一审判决已经生效。

【评析】

与普通商标相比，证明商标用来保证所使用商品的特定品质，有利于企业向市场推销商品，也有利于消费者选择商品，其保证了商品的质量，故法律法规对其注册、转让等方面有额外的限制。侵犯证明商标的行为会破坏相关公众通过商标来辨识商品或服务特殊品质的能力，不仅会对商标注册者造成负面影响，更会给该商标的商誉以及使用该证明商标的商品或服务的声誉造成不良影响。本案的争议焦点在于被告的行为是侵权行为还是对地理标志证明商标的正当使用，法院在审理中遵循以下审判思路：

一、地理标志证明商标的定义及内容

我国《商标法》第三条规定，经商标局核准注册的商标为注册商标，包括商品商标、服务商标和集体商标、证明商标；商标注册人享有商标专用权，受法律保护。证明商标作为特殊的注册商标，是由对某种商品或者服务具有监督能力的组织所控制，而由该组织以外的单位或者个人使用于其商品或者服务，用以证明该商品或者服务的原产地、原料、制造方法、质量或者其他特定品质的标志。

地理标志证明商标即标示某商品来源于某地区，并且该商品的特定质量、信誉或其他特征取决于其地理来源，由该地区的自然因素或人文因素所决定。申请地理标志证明商标有利于保护地方特产、推广区域商品市场，其外在价值在于其知名度，内在价值是该商品的生产加工地的自然和人文因素。首先，该地理来源并非仅仅是简单的商品产地信息，而是用于表明该商品具备特定质量、信誉或其他特征等的来源，能让人联想到商品的独特特征。其次，自然因素主要包括水质、土壤、地势、气候等，同样的品种离开了特定的地理气候环境，其品质特征往往迥然不同。人文因素包括用料、配方、工艺、历史传统等因素。

最后，地理标志证明商标由或文字，或字母，或图案或其组合组成，地名 + 品名是其核心，在标识图案中会显示有"中国地理标志证明商标""中国地理标志"等，从而使得消费者对相关商品的品质、声誉或其他特性产生一种信赖心理。其中，地名可以是标示商品或者服务特定地理来源的地理区域的名称或指称，也可以是因长期一致的使用而形成的标示特定地理区域的其他文字、短语或者符号，无须与具有相同名称的行政区划或者村落相一致，也无须与该地理区域的现行正式名称相一致。

根据《商标法》《商标法实施条例》《集体商标、证明商标注册和管理办法》等规定，证明商标申请人应当是对商品或者服务具有检测和监督能力，并具有法人资格的企业、事业单位或社会团体等组织。申请证明商标注册的，应当附送主体资格证明文件、使用管理规则并应当详细说明其所具有的或者其委托的机构具有的专业技术人员、专业检测设备等情况，以表明其具有监督该证明商标所证明的特定商品品质的能力。申请以地理标志作为证明商标注册的，还应当附送管辖该地理标志所标示地区的人民政府或者行业主管部门的批准文件。证明商标注册人本身不能使用证明商标，但是可以许可给他人使用。

"西湖龙井"是经国家工商行政管理部门履行一定的程序核准注册的地理标志证明商标，使用在第 30 类"茶叶"商品上，在其注册时依照流程由国家工商行政管理总局向社会公众公开了使用管理规则。使用者应遵守该规则使用该商标。

二、对地理标志证明商标的正当使用

《商标法》第十六条第二款规定，地理标志，是指标示某商品来源于某地区，该商品的特定质量、信誉或者其他特征，主要由该地区的自然因素或者人文因素所决定的标志。《商标法实施条例》第六条第二款规定，以地理标志作为证明商标注册的，其商品符合使用该地理标志条件的自然人、法人或者其他组织可以要求使用该证明商标，控制该证明商标的组织应当允许。以地理标志作为集体商标注册的，其商品符合使用该地理标志条件的自然人、法人或者其他组织，可以要求参加以该地理标志作为集体商标注册的团体、协会或者其他组织，该团体、协会或者其他组织应当依据其章程接纳其为会员；不要求参加以该地理标志作为集体商标注册的团体、协会或者其他组织的，也可以正当使用该地理标志，该团体、协会或者其他组织无权禁止。

根据上述规定可知，地理标志证明商标具有不同于一般商标的特殊性，它所标示的商品或服务所具有的特定品质本身就包括地理来源，是用来标示商品原产地、原料、制造方法、质量或其他特定品质的商标。证明商标的注册人负责对商品或服务的品质进行证明，其应当允许商品符合证明商标所标示的特定品质的自然人、法人或者其他组织正当使用该证明商标，不能剥夺虽没有向其提出使用该证明商标的要求，但其商品确实产于证明商标所标示产地、具有证明商标所代表的品质或使用了证明商标所证明的原料、制造方法的自然人、法人或者其他组织拥有正当使用该证明商标的权利。但同时，对于其商品并非产于证明商标所标示的产地、不具有证明商标所代表的品质、并非使用证明商标所证明的原料、制造方法的自然人、法人或者其他组织在商品上标注该商标的，证明商标的注册人则有权禁止，并依法追究其侵犯证明商标权利的责任。

西湖龙井作为我国传统名茶，其特定的品质主要由其茶叶产区的自然因素、采摘条件和制作工艺等所决定，原告作为"西湖龙井"商标的商标权人，在自然人、法人或其他组织的产品符合产地、工艺、品质的要求，而请求使用该证明商标的，应当允许。但对于不符合产地、工艺、品质要求的商品上标注该商标的，原告有权禁止，并依法追究其侵权责任。

同时，地理标志证明商标是由符合条件的多人共同使用的商标，其注册者需制定统一的管理规则并公之于众，让社会各界共同监督，以保护商品的特定品质，保护消费者的利益。原告制定的《"西湖龙井"地理标志证明商标使用管理规则》第五条要求"使用'西湖龙井'地理标志证明商标的商品的生产地域范围为杭州市政府划定的西湖龙井茶保护基地……"第六条对使用"西湖龙井"商标的商品的品质进行了规定，第七条为对使用"西湖龙井"商标的商品的采摘、加工工艺的要求。原告对涉案证明商标具有检测和监督的能力和义务，当事人需要提交材料证明其提供的商品或服务达到上述标准，在履行一定手续后，当事人就可以使用该证明商标，而对于在不符合上述要求的商品上使用证明商标的，原告有权禁止其使用并追究其责任。

三、对地理标志证明商标的侵权认定

由于地理标志证明商标的侵权行为是将该证明商标用于并不具有该证明商标所标识的产地、原料、制造方法和特定品质的商品上的行为，因此判断使用该证明商标的商品是否来自证明商标所标识的产地、是否具有证明商标所标识的原料、制造方法和特定品质就成为证明商标侵权认定的重要事实，而该事实则需根据当事人提交的证据加以认定。在证明商标侵权案件中，证明被诉侵权商品产地、原料、制造方法和特定品质的举证责任分配又成为一个关键的问题。

根据上述举证责任及其分配的基本原理，在地理标志证明商标侵权案件中，证明商标注册人作为主张权利存在的一方，需要就其权利产生的法律要件事实举证；被诉侵权使用证明商标的一方以自己的商品产自证明商标标识的产地，

其使用证明商标具有正当性进行抗辩，属于主张商标注册人权利受制的一方，作为主张权利受制的证明商标使用人，应就其抗辩主张成立的法律要件事实举证，即就其使用证明商标的商品确实来自证明商标所标识的产地承担举证责任。

四、被告在其产品及名片上使用与涉案商标相近似的商标是否构成侵权

本案被告辩称，其涉案的包装盒系被告几年前购进的样品，公证时顾客刻意看中标有西湖龙井茶叶的茶盒，并执意要求用其包装，是故意诱导被告用这个包装的，且其销售的是散装"虎"牌茶叶。法院认为，根据《商标法》第五十七条规定，未经商标注册人的许可，在同一种商品上使用与其注册商标近似的商标，或者在类似商品上使用与其注册商标相同或者近似的商标，容易导致混淆的，是侵犯注册商标专用权的行为。原告的证明商标的商品类别为第30类，核定使用商品为"茶叶"。被告在其所销售茶叶的包装袋、礼盒和茶叶罐的正中位置使用"西湖龍井"字样，属于商标性使用。经比对，被告使用的"西湖龍井"字样与涉案商标相比，区别仅在于简繁体、字体和横竖排列，故足以使相关公众误认为该商品是来源于特定产地并具有特定品质的商品，属于与涉案商标相近似的商标。此外，被控侵权商品本身或外包装上并无任何"虎"牌字样，被告也不能提供证据证明其产品来源于"西湖龙井"的指定生产区域以及产品符合"西湖龙井"的品质要求，因此被告在其产品上使用与涉案商标相近似的商标的行为构成侵权。

《商标法》第四十八条规定，商标的使用是指将商标用于商品、商品包装或者容器以及商品交易文书上，或者将商标用于广告宣传、展览以及其他商业活动中，用于识别商品来源的行为。原告指控被告在其名片上印制"虎牌西湖龙井"侵犯了其涉案商标权，对此法院认为，名片的作用在于在商业交往中的相互认识和自我介绍，同时也是向对方推销介绍自己的一种方式，属于《商标法》第四十八条所规定的"广告宣传行为"，被告在其名片上印制"虎牌西湖龙井"，目的在于让相关公众识别其销售的茶叶的来源。而根据被告当庭陈述，其销售的为中低端的散装茶，包括龙井、炒青、云雾等绿茶，被告未提供证据证明其店铺内销售的茶叶有"虎"牌西湖龙井，退一步说，即使被告店铺内有"虎"牌西湖龙井销售，被告仍需进一步证明该茶叶来源于"西湖龙井"的指定生产区域以及产品符合"西湖龙井"的品质要求。因此，被告在名片上使用"虎牌西湖龙井"字样，与原告涉案商标构成近似，是侵犯涉案注册商标专用权的行为。

（撰稿人：沈敬杰）

三

专利权民事纠纷案件

外观设计的客观比对与判断方法

——上海晨光文具股份有限公司与得力集团有限公司等侵害外观设计专利权纠纷案

【提要】

外观设计近似的判断常常受主观因素影响较大，影响司法公正及裁判尺度的统一。为使"整体观察，综合判断"原则在具体案件的适用中更加客观化，在外观设计侵权案件中，既应考察被诉侵权设计与授权外观设计的相似性，也应考察其差异性。应分别从被诉侵权产品与授权外观设计的相同设计特征和区别设计特征出发，就其对整体视觉效果的影响分别进行客观分析，避免主观因素的影响。未付出创造性劳动，通过在授权外观设计的基础上，改变或添加不具有实质性区别的设计元素以及图案和色彩，实施外观设计专利的，构成对外观设计专利权的侵犯。

【案情】

原告：上海晨光文具股份有限公司

被告：得力集团有限公司

被告：济南坤森商贸有限公司

案由：侵害外观设计专利权纠纷

一审案号：（2016）沪 73 民初 113 号

原告上海晨光文具股份有限公司（以下简称晨光公司）是名称为"笔（AGP67101）"的外观设计专利的专利权人，专利号为 ZL200930231150.3，申请日为 2009 年 11 月 26 日，授权公告日为 2010 年 7 月 21 日，目前处于有效状态。该授权外观设计（参见附图）由笔杆、笔帽组成，笔帽上设有笔夹。笔杆主体呈粗细均匀的细长状四周圆角柱体；顶端有正方形锥台突起，锥台中央有一圆孔；主体靠近笔头处内径略小，四周表面中心位置各有一凸状设计；笔头为圆锥状。笔帽主体呈粗细均匀的四周圆角柱体，长度约为笔杆长度的四分之一；顶端有正方形锥台突起。笔夹主体为扁平长方形片状；内侧面有波浪状突起；上端与笔帽顶端锥台弧形相连；下端为弧形；笔夹略长于笔帽，长出部分约占笔夹总长度的十分之一。专利简要说明记载，设计要点在于整支笔的形状，俯视图是最能反映设计要点的图片。2015年8月14日，国家知识产权局依原告请求就涉案专利出具了评价报告，作出"全部外观设计未发现存在不符合授予专利权条件的缺陷"的初步结论。2016年8月8日，国家知识产权局原专利复审委员会就被告得力集团有限公司（以下简称得力公司）针对涉案专利提出的无效宣告请求作出审查决定，认为授权外观设计与对比设计不构成实质相同，维持涉案专利权有效。

2015年11月30日，在淘宝网上"宝贝"栏目中搜索"得力A32160"，结果页面显示"共7件宝贝"，价格由1.0元/支到26.90元/盒（共12支）不等。北京市金杜律师事务所上海分所的委托代理人在标价为26.90元/盒的"得力坤森专卖店"中购买了4盒得力思达A32160波普风尚中性笔（以下代称被诉侵权产品）。上述过程由上海市黄浦公证处公证。上述"得力坤森专卖店"由被告济南坤森商贸有限公司（以下简称坤森公司）经营。被告得力公司确认其制造、销售过被诉侵权产品。

被诉侵权产品（参见附图）由笔杆和笔帽组成，笔帽上设有笔夹。笔杆主体呈粗细均匀的四周圆角柱体，靠近笔尖约三分之一处有一环状凹线设计；顶端有正方形锥台突起，锥台中央有一圆孔；主体靠近笔头处内径略小，四周表面中心位置各有一凸状设计；笔头为圆锥状。笔帽主体呈粗细均匀的四周圆角柱体，长度约为笔杆长度的四分之一；顶端有正方形锥台突起。笔夹主体为长方形；外侧面有长方形锥台突起，内侧面光滑；笔夹上端与笔帽顶端锥台弧形相连；下端平直；笔夹略长于笔帽，长出部分约占笔夹总长度的十分之一。

原告晨光公司诉称：其为涉案外观设计专利的专利权人，被诉侵权产品与涉案外观设计专利产品属于相同产品，且外观设计近似，两被告的行为构成对原告专利权的侵犯。故请求法院判令：1.两被告立即停止侵权行为；2.两被告销毁所有库存侵权产品以及制造侵权产品的专用设备、模具；3.被告得力公司赔偿原告经济损失180万元及为制止侵权所支付的合理费用20万元。

被告得力公司辩称：被诉侵权产品与原告外观设计不相同也不近似，被告行为不构成对原告专利权的侵犯。即使构成侵权，原告诉请的赔偿数额及合理费用也过高。

被告坤森公司未作答辩。

【审判】

上海知识产权法院经审理认为：被诉侵权产品与涉案外观设计专利产品属于相同产品，本案主要争议在于，被诉侵权设计与授权外观设计是否构成近似。在该问题的判断上，应分别考察被诉侵权设计与授权外观设计的相同设计特征与区别设计特征对整体视觉效果的影响，根据整体观察、综合判断的原则进行判定。

就相同设计特征来说，授权外观设计的笔杆主体形状、笔杆顶端形状、笔帽主体形状、笔帽顶端形状、笔帽相对于笔杆的长度、笔夹与笔帽的连接方式、笔夹长出笔帽的长度等方面的设计特征，在整体上确定了授权外观设计的设计风格，而这些设计特征在被诉侵权设计中均具备，可以认定两者在整体设计风格及主要设计特征上构成近似。

就区别设计特征来说，被诉侵权设计与授权外观设计所存在的四点区别设计特征，不足以对整体视觉效果产生实质性影响：笔夹内侧处于一般消费者不易观察到的部位；笔夹下端的弧形区别仅是整支笔乃至笔夹的细微局部差别；在笔夹整体形状、大小、与笔帽的连接方式及长出笔帽的长度比例等因素均相同的情况下，笔夹外侧的锥台突起对于整支笔的整体视觉效果影响有限；笔杆上的凹线设计只是横向环绕在笔杆上，面积很小，属于局部设计特征，对整体视觉效果的影响亦有限。

对于色彩和图案对近似认定的影响，授权外观设计的简要说明中并未明确要求保护色彩，因此，在确定其保护范围及侵权判定时，不应将色彩考虑在内。被诉侵权设计在采用与授权外观设计近似的形状之余所附加的色彩等要素，属于额外增加的设计要素，对侵权判断不具有实质性影响。

原告及被告得力公司均为国内较有影响的文具生产企业，在新产品的自主研发上更应投入更多的精力，对自身产品研发过程中涉及的法律风险也应有较为专业的认知。被告得力公司未付出创造性劳动，通过在原告授权外观设计的基础上，改变或添加不具有实质性区别的设计元素以及图案和色彩，实施原告外观设计专利，构成对原告外观设计专利权的侵犯。

综上，上海知识产权法院依照《中华人民共和国民法通则》第一百一十八条，《中华人民共和国专利法》第十一条第二款、第六十五条之规定判决被告得力公司立即停止制造、销售侵犯原告外观设计专利权产品的行为；被告坤森公司立即停止许诺销售、销售侵犯原告外观设计专利权产品的行为；被告得力公司赔偿原告经济损失50 000元及制止侵权的合理费用50 000元。

一审判决后，当事人均未上诉，案件已经生效。

【评析】

本案所涉产品为笔类产品，其外观看似大同小异，又为日常生活中常见，因此在侵权判断中更易受主观因素的影响。

外观设计专利是一种比较特殊的专利权。其与发明、实用新型专利在保护客体方面有很大的不同。发明和实用新型专利保护的都是技术方案，用于产生功能作用方面的效果，而外观设计专利保护的是产品外观的设计方案，用于产生视觉感受方面的效果。因此，对于外观设计的保护，国际上一直存在着通过著作权法保护和通过专利法保护两种模式。即使是在通过专利法保护外观设计的国家中，对于外观设计专利权的授权标准及侵权判断标准，做法也并不统一。在我国，《专利审查指南》及司法实践对于外观设计专利授权标准及侵权判定标准一直处于不断调整的状态。外观设计专利侵权案件较之发明及实用新型专利权侵权案件，常常呈现出看似简单实则复杂且易受主观因素影响的特点。不同的裁判者，由于个人经验及认知的差异，在是否构成近似的认定上，有时会得出截然相反的结论。

根据《最高人民法院关于审理专利权纠纷案件应用法律若干问题的解释》第十条、第十一条的规定，应以外观设计专利产品的一般消费者的知识水平和认知能力，根据授权外观设计、被诉侵权设计的设计特征，以外观设计的整体视觉效果进行综合判断。这通常被称为外观设计近似判断的"整体观察，综合判断"方法。但这是一个比较原则性的方法，在具体案件中如何把握、如何使不同裁判者在判断中减少主观因素的影响，得出相对客观的结论，本案在这方面进行了以下探索：

首先，分别确定被诉侵权产品与授权外观设计的相同设计特征和区别设计特征。

这一步在法庭调查阶段完成。应当注意引导当事人在比对时对相同设计特征和区别设计特征均进行陈述，避免仅仅注意区别设计特征，而忽略了对相同设计特征的归纳。因为如果仅仅关注区别设计特征，在判断被诉侵权产品与授权外观设计在整体视觉效果上是否存在差异时，主观上容易将区别设计特征放大，轻易认定被诉侵权设计与授权外观设计不构成近似。

其次，以一般消费者的知识水平和认知能力，分别分析相同设计特征和区别设计特征对整体视觉效果的影响。在此应注意以下几点：

一、在分析相同设计特征对整体视觉效果的影响时，首先应将由功能唯一限定或因其他原因已经成为惯常设计的元素排除在外。如汽车轮胎的圆形形状是由功能唯一限定的，不能将该形状对整体视觉效果的影响考虑在内。本案中，笔的整体形状是长圆柱体，这也已经成为惯常设计，也不应将其对整体视觉效果的影响考虑在内。需要注意的是，惯常设计不同于现有设计。现有设计是在申请日以前在国内外为公众所知的设计。现有设计中只有为一般消费者所熟知的、只要提到产品名称就能想到的相应设计，才构成惯常设计。例如，提到包装盒就能想到其有长方体、正方体形状的设计。

二、不能仅仅因为某个设计元素在现有设计中出现过，就排除其对整体视觉效果的影响，除非该元素由功能唯一限定或因其他原因已经成为惯常设计或被诉侵权产品与授权外观设计的相同点在单一现有设计中都已经存在。在我国当前已授权的外观设计专利中，完全抛弃现有设计而创造出的全新设计是很少的。多数外观设计专利是吸收现有设计中的某些元素，通过组合或是混搭形成新的设计。就本案所涉的笔类产品来说，笔的外观看似大同小异，但在整体造型及各部分的形状、大小等方面是有着各自的设计特点的。笔杆、笔帽、笔夹上的若干设计元素，在现有设计中都可能找到相同或近似的元素，不能因某个元素在现有设计中出现过就否定授权专利的稳定性，也不能因此不加区别地将其排除在对整体视觉效果产生影响的因素之外。当然这里有几个例外：一是该元素由功能唯一限定或因其他原因已经成为惯常设计（前文已述）。二是被诉侵权产品与授权外观设计的主要相同点在单一现有设计中均已存在，即构成现有设计抗辩。本案中，被诉侵权产品与授权外观设计相同的设计特征中，笔杆与笔帽的主体形状（粗细均匀的四周圆角柱体）、笔帽与笔杆的长度比例关系（笔帽长度约为笔杆长度的四分之一）在在先设计中是存在的，而且该在先设计也曾经被得力公司作为对比设计用于无效申请中。国家知识产权局原专利复审委员会审查后认为，授权外观设计与对比设计存在显著性区别，两者不构成实质性相同，故作出维持专利权有效的决定。授权外观设计经过国家知识产权局是否符合专利权授予条件的评价、专利无效审查等程序，在被告没有证据否定其有效性的情况下，法院不能因为某个或某些设计特征在现有设计中被披露过就否定其有效性，也不能将其不加区分地排除在对整体视觉效果产生影响的因素之外。本案授权外观设计与在先设计笔杆与笔帽的主体形状均为粗细均匀的四周圆角柱体，笔帽长度约为笔杆长度的四分之一，上述笔杆与笔帽的主体形状及笔帽与笔杆的长度比例关系对整体视觉效果的影响的确比较大，但在先设计的笔帽与笔杆上有若干条贯穿上下的棱线设计，这对笔杆及笔帽主体的视觉效果影响较大。此外，被诉侵权产品与授权外观设计，除了上述笔杆与笔帽的主体形状、笔帽与笔杆的长度比例关系相同之外，在笔杆及笔帽顶端的形状、笔夹与笔帽的连接方式、笔夹长出笔帽的长度等方面亦相同，而这些设计特征对整体视觉效果都有较大影响，而在在先设计中都不存在。故本案中，法院在考量对整体视觉效果产生影响的相同设计特征时，没有将笔杆与笔帽的主体形状及笔帽与笔杆的长度比例关系排除。在分别分析了相同设计特征和区别设计特征对整体视觉效果的影响之后，认定被诉侵权产品与授权外观设计在整体设计风格及主要设计特征上构成近似。

三、现有设计抗辩应与单独一项现有设计进行比对，不能与多个现有设计共同比对。如果授权外观设计已被国家知识产权局经过检索得出符合授予专利权条件的评价结论或经过无效宣告程序被认定为有效，则在侵权案件中通常无需对其有效性进行质疑，否则将使授权专利处于不稳定的状态。在被诉侵权产品与现有设计不相同，但有较大程度的近似时，在判断该近似是否构成实质性相同时，可以考虑以下几点：1. 被诉侵权产品与现有设计的区别是否是细微的、非显著性的；2. 被诉侵权产品是否是由现有设计转用得到的，且该具体的转用手法在相同或者相近种类产品的现有设计中存在启示；3. 被诉侵权产品是否是由现有设计或者现有设计特征组合得到的，且该具体的组合手法在相同或者相近种类产品的现有设计中存在启示。如果存在上述情况，则可以认定被告现有设计抗辩成立。

四、产品正常使用时容易被直接观察到的部位相对于其他部位，对整体视觉效果更具有显著影响；不容易观察到的部位及局部细微的变化，则对整体视觉效果不足以产生显著影响。如笔夹内侧的设计，其处于笔夹与笔帽之间的位置，一般消费者不容易观察到，不应认定为对整体视觉效果产生影响。本案中，被诉侵权产品笔夹内侧波浪状突起的区别设计特征就属该种情况。

五、区别设计特征在整体设计中所占大小比例可以作为对整体视觉效果是否产生显著影响的参考。本案中，被诉侵权产品的笔夹下端是平直的，而授权外观设计的笔夹下端为弧形；被诉侵权设计的笔杆靠近笔尖约三分之一处有一环状凹线设计，而授权外观设计没有凹线设计。法院认为，笔夹下端仅是笔的外观的细微局部，对整体视觉效果的影响极其有限；笔杆上的凹线设计位于笔杆靠近笔尖约三分之一处，只是横向环绕在笔杆上，面积也很小，属于局部设计特征，对整体视觉效果的影响亦有限。需要注意的是，区别设计特征在整体设计中所占大小比例仅仅作为对整体视觉效果是否产生显著影响的参考，不是决定因素。不能仅仅因为所占面积大就简单地认定对整体视觉效果产生显著影响，还应结合其他因素综合认定。本案中，被诉侵权设计的笔夹外侧有长方形锥台突起，而授权外观设计的笔夹外侧没有突起。笔夹外侧的长方形锥台突起虽然在笔夹上占据了较大面积，但笔夹对于笔的整体视觉效果的影响首先在于它的整体形状、大小、与笔帽的连接方式及长出笔帽的长度比例等，在这些因素均相同的情况下，法院认定，笔夹外侧的锥台突起对于整支笔的整体视觉效果影响有限，不足以构成实质性差异。

六、对于未将色彩、图案纳入保护范围的外观设计，不应将被诉侵权设计的色彩和图案对整体视觉效果的影响考虑在内。外观设计专利权的保护范围以表示在图片或者照片中的该产品的外观设计为准。形状、图案、色彩是构成产品外观设计的三项基本设计要素。外观设计请求保护色彩的，应当在简要说明中写明。未在简要说明中明确要求保护色彩的，在确定专利权保护范围及进行侵权判定时，不应将色彩考虑在内。

（撰稿人：徐飞）

附图：

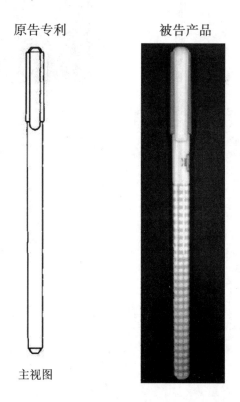

原告专利　　　　　　被告产品

主视图

俯视图

组件 1 左视图

先用权抗辩的司法认定

——盛纪（上海）家居用品有限公司诉上海统一星巴克咖啡
有限公司等侵害外观设计专利权纠纷案

【提要】

先用者在专利申请日前已经制造相同产品，并且仅在原有范围内继续制造
的，享有先用权，其主张的先用权抗辩成立。先用权人在原有范围内继续制造
相同产品不视为侵权，其制造相同产品的后续销售行为亦不构成侵权。

【案情】

原告： 盛纪（上海）家居用品有限公司
被告： 上海统一星巴克咖啡有限公司
被告： 增城市增豪不锈钢制品有限公司
案由： 侵害外观设计专利权纠纷
一审案号：（2015）沪知民初字第 504 号

盛纪（上海）家居用品有限公司（以下简称盛纪公司）系涉案"饮水杯
（0506－2）"外观设计专利权人，该专利申请日为 2014 年 5 月 26 日，授权公告
日为 2014 年 10 月 1 日。2015 年 6 月 29 日，盛纪公司在星巴克咖啡店公证购买
了"12oz 橙光不锈钢随行杯"一个。该产品标识的经销商为上海统一星巴克咖
啡有限公司（以下简称星巴克公司），制造商为增城市增豪不锈钢制品有限公
司（以下简称增豪公司），产品品号 435180，与涉案专利外观设计相比对，两
者外观相近似。

2013 年 11 月至 2014 年 2 月，星巴克咖啡公司（STARBUCKS COFFEE
COMPANY）、WOODMAX 公司、增豪公司之间的众多往来邮件，涉及一款星巴
克杯子的设计、开模、交付样品存在的问题等事宜，邮件附件中显示的杯子设

计图片与前述公证购买的被控侵权产品外观基本一致。

2014 年 2 月 24 日，星巴克咖啡公司向 WOODMAX 公司发送邮件订单订购 DIAMOND PHINNY 随行杯绿色 12 盎司和红色 12 盎司，数量分别为 10 680 只和 10 008 只。2014 年 2 月 25 日，WOODMAX 公司向增豪公司发送邮件订单，订单号、产品货号、颜色等均与前述订单相同，订单上附有的杯子图片与前述被控侵权产品实物外观基本一致，差异仅在于颜色不同。增豪公司于 2014 年 6 月 14 日完成上述订单产品的装箱、报关。

2015 年 2 月 2 日，星巴克公司向东莞沃美氏公司订购 12oz 橙光不锈钢随行杯 1248 个；同年 2 月 7 日，东莞沃美氏公司向增豪公司订购前述橙光不锈钢杯 1248 个，订单上附有的杯子图片与前述公证购买的被控侵权产品外观基本一致。上述订单产品于 2015 年 4 月 9 日交付，同年 6 月 9 日，东莞沃美氏公司向星巴克公司出具的增值税专用发票上载明"435180 12oz 橙光不锈钢随行杯"两批次共计 1260 只。

原告盛纪公司诉称：其系涉案外观设计专利的专利权人，被告星巴克公司销售的制造商为被告增豪公司的前述产品落入其涉案专利权保护范围，将星巴克公司、增豪公司诉至法院，请求判令两被告停止侵权、赔偿经济损失及合理费用共计 212 200 元。

被告星巴克公司辩称：被控侵权产品与涉案专利不相同也不相近似，未落入涉案专利保护范围；被控侵权产品采用的是现有设计，不构成侵权；被控侵权产品在专利申请日前已经生产，属于在先使用，不视为侵犯专利权；被控侵权产品具有合法来源，即使构成侵权，也不应承担赔偿责任。

被告增豪公司辩称：被控侵权产品与涉案专利不相同也不相近似，未落入涉案专利保护范围；被控侵权产品采用的是现有设计，不构成侵权；被控侵权产品在专利申请日前已经生产，属于在先使用，不视为侵犯专利权。

【审判】

上海知识产权法院经审理认为：原告是涉案"饮水杯（0506-2）"外观设计专利的专利权人，任何单位或者个人未经专利权人许可，不得为生产经营目的制造、许诺销售、销售、进口其专利产品。本案被控侵权产品采用的设计与授权外观设计经比对在整体视觉效果上无实质性差异，构成近似设计，被控侵权产品落入原告涉案外观设计专利权保护范围。但是，在案证据显示星巴克咖啡公司、WOODMAX 公司与增豪公司在专利申请日前相互协作配合，设计生产相关订单产品，增豪公司于 2014 年 2 月 25 日接受订单，并于 2014 年 6 月 14 日完成全部首批订单产品的生产、装箱、报关，即增豪公司在涉案专利申请日2014 年 5 月 26 日之前已经做好生产相关订单产品的准备，并制造出了相关产品。被控侵权产品与增豪公司在专利申请日前开始生产的首批订单产品外观基本一致，差异仅在于颜色不同。因颜色并非涉案专利的保护范围，并不影响两者与涉案专利相对应的设计部分系相同设计的认定，故被控侵权产品与增豪公司专利申请日前已经制造出的相关产品属于相同产品，且亦无证据显示增豪公司依据新的订单生产产品系超出原有范围。因增豪公司在涉案专利申请日前已经制造相同产品，并且仅在原有范围内继续制造，享有先用权，其主张的先用权抗辩成立。先用权人在原有范围内继续制造相同产品不视为侵权，其制造相同产品的后续销售行为亦不构成侵权。星巴克公司系被控侵权产品的销售商，提供证据证明其销售的产品来源于享有先用权的增豪公司，其销售产品的行为也不构成侵权。

综上，上海知识产权法院依照《中华人民共和国专利法》第五十九条第二款、第六十九条第（二）项，《最高人民法院关于审理侵犯专利权纠纷案件应用法律若干问题的解释》第八条、第十五条第三款的规定，判决：驳回原告盛纪公司的诉讼请求。

一审判决后，各方当事人均未上诉，一审判决现已生效。

【评析】

《专利法》第六十九条第（二）项规定了先用权，即在专利申请日前已经制造相同产品、使用相同方法或者已经做好制造、使用的必要准备，并且仅在原有范围内继续制造、使用的，不视为侵犯专利权。对于该条款的理解与适用，司法实践中一直存在较大分歧。本案的争议焦点也在于星巴克公司、增豪公司主张的先用权抗辩能否成立。

一、先用权的性质

先用权制度与专利在先申请制度密切相关。首先提出专利申请并获得专利授权的人不一定是首先作出发明创造、实施发明创造的人，而专利的垄断性决定了专利权被授予后，任何单位或个人未经专利权人许可，都不得实施其专利。在此情况下，为了弥补专利申请在先主义的不足，合理平衡先用权人与专利权人之间的利益关系，专利法规定了先用权制度，对专利权行使进行一定的限制。

关于先用权的性质，首先，先用权相对于特定的专利权而存在，只有专利授权后，才涉及是否存在与之相关的先用权；其次，先用权的权利主体并不特定，多个先用权人可以相互并存；再次，在权利行使方式上，先用权人可在原有范围内继续制造、使用，无权请求他人为一定行为或不为一定行为；最后，在权利行使效果上，不存在先用权被他人侵害或者后续的权利救济，仅是先用权人用来对抗专利权人的侵权指控。综上，先用权本质上是一种自用权，仅具有抗辩的功能，法律上亦不存在对该权利的救济，其在性质上更类似于抗辩权。

二、先用权与现有技术（设计）

先用权抗辩与现有设计抗辩均是对抗专利侵权指控的常见不侵权抗辩事由。两者在事实认定上存在交叉可能。先用者在专利申请日前制造相同产品、使用相同方法的行为如未公开，则先用者只能主张先用权抗辩；如在专利申请日前因使用行为（如销售行为）已导致相同产品或方法的公开，则该产品或方法已同时构成现有技术，先用者可同时主张先用权抗辩和现有技术抗辩。

因两者系不同抗辩事由，司法实践中亦应遵循不同的审理路径。先用权抗辩系权利行使的法定限制事由，侵权指控不能成立的例外情形；现有技术抗辩则属合理使用情形，被控侵权行为本质上不构成侵权，而非侵权的例外规定。两者认定抗辩能否成立的条件不同。先用权抗辩应当考察四个条件，即先用权人是否在专利申请日前已经制造出相关产品（使用相关方法）或做好制造（使用）的必要准备、相关产品是否属于相同产品、先用技术是否系先用权人以合法手段获得、先用权人是否在原有范围内继续制造；现有技术抗辩则应当考察两个条件，即对比技术相对于涉案专利是否构成现有技术，被控侵权产品是否采用了现有技术。两者比对规则不同，侵权成立是先用权抗辩适用的前提，故先用权抗辩需涉及两层技术比对，先是被控侵权产品采用的技术方案与专利权利要求的比对，两者构成相同或等同后才涉及第二层比对，也即被控侵权产品与专利申请日前的在先产品是否属于相同产品；现有技术抗辩则不必然以侵权成立为前提，可直接比对被控侵权产品与现有技术从而认定现有技术抗辩成立，而不必然要求进行被控侵权技术方案与专利的侵权比对。两者抗辩成立的效果不同。先用权抗辩成立后，专利权人如有证据证明先用者超出原有范围制造相同产品，仍可主张先用者构成专利侵权；现有技术抗辩成立后，专利权人指控相同被控侵权产品构成专利侵权的主张不能成立。

三、先用权抗辩认定的考量因素

1. 原有范围认定。先用权制度的设计初衷是弥补申请在先主义的不足，对原有范围的过宽解释，一定程度上会影响专利申请制度，因此，相关司法解释倾向于限制性解释，以生产规模来界定原有范围，其本质上更类似于量的限制。

除此之外，原有范围的认定亦存在实施主体的限定性，先用权人在申请日后将其技术另行转让或者许可他人实施，被诉侵权人主张该实施行为属于在原有范围内继续实施的，不予支持，但该技术或设计与原有企业一并转让或者承继的除外。关于原有范围的举证责任分配，先用权抗辩系先用权人主张存在先用权的积极抗辩事实，用以对抗专利权人的侵权指控，应由抗辩提出者承担举证责任。

本案中，增豪公司、星巴克公司并没有提供证据证明增豪公司在专利申请日前的确切生产规模，但其提供的证据可以证明，增豪公司依据 2014 年 2 月也即涉案专利申请日前的订单于 2014 年 6 月向星巴克咖啡公司交付产品 20 688 个，被控侵权产品购买于 2015 年 6 月 29 日，增豪公司依据 2015 年 6 月 9 日的增值税专用发票向星巴克公司交付产品仅为 1260 个，从数量来看，1260 个在 20 688 个的范围之内，且实际制造商均为增豪公司，并未发生实施主体的变更，故认定增豪公司的制造行为超出原有范围的依据不足。

2. 相同产品认定。相同产品的过宽或过窄解释均将有悖于先用权制度的设立初衷，影响该制度的实施效果，对相同产品的理解应回归专利制度的本源。专利权系对技术方案的专有实施权，对先用权人的保护亦是基于对在先技术方案的保护，故相同产品的讨论亦离不开相关技术方案的认定，与产品的名称、型号等外在称谓并无实质关联。相同产品应指被控侵权产品与专利申请日前已经制造出的相关产品属于相同专利产品，包括两者系同一产品，或者虽不是同一产品，但两者与涉案专利相对应的部分系实质相同。在此，首先，相同产品指的是被控侵权产品与专利申请日前已经制造出的相关产品的比对；其次，比对的标准是两者与涉案专利相对应的设计特征系完全相同或者无实质性差异，这其中既包括两者系同一产品，采用的所有设计特征均相同，也包括两者虽不是同一产品，但均包含了与涉案专利相对应的相同的设计特征。

本案中，经比对，被控侵权产品与 2013 年 11 月至 2014 年 2 月邮件附件中的杯子设计图片、2014 年 2 月 25 日 WOODMAX 公司向增豪公司发送的订单上所附杯子图片外观均基本一致，也即被控侵权产品与增豪公司在专利申请日前开始生产的首批订单产品外观基本一致，差异仅在于颜色不同。颜色并非涉案专利的保护范围，并不影响两者与涉案专利相对应的设计部分系相同设计的认定，故认定被控侵权产品与增豪公司专利申请日前已经制造出的相关产品属于相同产品。

3. 相关产品于专利申请日前已经制造且先用技术系合法取得。先用者应在专利申请日前已经制造相同产品、使用相同方法或者已经做好制造、使用的必要准备，其中，已经制造相同产品、使用相同方法相对容易界定，产品的生产记录、销售订单等均可作为证据予以证明；而对于"已经做好制造、使用的必要准备"的理解，应同时包括技术准备和生产准备。另外，技术来源应具有合法性，以非法获得的技术或者设计主张先用权抗辩的，不予支持。

本案中，综合在案证据，可以认定星巴克咖啡公司、WOODMAX 公司与增豪公司在专利申请日前相互协作配合，设计生产相关订单产品，增豪公司亦已于 2014 年 2 月 25 日接受订单，2014 年 6 月 14 日完成全部首批订单产品的生产、装箱、报关，由此可以认定增豪公司在涉案专利申请日 2014 年 5 月 26 日之前已经做好生产相关订单产品的准备，并制造出了相关产品，且技术来源合法。

4. 先用权抗辩主体。先用者可以主张先用权抗辩，此处的先用者一般指的是制造者，其可主张抗辩的行为不仅包括制造相同产品、使用相同方法的行为，同时也应包括制造、使用行为的后续销售、许诺销售行为。除制造商享有先用权外，侵权诉讼中销售商亦可同时主张先用权抗辩。本案中，增豪公司在涉案专利申请日前已经制造相同产品，并且仅在原有范围内继续制造，享有先用权，其主张的先用权抗辩成立。先用权人在原有范围内继续制造相同产品不视为侵权，其制造相同产品的后续销售行为亦不构成侵权。星巴克公司系被控侵权产品的销售商，提供证据证明其销售的产品来源于享有先用权的增豪公司，亦可主张增豪公司享有先用权，其销售产品的行为也不构成侵权。

（撰稿人：陈瑶瑶）

法院采信单方鉴定结论的条件

——山特维克知识产权股份有限公司诉
浙江美安普矿山机械股份有限公司
侵害发明专利权纠纷案

【提要】

在专利侵权纠纷案件审理过程中，专利权人由于被控侵权产品销售渠道或自身取证能力等因素限制，有时无法获取被控侵权产品的实物，只能通过摄影摄像等方式提交证据，在此情形下，如何通过对照片录像进行分析进而做出侵权比对判断甚至推断是审判实践中需要解决的问题。本案虽然没有被控侵权产品实物，但是根据专利权人提供的照片、录像，结合技术人员的专业知识明确了被控侵权的全部技术方案，最终支持了原告的诉请，体现了法院对知识产权的保护力度。

【案情】

原告：山特维克知识产权股份有限公司

被告：浙江美安普矿山机械股份有限公司

案由：侵害发明专利权纠纷

一审案号：（2015）沪知民初字第 748 号

原告山特维克知识产权股份有限公司向法院提出诉讼请求：1. 被告立即停止侵害原告享有的 ZL03820653.6 号"一种粉碎机及粉碎原料的方法"发明专利权，包括停止制造、销售及许诺销售被控侵权产品；2. 被告赔偿原告经济损失 100 万元；3. 被告赔偿原告合理费用 364 580 元。事实和理由：原告于 2003 年 8 月 27 日向中国国家知识产权局申请了名称为"一种粉碎机及粉碎原料的方法"的发明专利申请，该发明专利于 2007 年 10 月 10 日获得授权，至今有效。

原告于 2014 年 11 月 26 日在上海新国际博览中心举办的"bauma China 2014 中国国际工程机械、建材机械、工程车辆及设备博览会"进行市场调查时发现，被告在该博览会上展出的 GS300 立轴式冲击粉碎机（以下简称被控侵权产品）涉嫌侵犯原告享有的上述发明专利权，同时，原告发现被告公司网站（www. mpcrusher. com）上列出的"美安普产品"目录中也载明其销售的产品包含 GS300 立轴式冲击粉碎机。原告对被控侵权产品进行剖析后认为，被控侵权产品完全落入原告专利的保护范围。上海硅知识产权交易中心有限公司司法鉴定所也出具了《司法鉴定意见书》认为被控侵权产品对应的技术特征与原告专利的权利要求 1 - 7 的全部技术特征相同。原告认为，被告未经许可擅自使用原告的发明专利制造、销售、许诺销售、使用被控侵权产品，侵害了原告享有的发明专利权，应当承担停止侵权、赔偿损失的民事责任。

被告浙江美安普矿山机械有限公司辩称：被控侵权产品的技术特征与原告专利的技术特征不完全相同，被控侵权产品使用的转子是四通道的，被控侵权产品的"L 形挡板"的角度是 100°而非原告专利所述的 90°。被告请求法院驳回原告的全部诉讼请求。

2014 年 11 月 26 日，经原告申请，上海市长宁公证处公证员与原告的代理人来到上海新国际博览中心举办的"bauma China 2014 中国国际工程机械、建材机械、工程车辆及设备博览会"现场。原告的代理人在标有"衢州美安普矿山机械有限公司"字样的展台处取得宣传册两本，名片一张，原告的代理人使用该公证处照相机对该展台的现场状况、展示物品进行了摄影、摄像。上海市长宁公证处对上述过程进行了现场监督并制作了（2014）沪长证字第 8107 号公证书予以证明。根据该公证书记载，原告的代理人对本案被控侵权产品的外观和内部构造进行了拍照和摄像。被告确认被控侵权产品是其生产的。

2015 年 9 月 9 日，汇业律师事务所委托上海硅知识产权交易中心有限公司司法鉴定所对"衢州美安普矿山机械有限公司制造的型号为 GS300 立轴式冲击破碎机是否与山特维克知识产权股份有限公司授权公告号为'CN100341627C'的发明专利的专利权利要求 1 - 7 所记载的全部技术特征相同或等同"事项进行鉴定。鉴定材料包括：1. CN100341627C 专利授权文本纸质版一份；2.（2014）沪长证字第 8107 号公证材料一份（内含展会现场取证视频及图片光盘一份）。2015 年 10 月 29 日，上海硅知识产权交易中心有限公司司法鉴定所出具沪硅所［2015］鉴字第 011 号侵权司法鉴定意见书，其鉴定意见为 GS300 立轴式冲击破碎机对应的技术特征与 CN100341627C 发明专利的权利要求 1 - 7 所记载的全部技术特征相同。鉴定人叶枝灿出庭接受质询，该鉴定人明确表示虽然此次鉴定的主要鉴材是照片和视频资料，但可以从中看出被控侵权产品具有 L 形方向导杆，虽然无法看到是否 90 度但可以推导出该 L 形方向导杆的技术效果与涉案专利记载的相应技术特征的技术效果相同。

【审判】

上海知识产权法院认为，权利要求 4 在权利要求 1、2、3 的基础上增加了技术特征："L"形方向导杆的水平腿指向转子的旋转方向，这样在具有向上分量和关于转子成切向分量的方向中，由转子产生的任何灰尘将被方向导杆的垂直腿阻拦。经比对，被控侵权产品具有 L 形方向导杆，其水平腿位于六边形内外料斗之间，与转子成切线方向，因此与转子旋转方向一致，其垂直腿与上方形成相对密封结构，故可以阻拦转子产生的灰尘，法院认为，首先，被告没有证据证明被控侵权产品的"L"形方向导杆的角度是 100 度而非 90 度，从原告提供的被控侵权产品的图片和录像资料中也无法看出角度上的明显差异；其次，即使被控侵权产品的"L"形导向杆的角度为 100 度，与 90 度相比，也属于以基本相同的手段实现基本相同的功能、达到基本相同的效果的等同特征，即两者均可以实现"积聚原料形成坡体""阻拦转子产生的灰尘"等功能，被告也没有证据证明使用 100 度的导向杆能产生其他显著不同的功能及效果；最后，根据专利说明书的最后一段记载"然而也可能形成一个例如钢板、瓷砖或者类似板的预制坡体，所述坡体在粉碎机启动之后立即具有一个关于转子的期望切向倾斜度"，L 形方向导杆的角度也未被限定为必须是 90 度。因此，上海知识产权法院认为，被控侵权产品具有权利要求 4 增加的这一技术特征。此外，法院对于被告的现有技术抗辩亦未支持，在赔偿金额的确定方面，法院适用法定赔偿规则，考虑了被控侵权产品出口至越南的合同价格这一因素。

上海知识产权法院于 2016 年 11 月 4 日作出（2015）沪知民初字第 748 号民事判决，判决被告浙江美安普矿山机械有限公司立即停止对原告山特维克知识产权股份有限公司享有的名称为"一种粉碎机及粉碎原料的方法"的发明专利权（专利号为 ZL03820653.6）的侵害，并赔偿原告经济损失 50 万元以及合理费用 12 万元。宣判后，双方当事人均未提出上诉，判决已发生法律效力。

【评析】

本案主要涉及两个需要讨论的问题，一是对于单方鉴定（尤其是无实物鉴材），法院应当在何种条件下予以采信；二是在影像资料中无法显示的技术特征如何认定是否落入专利权保护范围。

一、采信单方鉴定（尤其是无实物鉴材）的条件

通常来说，在专利侵权案件的审理过程中，关于技术问题的事实查明，由原告向法院提出申请，再由法院向双方当事人协商确定或者法院指定的有鉴定资格的鉴定机构发出鉴定委托，然后整个鉴定程序会在法院的主持下逐步推进，包括确定鉴材的范围和内容、鉴定人员、召开现场鉴定会以及落实时间进度等，最终由鉴定机构向法院出具鉴定书，法院会在组织双方当事人对鉴定书进行质证后做出是否采信鉴定结论的裁判。近年来，随着专利案件诉讼的日益专业化，不少当事人选择在调查取证阶段就自行委托专业的知识产权司法鉴定机构进行侵权定性方面的鉴定，一方面可以提前判断是否有胜诉的可能性；另一方面也可以在诉讼中将其作为重要证据以支持己方的论点。事实上，从受理专利侵权纠纷案件之初至今，法院对于单方鉴定的态度也发生了阶段性的变化，从一开始基本上排斥，到有选择地接受部分鉴定结论，再到借助技术支持并全面听取原被告双方意见后接纳单方鉴定作为定案证据，这表明在专利审判领域，技术调查官、技术咨询专家、专家陪审员等制度的建立已经给法官在查明技术事实方面带来信心，同时，也减少了不必要的鉴定费用成本，给当事人减轻了负担。

当然，对于单方鉴定的接纳也必须符合一定的条件，不排除某些单方鉴定在鉴定材料、逻辑推理等方面存在问题进而导致鉴定结论令人无法接受。根据《民事诉讼法》以及《民事诉讼证据规则》的相关规定，鉴定意见是法定的证据种类之一，其是否能成为定案依据当然需要法院进行审查。审判人员对鉴定人出具的鉴定书，应当审查是否具有下列内容：（一）委托人姓名或者名称、委托鉴定的内容；（二）委托鉴定的材料；（三）鉴定的依据及使用的科学技术手段；（四）对鉴定过程的说明；（五）明确的鉴定结论；（六）对鉴定人鉴定资格的说明；（七）鉴定人员及鉴定机构签名盖章。单方鉴定作为一方当事人自行委托有关部门作出的鉴定结论，另一方当事人有证据足以反驳并申请重新鉴定的，人民法院应予准许。在本案中，原告向法院提交的其单方委托鉴定的鉴定报告在上述第（一）、（四）、（五）、（六）、（七）等方面均不存在瑕疵，但在第（二）、（三）两个方面，由于实物鉴材的缺失，法院在咨询了相关技术领域专家后对此进行了进一步的评判：1. 一般来说，与外观设计专利不同，在涉发明专利以及实用新型专利的专利侵权纠纷案件中，产品图片不能反映被控侵权产品的技术特征，因此在鉴定中需要以产品实物作为鉴材进行勘验比对，而且该实物鉴材还必须是原、被告认可为被控侵权产品的实物。在本案中，由于客观原因原告无法获取实物鉴材，但提交了以公证形式获取的在展会现场拍摄被控侵权产品内外结构的视频及图片，法院认为，上述公证获取的视频、图

片具有客观性，其内容反映了产品实物的大部分技术特征，与被告公司网站上的相关产品资料相互印证，可确认其真实性，因此可以作为实物鉴材的一种替代。2. 虽然视频、图片的内容对于部分技术特征无法做到完整呈现，但是鉴定人员结合被告公司网站上的技术参数、产品部件之间的装配关系以及机械学原理，对相关技术特征的比对都做出了符合逻辑的推理。3. 对于原告提交的单方鉴定，被告在当庭质询鉴定人的过程中，并未提出有力的反驳意见以及申请重新鉴定。综上，法院认为，该单方鉴定的依据以及技术手段和逻辑推理具有说服力，最终的鉴定结论也令人信服。

由此可见，除了符合法律规定的一般要求，法院采信单方鉴定的条件还在于：1. 鉴材的真实性与关联性必须经过严格的审查。以公证获取或对方当事人自认的情形为优先，并且通常要求被控侵权产品的实物，在有合理原因无法提供实物的情况下，能清晰显示技术特征的视频或图片也可以作为替代。2. 要求鉴定人员接受法院的技术调查。这是为了防止单方鉴定中的鉴定机构为了迎合委托人的鉴定目的，简单陈述对比结论，得出难以令人信服的鉴定结论。具体表现，法院对推理过程提出更高要求，要求鉴定人进行详细说明、罗列依据，参与法院组织的技术查明程序，回应（口头或书面）法院聘请的技术调查官、咨询专家等的提问（不仅限于庭审程序）。3. 诉讼相对方对于单方鉴定没有提出有力的反驳意见。在不少案件中，大部分被告的应诉态度较为消极，既没有提出有力的反驳理由也不肯积极参与新的鉴定程序，在这种情况下，采信单方鉴定对于案件的审理是比较重要的。

二、与无法查明的技术特征有关的侵权推定问题

关于无实物证据的侵权推定，主要存在两个情况：

1. 视频、图片资料显示部分技术特征。也即只能在视频资料中看到技术特征的外观但无法测量具体的数值。在本案中，关于"L"形方向导杆这一技术特征，鉴定人在接受庭审质询时明确表示虽然此次鉴定的主要鉴材是照片和视频资料，但可以从中看出被控侵权产品具有 L 形方向导杆，虽然无法看到是否是 90 度但可以推导出该 L 形方向导杆的技术效果与涉案专利记载的相应技术特征的技术效果相同。对此，法院在进行了专家咨询以及仔细阅读专利说明书后，认可了鉴定人的意见，认为即使被控侵权产品的"L"形导向杆的角度不是垂直的 90 度，但整体仍然呈 L 形，可以实现"积聚原料形成坡体""阻拦转子产生的灰尘"等功能，属于以基本相同的手段实现基本相同的功能、达到基本相同的效果的等同特征。

2. 从视频、图片资料中无法看出的技术特征。在本案中，涉案专利权利要

求1记载包括："第一喂给装置（56，90，96），用于将第一原料流垂直地喂给到转子"这一技术特征，根据专利说明书的记载，56是内部料斗、90是滑动节流阀、96是内部料斗入口，而视频、图片资料中并未显示有"滑动节流阀"。对此，有观点认为，"第一喂给装置"属于功能性技术特征，其结构已经在专利要求书中明确，因此，被控侵权产品不具有"第一喂给装置"这一技术特征。对此，法院在咨询了技术调查官后，认为虽然"滑动节流阀"这一机构未在影像资料中出现，但结合相关法律规定以及专利说明书的记载，仍然可以推定被控侵权产品具有该技术特征，理由如下：（1）根据《中华人民共和国专利法实施细则》第十九条第四款的规定，权利要求中的技术特征可以引用说明书附图中相应的标记，该标记应当放在相应的技术特征后并置于括号内，便于理解权利要求。附图标记不得解释为对权利要求的限制。因此，滑动节流阀（90）仅是为了与说明书实施例附图相对应，属于一种更优的技术方案，而非必需的选择，也即为了实现将"第一原料流垂直地喂给到转子"这一功能，第一喂给装置除了必须具有内部料斗（56）和内部料斗入口（96）以外，还可以（非必须）具有滑动节流阀这一机构；（2）关于"第一喂给装置"是否为功能性特征。根据《最高人民法院关于审理侵犯专利权纠纷案件应用法律若干问题的解释（二）》第八条规定，功能性特征，是指对于结构、组分、步骤、条件或其之间的关系等，通过其在发明创造中所起的功能或者效果进行限定的技术特征，但本领域普通技术人员仅通过阅读权利要求即可直接、明确地确定实现上述功能或者效果的具体实施方式的除外。法院在阅读了专利说明书的背景技术以及发明内容后，认为涉案专利的发明点在于第二喂给装置，而第一喂给装置属于本领域的现有技术，因此，不应当将其作为功能性技术特征来理解。在影像资料中显示有内部料斗（56）和内部料斗入口（96），鉴定人亦表示可以看到第一喂给装置，法院对此也予以确认。

综上，法院认为，在无实物证据的专利侵权案件中，即使影像资料无法显示某些技术特征，但法院可以借助鉴定意见、技术调查等技术支持以及对于专利权利要求的解读，最终推定专利侵权事实的存在，作出公正的判决。

（撰稿人：胡宓）

四

不正当竞争民事纠纷案件

电竞游戏赛事网络直播行为的
不正当竞争之认定

——上海耀宇文化传媒有限公司与广州斗鱼网络科技有限公司
著作权侵权及不正当竞争纠纷案

【提要】

随着电子竞技游戏产业日益发展，涉及该行业的不正当竞争纠纷日益增多，《反不正当竞争法》规定的具体不正当竞争行为的滞后性、局限性问题日益突出。本案通过对《反不正当竞争法》第二条原则条款的适用，明确未经授权许可，擅自对网络游戏赛事进行实时直播，免费坐享他人投资并组织运营赛事所产生的商业成果，为自己谋取商业利益和竞争优势，其实际上是一种"搭便车"行为，违反《反不正当竞争法》中的诚实信用原则，违背公认的商业道德，损害比赛组织运营者的合法经营利益，构成不正当竞争。

【案情】

原告（被上诉人）：上海耀宇文化传媒有限公司

被告（上诉人）：广州斗鱼网络科技有限公司

案由：著作权侵权及不正当竞争纠纷

一审案号：（2015）浦民三（知）初字第 191 号

二审案号：（2015）沪知民终字第 641 号

DOTA2（刀塔2）是美国维尔福公司（Valve Corporation）开发的一款风靡全球的电子竞技类网络游戏，该游戏在中国大陆地区的代理运营商为完美世界（北京）网络技术有限公司。2014 年，被上诉人（原审原告）上海耀宇文化传媒有限公司（以下简称耀宇公司）与游戏运营商签订战略合作协议，共同运营2015 年 DOTA2 亚洲邀请赛。耀宇公司通过协议约定获得该赛事在中国大陆地区的独家视频转播权，并负责赛事的执行及管理工作（包括选手管理、赛事宣传、场地租赁及搭建布置、设备租赁及购置、主持人聘请、赛事举行、后勤保障以及节目拍摄、制作、直播、轮播和点播等），双方还约定合作赛事的执行费用总计11 700 704元，耀宇公司承担8 200 704元。

耀宇公司在2015年1月至2月举办涉案赛事，赛事分为预选赛、决赛。2015年1月举行120场预选赛，该阶段各参赛队伍通过互联网及计算机进行比赛。通过预选赛，名次靠前的和其他受邀参赛队伍集中至上海，于2015年2月5—9日参加在耀宇公司提供的比赛场所进行线下主赛事即决赛。在上述赛事进行期间，耀宇公司通过火猫TV网站对比赛进行了全程、实时的视频直播。同时，耀宇公司还授予虎牙独家直播/转播的权利（除火猫TV外），并收取授权费用600万元。

斗鱼公司未经授权，以通过客户端旁观模式截取赛事画面配以主播点评的方式实时直播涉案赛事。耀宇公司指控斗鱼公司在2015年1月6—28日共播出了80场涉案赛事预选赛阶段的比赛，而斗鱼公司辩称仅直播了8场预选赛。2015年1月15日耀宇公司办理证据保全公证过程中约1小时的时间内，斗鱼公司同时直播了DK与TongFu、HGT与Inv之间的2场比赛，还预告在当日将直播另外4场比赛。

耀宇公司认为，斗鱼公司未经授权，截取赛事画面实时直播涉案赛事，侵犯了耀宇公司的合法权益。故耀宇公司诉至上海市浦东新区人民法院，请求判令斗鱼公司：1. 立即停止侵权行为；2. 赔偿耀宇公司经济损失800万元以及维权的合理开支211 000元（包括律师费20万元、公证费11 000元）；3. 在《新民晚报》刊登消除影响的声明。

斗鱼公司辩称，涉案游戏的客户端具有对外公开的旁观者观战功能，该功能通过软件对同一场比赛截取了十个不同视角的比赛画面供旁观者观看，且不限制比赛画面的流出，斗鱼公司直播的赛事画面即来源于该功能中的某个观战视角的比赛画面，因视角不同而与耀宇公司直播的画面不同。斗鱼公司没有实施侵权行为或者不正当竞争行为，故请求法院驳回耀宇公司的全部诉讼请求。

【审判】

上海市浦东新区人民法院认为，斗鱼公司明知涉案赛事由耀宇公司举办、并付出了较大的办赛成本，在未取得任何授权许可的情况下，向其用户提供了涉案赛事的部分场次比赛的视频直播，其行为直接损害了耀宇公司的合法权益，损害了网络游戏直播网站行业的正常经营秩序，违反了诚实信用原则和公认的商业道德，构成对耀宇公司的不正当竞争。据此，依照《中华人民共和国反不正当竞争法》第二条第一款、第九条第一款、第二十条，《中华人民共和国侵权责任法》第十五条第一款第（六）项和第（八）项、第二款的规定，判决：一、被告赔偿原告经济损失人民币 100 万元和维权的合理开支人民币 10 万元，合计人民币 110 万元；二、被告在"斗鱼"网站（网址为 www.douyutv.com）的首页显著位置刊登声明，消除对原告实施不正当竞争行为所造成的不良影响；三、驳回原告的其余诉讼请求。

斗鱼公司向上海知识产权法院提起上诉称：目前国内的游戏直播网站大部分都采取通过客户端截取比赛画面然后将画面转给观看玩家，并配上自己平台的解说和配乐从而进行直播，游戏厂商对此亦未提过异议，本案所涉游戏客户端并无任何禁止截取画面转播的提示，根据法无明文规定不可为即可为的民法原则，斗鱼公司通过客户端截取部分比赛画面，再配上自己独创性的评论在网上从特定观战者角度对涉案赛事进行直播，本质上是对涉案赛事进行报道，该行为没有超出游戏客户端旁观者的合理使用范围。原审适用《反不正当竞争法》第二条错误。

耀宇公司答辩称：游戏直播网站主办或直播、转播电子竞技游戏应取得游戏厂商和授权方许可并支付费用，这是国际国内通常做法和商业惯例。通过客户端观看比赛画面，只能为个人目的使用，不得用于商业用途。斗鱼公司不正当竞争行为影响了被上诉人与广告商、授权方之间的签约能力，并分流了被上诉人网站用户关注度和网站流量，侵害了被上诉人的经济利益。

二审法院认为，本案耀宇公司在与成都完美公司的协议中约定被上诉人获得赛事在中国大陆地区的视频转播权独家授权，负责赛事的执行及管理工作（包括选手管理、赛事宣传、场地租赁及搭建布置、设备租赁及购置、主持人聘请、赛事举行、后勤保障以及节目拍摄、制作、直播、轮播和点播等），承担执行费用等。耀宇公司一系列的人力、物力、财力的投入，其有权对此收取回报，通过视频转播赛事增加网站流量、扩大提高广告收入、提升知名度、加强网络用户黏性，使直播平台经济增值。因此，网络游戏比赛视频转播权需经比赛组织运营者的授权许可是网络游戏行业中长期以来形成的惯常做法，符合谁投入谁收益的一般商业规则，亦是对比赛组织运营者的正当权益的保护规则，符合市场竞争中遵循的诚实信用原则。斗鱼公司未对涉案赛事的组织运营进行任何投入，也未取得视频转播权的许可，却免费坐享耀宇公司投入大量人力、物力、财力组织运营的赛事所产生的商业成果，为自己谋取商业利益和竞争优势，其实际上是一种"搭便车"行为，夺取了原本属于耀宇公司的观众数量，导致其网站流量被严重分流，影响其广告收益能力，损害其商业机会和竞争优势，弱化其网络直播平台的增值力。因此，斗鱼公司的行为违反了《反不正当竞争法》中的诚实信用原则，违背了公认的商业道德，损害了耀宇公司合法权益，破坏了市场竞争秩序，具有明显的不正当性。据此判决驳回上诉，维持原判。

【评析】

本案系全国首例电子竞技游戏赛事网络直播纠纷案件，而电子竞技游戏产业是我国近年来才迅猛发展的行业，因而该行业内竞争者之间竞争自由的界限及如何进行知识产权保护等均是引人关注的热点问题。

一、市场竞争的自由与规制

电子竞技游戏行业内的竞争与一般市场竞争一样，既要鼓励业内竞争对手间的自由竞争以促进行业的蓬勃发展，但又要防止对竞争的放任自流，以免扰乱、破坏整个市场秩序。自由竞争，简单而言就是指所有市场参与者在完全没有外力干预情况下所进行的市场竞争。一般而论通过自由竞争可以使市场参与者优胜劣汰，资源配置得到进一步优化，竞争越充分激烈资源配置越优化，市场经济就越繁荣。但是鼓励市场自由竞争并不等于放任无序的、恶性的不正当竞争行为。

竞争的自由必须以公平为原则，公平是对于自由竞争的伦理规范，是对竞争自由的适度规制和矫正。我国《反不正当竞争法》第二条第一款规定，经营者在市场交易中，应当遵循自愿、平等、公平、诚实信用的原则，遵守公认的商业道德，这也是公平竞争对市场竞争主体的基本要求。而公认的商业道德，是指特定商业领域普遍认知和接受的行为标准，具有公认性和一般性。① 公平、诚实信用等原则构成最基本的竞争原则，公认的商业道德则是在这些原则的基础上所形成的各种具体商业惯例。我国《反不正当竞争法》第二条第一款所确立的这些原则，其实质就是市场竞争主体在市场竞争中应遵守的一种公平的竞争秩序。

二、对本案不正当竞争行为的认定

最高人民法院于 2011 年发布的《最高人民法院知识产权案件年度报告

---

① 参见《最高人民法院知识产权案件年度报告（2010）》，第 25 项。

（2010）》就山东省食品进出口公司等与马达庆等不正当竞争纠纷案件进行分析点评，为类似案件处理提供了指导性意见。最高人民法院认为，适用《反不正当竞争法》第二条第一款和第二款认定构成不正当竞争应当同时具备以下条件：一是法律对该种竞争行为未作出特别规定；二是其他经营者的合法权益确因该竞争行为而受到了实际损害；三是该种竞争行为因确属违反诚实信用原则和公认的商业道德而具有不正当性或者说可责性。最高人民法院在该案评析中还指出，在正常情况下能够合理预期获得的商业机会，可以成为法律特别是《反不正当竞争法》所保护的法益，但只有当竞争对手不遵循诚实信用原则和违反公认的商业道德，通过不正当手段攫取他人可以合理预期获得的商业机会时，才为《反不正当竞争法》所禁止。据此可见，竞争行为的不正当性，如是否不正当利用他人竞争优势或者破坏他人竞争优势，是司法实践中具体案件判断的关键；第二项要件中的"其他经营者的合法权益……受到了实际损害"目的是揭示不正当竞争的侵权性质，就不正当竞争行为构成而言，"损害"也应包括合理预期收益损失或合理预期商业机会流失等情况。

电竞赛事作为新晋体育竞赛项目，同样需要组织者投资、策划、运营、宣传、推广、管理等。本案耀宇公司通过协议约定获得赛事在中国大陆地区的视频转播权独家授权，并负责赛事的执行及管理工作，对赛事投入一系列的人力、物力、财力，其有权对此收取回报，通过视频转播赛事增加网站流量等使直播平台经济增值。正如上文所述，电子竞技游戏网络直播平台通过组织运营转播游戏比赛吸引网络用户，提高网络用户流量，增加网络用户黏性，吸引相关广告商投放广告。电竞赛事的转播权对于网络直播平台来讲，是其创造商业机会、获得商业利益、提升网站流量和知名度的经营项目之一。耀宇公司以此谋求商业利益的行为应受法律保护，他人不得以不正当的方式损害其正当权益。

电子竞技游戏比赛网络视频转播权需经比赛组织运营者的授权许可是网络游戏行业中长期以来形成的惯常做法，符合谁投入谁收益的一般商业规则，亦是对比赛组织运营者的正当权益的保护，符合市场竞争中遵循的诚实信用原则。本案双方当事人均系专业的电竞网络游戏视频直播网站经营者，双方具有直接的竞争关系。斗鱼公司明知涉案赛事由耀宇公司举办、耀宇公司享有涉案赛事的独家视频转播权、耀宇公司付出了较大的办赛成本，应知电子竞技游戏比赛网络视频转播权须经相关方授权许可的商业惯例的情况下，未对赛事的组织运营进行任何投入，也未取得视频转播权的许可，却免费坐享耀宇公司投入巨资，花费大量人力、物力、精力组织运营的涉案赛事所产生的商业成果，为自己谋取商业利益和竞争优势，其实际上是一种"搭便车"行为，夺取了原本属于耀宇公司的观众数量，导致耀宇公司网站流量严重分流，影响了耀宇公司的广告收益能力，损害耀宇公司竞争优势，弱化耀宇公司网络直播平台的增值力。斗鱼公司的行为违反了《反不正当竞争法》中的诚实信用原则，也违背了公认的商业道德，损害了耀宇公司合法权益，破坏了行业内业已形成的公认的市场竞争秩序，具有明显的不正当性，应为《反不正当竞争法》所禁止。

（撰稿人：陆凤玉　朱永华）

为说明商品销售商变化而使用他人商标
是否构成商标侵权和虚假宣传的认定

——开德阜国际贸易（上海）有限公司与阔盛管道系统（上海）有限公司、上海欧苏贸易有限公司虚假宣传纠纷案

【提要】

经营者为说明品牌代理销售商的变化，在善意、合理的限度内使用他人注册商标，属于商标正当使用，不构成商标侵权；在如实、详细告知消费者商品销售代理商及品牌变化的情况下，在宣传中使用他人商标不会导致相关公众产生误解，不构成虚假宣传。

【案情】

原告（上诉人）： 开德阜国际贸易（上海）有限公司

被告（被上诉人）： 阔盛管道系统（上海）有限公司

被告（被上诉人）： 上海欧苏贸易有限公司

案由： 虚假宣传纠纷

一审案号：（2013）徐民三（知）初字第 1017 号

二审案号：（2015）沪知民终字第 161 号

原告开德阜国际贸易（上海）有限公司（以下简称开德阜公司）系"洁水"文字商标的商标权人，该商标于 2002 年获得核准注册，核定使用商品为第 17 类塑料管等。2006 年 4 月 6 日，开德阜公司与案外人德国阿垮瑟姆公司签订独家销售协议，开德阜公司享有阿垮瑟姆公司水管类产品在华的独家经销权。德国阿垮瑟姆公司在中国注册有" 〔图标〕 ""aquatherm"两个商标，核定使用在第 19 类下水道装置等。2013 年 6 月 30 日，开德阜公司与阿垮瑟姆公司终止合作协议，开德阜公司不再代理销售阿垮瑟姆公司的产品。2013 年 7 月 1

日，被告阔盛管道系统（上海）有限公司（以下简称阔盛公司）成为阿垮瑟姆公司产品在华新代理商。原告开德阜公司在 2013 年 7 月 1 日之前，其注册的"洁水"商标仅用于推广销售阿垮瑟姆公司的产品。2013 年 7 月 1 日之后，开德阜公司继续持有"洁水"商标，该商标用于推广其他生产商的水管产品。阔盛公司在取得阿垮瑟姆公司产品的经销权之后，授权被告上海欧苏贸易有限公司（以下简称欧苏公司）在上海区域独家销售阿垮瑟姆公司的产品。两被告在网络上的宣传文章以及宣传单上使用了"原德国洁水、现德国阔盛""德国阔盛（原德国洁水）—不变的品质"" aquatherm（原德国洁水）德国阔盛"等宣传用语，在使用上述宣传用语时，同时还有"原代理商曾以德国'洁水'在华推广，从 7 月 1 日起德国厂方正式启用中文标识'阔盛'，用于中国市场推广""德国 aquatherm Gmbh 从 2013 年 7 月 1 日起正式启用官方持有的中文标识'阔盛'用于中国区市场推广。原在华使用的中文标识'洁水'系原代理商所持有，现已和德国阔盛 aquatherm Gmbh 公司及其产品无任何关联"等表述。

原告开德阜公司认为被告阔盛公司、欧苏公司使用的"原德国洁水、现德国阔盛""德国阔盛（原德国洁水）—不变的品质"等类似的宣传用语中含有"洁水"商标，构成对原告的商标侵权，同时上述宣传用语会使消费者产生误解，构成虚假宣传。故诉至法院，请求判令两被告停止商标侵权和虚假宣传行为，赔偿原告经济损失及合理费用共计 500 万元。

【审判】

上海市徐汇区人民法院认为，阔盛公司、欧苏公司在推广宣传中使用"洁水"商标属于合理使用，不会导致相关公众产生混淆。两被告的上述表述与事实相符，未作虚假陈述，且从宣传资料的整体来看，相关公众施以一般注意力阅读上述内容后，不会对被控的宣传用语产生歧义，亦不会对两者关系产生误解，不构成虚假宣传。一审判决驳回原告的全部诉讼请求。

一审判决后，原告不服，上诉于上海知识产权法院。

上海知识产权法院认为，基于"洁水"商标已经与阿垮瑟姆公司产品建立了稳定联系的事实，阔盛公司、欧苏公司在宣传活动中有必要向消费者告知"洁水"商标所指向的产品已经发生变化，两被告使用"洁水"商标主观上是善意的，且使用方式没有超出合理的限度，不会造成消费者对产品的来源产生混淆。阔盛公司、欧苏公司使用"德国阔盛（原德国洁水）—不变的品质""原德国洁水，现德国阔盛"等类似宣传用语，在纯粹的文字表述上确有不准确之处，但消费者在整体阅读宣传内容后，不会对"洁水"商标本身是否发生了变更、阔盛公司所销售商品的来源等产生误解，没有产生引人误解的效果。二审驳回上诉，维持原判。

【评析】

本案的特殊之处在于，原告作为销售代理商注册了"洁水"商标，但仅将该商标用语推广阿垮瑟姆公司的产品，被告基于品牌代理关系的变化在宣传用语中使用"洁水"商标是否属于商标的正当使用，使用被控的宣传用语是否构成虚假宣传，需要进一步的分析。

一、商标正当使用的认定

我国《商标法》第五十九条规定，注册商标中含有的本商品的通用名称、图形、型号，或者直接表示商品的质量、主要原料、功能、用途、重量、数量及其他特点，或者含有的地名，注册商标专用权人无权禁止他人正当使用。该条是我国立法上关于商标描述性正当使用的规定。所谓商标的正当使用，是指经营者为了说明自己所提供的商品或服务，便于消费者辨认，可以不经商标权人的许可而对其商标进行使用。允许商标正当使用的本质是商标权人利益与公共利益之间的平衡，商标的基本功能在于区别商品或服务来源，商标权人只享有在核定商品或服务类别上使用注册商标，并禁止他人在核定商品或服务类别上使用与其注册商标相同或近似的标识，其并不享有对商标符号的垄断。因此，对于经营者在商业活动中使用他人商标是否构成商标侵权的判断，应当考虑具体使用行为是否破坏了商标与商品或服务之间的联系功能，即是否会导致相关公众就商品或服务的来源产生混淆。如果在商业活动中使用他人商标只是为了描述或说明某种客观情况，且并不会导致相关公众就商品或服务的来源产生混淆，则该行为并非商标法意义上的商标使用行为，而是一种正当的商标使用行为，商标权人无权对此予以禁止。

从我国商标法关于商标正当使用的规定来看，商标的正当使用应当限定在善意、合理的范围内，判断是否构成商标正当使用，应当考虑使用他人商标是否是善意的，商标的使用方式是否合理并对消费者产生混淆等因素。首先，使用商标行为是否是善意的。对于使用商标是否善意的判断，可以从使用他人商标是否具有必要性的角度来考虑。通常来说，经营者如果不使用他人商标，也可以清楚地描述自己商品或服务特点，则使用他人商标是不必要的，尤其是对于具有较高知名度的商标，其使用行为往往不具有善意。本案中，在 2013 年 7

月 1 日之前，原告将其注册的"洁水"商标仅用于推广销售阿垮瑟姆公司的产品，经过长期使用，该商标与阿垮瑟姆公司的产品建立了稳定、唯一的联系，在相关消费者的认知当中，"洁水"商标指向的即阿垮瑟姆公司的产品。在 2013 年 7 月 1 日之后，阿垮瑟姆公司产品在华的经销商已由原告变更为被告阔盛公司，而原告继续保留"洁水"品牌与其他供应商开展新的合作。基于"洁水"商标已经与阿垮瑟姆公司产品建立了稳定联系的事实，两被告在宣传活动中有必要向消费者告知"洁水"商标所指向的产品已经发生变化，阔盛公司目前推广的产品即是之前"洁水"商标所指向的产品这一事实。因此，两被告在宣传用语中使用到"洁水"商标其主观上并非攀附上诉人的商誉，而是描述客观事实的必要。其次，商标的使用方式是否合理并对消费者产生混淆。经营者使用他人商标在描述自己商品或服务具有某种特点时，在使用方式上应当合理，如果使用方式上超出合理限度，导致相关消费者就商品的来源产生混淆或误认，则不构成商标的正当使用。本案中，由于"洁水"商标仅指向阿垮瑟姆公司的产品，其具有特定的指向，且这种指向已经在消费者中形成了认知，两被告使用"原德国洁水，现德国阔盛"等类似表述尚未超出合理范围。同时，两被告使用被控商标侵权的宣传用语时，还陈述了产品代理商和品牌变化的背景，消费者在阅读两被上诉人的宣传用语时，通常会理解为阔盛公司所销售的产品是原"洁水"商标所指向的产品，即阿垮瑟姆公司的产品，而并不会就商品的来源产生混淆。

二、虚假宣传行为的认定

《反不正当竞争法》第九条规定，经营者不得利用广告或者其他方法，对商品的质量、制作成分、性能、用途、生产者、有效期限、产地等作引人误解的虚假宣传。《反不正当竞争法》所规制的虚假宣传是"引人误解"的虚假宣传，只有宣传内容产生了引人误解的效果，才会损害公平竞争的市场秩序和消费者的合法权益，而不产生误导效果的虚假宣传实质上不具备竞争法意义上的责难性。

虚假宣传中的引人误解的认定与商标侵权中混淆的认定并不完全相同。商标法意义上的混淆通常是指商品或服务来源意义上的混淆，即消费者将此商品与彼商品误认为具有相同的来源，或误认为商品的生产经营者具有特定的关联关系。而虚假宣传中的引人误解范围相对更广，所有可能误导消费者交易决定的因素都可以构成引人误解。本案中，由于原告目前仍是"洁水"商标的商标权人，且该商标本身并未进行过变更，两被告使用"原德国洁水，现德国阔盛"等类似宣传用语，在纯粹的文字表述上确有不准确之处，但对"引人误解"的虚假宣传行为的认定，应当根据日常生活经验、相关公众的一般注意力、发生误解的事实和被宣传对象的实际情况等因素进行综合判断。

首先，对于两被告宣传用语应在整体上进行解读。消费者在接受商业宣传时通常是整体接受的，在就宣传内容是否会产生引人误解的判断上，应当以宣传内容在整体上是否可能给相关公众造成误解为准，不应将可能产生误解的某一词语或某几句话进行断章取义。因为即使部分宣传内容在隔离分析时会产生歧义，但消费者在整体接受后可以消弭有关的歧义内容，则实质上并没有产生引人误解的效果。如前所述，本案两被告在使用被控侵权宣传用语的同时，还详细陈述了产品代理商和品牌变化的背景等情况。因此，对于原告所主张的上述构成虚假宣传用语的认定，不能脱离具体的语境进行孤立的判断，而应放置在整体的宣传内容中进行合理解读。其次，根据相关公众的一般注意力、已有的认知经验，以及被宣传对象的实际情况进行判断。宣传内容是否具有虚假宣传的效果，与相关公众自身已有的知识、经验具有密切关系。由于两被告在使用被控侵权宣传用语时，已经详细陈述了产品代理商和品牌变化的背景等情况，加之消费者对该品牌产品具有一定的认知经验，故相关公众施加一般的注意力即应知晓宣传内容的真实含义，并不会对"洁水"商标本身是否发生了变更、阔盛公司所销售商品的来源等产生误解。

需要强调的是，如果两被告单独使用"原德国洁水，现德国阔盛"等类似用语作为宣传语，由于原告目前仍在使用"洁水"商标销售他人商品，被告单独使用上述宣传用语则可能产生歧义，对于不了解品牌变化背景的消费者以及新进入该领域的消费者，可能会认为洁水商标本身变更为阔盛商标，原洁水商标已经不再使用，此种情形则涉嫌构成虚假宣传。但两被告在使用上述宣传语的同时，已如实告知了有关品牌变化的情况，不会产生引人误解效果，不构成《反不正当竞争法》意义上的虚假宣传。

（撰稿人：范静波）

提供他人视频内容时
绕开片前广告构成不正当竞争

—— 深圳聚网视科技有限公司与北京爱奇艺科技有限公司其他
不正当竞争纠纷一案

【提要】

随着互联网技术的发展，《反不正当竞争法》规定的具体不正当竞争行为的滞后性、局限性问题日益突出。本案通过对《反不正当竞争法》第二条原则条款的适用，明确聚网视公司开发并运营的"VST 全聚合"软件实现的无需观看片前广告即可直接观看爱奇艺公司视频的功能，违背了诚实信用原则，损害了爱奇艺公司依托其正当商业模式获取商业利益的合法权益，构成不正当竞争。作为全国首例视频聚合不正当竞争案，本案对于类似诉讼的审理具有一定的借鉴意义。

【案情】

原告（被上诉人）：北京爱奇艺科技有限公司

被告（上诉人）：深圳聚网视科技有限公司

案由：其他不正当竞争纠纷

一审案号：（2015）杨民三（知）初字第 1 号

二审案号：（2015）沪知民终字第 728 号

北京爱奇艺科技有限公司（以下简称爱奇艺公司）系国内知名视频网站爱奇艺的经营者。其商业模式主要为"广告＋免费视频"（即用户观看一定时间的广告，爱奇艺公司向其提供免费视频播放）或者向用户收取一定费用使其成为会员用户，会员用户无需观看广告就可直接观看视频。爱奇艺公司通过视频前广告所收取的广告费或者通过会员用户收费获取收益，以支付视频版权、带宽、推广等支出并实现盈利。深圳聚网视科技有限公司（以下简称聚网视公司）开发运营的"VST全聚合"软件通过破解爱奇艺公司的验证算法，取得有效密钥后实现绕开片前广告，直接播放正片的目的。爱奇艺公司认为，"VST全聚合"软件聚合了包括爱奇艺在内的多家大型知名视频网站的视频内容，而聚网视公司却无需支付视频版权、带宽等营运费用，这种行为致使爱奇艺网站在用户中的受关注度下降，降低了广告主在爱奇艺公司处投放广告的曝光率，损害了爱奇艺公司的利益，故其依据《反不正当竞争法》第二条主张聚网视公司上述行为构成不正当竞争，要求赔偿经济损失和合理费用。

【审判】

上海市杨浦区人民法院经审理认为：基于爱奇艺公司、聚网视公司之间的竞争关系，爱奇艺公司对于其视频内容采取了加密措施，以及聚网视公司的"VST全聚合"软件实现的绕开爱奇艺片前广告直接播放正片的事实，认定聚网视公司行为构成不正当竞争。聚网视公司通过破解爱奇艺公司验证算法取得有效KEY值生成请求播放视频正片的SC值，从而绕开爱奇艺公司片前广告，实现无需观看片前广告即可直接播放正片，虽然未直接去除片前广告，但客观上实现了无需观看广告即可观看正片的目的，聚网视公司的行为直接干预并严重损害爱奇艺公司的经营，其在无需支付版权费用、带宽成本的前提下，使那些不愿意观看爱奇艺官网的片前广告又不愿意支付爱奇艺公司会员费的网络用户转而使用自己的软件，挤占了爱奇艺公司的市场份额，不正当地获取竞争优势，直接造成爱奇艺公司的广告费以及会员费收入的减少，违反了诚实信用原则和公认的商业道德，属于《反不正当竞争法》第二条的规制范围。据此，认定聚网视公司采用技术手段绕开片前广告，直接播放来源于爱奇艺公司视频的行为构成不正当竞争，并判决聚网视公司赔偿爱奇艺公司经济损失和合理费用36 000元。

一审判决后，被告聚网视公司不服，提起上诉。

上海知识产权法院经审理认为，爱奇艺公司依托"广告+免费视频"或者收取会员费的经营模式，谋求商业利益的行为属于受法律保护的经营行为。聚网视公司凭借技术手段绕开广告直接播放爱奇艺公司视频，使其用户在无需付出时间成本和费用成本的情况下，观看爱奇艺公司的视频，这将导致部分爱奇艺公司用户转而成为聚网视公司的用户且会导致爱奇艺公司广告点击量的下降。聚网视公司让其用户观看爱奇艺网站视频时，但其并未支付版权费等营运成本，相应的成本皆由爱奇艺公司承担。爱奇艺公司在支付成本的同时，还面临用户数量减少和广告点击量下降导致的商业利益的损失。作为技术实施方的聚网视公司是应当知道实施该技术会出现自己得利他人受损的后果，仍实施该技术，违背了诚实信用原则和公认的商业道德，损害了爱奇艺公司合法的经营活动。对原审法院认定聚网视公司采用技术手段绕开片前广告，直接播放来源于爱奇艺公司视频的行为构成不正当竞争的判决，予以维持。

【评析】

本案爱奇艺公司依据《反不正当竞争法》第二条一般条款主张聚网视公司在提供来源于爱奇艺公司视频内容时屏蔽视频前广告的行为构成不正当竞争，因此，对于上述行为是否构成不正当竞争行为需考量以下因素：

1. 该行为在其他法律、法规中是否有特别的规定

适用《反不正当竞争法》第二条的前提是该行为不仅在《不正当竞争法》中没有具体规定，而且在其他法律、法规中也没有具体规定。有观点认为，《著作权法》第四十八条明确规定未经著作权人或者与著作权有关的权利人许可，故意避开或者破坏权利人为其作品、录音录像制品等采取的保护著作权或者与著作权有关的权利的技术措施的行为为侵权行为。聚网视公司通过破坏爱奇艺公司采取的对其视频加密的技术手段，向其用户提供来源于爱奇艺公司视频内容时屏蔽视频前广告，因此，爱奇艺公司可以依据上述《著作权》的规定维护自己的合法权益，不应适用《反不正当竞争法》第二条予以规制。著作权保护技术措施是指用于防止、限制未经权利人许可通过信息网络向公众提供作品、表演、录音录像制品的有效技术、装置或者部件。本案中，聚网视公司通过破解爱奇艺公司验证算法取得有效 KEY 值生成请求播放视频正片的 SC 值，从而绕开爱奇艺公司片前广告，实现了无需观看片前广告即可直接播放正片的行为，是破坏了爱奇艺公司对其视频所设置的技术保护措施。如果爱奇艺公司是针对破坏技术措施行为提起侵权诉讼，其可以根据现行《著作权法》和《信息网络传播权保护条例》获得救济。

但本案中，爱奇艺公司并没有针对破坏技术措施行为行使诉权，其在本案中主张保护的是其依托"广告＋免费视频"或者通过收取会员费的商业模式谋取商业利益的经营活动，破坏技术措施只是聚网视公司侵害爱奇艺公司经营活动的手段，取得的是绕开爱奇艺公司片前广告、直接播放正片的结果，损害的是爱奇艺公司依托上述经营活动所产生的商业利益，包括广告收益和会员费收益。而《著作权法》技术保护措施所保护的对象本身是该法明确赋予著作权人的专有权利，如复制权、信息网络传播权等，因此，破坏技术措施所涉救济范

围也仅涵盖著作权专有权利范围，并不能延伸到依托商业模式所产生的商业利益，因此，爱奇艺公司主张的聚网视公司提供来源于爱奇艺公司视频内容时屏蔽视频前广告的行为并非《著作权法》予以特别规定的行为，因此，本案符合《反不正当竞争法》第二条适用条件。

2. 通过破解技术措施实现跳过广告直接播放视频的行为是否构成不正当竞争

爱奇艺公司向一般用户提供"广告+免费视频"以及向会员用户收取会员费用后提供无广告的视频播放的商业模式，并不违反《反不正当竞争法》的基本原则和法律禁止性的规定，其采用上述商业模式谋求商业利益的经营行为，应受到《反不正当竞争法》的保护。聚网视公司通过爬虫技术并实施破解爱奇艺公司加密技术取得爱奇艺公司的播放密钥，获得爱奇艺公司正片的真实地址，直接播放正片，其虽未积极实施屏蔽广告行为，但却达到跳过爱奇艺公司广告的效果，聚网视公司作为涉案软件的开发运营者是知晓其所谓的技术会跳过爱奇艺公司片前广告的，但仍积极追求该结果，其目的是在不支付版权、带宽等必要成本的前提下，通过"搭便车"行为，利用网络用户不愿支付时间成本又不愿支付金钱对价的消费心理，使爱奇艺公司用户成为聚网视用户。在影响爱奇艺公司广告收益和会员费收入的情况下，谋取自身竞争优势。因此，聚网视公司的行为违背了诚实信用原则和公认的商业道德，损害了爱奇艺公司的合法权益，应为《反不正当竞争法》第二条所规制的不正当竞争行为。

（撰稿人：杨韡）

企业英文名称的司法保护

——江苏天容集团股份有限公司诉湖南昊华化工有限责任公司 擅自使用他人企业名称纠纷案

【提要】

中国企业在对外贸易中实际使用的、与中文企业名称存在对应关系、已具有识别市场经营主体作用的英文名称，可以视为《中华人民共和国反不正当竞争法》第五条第三项规定的企业名称。擅自在出口商品上使用他人英文企业名称，对他人造成损害的，属于不正当竞争行为。

不正当竞争行为的损害赔偿额，可以根据权利人在被侵权期间因被侵权所受到的损失予以确定。权利人因被侵权所受到的实际损失可以根据侵权商品的销售量乘以权利人商品的单位利润所得之积计算。在查明侵权商品销售量年度区间分布时，可以侵权商品年度销售量乘以权利人商品该年度单位利润所得之积计算。权利人商品的利润一般应按照营业利润计算，在销售利润的基础上扣除相应的销售费用、管理费用、财务费用、营业税金及附加。

【案情】

原告：江苏天容集团股份有限公司

被告：湖南昊华化工有限责任公司

生效案号：（2015）浦民三（知）初字第 1887 号

原告江苏天容集团股份有限公司（以下简称天容公司）于 1998 年 9 月 29 日成立。天容公司原企业名称为溧阳市力华化学有限公司，于 2003 年 3 月 4 日更名为江苏溧化化学有限公司，于 2006 年 8 月 16 日更名为江苏天容集团有限公司，于 2006 年 8 月 25 日更名为江苏天容集团股份有限公司。

天容公司的《对外贸易经营者备案登记表》载明，其英文企业名称为

"JIANGSU TIANRONG GROUP CO., LTD"。印度政府农业部（农业合作司）植物保护、检疫和储存局中央农药登记委员会于 2015 年 10 月 9 日出具的文件载明，天容公司生产的杀螟丹原药（最少有效含量98%）已通过印度政府的登记，该文件中天容公司的英文企业名称为"JIANGSU TIANRONG GROUP CO., LTD"。

2014 年 5 月 6 日，浦东市场监督管理局查扣了湖南昊华化工有限责任公司（以下简称昊华公司）生产的欲出口至印度的杀螟丹原药16 000千克，该批杀螟丹外包装上标注了"Manufacturer：M/s. Liyang Chemical Factory, China（Jiangsu Tianrong Group Company, Ltd., China）"，包装袋上没有其他商标、企业名称等标识。

昊华公司的副总经理张某于 2014 年 6 月 19 日回答浦东市场监督管理局的询问时称：昊华公司经人介绍，于 2014 年 3 月 10 日与印度托比克有限公司签订合同，约定昊华公司向该印度公司销售16 000千克杀螟丹原药。由于昊华公司没有获得印度官方的登记，而天容公司通过了登记，为使昊华公司生产的杀螟丹通过印度海关，昊华公司应印度客户的要求在商品外包装上标注了天容公司的英文企业名称。昊华公司向印度市场出口农药已有六七年的时间，以前都是通过新加坡生达化工有限公司（Sundat（s）PTE Ltd.）出口，这家新加坡公司在印度已办理登记手续，所以标注的是新加坡公司的名称。

浦东市场监督管理局于 2014 年 7 月 5 日做出的浦市监案处字［2014］第150201402201 号行政处罚决定书载明：昊华公司使用天容公司英文企业名称，违反了《产品质量法》第三十条、第三十七条的规定，属冒用他人厂名的行为。责令昊华公司改正，并作处罚如下：没收杀螟丹原药16 000千克（640包）；罚款 30 万元。

在本案审理过程中，法院依天容公司申请向上海海关调取了昊华公司出口杀螟丹的报关资料。根据上海海关提供的昊华公司在 2012 年 6 月至 2014 年 1 月期间的报关资料，在此期间，昊华公司部分批次的商业发票和装箱单的唛头栏标注的生产企业名称为天容公司的英文企业名称，部分批次的商业发票和装箱单的唛头栏标注的生产企业名称为"SUNDAT（S）PTE. LTD., SINGAPORE"（新加坡生达化工有限公司）。原、被告确认，商业发票和装箱单上标注的生产企业名称为天容公司英文企业名称的杀螟丹共计3 971 920美元，双方确认按 1 美元兑换人民币 6.1565 元计算人民币金额。

天容公司 2012 年度至 2014 年度的审计报告载明，其主要产品包括杀虫双系列、杀螟丹系列、精噁除草剂系列及其他除草剂系列，审计报告中单列了杀螟丹的营业收入、营业成本等数据。昊华公司的 2012 年度至 2014 年度的审计报告中，只有公司营业收入、营业成本等数据，没有单列杀螟丹的营业收入和营业成本。

原告天容公司诉称：杀螟丹原药是一种有中等毒性的杀虫剂，按照印度的法律规定，须获印度官方登记后方可进入印度市场。天容公司的杀螟丹原药已办理了印度官方的登记手续，而昊华公司的杀螟丹未办理印度官方的登记手续，昊华公司为向印度出口杀螟丹原药，擅自使用了天容公司的英文企业名称。在2012年6月至2014年1月期间，昊华公司曾冒用天容公司英文企业名称向印度出口杀螟丹原药货值24 453 125.48元。经估算，2014年，天容公司的杀螟丹原药毛利率为42.62%，以此为依据，昊华公司因出口涉案商品获利10 421 922.08元。此外，天容公司为本案支出律师费50万元。昊华公司擅自使用天容公司的企业名称，给天容公司造成损失，构成不正当竞争，应当承担损害赔偿责任。请求法院判令：昊华公司赔偿天容公司经济损失10 421 922.08元及支出的律师费50万元。

被告昊华公司辩称：昊华公司此前通过新加坡生达化工有限公司向印度出口杀螟丹。此次应印度客户的要求，在包装袋上使用了天容公司的英文企业名称，这批货物已被浦东市场监督管理局查扣。昊华公司此前出口印度的杀螟丹包装袋上没有标注天容公司的英文企业名称，仅在部分批次的商业发票和装箱单上使用了天容公司的英文企业名称。昊华公司使用天容公司的英文企业名称仅是为了出口，并未使销售对象误认为涉案商品是天容公司生产的，也未影响天容公司的商品出口，没有给天容公司造成经济损失。天容公司的英文企业名称未经企业登记主管机关依法登记注册，不属于《反不正当竞争法》所保护的企业名称。

【审判】

上海市浦东新区人民法院经审理认为，天容公司的英文企业名称与其中文企业名称存在对应关系，且天容公司在经营活动中实际使用该英文名称，该英文企业名称已具有识别市场经营主体的作用，属于《反不正当竞争法》第五条第三项规定的企业名称，依法受《反不正当竞争法》的保护。昊华公司在出口印度的杀螟丹上使用了天容公司的英文企业名称，主观上具有仿冒的故意，客观上引人误认为是天容公司的商品，挤占了天容公司的出口市场份额，给天容公司造成损害。昊华公司的行为不仅损害了天容公司的合法权益，也扰乱了正常的对外贸易市场秩序，属于《反不正当竞争法》第五条第三项所规定的擅自使用他人企业名称的不正当竞争行为。

不正当竞争行为的损害赔偿额，可以根据权利人在被侵权期间因被侵权所受到的损失，即侵权商品的销售量乘以权利人相同商品的单位利润所得之积计算。根据天容公司的年度审计报告，可以计算出天容公司杀螟丹产品的营业利润率。法院根据昊华公司出口的杀螟丹的金额及天容公司该商品的营业利润率，计算出天容公司经济损失3 125 069.20元。

上海市浦东新区人民法院据此判决：昊华公司赔偿天容公司经济损失3 125 069.20元及合理费用20万元。判决后，双方当事人均未上诉，昊华公司主动支付了判决确定的赔偿金。

【评析】

一、企业在对外贸易中使用的英文企业名称获得《反不正当竞争法》保护的条件

我国企业在开展国内经营活动时通常使用中文名称，但在对外贸易经营活动中，则通常需要使用英文名称。《企业法人登记管理条例》第十条规定："企业法人只准使用一个名称。企业法人申请登记注册的名称由登记主管机关核定，经核准登记注册后在规定的范围内享有专用权。"目前，企业法人登记主管机关并不受理中国企业英文企业名称的核准登记。根据《对外贸易法》第九条的规定："从事货物进出口或者技术进出口的对外贸易经营者，应当向国务院对外贸易主管部门或者其委托的机构办理备案登记；但是，法律、行政法规和国务院对外贸易主管部门规定不需要备案登记的除外。备案登记的具体办法由国务院对外贸易主管部门规定。对外贸易经营者未按照规定办理备案登记的，海关不予办理进出口货物的报关验放手续。"对外贸易经营者在备案时需提交《对外贸易经营者备案登记表》，该表中有一栏是"经营者英文名称"，对外贸易经营者可自行确定英文名称，有关部门在备案登记时不会进行实质审查。

本案的主要争议焦点是中国企业在对外贸易中使用的英文企业名称是否属于《反不正当竞争法》第五条第三项规定的企业名称。《最高人民法院关于审理不正当竞争民事案件应用法律若干问题的解释》（以下简称《不正当竞争解释》）第六条第一款规定：企业登记主管机关依法登记注册的企业名称，以及在中国境内进行商业使用的外国（地区）企业名称，应当认定为《反不正当竞争法》第五条第三项规定的"企业名称"。具有一定的市场知名度、为相关公众所知悉的企业名称中的字号，可以认定为《反不正当竞争法》第五条第三项规定的"企业名称"。根据该解释，《反不正当竞争法》所保护的企业名称包括

三类情形：一是企业登记主管机关依法登记注册的企业名称；二是在中国境内进行商业使用的外国（地区）企业名称；三是具有一定的市场知名度、为相关公众所知悉的企业名称中的字号。

《反不正当竞争法》保护的企业名称是否仅限于上述三类，有两种相反的观点。一种观点认为，除法律、司法解释明确规定的情形外，其他标识企业身份的名称不能认定为企业名称。另一种观点认为，司法解释列举了几种可认定为企业名称的情形，但并不排除其他可以认定为企业名称的情形。我们认为，第二种观点显然更为合理。企业名称是市场主体的名称和企业重要的营业标识，消费者或者其他经营者可以通过不同的营业标识识别经营主体。《反不正当竞争法》保护企业名称的目的是制止造成市场混淆的不正当竞争行为。企业在经营活动中正当使用的企业名称，不管是中文企业名称还是外文企业名称，只要其具有标识经营主体的作用，其企业名称就应当受法律保护。

司法实践中，对《反不正当竞争法》中所称的企业名称包括哪些类型，亦存在逐步扩大范围的趋势。最高人民法院于 2006 年发布《不正当竞争解释》规定了企业字号获得反不正当竞争法保护的条件，但没有将企业简称纳入保护范围。最高人民法院于 2009 年发布《关于当前经济形势下知识产权审判服务大局若干问题的意见》中指出："对于具有一定市场知名度、为相关公众所熟知、已实际具有商号作用的企业名称中的字号、企业或者企业名称的简称，视为企业名称并给予制止不正当竞争的保护。"最高人民法院在（2008）民申字第758号山东起重机厂有限公司与山东山起重工有限公司侵犯企业名称权纠纷案，及天津中国青年旅行社诉天津国青国际旅行社擅自使用他人企业名称纠纷案（指导案例29号）中均明确，具有一定市场知名度、为相关公众所知悉，已实际具有商号作用的企业名称简称，可以视为企业名称予以保护。由此可见，《反不正当竞争法》第五条第三项规定的企业名称不限于经企业登记主管机关依法登记注册的企业名称，虽然《反不正当竞争法》及司法解释未明确规定英文名称可以获得《反不正当竞争法》的保护，但亦不能由此推论英文名称不受《反不正当竞争法》的保护。

对外贸易是我国经济的重要组成部分，中国企业在对外贸易中使用的企业名称逐渐成为重要的商业标识，承载着企业的商誉。天容公司进行对外贸易经营者备案登记时所用的英文名称为"JIANGSU TIANRONG GROUP CO.，LTD"。天容公司生产的杀螟丹农药在印度有关部门进行登记时也使用这一英文企业名称。"天容"是原告的字号，"TIANRONG"系"天容"的汉语拼音，"JIANGSU TIANRONG GROUP CO.，LTD"与天容公司的中文企业名称存在对应关系，且天容公司在经营活动中实际使用该英文名称，该英文企业名称已具有识别市场经营主体的作用，属于《反不正当竞争法》第五条第三项规定的企业名称，依法受《反不正当竞争法》的保护。天容公司和昊华公司均为从事杀螟丹原药生产、出口企业。由于昊华公司生产的杀螟丹尚未通过印度农业部门的登记，其无法以自己的名义向印度出口杀螟丹。昊华公司在出口商品上使用天容公司的英文名称，主观上具有仿冒的故意，客观上引人误认为是天容公司的商品，挤占了天容公司的出口市场份额，给天容公司造成损害。昊华公司的行为不仅损害了天容公司的合法权益，也扰乱了正常的对外贸易市场秩序，属于《反不正当竞争法》第五条第三项所规定的擅自使用他人企业名称的不正当竞争行为。

二、损害赔偿额的确定

《最高人民法院关于审理商标民事纠纷案件适用法律若干问题的解释》第十四条规定，《商标法》第五十六条第一款规定的侵权所获得的利益，可以根据侵权商品销售量与该商品单位利润乘积计算；该商品单位利润无法查明的，按照注册商标商品的单位利润计算。第十五条规定，《商标法》第五十六条第一款规定的因被侵权所受到的损失，可以根据权利人因侵权所造成商品销售减少量或者侵权商品销售量与该注册商标商品的单位利润乘积计算。参照上述规定，本案可以根据侵权商品销售量与该商品的单位利润乘积确定赔偿金额。本案中，双方确认了侵权商品的销售量，但对于该商品的单位利润存在争议。

利润有营业利润和销售利润之分，《商标法》和《反不正当竞争法》没有明确规定赔偿利润是指营业利润还是销售利润。2001年7月1日施行的《最高人民法院关于审理专利纠纷案件适用法律问题的若干规定》第二十条第三款规定："侵权人因侵权所获得的利益可以根据该侵权产品在市场上销售的总数乘以每件侵权产品的合理利润所得之积计算。侵权人因侵权所获得的利益一般按照侵权人的营业利润计算，对于完全以侵权为业的侵权人，可以按照销售利润计算。"此后修订的专利纠纷案件司法解释一直沿用了该规定。我们认为，在商标侵权及仿冒类不正当竞争纠纷中，亦可参照上述规定，即侵权人因侵权所获得的利益一般按照侵权人的营业利润计算，对于完全以侵权为业的侵权人，可以按照销售利润计算。财务费用、管理费用等一般在企业支出中占有相当大的比例，而正常情况下这些费用确实为被告的实际支出，因此应当将其从被告侵权获利中相应扣减，即一般性的侵权行为以营业利润计算，对当事人比较公平，也符合侵权人获利的实际。因本案被告除了销售侵权商品，还有其他正常的经营业务，涉案商品的货值仅占其营业收入的一小部分，被告并非以侵权为业，故本案按照营业利润计算赔偿金额更为合理。

　　在计算赔偿金额时，是选择使用被告产品的利润率还是原告产品的利润率，这主要取决于原告的主张及双方举证的情况。侵权商品销售量与该被告销售该商品的单位利润的乘积，可以计算出被告的侵权获利。而侵权商品销售量与原告销售该商品的单位利润的乘积，可以计算出原告的损失。该计算方式推定被告每销售一件侵权产品，就挤占了原告一件产品的市场份额，原告就少销售了一件产品。本案中，原、被告均提交企业的年度审计报告。昊华公司的年度审计报告中只有整个公司的利润表，报告中未单列杀螟丹的营业收入和营业成本，根据其年度审计报告，无法计算出杀螟丹的利润率。天容公司的年度审计报告中不仅有公司的利润表，还单列了杀螟丹的营业收入和营业成本，能够据此计算出天容公司杀螟丹的利润率。因昊华公司杀螟丹的单位利润无法确定，故可根据天容公司杀螟丹的单位利润计算赔偿金额。

（撰稿人：邵勋　袁田）

招投标瑕疵是否构成串通
投标不正当竞争的认定

——天津市中力神盾电子科技有限公司与上海联电实业
有限公司等串通投标不正当竞争纠纷案

【提要】

当中标人的投标文件及招标程序存在一定瑕疵时，不应据此直接推定中标人与招标人之间存在串通投标情形，仍应从招投标活动的制度价值出发，以是否导致招标目的落空为判断标准，就上述瑕疵是否足以导致中标无效进行审查。本案招投标中存在的瑕疵并不足以导致中标无效，更不足以推定中标人和招标人之间存在串通投标的故意，故不存在串通投标的不正当竞争行为。

【案情】

原告（上诉人）： 天津市中力神盾电子科技有限公司

被告（被上诉人）： 上海联电实业有限公司

被告（被上诉人）： 上海建工集团股份有限公司

被告（被上诉人）： 上海市安装工程集团有限公司

被告（被上诉人）： 上海中心大厦建设发展有限公司

被告（被上诉人）： 中国技术进出口总公司

案由： 串通投标不正当竞争纠纷

一审案号：（2014）浦民三（知）初字第 216 号

二审案号：（2015）沪知民终字第 182 号

原告天津市中力神盾电子科技有限公司（以下简称中力神盾公司）与被告上海联电实业有限公司（以下简称联电公司）同为涉案项目"上海中心大厦项目机电系统分包工程浪涌保护器智能监控系统专业供应"的投标人，上海建工集团股份有限公司（以下简称建工集团）、上海市安装工程集团有限公司（以下简称安装工程公司）、上海中心大厦建设发展有限公司（以下简称上海中心大厦公司）为该项目的招标人，被告中国技术进出口总公司（以下简称技术进出口公司）为该项目的招标代理单位。

根据该项目招标公告及招标文件，招标的要求包括作为制造商的投标人实收资本或履约能力不低于人民币 200 万元，近五年内在中国境内应有三个以上类似项目业绩；投标人须在投标时提供由地（市）级银行出具的愿意为投标人开具相当于中标合同金额 10% 履约保函和 15% 预付款保函的承诺书（保函在中标后开具）；"电力供应"部分规定了电气设备的电压，其中频率为 50Hz；上一级开关型 SPD（即浪涌保护器或避雷器）与次级限压型 SPD 的电缆线隔距应大于 10m；对四级 SPD 的技术参数分别作了规定，其中前三级 SPD 的最大工作电压 Uc 均为 420V，通流量 In 依次为 ≥80KA、40KA、20KA，电压保护水平 Up 依次为 ≤3.0KV、2.4KV、1.7KV，波形均采用 8/20μs，并要求采用熔断组合型 SPD。开标时间为 2012 年 8 月 6 日上午 9：00，书面提问截止时间为 2012 年 7 月 10 日上午 12 时前，如有需要将举行招标答疑会，书面答疑文件发出时间不晚于投标截止日前 15 日。该项目的评标采用综合评估法。

2012 年 7 月 10 日，被告联电公司及另一家投标单位就招标文件中的相应内容向被告技术进出口公司进行提问。同年 8 月 2 日，技术进出口公司向包括原告中力神盾公司和联电公司在内的各投标人送达了招标补充文件，将开标时间改为 2012 年 8 月 21 日下午 1 时，并表示招标技术文件中的"雷电防护等级为 A 级"和"防雷工程设计施工甲级资质"不是对投标单位的要求。

联电公司的投标文件中包括了投标产品的检测报告、近三年财务报表、最近 5 年完成类似项目简介等内容。其投标的第一级产品的 Uc 为 385V DC，第二级产品的试验类别为 Ⅰ级试验，Uc 为 385V，In 为 12.5KA，第三级产品的 Uc 为 385V，Up 为 1.75KV，均采用熔断器进行保护。

2012 年 8 月 21 日，该项目的评标委员会经初审和详细评审，将联电公司（第一名）和中力神盾公司（第二名）推荐为中标候选单位。后招标方公示联电公司为第一中标候选人，但未公示第二中标候选人。

中力神盾公司对上述评标结果不服，向招标方提出异议，并向上海市机电设备招投标工作领导小组办公室进行投诉。评标委员会经评议出具会议纪要，对该异议的处理结果为"维持原评标结果不变"，对中力神盾公司所提异议进行了具体回应，其中包括原告在本案中提出的联电公司的注册资本、履约能力、保函及三级产品的技术指标问题。2013 年 7 月 11 日，上述办公室对中力神盾公司的投诉作出处理意见：1. 上海中心大厦机电系统分包工程浪涌保护器智能监控系统专业供应项目的招投标过程符合法定程序。2. 招标文件存在表述不够严密等问题，但不影响评标委员会作出的评审和评标结果。中力神盾公司对此提起行政诉讼，后撤诉。

2013年7月1日，被告建工集团、安装工程公司、上海中心大厦公司向联电公司发出中标通知书，并向中力神盾公司发出未中标通知书。

原告中力神盾公司诉称：其系国内著名的专业生产防雷设备的企业，是国家防雷标准的主编单位之一，此次投标的产品全部满足招标文件的要求。其经调查得知，被告联电公司在注册资金、履约能力、近5年内的项目条件、第一级产品取得型式试验报告的时间、未按要求提供履约保函和预付款保函承诺书、没有产品的强制备案表等方面不符合招标文件要求；同时，投标文件未实质响应招标文件要求、投标产品未达到招标文件技术要求，包括：第一级产品是直流设备而非招标要求的交流设备、第一级产品为开关型而非招标要求的限压型产品、三级产品的最大持续工作电压均不符合要求、第二级产品为Ⅰ级试验产品而非招标要求的Ⅱ级试验产品且标称放电电流不符合要求、第三级产品的电压保护参数不符合要求、产品不是招标要求的熔断组合型SPD（即浪涌保护器）、防雷资质等级不合要求。此外，第一被告投标时注册资金远低于原告注册资金和本次项目金额，防雷资质低于原告，第一级产品没有任何工程业绩，在这些项目上得分应比原告低，打分不合理。其余四被告未进行资格预审，仅公示一位中标候选人，违反了相应法律规定；配合联电公司延后开标时间，以使其取得产品检测报告和进行强制备案。根据上述情形可推断五被告间存在串通投标的不正当竞争行为。故诉至法院，请求判令：确认本次上海中心大厦项目机电系统分包工程浪涌保护器智能监控系统专业供应工程招标活动中的中标结果无效。

被告联电公司辩称：1. 其具备投标资格。（1）虽其注册资本是100万元，但在投标文件中提供了本公司近三年财务报表及近5年完成的类似项目简介，满足招标文件关于200万履约能力和近5年项目的要求。（2）其投标的产品均有型式试验报告并经气象局备案，招标文件并未要求提供强制备案表。其中，招标文件中第一级产品的参数是按照老国标，而第一被告的同级产品是按照新国标，故其在拿到招标文件后又按照老国标去做了产品测试，于2012年8月17日取得型式试验报告，并在同年8月21日进行了强制备案，未超过投标截止日。（3）提供银行履约保函及预付款保函承诺书的要求出现在招标公告中，招标文件未提此要求，仅指出保函需在中标后开具。2. 其投标的产品满足招标文件的技术要求。（1）招标文件第5节所谓的交流设备是指用电环境，并非要求提供交流产品。直流的浪涌保护器亦可对交流系统提供保护，原告的主张系理解错误。（2）根据招标文件 2.2.1 条的表述，第一级产品可以为开关型。（3）招标文件要求第一、二、三级产品的最大持续工作电压为 420V，但最大持续工作电压并非越高越好。在满足国标要求的情况下，防雷产品的最大持续工作电压越低，对被保护设备的保护越好，但防雷产品的损耗会比较大；反之，若防雷产品的最大持续工作电压越高，则防雷产品损耗越小，但被保护设备的损耗越大。联电公司投标的产品系在满足国标情况下作出的最优选择，且得到了评标委员会的认可。（4）招标文件中第二级产品的参数是根据 Ⅱ 级试验，而其投标的为 Ⅰ 级试验产品，根据国家标准 GB 50343 – 2004 的表 5.4.1 – 2 和 GB 50343 – 2012 的表 5.4.3 – 3，Ⅰ 级试验的标称放电电流 12.5KA，等同于 Ⅱ 级试验的 50KA，满足招标文件"≥40KA"的要求。（5）根据国家标准 GB 50057 – 2010 的表 6.4.4 和 GB 50343 – 2012 的表 5.4.3 – 1，用电设备的耐冲击电压是 2.5KV，在保留 20% 裕量的情况下，第三级 SPD 的电压保护水平只要小于 2KV 就满足国标。其产品为 1.75 KV，满足国标要求，虽不满足招标文件"≤1.7KV"的要求，但得到了评标委员会综合评标的认可。同时，GB 18802.1 – 2002 还对保护电压提供了优先值，与本案招标要求最近的优先值是 1.8KV，故相应产品应标 1.8KV，标 1.7KV 或 1.75KV 理论上均不合规。（6）教科书、行业内和标准中都无原告所谓熔断组合型产品的说法，联电公司是按正常做法将熔断器和避雷器用线接在一起，符合招标文件要求。（7）招标方在补充文件中已明确防雷资质等级是针对设计、施工而非产品，不是对本案投标单位的要求。本案专家评标是综合性评标而非简单核对参数，原告主张被告弄虚作假串通投标的事实不存在，系主观臆测。

被告建工集团、安装工程公司、上海中心大厦公司共同辩称：1. 原告提出的各项异议均已由评标委员会复审，结论是维持原评标结果，行政管理部门也予以确认。2. 招标方针对投标人所提问题做出答疑后，按照法律规定必须顺延开标时间，原告所称的配合延迟开标时间并无事实依据。3. 原告未提供任何证据证明招标人与中标人之间存在串通投标的意思联络。系争招标项目采用综合评标法，选取的是最大限度满足的单位，并非要求与招标文件一字不差，而联电公司完全符合中标条件。4. 防雷资质不是对投标单位的要求，该项也未计入专家打分。5. 涉案招标采取资格后审而非原告所谓的资格预审。如果第一中标候选人因相关原因不符合中标条件，招标方会选择重新招标，不会确定第二中标候选人中标，对第二中标候选人是否公示与本案无关。

被告技术进出口公司辩称：1. 法律并未要求必须通过资格预审的方式进行资格审查，涉案招标采取的是资格后审。2. 其仅公示第一中标候选人是作为拟中标人进行公示，不需要公示全部中标候选人。3. 开标时间顺延是因为招标单位就投标人所提问题发送澄清文件后，距离投标截止时间不足 15 日，根据法律规定必须顺延。

【审判】

上海市浦东新区人民法院经审理认为：本案原告并未提交证据直接证明各被告之间存在串通投标行为，而系以被告联电公司不具备投标资格、投标产品不满足招标文件技术要求，其余四被告明知上述情况仍让其参与投标、配合延迟开标时间并确认其中标、招标程序不符合法律规定为由，推定各被告之间存在串通投标的不正当竞争行为。故本案审查的重点在于原告主张的上述情形是否属实；若属实，是否属于《招标投标法实施条例》（以下简称《实施条例》）规定的串通投标的情形。首先，关于开标时间变更问题。招标方在招标文件规定的范围内，根据投标人的提问向各投标人发出答疑文件，并根据《招标投标法》和《实施条例》的规定，在答疑文件发出时间距投标截止日不足 15 日时进行顺延，不违反法律规定，也无明显不合理之处。其次，关于招标程序的问题。根据《实施条例》第十五条第二款和第二十条的规定，招标人对潜在投标人进行资格审查有资格预审和资格后审两种方式，并非如原告所称必须进行资格预审。本案中，招标文件中规定了对潜在投标人的资格要求，开标后评标委员会对投标人的资格进行了审查，可见采取的是资格后审。评标委员会推荐联电公司和原告分别为第一和第二中标候选人，但招标人仅公示了第一中标候选人，违反了《实施条例》的规定，但该行为并非《招标投标法》规定的可导致中标结果无效的情形，更不足以认定各被告之间串通投标。再次，关于原告提出的联电公司不具备投标资格的情形。经审查，联电公司的投标文件中包含有相应资质文件，评标委员会在复评时亦进行了认可，故原告认为联电公司不具备投标资格的情形并不属实。最后，关于原告主张的联电公司投标产品不满足招标文件技术要求的情形。国家标准对涉案产品技术性能的相关参数值进行了规定，现联电公司投标产品的技术参数均满足国家标准的要求。虽部分参数值与招标文件要求不完全相同，但评标委员会根据评标细则及其专业知识，对各投标人投标的浪涌保护器及智能监控系统等多项指标进行审查和综合评分，得出联电公司满足投标资格且综合得分排名第一的结论。在原告提出异议后，评标委员会经复评，仍对联电公司投标产品的技术性能予以认可，作出维持原评标结果的结论。原告关于只要参数与招标文件不同则不应中标的观点，与综合评标法的内涵不符。原告以其质疑来推断招标人与中标人存在串通投标的不正当竞争行为，缺乏事实和法律依据。综上，原告并无证据证明各被告实施了相互勾结、排挤竞争对手的不正当竞争行为，其指控的情形也不足以推断各被告之间存在串通投标的不正当竞争行为。因此，原告的诉讼请求缺乏事实依据。

综上，上海市浦东新区人民法院依照《中华人民共和国反不正当竞争法》第十五条、《中华人民共和国民事诉讼法》第六十四条第一款之规定，判决：驳回原告中力神盾公司的诉讼请求。

一审判决后，原告中力神盾公司不服，提起上诉。

上海知识产权法院经审理后认为，一审判决认定事实清楚，适用法律正确，判决并无不当，判决驳回上诉，维持原判。

【评析】

涉案招投标过程中存在一定瑕疵，是否可根据该瑕疵直接认定招标人与中标人存在串通行为，进而导致中标无效的法律后果，为本案的争议焦点。

一、瑕疵招投标不等同于串通投标

在招投标过程中，招标人、投标人均应遵守《招标投标法》及其实施条例的规定；同时，作为一种民事行为，根据意思自治原则，事先公布的招标文件对招投标人而言即为其在招投标活动中所应严格执行的"宪法"。当中标人的投标文件在某些方面与招标文件的要求不符（以下称瑕疵招投标），但并不存在《招标投标法实施条例》规定的具体串通投标行为的情况下，是否可以根据该种瑕疵直接推定招标人与中标人之间构成串通投标不正当竞争？

笔者认为，《招标投标法》及其实施条例规定了具体串通投标行为，其法律后果系导致中标无效。当招投标过程中存在一定瑕疵但并不属于法律规定的串通投标行为时，从中标无效的判断标准上来看，并非任意瑕疵招投标行为均可导致中标无效。串通投标的客观方面为串通行为，主观方面为故意，而瑕疵招投标仅为一种客观事实，不足以据此直接认定招标人与中标人之间存在串通投标的故意。因此，不应根据招投标瑕疵直接推定招标人与中标人之间构成串通投标的不正当竞争，需结合该瑕疵对招标目的的影响判断。既不能操之过严，将轻微瑕疵行为均认定为不正当竞争行为；亦不可失之过宽，以免放纵相应的投机、违规行为，使《反不正当竞争法》失去其应有的约束力。例如，被告人徐某等串通投标罪[①]一案中，招标公告中明确当投标人为代理商时，必须获得生产商出具的唯一授权代理证明文件，被告人伪造代理证明，使仅有的三个投

---

① 上海市崇明县人民法院（2012）崇刑初字第91号刑事判决书。

标公司在其统一意志下一起投标报名，导致各投标者之间缺失竞争，直接破坏了招投标活动的价值，属于串通投标行为。而在北京希尔信息技术有限公司诉江苏金智教育信息技术有限公司等串通投标不正当竞争纠纷一案①中，金智科技公司投标的计算机软件著作权属于其关联公司，其仅享有使用权，不符合招标文件的要求，且并未在投标文件中提交许可使用协议。法院认定该行为虽存在一定瑕疵，但以影响承揽人开发能力的关键在于获得相关计算机软件的使用权、仅拥有软件的所有权并无实质意义为由，认为上述瑕疵并不足以导致中标结果无效的法律后果，认定不存在串通投标行为。

二、应以是否导致招标目的落空为判断标准

招标投标活动的本质在于要求当事人遵循公开、公平、公正以及诚实信用原则，在同等条件下通过市场竞争实现优胜劣汰，最佳配置使用人、财、物力。招投标作为一种制度的基本价值在于通过竞争性缔约机制的引入，给投标人以公平竞争的机会，从而使最优的投标人脱颖而出，使招标人以较低的价格获得最优的商品或服务。串通投标行为直接违反了上述基本价值，使得招标活动的目的不能实现。但瑕疵招投标并不一定会导致招标的目的无法实现，故从招投标的制度价值角度考虑，瑕疵招投标并不意味着可直接推定中标人与招标人之间存在串通投标行为，关键在于该行为是否导致招标目的落空，这也是串通投标不正当竞争案件的审查重点。

本案招标项目的标的为浪涌保护器智能监控系统，主要包括浪涌保护器以及其监控系统，故招标目的在于选出最优的防雷产品及与其相应的智能监控系统。防雷方案为一项系统工程，决定防雷效果的关键因素包括各级 SPD 的技术参数、安装位置、监控系统的设计等。在原告列举的众多第一被告不符合招标文件要求、招标程序违反法律的事实中，确实存在瑕疵的情形包括：第一被告未提交保函承诺书、三级产品的最大持续工作电压及第三级产品的电压保护参数不符合招标要求、招标方仅公示了一位中标候选人。其余情形经审查，系原告对招标文件或法律规定理解错误所致。从该次招标目的即选择最优防雷产品及监控系统方面看，上述瑕疵招投标情形中的未提交保函承诺书和仅公示一位中标候选人与招标的目的关联度较低，属轻微瑕疵，不足以推定串通投标行为的存在。两类技术指标的不符与招标目的息息相关，但是否足以推定串通行为还需结合其对招标目的的影响程度来判断。国家标准对涉案产品技术性能的相关参数值进行了规定，在满足国家标准的情况下，影响防雷效果的关键在于参

---

① 北京市石景山区人民法院（2012）石民初字第 609 号民事判决书。

数值及各参数之间的配合。原告关于只要参数与招标文件不同则不应中标的观点，与涉案项目综合评标法的内涵不符，仅根据个别参数的差别来推定防雷效果也不符合事实。现第一被告投标的产品技术性能完全满足国家标准的规定，评标委员会根据评标细则及其专业知识，在对各投标人投标的浪涌保护器及智能监控系统等多项指标进行审查和综合评分后，认为第一被告投标产品的部分参数值与招标文件要求不完全相同，但满足涉案项目的要求，且综合排名第一。在原告提出异议后，评标委员会经复评，仍对第一被告投标产品的技术性能予以认可。据此，法院认定，原告根据上述情形推断招标人与中标人存在串通投标的不正当竞争行为缺乏事实和法律依据。

（撰稿人：叶菊芬）

工具类软件拦截他人视频前
广告行为的法律性质认定

——北京爱奇艺科技有限公司与上海大摩网络科技有限公司
不正当竞争纠纷案

【提要】

视频分享网站基于"广告＋免费视频"的商业模式而产生网站运营者与用户之间的约定利益应受法律保护。第三方工具类软件经营者不得使用技术手段破坏他人基于正当商业模式而获得的法定或约定利益。若工具类软件违反商业道德与诚实信用原则，使用技术手段拦截视频分享网站中的视频前广告以获取自身竞争优势，干扰视频分享网站的正常运营，损害了网站运营者的合法权益，则构成不正当竞争，应当承担相应民事责任。

【案情】

原告（被上诉人）： 北京爱奇艺科技有限公司

被告（上诉人）： 上海大摩网络科技有限公司

案由： 其他不正当竞争纠纷

一审案号：（2015）闵民三（知）初字第 271 号

二审案号：（2016）沪 73 民终 33 号

原告北京爱奇艺科技有限公司（以下简称爱奇艺公司）成立于 2007 年，主要经营范围为互联网信息服务业务等，其运营的"爱奇艺"网站（www. iqiyi. com）向网络用户提供视频播放服务，并在业内取得了较好业绩与较高知名度。原告运营该网站的商业模式主要为：一方面，花费大量资金购买正版视频节目著作权并为带宽、推广宣传等项目支付费用；另一方面，通过两种收入来源维持网站正常运营。具体如下：一是"广告＋免费视频"模式中的广告收入，即在播放视频前播放商业广告以收取广告费，用户通过观看片前广告进而获得免费观看视频的对价；二是"付费会员＋免费视频"模式中的会费收入，即用户付费注册成为会员，会员在有效期内享有跳过广告直接观看视频节目的会员权益。对于前种收入来源，原告方与客户签订的网络广告发布合同中通常约定按 cpm 计费，即按访问视频前广告的人次进行收费。

被告上海大摩网络科技有限公司（以下简称大摩公司）成立于 2012 年，主要经营范围为计算机软硬件设计、开发等。被告在其运营的网站 www. ad - safe. com 中向用户免费提供"ADSafe"净网大师软件（以下简称涉诉软件）的下载服务。该涉诉软件系被告研发，系全方位智能拦截软件，宣传语为"干净的感觉真好"，著作权归被告所有。据被告网站首页的软件简介显示，涉诉软件的主要功能之一为"看视频不等待"，使用该功能"可以跳过 30 秒、60 秒、90 秒的视频等待，杜绝一切干扰"，该功能由用户自行决定是否勾选启用。

2014 年 9 月 19 日、2015 年 4 月 24 日，原告通过两次公证取证，证明在安装涉诉软件并启用其"看视频不等待"功能时，可在"爱奇艺"网站电脑端、安卓端中，跳过原本在视频前播放的时长约为 60 秒的广告，直接播放视频内容。

庭审中，原告陈述其网站中的视频与广告的播放机制：当用户点击视频播放页面时，该页面会加载一个主播放器。该主播放器分为两个部分，即广告播放器与视频播放器。用户点击播放视频后，主播放器先行加载广告播放器并向服务器请求广告数据，后根据获取的广告数据开始播放广告；广告播放完毕后将发送特定信号，主播放器收到特定信号后加载视频播放器开始播放视频内容。同时，被告陈述涉诉软件"看视频不等待"功能的运行原理：用户点击视频后会产生网络数据处理层，若用户安装了涉诉软件并选择启用"看视频不等待"功能，涉诉软件就会阻止答复视频播放器中的广告数据请求而仅答复播放视频内容请求，进而实现在用户设备上跳过广告直接播放视频内容的效果。

原告爱奇艺公司诉称：大摩公司通过宣传引诱用户下载并启用"看视频不等待"功能，使得用户不用收看爱奇艺公司网站的视频前广告，直接获取视频内容，该行为损害了爱奇艺公司播放广告应取得的合法权益，构成不正当竞争。据上，请求判令被告停止侵权、消除影响，并赔偿原告经济损失人民币 200 万元（以下币种均为人民币）、合理费用 8.35 万元。

被告大摩公司辩称：首先，被告研发、运营涉诉软件的目的并非针对原告，也不是为了损害他人权益和谋求不正当商业利益，而是提供更好满足消费需求、便于消费者选择中立性技术工具。涉诉软件是否安装、如何使用，均由用户自行决定，故被告仅向用户提供了涉诉软件，但未实施跳过视频前广告的行为。

其次，原告"广告＋免费视频"的商业模式不属于受法律保护的法定利益，即使原告因用户使用涉诉软件而导致收益下降，也是市场发展、用户自行选择的结果，被告向用户提供涉诉软件的行为不构成不正当竞争。最后，即使被告构成不正当竞争，被告未诋毁原告商誉或侵害原告人身权等权利，原告也未提供证据证明其损失及被告获利，故不同意承担消除影响及赔偿损失的民事责任。

【审判】

上海市闵行区人民法院经审理认为，本案争议焦点在于：一、原告"广告＋免费视频"的商业模式是否正当，是否应予保护；二、被告运营的具有"看视频不等待"功能的涉诉软件，是否系被告基于公共利益而研发的中立性技术工具，若不是，则是否构成侵权。关于争议焦点一，法院认为，"广告＋免费视频"的商业模式，并非原告独享，不属于法律保护的范围。然而，该商业模式实可视为用户与原告达成的观看视频节目"协议"，原告发出"广告＋免费视频"的要约，用户一旦选择进行点播即可视为承诺，双方达成一致意思表示，用户点播后即对双方产生约束力。经查，该"协议"中播放的商业广告并非恶意或不合法广告，故基于该"协议"而产生的原告与用户之间的约定利益应受法律保护，他人不得损害。关于争议焦点二，法院认为，被告研发运营涉诉软件具有营利性，原、被告向网络用户提供的服务虽不同但相关联，两者具有竞争关系。本案原告争讼内容为涉诉软件中的"看视频不等待"功能，被告明知或应知该功能主要拦截对象为视频分享网站正常播放的视频前商业广告，且在运营时抓住用户既不愿支付时间成本也不愿支付金钱成本的消费心理，通过广告宣传、免费下载、用户可添加规则源等手段引诱用户下载涉诉软件，进而提高涉诉软件下载量，积聚人气，提升被告知名度来取得自身竞争优势。被告的上述行为，从短期看，直接损害原告与用户之间的约定利益，给原告造成商业损失；从长远看，视频分享网站因收益受到严重影响将无法承受购买正版视频的著作权费，在无利可赚的情况下将无人经营视频分享网站，最终损害广大消费者的利益。因此，被告研发运营涉诉软件的"看视频不等待"功能并非基于保护消费者等公共利益的需要，不具有保护公共利益的必要性、合理性，违背了商业道德与诚实信用原则，损害了原告合法利益而为自己获益，构成不正当竞争。

综上，上海市闵行区人民法院依照《中华人民共和国反不正当竞争法》第二条、第二十条，《中华人民共和国侵权责任法》第九条第一款、第十五条第一款第（一）和（六）项的规定，判决：被告大摩公司立即停止侵权，并赔偿原告爱奇艺公司经济损失200 000元、合理开支33 500元。

一审判决后，被告大摩公司不服，提起上诉。

上海知识产权法院经审理后认为，一审判决认定事实清楚、适用法律正确，审判程序合法，所作判决并无不当，判决驳回上诉，维持原判。

【评析】

本案系工具类软件使用技术手段拦截他人网站视频前广告所引发的新类型不正当竞争纠纷案件。涉案被诉行为并非《反不正当竞争法》中所列举的具体不正当竞争行为，故审理难点在于如何准确适用《反不正当竞争法》第二条原则性条款对互联网环境中新出现的竞争行为予以规范、调整。本案明确了商业模式本身不受法律保护，但因正当商业模式而产生的法定或约定利益受法律保护；同时，根据传统侵权行为的构成要件，从行为主体、行为违法属性及损害后果的角度对互联网环境中的被诉行为是否构成不正当竞争进行了认定，准确把握了《反不正当竞争法》的立法精神和适用条件，具有一定的借鉴意义。

一、行为主体间是否存在竞争关系

最高人民法院在审理有关不正当竞争案件的司法政策中曾指出，竞争关系是取得经营资格的平等市场主体之间在竞争过程中形成的社会关系，存在竞争关系是认定构成不正当竞争的要件之一。

首先，原、被告双方均为经营者，从事市场经营活动。市场经营活动最大的特点在于"以营利为目的"。其中，营利不等于赢利，且营利的方式多种多样，有眼前利益，也有长远利益。例如，在互联网行业中，软件开发者投入人力、物力研发软件，前期投入资金，免费向用户提供，进而吸引用户下载，集聚人气、提高网站知名度来提升网站价值的行为本身即具有营利性。

其次，原、被告间抑或存在经营范围重合的同业竞争情形，抑或存在诸如经营结果"损人利己""搭便车"等关联关系的竞争情形。例如，本案中，虽然原、被告双方向用户提供不同的网络服务内容，但被告涉诉软件"看视频不等待"功能针对的目标对象是不特定地落入其运行原理的视频分享网站，若无原告类的视频分享网站，则被诉"看视频不等待"功能将成为无本之木、无源之水，不存在运营的基础和价值。因此，原、被告虽然向用户提供的服务不同，但两者相关联，存在利用与被利用的关系，属于为《反不正当竞争法》所调整的竞争关系。

最后，原、被告间存在特定、具体的竞争关系。在实务中，被诉竞争行为可能针对特定的经营者，也可能针对不特定的经营者。对于后种情形，只要侵权人、侵权行为、损害后果是具体且特定的，并存在损害与被损害的侵权因果关系，从原则上讲，任何受损的不特定经营者均可成为主张权利的适格主体。

二、被诉行为是否具有竞争不当性

市场经济要求竞争公平、正当、有序，互联网经济的健康发展则更需要有序的市场环境和明确的市场竞争规则作为保障。在认定被诉行为是否为不当的竞争行为时，可主要从以下两方面进行考量：一是是否属于一种市场竞争行为；二是是否违反诚实信用原则或公认的商业道德。

一方面，具体到互联网环境中，市场竞争行为的本质没有变，依然在于获取交易机会，提升自身的竞争优势。例如，本案中被告通过宣传其运营软件的"看视频不等待"功能，获取与视频分享网站用户的交易机会，进而扩大涉诉软件用户数量，提升自身竞争优势，故可以认定被诉行为系一种市场竞争行为。

另一方面，互联网环境中技术更新快，竞争方式、手段纷繁复杂，但需要明确，竞争行为的不当性，主要体现在技术使用行为是否违反诚实信用原则或公认的商业道德，并非对技术本身进行评价。具体来讲，虽然技术创新本身值得鼓励，但不能否认，任何一项技术既可能被用于合法的、不受争议的用途，也可能被用于非法的用途，侵犯他人权益。因此，只有当有证据能证明技术研发者为了自身利益，在开展经营活动时故意引诱、教唆、帮助他人实施侵权行为时，才应承担侵权责任。本案中，被告研发了涉诉软件的"看视频不等待"功能，利用用户既不愿支付时间成本也不愿支付金钱成本的消费心理，引诱用户下载、使用涉案软件，目的在于依托原告多年经营所取得的用户群，为自身增加市场交易机会，取得市场竞争优势，其行为本质具有不当利用他人市场成果来谋求自身竞争优势的性质，违反了诚实信用原则与公认的商业道德，具有不当性。

三、被诉行为是否产生了损害后果

互联网技术蓬勃发展，商业模式纷繁多样，竞争激烈。对于《反不正当竞争法》未作特别规定予以禁止的行为，在适用原则性条款时应遵循审慎原则，即只有在给其他经营者的合法权益造成损害，不制止不足以维护公平竞争秩序的情况下，才可以适用原则性条款予以制止。

一方面，法律保护的经营者合法权益的来源必须合法、正当。互联网环境中，市场竞争中的权益来源多基于其商业模式。虽然，商业模式本身不受法律保护，但只要商业模式本身并未违反《反不正当竞争法》的原则性精神和禁止性规定，经营者以此获得的法定或约定商业利益应受保护，他人不得以不正当的方式进行损害。例如，本案中原告向用户推出"广告＋免费视频"的商业模式，是原告与消费者之间为适应网络环境而逐渐形成的提供服务和消费的有效便捷办法，该经营模式没有法律明文规定须加以保护，也非原告独享，确实没有法定利益。然而，在该商业模式下，用户选择"广告＋免费视频"方式观看视频，则实可视为用户与原告达成了一份观看视频的协议，双方应当受协议约束，基于该模式原告与用户产生了约定利益，正当、合法，他人不得损害。

另一方面，法律还保护消费者及公共利益，被诉竞争行为不得对此进行损害。例如，本案中的涉诉软件"看视频不等待"功能，貌似对用户有利，用户可不用付费直接观看不带有视频广告的视频节目，但从长远来看，视频分享网站因收益受到严重影响，将无法承受购买播放视频节目著作权费用，在无利可赚的情况下，将无人去经营视频分享网站，最终损害了广大视频消费者利益。因此，在认定是否有损消费者利益或社会公共利益时，还应从市场竞争的长远发展角度考虑，进而有效发挥司法在知识产权保护中的主导作用，进一步营造稳定、公平的市场竞争秩序与良好的营商环境。

（撰稿人：顾亚安　陈亦雨）

擅自公开竞争对手裁判文书
信息的法律性质认定

——扬州市龙卷风餐饮企业管理有限公司与上海圣敏餐饮管理有限公司不正当竞争纠纷案

【提要】

裁判文书未生效时，所涉的事实和法律认定属于司法未决问题。经营者将涉及竞争对手的未生效裁判文书通过互联网等渠道公之于众，并对此作出夸大、曲解、断章取义的表述，会导致相关公众产生误解，进而损害竞争对手的商誉，破坏其正常经营活动，构成商业诋毁。裁判文书生效后，若经营者公开宣传的内容未能如实反映生效文书所查明的事实和认定的结论，导致公众对其竞争对手产生误解，损害了竞争对手的商誉，则也属捏造、散布虚伪事实的行为，构成商业诋毁。

【案情】

原告（被上诉人）：扬州市龙卷风餐饮企业管理有限公司

被告（上诉人）：上海圣敏餐饮管理有限公司

案由：其他不正当竞争纠纷

一审案号：（2015）闵民三（知）初字第 1291 号

二审案号：（2016）沪 73 民终 132 号

原告扬州市龙卷风餐饮企业管理有限公司（以下简称龙卷风公司）与被告上海圣敏餐饮管理有限公司（以下简称圣敏公司）均从事包括龙卷风土豆零食在内的餐饮业特许经营加盟业务，双方许可经营的门店均销售龙卷风土豆产品。

2013 年 7 月 2 日，被告圣敏公司成立，经营范围为餐饮企业管理，食用农产品（不含生猪产品）的销售等。经案外人卡福系统株式会社授权，被告获得"storm potato"男版、女版作品在中国境内的独家使用许可权。根据作品登记证所载内容显示，上述作品的创作完成时间均为 2009 年 8 月 27 日，首次发表时间均为 2009 年 10 月 23 日。后又经案外人李奉九、朴妽浩、柳俊模授权，被告于 2013 年 6 月 17 日获得串扦土豆片外观设计专利在中国境内的许可使用权。

2014 年 2 月 24 日，原告龙卷风公司成立，法定代表人为李彩章，经营范围为预包装食品兼散装食品零售；餐饮企业管理。原告公司成立当日，李彩章出具授权书一份，授权原告使用其于 2012 年 8 月 21 日从案外人苏保付处获得独占许可使用权的第 8867370 号"龙卷风"商标，该商标核定使用商品为第 29 类，有效期自 2012 年 8 月 21 日至 2022 年 8 月 20 日。2014 年 10 月 11 日，其法定代表人李彩章对其个人创作的图案标识进行著作权登记，登记证书上显示创作完成时间 2013 年 10 月 8 日，首次发表时间 2014 年 1 月 22 日。2015 年 1 月至 4 月，李彩章获得串扦火腿肠（龙卷风）、串扦红薯（龙卷风）、串扦土豆（龙卷风）三项外观设计专利，并获得薯塔机（大）外观设计专利的授权。

2015 年 2 月 13 日，原告向江苏省扬州市扬州公证处申请证据保全公证。根据公证书所附光盘内容显示，在被告运营管理的网站页面中包含以下信息：网页中有"假冒品牌："字样，在"假冒品牌："下方罗列了一些图案标识，其中有原告企业形象标识，即李彩章个人创作的图案标识加"STORM POTATO"字样。

2015 年 3 月 13 日，原告再次向江苏省扬州市扬州公证处申请证据保全公证。根据公证书所附光盘内容显示，点击被告运营管理的网站页面中的"龙卷风土豆"栏下的"假冒品牌"，进入相应界面，显示如下信息：网页上方有"打假成功案例！维护消费者的权利！"字样；在上述字样下方，显示有被告的相关信息；在上述被告的相关信息下方，显示有原告的相关信息，即李彩章个人创作的图案标识，在该标识上印有"STORM POTATO""假冒品牌"字样，同时在该标识右边显示有"被告品牌＆企业：""品牌：STORM POTATO""企业：扬州市龙卷风餐饮企业管理有限公司""被告人：李彩章"四行字样；在上述原告的相关信息下方，显示有（2014）扬广知民初字第 70 号民事判决书。

2015 年 2 月 11 日，江苏省扬州市广陵区人民法院对圣敏公司与龙卷风公司、李彩章不正当竞争纠纷一案作出（2014）扬广知民初字第 70 号民事判决。判决书中载明："李彩章曾与圣敏公司合作，签订过许可合同，知晓圣敏公司加盟店的装饰装潢和形象设计等细节。后李彩章成立龙卷风公司并以公司名义自行经营同类商品和发展自己的加盟商。龙卷风公司经营或授权的相关店面的装饰装潢和形象设计在整体上与圣敏公司的加盟店风格形象构成近似，个别细节上完全一致或高度近似，足以造成消费者认识上的混淆，误认为龙卷风公司经营的商品来源于圣敏公司或与圣敏公司有密切关联。龙卷风公司以使用近似装潢的方式来攀附圣敏公司商品的知名度，构成不正当竞争，应立即停止侵权……"一审判决后，龙卷风公司、李彩章不服，提出上诉。江苏省扬州市中级人民法院经审理后于2015年9月1日作出判决，驳回上诉、维持原判。

原告龙卷风公司诉称：自2014年7月起，被告将一份未生效判决书发布在其企业网站上，并将原告的企业名称、法定代表人、商标突出显示于该网站的"假冒品牌"一栏中，以此捏造原告假冒被告品牌并被法院判决的虚假事实。然而，该判决所涉原被告间的不正当竞争纠纷正在二审审理过程中，被告将该未生效裁判文书发布在网站上混淆视听，造成相关公众误以为原告的品牌及产品系假冒伪劣。随后，虽然被告补充提供了该案二审已生效判决书，但该判决书认定原告对被告的不正当竞争仅限于原告的店铺装潢与被告相似，这与被告在其网站上宣传"原告系假冒品牌"的关联性及法律后果有着较大差别。原告认为，被告不仅对自己的产品作引人误解的虚假宣传，而且捏造事实诋毁原告，是一种恶意竞争的行为，对原告的商业信誉和商品声誉造成了严重的损害。据上，请求判令被告停止侵权，消除影响，并赔偿原告经济损失80 000元、公证费2040元、律师费6000元。

被告圣敏公司辩称：被告在其官网上公布自己的维权打假成果是维护自身品牌的一种措施，对所涉法律文书的引用正当合理。基于一审判决书的内容，被告认为假冒品牌是对侵犯商标权、不正当竞争的通俗说法。被告认为，品牌的内涵远大于商标，应包括专利、店铺装潢等，装潢设计系被告品牌的核心价值所在，故原告对被告知名商品装潢的侵犯，即是对被告品牌标识的侵犯。因此，被告将上述判决书在未生效时刊登上网是向客户说明案件进展情况；在已生效时刊登上网并对此进行"假冒品牌"的陈述行为，并非恶意诋毁原告，而系对自身品牌进行维权的正当合法行为，故请求法院驳回原告的所有诉请。

【审判】

上海市闵行区人民法院经审理认为：一方面，未生效裁判文书所涉的事实和法律认定属于司法未决问题。本案中，圣敏公司在一审裁判文书尚未生效的情况下，以"假冒品牌！打假成功案件！"为标题，将未生效判决书予以公开散布，会导致相关公众产生误解，认为龙卷风公司破坏竞争对手的正常经营活动，损害龙卷风公司的商誉，构成商业诋毁。另一方面，涉案裁判文书的内容为判决龙卷风公司停止使用与圣敏公司许可加盟店近似的装饰装潢，并未对龙卷风公司品牌是否为"假冒品牌"进行认定。涉案判决生效后，圣敏公司在其官网上所作的表述未能如实反映生效判决所查明的事实和裁判的内容，超越了裁判文书认定的侵权范围，没有事实依据，属于捏造虚伪事实。本案中，尽管圣敏公司将涉案裁判文书附在涉案网页下方，但浏览该网页的社会公众并不必然会完整浏览该文书；相反，社会公众会认为圣敏公司之行为系对该判决书的提炼、概括，从而误认为龙卷风公司的品牌是"假冒品牌"。并且，圣敏公司的上述内容均发布在其官方网站上，互联网互联互通的特性决定了任何网络用户对于上述内容都存在浏览的可能。因此，上述行为降低了相关公众对龙卷风公司的评价和信任，损害了其商誉，构成商业诋毁。

综上，上海市闵行区人民法院依照《中华人民共和国反不正当竞争法》第十四条、第二十条，《中华人民共和国侵权责任法》第十五条第一款第（一）项、第（六）项、第（八）项和第二款，《最高人民法院关于审理不正当竞争民事案件应用法律若干问题的解释》第十七条第一款之规定，判决：圣敏公司立即停止侵权，消除影响，并赔偿龙卷风公司经济损失30 000元及公证费2040元、律师费5000元，合计人民币37 040元。

一审判决后，被告圣敏公司不服，提起上诉。

上海知识产权法院经审理后认为，一审判决认定事实清楚、适用法律正确，审判程序合法，所作判决并无不当，判决驳回上诉，维持原判。

【评析】

经营者公布有关竞争对手的判决信息，尤其是未生效判决信息，是否构成商业诋毁，是不正当竞争纠纷中较为新颖的司法实务问题。根据我国《反不正当竞争法》第十四条规定，经营者不得捏造、散布虚伪事实，损害竞争对手的商业信誉、商品声誉。故认定公布竞争对手未生效或已生效判决内容是否构成商业诋毁，可从以下几方面考虑。

一、双方当事人是否存在竞争关系

对于竞争关系的认定可结合营业执照上的经营范围与实际经营情况进行认定。结合本案，原、被告同为餐饮企业管理公司，在国内开展餐饮品牌的加盟业务，双方许可加盟的门店中均经营龙卷风土豆产品，故存在同业竞争关系，符合我国《反不正当竞争法》对于商业诋毁行为主体认定的要求。

二、"捏造、散布虚伪事实"的行为是否存在

公开法院的判决文书内容应当具备两个前提，一是该判决书已经生效。因为在判决书未生效期间，判决所争议的事实属于司法未决事实，所争议的焦点亦属于司法未定之论。二是必须公允、正当、客观地公布判决书的内容，不能有任何的断章取义、夸大或曲解，否则就有违公平正义的司法理念。如果判决书未生效就不适当地加以公开宣传，或判决书已经生效但公开宣传的内容未能如实反映判决书所查明的事实和认定的结论，那么就应被认定为捏造、散布虚伪事实的行为。结合本案，在涉案判决未生效与生效两个时间段，被告的涉案网页中指称原告为"假冒品牌"，涉案判决为"打假成功案例"。然而，品牌是一个复合概念，包含内外两层含义：对外是指外在的、具象的有形标识，可直接给予社会公众较强的感觉上的冲击，包括名称、商标、包装、装潢等；对内是社会公众的心理感受，是一种使用后的印象、体验和评价。因此，装潢侵权是对品牌的一种侵犯，但不能理解为装潢侵权即假冒品牌，不能将二者绝对等同起来。尽管被告将（2014）扬广知民初字第 70 号民事判决书附在涉案网页下方，但浏览该网页的社会公众并不必然会完整浏览该判决书，反而会误认为被告之陈述系对裁判文书的提炼、概括，从而误导社会公众认为原告的品牌是"假冒品牌"，且系在该判决中所查明的事实及认定的结论。同样"打假成功案例"的含义甚为广泛，无法让浏览该网页的社会公众准确理解为原告实质上是侵犯了被告许可加盟店的装饰装潢。因此，被告在自己的网站中指称原告为"假冒品牌""打假成功案例"的行为，是对该判决书所查明事实及认定结论的夸大或曲解，仍属于捏造、散布虚伪事实的行为。

三、竞争对手的商誉是否受到损害

禁止商业诋毁的立法目的即是要规制经营者通过不正当评价来损害他人商誉的行为。经营者在市场交易中，应当遵循公平竞争、诚实信用的原则，依据真实的事实对其他经营者进行客观、公允的评价。结合本案，原告虽然在他案中被认定为侵犯了被告的装饰装潢，但是该判决中并没有认定原告的品牌是假冒品牌，原告仍可以以其自身品牌开展加盟业务。被告在网站指称原告为"假冒品牌"的行为，极易会使原告已有的加盟商、潜在的加盟商或消费者等相关公众产生不恰当的理解，从而对原告的品牌产生怀疑和不信任，进而改变相关公众的加盟或消费选择。品牌是一个企业的生命线，假冒品牌比装潢侵权所带来的不良评价及消极影响更加严重。所以，被告的行为会使相关公众对原告的企业形象和产品质量产生过度的不良印象，使原告的社会评价度产生不必要的

降低，不正当地损害了原告的商业信誉和商品声誉。

综上，该类案件审理的关键在于判断该行为是否会引人误解，使公众产生不正当的评价，从而贬损了竞争对手的商誉。本案从立法目的出发，对不正当竞争行为中的商业诋毁进行要件式分析，从而得出审判结论，具有一定的典型意义。

（撰稿人：牟鹏　陈亦雨）

五

知识产权刑事案件

经营场所提供者容留销假
行为的刑事责任认定

——李如国等销售假冒注册商标的商品罪案

【提要】

经营场所提供者明知商户涉嫌销售假冒注册商标商品的犯罪行为，仍然为其提供租赁场所，并以放任商铺藏匿假冒商品，预先提供消息以逃避查处等方式容留商户销假的，应当对经营场所提供者以销售假冒注册商标的商品罪的共犯定罪处罚。

【案情】

公诉机关：上海静安区人民检察院

被告人：李如国、万建平

案由：销售假冒注册商标的商品罪

一审案号：（2015）普刑（知）初字第 50 号刑事判决书

二审案号：（2016）沪 03 刑终 46 号

上海韩城企业管理有限公司（以下简称韩城公司）于 2003 年注册，负责南京西路 580 号南证大厦（亦称"淘宝城"）的对外出租及日常物业管理。2010 年 11 月至 2013 年 5 月间，租赁"淘宝城"商铺经营的商户因犯销售假冒注册商标的商品罪被判有罪的案件共计 33 件，涉案金额共计人民币 3 亿余元。被告人李如国作为韩城公司实际控制人，明知"淘宝城"内商铺售假活动高发且多次被行政、司法机关查处，仍通过韩城公司及管理团队为商户提供租赁场所，容留商铺售假，并从中牟取个人不法利益，其间，被告人李如国以现金收款不入账的方式牟利，每月收取商铺扩大经营费，两年内合计 937500 元。为吸引游客购物，被告人李如国还授意以向"黄牛"高额收取大厅花车租金的形式，允许交钱的"黄牛"拉客进"淘宝城"消费。被告人万建平明知"淘宝城"内多家店铺销假，为规避检查，在店铺老板的要求下，先后为多家售假店铺进行装修，并在上述店铺内装修暗格、电子遥控门等设施用于藏匿及暗中销售假冒注册商标的商品。经查，上述商铺销售假冒注册商标的商品共计3827件，价值共计人民币27 463 290元。

此外，被告人李如国指使他人对店铺进行装修，并自行安排营业员进行销售，经查获并扣押待销售的假冒"PRADA""CHANEL"等注册商标的价值共计人民币606 930元。

公诉机关指控：被告人李如国明知是假冒注册商标的商品仍予以销售，待销售金额巨大，且明知他人侵犯知识产权犯罪，而为其提供经营场所，待销售金额巨大，应当以销售假冒注册商标的商品罪追究其刑事责任。被告人万建平明知他人销售假冒注册商标的商品仍为其提供装修帮助，应当以销售假冒注册商标的商品罪追究其刑事责任。

被告人李如国、万建平及其辩护人对起诉书指控的犯罪事实和罪名均无异议，但认为李如国虽为韩城公司实际控制人，但"淘宝城"被判刑事案件并非经过李如国之手，且并无直接证据证明李如国对租户的所为知晓，所收的扩大经营费非李如国直接使用，李如国在该节事实中起次要作用。建议对李如国减轻处罚。

被告人万建平的辩护人认为，万建平并未介绍商品售卖，未从涉案店铺的售假行为中分得好处，因为帮助店铺装暗格和不装暗格的装修价格相同。建议法庭对被告人万建平减轻处罚。

【审判】

上海市普陀区人民法院经审理认为，被告人李如国作为韩城公司的股东和实际控制人，就韩城公司违法的财务管理、记账方式以及对"淘宝城"进行店铺出租、物业管理和市场经营的管理模式起到决定性作用，对"淘宝城"内历年来大量存在售假活动主观是明知的。被告人李如国利用其控制地位，以决策、授意和默许的方式，通过韩城公司及管理团队为商户提供租赁场所，容留商铺售假，放任商铺以装修暗格方式藏匿假货，并向商铺预先提供消息以逃避查处，对造成"淘宝城"内售假频发、装修藏匿、"黄牛"拉客、导游带团的不良业态负有直接责任。被告人李如国明知他人实施销售假冒注册商标商品的犯罪，待销售金额巨大，而为其提供经营场所等便利条件及帮助，构成共犯，应对已经刑事判决的"淘宝城"店铺售假犯罪行为承担共同犯罪的刑事责任，根据被告人李如国在共同犯罪中的作用，不能认定为从犯。并且，被告人李如国在明知经营箱包的商铺大量存在售假的情况下，决定每月向店铺收取扩大经营费，变相从商铺的售假行为中直接牟利，其违法所得应予追缴。被告人李如国明知是假冒注册商标的商品仍自行经营店铺予以销售，待销售金额巨大，该行为亦构成销售假冒注册商标的商品罪。根据相关司法解释的规定，销售明知是假冒注册商标的商品，销售金额数额巨大的，依法应当判处三年以上七年以下有期徒刑，并处罚金。鉴于涉案被查获商品均系待销售商品，因经营者意志以外的原因尚未进行销售，依法按照犯罪未遂认定，可以比照既遂犯从轻处罚。被告人李如国在庭审中能如实供述自己的罪行，依法可以从轻处罚。被告人李如国自愿通过家属预缴人民币 10 万元作为罚金，本院在量刑时酌情予以考虑。

被告人万建平明知他人销售假冒注册商标的商品，仍为其提供装修帮助，用于藏匿假冒商品、逃避查处，其行为已构成销售假冒注册商标的商品罪，依法应当按照销售假冒注册商标的商品罪的共犯论处。被告人万建平的装修帮助行为，可以认定为其在共同犯罪中起到次要作用，构成从犯，依法予以减轻处罚。鉴于涉案店铺被查获商品待销售金额巨大，因经营者意志以外的原因尚未进行销售，依法按照犯罪未遂认定，可以比照既遂犯从轻处罚。被告人万建平在庭审中能如实供述自己的罪行，依法可以从轻处罚。

综上，上海市普陀区人民法院依照《中华人民共和国刑法》第二百一十四条，第二十三条，第二十五条第一款，第二十七条，第六十七条第三款，第五十三条，第六十四条，第七十二条第一款、第三款，第七十三条第二款、第三款及《最高人民法院、最高人民检察院关于办理侵犯知识产权刑事案件具体应用法律若干问题的解释》第二条第二款、第十二条第一款、第十六条之规定，判决：一、被告人李如国犯销售假冒注册商标的商品罪，判处有期徒刑三年六个月，并处罚金人民币一百万元。二、被告人李如国的违法所得依法予以追缴。三、被告人万建平犯销售假冒注册商标的商品罪，判处有期徒刑一年十一个月，缓刑一年十一个月，并处罚金人民币两万元。

一审判决后，被告人李如国提出上诉。

上海市第三中级人民法院经审理后驳回上诉，维持原判。

【评析】

一、经营场所提供者容留销售假冒注册商标商品犯罪应当受刑法规制

本案中，被告人李如国的行为应当从两个层面进行分析：一方面，其明知

是假冒注册商标的商品仍自行经营店铺予以销售，且金额巨大，根据相关司法解释的规定，构成了销售假冒注册商标的商品罪；另一方面，其作为韩城公司的实际控制人，以决策、授意和默许的方式，通过韩城公司及管理团队为商场内商户提供租赁场所，容留商铺售假，并协助逃避工商检查。对于后一行为是否构成刑事犯罪并由刑法调整，相关法律并无直接规定，实践中也存在诸多争议。

有观点认为，被告李如国作为经营场所提供者和管理者，明知部分商户存在销售假冒注册商标的商品行为，却向其提供租赁场所，应认定为商标间接侵权行为。在这种情况下，基于刑法的谦抑性，不宜轻易将其纳入刑事处罚范畴。法院经审查后认为，从现有刑法条款来看，对于场所提供者协助销假行为责任认定并未设置相应的罪名，亦无直接的法律规定，但并不意味着此类行为可以降格至民事侵权范畴进行处分。首先，从行为目的上看，经营场所提供者明知商户存在销假行为，不仅不加制止，并意图通过容留销假获取不法利益，其主观上甚至等价于"直接销售"的犯罪故意。本案中，被告人李如国向商户提供经营场所期间，收取"淘宝城"部分商铺的经营箱包费用即扩大经营费合计达人民币93万余元，其目的并不在于维护正常的市场交易秩序，而是充当违法行为"保护伞"。其次，从行为对象上看，商户所涉销假行为并非一般的民事侵权，其销假次数、金额及范围达到了构成刑事犯罪的标准。本案中，涉案商户因犯销售假冒注册商标的商品罪被判处有罪判决的共计33件，涉案金额高达人民币3亿余元，远非一般的商标侵权行为所能比拟，在这种情况下，被告人李如国放任他人为商户销假装修暗格、预先提供消息以逃避监管，该行为等价于销售假冒注册商标的商品罪共犯中的"技术协助"。最后，从行为后果上看，场所提供者虽非直接的销假行为实施者，但其在制止犯罪行为上的不作为，客观上造成销假犯罪行为泛滥，并长期得不到遏制。综上，该行为与一般的商标间接侵权存在明显的区别，应当受到刑罚规制。

二、经营场所提供者容留销假入刑的路径选择

根据《最高人民法院、最高人民检察院、公安部关于办理侵犯知识产权刑事案件适用法律若干问题的意见》第十五条规定："明知他人实施侵犯知识产权犯罪，而为其提供互联网接入、服务器托管、网络存储空间、通讯传输通道、代收费、费用结算等服务的，以侵犯知识产权犯罪的共犯论处。"但实务中，侵犯知识产权犯罪共犯并不仅仅局限于上述行为，通常还包括生产、出租、运输、生活照顾及其他提供资金资助等辅助行为。在上述侵犯知识产权犯罪中，一方面要求存在直接的犯罪实施行为，另一方面，帮助犯实施了其他辅助行为，

客观上促进了实行行为的发生，且有助于加强共同犯罪人的犯罪意图。就本案而言，涉案商户因犯销售假冒注册商标的商品罪被判处有罪判决的共计 33 件，而被告人李如国作为涉案经营场所的实际控制人，长期出租经营场所放纵、容留商户售假并从中牟利，应当以销售假冒注册商标的商品罪帮助犯处理。

具体对于帮助行为的判断上，应该考虑其他犯罪行为人是否已经实施了犯罪行为。本案中，被告李如国明知他人通过商铺实施销售假冒注册商标商品犯罪行为，仍然放任商铺以装修暗格方式藏匿假货，并向商铺预先提供消息以逃避查处，对造成"淘宝城"内售假频发、装修藏匿、"黄牛"拉客、导游带团的不良业态负有直接责任，构成了销售假冒注册商标的商品罪的帮助犯。

三、个人犯罪与单位犯罪实质性区分

本案中，被告人李如国辩称，其虽为韩城公司实际控制人，但"淘宝城"被判刑事案件并非经过其之手，应当构成单位犯罪。根据《刑法》对单位犯罪的基本解释，单位犯罪是指公司、企业、事业单位、机关、团体为单位谋取非法利益或者以单位名义、经单位集体研究决定实施的行为。在认定单位犯罪时，不能脱离单位意志的整体性和单位利益的团体性两个特征。根据《最高人民法院关于审理单位犯罪案件具体应用法律有关问题的解释》第三条规定，盗用单位名义实施犯罪，违法所得由实施犯罪的个人私分的，依照刑法有关自然人犯罪的规定定罪处罚。本案中，被告李如国作为韩城公司的股东之一，但自始至终未见该公司召开股东会决议、董事会决议等，从现有证据可以看出，被告人李如国统管韩城公司财政、人事、店铺租赁，对"淘宝城"的经营管理拥有绝对控制权，在经营过程中收取扩大经营费、不与商铺经营者签订租赁协议的决定均由李如国一人作出，并非出自单位的整体意志。从款项流向来看，实际上李如国借韩城公司名义收款，而钱款均打入李如国个人账户，其违法行为所获利益只是由其个人获得。因此，无论从单位意志的整体性还是从单位利益的团体性看，本案均无确实充分的证据证明系单位犯罪，应当认定为李如国个人犯罪。

（撰稿人：华碧芳　王萌）

以货标分离的方式假冒
注册商标的行为性质的认定

——以李某某、徐某某假冒注册商标罪案为视角

【提要】

本案系涉外侵犯知识产权刑事案件，对司法实务中颇具争议的货标分离的行为进行了准确定性。从商标权人的商标专用权而言，在境外人员实施货标结合行为之前，其商标专用权被假冒和侵犯，故应认定境内外人员均系假冒注册商标罪的实施者，构成假冒注册商标罪。

【案情】

公诉机关：上海市闵行区人民检察院

被告人：李某某、徐某某

案由：假冒注册商标罪

一审案号：（2014）闵刑（知）初字第 72 号

2010 年 5 月起，被告人李某某伙同徐某某等人为牟取非法利益，由被告人李某某负责联系客户、安排订单，由被告人徐某某辅助李某某跟进订单及代为付款、记账等，在国内采购假冒 UGG、HUNTER、Ray·Ban 等注册商标的雪地靴、雨靴、眼镜等商品，并采用谎报品名、货标分离的方式，通过 EMS、DHL 等物流公司跨境寄售至英国。2013 年 1 月，被告人李某某、徐某某根据英国客户要求，通过货标分离寄售的方式，将假冒 Ray·Ban、CHANEL 注册商标的太阳眼镜寄售至英国，并利用西联汇款及现金等方式收取货款折合人民币 12 万余元（以下币种均为人民币）。2013 年 2 月，上海海关在对上述包裹清关检验时，查获 Ray·Ban 注册商标标识 12 357 个，CHANEL 注册商标标识 2000 个、CHANEL 眼镜布 800 块。经商标权利人鉴定，上述标识及货品均系假冒产品。

2013 年 11 月 19 日、2014 年 3 月 26 日，被告人李某某、徐某某分别经公安机关电话通知后，主动投案并如实供述了犯罪事实。经查实，2010 年 5 月 4 日至 2013 年 2 月 1 日，李某某、徐某某相关账户的销售金额折合人民币共计 425 万余元。

公诉机关指控被告人李某某、徐某某的行为已构成销售假冒注册商标的商品罪，且属共同犯罪，提请本院依照《中华人民共和国刑法》第二百一十四条之规定予以判处。

被告人李某某、徐某某在开庭审理中对上述事实均无异议。

被告人李某某的辩护人认为：在 425 万元非法经营数额中，部分商品没有配备注册商标的标识，系英国客户直接购买标识；被告人李某某系根据英国客户的要求，将假冒注册商标的商品销售予特定的两个英国客户，并非直接销售给不特定人群，其行为系提供中介服务，在整体犯罪中起辅助作用，对中国的市场经济未造成实际损害，社会危害性较小。

被告人徐某某的辩护人认为：被告人徐某某系自首，仅领取工资，没有额外获利，在犯罪中起辅助作用，属于从犯；被告人徐某某于 2011 年后参与犯罪，其仅应对其参与的犯罪承担法律责任。

【审判】

上海市闵行区人民法院经审理查明：2010 年 1 月至 2013 年 1 月，被告人李某某采购并销售假冒 UGG、HUGO BOSS、Ray·Ban、POLO、ARMANI JEANS、GUCCI、BOSS、DIOR、MARC JACOBS、CHANEL 等注册商标的商品（含标识）计人民币992 029.40元，美元26 611.20元。具体有 13 节事实，均有相应的电子邮件（含合同订单）、公司电子台账、银行账目明细及相关商标权利人的商标注册资料等予以佐证。根据被告人李某某公司的电子账目、被告人李某某个人中国银行账目明细以及上海财瑞会计师事务所有限公司出具的司法鉴定意见书，公诉机关指控被告人李某某已销售假冒注册商标的商品的金额，共达人民币 425 万余元人民币，被告人李某某也基本予以认可，但本院认为，除上述已查明的 13 节共计金额 117.3 万余元的犯罪事实，其余指控金额存在或缺乏对应的合同订单，或相对应的商品无商标注册资料，或未使用注册商标等情形，不能形成完整的证据链予以佐证，故本院无法予以查实或予以认定。被告人徐某某自 2011 年 3 月后辅助被告人李某某跟进订单、代为付款并予记账，其参与的犯罪数额为人民币949 964.40元。

被告人李某某接受境外特定客户的订单，采购假冒注册商标的商品，其伙同被告人徐某某，通过合同订单，明确需要的假冒注册商标的商品款式，并以货物和标识分离的方式寄售予境外客户。本院认为，被告人李某某、徐某某的行为系根据分工，在中国境内分别订制商品、假冒注册商标的标识，实际是指使他人制造、生产假冒注册商标的商品或标识，因明知上述行为的违法犯罪性，故通过货物和标识分离的方式寄送至境外以逃避海关监管，再由境外人员完成商品与标识的组合成为假冒注册商标的商品后予以销售，即是在未经注册商标权利人许可或授权的情况下，在同种商品上使用与权利人注册商标相同的商标而牟取非法利益，而并非直接采购已经作为成品的假冒注册商标的商品后予以销售。被告人李某某、徐某某的犯罪行为发生在中国境内，均应构成假冒注册商标罪。关于非法经营金额，被告人李某某应以其制造、储存、运输、销售侵权产品的实际销售价格计算，共计人民币1 173 733.30元；被告人徐某某参与的非法经营数额为人民币949 964.40元。

综上，本院认为，被告人李某某、徐某某违反中华人民共和国商标管理法规，为牟取非法利益，未经注册商标权利人许可，在同一种商品上使用与其注册商标相同的商标，情节特别严重，其行为均已构成假冒注册商标罪，且属共同犯罪，应依法予以惩处。被告人李某某在共同犯罪中起主要作用，系主犯；被告人徐某某在共同犯罪中起次要、辅助作用，系从犯，应当从轻处罚。被告人李某某、徐某某自动投案并如实供述犯罪事实，系自首，可以减轻处罚。公诉机关指控的罪名不当，本院予以纠正。

据此，依照《中华人民共和国刑法》相关规定，判决：一、被告人李某某犯假冒注册商标罪，判处有期徒刑一年六个月，并处罚金人民币五十万元及驱逐出境；二、被告人徐某某犯假冒注册商标罪，判处有期徒刑一年，缓刑一年，并处罚金人民币二万元；三、查获的假冒注册商标的商品及标识予以没收；四、违法所得予以追缴。

【评析】

本案系被告人从不同渠道分别订制、采购商品及假冒注册商标的标识，通过货标分离的方式寄送至境外，由境外人员完成组装并销售，判决结果明确了被告人的行为系假冒注册商标的行为。本案中部分指控金额由于缺乏相关证据，无法形成完整的证据链，故人民法院对该部分金额未予认定，具有重大示范意义。

本案的争议焦点在于通过货标分离的方式进行销假的行为应当如何定性。审理中关于上述问题存在两种观点，一种观点认为被告人李某某、徐某某根据分工，在中国境内分别订制商品、假冒注册商标的标识，因明知上述行为的违法犯罪性，故通过货物和标识分离的方式寄送至境外以逃避海关监管，由境外人员最终完成商品与标识的组合后将假冒注册商标的商品予以销售，被告人李某某、徐某某的犯罪行为发生在中国境内，构成假冒注册商标罪；另一种观点认为被告人李某某、徐某某主观上仅从是商品的流通环节牟利，故构成销售假冒注册商标的商品罪。

《中华人民共和国刑法》第二百一十三条对假冒注册商标罪规定"未经注册商标人许可，在同一种商品上使用与其注册商标相同的商标，情节严重的……"；在第二百一十四条将销售假冒注册商标的商标罪规定为"销售明知是假冒注册商标的商品，销售金额数额较大的……"；根据《最高人民法院、最高人民检察院关于办理侵犯知识产权刑事案件具体应用法律若干问题的解释（一）》第八条第二款规定："《刑法》第二百一十三条规定的'使用'，是指将注册商标或假冒的注册商标用于商品、商品包装或者容器以及产品说明书、商品交易文书，或者将注册商标或者假冒的注册商标用于广告宣传、展览以及其他商业活动的行为"，而刑法关于销售假冒注册商标的商品罪的规定则主要是从流通环节进行规制，即行为人本身并无制作或者另行购入非法制作的注册商标标识的行为，仅是销售成套的假冒注册商标的商品行为。

结合本案案情，被告人李某某、徐某某的行为系根据分工，在中国境内分别订制成套的商品以及假冒注册商标的标识，每件订购的商品及假冒注册商标的标识均存在一一对应的关系，被告人李某某、徐某某因明知上述行为的违法犯罪性，为逃避海关监管，故通过将货物和标识分离的方式寄送至境外，由境外人员完成商品与标识的组合后将假冒注册商标的商品予以销售，换言之，被告人李某某、徐某某于通过货标分离的方式寄送商品前实施了商品及假冒注册商标标识的订购行为，并根据订单将二者的数量、型号进行了匹配，从商标权人的角度而言，其商标专用权被假冒和侵犯在此时已经被确定，构成法律规定的"使用"行为，而境外人员为了完成假冒注册商标商品的销售行为，必然将非法制造的注册商标标识粘贴于相关商品之上。故本案被告人李某某、徐某某是假冒注册商标行为的实施者。李某某、徐某某的行为系在未经注册商标权利人许可或授权的情况下，在同种商品上使用与权利人注册商标相同的商标而牟取非法利益，而并非直接采购已经作为成品的假冒注册商标的商品后予以销售，故构成假冒注册商标罪。

（撰稿人：田力烽　季秋玲）

计算机软件著作权侵权认定中
"实质性相似"的理解与认定

——被告人汪洁等侵犯著作权罪案

【提要】

对计算机软件实质性相似的认定，应根据行业惯例和软件特点，在排除公共文件和第三方文件的基础上，对软件的服务器端以及客户端程序进行比对，如果经比对两款软件文件相似度比例高，且出现了相同的个性化信息，除了解释为复制而无其他，则应当认定构成实质性相似。

【案情】

公诉机关：上海市徐汇区人民检察院

被告人（上诉人）：汪洁

被告人（上诉人）：万臻

被告人（上诉人）：孙国龙

被告人（上诉人）：娄波

被告人：金文兵

被告人：沈良君

被告人：黄文峰

被告人：安明浩

案由：侵犯著作权罪

一审案号：（2013）徐刑（知）初字第 20 号

二审案号：（2014）沪一中刑（知）终字第 7 号

2006 年 9 月，上海乌龙网络技术发展有限公司（以下简称乌龙公司）注册成立，以通过互联网运营英语学习软件为主要经营活动。2008 年 10 月，乌龙公司对其所拥有全部权利的《乌龙学苑1.0版》英语教育网络学习软件在国家版权局进行了计算机软件著作权登记。2009年起，乌龙公司进行了股权变更及增资扩股，被告人汪洁为公司法定代表人。至2011年，乌龙公司又陆续开发并运营《乌龙学苑2.0版》及《乌龙学苑3.0版》英语学习软件，上述两款软件均未重新作软件著作权登记。

2012年2月，上海家翊星信息科技有限公司（以下简称为家翊星公司），工商登记股东为许灿及娄波，法定代表人为许灿，实际控制人及经营负责人系汪洁及万臻，万臻担任总经理。被告人汪洁及万臻在该公司成立前后，招聘了多名乌龙公司前员工进入家翊星公司，被告人汪洁安排被告人金文兵、孙国龙、沈良君、黄文锋、安明浩等复制《乌龙学苑3.0版》软件服务器端及客户端程序下的大量文件，制成《家育星》软件，汪洁直接对制作《家育星》软件提供策划及指导，万臻负责公司的日常行政管理工作，之后以家翊星公司的名义通过互联网运营《家育星》软件，并以招揽代理商及向代理商出售该软件的点卡获利。在上述活动中，金文兵、沈良君、黄文锋主要从事运营《家育星》软件的网页及维护、孙国龙主要从事服务器的架设及维护、安明浩曾参与家翊星公司前期成立工作及上述软件的测试活动，还参与后续软件推广及营销活动，被告人娄波除投入家翊星公司成立的部分资金外，还参与《家育星》软件制作的前期策划及后续营销活动。

根据上海辰星电子数据司法鉴定中心作出的鉴定意见，《乌龙学苑3.0版》与《家育星》软件在各自服务器端程序及客户端程序上均存在实质性相似；经司法审计，2012年5月至同年12月期间，被告人汪洁、万臻、金文兵、孙国龙、沈良君、黄文锋、娄波、安明浩等以家翊星公司名义运营《家育星》软件获取的非法经营额为人民币1 060 273元。

公诉机关认定，被告人汪洁、万臻、金文兵、孙国龙、沈良君、黄文锋、娄波、安明浩结伙以营利为目的，未经著作权人许可，复制发行其计算机软件，非法经营数额达人民币106万余元，属于有其他特别严重情节，其行为均已触犯《中华人民共和国刑法》第二百一十七条第（一）项、第二十五条第一款之规定，应当以侵犯著作权罪追究其共同犯罪的刑事责任。

【审判】

上海市徐汇区人民法院经审理认为：著作权人有权对软件行使修改权并对修改后的软件继续享有著作权，《乌龙学苑3.0版》软件，系乌龙公司在其享有著作权的《乌龙学苑 1.0 版》《乌龙学苑 2.0 版》软件基础上进行修改后的升级版，乌龙公司对《乌龙学苑 3.0 版》软件享有著作权。根据家翊星公司的实际出资以及日常经营管理情况，可以认定被告人汪洁、万臻系家翊星公司的实际控制者和所有者，其在未经乌龙公司同意的情况下，指使原为乌龙公司员工或代理商的被告人娄波、金文兵、孙国龙、沈良君、黄文锋、安明浩，通过复制乌龙公司享有著作权的《乌龙学苑 3.0 版》软件相关文件的方式，制成《家育星》软件并投入运营。经比对，该两款软件虽然并非完全一致，但主体结构、功能实质性相同，系实质性相似，构成刑法意义上的非法复制行为，应当以侵犯著作权罪定罪处罚。其中，被告人汪洁、万臻在共同犯罪中起主要作用，是主犯，被告人娄波、金文兵、孙国龙、沈良君、黄文锋、安明浩在共同犯罪中起次要、辅助作用，系从犯，且犯罪情节较轻或轻微，依法应当减轻或者免除处罚。被告人汪洁、万臻、金文兵、沈良君、黄文锋、安明浩在审理中虽对自己的行为性质有所辩解，但可认定就事实能如实供述，依法可予以从轻处罚；被告人娄波、孙国龙系自首，依法可予以从轻处罚。

依照《中华人民共和国刑法》第二百一十七条第一项，第二十五条第一款，第二十六条第一款，第二十七条，第五十三条，第六十四条，第六十七条第一款、第三款，第七十二条第一款、第三款，第七十三条第二款、第三款及《最高人民法院、最高人民检察院关于办理侵犯知识产权刑事案件具体应用法律若干问题的解释》第五条第二款规定，判决：被告人汪洁犯侵犯著作权罪，判处有期徒刑三年，并处罚金人民币十万元；被告人万臻犯侵犯著作权罪，判处有期徒刑三年，缓刑三年，并处罚金人民币五万元；被告人娄波犯侵犯著作权罪，判处有期徒刑六个月，缓刑一年，并处罚金人民币一万元；被告人金文兵、孙国龙、沈良君、黄文锋、安明浩犯侵犯著作权罪，免予刑事处罚；各被告人处查扣的电脑、硬盘、《家育星》软件学习卡等与本案犯罪有关的物品予以没收。

一审判决后，被告人汪洁、万臻、孙国龙、娄波不服，向上海市第一中级人民法院提起上诉。

上海市第一中级人民法院经审理后认为，一审判决事实清楚，证据确实、充分，定罪准确，审判程序合法，故裁定驳回上诉，维持原判。

【评析】

本案系一起典型的员工为谋求私利，组织成立新公司窃取、复制并发行原公司计算机软件，从而侵犯权利人计算机软件著作权的新类型犯罪案件。我国刑法规定，侵犯著作权罪的客观表现为复制发行。与一般作品简单的机械复制不同，计算机软件的复制行为通常具有一定的专业性和隐蔽性，技术含量较高，需要法院从法律和技术方面对软件的同一性做出认定，进而确定是否侵犯著作权。关于计算机软件的侵权判定，目前从法律层面上各国还未有明确的统一标准，实践对此亦在不断探索，就现阶段来说，"实质性相似＋接触＋排除合理解释"原则是我国司法实践中比较通行的判定标准之一，即如果被控软件与权利软件相同或者实质性相似，同时有证据证明被诉侵权人（或者被告人）接触了权利软件，且其对两款软件的实质性相似无法作出合理解释，即可判定侵权或犯罪行为成立。本案中，被告人均系乌龙公司前员工，且其均承认《家育星》软件确系在复制乌龙学苑部分软件的基础上得以制成，因此，"接触"与"排除合理解释"并不难认定。本案的关键在于被告人的"复制"行为是否使涉案两款软件达到"相同"或"实质性相似"，从而构成对乌龙学苑软件著作权的侵犯。对此，法院的判决明确，对计算机软件实质性相似的认定，应当根据行业惯例和软件特点，在排除公共文件和第三方文件的基础上，对软件的服务器端以及客户端程序文件进行比对，如果经比对两款软件文件相似度比例高，且出现了相同的个性化信息，除了解释为复制而无其他，则应当认定构成实质性相似从而构成刑法意义上的复制。

一、实质性相似的认定应区分思想与表达

计算机软件作品同样遵循的是著作权法思想表达二分法的保护原则，将思想与表达进行抽离后，实质性相似的认定是对两个软件作品表达方式进行比对后做出的综合判断。鉴于计算机软件有其特殊性——既是技术方案，亦是思维成果，兼有"实用功能"与"文字作品"的双重属性，故而导致计算机软件的思想和表达经常互相渗透，难以进行明确的划分。美国联邦第二巡回法院在Computer A Ssociates International Inc 诉 Altai, Inc 一案中，确定了抽象、过滤、比较三步法，尝试将两者进行区分。所谓抽象，即是将两款软件中不受著作权法保护的思想抽离出来；所谓过滤，是将两款软件中相似的但属于公共领域的内容过滤掉；最后，将经过抽象和过滤后的剩下内容进行比对，以此确定是否构成实质性相似。这一方法为后来多数法院所沿用，对于我国的司法实践也有重要的借鉴意义。本案中，在对两款软件进行实质性相似比对之前，法院确定，应当首先将两款软件进行解析，然后将其中的公共文件以及第三方文件剔除，最后再进行比对，这一做法，即可视为系对于抽象、过滤、对比这一方法的实

际运用，不仅确定了计算机软件的保护范围，也保证了实质性相似比对的针对性和准确性。

二、实质性相似的比对对象应根据行业惯例和软件特点进行确定

两款软件是否实质性相似，不能仅从用户界面、软件功能等方面来看，而应当根据软件的特点和行业惯例，科学地确定实质性相似的比对对象。根据《计算机软件保护条例》的规定，计算机软件的保护范围分为计算机程序及其相关文档，因此计算机软件的实质性相似也应当分为两类：一是文档部分实质性相似，二是程序部分实质性相似。由于文档类似于文字作品，其是具体可见的，无需经过专业鉴定比对即可确定是否相同或类似，且根据本案的实际情况，涉案软件的著作权登记申请表上明确载明，整套软件分为客户端程序和服务器端程序两部分，因此，从涉案软件的特点出发，该两款计算机软件的实质性相似比对应当是对客户端程序和服务器端程序进行比对。此外，根据行业惯例，在对类似的计算机软件进行比对时，采取就软件客户端程序进行比对的方法居多，因此，法院结合涉案软件特点以及行业惯例，确定两款软件的客户端程序和服务器端程序为比对对象，可以反映出两款软件的核心和全貌，是科学的，也是合理的。本案中，被告人辩解未被列入比对对象的语音包等内容，虽然也系软件的组成部分，但其对两款软件实质性相似的判断无实质性影响，因而无须再对其进行比对。

三、实质性相似应结合相似度比例以及个性化特征进行综合认定

在确定实质性相似的比对对象为两款软件的客户端和服务器端程序后，应对客户端程序以及服务器端程序下的文件以及文件目录分别进行整体比对，文件以及文件目录相似度比例越高，则两款软件构成实质性相似的概率就越大。本案中，无论是客户端程序还是服务器端程序下的文件以及文件目录，经过比对，其相似度比例均达到了70%以上，远远超出了正常软件的相似度范围，复制的可能性极高。然而，对于两款软件程序文件中多少比例的文件以及文件目录相似可以认定为构成实质性相似，行业并没有统一的标准，故仅仅依靠程序文件相似的比例，并不能轻易作出两款软件具有实质性相似的结论。对于计算机软件的实质性相似判断，需要在量化的基础上结合其他因素进行综合性的判断。实践中，在编写程序时，开发者往往会在软件程序中加入一些个人或者开发状况的信息，如开发者的姓名、邮箱、公司等的签名信息等。这些信息一般来说具有特定含义，具有唯一性。如果在对两款软件进行比对时，出现了相同

的个性化信息，则排除合理解释，可以证明两个软件之间具有复制的盖然性。本案中，法院正是考虑到被诉侵权的《家育星》软件中存有"乌龙学院""汪洁"以及带有乌龙名称的网址等属于《乌龙学苑》软件独有的个性化信息，结合两款软件具有极高的相似度比例，对两款软件的实质相似性做出了最终确认，从而判定被告人构成了侵犯著作权罪。

（撰稿人：王利民　刘秋雨）

假冒注册商标罪中"非法经营数额"的司法认定与思考

——被告单位上海祥运箱包有限公司等假冒注册商标罪案

【提要】

在现有证据无法证实假冒注册商标的商品标价或售价的情况下，不应简单地以被侵权产品的市场中间价作为非法经营额的认定标准，而应充分考虑现实中假货与正品价格的巨大差距，从罪责刑相一致这一角度出发，合理确定侵权产品的销售价格，从而准确地对被告人进行定罪量刑。

【案情】

公诉机关：上海市松江区人民检察院

被告人（上诉人）：黄云火

被告单位：上海祥运箱包有限公司

被告人：朱海勇

被告人：姚天观

一审案号：（2014）徐刑（知）初字第35号

二审案号：（2015）沪三中刑终字第4号

2011年5月至2011年12月，被告人朱海勇在经营上海伟塑新型建材有限公司（以下简称伟塑公司）期间，未经商标权利人浙江伟星新型建材股份有限公司同意并授权，以提供模具、来料加工的形式委托由被告人黄云火经营的、被告人姚天观为具体生产负责人的被告单位上海祥运箱包有限公司（以下简称祥运公司）生产假冒注册商标伟星的 PP–R 塑料管件。被告单位祥运公司及被告人黄云火、姚天观共计为被告人朱海勇加工生产各类塑料管件三十九万余件，剔除注明为飞马牌的塑料管件后，可认定假冒注册商标伟星的 PP–R 塑料管件的数量为二十一万余件，其正品的市场中间价达三百余万元。2012 年 8 月 17 日，公安机关从被告人朱海勇的厂房内查获经鉴定为假冒注册商标伟星的 PP - R 塑料管材 5400 米、塑料管件 12 710 件、标有"伟星管业"字样的合格证 1 箱及便携机 1 台。

另查，被告人朱海勇因 2011 年年初生产、销售假冒注册商标伟星的塑料管材及配件，于 2012 年 6 月 6 日被临海市公安局刑事拘留，同年 7 月 13 日被逮捕，2013 年 4 月 26 日被浙江省临海市人民法院以假冒注册商标罪判处有期徒刑一年二个月，并处罚金人民币十四万元，2013 年 8 月 5 日刑满释放当日，因本案被上海市公安局松江分局刑事拘留，2013 年 9 月 11 日变更强制措施为取保候审。2014 年 2 月 24 日，被告人姚天观经公安机关电话通知到案，2014 年 2 月 27 日，被告人黄云火经公安机关电话通知到案。

公诉机关认定，被告人朱海勇伙同被告单位祥运公司的负责人被告人黄云火及其他直接责任人员被告人姚天观，未经注册商标所有人许可，在同一种商品上使用与其注册商标相同的商标，情节特别严重，其行为已触犯《中华人民共和国刑法》第二百一十三条、第二百二十条、第二十五条第一款，犯罪事实清楚，证据确实、充分，应以假冒注册商标罪追究其刑事责任。

被告人朱海勇及其辩护人辩称，公诉机关指控的侵权产品的数量无充分证据加以证明，被告单位祥运公司的生产统计表不能证明生产数量为二十多万件；关于侵权产品的价值，公诉机关是按正品的 3.6 折计算，缺乏依据，应该按被告人实际销售时的 2.2 折计算更加合理。

被告人黄云火及其辩护人辩称，对侵权产品的总数量有异议，被告单位统计表中的部分产品不是伟星牌的，即使统计表注明是伟星牌的，但实际产品是否标注了"伟星"字样也无法查清；对起诉时认定的犯罪金额有异议，侵权产品的价值应该按实际销售时的正品的 2.2 折计算。

【审判】

上海市徐汇区人民法院经审理认为：本案中各方对被告人朱海勇委托被告单位祥运公司加工伟星牌塑料管件的事实均无异议，争议焦点主要在于具体的数量以及非法经营数额。根据祥运公司销售统计表的记载，被告单位为被告人朱海勇加工的全部塑料管件的数量为 392 992 件，剔除销售统计表中明确注明为其他品牌塑料管件的数量，应认定假冒伟星品牌的塑料管件的数量为 217 577 件。被告人朱海勇辩称该总数中包含了部分未假冒伟星商标的塑料管件，但并无确实充分的证据证实，且公安机关在其厂房内查获的假冒塑料管件均标注有伟星商标，故对该项辩解不予采纳。关于非法金额数额，由于被告人未提供其实际销售价，故公诉机关起诉时按被侵权产品的市场价乘以批发折扣 3.6 折认定，但考虑到现实中，侵权产品的销售价格，无论是批发还是零售，一般情况下均会实际低于同类正品，另被告人朱海勇同时期在因生产销售假冒伟星牌注册商标的塑料管材及配件被浙江省临海市人民法院处以刑罚的另案中，系以伟星正品 2.2 折的价格计算销售侵权产品，故从有利于被告人的角度出发，在本案中酌情按被侵权产品市场价格的 2.2 折计算非法经营额，计六十七万余元。综上，被告人朱海勇伙同被告单位祥运公司的负责人被告人黄云火及其他直接责任人员被告人姚天观，未经注册商标所有人许可，在同一种商品上使用与其注册商标相同的商标，侵权产品的数量达二十一万余件，非法经营额达六十七万余元，均属情节特别严重，其行为已构成假冒注册商标罪，应予处罚，公诉机关指控成立。各被告人及被告单位系共同犯罪，被告人朱海勇系主犯，被告单位祥运公司及被告人黄云火、姚天观系从犯，依法应当减轻处罚。被告人朱海勇在判决宣告以后，刑罚执行完毕以前，又发现其在判决宣告以前还有其他罪没有判决，系漏罪，依法应当数罪并罚。被告单位祥运公司及被告人黄云火、姚天观系自首，依法可以从轻处罚。

依照《中华人民共和国刑法》第二百一十三条，第二百二十条，第二十五条第一款，第二十六条第一款、第四款，第二十七条，第五十三条，第六十四条，第六十七条第一款，第六十九条，第七十条，第七十二条第一款、第三款，第七十三条第二款、第三款及《最高人民法院、最高人民检察院关于办理侵犯知识产权刑事案件具体应用法律若干问题的解释》第一条规定，判决：被告单位上海祥运箱包有限公司犯假冒注册商标罪，判处罚金二万元；被告人朱海勇犯假冒注册商标罪，判处有期徒刑三年六个月，并处罚金十万元，与前罪原判有期徒刑一年二个月并处罚金十四万元合并，决定执行有期徒刑四年，并处罚金二十四万元；被告人黄云火犯假冒注册商标罪，判处有期徒刑一年，缓刑一年，并处罚金一万元；被告人姚天观犯假冒注册商标罪，判处有期徒刑九个月，缓刑一年，并处罚金五千元；被告单位上海祥运箱包有限公司、被告人朱海勇、黄云火、姚天观的违法所得予以追缴；查获的假冒注册商标的商品、商标标识及作案工具等与本案犯罪有关的物品予以没收。

一审判决后，被告人黄云火不服提起上诉，后在上海市第三中级人民法院审理期间撤回上诉，一审判决已生效。

【评析】

在假冒注册商标罪的司法实践中，就如何认定非法经营数额存在着不同做法和理论争议。《最高人民法院、最高人民检察院关于办理侵犯知识产权刑事案件具体应用法律若干问题的解释》（以下简称《知识产权解释》）对"非法经营数额"作了明确定义，并规定已销售的侵权产品的价值，按照实际销售的价格计算。制造、储存、运输和未销售的侵权产品的价值，按照标价或者已经查清的侵权产品的实际销售平均价格计算。侵权产品没有标价或者无法查清其实际销售价格的，按照被侵权产品的市场中间价格计算。依据上述规定，"非法经营数额"应按照以下先后顺序认定：（1）标价或已查清的侵权产品的实际销售平均价格；（2）被侵权产品的市场中间价格。上述认定方法不是任选的，而是递进的，只有按照前种方法无法认定时，才适用后种方法进行计算。然而实践中，被告人往往没有完整、正规的财务账册，涉案商品的标价也无法查清，在此情况下，多数案件会采用"被侵权产品的市场中间价格"进行计算，由此便引发了对该种做法的诸多争议。

一、对"市场中间价"法的评价

毋庸置疑，以"被侵权产品的市场中间价"计算非法经营数额既可以节约侦查和司法成本，又可以防止打击不力，对犯罪者起到强大的震慑作用，但在未穷尽一切手段确定侵权产品实际销售价格的情况下，不宜贸然将"被侵权产品的市场中间价格"作为计算非法经营数额的标准，主要理由如下。

其一，该种做法有违"刑法谦抑"之精神。在侵权产品明显低于正品市场价格销售（即"以假售假"）的情况下，如果以"被侵权产品的市场中间价格"作为假冒商品的货值认定标准，其实际是以一个被告人不可能的销售价格来计算其预期销售金额。实践中，民事案件尚不能贸然以正品价格来论侵权人因侵权所获利益，更多是根据权利人的权利状态、侵权的恶意程度、后果及影响等因素综合确定侵权赔偿额，在更强调证据证明力、证明标准的刑事案件中更应持谨慎态度。仅依据查获的侵权产品数量以及正品价格对其苛以刑罚，有时会显得不科学也不公平，亦与"刑法谦抑"精神背道而驰。

其二，该种做法不符合"量刑平等"之原则。"平等适用法律"是我国刑法确立的基本原则之一，它蕴含着"定罪平等""量刑平等"和"行刑平等"三大要求。在被告人"以假售假"、消费者"知假买假"的情况下，如果教条地按司法解释之规定，能查清实际销售价格的，以较低的销售价格计算非法经营额，无法查清实际销售价格或标价的，则按照相差甚远的"被侵权产品市场中间价格"来计算非法经营额，那么在销售同样数量假冒商品的情形下，不同被告人将会因法院是否能查清实际销售价格而面临不同的刑罚处罚，这明显有违"量刑平等"之要求。

二、对"市场中间价"适用之建议

从知识产权刑事保护的实际需要来看，"市场中间价"确实有其存在的必要性与合理性，但应有严格的适用条件，必须符合主客观一致原则。在假冒注册商标罪中"以假充真"的，假冒商品的售价与被侵权产品的市场价格几乎没有差异，若侵权产品没有标价或者无法查清其实际销售价格的，则应按照被侵权产品的市场中间价格计算，当然还需先证明被告人确系"以假充真"，通过取证被告人的销售地点、销售方式、销售渠道等证明被告人确系以侵权产品冒充正品销售，以此达到混淆消费者之非法目的。在"以假售假"情形下，假冒商品的实际售价与被侵权产品的市场价格往往差异巨大，假冒注册商标罪又鲜有未遂的情形，无法在金额与实际价值不符的情况下按未遂情节加以调整，故实际销售价格应成为侵权产品货值金额的首选计算标准。无实际销售价格的，应以侵权产品的销售标价为准。如果侵权产品既无标价，也无进货、销售记录，则可通过讯问被告人获取其以往的销售价格、结合证人证言查询销售情况、通过市场调查、委托评估等获取侵权产品的市场中间价等方式，相互印证，从而确定被告人的实际销售价格，罚当其罪。本案中，法院即是根据被告人自述的以往商品的销售价格，再通过调查同期其他案件中其销售同类产品的价格，最终对涉案侵权产品的销售价格进行了认定，从而正确地对被告人进行了定罪量刑，体现了法院在司法裁判中一贯秉承的"有利于被告人"和"量刑平等"原则。

（撰稿人：王利民　刘秋雨）

知识产权行政案件

计算机软件商业秘密构成
法定要件之举证责任

——上海牟乾广告有限公司诉上海市静安区市场监督管理局、
上海商派网络科技有限公司、酷美（上海）信息技术有限公司
行政处罚上诉案

【提要】

本案是上海市高级人民法院知识产权庭受理的首例行政案件，涉及对计算机软件商业秘密的法律保护。计算机软件可以从著作权或商业秘密之不同路径寻求法律保护，但两种权利的法定构成条件完全不同。行政案件中，第三人主张其软件构成商业秘密，而行政机关也认定软件构成商业秘密并进行查处时，应对该软件符合《反不正当竞争法》第十条第三款规定之条件进行举证。如行政机关未能举证证明其已对计算机软件符合"不为公众所知悉"之要件进行审查，即使该软件符合商业秘密的其他构成要件，其所做出的相应行政处罚亦缺乏事实和法律依据。人民法院对该行政处罚错误部分依法予以撤销，充分体现了我国知识产权保护"司法主导"原则。

【案情】

上诉人（原审被告）：上海市静安区市场监督管理局（以下简称静安市场监管局）。

上诉人（原审第三人）：上海商派网络科技有限公司（以下简称商派公司）。

上诉人（原审第三人）：酷美（上海）信息技术有限公司（以下简称酷美公司）。

被上诉人（原审原告）：上海牟乾广告有限公司（以下简称牟乾公司）。

案由：行政处罚决定纠纷

一审案号：（2016）沪73行初1号

二审案号：（2016）沪行终738号

原告牟乾公司由上海管易软件科技有限公司（以下简称管易公司）变更名称而来。商派公司和酷美公司认为管易公司网站上进行虚假宣传，同时恶意高薪聘请其员工，获取其软件源代码及相关文档，上述行为构成虚假宣传和商业秘密侵权，故向上海市工商行政管理局闸北分局（以下简称闸北工商分局）进行举报。接报后，闸北工商分局对管易公司的电脑数据和相关网页进行了取证，并委托上信司法鉴定所对取证数据与商派公司提供的光盘数据进行比对。后该所出具司法鉴定意见书认为：管易公司电脑中文件"可以认定的部分"与商派公司提供的相关软件代码相同，可视为来自同一来源；并存在相同的相关文档。据此，上海市闸北区市场监督管理局（闸北工商分局与相关局职能整合组建成，以下简称闸北市场监管局）对管易公司作出行政处罚决定：一、管易公司在网站发布不实信息的行为构成虚假宣传，责令其停止违法行为、消除影响和罚款人民币一万元整的处罚。二、商派公司和酷美公司共同研发了涉案软件，管易公司招聘了原商派公司和酷美公司参与软件研发并签订保密协议的相关人员，且在上述人员的工作电脑中存有从商派公司处获取的涉案软件和文档。结合司法鉴定意见书，可以认定管易公司实施了侵犯商业秘密行为，决定对其作出责令停止违法行为，罚款人民币贰万元整的处罚。综上，合并执行处罚：一、责令停止虚假宣传行为，消除影响；二、责令停止侵犯商业秘密行为；三、罚款人民币叁万元整。

牟乾公司不服该处罚决定，向上海知识产权法院提起行政诉讼。

【审判】

上海知识产权法院经审理认为，闸北市场监管局就牟乾公司虚假宣传行为所作的行政处罚决定正确，予以维持。但因商派公司和酷美公司未指明涉案信息中秘密点范围，误将软件程序及文档都作为商业秘密的保护对象。而闸北市场监管局也未确定技术信息的范围，无法对其是否达到"不为所属领域的相关人员普遍知悉和容易获得"的商业秘密程度进行判断。故闸北市场监管局对于管易公司构成商业秘密侵权的认定应当予以撤销。据此，判决：一、撤销行政处罚决定中因认定管易公司侵犯商业秘密所作的行政处罚决定，即"责令停止违法行为""罚款人民币贰万元整"；二、驳回原告其余诉请。

一审判决后，静安市场监管局（因上海市闸北区与静安区两区合并，静安市场监管局承继原闸北市场监管局的职责）、商派公司、酷美公司均不服，分别提起上诉。

上海市高级人民法院经审理认为，涉案信息是否构成商业秘密，需对其是否符合商业秘密的四个法定要件进行审查。在行政诉讼中，认定商业秘密侵权行为存在并由此作出行政处罚的行政机关，应当承担民事诉讼中权利主张人的举证义务，即对其认定的商业秘密符合法定要件承担举证责任。本案中，静安市场监管局应当首先证明涉案信息处于"不为公众所知悉"的状态，即客观上无法从公共渠道直接获取，不能仅仅从持有人已采取了保密措施即推定相关信息必然不为其所属领域的相关人员普遍知悉和容易获得。只有当涉案信息符合秘密性要件后，行政机关才可进一步对于其是否具有价值性、实用性以及持有人是否采取了必要的保密措施等要件进行认定，以确定本案是否存在商业秘密。静安市场监管局在未能证明涉案信息系"不为公众所知悉"的情况下，对其是否具有价值性、实用性以及持有人是否采取了必要的保密措施作出认定，并对涉案信息与被控侵权软件进行比对，没有意义；况且其也未能证明司法鉴定意见书已经对两者进行了完整的比对。因此，闸北市场监管局因认定管易公司侵犯他人商业秘密进而作的行政处罚决定，缺乏事实和法律依据，应予撤销。综上，二审法院依法判决驳回上诉，维持原判。

【评析】

本案涉及的主要法律问题是，软件复制及使用行为是否必然构成侵犯软件商业秘密的行为？

本案中，行政机关查明被处罚人公司电脑中存有复制了第三人源程序和文档的文件，若第三人的源程序和文档构成作品，则被处罚人未经许可擅自复制并使用上述软件的行为，涉嫌构成对他人作品著作权的侵害。但该不当复制并使用软件的行为，只有在当软件同时构成作品和商业秘密的情况下，才会产生著作权和商业秘密侵权责任的竞合。换而言之，如果软件构成作品但不构成商业秘密，则即便行为人侵犯了其著作权，也不会同时构成商业秘密侵权。

一、商业秘密的定义

当计算机软件符合独创性、有形性、可复制性之智力成果的情况下，即构成作品。而根据我国《反不正当竞争法》第十条第三款规定，商业秘密是指不为公众所知悉、能为权利人带来经济利益、具有实用性并经权利人采取保密措施的技术信息和经营信息。即商业秘密是具有秘密性、价值性、实用性并经持有人采取保密措施的技术信息和经营信息。若软件权利人欲以商业秘密为途径寻求法律救济，则必须同时具备上述四个法定要件，缺一不可。

计算机软件要符合商业秘密法定要件，首先必须具有秘密性。《最高人民法院关于审理不正当竞争民事案件应用法律若干问题的解释》第九条第一款规定，有关信息不为其所属领域的相关人员普遍知悉和容易获得，应当认定为《反不正当竞争法》第十条第三款规定的"不为公众所知悉"，故商业秘密的秘密性要件是指该信息不被该行业普遍知悉且客观上无法从公共渠道直接获取。

二、软件商业秘密构成的举证责任

根据《最高人民法院关于审理不正当竞争民事案件应用法律若干问题的解释》第十四条的规定，当事人指称他人侵犯其商业秘密的，应当对其拥有的商业秘密符合法定条件、对方当事人的信息与其商业秘密相同或者实质相同以及对方当事人采取不正当手段的事实负举证责任。其中商业秘密符合法定条件的证据，包括商业秘密的载体、具体内容、商业价值和对该项商业秘密所采取的具体保密措施等。

三、行政案件中行政机关应当对涉案信息构成商业秘密承担举证责任

根据前述规定，在涉及软件的商业秘密侵权民事案件中，原告应当承担证明其软件符合商业秘密法定要件的举证责任。而在商业秘密行政案件中，做出具体行政处罚行为的行政机关对其处罚决定的合法性进行证明，即对其认定的商业秘密符合法定的秘密性、价值性、实用性并经持有人采取保密措施之要件承担举证责任。

本案中，行政机关应当举证证明软件整体处于"不为公众所知悉"的状态，即不为其所属领域的相关人员普遍知悉和容易获得，不能仅仅以权利主张人对软件采取了保密措施，即推定该信息必然不为其所属领域的相关人员普遍知悉和容易获得。本案中，鉴定机构出具的《司法鉴定意见书》之"委托鉴定事项"仅针对证据固定、鉴定对象的相关文件之内容同一性比对以及文件之真实性鉴定，具体鉴定过程也并未涉及涉案源程序及文档是否"不为公众所知悉"的事实状态的认定。行政机关仅以第三人对软件采取了保密措施，即推定该信息必然不为其所属领域的相关人员普遍知悉和容易获得，缺乏事实和法律依据。因此，行政机关在本案中并未能够提供证据证明涉案源代码和文档整体符合商业秘密的秘密性要件。

虽然，行政机关证明了涉案源代码和文档符合价值性、实用性以及采取保密措施之商业秘密法定要件，但未能证实其满足秘密性要件，且在信息同一性

的比对中还存在瑕疵，故其认定商业秘密侵权成立的处罚决定，缺乏事实依据，应被撤销。

四、行政案件与民事侵权诉讼的关系

在不服行政处罚而涉及行政诉讼的上诉案件中，二审法院的审理范围仅限于对一审判决及行政机关相关行政处罚的审查，并不涉及对被处罚人是否侵犯他人软件作品著作权之民事责任的认定。因此，如第三人认为被处罚人复制并使用其软件的行为另涉及著作权侵权，可另行提起民事侵权诉讼，本案行政案件的处理结果，并不影响相关权利人民事权利的行使，也不影响民事著作权侵权案件的认定。

（撰稿人：王静）

七

知识产权诉讼程序案件

权利人未报案的刑事程序是否
产生民事诉讼时效中断效力

——勃贝雷有限公司诉陈凯、鲁秋敏侵害商标权纠纷案

【提要】

权利人未报案的刑事程序并不当然产生诉讼时效方面的法律后果，但是，权利人配合公安部门调查案件相关事实，这一事由对权利人产生两个法律后果：一是产生诉讼时效开始起算的法律后果，因为其已知道侵权行为的存在；二是产生诉讼时效中断的法律后果，因为其在积极配合公安部门调查的同时，有理由信赖自己的权利已处于公权力保护之中，且侵权的具体事实及权利受保护程度有赖刑事程序的结果而定。因此，上述事由应属于"其他与提起诉讼具有同等诉讼时效中断效力的事项"。

【案情】

原告（被上诉人）：勃贝雷有限公司

被告（上诉人）：鲁秋敏

被告：陈凯

案由：侵害商标权纠纷

一审案号：（2014）杨民三（知）初字第381号

二审案号：（2015）沪知民终字第6号

勃贝雷有限公司系第75130号及第G733385号"BURBERRY"注册商标权利人。2009年10月起，陈凯伙同鲁秋敏通过他人注册淘宝网店，对外低价销售假冒"BURBERRY"注册商标的服装，相关部门在行政执法中发现该侵权行为而案发并对其提起了刑事公诉，后被法院于2012年8月24日以销售假冒注册商标的商品罪判处刑罚。勃贝雷有限公司于2012年3月21日在公安机关要

求其确认查获物品是否系假冒注册商标商品并出具价格证明时，获悉陈凯、鲁秋敏的侵权行为及被立案侦查的情况。2014 年 8 月 15 日，勃贝雷有限公司提起本案一审民事诉讼，要求判令陈凯、鲁秋敏停止侵权，连带赔偿原告经济损失及合理支出人民币 100 万元。

上诉人鲁秋敏不服一审判决，提起上诉称：勃贝雷有限公司最晚应于 2014 年 3 月 20 日前提起诉讼，故其 2014 年 8 月 15 日起诉已过诉讼时效，原审法院并未正确适用法律。原审法院既已认定鲁秋敏及陈凯自 2012 年 3 月 20 日起已停止侵权行为，根据《最高人民法院关于审理商标民事纠纷适用法律若干问题的解释》（以下简称《商标案件适用法律解释》）第十八条规定，对于侵权损害赔偿数额应自勃贝雷有限公司向人民法院起诉之日起向前推算二年期间的获利计算。而本案起诉之日至向前推算二年之间，不存在侵权行为和侵权获利，也就无需赔偿损失。故鲁秋敏请求本院撤销原审判决，依法改判。

被上诉人勃贝雷有限公司辩称，其一审起诉未过诉讼时效。其于 2012 年 3 月 21 日得知侵权行为并向公安机关提供相关材料后，基于对刑事司法的信赖及实践中存在的先刑后民的惯常做法，没有在当时提起民事诉讼。但此时刑事程序已经存在，故诉讼时效应中断，并在刑事程序终结后重新计算。涉案刑事判决生效日期是 2012 年 9 月 3 日，故其于 2014 年 8 月 15 日起诉未过诉讼时效。

原审被告陈凯对原审判决无异议。

【审判】

上海市杨浦区人民法院经审理认为：勃贝雷有限公司虽于 2012 年 3 月 21 日获悉被告陈凯、鲁秋敏侵权并被公安机关立案侦查，但两被告能否被认定为侵权主体、侵权行为相关证据等，需等待刑事判决生效后才能确定。本案诉讼时效期间应从该刑事判决书生效之日起计算，故勃贝雷有限公司的起诉并未超过诉讼时效，陈凯、鲁秋敏应对其侵犯他人注册商标权行为承担相应的民事责任。上海市杨浦区人民法院依照《中华人民共和国侵权责任法》第八条，《中华人民共和国商标法》（2001 年修正）第五十二条第（一）项和第（二）项、第五十六条第一款，《最高人民法院关于审理商标民事纠纷案件适用法律若干问题的解释》第九条第一款、第十条、第十七条、第十八条、第二十一条第一款之规定，判决：陈凯、鲁秋敏连带赔偿勃贝雷公司经济损失人民币 15 万元及合理费用人民币 1.5 万元；驳回勃贝雷公司的其余诉讼请求。

一审判决后，被告鲁秋敏不服，提起上诉。

上海知识产权法院经审理认为，因商标权利人未进行刑事报案，故涉案刑事程序并不当然产生诉讼时效方面的法律效果。但被上诉人接到公安部门要求出具价格证明及进行真假货品鉴别时，诉讼时效期间即开始起算。但同时，其有合理理由信赖正在进行的刑事侦查可使其权利得到保护。且原审被告侵权的具体行为、规模、侵害后果等，必然依仗刑事裁判的最终认定而确定。故该情形属于"其他与提起诉讼具有同等诉讼时效中断效力的事项"，诉讼时效期间随之中断。因此，被上诉人起诉未超过诉讼时效，侵权人应承担民事责任。至于按起诉之日倒推二年期间的侵权获利计算损失的规定适用于侵权行为处于持续状态，权利人知道侵权行为后超过二年起诉的情况，而本案不适用这一规定。故上诉人的上诉理由不成立。原审法院认定事实清楚，审判程序合法，判决结果并无不当，应予维持，但适用法律不全面，应予补正。

【评析】

本案是因销售假冒注册商标商品的刑事犯罪引起的侵害商标权民事纠纷，本案当事人对刑事判决认定的犯罪事实及原审法院认定的侵权事实并无异议，双方分歧主要在于被上诉人向原审法院起诉时是否已经超过诉讼时效，以及赔偿损失是否适用《商标案件适用法律解释》中依起诉日倒推二年期间的侵权获利为据计算的规定。

一、本案是诉讼时效起算问题还是诉讼时效中断问题

诉讼时效是指权利人不行使权利的事实状态持续经过法定期间，其权利即发生效力减损的制度。即权利人因诉讼时效期间届满，在义务人行使诉讼时效抗辩权时，丧失请求法院保护的权利。根据我国《民法通则》第135条及《商标案件适用法律解释》第18条规定，商标权利被侵害的权利人向人民法院请求保护的诉讼时效期间为二年，自商标注册人或利害权利人知道或者应当知道侵权行为之日起计算。

诉讼时效是一项对权利人行使权利的时间作限制的制度，其设立目的是督促权利人行使权利，维护交易关系的稳定，而并不是免除债务人债务，更不是保护债务人的不当利益。因此，《最高人民法院关于审理民事案件适用诉讼时效制度若干问题的规定》（以下简称《诉讼时效规定》）明确规定了当事人未提出诉讼时效抗辩时，法院不应主动释明及适用诉讼时效规定裁判；该规定还对诉讼时效抗辩提出的时间和阶段也作了限定。诉讼时效期间届满，权利人丧失的是得到法院强制力保护的权利，并不丧失实体权利。

不仅如此，为了平衡当事人之间的利益，法律对诉讼时效还设置了障碍制

度，诉讼时效中断、中止即是诉讼时效的障碍制度。本案的争议看似是商标侵权之诉的诉讼时效期间起算点的确定问题，但实质则是对上诉人及原审被告的刑事追诉程序是否构成诉讼时效中断事由的问题。因为，我国法律明确规定了诉讼时效期间自权利人知道或应当知道权利被侵害起计算。可见，诉讼时效起算点的规定是明确的，不存在歧义，也不应有争议。双方的争议实际是诉讼时效是否要重新起算的问题，而只有在发生中断情形时，才有诉讼时效期间重新计算的可能，所以本案争议的实质是是否发生诉讼时效中断的事由。

我国《民法通则》第 140 条规定："诉讼时效因提起诉讼、当事人一方提出要求或者同意履行义务而中断。从中断时起，诉讼时效期间重新计算。"最高人民法院《诉讼时效规定》从第 11 条到第 19 条规定了诉讼时效中断的具体情形。其中，第 15 条规定了刑民交叉案件的诉讼时效中断问题。值得注意的是，该条明确指明了适用于"权利人向……报案或控告"的情形，本案原审被告侵犯注册商标专用权的犯罪行为并非由权利人发现而"报案或控告"，而是公安机关发现违法行为后主动进行刑事侦查，故本案不能直接适用该条规定。《诉讼时效规定》第 13 条则规定了可以认定为与提起诉讼具有同等诉讼时效中断效力的事项，但就其列举的 8 项事由，与本案也不一致。那么，可否适用该条第（9）项"其他与提起诉讼具有同等诉讼时效中断效力的事项"的规定？

本案中，作为权利人的被上诉人原先并不知道自己的权利被侵害，在其被要求出具价格证明及进行真假货品鉴别时才知道权利受到侵害，与此同时也获知了上诉人及原审被告已经处于被刑事侦查的状态。这一事件本身可以做这样的解读：1. 作为权利人知道自己的权利受到侵害，诉讼时效期间依法起算；2. 作为商标权利人以自己的积极行为配合公安机关作出相关鉴别，也表明对权利保护的积极态度；3. 在侵权行为已被纳入刑事程序的情况下，权利人有合理理由信赖其民事权利能得到保护；4. 从客观上说，上诉人及原审被告侵权的具体行为、规模、侵害后果等，必然依仗刑事裁判的最终认定而确定。被上诉人的民事权利能保护到何种程度，也与刑事诉讼的结果有很大关联。因此，该刑事程序虽并非由权利人报案或控告引起，但该刑事程序的存在及持续具有诉讼时效中断的效力，属于与提起诉讼具有同等诉讼时效中断效力的事项。被上诉人在接到公安部门通知并出具价格证明、进行真假货品鉴别时，已知道权利受到侵害，诉讼时效期间即开始起算；但同时，其得知两侵权人的行为已进入刑事侦查程序，基于前述已分析的理由，诉讼时效期间随之中断。待刑事程序结束，诉讼时效中断的事由即被排除，诉讼时效期间重新起算，故被上诉人起诉未超过诉讼时效，侵权人应就其侵权行为依法承担民事责任。

所以，本案应适用诉讼时效中断的相关规定而不是诉讼时效起算的规定。

二、本案是否适用依起诉日倒推二年期间侵权获利计算损失的规定

上诉人不服原审判决的另一个理由是，根据最高人民法院《商标案件适用法律解释》第 18 条规定，赔偿损失应按起诉之日倒推二年期间的侵权获利计算。在该段时间内，两原审被告因刑事案件案发已经停止了销售假冒注册商标商品的行为，既然没有侵权行为也就没有侵权获利，也就不需要承担赔偿责任。简言之，即使原审原告的起诉未过诉讼时效，如适用这条规定，其也不需要赔偿。因为，自起诉日倒推二年，两被告早已停止侵权行为，何来侵权获利？则赔偿额的计算也无所依凭。

上诉人所引用的规定是《商标案件适用法律解释》第 18 条的部分内容，即 "……注册人或者利害关系人超过二年起诉的，如果侵权行为在起诉时仍在持续，在该注册商标专用权有效期限内，人民法院应当判决被告停止侵权行为，侵权损害赔偿数额应当自权利人向人民法院起诉之日向前推算二年计算"。可见，该规定适用于侵权行为处于持续状态的情况下，权利人知道侵权行为后超过二年起诉的，赔偿数额的计算按起诉之日倒推二年期间的侵权获利为依据计算。这条规定仅针对知道持续存在的侵权行为后超过二年起诉的情况，不涉及任何诉讼时效中断情形。而本案由于诉讼时效中断，权利人是在诉讼时效中断后二年内起诉，故不属于适用这一规定的情形。

综上，二审法院适用《民法通则》第 140 条、《诉讼时效规定》第 13 条第(9) 项规定，认定本案中的刑事程序属于 "其他与提起诉讼具有同等诉讼时效中断效力的事项"，产生诉讼时效中断的效力，被上诉人的起诉未超过诉讼时效，其诉请应获得法院保护。既维持了一审判决，又详尽补充了判案理由及法律依据，正确、全面地适用了法律规定和司法解释。

（撰稿人：陈惠珍）

侵害共有著作权案件的行为保全

——亚拓士软件有限公司与娱美德娱乐有限公司、上海恺英网络科技有限公司诉前停止侵害著作权纠纷案

【提要】

对不能分割使用的计算机软件享有共有著作权的权利人对外授权许可他人使用著作权时，应当与其他共有权利人协商一致。未经协商擅自对外授权，所签合同涉嫌侵犯共有著作权，其他共有权利人申请法院禁止该合同履行，符合情况紧急和及时止损的法定要件。

【案情】

申请人（复议被申请人）： 亚拓士软件有限公司

被申请人（复议申请人）： 娱美德娱乐有限公司

被申请人（复议申请人）： 上海恺英网络科技有限公司

案由： 侵害计算机软件著作权纠纷

案号：（2016）沪 73 行保 1 号

复议案号：（2016）沪 73 行保复 1 号

申请人亚拓士软件有限公司（以下简称亚拓士公司）与被申请人娱美德娱乐有限公司（以下简称娱美德公司）均为韩国公司，其共同拥有 Mir2（传奇）游戏软件的著作权，该游戏在中国大陆已正常运营 15 年。娱美德公司于 2016 年 6 月 28 日与被申请人上海恺英网络科技有限公司（以下简称恺英公司）签订了涉案软件的移动游戏和网页游戏授权许可合同，合同金额 300 亿韩元。恺英公司的关联公司就此合同进行了网上公告，娱美德公司在合同签订后向亚拓士公司发送了书面通知。

亚拓士公司申请称：娱美德公司未与其协商擅自行使不可分割的共有著作

权，违反《中华人民共和国著作权法》第十三条及《中华人民共和国著作权法实施条例》第九条之规定。为防止授权行为对申请人合法权益及目前游戏运营秩序造成不可挽回的损失及严重不良影响，请求法院禁止两被申请人实际履行其未经与申请人协商签署的合同，并提供现金人民币 5000 万元作为担保。

【审判】

上海知识产权法院认为，申请人与被申请人娱美德公司共同拥有涉案游戏软件的著作权，娱美德公司若未与申请人协商一致而签订对外授权许可合同，涉嫌侵害申请人作为共有著作权人的权利。鉴于两被申请人签订合同后可能投入商业运营，如不及时制止将会对共有著作权人的权利造成难以弥补的损害，遂裁定两被申请人立即停止履行涉案合同。

本案裁定后，两被申请人不服，提出了复议申请。其复议称：本案不具备采取诉前行为保全应具备情况紧急、不保全将无法弥补损失的条件。因为亚拓士公司与娱美德公司曾达成"和解笔录"，双方都可单独与海外第三方签署授权许可协议；共有著作权人事先协商一致并非行使著作权的法定前提；娱美德公司已善意通知，亚拓士公司未在合理时间内提出异议和反对许可的正当理由；在娱美德公司承诺分享许可收益的情况下，亚拓士公司不可能遭受不可弥补的损害。恺英公司已开始履行涉案合同并将合同事宜通过其母公司（上市公司）向社会进行了公告，若授权许可合同停止履行，将影响正常经营并波及股价而损害社会公共利益。

上海知识产权法院复议认为：复议申请人提供的"和解笔录"并未明确娱美德公司就涉案软件拥有单独对外授权许可的权利。涉案合同若履行，必然对共有著作权人产生实际损害后果；及时制止一个可能侵害他人权利的合同的履行，也有利于合同当事人及时止损；维持公司业绩形象不应建立在可能侵害他人权利的基础之上，行为保全裁定会影响股价而侵害公共利益的观点难谓合理合法。故裁定驳回两复议申请人的复议请求。

【评析】

共有权利人对不可分割使用的计算机软件著作权的行使应协商一致，这既是相关法律规定的前置程序，也是民事主体应当遵循的平等、诚实、信用原则的基本要求。只有经过协商未能达成一致，又没有合理理由的，才符合"任何一方可行使除转让以外的其他权利"的条件。若未经协商擅自对外授权，所签合同可能因侵犯共有权利而无效。禁止无效合同履行可防止著作权侵权行为的实际发生或损失的进一步扩大，符合诉前停止侵权的行为保全相关规定要求的情况紧急和防止难以弥补的损害发生的条件。故共有权利人的这一申请应当予以支持。本案对侵害共有著作权权利的行为保全案件的处理具有参考价值。

（撰稿人：陈惠珍）

侵害计算机软件著作权案件的诉前证据保全

——申请人欧特克公司、奥多比公司与被申请人上海风语筑展览有限公司诉前证据保全案

【提要】

法院依法采取保全措施后，申请人向法院提起诉讼。案件审理中，法院以证据保全结果为基础，基本固定案件事实，以当事人的诉求为切入点，逐步拉近各方差距，力促双方达成和解。当事人最终以"赔偿 + 软件正版化"方式达成和解，且和解协议已全部履行完毕。

【案情】

申请人：欧特克公司

申请人：奥多比公司

被申请人：上海风语筑展览有限公司

案由：侵害计算机软件著作权纠纷

案号：（2015）沪知民保字第 1 号、第 2 号

欧特克公司、奥多比公司系两家美国软件公司，其提供了上海风语筑展览有限公司商业使用两公司 AutoCAD、Photoshop、Acrobat 等系列计算机软件的侵权线索。鉴于其客观上无法获得相关证据，且证据极易藏匿或毁灭，故申请人请求上海知识产权法院进行诉前证据保全。

【审判】

上海知识产权法院审查认为，申请人提供了被申请人侵权的初步线索，申请保全的证据属于法律规定的可能灭失或者以后难以取得的情形，且申请人亦

因客观原因不能自行收集上述证据，符合诉前证据保全的条件。遂裁定对被申请人经营场所内的计算机以及其他设施设备上的上述系列软件的相关信息进行证据保全，并充分发挥与上海市第三中级人民法院"合署办公"的制度优势，及时、有效完成对近400台电脑的证据保全，顺利完成了保全裁定的执行。

【评析】

加大知识产权司法保护不仅体现于实体方面的法律制度建设及实施，还应体现于诸如临时禁令、证据保全等程序制度的执行。本次诉前证据保全措施的依法适用，不仅及时固定了相关证据，也充分展示了知识产权司法保护的力度。

（撰稿人：吴盈喆）

网络不正当竞争诉前行为保全的司法审查

——浙江淘宝网络有限公司与上海载和网络科技有限公司等
申请诉前停止侵害知识产权纠纷案

【提要】

该案是新民事诉讼法规定行为保全制度后，全国法院就电商领域的不正当竞争行为首次作出诉前行为保全裁定的案件。法院根据《民事诉讼法》及相关知识产权实体法的规定，参考 TRIPs 协议及域外司法实践，归纳出诉前行为保全的适用条件：（1）申请人具有胜诉可能性；（2）不采取保全措施会对申请人造成难以弥补的损害；（3）采取保全措施不损害社会公共利益。作为一种司法临时保护措施，该案诉前行为保全提高了司法救济的及时性和有效性。

【案情】

申请人：浙江淘宝网络有限公司

被申请人：上海载和网络科技有限公司

被申请人：载信软件（上海）有限公司

案由：申请诉前停止侵害知识产权纠纷

案号：（2015）浦禁字第 1 号

申请人浙江淘宝网络有限公司（以下简称淘宝公司）于 2015 年 10 月 23 日提起诉前行为保全申请，称：其系"淘宝网"（www.taobao.com）的所有者及实际运营者，被申请人上海载和网络科技有限公司（以下简称载和公司）系"帮 5 买"网站（www.b5m.com）的所有者及经营者，二者均系网络交易平台，具有直接竞争关系。载和公司在"帮 5 买"官网提供"帮 5 淘"网页插件的下载，该插件由被申请人载信软件（上海）有限公司（以下简称载信公司）开发并提供技术支持。用户安装该插件后，使用 IE、百度、搜狗等主流浏览器在

"淘宝网"购物时，会在"淘宝网"页面中出现"帮5买"网站的广告栏和搜索栏，在商品详情页的原有标价附近以醒目方式出现"现金立减"或"帮5买扫一扫立减1元"等链接，用户点击该链接则跳转到"帮5买"网站页面，并在该网站完成下单、支付等交易流程。

申请人认为，被申请人载和公司的行为系利用"淘宝网"品牌的知名度与美誉度谋取不正当利益，不仅劫取了原本应由申请人享有的商业利益，更对"淘宝网"的市场形象带来了极大的负面评价，已构成不正当竞争行为。被申请人载信公司作为"帮5淘"插件的开发者及技术服务支持者，未尽注意义务，为载和公司的不正当竞争行为提供帮助，应承担连带责任。为阻止两被申请人继续实施不正当竞争行为，申请人曾对"淘宝网"进行安全升级，但该技术措施被两被申请人破解。后申请人向上海市浦东新区市场监督管理局举报，请求行政部门对被申请人实施的不正当竞争行为进行处理，已立案。但被申请人仍在疯狂实施其不正当竞争行为。经统计，2015年7月至8月，被申请人以"帮5淘"插件嵌入"淘宝网"的方式，独立访问"淘宝网"多达5306万余次，用户在"淘宝网"页面上误点"帮5买"所嵌入的链接达7859万余次，劫取了原本属于申请人的巨额商业利益，造成"淘宝网"多达上亿元人民币的可预期收入损失。考虑到不正当竞争案件的审理周期，行政举报案件的处理周期，以及原告在"双十一"期间所计划进行的商业推广活动，如果不能及时制止两被申请人的不正当竞争行为，将给申请人造成不可弥补的损害。据此，申请人申请法院责令两被申请人停止继续以"帮5淘"网页插件的形式对申请人实施不正当竞争行为。

申请人提交了"帮5买"网站及其备案、被申请人实施涉嫌侵权行为、申请人用户投诉情况、淘宝论坛及其他第三方网站上网友讨论情况、申请人监控"帮5买"标识在其网站被点击次数的证据保全公证书，以及申请人向上海市浦东新区市场监督管理局举报材料及该局予以立案的举报答复书等证据材料，并提供了担保。

【审判】

上海市浦东新区人民法院经审理认为，诉前行为保全应满足以下条件：（1）申请人具有胜诉可能性；（2）不采取保全措施会对申请人造成难以弥补的损害；（3）采取保全措施不损害社会公共利益。本案中，根据申请人提供的证据材料，可初步证明"帮5淘"插件的发行者为被申请人载信公司，被申请人载和公司以"帮5淘"插件嵌入"淘宝网"购物页面的方式，使得"淘宝网"

购物页面出现"现金立减"等标志，从而导致原本欲在"淘宝网"进行交易的用户被引导至"帮5买"网站，并进而与被告载和公司达成交易。结合上述条件进行分析，首先，"淘宝网"与"帮5买"网站均为购物网站，二者具有直接竞争关系。载和公司的上述行为使其无须付出相应的宣传推广费用即可借助申请人的平台获得用户和交易机会，涉嫌不正当地利用"淘宝网"的知名度和用户基础。因此，两被申请人的行为有可能构成不正当竞争。其次，"淘宝网"的交易量巨大，且具有购物狂欢节之称的"双十一"即将到来，若不及时制止上述被控侵权行为，可能对申请人的竞争优势、市场份额造成难以弥补的损害。最后，采取保全措施不会损害社会公共利益，且申请人已提供有效担保。本案符合作出诉前行为保全的条件。综上，上海市浦东新区人民法院依照《中华人民共和国民事诉讼法》第一百零一条、第一百五十四条第一款第（四）项，《最高人民法院关于适用〈中华人民共和国民事诉讼法〉的解释》第一百七十一条的规定，裁定：载和公司、载信公司立即停止将"帮5淘"网页插件嵌入淘宝公司"淘宝网"网页的行为。

两被申请人不服，提起复议，主要理由是：1. 载和公司经营的"帮5买"网站并不销售商品，而是为注册会员提供在"淘宝网""天猫商城"等网站购物后的运费和减价补贴，与"淘宝网"不构成竞争关系。2. "帮5淘"插件由载信公司开发，"帮5买"网站为自愿安装该插件的注册会员提供代购服务，会员的购买行为实际上均是与"淘宝网"等购物网站之间的交易，故不仅不影响商家的利益，还因其对注册会员的补贴付出促进了"淘宝网"购物量的增加。3. 互联网作为新兴产业，鼓励中小微企业合法经营，在案件未实体审理的情况下对其作出禁令，不符合社会公共利益。

针对被申请人的复议理由，上海市浦东新区人民法院认为，根据现有证据，"帮5买"网站除提供商品信息搜索服务外，还就该网站出现的商品提供购买服务，可见该网站属于购物网站。至于该商品由网站经营者直接供货还是提供其所谓的代购服务，均不影响该网站的性质认定。因此，本案当事人之间具有竞争关系。申请复议人将"帮5淘"网页插件嵌入"淘宝网"网页的行为，容易导致用户就"帮5买"网站与"淘宝网"的关系产生误认，有可能构成不正当竞争。故对上述复议理由不予支持。据此，上海市浦东新区人民法院决定：驳回载和公司、载信公司的复议申请，维持原裁定。

【评析】

行为保全，又称临时禁令。"禁令"（Injunction）一词从英美法移植而来，意指法院作出的要求当事人为或者不为特定行为的命令。临时禁令则是指法院在对案件争议作出终局裁判前，责令当事人作出一定行为或禁止其作出一定行为的制度。临时禁令在 TRIPs 协议第 50 条中被称为"临时措施"（Provisional Measures）。为满足加入世界贸易组织的条件和遵守 TRIPs 协议的要求，我国 2000 年修改的《专利法》和 2001 年修改的《商标法》、《著作权法》均规定了诉前停止侵权行为制度，最高人民法院随后还出台了相关司法解释，但针对不正当竞争行为无此类规定。直至 2012 年《民事诉讼法》修改，统一规定了行为保全制度，将适用范围扩展到整个民事诉讼领域，并根据提起申请的阶段不同，分为诉前行为保全和诉中行为保全。本案是新《民事诉讼法》规定行为保全制度后，法院针对电商领域的涉嫌不正当竞争行为首次发出诉前行为保全裁定。

当事人申请诉前行为保全时，案件是否侵权尚无最终定论。若不准许或发布不及时，可能造成权利人市场份额的减少；若发布不当，又可能会给被控侵权人带来损失。在互联网领域的知识产权案件中，一方面，鉴于涉嫌侵权行为往往能在短时间内造成巨大的损害后果且持续扩大损害范围，是否做出行为保全裁定对于当事人的利益影响则更为重大。另一方面，实践中被控侵权人往往通过管辖权异议、上诉等方式拖延诉讼进程，导致救济周期过长，可能造成知识产权人"赢了官司输了市场"的尴尬局面。对于有的权利人来说，及时制止正在发生的侵权行为比在旷日持久的诉讼后获得经济赔偿更为重要，故行为保全成为十分重要的救济手段。但同时，行为保全制度也是一把双刃剑，运用得当会加大知识产权保护力度，反之则会阻碍科技文化的发展，故如何把握诉前行为保全的适用条件至关重要。

《民事诉讼法》规定，诉前保全的条件为"情况紧急，不立即申请将会使其合法权益受到难以弥补的损害"，并不涉及对于被控行为是否侵权的判断；《著作权法》等法律则规定诉前行为保全应满足"有证据证明正在实施或者即将实施侵权行为"及"如不及时制止将会使权利人的合法权益受到难以弥补的损害"两个条件。笔者认为，若法院不对被控侵权人实体上的侵权可能性作出任何判断，即依权利人单方申请作出行为保全，则有违民事诉讼的公正性原则。故应将权利人的实体"胜诉可能性"作为诉前行为保全的条件。同时，TRIPs 协议还要求成员国司法当局在保护权利人合法权益的同时，兼顾被申请人和社会公众的利益。因此，在本案的审查中，诉前行为保全应满足以下条件：（1）申请人具有胜诉可能性；（2）不采取保全措施会对申请人造成难以弥补的损害；（3）采取保全措施不损害社会公共利益。

一、关于"胜诉可能性"

顾名思义，"胜诉可能性"涉及一种盖然性的判断。申请人虽无须证明胜诉的必然性，但仍应证明侵权行为存在的可能性。然而，申请人提供的证据应达到怎样的证明标准，其胜诉的可能性达到何种程度法院才可支持其保全申请，向来争议较大。若标准过宽，则容易造成权利滥用，使得行为保全制度沦为打击竞争对手的工具；反之，若标准过严，会导致过于限制行为保全制度的适用范围，无法发挥制度功能，不利于司法救济的及时性和有效性。

从比较法的角度看，英国法院对该条件采取实质性争议标准，只要能排除滥诉和明显不可能胜诉的情形即可；美国对于侵权成立要求优势证据，但对于权利有效性和可执行性等问题则采取推定成立的态度；德国、日本和我国台湾地区只要求申请人对请求权进行释明，同时允许以担保的方式弥补释明内容的欠缺。

借鉴上述经验，在审查权利人的"胜诉可能性"时，主要是审查两点：一是申请人为其主张的知识产权的权利人，具有可受保护的权利或利益，需提交相关权属证据；二是被申请人的行为有构成侵权的可能性，需提交被申请人正在实施或者即将实施侵权行为的证据。在排除明显没有胜诉可能性的情形后，对于"胜诉可能性"的判断应采取一个相对灵活的标准，在保护权利人及避免保全错误之间寻求平衡，并结合是否造成难以弥补的损害、双方利益及公共利益的平衡、申请人是否提供有效担保等其他因素综合考虑，整体判断。

本案中，申请人要求保护的利益系其作为互联网购物平台的竞争优势。网络购物平台赖以生存的基础是用户流量，申请人通过多年的经营和宣传推广，使得其网络购物平台"淘宝网"获得了极大的用户流量和极高的知名度、美誉度，成为行业内的龙头。用户流量及平台信誉对网络购物平台而言，具有极大的商业价值，属于可受《反不正当竞争法》保护的商业利益。根据申请人提交的证据，法院基于以下几点认定被申请人的行为有可能构成不正当竞争：首先，被申请人的网站除提供商品搜索功能外，还直接提供网络购物功能，与申请人具有竞争关系；其次，网络用户在电脑上安装被申请人的插件后，登录"淘宝网"页面时会出现被申请人网站的广告条和搜索框，更在"淘宝网"的价格标签及购买按钮下插入风格相似的优惠购买按钮，用户点击后则跳转至被申请人网站达成交易，可能使用户误以为被申请人与"淘宝网"存在关联关系。基于上述情形，虽尚难以认定被申请人的行为必然构成不正当竞争行为，但其通过技术手段嵌入申请人网页，引导用户与自己发生交易，且易使用户产生混淆，该行为具有不正当竞争的表面特征，有可能构成不正当竞争行为。故法院认定本案申请人具有"胜诉可能性"。

二、关于"难以弥补的损害"

关于如何把握"难以弥补的损害"，有观点认为，如果申请人能够证明其胜诉可能性，则法院可推定其将受到难以弥补的损害①。但笔者认为，只有存在事后赔偿难以弥补的损害，才有必要允许当事人在法院作出终局裁判前，申请法院责令对方作出或不作出一定行为，否则大可等待法院的终局裁判。在这个意义上，"难以弥补的损害"条件具有独立的意义，是行为保全制度的正当性基础。"胜诉可能性"仅为诉前行为保全的充分条件，"难以弥补的损害"则为诉前行为保全的必要条件，二者缺一不可。

通常情况下，有以下情形可以认定为将造成难以弥补的损害：（1）侵权行为涉及著作人身权内容或者涉及商誉；（2）侵权行为的发生或将继续严重抢占申请人的市场份额，影响申请人的重大利益；（3）侵权行为如不及时制止，将严重扩大侵权行为的范围和损害后果；（4）被申请人缺乏足够的偿付能力②。在反不正当竞争案件中，"难以弥补的损害"主要是指申请人的竞争优势、市场份额等因被申请人的被控不正当竞争行为遭受难以恢复的损害。例如，在申请人美国礼来公司等与被申请人黄孟炜行为保全申请案中③，被申请人承认下载了属于申请人的保密文件，并承诺允许申请人的指定人员检查和删除上述文件，但拒绝履行该义务。被申请人的拒绝行为使得申请人的商业秘密存在被披露的危险，而一旦披露，申请人依据商业秘密而享有的竞争优势将荡然无存，因此此处存在难以弥补的损害。

本案中，申请人主张的竞争优势主要体现为网络购物平台"淘宝网"的用户流量。被申请人的行为涉嫌利用"淘宝网"的知名度和用户基础，并容易导致用户产生混淆。"淘宝网"交易量巨大，当事人提出申请时又正值具有购物狂欢节的"双十一节"来临之际，如果涉嫌侵权行为不能有效制止，可能导致申请人的竞争优势、市场份额发生变化。一旦被申请人通过被控侵权行为抢夺了申请人的市场份额，即便事后法院认定被申请人行为构成不正当竞争，并进而判决其停止不正当竞争行为，申请人的竞争优势和市场地位在短时期内也难以恢复。基于此，法院认定本案满足"难以弥补的损害"条件。

---

① 张广良：《知识产权侵权民事救济》，法律出版社2003年版，第49页。
② 北京市高级人民法庭知识产权庭编：《知识产权诉讼实务研究》，知识产权出版社2008年版，第409页。
③ 中华人民共和国上海市第一中级人民法院（2013）沪一中民五（知）初字第119号民事裁定书。

三、关于"不损害社会公共利益"

所谓社会公共利益，是指一定社会条件下或特定范围内，与不特定多数主体利益相一致的利益。知识产权具有私人产品和公共产品的双重属性，如何合理地确定其保护范围，不仅关系到权利人的利益，也关系到公共利益。为此，知识产权立法在赋予知识产权人以专有使用权的同时，又通过适当的限制，来保证社会公众对知识产权的合理利用，如著作权领域内的合理使用制度、专利权领域内的强制许可制度等。也正基于此，在考虑是否作出诉前行为保全这一直接影响一方当事人利益的措施时，亦应对公共利益进行权衡。在不正当竞争案件中，公共利益往往是指众多消费者的利益。本案中，被申请人的行为有可能导致消费者产生混淆，与公共利益相悖，本案适用诉前行为保全并不会损害消费者的利益或其他公共利益。

鉴于诉前行为保全毕竟是在一定程度上牺牲了被申请人的程序保障利益和行动自由，为确保保全错误的情形下被申请人能得到救济，法院要求申请人提供一定的担保，以平衡双方的利益。在担保金额的确定上，法院综合考虑了申请人胜诉可能性的高低、被申请人停止有关行为可能遭受的损失等因素。

综上，法院就本案作出诉前行为保全的裁定，在被申请人不服提起复议后，法院召开听证充分听取双方意见，仍旧以上述条件作为审查要点，作出驳回被申请人复议，维持原裁定的决定。

（撰稿人：叶菊芬）

I

Civil Cases on
Copyright Infringement

Examination and Identification of Fair Use in Judicial Practice

—Dispute over Copyright Infringement Between Shanghai Animation Film Studio and Zhejiang New Film Age Culture Communication Co. , Ltd. *et al.*

[Summary]

In examining and judging whether the use of the cartoon characters of Calabash Boys and Sergeant Black Cat constitutes a fair use, it is decided that such use in the movie posters involved is transformative use, which means that the use of the original works is not limited to represent the literary and artistic value of the works themselves, but to render in them new values, functions or nature when they are used in the new works, thus changing their original functions or purposes. In judging whether transformative use constitutes fair use, we should consider the components constituting fair use as stipulated in the Copyright Law, that is, in the case of transformative use, it shall constitute fair use only when the work is still in normal use and the legitimate interests of the copyright owner are not damaged inappropriately.

[Case Review]

Plaintiff (Appellant):Shanghai Animation Film Studio

Defendant (Respondent): Zhejiang New Film Age Culture Communication Co. , Ltd.

Defendant (Respondent): Huayi Brothers Shanghai Cinema Management Co. , Ltd.

Cause of Action: Copyright Infringement

First-Instance Case No.: (2014) No. 258

Second-Instance Case No.: (2015) No. 730

There had been dispute and a lawsuit concerning the ownership of the copyright of Calabash Boys, the artwork involved. In March 2012, in Judgment No. 62 (2011), Shanghai No. 2 Intermediate People's Court rendered a final judgment on the dispute over copyright ownership between Hu Jinqing, Wu Yunchu and Shanghai Animation Film Studio (hereinafter referred to as SAFS). Shanghai No. 2 Intermediate People's Court investigated and found that at the end of 1985, appointed by their employer SAFS, Hu Jinqing and Wu Yunchu drafted the characters of Calabash Boys. The seven Calabash Boys have the same style and their common features are: square face, thick and short eyebrows, bright eyes, solid body, a calabash on the head, gourd-leaf-collar around the neck, wearing waistcoats and shorts, with gourd-leaf-apron around the waist. The colors of their clothes are red, orange, yellow, green, cyan, blue and purple. Considering the background, historical conditions, laws and regulations, and the rules and regulations of the institution when the Calabash Boys was created, the court decided that the work created by Hu Jinqing and Wu Yunchu was job-related work under the specific historical conditions and its copyright, except the claim to authorship, was enjoyed by SAFS.

In May 2014, in Judgment No. 223 (2014), Fujian Higher People's Court made a final judgment on the dispute between SAFS, Fujian Sergeant Black Cat Children's Products Co., Ltd. and Fujian Nanhua Group on infringement of other copyright. After investigation, Fujian Higher People's Court found that SAFS filmed the cartoon Sergeant Black Cat in the 1980s. The actual creator of Sergeant Black Cat (i. e., the work involved) was Dai Tielang, then the director of SAFS. Sergeant Black Cat is dressed in black uniform, with red epaulets. It has a round head and wears a white-black cap (white on top of black), and between the two colors there is a yellow circle pattern with a blue arrow on it. The upper half of its face is black, and the two raised ears are also black. The lower half of its face is uniquely white. The outer circle of its eyes is golden yellow and the inner circle is black. It has straight long beards, wears white gloves and is equipped with a pistol at the waist, fixed with a white strap. The court ruled that the cartoon Sergeant Black Cat was copyrighted by SAFS. Under the planned economic system at that time, all the people involved in the production of the film were the staff of SAFS. Therefore, in the absence of evidence to the contrary, SAFS enjoyed the copyright of the artwork Sergeant Black Cat (i. e. , the work involved in the case).

Invested and produced by Zhejiang New Film Age Cultural Communication Co. , Ltd. (hereinafter referred to as New Film Age), the film *The Struggle of 80's* was officially released on February 21, 2014. The film poster in dispute shows as follows: the upper two-thirds' space is predominant with the images of the hero and heroine as well as their names, while the background is scattered with multiple drawings, such as young pioneers in white and green school uniforms attending flag-raising ceremony, classroom activities, and after-school games, etc. ; household appliances such as a black-and-white TV set and a floor lamp; daily necessities such as a sewing machine, a 28-type bicycle, a hot water bottle and a spittoon; cultural and educational supplies such as desks and pencil boxes; toys such as tin frogs, gyroscopes and marbles; snacks such as fig fruit, as well as the involved cartoon characters of the Calabash Boy and the Sergeant Black Cat, which stand beside the hero and the heroine. The drawings in the background are significantly smaller than the hero and the heroine. The size of the Calabash Boy and the Sergeant Black Cat is basically the same as that of other drawings in the background. The lower one third of the poster is mainly occupied by the name of the movie: *The Struggle of the 80's*, together with the information of the producer, the production company and actors. There are also the words reading "Released on February 21, 2014. "

On March 7, 2014, the certification of evidence preservation filed by SAFS showed that on February 22, 2014, Huayi Brothers Shanghai Cinema posted on Weibo, the Chinese version, the film poster involved. The post reads: " *The Struggle of the 80's*" tells the story of the young graduates who were born after the 1980s abandoning the comfortable living environment in cities and the promising future provided by their parents, and choosing to go to the countryside where conditions were much tougher and start their own business there. One of the highlights of the film is how the self-made parents raise their children. Below the text there is the poster involved. Then, when you searched "*The Struggle of the 80's poster*" on www. baidu. com, the results showed that the poster involved had appeared in many media websites such as 1905. com, xinhuanet. com, yule. sohu. com, www. qq. com and ent. 163. com.

After comparison in court, the infringing images in the poster involved were basically identical with the artistic characters of the Calabash Boys and the Sergeant Black Cat claimed by SAFS. SAFS alleged that New Film Age had made the following modification without authorization: there were two white bars on the epaulets of SAFS's Sergeant Black Cat, but they disappeared in the poster involved; and there were two leaves on the calabash on the head of SAFS's Calabash Boy and two leaves on his collar, yet there was only one leaf on the head and zero on the collar in the poster involved.

The Struggle of the 80's was officially released upon examination and approval by the Film Administration of the State Administration of Radio, Film and Television. It contained no content relating to the Calabash Boys or Sergeant Black Cat.

According to the relevant state regulations concerning film script (outline) filing, film management and the notice for submitting feature films (film, digital) for examination, the materials required to be submitted include a number of relevant stills or posters (1 - 2 copies) and a compact disc. New Film Age had prepared two posters on the film, one being the poster involved and the other had nothing to do with the Calabash Boys or Sergeant Black Cat. The poster involved was provided by New Film Age to Huayi Brothers Cinema Management (Shanghai) Co., Ltd. (hereinafter referred to as Huayi Brothers), which used it on its Weibo account for the film promotion.

Plaintiff SAFS alleged that it owned the copyright of the artistic characters of the Calabash Boys in the animated film *The Calabash Brothers* and the copyright of the artistic character of Sergeant Black Cat in the namesake animated film. In the poster of the film *The Struggle of the* 80's produced by Zhejiang New Film Age Cultural Communication Co., Ltd., the company used the characters of the Calabash Boy and Sergeant Black Cat, the copyrights of which were owned by SAFS, and changed them without authorization. Huayi Brothers Cinema Management (Shanghai) Co., Ltd. also posted the poster involved on its official Weibo account. SAFS claimed that New Film Age had infringed its right to modify, copy, distribute and disseminate on the Internet by using the characters of the Calabash Boy and Sergeant Black Cat without authorization; Huayi Brothers' behavior had constituted an infringement on its right to disseminate on the Internet, and constituted joint infringement with New Film Age. Therefore, SAFS appealed to and requested the court to order: 1. New Film Age and Huayi Brothers to make a public apology in the prominent position of Shanghai Morning Post or other paper media of the same level to eliminate the impact; 2. New Film Age and Huayi Brothers to stop infringing on SAFS's copyrighted Calabash Boys and Sergeant Black Cat; 3. New Film Age and Huayi Brothers to jointly and severally compensate SAFS for economic losses and litigation costs totaling RMB 531,750.

Defendant New Film Age argued that: a) the existing evidence could not prove that SAFS owned the copyrights of characters of the Calabash Boys and Sergeant Black Cat; b) even if SAFS owned the copyrights, the poster involved mainly showed a young man and woman born in the 1980s, and the small patterns in the background, such as a sewing machine, a hot water bottle, the Calabash Boy and Sergeant Black Cat, were only to indicate the characteristics of the age (i. e. , the 1980s) where the protagonists grew up; c) in terms of use, the use of the Calabash Boy and Sergeant Black Cat in the poster was fair use as the characters were different from those in the animated films produced by the plaintiff and they only took up small room in the poster; d) there were two posters of the film and the other poster was cartooned. The circulation of the poster involved was very small. Even if it constituted infringement, the amount of compensation for photo copyright should be much lower.

Defendant Huayi Brothers argued that: a) the existing evidence could not prove that SAFS owned the copyright of the character of Sergeant Black Cat; b) even if SAFS enjoys the copyright, Huayi Brothers' use of the poster to promote the film was fair because the film was legally released, and the poster involved, which was provided by the producer to the issuer after examination, was also official. The poster had a legal source, so Huayi Brothers did nothing wrong in using it; c) as symbols of the 1980s, the artworks involved were public welfare in nature, and their appearance in the poster was inconspicuous, hence causing no harm to the interests of the plaintiff; d). even if it constituted an infringement, the amount of compensation for photo copyright should be much lower.

[Judgment]

After hearing, Shanghai Putuo District People's Court held that: a) the Calabash Boys and Sergeant Black Cat were published artworks; b) New Film Age's citation of other people's works was to illustrate a specific problem, that is, the age characteristics of the protagonists in the film involved; c) in terms of the proportion of the cited works in the whole work, the cited works were used in the background and only occupied a small area of the poster, and they were not highlighted. Therefore, such citation was appropriate; d) the use of allegedly infringing poster did not affect the normal use of SAFS's works. Therefore, the court found that New Film Age's use of the artworks of the Calabash Boy and Sergeant Black Cat in its film poster was fair use as stipulated in the Copyright Law.

To sum up, Shanghai Putuo District People's Court dismissed SAFS's requests.

Refusing to accept the first judgment, Plaintiff SAFS appealed to Shanghai Intellectual Property Court.

After hearing, Shanghai Intellectual Property Court held that, according to the Copyright Law of the People's Republic of China, in order to introduce, comment on a work or illustrate a problem, appropriate citation of other people's published works constitutes fair use. "To illustrate a problem" means that the citation of a published work is to illustrate other problems, not to show the artistic value of the cited work itself, and the original artistic value and function of the cited work are transformed in the new work; and it still constitutes fair use even if it is not necessary to cite a work in the new work.

In this case, the Calabash Boys and Sergeant Black Cat were the most famous cartoon characters in the 1980s. They are deeply engraved in the memories of people who were children in the 1980s and are naturally part of their childhood memories. Apart from the Calabash Boy and Sergeant Black Cat, the poster involved also cited many other representative images, scenes and objects familiar to the children in the 1980s, such as a black-and-white TV set, a floor lamp, a sewing machine, a 28 – type bicycle, a hot water bottle, a spittoon, desks, pencil boxes, a tin frog, a spinning top, marbles, fig fruit and young pioneers in white and green school uniforms attending the flag-raising ceremony, classroom activities and after-school games. These elements covered children's daily necessities, cultural and educational supplies, toys, snacks and life and learning scenes in the 1980s. The whole film poster presented to the audience the daily life experiences of children in the 1980s. Therefore, the use of the Calabash Boy and Sergeant Black Cat in the poster was no longer a pure reproduction of the artistic beauty and function of those art works, but a reflection of the common experience of a generation growing up in the 1980s, when the animations were a hit. They suggested the age characteristics of the protagonists of the film. Therefore, the use of the Calabash Boy and Sergeant Black Cat in the poster rendered in the artworks new value, significance and function. Their original artistic value and function were transformed significantly. It met the condition of "to illustrate a problem" as stipulated in the Copyright Law.

In conclusion, with a view to illustrating the specific problem of the age characteristics for children in the 1980s, New Film Age appropriately used the representative cartoon characters of the Calabash Boy and Sergeant Black Cat at that time, together with other typical elements of that age, in the film poster involved and put them in the background. Such use constituted fair use. Accordingly, Shanghai Intellectual Property Court rejected the appeal and upheld the original judgment.

[Case Study]

This case concerns copyright infringement and the key to solving this case lies in deciding whether the alleged infringement constitutes fair use. Therefore, it involves the criteria for judging fair use and other relevant factors that need to be considered in judicial practice.

Fair use refers to the legal act of using other people's copyrighted works for legitimate purposes under the conditions prescribed by law, without obtaining permission from the copyright owner or paying remuneration to the copyright owner. Article 22 of the Copyright Law of the People's Republic of China lists in detail twelve acts that can be deemed as fair use. In those circumstances, one can use others' copyrighted work without permission of or payment to the copyright owner, but the author's name and the name of the work should be specified, and other rights enjoyed by the copyright owner in accordance with the Copyright Law should not be infringed. Article 21 of the Regulations for the Implementation of the Copyright Law (Regulations) stipulates that, in accordance with the relevant provisions of the Copyright Law, where a published work can be used without permission of the copyright owner, the normal use of that work shall not be affected, and the legitimate interests of the copyright owner shall not be hurt unreasonably. Therefore, all statutory requirements should be considered when examining and judging whether an act constitutes fair use. For example, Article 22 (2) of the Copyright Law prescribes the purpose and nature of use, which is to "introduce, commenting on a work or illustrate a problem. " It requires that the original work be rendered with new content or meaning and generate aesthetic or artistic expressions which are different from those in the original work. When considering this requirement, we should focus on whether the use of the original work constitutes transformative use, because the higher the degree of transformation, the more likely it is to constitute fair use. Both the Copyright Law and the Regulations require that the original works cited be published works, which is an examination of the nature of the original works. Also, other relevant provisions, such as " appropriate quotation" stipulated in Article 22 of the Copyright Law and " shall not affect the normal use of the work or hurt the legitimate interests of the copyright owner " stipulated in Article 21 of the Regulations, propose consideration of factors such as the quantity and content of the quotation and the consequence of the quotation (i. e. , the impact on the market or value of the original work).

When examining the purpose and nature of the use, we should pay attention to whether the content of the original work has been transformed in the process of use. If new information, new aesthetics and new understanding are produced out of the original work, such use shall be fair use. In this case, the images of Calabash Boy and Sergeant Black Cat, together with the pictures of a black-and-white TV set and a floor lamp, make up the background of the poster. Whether they are to fit the theme of the poster or indicate the age and identity characteristics of the protagonists, the works have been injected with new contents, meanings and information, presenting completely different aesthetic and artistic expressions. In other words, the use of the artworks of Calabash Boy and Sergeant Black Cat involved in the case in the film poster has produced new value, meaning and function. Their original artistic value and function have been transformed, and the degree of transformation is rather high. The use of Calabash Boy and Sergeant Black Cat in the poster is no longer to simply reproduce the artistic aesthetics and functions of the works themselves, but to reflect the shared experience of a generation who were children in the 1980s, when the animated films Calabash Boys and Sergeant Black Cat were such a hit. They also suggest the age characteristics of the main characters in the film.

When examining the nature of the original work, if the original work has already been published, the citation of it is more likely to constitute fair use. In this case, the artworks of Calabash Boy and Sergeant Black Cat are characters from animated films, which were released in the 1980s. Therefore, the works involved are published works.

When judging whether the use is appropriate, we should consider the relevant factors regarding "the purpose and nature of the use" (i. e. , to "introduce, comment on a work or illustrate a problem") and decide if the new work has transformed the original work instead of simply replacing it. Then we should judge further whether such use constitutes fair use or not. In some cases, using other people's entire work may also constitute fair use. In this case, although the two characters of Calabash Boy and Sergeant Black Cat are presented in the film poster as a whole, they serve as the background with 20 other elements that show the characteristics of the 1980s. In terms of the proportion of the cited works in the whole work, the cited works are in an auxiliary, supporting and subordinate position. Taking an overall view of the poster involved, the hero and heroine of the film are in a dominant position, accounting for about one-half of the whole poster. The works involved occupy a relatively small area of the poster and are in harmony with other background patterns. The images of Calabash Boy and Sergeant Black Cat are not highlighted. The poster is not to show the original artistic charm and aesthetic value of Calabash Boy and Sergeant Black Cat. Instead, they are used to reflect an era, i. e. , the 1980s, when Calabash Boys and Sergeant Black Cat were very popular among the children. Moreover, animation images are unlikely to be used in part. That is why the two works involved are used as a whole in the film poster. In this case, this factor needs to be identified by taking into account other factors.

As for the consequences of the use, the considerations are mainly as follows: the impact on the potential market of the original work, the replacement of the original work by the infringing work in the name of fair use, and the replacement or abandonment of the original work in the market because of the emergence of the new work. In this case, the film in question was released for one to two weeks, starting February 21, 2014. Except for the use in the poster, nothing regarding the Calabash Boys or Sergeant Black Cat appeared in the film or the promotional materials. Therefore, the use of Calabash Boy or Sergeant Black Cat in poster by the New Film Age to help illustrate the age characteristics of the main characters of the film did not affect the normal use of the works of SAFS. They did not develop a competitive relationship in the market, and it will not result in the replacement or abandonment of the original works in the market.

In practice, comprehensively examining the various elements of fair use and focusing on whether the use of the original work constitutes transformative use can help us grasp the essence of fair use and clarify the criteria for judging whether the infringement constitutes fair use.

(Writers: Lu Fengyu & Zhu Yonghua)

Does Deep Linking Constitute Infringement of the Right to Communicate over Information Networks?

—Appeal Concerning Infringement of the Right to Communicate Works over Information Networks Between Shanghai Hode Information Technology Co. , Ltd. and Beijing Qiyi Century Technology Co. , Ltd.

[Summary]

In the current judicial practice, there are different criteria for judging whether deep linking constitutes infringement of the right to communicate over information networks, including: 1. Server; 2. Users' perception; 3. Substantive substitution. In this case, the court of first instance adopted criterion 3. Substantive substitution, which was opposed by the court of second instance. According to the statutory principle of intellectual property rights, the court of second instance held that when deciding whether the infringement of the right to communicate over information networks is committed, the court should examine and judge whether the alleged behavior is controlled by the right to communicate over information networks. According to the Regulations on the Protection of the Right to Communicate Works to the Public over Information Networks and relevant judicial interpretations, the court of second instance found that the following conditions should be met to constitute infringement of the right to communicate over information networks: 1. There is no permission of the right owner; 2. The defendant put the work on the information network; 3. The public can access the work at the time and place chosen by the themselves.

[Case Review]

Plaintiff (Appellant):Beijing Qiyi Century Technology Co. , Ltd.

Defendant (Respondent):Shanghai Hode Information Technology Co. , Ltd.

Cause of Action:Dispute over infringement of the right to communicate works to the public over information networks

First-Instance Case No. :(2014) PMS(Z)CZ No. 1137

Second-Instance Case No. :(2015) HZMZZ No. 213

Beijing Qiyi Century Technology Co. , Ltd. ("Qiyi") was authorized exclusively to obtain the right to communicate variety shows including Happy Camp over information networks. The nature of the authorization included the right of exclusive communication over information networks and the right to safeguard such right. The authorized use was limited to the Internet (PC) and mobile wireless (IPAD, mobile phones, etc.). The authorized region was the mainland of China. The authorization period was from January 1, 2014 to December 31, 2014, during which Qiyi could air *Happy Camp* broadcast on Hunan TV channel every Saturday at 20:15. The period of use was two years (January 1, 2014 – December 31, 2015). During the authorization period, the authorized party had the right to defend its rights in its own name (including and not limited to letters, complaints, lawsuits, etc.).

Shanghai Hode Information Technology Co. , Ltd. ("Hode") is the operator of "Bilibili" website (www. bilibili. com). Registered users can upload videos from Sina, Youku and Tencent to Bilibili for others to watch and comment on. Specifically, a user copies and pastes or types in the address of the webpage where the video is played to the uploading page of Bilibili, and fills in the fields such as title and tag. Bilibili's internal software then extracts the code of the video on that website. The user can also provide the code directly. After receiving the code, Bilibili will send a request to the server of the website where the video is located. Once getting a reply, Bilibili will extract the video data and have it played in the player on its website. The source address of the video, not Bilibili's address, will be shown if one checks the access address of a video uploaded to and played on Bilibili using a plug-in called Live HTTP headers.

According to the records of Bilibili's website management system, the allegedly infringing video in this case came from tv. le. com. The video link was provided by

Bilibili's registered user named "Qing Huai Jiang" on July 20, 2014. The link was deleted on Bilibili on October 28, 2014. Qiyi acknowledged that it had no cooperative relationship with tv. le. com in respect of the work involved.

After hearing, the court of first instance ordered Hode to compensate Qiyi RMB 3000 yuan for economic losses and RMB 2500 yuan for reasonable expenses. Refusing to accept the judgment, both Qiyi and Hode appealed.

Qiyi appealed for revocation of the original judgment and for a compensation of RMB 100,000 yuan for its economic losses. It appealed on the following grounds: 1. Although Hode did not directly upload the program involved, it provided the program by interfering with the link service. Its infringement was severe in nature and obviously in bad faith with the provision of online broadcasting within hours after the premiere of the program involved; 2. Qiyi had spent a huge amount of money for the authorization. The usage fees for each episode of *Happy Camp* was as high as several hundred thousand yuan, so the compensation amount decided in the original judgment was far less than the reasonable licensing fees. Qiyi also paid for the notarization and the lawyers to stop infringement. Therefore, the compensation of RMB 3,000 for economic losses and RMB 2,500 for reasonable expenses in the original judgment is obviously too low.

To Qiyi's appeal, Hode responded that the amount of compensation in the original judgment was too high. Bilibili, the website involved operated by Hode, is a famous sharing website, which produced no yields and was not implanted with ads. Variety shows are updated on a weekly basis, and no one watches them after one week. Also, expenditure there is no evidence about the licensing fees claimed by Qiyi.

Hode appealed for a retrial or for the dismissal of Qiyi's requests in the original trial. It appealed on the following grounds: 1. The link address of the allegedly infringing video was uploaded by a network user. Hode (the Appellant) did not interfere with and choose manually the user's uploading. Hode only provided the link service, not the infringing work. Hode did not directly commit infringement, so there is no direct infringement; 2. The original judgment is a subjective assumption in holding that Hode's act would inevitably harm the interests of the Qiyi, the licensee. There is no sufficient factual basis for the judgment and the amount of compensation is too high.

To Hode's appeal, Qiyi responded that Hode, which is not a link service provider, had committed direct infringement with the act of deep linking.

[Judgment]

After hearing, Shanghai Pudong New Area People's Court held that: Internet users can watch the video involved directly on Bilibili (the website operated by Hode), with no access to the interface of the linked website. At this stage, the server storing the video in the linked website became a remote server controlled by Hode and was used by Hode for free. Hode's website had essentially replaced the linked website to communicate the work to the public, who were offered the possibility of accessing the work involved at a time or place chosen by themselves. Therefore, it should be recognized that Hode's act constituted provision of works, which infringed Qiyi's right to communicate works over information networks. Accordingly, Shanghai Pudong New Area People's Court, in accordance with Article 10 (1) (12), Article 48 (1), and Article 49 of the *Copyright Law of the People's Republic of China*, Article 25 (1), (2) and Article 26 of the *Interpretation of the Supreme People's Court Concerning the Application of Laws in the Trial of Civil Disputes over Copyright*, made the judgement that Hode shall compensate Qiyi RMB 3,000 for its economic losses and RMB 2,500 for reasonable expenses incurred for stopping the infringement.

Refusing to accept the judgment of first instance, Qiyi and Hode appealed.

After hearing, Shanghai Intellectual Property Court held that the program involved actually came from tv. le. com and its transmission was controlled by tv. le. com. Hode provided search and link services for the transmission of such program through technical means. It did not put the work in the network, which did not constitute provision of works and was therefore not a direct infringement. Hode did not redirect the program involved to the linked website and guide users to watch the program there, nor did it remind users that the program involved originated from other websites. For that, Hode should bear a higher duty of care for the authorization of videos. Considering the factors such as the popularity of the program involved and the uploading time, it should have known subjectively that the program involved was highly likely to be infringed. However, it helped expand the consequences of infringement of the program involved. Therefore, Hode infringed Qiyi's right to communicate over information networks, and its act constituted contributory infringement. Hode should bear the liability for compensation. There is nothing wrong with the original judgment. Accordingly, the court rejected the appeal and upheld the original judgment.

[Case Study]

This case concerns the dispute over the infringement of the right to communicate works over information networks. China's statutory provisions on " the right to communicate works over information networks" are directly derived from Article 8 of the World Intellectual Property Organization Copyright Treaty (WCT). It refers to the provision of works, performances or audio and video products to the public by wired or wireless means, so that the public would have the right to access such works, performances or audio and video products at the time and place chosen by themselves. Without permission of the right holder, network users and network service providers' provision of works shall constitute an infringement on the right to communicate over information networks. Under the *Copyright Law of the People's Republic of China*, the communication of works over information networks is limited to "provision (of works) ," but it does not define which behavior can be deemed as "provision. " The *Provisions of the Supreme People's Court on Several Issues Concerning the Application of Laws in the Trial of Civil Disputes over Infringement of the Right to Communicate Works over Information Networks* enumerate and generalize the behaviors of "provision," and make it clear that the "behavior of provision" is the act of putting the works in the information network, which constitutes direct infringement.

Ⅰ. Criteria for Judgment on Infringement Caused by Non-redirecting of Deep Linking in Current Judicial Practice

In this case, Qiyi and Hode had no objection to the fact found in the original trial that the program involved was not stored on the server of Hode, i. e. , Hode did not upload the program directly to its server, it got the link of the program from tv. le. com. Therefore, Hode set up deep linking which would redirect to a third-party website for the program involved, providing search and link services for the communication of such program. It became a provider of network services.

In the current judicial practice, there are different criteria for judging the infringement of the right to communicate works over information networks caused by deep linking, including: 1. Server. This is an objective criterion. If the information is stored on the server of the linking website, the website is communicating information on the information networks. Without the permission of the right holder, such communication, if going beyond the statutory scope of use, shall constitute direct infringement on the right to communicate works over the information networks; if the linking website does not store the information and it only provides search and link services to the public using non-redirecting of deep linking, then the websites is providing network services, which does not constitute a direct infringement on the right to communicate works over the information networks. In some cases, the behavior of the network service provider of the linking website does not constitute a direct infringement on the right to communicate works over the information networks, but if it objectively contributes to the communication of works on the linked website, it may be liable for indirect infringement. In that case, it is necessary to further examine and determine whether the linking website has committed an indirect infringement and, if yes, whether it should be liable for compensation. 2. User's perception. This is a subjective criterion based on the information source perceived by users. Specifically, as long as the network service provider provides network technologies in a way which makes users feel that the website is providing information or that they can access the works directly from the website, the website's behavior shall be deemed as providing works. Applying this criterion, by setting up deep linking with no redirecting, the network service provider will make the general public intuitively feel that the information they have accessed comes from the linking website, and it is impossible for them to tell that the information actually comes from the linked website. Although the linking website does not store the information on its server, it makes the users feel that it provides content services rather than technical services, thus constituting direct infringement on the right to communicate works over the information networks. 3. Substantive replacement. According to this criterion, the result of setting up deep linking with no redirecting is that users can access the information directly on the linking website without going through the interface of the linked website. The server of the linked website where the information is stored is now equivalent to a remote server controlled by the linking website, and the linking website has in essence replaced the linked website to communicate works to the public. Moreover, the linking website uses the broadband and the web-disk of the linked websites for free, which makes it possible for users to access the work at the time or place they choose. To a certain extent, it obtains the benefits of communication that should have obtained by the linked website. Although the linking website does not store information on its server, it plays information on its own website without authorization, which constitutes substantial replacement of the linked website. Therefore, it is concluded that the linking website has implemented the act of providing works, which infringes the right of the right holder to communicate works over information networks. The court of first instance in this case adopted this criterion, holding that network users can watch the video involved directly on Hode's website without accessing the interface of the linked website, and the server of the linked website where the video was stored became a remote server controlled by Hode at this stage, and was used by Hode for free. Hode had essentially replaced the linked website to communicate the work to the public, which makes it possible for the public to access the work involved at a time or place chosen by themselves. Therefore, the court found that Hode's behavior constituted provision of works, which infringed the right of Qiyi to communicate the work over information networks.

Ⅱ. Reasons for Choosing the Criterion of Server in the Trial of Second Instance

According to the legal principle of intellectual property rights, when deciding whether the right to communicate the works over information networks is infringed or not, the court should examine and judge whether the behavior under litigation is controlled by the right to communicate the works over information networks. The existing laws stipulate that the behavior controlled by the right to communicate the works over information networks should have the feature of providing works to the public, that is, putting works in the information network. There is no such criterion as user's perception, so there is no legal basis for adopting this criterion. The court of first instance adopted the criterion of substantive replacement, holding that Hode's website had essentially replaced the linked website to communicate the work to the public and it had manually interfered with the link service, thus constituting provision of works. However, the court of second instance held that although Hode's website did not redirect the public to the linked website to watch the program involved, it did not change the fact that the program involved originated from tv. le. com. Hode's communication of the program involved depended on the existence of the program involved on tv. le. com, which was the premise of Hode's linking. Hode's linking should not be regarded as a substantial replacement of tv. le. com to put the work in the information network, thus constituting provision of works. Under such circumstance, the criterion of substantive replacement has gone beyond the existing relevant provisions on the right to communicate works over information networks. Therefore, the court of second instance adopted the criterion of server in accordance with the current legal provisions, holding that the following conditions should be met for constituting infringement on the right to communicate works over information networks: 1. without the permission of the right holder; 2. the defendant puts the work in the information network; 3. the public can access the work at the time and place chosen by themselves. In addition, Article 5 of the *Provisions of the Supreme People's Court on Several Issues Concerning the Application of Laws in the Trial of Civil Disputes over the Right to Communicate Works over Information Networks* stipulates that if a network service provider substantially replaces other network service providers in providing relevant works to the public by providing snapshots and thumbnails of web pages, the people's court shall decide that it constitutes provision of works. It should be noted here that the thumbnails and snapshots provided by a search and link service provider are cached in the provider's server by copying. Even if the relevant content is deleted by the linked website, the existence of thumbnails and snapshots of web pages will not be affected. Web users can still see them. Therefore, there is a difference between this case and the provision of thumbnails and snapshots prescribed by the Supreme People's Court.

In this case, Hode provided search and link services for the communication of the program involved through technical means. It did not put the program in the network nor directly provide the program. Therefore, Hode's behavior did not constitute provision of works, nor did it constitute direct infringement. However, the program involved "Happy Camp" is a famous variety show in China, and the uploading time is July 20, 2014. From title of the program "Happy Camp 20140719 Guys from the Tiny Times" uploaded to Hode's website, it can be found that it was uploaded the next day after premiere. Hode should have known that there was a great possibility of infringement, yet it took no measures to prevent or avoid such infringement, thus helping to expand the consequences of infringement of the program involved. Therefore, Hode's behavior infringed the Qiyi's right to communicate works over information networks.

(Writers: Lu Fengyu & Liu Le)

Examination and Identification of Network Service Providers and Network Content Providers

—Zhou Weihai v. Shanghai Yiyou Information Technology Co. , Ltd. & Shanghai Chuangzheng Information Technology Co. , Ltd. over Copyright Infringement

[Summary]

The examination and identification of network service providers and network content providers should take into full consideration the website's business, content arrangement, publicity information, self-introduction and profit model. The website's use of the infringing work is for its main business, not just for communicating the work to the public. Therefore, the website should be deemed as a content provider.

[Case Review]

Appellant (Defendant in the original trial): Shanghai Yiyou Information Technology Co. , Ltd.

Respondent (Plaintiff in the original trial): Zhou Weihai

Defendant in the original trial: Shanghai Chuangzheng Information Technology Co. , Ltd.

Cause of Action: Infringement of Copyright

First-Instance Case No. : (2014) No. 427

Second-Instance Case No. : (2015) No. 287

Zhou Weihai (周维海) submitted 37 film negatives and the digital photos of some tourist attractions in Yancheng, Jiangsu Province. These photos were also published under the column of Yancheng tourist attractions on Zhou Weihai (周为海) – Sina Blog (周为海 is 周维海's pen name). The 37 photos were: Jinghui Temple, Yuan's House in Yandu, Yancheng New Fourth Army Memorial Hall, Dazong Lake Scenic Spot, Former Residence of Hu Qiaomu, Former Residence of Lu Bingshu, Shi Nai'an Memorial Hall 1, Shi Nai'an Memorial Hall 2, Dong Xiaoxian Temple 1, Dong Xiaoxian Temple 2, Dong Yong's Tomb, Ancient Qingfeng Bridge 1, Ancient Qingfeng Bridge 2, Yancheng Yongning Temple – the Bell Tower, Yancheng Yongning Temple – the Old Monk's Memorial Tablet in Mingshan, Yancheng Yongning Temple – Tianwang Temple, Yancheng Yongning Temple – Dabei Temple, Yancheng Yongning Temple – Nianfo Hall, Yancheng Yongning Temple – Sutra Library, Yancheng Ziyun Mountain, Fangongdi Ruins 1, Fangongdi Ruins 2, Fangongdi Ruins 3, Fangongdi Ruins 4, Fangongdi in Caoyan, Haichunxuan Pagoda, Yancheng Peony Garden 1, Yancheng Peony Garden 2, Yancheng Luxiufu Memorial Hall 1, Yancheng Luxiufu Memorial Hall 2, Yancheng Luxiufu Memorial Hall 3, Dafeng Elk Reserve, Former Residence of Qiao Guanhua 1, Former Residence of Qiao Guanhua 2, Sancang Martyrs Cemetery – Suyu Memorial Hall, Xixin Temple – Yufo Tower, Xixin Temple – Wanfo Pagoda.

Earsgo is a travel information website operated by Shanghai Yiyou Information Technology Co., Ltd. ("Yiyou"), which provides services such as voice guide and information about the scenic spots for tourists and travel agencies. The website covers the following sections: domestic scenic spots, foreign scenic spots, category of scenic spots, and travel routes. The business scope of Yiyou includes: information technology, network technology, technical development, transfer, consultation and services regarding computers, and consultation on travel (no involvement in travel agency business). On March 18, 2014, when searching "Yancheng" on www. earsgo. com, it led you to the page of "Introduction to Yancheng Scenic Spots (pics & text)." By clicking on these scenic spots, the 37 photos involved could be found on the pages followed. By comparison, the 37 photos on earsgo, the 37 photos on Zhou Weihai's Sina blog were identical to the 37 pieces of works advocated by Zhou Weihai. Zhou Weihai sued Yiyou for infringement of copyright.

The Plaintiff Zhou Weihai claimed that he had independently created 37 photographic works including Jinghui Temple and published them on his personal blog. In March 2014, the Plaintiff found that the two Defendants had used, without the Plaintiff's authorization, the above photographs on their co-operated website: Earsgo (www. earsgo. com), without the author's name or any payment. The Plaintiff claimed that the two Defendants' behavior had infringed his copyright, so he requested the court to order that: 1. the two Defendants stop further infringement; 2. the two Defendants publish a statement on the front page of Earsgo, apologizing for the infringement and eliminating the effect. The statement shall last no less than one year; 3. the two Defendants compensate the Plaintiff RMB 110,000 (the same currency as below) for economic losses; 4. the two Defendants compensate the Plaintiff RMB 3,200 for reasonable expenses on litigation. During the trial, the Plaintiff proposed that as the Defendants had removed the photos involved from Earsgo, he would abandon the first claim.

The Defendant Yiyou argued that it objected to the Plaintiff's claims on the following grounds: 1. it objected to the Plaintiff's enjoyment of the copyright of the works involved. The film negatives could be reproduced, the digital photos could be copied from anywhere, and the works published on the blog cannot prove the Plaintiff's enjoyment of the copyright of the works involved. 2. Yiyou is a network service provider providing space for information storage, and the works claimed by the Plaintiff were uploaded by a member of Earsgo. According to relevant laws, if the right holder believed that the works involved in the Defendant's services had infringed his copyright, he should inform the defendant and present relevant evidence in advance. Yet the Plaintiff did not do that before filing an action. 3. According to the relevant legal provisions, Yiyou complies with the exemption clauses for network service providers.

The Defendant Chuangzheng argued that: 1. it does not agree that the Plaintiff enjoys the copyright of the works involved, with the same reasons provided by Yiyou. 2. Chuangzheng did not receive any notice from the Plaintiff. 3. Chuangzheng only dealt with the ICP filing for Yiyou. It is not an organizer of Earsgo, nor does it engage in the construction and operation of the website. Chuangzheng used to rent the server to Yiyou. Later the server was owned by Yiyou. Now it only provides telecom hosting service to Yiyou.

[**Judgment**]

At first instance, Shanghai Putuo District People's Court held that the copyright of photographic works belongs to the author. In this case, the film negatives, digital photos and notarial certificates provided by the Plaintiff were sufficient to prove that the author of the works involved is the Plaintiff, whose copyright in the works involved is protected by the law of China. Without permission, the defendant Yiyou used the Plaintiff's 37 works involved on its website Earsgo, with no mention of the Plaintiff's name or payment. Its act had constituted an infringement on the Plaintiff's copyright. It should bear the corresponding civil liabilities of stopping infringement, eliminating influence, apologizing for compensation, and compensating for losses. There is insufficient evidence to support the Plaintiff's claim that the Defendant Chuangzheng is a co-operator of Earsgo, which shall be dismissed by the court. As for Yiyou's defense that it is a network service provider which provides space for information storage, and is therefore compliant with the exemption clauses for that capacity: in this case, Earsgo, a professional travel marketing platform operated by the Defendant Yiyou, provides various travel-related information services for tourists and travel agencies. Although Yiyou provided screenshots of related webpages of the backstage operation of Earsgo, they are not enough to prove that Earsgo only provides space for information storage. Therefore, the Yiyou's use of the works involved on Earsgo without the permission of the Plaintiff constituted infringement. Or, assuming that Yiyou's defense was established, according to the relevant laws of China, network service providers, who provide space for information storage to enable their clients to communicate works, performances, audio and video products to the public over the information networks, shall not be liable for compensation if they: (1) clearly indicate that the information storage space is provided for their clients, and make public the name, contact person and network address of the client; (2) do not change the works, performances, audio and video products provided by their clients; (3) do not know or have no justified reason to know about the infringement of the works, performances and audio and video products provided by the clients; (4) do not gain economic benefits directly from the works, performances, audio and video products provided by the clients; (5) delete the works, performances, audio and video products which are claimed by the right holder as infringing in accordance with the provisions hereunder upon receipt of notice from the right holder. In this case, according to the facts ascertained, members of Earsgo did not sign in with a real name. The registration would be successful with a valid e-mail address. Yiyou could not provide the real name, identity information and effective contact information of the member who, as it argued, had uploaded the works involved; Earsgo is not a non-profit website, and the Earsgo coins used on the website can be traded with money. The website provides "advertising services" and some membership services are paid services; after receiving the Plaintiff's complaint and relevant evidence materials, Yiyou did not immediately delete the works involved, nor did it provide relevant evidence to prove that it had transferred the above materials to the member who, as it argued, had uploaded the works involved. Therefore, even if Yiyou's defense that it is a network service provider of information storage space was established, it did not comply with the exemption clause.

Accordingly, Shanghai Putuo District People's Court, in accordance with Article 3 (5), Article 9 (1), Article 10 (1) (ii), (xii), Article 10 (2), Article 47 (7), Article 48 (1) and Article 49 of the *Copyright Law of the People's Republic of China*, Article 14, Article 15, Article 22 of the *Regulation on the Protection of the Right to Communicate Works to the Public over Information Networks* and Article 7 of the *Interpretation of the Supreme People's Court Concerning the Application of Laws in the Trial of Civil Disputes over Copyright*, made the following judgment: the Defendant Yiyou shall make an apology on the front page of Earsgo (www. earsgo. com) for one month and compensate Zhou Weihai RMB 37,000 for his economic losses and RMB 3,000 for reasonable expenses.

Refusing to accept the judgment, Yiyou filed an appeal.

Shanghai Intellectual Property Court, the court of second instance, found the following facts: on the upper left of the website of Earsgo, there is a phrase saying "Global Voice Tour Guide No. 1." Under the column "About Us" on the website, it states that the Appellant is a high-tech start-up enterprise specializing in e-travel, mainly providing Chinese-English voice guide services for global tourist attractions. Earsgo uses advanced information network, voice and integration technology to create a real-time network voice guide service, providing convenient and easy voice guide for a vast number of tourists. Earsgo Membership Card, Earsgo Interface Service for Attractions, and Earsgo Voice Guide System for Attractions are listed under the column of "Product Profile." The court of second instance held that, first of all, according to the contents under "About Us" and "Product Profile" as well as the slogan on the website of Earsgo, it can infer that Earsgo, which is operated by Yiyou, is a travel service website providing voice guide and other services at scenic spots. Second, the photos involved appear at the upper part of the page introducing a corresponding scenic spot, below the photo is the text introduction of the scenic spot. These photos are used to introduce and display the scenic spots. Yiyou's use of those photos were also for the introduction and display of the corresponding scenic spots on Earsgo. It did not simply provide network space for users to browse and download those photos. Therefore, what Earsgo provided is not information storage space as prescribed under the *Copyright Law*. Its members had uploaded photos of the scenic spots to introduce and display the scenic spots, rather than communicate works to the public. Accordingly, the court dismissed the appeal and upheld the original judgment.

[**Case Study**]

Ⅰ. Identification of network content providers and network service providers and their infringement

According to the *Copyright Law*, the right of communication over information networks refers to the right to provide works to the public by wired or wireless means, so that the public can access the works at a time and place chosen by themselves. Without permission of the right holder, the provision of works, performances, audio and video products by network users and network service providers over information networks, unless otherwise provided under laws and administrative regulations, shall be decided by the people's court as infringement upon the right to communicate works over information networks. The people's court shall determine that the provision specified in the preceding paragraph has been done if works, performances, audio and video products are placed on the information networks by being uploaded to a network server, placed in a shared document, and via file-sharing software, so that the public can download, browse or access them by other means at a time and place chosen by themselves. The people's court shall not consider it a contributory infringer if the network service provider can prove that it only provides network services such as automatic access, automatic transmission, information storage space, search, link, document sharing, etc. If a network service provider can prove that it only provides network services without fault, the people's court shall not consider it an infringer. Whether the network service provider has fault or not is the key to determine whether it has committed infringement. The fault of network service providers includes that they know or should have known network users' communication of works over information networks. Specifically, for providers of information storage space, whether they should have known the infringement of network users on the right of communication over information networks should be decided by taking into consideration the following factors: whether the specific fact of the infringement of network users is obvious, whether the works are edited, recommended, or used to generate economic benefits, and whether appropriate measures are taken. Therefore, in the case of disputes over the right to communicate works over information networks, investigation should be made first to decide the defendant is a network content provider or a network service provider, i. e. , the infringing act is provision of network content or network service, and the defendant provides network content or network service.

II. Examination and identification of the providers of information storage space service

The network service providers of information storage space refer to the network service providers that provide storage space for network users with their own servers and allow them to upload information for other network users to browse or download, such as BBS service, FTP service, personal home page, MSN space and personal blog space, in order for network users to share information. In judicial practice, the examination and identification of service providers of information storage space should take into consideration the website's business, content arrangement, publicity information, self-introduction, profit model and how the works involved were communicated to the public. A website providing information storage space generally takes the provision of information storage space as its main business. It mainly provides a network platform for information sharing, not the information content, nor does it operate other business.

Ⅲ. Website operators who use pictures uploaded by network users for publicity of their main business should not be identified as providers of information storage space services.

After investigation, the following facts were ascertained: first, the slogan on the website of Earsgo is "Global Voice Tour Guide No. 1"; under the column "About Us" on the website, it states that Yiyou is a high-tech start-up enterprise specializing in e-travel, mainly providing Chinese-English voice guide services for global tourist attractions. Earsgo uses advanced information network, voice and integration technology to create a real-time network voice guide service, providing convenient and easy voice guide for a vast number of tourists; Earsgo Membership Card, Earsgo Interface Service for Attractions, and Earsgo Voice Guide System for Attractions are listed under the column of "Product Profile." Such information can prove that Earsgo, operated by Yiyou, is a travel service website providing voice tour guide and other services at scenic spots. The price displayed in Earsgo coins of voice tour guide for scenic spots on the website also confirms that. Second, the pictures involved appear on the upper part of the page introducing the corresponding scenic spot, and below the picture is the text introduction of the scenic spot. These pictures were used to introduce and display the corresponding scenic spots. Even if these pictures, as argued by Yiyou, were uploaded by a member of Earsgo, Yiyou's use of these pictures was to introduce and display the corresponding attractions on Earsgo rather than provide network space for users to browse and download. Therefore, what Earsgo provided is not information storage space as prescribed under the *Copyright Law*. Its members had uploaded photos of the scenic spots to introduce and display the scenic spots, not just communicate works to the public for information sharing. Therefore, Yiyou infringed Zhou Weihai's copyright by using and communicating the pictures involved without the permission of the right holder.

(Writers: Lu Fengyu & Yang Qingqing)

Copyright Protection of Works of Applied Art

—Blue Box International Limited v. Dumex Baby Food Co. , Ltd. *et al.* over Infringement of the Right to Reproduce and Distribute Works

[Summary]

The product involved in the dispute between Blue Box International Limited (the Plaintiff) and four Defendants including Dumex Baby Food Co. , Ltd. over the infringement of the right of reproduction and distribution of works has issues on the aesthetics of a work of applied art and the physical separation and conceptual separation of practical functions, which were carefully analyzed and elaborated in the judgment. This case can serve as an example of accurately identifying works of applied art and defining their scope of protection. Whether the different defendants in a joint action committed contributory infringement of copyright should be investigated from the subjective fault and specific behavior of the perpetrator. According to the different behaviors of the four Defendants, the court ordered them to bear different responsibilities.

[Case Review]

Plaintiff (Respondent):Blue Box International Limited
Defendant: Dumex Baby Food Co. , Ltd. (Defendant No. 1 or Dumex)
Defendant:Shanghai Lovhome Household Supplies Co. , Ltd. (Defendant No. 2 or Lovhome)
Defendant:Shanghai Esto Trade Development Co. , Ltd. (Defendant No. 3 or Esto)

Defendant (Appellant): Zhejiang Klupp Machine Co. , Ltd. (Defendant No. 4 or Klupp)

Cause of Action: Infringement of the right of reproduction and distribution of works

First-Instance Case No. : (2014) PMS(Z)CZ No. 67

Second-Instance Case No. : (2015) HYZMW(Z)ZZ No. 30

The Plaintiff is a Hong Kong company. In early 2010, the Plaintiff intended to develop a medium-and-high-grade riding toy car, which could serve as a scooter, a storage box and a trolley case, at a price of about US \$ 25, and assigned its employee Ma Hansen to design it. In the design process, for safety reasons, the designer gave up the idea of scooter; after considering animal images such as tiger, monkey and kitten, the designer finally decided bear. By January 2011, the design and sample production had been completed, and the product was named "Little Bear Amusement Luggage Trolley. " The luggage trolley consists of a panel with the pattern of a bear's face and a four-wheeled box (which is also the body). On the bear's face there are two large round eyes and a spiral pattern on the left cheek (for dimple). The bear's mouth tilts towards the right cheek, and it has two semicircular ears on its head. When the bear-face panel is pulled open and the box is flat, the four wheels can be landed on the ground for riding; when the panel is pulled up, the bear's ears can be used as a handle that the kid can grip when riding. Close the panel, lift the box and pull out the handle, you can get a wheeled luggage box. On January 7, 2011, the Plaintiff and Blue Box Dongguan, the outsider, reached a cooperation agreement, under which Blue Box Dongguan would produce and sell the products by itself or by entrusting a third party in accordance with the Plaintiff's design drawings. Later, Blue Box Dongguan authorized Magic Stone, another outsider, to be the sole partner of "BLUE-BOX" in China. On December 8, 2011, on the cover of a brochure distributed at the banquet "2011 Hong Kong Toy Industry Outstanding Achievement Award Ceremony, the 25th Anniversary of Hong Kong Toy Association and the Inauguration Ceremony of the Executive Committee," the picture of "a boy riding an amusement luggage trolley" was provided by the Plaintiff. The luggage trolley in the picture is the same as the product involved. From March to April 2012, Magic Stone participated in the Beijing Toy Show, where the product involved was exhibited.

On August 10, 2012, outsider Hu Kedi (an employee of Defendant No. 4) applied to China National Intellectual Property Administration (CNIPA) for a patent for the design of a toy trolley case, and he was granted a patent certificate in December of the same year. The view of the toy trolley case attached to the certificate is identical with that of the Plaintiff's "Little Bear Amusement Luggage Trolley." On October 31, 2012, Fang Jiading, the legal representative of Defendant No. 4, applied to CNIPA for a patent for utility model. The name of utility model is toy trolley case. In April 2013, he was granted the patent certificate. The usage in the instructions and the structure of the toy trolley case in the drawings attached to the certificate are identical with those of the Plaintiff's "Little Bear Amusement Luggage Trolley."

In September 2013, the Plaintiff applied to the National Copyright Administration of China (NCAC) for the registration of the product involved, with the author being Ma Hanson and the right holder the Plaintiff. The certificate of the ownership of copyright in the registration states that "This work is a service creation, and its copyright belongs to the unit (company)," with the signatures of Ma Hansen and the legal representative of the Plaintiff and the seal of the Plaintiff.

On January 23, 2013, Zhuang Jing, the Plaintiff's attorney, accompanied by the notary of Shenzhen Notary Office, Guangdong Province, went to Wal-Mart at Overseas Chinese City, Nanshan District, Shenzhen, where she bought four cans of Dumex milk powder and was given a child's walker for free. By comparison in court, this children's walker and the "Little Bear Amusement Luggage Trolley" advocated by the Plaintiff were almost identical in appearance, structure, use and the image of bear, except for the difference in colors. The supplier marked on the gift box is Defendant No. 2, and the manufacturer is Defendant No. 4. On January 29, 2013, with the witness of the notary, Zhuang Jing clicked "Dumex 1000-day Resistance Plan" and the "Video on the Operating Method of the Bear Luggage Trolley" on the next page on www.lovhome.com, the website of Defendant No. 2, and videotaped the whole process.

On September 26, 2013, Ni Ye, the Plaintiff's attorney, saved and extracted, under the witness of the notary of Shanghai Oriental Notary Office, the related e-mails from Jiang Xiangwen's computer, who was an employee of Magic Stone. The main contents of the mails are as follows: From April 5 to 11, 2012, Jiang Xiangwen negotiated with Sun Yan, an employee of a company in Liaoning Province, about 30,000 "Little Bear Amusement Luggage Trolleys" at a unit price of RMB 98. In the product information sent by Jiang Xiangwen, the retail price of the commodity is RMB 349. On the same day and November 4, 2013, Ni Ye saved and extracted, under the witness of the notary, Jiang Xiangwen's e-mails and QQ messages. The notary office produced two notarial certificates accordingly, which mainly covered the QQ conversations between Jiang Xiangwen (QQ No. : 1653502643, Name: " im Maggie (magic stone)" or " Maggie Magic Stone (Shanghai)") and " FRANK-Esto" (Zhou Minlin, Frank, Shanghai Lovhome Household Supplies Co. , Ltd. , Shanghai Esto Trade Development Co. , Ltd, Address: 8F, Building 1, 2007 Hongmei Road, Xuhui District, Shanghai, Tel: 021 – 60406051, Fax: 021 – 60406021, QQ: 1710209702 E-mail: frank@ lovhome. com) on March 28, July 11, and August 24, 2012. The messages included: Jiang Xiangwen successfully sent the document " Introduction to Magic Stone Products. ppt" to " FRANK-Esto"; Jiang Xiangwen successfully sent the document " Sample List-Esto 120711. xls" to " FRANK-Esto"; " FRANK-Esto" returned a receipt reading " We now receive the following samples from Magic Stone (Shanghai) Co. , Ltd. : ... Little Bear Amusement Luggage Trolley ... Quantity: 2, Borrower: Shanghai Esto Trade Development Co. , Ltd. (affixed with the company's electronic seal), Received by: FRANK ZHOU".

On February 28, 2014, Ni Ye, the Plaintiff's attorney, applied to the court for an inquiry order, and obtained Zhou Minlin's pension insurance information from Shanghai Social Insurance Administration Center. The result showed that " From July 2011 to now, Shanghai Esto Trade Development Co. , Ltd. has been paying social insurance for Zhou Minlin, who left the company in June 2012 and returned in July 2012. " In addition, the information on Zhou Minlin's business card provided by the Plaintiff was the same as that of " Zhou Minlin" and " Frank" shown in the aforementioned notarial certificates. The business card also indicated the information about Defendants No. 2 and No. 3.

The Plaintiff claimed that in February 2010, it assigned its employee to design the" Little Bear Amusement Luggage Trolley," which was launched in 2011. The toy is a work of applied art and the copyright is enjoyed by the Plaintiff. In 2012, Magic Stone (Shanghai) Trade Co. , Ltd. (" Magic Stone"), the Plaintiff's agent in Shanghai and an outsider of this case, participated in the Beijing Toy Show, where the toy was also exhibited. In January 2013, the Plaintiff found that the " children's walker" gifted by Defendant No. 1 for the sale of Dumex milk powder was almost identical to the Plaintiff's " Little Bear Amusement Luggage Trolley" in terms of the overall design and visual effect, especially the most prominent panel design. The packaging of the "children's walker" also showed that the Defendant No. 2 was the supplier and Defendant No. 4 was the manufacturer. The Plaintiff also found that Defendant No. 2 and Defendant No. 3 were affiliated companies, and Defendant No. 3 had asked its employee Zhou Minlin to ask Magic Stone for the product profile of the "Little Bear Amusement Luggage Trolley" and obtained two samples on July 13, 2012. The Plaintiff claimed that its "Little Bear Amusement Luggage Trolley" is a three-dimensional work of art protected by the Copyright Law, and it enjoys the copyright for the product as a whole. After receiving the samples through Defendant No. 3, Defendant No. 2 entrusted Defendant No. 4 to reproduce the product and offered it to Defendant No. 1 for distribution. The four Defendants had jointly infringed upon the Plaintiff's copyright, so the Plaintiff requested the court to order that: the four Defendants immediately stop the infringement, jointly and severally compensate the Plaintiff RMB 500,000 for economic losses and RMB 150,000 for reasonable expenses on investigation and stopping the infringement.

[Judgment]

After hearing, Shanghai Pudong New Area People's Court held that art works are protected under the Copyright Law of China. The product involved in this case possesses the animal pattern for enjoyment and the practical functions of riding, storing and towing. The aesthetics of the pattern shows originality and reaches a considerable height, and can be separated from the practical functions physically and conceptually under different ways of use, which makes the product a work of applied art. Works of applied art are protected as artworks under the Copyright Law of China, but the scope of protection is limited to the parts in the works which have artistic beauty and constitute works of art. The Copyright Law does not protect practical functions. Therefore, in this case, as a work of applied art, the product involved shall be protected in part, i. e. , the bear-face panel or the pattern of the bear's face, rather than as a whole according to China's Copyright Law.

The pattern of the bear's face in the product involved is a work created by Ma Hansen for fulfilling the task assigned by the Plaintiff. The copyright ownership certificate signed by Ma Hansen and the Plaintiff proves that the copyright of the work involved belongs to the Plaintiff. The Plaintiff is a legal person in Hong Kong, and the work involved was created in Hong Kong. However, the products attached to the Plaintiff's copyrighted work have been made public in the mainland market through the promotion of its partners, i. e. , the work has been published in the mainland of China. Therefore, the Plaintiff has the right to claim protection in accordance with the *Copyright Law of the People's Republic of China*.

The work claimed by the Plaintiff is the bear-face pattern on the "Little Bear Amusement Luggage Trolley," and the infringing work is the bear-face pattern on the "Children's Walker" of the Defendant. By comparison, it is found that they are almost identical. Given that the Plaintiff finished the design and created the product involved before the Defendant, it can be found that the "Children's Walker" is reproduction of the Luggage Trolley. The infringing product was produced by Defendant No. 4 and sold to Defendant No. 2, which re-sold it to Defendant No. 1, and Defendant No. 1 offered it to consumers for free. Therefore, Defendant No. 4 directly infringed the Plaintiff's copyright by reproducing and distributing the Plaintiff's work without permission, which, and should bear the civil liability of stopping the infringement and making due compensation. Considering the relationship between Defendants No. 2, No. 3 and Zhou Minlin, Defendant No. 2 should have known that Zhou had obtained the product and related information from the Plaintiff, yet it still bought the infringing product in batches and sold them to Defendant No. 1. Therefore, Defendant No. 2 had fault in distributing the infringing product and should bear corresponding civil liability. The Plaintiff claimed that Defendants No. 2 and No. 4 jointly committed the infringement, but it did not provide evidence. Since Defendant No. 4 might obtain information about the Plaintiff's product via other channels, the Plaintiff's claim that Defendant No. 2 should bear joint and several liability was dismissed. As Defendant No. 2's infringement of the distribution right was based on the reproduction and distribution of Defendant No. 4, Defendant No. 4 became the wrongdoer and should bear joint and several liabilities with Defendant No. 2. Although Defendant No. 3 had obtained the Plaintiff's product, it did not infringe the Plaintiff's copyright by providing Defendant No. 2 with information about the Plaintiff's product, so the Plaintiff's claim for Defendant No. 3 to bear civil liability was dismissed. Defendant No. 1 infringed the Plaintiff's distribution right by purchasing the infringing product as a gift for consumers and should bear the civil liability for stopping the infringement.

However, the producer of the infringing product was identified, and it is difficult to ascertain that Defendant No. 1 was a wrongdoer because it knew or ought to know that the product it used as a gift was an infringing product. Therefore, Defendant No. 1's defense that its gift had come from a legal source was established, and the Plaintiff's claim that Defendant No. 1 should bear joint and several liabilities for compensation was dismissed.

Accordingly, Shanghai Pudong New Area People's Court decided that: Defendants No. 1 and No. 2 immediately stop infringing upon the Plaintiff's right to distribute the "Bear-Face Pattern" of the "Little Bear Amusement Luggage Trolley"; Defendant No. 4 immediately stop infringing upon the Plaintiff's right to reproduce and distribute the "Bear-Face Pattern" of the "Little Bear Amusement Luggage Trolley"; Defendant No. 2 compensate the Plaintiff RMB 50,000 for economic losses and RMB 15,000 for reasonable expenses, and Defendant No. 4 shall be jointly and severally liable for that; Defendant No. 4 compensate the Plaintiff RMB 200,000 for economic losses and RMB 60,000 for reasonable expenses. The Plaintiff's other claims were dismissed.

Refusing to accept the judgment, Defendant No. 4 appealed.

After hearing, Shanghai No. 1 Intermediate People's Court held that there is nothing wrong about the original judgment as the facts were found clearly, the law was applied correctly, and the procedure was in accordance with law. The appeal should be rejected for lack of factual and legal basis. According to Article 170 (1) (i) of the *Civil Procedure Law of the People's Republic of China*, the court dismissed the appeal and upheld the original judgment.

[Case Study]

This case involves the identification and protection of works of applied art, and whether the four Defendants committed joint infringement and their respective liability. Therefore, the main focuses of this case are: 1. whether the Plaintiff's claim for copyright protection of the product involved can be established, and if yes, how much the protection scope is; 2. if the Plaintiff's claim for the right regarding the work is established, whether its claim for infringement liability of the four Defendants can be supported.

Ⅰ. Whether the product involved is protected under China's Copyright Law and the scope of protection

This case concerns the protection of works of applied art. While the *Copyright Law* of China does not specify whether to protect the copyright of works of applied art, the *Berne Convention*, an international treaty to which China is a party, allows member states to protect works of applied art in accordance with the copyright law. In the *Regulations on Implementing International Copyright Treaties*, China also explicitly requires the protection of foreign works of applied art. In the administrative enforcement and judicial practice of the *Copyright Law* in China, the copyright law is also applicable to protect works of applied art. Yet such protection is conditional: one lies in the protection conditions of works of applied art, that is, the identification conditions of works of applies art; the other lies in the scope of protection of works of applied art. This is mainly to conform to the basic principles of the Copyright Law, and reflect the strict functional boundaries of different legal systems.

As for the identification conditions of works of applied art, it is generally believed that the following conditions should be met: first, the practical function and artistic beauty of the work of applied art can be independent of each other; second, the independent art design has originality; third, the art design has reached a certain artistic height. The product involved in this case has animal pattern for artistic enjoyment, the practical functions for riding, storing and towing, and the originality and artistic beauty of the pattern has reached a certain height, so it is a work of applied art. First, the practical functions and the artistic beauty of the product involved can be independent of each other. The product involved is composed of two parts: the body of the wheeled amusement trolley (also the body of the wheeled suitcase) and the bear-face panel (also the head of the amusement trolley). On the whole, it is a practical toy, but its bear-face panel possesses strong artistic beauty. As a wheeled suitcase, the practical case and the beautiful bear-face panel can be physically distinguished and independent of each other. When the bear-face panel is pulled up, the wheeled suitcase becomes a trolley for young children to ride on. Accordingly, the bear-face panel becomes a handle, which means that it has the function as a handle of the trolley. At this point, the handle and the body (i. e. , the suitcase) can still be separated physically, but for the handle itself, the bear-face pattern and the practical function are inseparable physically, they can, however, be separated conceptually. Because the practical function of the handle will not be affected no matter which animal image or pattern it is designed, even with no pattern. Second, the design of the aesthetic part which can exist independently has originality, and the artistic beauty has reached a certain height. The bear-face panel on the product involved is a three-dimensional plastic design of the bear's head, which is a cartooned and artistic expression of the bear. The design of the smart eyeballs, the dimple on one side of the face and the mouth tilting to the other side makes the bear playful and lively and easy to be loved by children. The design not only reflects the originality of the creator, but also achieves a high artistic level. The whole bear-face pattern has become a work of art.

On the scope of protection of works of applied art under the *Copyright Law*. Based on the basic principle that *Copyright Law* does not protect practical functions, the scope of protection of works of applied art under the *Copyright Law* is limited. Under the *Copyright Law of China*, works of applied art are protected as works of fine art, but the scope of protection is limited to the parts of works of applied art which have artistic beauty and constitute works of fine art. Therefore, in this case, as a work of applied art, the product involved shall only be protected for its bear-face pane, not the whole "Little Bear Amusement Luggage Trolley," according to the *Copyright Law* of China.

The purpose of setting up conditions for the identification of works of applied art and limiting the scope of protection under the *Copyright Law* is to better reflect the functions of the *Copyright Law* and to define the boundary with the system of design patents. The judgment of this case has made a detailed analysis and accurate definition of the conditions for the identification of works of applied art and the scope of protection of works of applied art under the Copyright Law, suggesting a good grasp on the system of the *Copyright Law*.

II. Determination of the nature of the Four Defendant's Behaviors and their Responsibility

The Plaintiff claimed that after Defendant No. 3 obtained the Plaintiff's product, it was provided by Defendant No. 2 to Defendant No. 4 for reproduction and distribution. After purchasing the infringing product, Defendant No. 1 distributed it to Defendant No. 1, which then distributed it by way of complimentary. Therefore, the four Defendants committed joint infringement and should bear joint liability for that. After hearing, the court determined the nature of the four Defendants' behaviors and the liability they should bear respectively.

According to the facts ascertained by the court, the infringing product involved was produced by Defendant No. 4 and sold to Defendant No. 2, which re-sold it to Defendant No. 1, which gave it to consumers as a gift. The flow of the infringing product is clear, but it is not easy to determine the nature of the four defendants' behaviors and their responsibility. It is even more difficult for the court to identify and support the Plaintiff's claim that the four defendants had the joint intent of infringement and should bear joint and several liabilities. The reasons are as follows: first, it is difficult to identify the subjective mental state of joint intent; second, the infringement of the intangible intellectual property rights and the infringement of tangible property have different characteristics. The right carrier of tangible property is unique, so it is easy to determine the actor's subjective fault and participation in specific acts; while the right carrier of intangible property such as intellectual property is multiple, the right holder's access to the right carrier is not necessarily related to infringement, and the law also provides for exemption under certain circumstances. Therefore, in the judgment of intellectual property infringement, it is difficult to determine the actor's fault and participation in the act.

In this case, the behavior of Defendant No. 4 is relatively clear, and it is easy to determine its responsibility because it is the source of the infringing product and it should also be responsible for the subsequent circulation of the product. Therefore, the court decided that Defendant No. 4 should bear the civil liability for infringement of reproduction and distribution right, and also the joint and several liabilities for the infringement of distribution right by Defendant No. 2. As the distributor of the infringing product, Defendant No. 1 must first assume the responsibility of stopping the infringement. As for whether it should assume other responsibilities, the decision would be made according to the facts found in the case. In this case, Defendant No. 1's purchase of product through Defendant No. 2 is not enough to confirm that it knew or ought to know that the product is an infringing product. Therefore, the exemption clause is applicable here and Defendant No. 1 shall not be liable for compensation.

What is difficult to determine is the behaviors Defendants No. 2 and No. 3 and their responsibility. Although the Plaintiff's evidence is sufficient to prove that Defendants No. 2 and No. 3 are affiliated companies, and Zhou Minlin's acquisition of the Plaintiff's sample product and his relationship with Defendants No. 2 and No. 3 have also been identified, it cannot be concluded that Defendants No. 2 and No. 3, Defendants No. 2 and No. 4 have common intent of infringement. According to the available evidence, as the infringement found in this case was later than the time when the Plaintiff's product was released in the domestic market, the possibility of Defendant No. 4 accessing and obtaining information about the Plaintiff's product through other ways cannot be ruled out. It is difficult to determine that Defendant No. 2 provided the sample product directly to Defendant No. 4. However, it is sufficient for the court to regard Zhou Minlin as a contact point, and found that Defendant No. 2 obtained the Plaintiff's product and related information through this contact point. On this basis, the court found that Defendant No. 2 should have a duty of scrutiny and care when purchasing the infringing product from Defendant No. 4. However, Defendant No. 2 purchased the infringing product in batches and sold them without performing such duty. Therefore, Defendant No. 2 should bear the liability for infringement. Although Defendant No. 3 obtained the Plaintiff's product, it cannot be determined that Defendant No. 3's behavior constituted infringement of copyright only because Defendant No. 2 acquired information about the Plaintiff's products through Defendant No. 3. Therefore, the Plaintiff's claim that Defendant No. 3 should bear civil liability lacks factual basis.

(Writer: Chen Huizhen)

The Basic Method of Determining the Substantial Similarity Between Works of Fine Art

—Animation International Ltd. v. Shanghai Yaya Information Technology Co. , Ltd. *et al.* over Infringement of the Right to Reproduce and Adapt Works

[**Summary**]

In the process of determining whether the allegedly infringing work is plagiarism of the work of fine art of the right holder, it is difficult to determine the existence of substantial similarities between the two works in judicial practice. To solve this problem, the three-step approach is applied in this case: first, if the plaintiff claims that the infringing work is plagiarism of part of its work, the more quintessential and creative that part is, the greater the possibility of infringement is decided. Second, use the abstract-filter-contrast method as the main test method. After properly examining the works of the plaintiff and the defendant, the sameness or similarities between the two works in terms of lines, shapes, shades and colors are first determined, then the ideological parts are removed, and then the existence of the remaining elements in the public domain is examined. Finally, we can judge whether the two works are substantially similar according to the same or similar parts under protection after such filtering. Third, by comparing the two as a whole, we can judge whether the two works are substantially similar.

[**Case Review**]

Plaintiff: Animation International Ltd. ("Animation")

Defendant: Shanghai Yaya Information Technology Co. , Ltd. ("Yaya")

Defendant: Shanghai Yibaimi Network Technology Co. , Ltd. ("Yibaimi")
Cause of Action: Infringement of the Right to Reproduce and Adapt Works
First-Instance Case No. : (2014) PMS(Z)CZ No. 1097
Second-Instance Case No. : (2015) HZMZZ No. 614

Shanghai Pudong New Area People's Court found that the manga series *Doraemon* was first published in Japan on Dec. 1, 1969. The character "Doraemon" is a cat-like robot with a large and round head and a relatively small body. Its round eyes, above the line between its head and face, are close to each other. Its round nose is closely under the eyes. It has a large mouth, which almost spans the whole face. It has three whiskers on both cheeks, and a collar, along with a bell, around the neck. It has a big pocket on the belly. It has round hands, oval feet, and a spherical tail at its back (see Figure 1 for details). The character of "Doraemon" is very popular all over the world. In the Chinese-version animation and publications of "Doraemon," there are the characters of "哆啦A梦" in artistic font. The characters are written in blue, with rough and round strokes. And there is a red ellipse at the bottom of each character. The point at the top of the character "啦" is represented by the yellow bell in the cartoon character of "Doraemon," and the strokes at the upper part of the character "梦" are represented by two smiling and blinking eyes. The whole font has a black outline (see Figure 2 for details). The Plaintiff Animation, authorized by the copyright owner of the cartoon character of "Doraemon," has obtained the right to conduct and expand the commodity authorization business on the cartoon character of "Doraemon" in the name of the Plaintiff in mainland of China, and to take legal action when infringement occurs.

The two Defendants jointly operated an application software called "Dingdong Community (叮咚小区)" and used the graphics and character graphics of the application software for promotion. The graphics of the application software is a square with four round corners. The whole picture consists of four parts: the upper red part and the lower blue part are divided by an arc; in the blue part there is a white semicircle; there is a yellow doorbell between the red part and the blue part, and the doorbell has a blue outline (see Figure 3 for details). The font of "叮咚小区" is thick, round and blue, with a blue outline. There is a yellow doorbell, which is the same as the one on the graphics of the application software, above the space between "咚" and "小" (see Figure 4 for details).

In 2014, the Defendant Yibaimi and EMC² China signed the Brand Construction

Service Contract for Dingdong Community, under which Yibaimi entrusted EMC^2 China with the work of brand appeal, slogan and brand-related design for the "Dingdong Community Project." In the article published on Dingdong Community's WeChat account, the Defendant Yaya said that "On March 21, 'Dingdong Community' was officially launched. Meanwhile, its blue-and-white LOGO covers all major rail transit stations in Shanghai. Such color combination reminds people of the omnipotent cat-robot Doraemon. Dingdong Community is just like Doraemon's magic pouch, which includes services such as meter reading for water, electricity and gas, utilities charging, Best Tone (114), pet matching, forum for discussion, discounts at nearby stores, second-hand market, carpooling, and housekeeping."

The Plaintiff claimed that in the ad promoting the application software "Dingdong Community," which was developed and operated by the two Defendants, a number of elements of the character "Doraemon" were used without authorization. The two Defendants' behaviors infringed the Plaintiff's right to reproduce and adapt the cartoon character "Doraemon" and the character graphics of "哆啦 A 梦." Therefore, the Plaintiff requested the court to order the two Defendants to: 1. immediately stop using the elements of the character "Doraemon"; 2. make a statement in *Legal Daily* to clarify the facts and eliminate the impact; 3. compensate the Plaintiff RMB 2 million for economic losses and RMB 50,000 for reasonable expenses.

During the trial, the Plaintiff acknowledged that the works it claimed were: 1. the trunk of the cartoon character "Doraemon," which includes creative elements such as the red collar (narrow and long), the yellow bell (made up of two small semicircles, the upper semicircle is smaller than the lower one; the two semicircles are separated by two lines in the middle, and a black line in the lower semicircle indicates that the bell inclines 180 degrees), the white abdomen (a large semicircle), the pouch (a semicircle) and the blue body (see the trunk in Figure 1); 2. the character graphics of "哆啦 A 梦" (Figure 2). The font of the character graphics is fat. The head and strokes of some characters are transformed into an oval. The last stroke of the four characters is transformed into four ovals, which are on the same line. There is a yellow bell with an inclination of 135 degrees on the upper right of the character "啦," and a pair of smiling eyes in the middle of the character "梦." The four characters are generally in blue, with a white outline. The chubby, funny character graphics are consistent with personality of the cartoon character "Doraemon." The Plaintiff claimed that the graphics of the two Defendants' application software "Dingdong Community" (Figure 3) and the character graphics of "叮咚小区" (Figure 4) were substantially similar to the two works claimed by the Plaintiff respectively, thus constituting infringement.

The Defendant Yaya argued that the application software "Dingdong Community" involved was not operated by it, so it had nothing to do with the case. Therefore, it requested the court to dismiss the charges against it.

The Defendant Yibaimi argued that the determination of copyright infringement should adhere to the principle of protecting the originality of the work, and the originality of the cartoon character "Doraemon" is embodied in its overall image, especially its head, body and whiskers. Those elements, rather than the collar, bell and pouch advocated by the Plaintiff, represent the originality of the work. Besides, the art rules governed by color, point of view, shape and aesthetic habits are not protected under the Copyright Law, so the Plaintiff has no right to claim for those parts. In this case, the graphics of the Defendant's application software "Dingdong Community" are original in composition and detailed expression, and is completely different from "cat" image in the Plaintiff's cartoon character "Doraemon"; the character graphics of "叮咚小区" are created by the Defendant independently, which is not substantially similar to the character graphics of "哆啦 A 梦." Therefore, the copyright infringement claimed by the Plaintiff cannot be established; the Defendant requested the court to dismiss the Plaintiff's claims.

[Judgment]

After hearing, Shanghai Pudong New Area People's Court held that the Plaintiff, authorized by the right holder, could bring a lawsuit against the copyright infringement of the cartoon character "Doraemon." However, in this case, there is insufficient evidence to prove that the Plaintiff has obtained the copyright for the character graphics of "哆啦 A 梦," and that the Plaintiff can claim copyright infringement on such character graphics against the two Defendants.

As to whether the graphics of the application software "Dingdong Community" is substantially similar to the trunk of the cartoon character "Doraemon," the court held that the level of originality of the trunk of the cartoon character "Doraemon" claimed by the Plaintiff is rather low, and by comparing the same and similar points between it and the graphics of the application software "Dingdong Community" (excluding those in the ideological and common areas), it cannot be concluded that the two are substantially similar. Moreover, there are many differences and significant visual differences between the Plaintiff's work and the Defendants' work. Such protection of the Plaintiff's work will hinder others' freedom of creation to the extent permitted by law.

As to whether the character graphics of "叮咚小区" used by the two Defendants are substantially similar to the character graphics of "哆啦A梦," the court held that the same and similar points between the character graphics of "叮咚小区" used by the two Defendants and the character graphics of "哆啦A梦" belong to the common area in the creation of artworks. They are not original. Besides, there are great visual differences between them. Therefore, the two are not substantially similar.

To sum up, the Plaintiff cannot prove that it has obtained the copyright of the character graphics of "哆啦A梦" and that it has the right to protect the copyright; the graphics of the application software "Dingdong Community" run by the two Defendants and the character graphics of "叮咚小区" are not substantially similar to the trunk of the cartoon character "Doraemon" and the characters graphics of "哆啦A梦" claimed by the Plaintiff. The two Defendants' behaviors do not constitute an infringement on the copyright of the Plaintiff's works. Also, the two Defendants' works are not new works created based on the Plaintiff's works, so there is no infringement upon the Plaintiff's right to adapt the works. Since the two Defendants' behaviors do not constitute copyright infringement, all the claims of the Plaintiff should be dismissed. In accordance with the provisions of Article 10 (1) (ⅴ) and 10 (1) (ⅹⅳ) and Article 11 of the *Copyright Law of the People's Republic of China*, the court decided to dismiss all the plaintiff's claims. After the judgment, the Plaintiff Animation filed an appeal, which was later withdrawn in the second instance.

[Case Study]

The determination of plagiarism between works of fine art generally follows the criteria of "access" + "substantial similarity." As for "access," the plaintiff only needs to prove that its work is completed before the completion of the allegedly infringing work, and that the defendant has the possibility of accessing the plaintiff's work. In practice, this criterion can easily be decided by the judge. By contrast, in practice, there are many methods to determine whether two works are "substantially similar." Because of the differences of the judges' understanding of the works, the application of different test methods and judgment scales, and the lack of objective standard basis, it has always been difficult and controversial in judicial practice to determine substantial similarity between works of fine art.

In judicial practice, there are two main methods for the comparison of substantial similarities between works. One is the abstract-filter-contrast method, which is to divide the work into different levels of abstraction, eliminate the general ideological mode, and compare the remaining protected factors. The other is the holistic comparison method, which compares the two works without any filtering, and whether they are substantially similar will be determined based on the overall impression and perception. Comparing the two methods, we can find that the former is more abstract and stricter than the latter, which may lead to an unfavorable result on copyright protection. The second method, which is based on the overall perception and impression, may bring some ideological elements or common area-related content into the comparison, which will lead to the tendency to expand copyright protection. Therefore, both methods have their own basis and advantages and disadvantages. It is worth exploring and researching how to use these two methods reasonably in order to achieve a balance between copyright protection and promoting new creation.

In this case, the Plaintiff claimed that the graphics of the application software "Dingdong Community" operated by the two Defendants are substantially similar to the trunk of the cartoon character "Doraemon," and the character graphics of "叮咚小区" to those of "哆啦A梦," which led to the conclusion that the two Defendants infringed the Plaintiff's copyright. The cartoon character "Doraemon" was published long before the launch of the application software "Dingdong Community," and the character is popular all over the world. Therefore, the possibility of the two Defendants' access to the cartoon character is undisputed. As a result, the focus of this case lies in comparing the works and determining whether they are substantially similar. When comparing the above-mentioned works, the court adopted the following steps:

Ⅰ. If it is necessary to determine that the allegedly infringing work is plagiarism of part of the work claimed by the Plaintiff, the larger extent the allegedly infringing part occupies the essence of the plaintiff's work and the higher the originality of the plaintiff's work is, the more likely the infringement is determined.

Compared with other similar cases, this case is different in that the Plaintiff claimed that the Defendant's work is substantially similar to the trunk, not the whole, of its cartoon character "Doraemon." Therefore, the court concluded that the cartoon character "Doraemon" shows a cute, chubby and witty cat-like robot, and the blue-and-white round face, the round eyes, the red nose, the three whiskers on both sides and the cat face without ears are undoubtedly the most original points in this work of art. Those points fully reflect the characteristics of the cat-like robot that the author intends to express. Compared with the cat's face, the trunk of Doraemon is less original. The red collar, white pouch, yellow bell and blue body are quite common, and the lines are also quite simple. The trunk of "Doraemon" alone cannot fully express the artistic image and aesthetic effect that the author wants to pursue for the cat-like robot. Therefore, as part of the artwork, the trunk of "Doraemon" has a low level of originality. A higher standard for substantial similarity will be required to determine that the Defendants' work constitutes infringement.

Ⅱ. Taking abstract-filter-contrast as the main test method

Comparing the same and similar points between the trunk of the cartoon character "Doraemon" and the graphics of the application software "Dingdong Community," it can be found that both works used the colors of red, blue, yellow and white. As the combination of these four colors can bring people the sensation and feeling of beauty, loveliness and peace, the selection and combination of these four colors are commonly seen in the works of fine art, especially in the creation of cartoon characters such as Conan, Superman, and Donald Duck. Therefore, for the Plaintiff, the selection of the four colors is not creative and cannot be monopolized by it. In composition, the trunk of "Doraemon" is shown as a collar worn around the neck, a bell tied to the collar, under which there is a circular abdomen and a semicircular pouch. The rest is part of a body. On the whole it is the trunk of a cartoonized human body. The graphics of the application software "Dingdong

Community" is a square with four rounded corners, a shape which is commonly used in application software nowadays. Comparing the same or similar elements between the two, it can be found that there is a semicircular pouch in the lower part of the trunk of "Doraemon" and there is also a semicircle at the lower half of the graphics of "Dingdong Community," but a semicircular pouch or a semicircle itself is not original. The use of a semicircle, a very simple art form, to represent the pouch should belong to the common area and should not be monopolized by the Plaintiff. The red collar in the trunk of "Doraemon" is similar to the red arc in the upper half of "Dingdong District," but this choice is very simple and common. It is not original and cannot be monopolized by the Plaintiff. The blue trunk of "Doraemon" is similar to the blue background of "Dingdong District," but the blue background is also commonly seen in art works. Therefore, it is not original, either.

Ⅲ. Taking holistic comparison as the secondary test method

The court found that there were also many differences in the overall visual effect between the two: (1) in the selection of colors: the abdomen and the pouch on it of the cartoon character "Doraemon" are white, while there is only a white semicircle in the lower part of the graphics of the application software "Dingdong Community," and the background of the white semicircle is blue. Also, the trunk of the cartoon character "Doraemon" has a black outline, while there is no black outline between the color blocks of the application software "Dingdong Community." The visual effects of the two are different; (2) in composition: comparing the upper half of the two, there is a long and narrow collar above the trunk of "Doraemon" and there is a round bell on the collar. The upper half of the application software "Dingdong Community" is marked out by an arc, which is wider than the collar of "Doraemon." There is a circular doorbell in the middle of the arc, and the shape of the doorbell is completely different from that of the bell in "Doraemon." Besides, there is a circular abdomen in the trunk of "Doraemon," while there is no corresponding part in the graphics of the application software "Dingdong Community." So many differences between the two in composition resulted in significant visual differences; (3) in terms of lines: the lines of the trunk of "Doraemon" are relatively soft and round, reflecting a plump and cute cartoon character, while regular straight lines and circles are used in the graphics of "Dingdong Community," reflecting a concise and clear application software, so there are also significant differences in the use of lines between the two; (4) Most importantly, there were also big differences in the overall visual effects of the two. The trunk of "Doraemon" has the white round abdomen, which occupies a large proportion in the whole picture, plus the round and plump body, creating an overall visual effect of a chubby and cute cat-like robot, while the graphics of "Dingdong Community" is a common square with rounded corners. The two are obviously different from each other. The yellow circular part in the middle, which is also the most original part of the two works, presents a three-dimensional bell and a plane doorbell, which are obviously different. The ultimate difference in the overall visual effect caused by these different elements is that the trunk of the cartoon character "Doraemon" gives the viewer a picture of a cute chubby cat-like robot body with a collar, a bell and a pouch, while the graphics of the application software "Dingdong Community" gives the viewer a feeling of pleasant and convenient life in the community with a smiling face and a doorbell, but it will not produce the visual effect of a cat-like robot body.

The court concluded that the trunk of the cartoon character "Doraemon" claimed by the Plaintiff had a low level of originality, and that the same and similar points between it and the graphics of the application software "Dingdong Community" (excluding those in the ideological and common areas) were not enough to prove that they were substantially similar. Also, there were many differences and visual disparity between the Plaintiff's and the Defendants' works. Protection of the Plaintiff's work will hinder others' freedom of creation permitted by law.

Ⅳ. When the work is simple, the holistic comparison method can be used as the main test method.

Compared with the two works mentioned above, the character graphics of "哆啦A梦" and "叮咚小区" are relatively simple. Therefore, the holistic comparison method was used to determine whether they were substantially similar. The court held that the same and similar points between the character graphics of "叮咚小区" and those of "哆啦A梦" lied in the use of the colors of blue and yellow and the thick and rounded fonts with descriptive edges. Such use is to show the visual effects of simplicity, loveliness, peace and tranquility. These elements are commonly used in the creation of character graphics. Instead of being original, they belong to the common area and can be used by everyone. Besides, there are some major differences between the two：there are red ovals at the bottom of the four characters "哆啦 A 梦," a pair of smiling and blinking eyes in the middle of the character "梦," while those elements do not exist in the character graphics of "叮咚小区"; in the character graphics of "叮咚小区," there is a plane yellow doorbell in the middle above the characters "咚" and "小," while there is a three-dimensional yellow bell above the character "啦" in the character graphics of "哆啦 A 梦." Therefore, the two were not substantially similar because of the significant detailed and visual differences.

In conclusion, when comparing the substantial similarities between the Plaintiff's and the Defendants' works, the court first determined whether the part of the work claimed by the Plaintiff was the quintessence of the work and the degree of originality of that part. Then the court took abstract-filter-contrast as the main test method, and holistic comparison as the secondary, overcame the limitations of the two methods to achieve a balance between copyright protection and promotion of creation, and finally drew a conclusion that the works of the two parties did not constitute substantial similarities, achieving a good result. Although the above methods are not applicable to all cases involving substantial similarities, the trial of this case undoubtedly provides some ideas for the trial of such cases.

(Writer：Yang Jie)

Figure 1：The Character of Doraemon

Figure 2：The Character of 哆啦 A 梦

Figure 3：The Character of Dingdong Community

Figure 4：The Character of 叮冬小区

Limited Protection and
Restrictions of Allegedly Infringing Works

—Yin Wenjun v. Shanghai Siyuan Education over the Infringement of the Right of Authorship and the Right to Reproduce the Work and Get Remuneration

[Summary]

The "work" re-created by the author through quoting a prior work in batches without the prior right holder's permission will lead to the overlap or conflict between the copyright and the prior rights. However, the Copyright Law does not deprive the protection of such "infringing deductive works." If, compared with an infringing work which has been decided by the court, an "tort deductive work" is original apart from the allegedly infringing part, it should still be protected under the Copyright Law, but there will be some difference in calculating the amount of compensation.

[CaseReview]

Plaintiff (Respondent): Yin Wenjun

Defendant (Appellant): Shanghai Siyuan Education

Cause of Action: Infringement of the right of authorship and the right to reproduce the work and get remuneration

First-instance Case No.: (2013) XMS(Z)CZ No. 936

Second-instance Case No.: (2015) HYZMW(Z)ZZ No. 14

On August 23, 2011, the Plaintiff Yin Wenjun signed a book publishing contract with China Welfare Institute Publishing House, under which the 8,000-character book to be published is called *Fun with Chinese Characters*.

In September 2011, the textbook *Fun with Chinese Characters* was first published by China Welfare Institute Publishing House. The book, which contained 10,000 characters, was compiled by Yin Wenjun. The price of the book was RMB 80 yuan (five volumes). The first three volumes were called *Fun with Learning Chinese Characters*, the fourth volume was called *Chinese Pinyin*, and the fifth *Calligraphy*.

On August 13, 2001, Shanghai Qihang Education School was established and registered with the approval of Shanghai Xuhui District Civil Affairs Bureau. On August 3, 2009, it was renamed as Shanghai Siyuan Education ("Siyuan Education") with the approval of Shanghai Xuhui District Civil Affairs Bureau and Shanghai Xuhui District Social Organizations Administration Bureau. The initial capital is RMB 600,000 and the business scope is non-academic secondary education. The website of the Defendant Siyuan Education for children's education is www. siyuanchild. com. It had five campuses: Xuhui Campus, Longbai Campus, Dahua Campus, Pudong Yaohan Campus and Southern Campus, which all offered courses of Chinese character learning, Chinese Pinyin and calligraphy.

The Plaintiff Yin Wenjun, one of the founders of Wenguang School, asked her colleagues Li Qingchuan and Xu Ling in April 2013 to apply for the courses of Chinese character learning, Chinese Pinyin and calligraphy on the Defendant's Longbai Campus and Southern Campus respectively. After paying the fees, the Plaintiff obtained the allegedly infringing textbooks on Chinese character learning, Chinese Pinyin and calligraphy.

On May 14, 2009, outsiders Chen Shuhong and Yu Yongquan sued Wenguang School on the grounds that Wenguang School's textbook *Fun with Learning Chinese Characters* (Wenguang's textbook) had plagiarized the outsiders' work *Fun with Learning Chinese Characters*. On November 6 of the same year, Shanghai Pudong New Area People's Court held that the textbook complied by outsiders Chen Shuhong and Yu Yongquan contained 8,673 characters, Wenguang's textbook contained 4,197 characters, of which 4,004 characters, or 95. 4%, came from the outsiders' textbook, thus constituting infringement. The court made the civil judgment (2009) PMS(Z)CZ No. 153, which was upheld by Shanghai No. 1 Intermediate People's Court on January 12, 2010 and has already entered into force.

The *Fun with Learning Chinese Characters* claimed by the Plaintiff and the Wenguang's textbooks were both textbooks for teaching children characters. Their main contents were about illustrating a Chinese character with a line of nursery rhyme. Their differences lied in the course allocation and the order of character learning. The Plaintiff's *Fun with Learning Chinese Characters* had 80 hours of lessons, including 521 lines of nursery rhymes for 521 characters, 265 of which also appeared in Wenguang's textbook. Eighteen of the 265 lines of nursery rhymes were identical. The Plaintiff confirmed that she did not enjoy the copyright of twelve lines included in them. The 12 characters were "尖, 晶, 多, 李, 庄, 奈, 宵, 选, 叽, 他, 转, 剃." The Plaintiff claimed that the other six lines of nursery rhymes, corresponding to the characters "舌, 乒, 乓, 兵, 右, 凡," were original. There were some differences in the following aspects in the remaining 247 lines of rhymes between the two textbooks: for lines where the expressions were basically the same, some characters had been added or replaced; for lines where the expressions were similar, some characters had been used differently; for lines where the main meanings and expressions were different. There were 208 lines corresponding to the first two scenarios and 39 to the third.

The allegedly infringing textbook was also about teaching children characters. Comparing with the textbook claimed by the Plaintiff, it can be found that the two were different in course arrangement and the order of characters. In terms of content, the allegedly infringing textbook had 31 pages, involving 276 lines of nursery rhymes, and Page 9 was duplicate with Page 11. During the trial, the Plaintiff claimed that 127 nursery rhymes in the allegedly infringing textbook constituted infringement. Among the 127 nursery rhymes, 5 were repeated, 117 were identical with those in the Plaintiff's textbook, and 10 similar to those in the Plaintiff's textbook. According to the comparison between the Plaintiff's textbook and Wenguang's textbook, in those 10 nursery rhymes, the character "仇" was not included in Wenguang's textbook; the expression types of the rhymes corresponding to other characters, except for "果," were identical or similar to those in the Plaintiff's textbook and Wenguang's textbook. Among the identical 117 nursery rhymes, the Plaintiff acknowledged that she did not enjoy the copyright of 7 lines. The characters corresponding to 61 lines were not included in Wenguang's textbook. Other characters corresponding to 49 lines were included in Wenguang's textbook. According to the comparison between the Plaintiff's textbook and Wenguang's textbook, the expression types of 43 lines were identical or similar to those in the Plaintiff's textbook and Wenguang's textbook. The expression types of 6 lines were different from those in the Plaintiff's textbook and Wenguang's textbook.

Comparing the Plaintiff's *Chinese Pinyin* with the allegedly infringing Chinese Pinyin textbook, it can be found that both textbooks were about teaching children to learn Chinese Pinyin. In terms of content, both textbooks focused on syllables such as vowels, initials and nasals. The textbooks were basically identical in the page layout, the course arrangement and the selection of characters. There were 36 pages in the Plaintiff's *Chinese Pinyin*, involving about 500 characters, and 34 pages in the allegedly infringing Chinese Pinyin textbook, which involved approximately the same characters as those in the Plaintiff's textbook, with only 32 differences.

Comparing the Plaintiff's *Calligraphy* with the allegedly infringing calligraphy textbook, it can be found that both were exercise books designed for practicing handwriting. In terms of the page layout, both were covered with squares, the first vertical column and some horizontal lines were filled with printed Chinese characters for practicing. In the order of arrangement, both adopted the order from basic strokes to structural fonts to choosing characters to practice. The Plaintiff's *Calligraphy* had 20 pages, involving 146 strokes and characters. It also had a front page entitled "Calligraphy Exercise Book-Junior Class," which mainly introduced writing posture and how to hold the pen. The allegedly infringing calligraphy textbook had 19 pages, involving 136 strokes and characters, with no front page. The Plaintiff's *Calligraphy* chose the squares in the form of a 2x2 table and there were two diagonal lines in the 2x2 table used in the allegedly infringing textbook. The fonts in the two textbooks were also different. In the selection and arrangement of characters, 30 strokes or characters, or 22.06%, selected in the allegedly infringing textbook were not shown in the Plaintiff's textbook, and the order of 12 strokes or characters, or 8.82%, in the allegedly infringing textbook was inconsistent with that in the Plaintiff's textbook.

The Plaintiff Yin Wenjun claimed that she had compiled a set of textbooks (five volumes) called *Fun with Learning Chinese Characters*, which was published by China Welfare Institute Publishing House in September 2011. The first three volumes were called *Fun with Learning Chinese Characters* and the other two were called *Fun with Learning Chinese Characters-Chinese Pinyin* and *Fun with Learning Chinese Characters- Calligraphy Exercise Book*. The Defendant Siyuan Education, without the permission of the Plaintiff, used the Plaintiff's works as its textbooks: it adapted the essence of the Plaintiff's *Fun with Learning Chinese Characters* into its literacy textbook, slightly changed the Plaintiff's *Chinese Pinyin* and made it its pinyin textbook, and reprinted the Plaintiff's *Calligraphy* and made it its calligraphy textbook. The Defendant made huge profits by using the above-mentioned textbooks in its five campuses in Shanghai, which infringed upon the Plaintiff's right of authorship, right to reproduce and get remuneration for the set of textbooks *Fun with Learning Chinese Characters*. Therefore, the Plaintiff requested the court to order that: 1. the Defendant immediately cease the infringement; 2. the Defendant make a public apology to the Plaintiff in *Jiefang Daily*, *Wenhui Daily*, *Xinmin Evening News*, on the Defendant's website www. siyuanchild. com and the bulletin boards of the Defendant's Xuhui Campus, Longbai Campus, Dahua Campus, Southern Campus and Pudong Yaohan Campus to eliminate the impact; 3. the Defendant compensate the Plaintiff RMB 100, 000 for economic losses; 4. the Defendant compensate the Plaintiff RMB 13,779 for reasonable expenses (including RMB 5, 000 for lawyer fees, RMB 8,319 for registration, RMB 360 for copying and RMB 100 for transportation).

The Defendant Siyuan Education argued that, first, the textbooks involved in the case should not be regarded as works, and the Plaintiff does not enjoy their copyright. The textbooks involved are mainly about Chinese character spelling and Pinyin, which are the usual methods used in teaching. They belong to the common area and are anything but original. The Plaintiff cannot claim copyright in this regard. As a teacher of Wenguang School, the Plaintiff's textbooks involved in the case is job-related works, and the copyright of them, if any, should be owned by Wenguang School. In addition, the textbooks involved have originated from Wenguang School's textbook, which has been convicted of infringement by effective judgment. Therefore, the textbooks involved in the case do not constitute works, and the Plaintiff does not enjoy copyright in them. Second, the Defendant has the manpower and resources to compile its own textbooks. It did not use the allegedly infringing textbooks. The evidence provided by the Plaintiff cannot prove that the allegedly infringing textbooks were obtained from the Defendant. Third, even if the Defendant had committed the infringement as claimed by the Plaintiff, as the textbooks involved had been published for a long time and in a small number, the Defendant did not cause actual losses to the Plaintiff, so the amount of economic losses claimed by the Plaintiff had no basis. In summary, the Defendant requested the court to dismiss all the Plaintiff's claims.

[Judgment]

After hearing, Shanghai Xuhui District People's Court held that the selection and arrangement of Chinese characters in the *Fun with Learning Chinese Characters* formed a special combination, which had certain degree of originality; the author's interpretation of Chinese characters from the aspects of shape, pronunciation and meaning in *Fun with Learning Chinese Characters* also reflected originality. They were the author's intellectual achievements. According to the comparison between the Plaintiff's textbook and Wenguang's textbook, 56.62% of the nursery rhymes in the Plaintiff's textbook was original and the textbook can thus be considered a new work. As to whether the textbook has infringed on the copyright of others' work, it is not within the scope of the trial in this case. The court will not make any judgment on that, nor will that affect the Plaintiff's institution of an action against the party which has infringed her copyright. *Chinese Pinyin* and *Calligraphy* were both original with annotation of the Pinyin syllables and arrangement and induction of the phrases, stroke structures and writing methods. Therefore, the textbook *Fun with Learning Chinese Characters* was formed through the author's selection and annotation, which embodied the author's ideas. It had some original expressions and could be reproduced in tangible form. It should be protected under the *Copyright Law* of China. When the textbook was published, the author was the Plaintiff Yin Wenjun. Unless the defendant could provide evidence to the contrary, the court would find that the Plaintiff Yin Wenjun was the author of the textbook *Fun with Learning Chinese Characters* and enjoyed the copyright in the above works. Given that the defendant had no evidence to prove that it had used the textbooks compiled by itself in teaching, that there were witnesses' testimony and receipts to prove the Plaintiff's acquisition of the allegedly infringing textbooks, and that the allegedly infringing textbooks acquired by the Plaintiff were identical with the original ones held by the Defendant, it can be concluded that the allegedly infringing textbooks were obtained from the Defendant, i. e. , the Defendant had used the allegedly infringing textbooks in its daily business activities. Among the 127 nursery rhymes that the Plaintiff claimed were infringed by the Defendant, 62 were not shown in Wenguang's textbook, and 7 were different from those in Wenguang's textbook in terms of expression. Yet the expression of the 69 nursery rhymes in the allegedly infringing textbook was identical or similar to that in the Plaintiff's textbook. Therefore, the 69 nursery rhymes in the allegedly infringing textbook infringed the Plaintiff's copyright. For the other 58 nursery rhymes claimed by the Plaintiff for infringement, because these rhymes lack originality, and the substantially similar content in Wenguang's textbook had been convicted of infringement by an effective judgment, the Plaintiff cannot claim for those rhymes. Therefore, 25% of the contents in the allegedly infringing textbook was identical or similar to the nursery rhymes in which the Plaintiff enjoyed the copyright. It went beyond the degree of coincidence, so the court found that this part in the allegedly infringing textbook infringed upon the Plaintiff's copyright in *Fun with Learning Chinese Characters*. Second, the contents of the allegedly infringing textbooks *Chinese Pinyin* and *Calligraphy* were substantially similar to those of the Plaintiff's textbooks. Therefore, the court found that the *Chinese Pinyin* and *Calligraphy* textbooks used by the Defendant infringed the Plaintiff's copyright. The Defendant Siyuan Education, without the Plaintiff's permission, reproduced the contents of the Plaintiff's works and applied them in its daily business activities, and did not show the author's name. It infringed the Plaintiff's right of authorship, right to reproduce her works, and to allow others to use the works in the above ways and get remuneration for that. The infringement should be stopped. Considering that the scope affected by the Defendant's infringement is limited by its teaching activities, the declaration shall only be published on the Defendant's website www. siyuanchild. com. The court refused to support the Plaintiff's claim for elimination of influence because the Plaintiff did not submit evidence to prove that her personal reputation and social evaluation had been damaged by the infringement.

To sum up, Shanghai Xuhui District People's Court, in accordance with Article 10 (1) (ii), (v), (2), Article 11 (4), Article 47 (5), (7), Article 48 (1), Article 49 of the *Copyright Law of the People's Republic of China*, Article 2 of the *Regulation for the Implementation of the Copyright Law of the People's Republic of China*, Article 15 (1) (i), (vi), (vii), (2) of the *Tort Liability Law of the People's Republic of China*, Article 25 (1) (2) and Article 26 of the *Interpretation of the Supreme People's Court Concerning the Application of Laws in the Trial of Civil Disputes over Copyright*, made the following judgment: 1. The Defendant Siyuan Education shall immediately cease to infringe upon the Plaintiff Yin Wenjun's copyright in the textbook *Fun with Learning Chinese Characters* the day the judgment comes into effect; 2. Upon effectiveness of the judgment, the Defendant Siyuan Education will make an apology to the Plaintiff Yin Wenjun on the home page of www. siyuanchild. com. The apology shall last for 72 hours. (The contents of the statement must be examined by the court. If the Defendant fails to fulfill this, the court will publish the main content of the judgment in the relevant media, and the cost will be borne by the Defendant); 3. The Defendant Siyuan Education shall compensate the Plaintiff Yin Wenjun RMB 30, 000 for economic losses and reasonable expenses within 10 days from the date when this judgment comes into force; 4. The rest of the Plaintiff Yin Wenjun's requests are dismissed.

Refusing to accept the judgment, the Defendant Siyuan Education appealed.

After appealing with Shanghai No. 1 Intermediate People's Court, as the appellant failed to pay the fees within the time limit, the court found that the appeal was withdrawn by the appellant. The first instance decision has come into force.

[Case Study]

This case is not about protecting the rights of the prior copyright owner. Instead, it concerns the situation where the infringing work is used by a third party, whether the infringing work can be protected and to which extent it is protected by the *Copyright Law*.

I. Original "infringing works" are also considered works

According to the *Regulation for the Implementation of the Copyright Law of the People's Republic of China*, works under the *Copyright Law* refer to intellectual achievements that are original in the field of literature, art and science and can be reproduced in some tangible form. This article stipulates the object protected by the Copyright Law of China: works. Therefore, we first need to decide whether the infringing works claimed by the Plaintiff can constitute works as prescribed under the *Copyright Law*.

Infringing works refer to works that infringe other people's prior rights during the process of creation or use, including but not limited to works created by infringing other people's prior intellectual property rights. Infringing works can be divided into two types. One is the work formed by completely plagiarizing other people's work. Such work lacks originality and cannot constitute a work as prescribed under the *Copyright Law*. The infringing work cannot constitute a work if the infringed work is removed from it, so it certainly cannot be protected under the *Copyright Law*. The other is the work created on the basis of other people's work. It is not complete plagiarism. Even though the quotation of other people's prior work has gone beyond the reasonable scope, but if such quotation is removed, the infringing work still contains the part independently created by the author, and may even constitute an independent work. This type of infringing work should be considered original and can constitute the work under the *Copyright Law*.

Generally speaking, the intellectual property law protects intellectual achievements. The Plaintiff's works had infringed other people's prior copyright, but they also contained the author's original work. In this case, the *Fun with Learning Chinese Characters* claimed by the Plaintiff is a literacy textbook for kids containing the selection and arrangement of Chinese character and the interpretation of the characters through associative memory. The nursery rhymes for each character were arranged loosely in a certain order. Different choice of characters or combination may arise due to different shapes of the characters or different ways of memorizing and interpretation. Each nursery rhyme for each character also contained content created by the author independently. After comparing the Plaintiff's work with the prior work, it was found that 56.62% , or more than half, of the nursery rhymes in the Plaintiff's work was original. It belonged to the second type of infringing works. That part, if re-arranged, can form a new work completely different from the prior work. Therefore, the Plaintiff's work cannot be denied entirely just because it contained infringing content.

Ⅱ . The Degree of Protection of "Infringing Works"

Whether or not an author can use his or her own work and how he or she can use it have nothing to do with his or her acquisition of copyright. It depends on whether there are prohibitive provisions in the law. Granting protection of infringing works under the *Copyright Law* does not mean that the author of the infringing work can use the infringing work at will, because such use is definitely infringement of other people's copyright. Others can neither use the work at will, otherwise it will constitute infringement on the copyright of the author.

From the perspective of encouraging creation: the infringing work contained original content created by the author; when its copyright was infringed by a third party, the author should be protected. Therefore, in this case, the Defendant infringed the copyright enjoyed by the Plaintiff in the infringing work with 25% of the literacy textbook used by the Defendant being identical or similar to that of the Plaintiff's original content.

From the perspective of social public welfare: after all, such infringing works are different from those created independently. The degree of originality in infringing works is relatively low. Protection of such infringing works should be limited because of their use of others' prior works for benefits. In the case of infringement of infringing works by a third party, the amount of compensation should be lower than that for independently created works.

(Writer: Yuan Yang)

Limits of Infringement on the Right to Adapt Works and Identification of the Nature of Relevant Promotional Activities

—Perfect World (Beijing) Software Co. , Ltd. v. Shanghai Blaze Fire Network Technology Co. , Ltd. *et al.* over infringement of the right to adapt works, false publicity and unfair competition

[**Summary**]

The right of adaptation is the right to change works and create new works with originality. Changing a work generally means changing a work from one type to another without changing its content. Whether a game work constitutes the adaptation of a literary work depends on whether the characters, the relationship between the characters and the plot in the game are substantially similar to those in the literary work. In the case of infringement of the right of adaptation, because the game does contain elements of the relevant literary work, using the content of the relevant literary work for publicity does not constitute false publicity, but it may constitute unfair competition.

[**Case Review**]

Plaintiff (Appellant) :Perfect World (Beijing) Software Co. , Ltd.

Defendant (Respondent): Shanghai Blaze Fire Network Technology Co. , Ltd.

Defendant (Respondent) :Fujian Borui Network Technology Co. , Ltd.

Defendant (Respondent): Guangzhou i9Game Information Technology

Co. , Ltd.

　　Defendant (Respondent): Fujian Youlong Network Technology Co. , Ltd.

　　Cause of Action: infringement of the right to adapt works, false publicity and unfair competition

　　First-Instance Case No. : (2015) YMS(Z)CZ No. 55

　　Second-Instance Case No. : (2016) H73MZ No. 39

　　In December 2010, Guangzhou Publishing House and Flower City Publishing House jointly published four works (2nd edition, paper version): *The Legend of the Condor Heroes*, *The Return of the Condor Heroes*, *The Heavenly Sword and Dragon Saber* and *The Smiling*, *Proud Wanderer*. On the cover and title pages of those books, the author's signature is "Jin Yong," and the works are "Jin Yong's works." A brief introduction to Jin Yong is printed on the flap of the above-mentioned books, which reads "Born as Zha Liangyong. . . . "

　　On January 1, 2002, Zha Liangyong granted Ming Ho Publications Corporation Ltd. the exclusive right of *Works by Jin Yong* (including 12 works such as *The Legend of the Condor Heroes*, *The Return of the Condor Heroes*, *The Heavenly Sword and Dragon Saber* and *The Smiling*, *Proud Wanderer*) in China, excluding publishing and distributing the simplified Chinese version of the works in book form. The contract came into effect on January 1, 2002 when it was signed in Hong Kong and would expire until a written termination agreement is reached between the two parties.

　　On April 8, 2013, Ming Ho Publications Corporation Ltd. issued a license, stating that Zha Liangyong has the right to exclusively authorize Perfect World (Beijing) Software Co. , Ltd. ("Perfect World") the right to adapt the mobile terminal game software of his works *The Legend of the Condor Heroes*, *The Return of the Condor Heroes*, *The Heavenly Sword and Dragon Saber* and *The Smiling*, *Proud Wanderer* and the commercial development right of the adapted game software (including but not limited to the development, production, distribution, publicity, operation of the game software and their communication over information networks, as well as development, production and sales of derivatives based on the game software).

　　On April 30, 2013, Zha Liangyong and the Plaintiff Perfect World signed the *Mobile Terminal Game Software Adaptation Licensing Contract* respectively for the four works involved, which stated that the licensor Zha Liangyong authorized the right to adapt the mobile terminal game software of the above works to the Plaintiff, which would have the right to develop the mobile terminal game software and produce, promote and operate the "adapted software" in various languages (except Japanese) in all parts of the world. The period for the Plaintiff to acquire the exclusive right of adaptation in the Chinese mainland was three years.

On May 16, 2014, Wang Ping, the Plaintiff's attorney, came to Beijing Fangyuan Notary Office to apply for the notarization of evidence preservation in the process of checking the website of Liu Da Men Pai (*Six Sects*): visited http://www.6damenpai.com/ and came to the official website of Liu Da Men Pai, downloaded and installed the game "Six Sects" (Android version), and ran the game for demonstration; after searching on the website of China Copyright Protection Center, it showed that the copyright owner of the computer software named "Six Sects OL Software" is "Shanghai Blaze Fire Network Technology Co., Ltd.," the registration date is May 5, 2014; on www.duouoo.com, there were headlines reading "Mobile Game *Six Sects* Releases the Wild Wuxia Dream" and "Analysis of the Trade System of *Six Sects*." According to the news, "Since its launch on May 8, *Six Sects*, the first retrospective real-time wuxia mobile game distributed by Shanghai Blaze Fire, has been a hit among players... Nearly 1,000 users rushed into the second gate again... Only four days after the game was launched, the number of gold ingots consumed has exceeded 2 billion, which is equivalent to more than RMB 200 million ···" Shanghai Blaze Fire Network Technology Co., Ltd. ("Blaze Fire") admitted in court that the game involved was operated by it solely, and www.6damenpai.com was its website.

On December 16, 2014, Yu Mengfei, an attorney from Watson & Band (Shanghai), came to Shanghai Oriental Notary Public Office, where she used the computer to perform the following operations: visited http://www.6damenpai.com/ and entered the "News Center" page, clicked the post which was published on November 1, 2014 and entitled "Who do you remember from the *Six Sects* in 1990s." The content of the post read "飞雪连天射白鹿,笑书神侠倚碧鸳 (*Each character is the initial in the title of Jin Yong's 14 novels*)... Among the several versions of *The Heavenly Sword and Dragon Saber*, Ma Jingtao's version was the first to be known by people ··· Speaking of 'Brother', the Brother Jing played by Huang Rihua in *The Legend of the Condor Heroes* (1983) was one of the most classic figures in our childhood ···"; on the "News Center" page, clicked the post which was published on October 27, 2014 and entitled "My Impression of the *Six Sects in the* 1990s," and the content of the post read, "*Six Sects*, a derivative from the classics, recreates a wulin for the players, where you can learn the unparalleled skills like Zhang Wuji, defend Xiangyang like Guo Jing, or even create chaos like Dongfang Bubai. Join the *Six Sects* and start your journey in the wulin; clicked on the "News Center" page the post which was published on July 23, 2014 and entitled "The Heroes in the *Six Sects*." The content of the post read "I believe that all players who have read classic wuxia novels would have their favorite heroes or those they don't like much. For example, the scruffy, happy-go-lucky and righteous Linghu Chong, the righteous and evil Huang Yaoshi, the fierce, vicious and disgusting Abbess Miejue, or the unscrupulous and silly Jinlun Lama. Now in *Six Sects*, players can choose to challenge those heroes as he likes ... "; on the "*Six Sects* Game Database" page, clicked on "Introduction to the Sect," the introduction to the Shaolin Sect read "A significant power in the wulin, Shaolin was honored as the 'source of all martial arts'. The major skill of Shaolin Sect was Yijin Jing"; the introduction to Wudang Sect read "Founded by Zhang Sanfeng, Wudang was one of the two major powers in the wulin (martial artists' community) alongside Shaolin. The disciples of Wudang were famous for their chivalry. There were the famous 'Seven Heroes of Wudang'. The skills of Wudang were Taiji Fist and Taiji Swordplay; and the introduction to Emei Sect read "Emei Sect was founded by Guo Xiang, the daughter of Guo Jing, and the major skill was Nine Yin and Nine Yang …"; clicked on "Follow" on the home page, it showed that the game's Weibo account was named "Six Sects OL." It had 61,590 followers and had published 176 posts. In the Weibo account, it was certified as "Shanghai Blaze Fire Network Technology Co., Ltd." and in the profile, it read "Mobile Game *Six Sects*."

The Plaintiff notarized the interface, game process and recharge information of the game "Six Sects" (Android version): 1. Visited www. 6damenpai. com and downloaded and installed an application named "Six Sects," recharged it when using the application. The transaction information showed that the money was paid to "Shanghai Blaze Fire Network Technology Co., Ltd."; 2. Visited www. miitbeian. gov. cn and found that the organizer of the website www. 19196. com was "Fujian Youlong Network Technology Co., Ltd" ("Youlong"), downloaded the game involved on www. 19196. com and recharged, the transaction information showed that the money was paid to "Fujian Youlong Network Technology Co., Ltd.

("Youlong")"; 3. Downloaded and installed an application called "91 Assistant." Opened "91 Assistant" to search and install the application " Six Sects." After recharging, the transaction information showed that the money was paid to "Fujian Borui Network Technology Co. , Ltd" ("Borui"); 4. Downloaded and installed the software called "9Game," opened it to search and install " Six Sects." After recharging, the transaction information showed that the money was paid to "Guangzhou i9Game Information Technology Co. , Ltd" ("i9Game"). The Plaintiff also checked the number of downloads of the game on various platforms.

By comparison, the four works claimed by the Plaintiff were similar in different degrees to the game *Six Sects* in terms of content, characters, relationship between characters and plot development.

1. According to the notarized game process provided by the Plaintiff, the plot of the game *Six Sects* was basically the same as the first seven chapters of the literary work *The Smiling, Proud Wanderer.* The content after Chapter 7 of *The Smiling, Proud Wanderer* was not reflected in the notarized game process submitted by the plaintiff.

In the game involved, the following main characters in the literary work appeared: Yue Buqun (nicknamed "Gentleman Sword"), Ning Zhongze, Linghu Chong, Lao Denuo, Yue Lingshan from Mount Hua Sect; Dingyi, Yilin, etc. from North Mount Heng Sect; Zuo Lengchan, Fei Bin, etc. from Mount Song Sect; Yu Canghai, Luo Renjie, Yu Renyan, etc. from Qingcheng Sect; Qu Yang, Qu Feiyan, Monk Bujie, Lin Pingzhi and so on. The main martial arts involved were Mount Hua Swordplay, Tai Yue San Qing Feng, Duo Ming Lian Jian, Nine Swords of Dugu and Violet Mist Divine Skill.

2. Characters and Events Relevant to the Case in *The Heavenly Sword and Dragon Saber*

The Dragon Saber, the important clue in *The Heavenly Sword and Dragon Saber* first appears in the contest between Hai Shapai and Hai Dongqing. The reason why Miejue bears a grudge against the Ming Cult is that Gu Hongzi, Miejue's senior, challenges Yang Xiao, the Bright Left Messenger of the Ming Cult, to a martial arts contest and borrows Miejue's Heavenly Sword in the hope that it would give him an advantage. However, Gu loses to Yang Xiao and the sword is seized from him by Yang before he could even unsheathe it. Yang throws the sword to the ground and Gu dies in frustration.

In the game involved, the following main characters from *The Heavenly Sword and Dragon Saber* appeared: Zhou Zhiruo, an apprentice of Emei Sect, Zhang Sanfeng and his seven apprentices, Song Qingshu, son of Song Yuanqiao, Abbess Miejue, and Yang Xiao, the Bright Left Messenger of the Ming Cult. The martial arts involved included Wudang Swordplay, Wudang Heart Sutra, Emei Swordplay, Wind and Cloud Crossing Palm, Emei Heart Sutra, Nine Movements, Mie Swordplay and Jue Swordplay.

3. Characters and Events Relevant to the Case in *The Legend of the Condor Heroes* and *The Return of the Condor Heroes*

The Plaintiff's notarized game process listed the names of Fu Er, Dawu, Xiaowu, Brother Yelu, Master Guo and Rong Er in the game scene of the Battle of Xiangyang.

It was also found that on May 5, 2014, with the approval of the State Copyright Administration, Blaze Fire obtained the computer software copyright registration certificate for the software named "Six Sects OL Mobile Online Game Software [Six Sects OL Software] V1.0," and the development completion date was April 11, 2014.

The Plaintiff Perfect World claimed that the Plaintiff had obtained the exclusive right to adapt the mobile terminal game software in the Chinese mainland for the four works: *The Legend of the Condor Heroes*, *The Return of the Condor Heroes*, *The Heavenly Sword and Dragon Saber*, and *The Smiling, Proud Wanderer* and had the right to hold, by any legal means, any third party accountable for infringement and unfair competition in its own name within the authorization period. In May 2014, the Plaintiff found that the Defendant Blaze Fire, without legal authorization, had developed a mobile game called *Six Sects*, which used a lot of the original elements of the above works. In addition, Blaze Fire made extensive use of elements related to Jin Yong's works in promoting *Six Sects* on its official website. The other three Defendants were also involved in the actual operation of the mobile game *Six Sects* and gained benefit from it. In summary, the Plaintiff requested the court to order that: 1. the four Defendants immediately stop infringing Jin Yong's copyright; 2. the four Defendants immediately stop violating the principle of good faith and making false publicity; 3. Defendant No. 1 publish a statement to eliminate adverse effects; 4. the four Defendants jointly compensate the Plaintiff RMB 10,200,000 for economic losses (including reasonable expenses).

The Defendant Blaze Fire argued that: 1. Blaze Fire had created and completed the game involved independently and obtained the copyright registration certificate for the game on April 11, 2014. Blaze Fire operated the game in which it enjoyed the whole copyright on its server, and did not infringe any copyright as claimed by the Plaintiff; 2. Blaze Fire did not infringe the right to adapt the four works involved by Jin Yong. The adaptation claimed by the Plaintiff should refer to the act of changing the plot on the basis of the literary work when it is converted into a game, but there was no clear plot in the game involved; 3. Blaze Fire never announced that the game involved was adapted from Jin Yong's works. Moreover, the Plaintiff had no evidence to prove that the game involved had occupied its market share. Blaze Fire did not adapt the works or make false publicity; 4. The game involved was solely operated by Blaze Fire, the other three Defendants did not operate the game; 5. The *Copyright Licensing Contract* signed between the Plaintiff and Jin Yong should come into effect upon payment, while the Plaintiff could not prove that it had paid the licensing fee and thus enjoyed the right to adapt the four works involved.

The Defendant Borui argued that: 1. The game involved was not developed by Borui, and Borui did not participate in the operation of the game, nor did it infringe any copyright or make any false publicity; 2. As a platform operator, Borui could not judge whether the game involved had infringed the copyright of others. Blaze Fire provided the copyright registration certificate when uploading the game to the platform operated by Borui, which could only verify according to the certificate. There was no evidence to prove that Borui knew or ought to know that the game involved was an infringing work; 3. The Plaintiff did not warn Borui about the infringement or send it any letters before the proceedings. Borui had no subjective intention or negligence.

The Defendant i9Game argued that: 1. i9Game was not the operator of the game, and did not infringe any copyright or commit unfair competition; 2. i9Game had performed due diligence by requiring Blaze Fire to provide the copyright certificate when the game was uploaded to the platform operated by it. Also, the name of the game involved was *Six Sects*, not the name of any novel by Jin Yong, so it was unlikely that i9Game knew or should have known that the game involved was suspected of infringement; 3. i9Game's platform provided two technical services for the game involved: an account system and a recharge channel. It only charged on behalf of Blaze Fire, and the revenue finally went to Blaze Fire; 4. In the operation of the game involved, i9Game did not receive any notice on rights or infringement from the Plaintiff.

The Defendant Youlong argued in writing that: 1. Jin Yong did not enjoy copyright in the names of the relevant factions and historical figures in the game *Six Sects*. The Chinese wuxia factions and related figures were real. They were not created by Jin Yong; 2. Blaze Fire had obtained the copyright of the game software, and Youlong was unable to judge whether the game software would infringe on the legitimate rights and interests of a third party. It could only decide based on the computer software copyright registration certificate provided by Blaze Fire. Youlong had performed due diligence and had no subjective fault; 3. Youlong only provided players with a recharge channel; it did not make any profits from that and should not bear liability for infringement.

[Judgment]

After hearing, Shanghai Yangpu District People's Court held that Zha Liangyong was the author of the literary works *The Legend of the Condor Heroes*, *The Return of the Condor Heroes*, *The Heavenly Sword and Dragon Saber* and *The Smiling, Proud Wanderer*, so he enjoyed the copyright of the four works. The Plaintiff was authorized the exclusive right to adapt the mobile terminal game software of the four works involved case in the Chinese mainland and the commercial development right of the adapted game software. The Plaintiff had the right to hold any third party responsible for using such works without authorization or unfair competition against such works within the authorization period.

From the perspectives of characters, plots and details, the Defendant Blaze Fire's unauthorized adaptation of *The Smiling, Proud Wanderer* into a game infringed the Plaintiff Perfect World's exclusive right to adapt the work into a game and its rights and interests by operating the adapted game. According to the content of the game *Six Sects* shown in the Plaintiff's notarial certificate, the use of relevant elements in the literary work *The Heavenly Sword and Dragon Saber* was mainly reflected in the names of the characters such as Zhang Sanfeng and Song Yuanqiao from Wudang Sect, the relationship between the characters, and the event of Guhongzi, Abbess Miejue's senior, being killed by Yang Xiao's unkind remarks. However, from the perspective of plot development, the most important element in adaptation, it could be found that the existing notarized content of the game Six Sexts did not contain the same plot as that of the literary work *The Heavenly Sword and Dragon Saber*. For *The Legend of the Condor Heroes* and *The Return of the Condor Heroes*, the notarized content of the game only listed the names of the elders in the Beggars' Sect, Fu Er, Dawu, Xiaowu, Brother Yelu, Master Guo, Rong Er, etc. in the scene of the Battle of Xiangyang. There were no plots from the two works. Therefore, the existing evidence cannot prove that the game *Six Sects* constituted an adaptation of *The Heavenly Sword and Dragon Saber*, *The Legend of the Condor Heroes* and *The Return of the Condor Heroes*.

The game*Six Sects* did use the relevant elements of the four literary works involved, so the publicity made by the Defendant Blaze Fire using the elements of the four literary works involved did not constitute false publicity. However, by combining the four novels in its game *Six Sects* and using the elements of Jin Yong's novels in promoting the game, the Defendant Blaze Fire had exerted a negative impact on the development and operation of related games by the Plaintiff Perfect World. Robbing the players belonging to the Plaintiff, the Defendant committed unfair competition.

The "91 Assistant" operated by the Defendant Borui, the "9Game" operated by the Defendant i9Game and the www. 19196. com operated by the Defendant Youlong were all platforms for software uploading, storage and downloading. It was difficult for them to conduct substantial review of all uploaded software one by one. Moreover, the Defendant Blaze Fire had obtained the computer software copyright registration certificate for the game *Six Sects* developed by itself. The existing evidence cannot prove that the Defendants Borui, i9Game and Youlong have helped the Defendant Blaze Fire commit the infringement intentionally. The three Defendants have performed due diligence and should not be liable for compensation.

Accordingly, Shanghai Yangpu District People's Court, in accordance with Articles 2 and 20 of the *Anti-Unfair Competition Law of the People's Republic of China*, Article 10 (1) (xiv), Article 10 (2), Article 48 (i), Article 49 of the *Copyright Law of the People's Republic of China*, and Article 144 of the *Civil Procedure Law of the People's Republic of China*, made the following judgment: 1. the Defendant, Shanghai Blaze Fire Network Technology Co. , Ltd. , shall publish a statement on the top of its website for 72 consecutive hours to eliminate the impact of the infringement; 2. the Defendant, Shanghai Blaze Fire Network Technology Co. ,

Ltd. , shall compensate the Plaintiff, Perfect World (Beijing) Software Co. , Ltd. , RMB 500,000 for economic losses and reasonable expenses within 10 days from the date of the judgment coming into force; 3. the other requests of the Plaintiff, Perfect World (Beijing) Software Co. , Ltd. , shall be dismissed.

After the first-instance judgment was made, the Plaintiff appealed but later withdrew the appeal. The first-instance judgment has come into effect.

[Case Study]

Adaptation as prescribed under the Copyright Law refers to the creation of a new work by adapting the original work without changing the basic expression of the original work. Therefore, the key to judge whether an adaptation is constituted lies in whether the characters, the relationship between the characters and the plot development are substantially similar between the original and new work, and there is no general standard in judicial practice. In the case of infringement of the right of adaptation, whether the defendant's behavior constitutes unfair competition or not requires specific analysis of the judge according to the different circumstances in different cases. The focus in trying this case is to determine whether the four Defendants infringed the Plaintiff's exclusive right to adapt the literary works into games and whether they committed acts of unfair competition. The court had the following considerations in its trial:

I. Identification of the Boundaries of Infringing the Right to Adapt Works

The Copyright Law does not protect abstract ideas. It protects the concrete expressions of ideas in tangible ways such as words, music and art. The four works- *The Legend of the Condor Heroes*, *The Return of the Condor Heroes*, *The Heavenly Sword and Dragon Saber*, and *The Smiling, Proud Wanderer*-shared a process of developing from a general theme to a specific plot and finally to the expression of it in concrete words. This is a gradual shift from idea to expression, from abstract to concrete. The right of adaptation refers to the right to change the existing works and create new ones with originality. To change works generally means to change the type of works, not the content. In this case, as for whether the game *Six Sects* involved constituted infringement of the right to adapt the four works, the key is to determine whether the idea or expression of the original works is used in the game, i. e. , whether the characters, the relationship between the characters, the plot development in the game are substantially similar to those in the literary works.

First, on characters. According to the Notarial Certificate JFYNJZZ No. 11748 (2014) issued by Beijing Fangyuan Notarial Office, in the game *Six Sects*, the characters from Mount Hua Sect included Yue Buqun (nicknamed "Gentleman Sword"), Ning Zhongze (nicknamed "Heroine Ning"), Linghu Chong, Lao Denuo, Liang Fa, Shi Daizi, Gao Genming, Lu Dayou, Tao Jun, Ying Bailuo, Shu Qi, Yue Lingshan, and Cheng Buyou from the Sword faction. The names of these characters were exactly the same as those in *The Smiling, Proud Wanderer*. After the Plaintiff Perfect World sent out the letter on the Defendant's infringement, according to the Notarial Certificate No. 20218 (2014) issued by Shanghai Oriental Notarial Public Office, the Defendant Blaze Fire slightly changed the names of the characters in the game, but the pronunciation of the name remained the same, for example, "成不忧" was changed to "程不忧" (both read: Cheng Buyou), or changed the order of characters in the name, for example, Lao Denuo to Lao Nuode, Shi Daizi to Dai Shizi. The notarial certificate also showed that other characters in the game included Qu Yang, Qu Feifei, Zuo Lengchan and Fei Bing of Mount Song Sect, Dingyi and Yilin of (North) Mount Heng Sect, Master Mo, Liu Zhengfeng and Xiang Danian of (South) Mount Heng Sect, Yu Renyan, Yu Renhao and Luo Renjie of Qingcheng Sect, Lin Pingzhi (nicknamed "Xiao Linzi"), General Chief and son of the owner of Fuwei Escort Agency, and the lecherous Tian Boguang. Except that some characters in the names were replaced by a different character with the same pronunciation, the names of the above-mentioned characters were basically the same as those in *The Smiling, Proud Wanderer*. Also, the relationships among the characters, such as master-apprentice, senior-junior, rivalry and friendship, were also the same as those in *The Smiling, Proud Wanderer*.

Second, on plot development. As mentioned above, in the notarized game *Six Sects* provided by the Plaintiff Perfect World, the following plots: Lin Pingzhi, son of the owner of Fuwei Escort Agency, accidentally kills Yu Renyan, son of the leader of Qingcheng Sect; to secure the Bixie Swordplay Manual, Qingcheng Sect destroys Fuwei Escort Agency; Linghu Chong stops Tian Boguang from making sexual advances on Yilin, a nun from (North) Mount Heng Sect; Liu Zhengfeng of (South) Mount Heng Sect retires; Mount Song Sect accuses Liu Zhengfeng of collaborating with Qu Yang and massacres the Liu family; Liu Zhengfeng is saved by Qu Yang; Fei Bing from Mount Song Sect kills Qu Feifei, Qu Yang's granddaughter; Master Mo kills Fei Bing, are basically the same as those of the first seven chapters of *The Smiling, Proud Wanderer*.

Finally, on detail design. The following details in the game *Six Sects*: the reason why Xiao Linzi, the young master of Fuwei Escort Agency, kills Yu Renyan is that Yu makes sexual advances on Salaotou's granddaughter; Qingcheng Sect gives Liu Zhengfeng the property plundered from Fuwei Escort Agency as a gift of congratulations; Linghu Chong fights with Tian Boguang to save Yilin; to make Yilin leave first, Linghu Chong lies that he goes unlucky at the sight of a nun, were the same as those in *The Smiling, Proud Wanderer*.

Therefore, the existing evidence could prove that the game *Six Sects* constituted an adaptation of the first seven chapters of *The Smiling, Proud Wanderer*. As the Plaintiff Perfect World was authorized to have the exclusive right to adapt *The Smiling, Proud Wanderer* into a game and publish and operate the adapted software in the Chinese mainland, the Defendant Blaze Fire company's behavior constituted an infringement on the above rights of the Plaintiff Perfect World.

As for the Plaintiff Perfect World's claim that the game *Six Sects* constituted an adaptation of *The Heavenly Sword and Dragon Saber*, *The Legend of the Condor Heroes* and *The Return of the Condor Heroes*, the court held that, according to the notarized content of the game *Six Sects* provided by the Plaintiff, the use of relevant elements in *The Heavenly Sword and Dragon Saber* was mainly reflected in the names of the characters: Wudang Sect: Zhang Sanfeng, Song Yuanqiao, Yu Lianzhou, Yin Liting, Mo Shenggu, Song Qingshu; Emei Sect: Abbess Miejue, Ding Minjun, Ji Xiaofu and Zhou Yunruo; Ming Cult: Yang Xiao; Shaolin Sect: Jueyuan, the relationships between the characters, and the event of Guhongzi, Miejue's senior dying in frustration due to his loss to Yang Xiao. However, from the perspective of the storyline and context development, the most important elements in adaptation, the existing notarized content of the game *Six Sects* did not contain the same storyline as that of *The Heavenly Sword and Dragon Saber*. For *The Legend of the Condor Heroes* and *The Return of the Condor Heroes*, the notarized content of game *Six Sects* only showed a list of names in the scene of the Battle of Xiangyang: the elders of the Beggars' Sect, Fu Er, Dawu, Xiaowu, Brother Yelu, Master Guo, Rong Er, etc. There were no plots which were the same as those of the two works.

Therefore, the existing evidence cannot prove that the game *Six Sects* constituted an adaptation of *The Heavenly Sword and Dragon Saber*, *The Legend of the Condor Heroes* and *The Return of the Condor Heroes*.

II . Identification of the Nature of the Promotional Activities

The Defendant Blaze Fire's use of the relevant elements of the four literary works-*The Smiling*, *Proud Wanderer*, *The Heavenly Sword and Dragon Saber*, *The Legend of the Condor Heroes* and *The Return of the Condor Heroes*-in the game *Six Sects* constituted unfair competition against the Plaintiff Perfect World.

First, false publicity refers to the misleading promotion of the quality, components, performance, use, producer, validity period and origin of a commodity by an operator through advertising or other means. As mentioned earlier, the game *Six Sects* did use the relevant elements of the four literary works involved, so the Defendant Blaze Fire's promotion of the elements of the four literary works involved did not constitute false publicity.

Second, the authorization that the Plaintiff Perfect World had obtained from Zha Liangyong included the adaptation into game software for mobile terminal users based on the titles, stories, characters, martial arts and places in the works, and the launch and operation of the "adapted software." The Plaintiff was authorized to hold any party responsible for any infringement and unfair competition regarding the four literary works involved. Therefore, although the game *Six Sects* did not constitute an adaptation of the three works: *The Heavenly Sword and Dragon Saber*, *The Legend of the Condor Heroes* and *The Return of the Condor Heroes*, the Defendant Blaze Fire mixed the classical elements, plots and characters of the four works in the game. In its promotion of the game, there were the following statements: "The Zhang Wuji played by Ma Jingtao is absolutely an indelible figure from our childhood," "then the Brother Jing played by Huang Rihua in *The Legend of the Condor Heroes* (1983) is one of the most classic figures from our childhood," "The good-looking man who has a clear cut on what to love and what to hate will never be surpassed-that's what people think of Gu Tianle's Yang Guo from *The Return of the Condor Heroes*," "*Six Sects*, a derivative from the classics, recreates a wulin for the players, where you can learn the unparalleled skills like Zhang Wuji, defend

Xiangyang like Guo Jing, or even create chaos like Dongfang Bubai Join … the *Six Sects and start your journey in the wulin*," "*the scruffy, happy-go-lucky and righteous Linghu Chong, the righteous and evil Huang Yaoshi, the fierce, vicious and disgusting Abbess Miejue, or the unscrupulous and silly Jinlun Lama. Now in Six Sects*, players can choose to challenge those heroes as they like." Such statements, alongside the game content, would attract the fans of *The Smiling, Proud Wanderer, The Heavenly Sword and Dragon Saber, The Legend of the Condor Heroes* and *The Return of the Condor Heroes* to become players of the game *Six Sects*. Such seizure of the market share and the players belonging to the Plaintiff Perfect World exerted an adverse effect on the development and operation of the Plaintiff and disrupted the normal economic order in the market. Therefore, the Defendant Blaze Fire's behavior constituted unfair competition against the Plaintiff Perfect World.

Ⅲ. Identification of the Liability of the Network Service Providers

The "91 Assistant" operated by the Defendant Borui, the "9Game" operated by the Defendant i9Game and the website www. 19196. com operated by the Defendant Youlong are all platforms providing software uploading, storage and downloading services. The three Defendants are all network service providers. To judge whether a network service provider's behavior constitutes infringement, the key is to find whether it helps others with the infringement, making the infringement occur and the consequence expand. The criterion for judging whether a network service provider has fault is whether it has reached the level of care it should have, whether it knows or has reasonable reasons to know about the possible adverse consequences. Such criterion varies for different network service providers in different cases.

In this case, objectively speaking, the number of software uploaded to the public software platforms is huge, so it is difficult for the Defendants Borui, i9Game and Youlong to conduct a substantial review of all the uploaded software one by one. Also, the Defendant Blaze Fire had obtained the computer software copyright registration certificate for its game *Six Sects*, and provided it to the Defendants Borui, i9Game and Youlong when uploading the game client. Neither the name of the game nor the introduction of the game provided by Blaze Fire on the three platforms indicated any association to any literary works. Besides, the Plaintiff Perfect World did not send letters to the Defendants Borui, i9Game and Youlong to delete the game after discovering the suspected infringement of *Six Sects*. Therefore, the existing evidence cannot prove that the Defendants Borui, i9Game and Youlong have intentionally helped the Defendant Blaze Fire commit infringement. As the Defendants Borui, i9Game and Youlong subjectively have no fault, they should not be liable for compensation. In this case, the Defendant Blaze Fire should bear the liability for compensation.

(Writers: Huang Yang & Shen Jingjie)

Identification of Infringement by Private Cinemas and Copyright Protection

—Beijing iQIYI Science & Technology Co. , Ltd. v. Shanghai Wanmu Business Consulting Co. , Ltd. over Infringement of the Right to Communicate Works over Information Networks

[Summary]

Private cinema, as a new film watching mode emerging in line with the development of the market, provides consumers with privacy and personalized choices. However, it also causes many legal problems. The Defendant's business model in this case is that after obtaining the film involved, it put the video file on its server. When the user used the preset system to broadcast a film in the private cinema compartment, the film was communicated through the local area network set up at the Defendant's business premises. The Defendant's behavior infringed the right to communicate works over information networks, which is protected by the Copyright Law, not the right to show. This case is the first case in China to identify private cinema watching mode as infringement, which can serve as reference for the trial of similar cases.

[Case Review]

Plaintiff: Beijing iQIYI Science & Technology Co. , Ltd.

Defendant: Shanghai Wanmu Business Consulting Co. , Ltd.

Cause of Action: Infringement of the right to communicate works over information networks

First-Instance Case No. : (2016) H0110MC No. 4902

Ⅰ. Ownership and Authorization of the Films Involved

(1) About the film *SPL* Ⅱ: *A Time for Consequences*

On May 22, 2015, the Film Bureau of the State Administration of Press, Publication, Radio, Television and Television issued a license (No. 159 [2015]) for the release of film entitled *SPL* Ⅱ: *A Time for Consequences*. The film producers are Sil-Metropole Organisation Ltd., Sun Entertainment Culture Limited (Hong Kong, China), Bona Film Group Limited and Maximum Gain Kapital Group Limited (Hong Kong, China).

On June 12, 2015, Sil-Metropole Organisation Ltd., Bona Film Group Limited and Maximum Gain Kapital Group Limited (Hong Kong, China) confirmed in a copyright certificate that the sole copyright holder of the film *SPL II: A Time For Consequences* is Sun Entertainment Culture Limited (Hong Kong, China), and the licensing included the right to own the copyright, the right to sublicense and the right to protect the rights. The licensing period of the right to communicate the film over information networks was from August 28, 2015 to August 27, 2065.

On August 18, 2015, Sun Entertainment Culture Limited (Hong Kong, China) confirmed through the resolution made by the Board of Directors the contents of the Copyright Certificate attached to the resolution. The contents of the Copyright Certificate are: on June 12, 2015, Sun Entertainment Culture Limited (Hong Kong, China) granted Star Alliance Pictures (Wuxi) Co., Ltd. its exclusive rights to own the copyright, to sublicense and to protect the rights for the film *SPL* Ⅱ: *A Time For Consequences* in the territory of the People's Republic of China (excluding Hong Kong, Macao and Taiwan). The licensing period of the right to communicate the film over information networks begins on August 28, 2015 and ends on August 27, 2065.

On January 20, 2015, Star Alliance Pictures (Wuxi) Co., Ltd. issued a licensing letter, granting Beijing Qiyi Century Technology Co., Ltd. its exclusive right to communicate the film *SPL II: A Time for Consequences* over information networks in the Chinese mainland (excluding Hong Kong, Macao and Taiwan). The licensing period is seven years from the launch of the film online (June 18, 2015).

On January 20, 2015, Beijing Qiyi Century Technology Co., Ltd. issued a licensing letter, granting the Plaintiff its exclusive right to communicate the film *SPL*

II: *A Time for Consequences* over information networks in the Chinese mainland (excluding Hong Kong, Macao and Taiwan). The licensing period is the same as that enjoyed by the licensor.

(2) About the film *One Hundred Thousand Bad Jokes*

On December 9, 2014, the Film Bureau of the State Administration of Press, Publication, Radio, Television and Television issued a license (No. 037 [2014]) for the release of the film entitled *One Hundred Thousand Bad Jokes*. The film producers are Shanghai Toonmax Media Co. , Ltd. , Wanda Media Co. , Ltd. , and Beijing April Star Network Technology Co. , Ltd.

On January 20, 2015, Shanghai Toonmax Media Co. , Ltd. issued a licensing letter, granting Beijing Qiyi Century Technology Co. , Ltd. its exclusive right to communicate the film *One Hundred Thousand Bad Jokes* over information networks, the right to sublicense and to protect the rights in the Chinese mainland (excluding Hong Kong, Macao and Taiwan). The licensing period is from February 1, 2015 to January 31, 2065.

On January 20, 2015, Beijing Qiyi Century Technology Co. , Ltd. issued a licensing letter, granting the Plaintiff its exclusive right to communicate the film *One Hundred Thousand Bad Jokes* over information networks, the right to sublicense and to protect the rights in the Chinese mainland (excluding Hong Kong, Macao and Taiwan). The licensing period is from February 1, 2015 to January 31, 2065.

On January 27, 2015, Wanda Media Co. , Ltd. issued a copyright certificate, declaring that it was one of the copyright owners of the film *One Hundred Thousand Bad Jokes*, and that it granted Shanghai Toonmax Media Co. , Ltd. the right to communicate the film *One Hundred Thousand Bad Jokes* over information networks exclusively or sublicense a third party to do so. The licensing period shall be from the date of obtaining the film release license to the date of termination of the copyright protection period.

On January 27, 2015, Beijing April Star Network Technology Co. , Ltd. issued a copyright certificate, declaring that it was one of the copyright owners of the film*One Hundred Thousand Bad Jokes*, and that it granted Shanghai Toonmax Media Co. , Ltd. the right to communicate the film *One Hundred Thousand Bad Jokes* over information networks exclusively or sublicense a third party to do so. The licensing period shall be from the date of granting a film release license to the date of termination of the copyright protection period.

Ⅱ. Playing of the films involved in the Defendant's business premises

On October 28, 2015, upon the application of the Plaintiff, Jiang Minzheng and Liang Yongjie, notaries from Shanghai Changning District Notarial Office, and Wang Huizhong, the Plaintiff's attorney, came to Wanmu Cinema, which was located in Lotus International Plaza, on the north side of Humin Road, between Gufang Road and Lianhua Road. The notaries took pictures of the cinema. After entering a private room, the notaries turned on the computer there, searched *SPL II* on the computer, clicked on "play" and got two video clips by videotaping the playing process, and. The notaries also got a business card, a promotional leaflet and a receipt (RMB 600 for recharge) at the cinema.

On February 25, 2016, upon the application of Co-Effort Law Firm, Zhang Zhiming and Xu Liming, notaries of Shanghai Oriental Notarial Public Office, and Attorney Qian Zhen came to Wanmu Cinema (3F, Lotus International Plaza, No. 7866 Humin Road, Shanghai). After the three entered Rooms V4 and V7 together, the notaries used digital camera provided by the notarial office to take pictures of the playing devices in the rooms. Attorney Qian Zhen searched and played the film involved on the computers in the rooms. The notaries videotaped the process and got the video files. The specific steps are as follows: 1. After staff of Wanmu Private Cinema turned on the computer terminal in the room, the projection screen showed the playback interface; 2. The playback interface included columns such as "Homepage," "Latest," "Classics" and "Categories," clicked one by one and finally came to the "Categories" column; 3. Clicked on the "Mainland" option, clicked the letters S, P, L, and two films appeared: *SPL* and *SPL II*; 4. Clicked on *SPL II* and came to the "Introduction to the plot" page, and then click on the "Play Now" button in the "Introduction" page, then clicked on the "Play Now" button. When the film was being played, fast forwarded it to the middle and the end of the film, indicating that the film could be played in full. The release license number and the names of producers were also displayed at the beginning of the film; 5. When the film was being played, right-clicked and a dialog box popped up, which contained a column called "Properties." Clicked "Properties," there came a window called "Playing Info." This window contained columns such as "Playing Info," "File Info," "System Info." Clicked the columns one by one, and under the "File Info" column, it showed that location of the film in the LAN (local area network) was:

192. 168. 0. 249/G/Saat Po Long2-杀破狼 2 之杀无赦-2015/Saat. Po. Long2. 2015. 1080p. WEB-DL. X264. AAC-XJCTV. mkv; 6. Right-clicked on the playing page of the film, and the same dialog box as in Step 5 popped up. Clicked the "Open Folder" column in the dialog box to enter "My Computer" page, where the location of the film source in the LAN was shown; 7. Clicked 192. 168. 0. 249 at the bottom left on "My Computer" page, there came the network shared disks d, e, f, g and "users." Selected disk g, where the source of *SPL II* in the LAN could be found. Played it; 8. Repeated the above steps to play the film *One Hundred Thousand Bad Jokes* and confirmed that this film was also stored in the server terminal whose address was 192. 168. 0. 249. The notaries also secured a business card, a promotional material and a general machine-printed invoice by Shanghai Local Tax Bureau (RMB 1,000 in recharge). On March 15, 2016, the Notarial Office issued the notarial certificate No. 2647 (2016). The notaries recorded the videos on CD, printed the pictures taken on the spot, and copied the business card, promotional material and invoice. Those materials were all attached to the notarial certificate.

The Defendant stated that at Wanmu Private Cinema, each compartment was equipped with a computer terminal. After turning on the computer, consumers could search and play the film by operating on the pre-installed playing interface. The hard disk in the computer terminal at the compartments could not store films. The Defendant had stored the films involved in the hard disk of the server terminal whose address was 192. 168. 0. 249. Consumers used a unified playing interface to select and order the film. After being read by the LAN set up in the cinema, the film stored in the server terminal would be played.

Ⅲ. The Defendant's business conditions and charging standards

The Defendant was registered and established on July 18, 2013, with a registered capital of RMB 200,000. Its business scope mainly includes business consultation, corporate image planning, and computer graphic design and production.

There were more than 20 compartments at the Defendant's premises. The services were charged by hour. The price per hour varied from RMB 98 to 398 according to the size of the compartment. There was a 50% discount between 10 a. m. and 4 p. m. on weekdays. There was no discount after 4 p. m. on weekdays and during holidays. There was a discount of 40% to 70% on the basis of the above prices according to the amount of recharge of members.

The Plaintiff Beijing iQIYI Science & Technology Co. , Ltd. claimed that the Plaintiff was the legal operator of iQIYI. COM, a large online video platform in China, and spent a lot of money on copyright licensing. The Plaintiff was authorized to enjoy the exclusive right to communicate films such as *SPL II* and *One Hundred Thousand Bad Jokes* over information networks in the Chinese mainland. The Defendant Wanmu set up multiple luxury compartments in its Wanmu Private Cinema. Without permission to communicate the films involved over information networks, the Defendant provided paid video-on-demand service to consumers using computer terminals through the self-built LAN. The Plaintiff believed that the Defendant had infringed the Plaintiff's right to communicate the works involved over information networks by placing the works in its LAN, enabling the public to play them at the time and place chosen by themselves. As an exclusive licensee, the Plaintiff had the right to bring a lawsuit under its own name. Accordingly, the Plaintiff requested the court to order the Defendant make a compensation of RMB 500,000 for its economic losses and reasonable expenses on protecting its rights.

The Defendant Shanghai Wanmu Business Consulting Co. , Ltd. argued that it objected to the Plaintiff's request on the following grounds: one, consumers can directly visit the Plaintiff's video website on the computer terminal in the compartment to watch the two films involved. There was the possibility that after consumers watched the films online, the films involved were automatically cached in the Defendant's server terminal. Therefore, there is evidence to prove that the Defendant committed the infringement; two, even if the court found the Defendant's infringement, the amount of compensation claimed by the Plaintiff is too high. Consumers came to the Defendant's cinema not just for film watching, but also for the space services. The Defendant did not provide evidence to support its defense.

[Judgment]

After hearing, Shanghai Yangpu District People's Court held that according to the relevant provisions of the Copyright Law, the copyright of a film work is enjoyed by the producer; if there is no proof to the contrary, the citizen, legal person or other organization signed on the work shall be the author. The films involved *SPL II* and *One Hundred Thousand Bad Jokes* were protected by Copyright Law as they were produced on a certain medium, made up by a series of pictures with or without sounds, and played by appropriate devices or communicated by other means. The Plaintiff provided the release licenses and the licensing documents of the producers for the films *SPL II* and *One Hundred Thousand Bad Jokes* to prove that it had been authorized by the copyright owner to enjoy the exclusive right to communicate the two films over information networks, and have the right to bring a lawsuit in its own name for any infringement occurs within the licensing scope and the licensing period.

In this case, the computer terminal in the compartment of the Defendant's Wanmu Private Cinema was equipped with a unified playback interface. Although the computer terminal in each compartment did not store the films involved, consumers could connect to the server terminal through the LAN set up by the Defendant itself after choosing the films on the playback interface. The Defendant stored the films involved in the server terminal without permission, so that consumers could play them through the network at the time chosen by themselves. Such behavior infringed the Plaintiff's right to communicate works over information networks.

On the Defendant's argument that the films involved were automatically cached after consumers watched them on the Plaintiff's website, the court held that according to the notarized process, the films involved were indeed stored on the Defendant's server terminal. By operating on the Defendant's "Home Page," one could find the films involved in the database and play them. If the films had been cached after being played by consumers on the Plaintiff's website, they could not appear in the database. Therefore, Shanghai Yangpu District People's Court refused to accept the Defendant's defense.

Accordingly, Shanghai Yangpu District People's Court, in accordance with Article 15 (1) (vi) and Article 36 (1) of the *Tort Liability Law of the People's Republic of China*, Article 10 (1) (xii), Article 48 (i) and Article 49 of the *Copyright Law of the People's Republic of China*, Article 25 (1) (2) and Article 26 of the *Interpretation of the Supreme People's Court Concerning the Application of Laws in the Trial of Civil Disputes over Copyright*, and Article 3 of the *Provisions of the Supreme People's Court on Several Issues Concerning the Application of Law in Hearing Civil Disputes Involving Infringement of the Right of Communication over Information Networks*, decided that the Defendant Shanghai Wanmu Business Consulting Co., Ltd. shall compensate the Plaintiff Beijing iQIYI Science &

Technology Co. , Ltd. RMB 30,000 (including reasonable expenses of RMB12, 000) within 10 days from the effective date of this judgment.

After the first trial, neither parties appealed.

[Case Study]

The dispute in this case over copyright infringement caused by a private cinema broadcasting other people's films is the first case of its kind in Shanghai. The court eventually found that the Defendant's behavior infringed the Plaintiff's right to communicate works over information networks, not the right to show or other rights. The result of this case and how it was handled can serve as reference for the trial of similar cases in the future.

I . Which copyright of the Plaintiff was infringed by the Defendant?

According to the court's investigation of the Defendant's business premises, the Defendant's business model was to place the video files in the server after obtaining the films involved. When customers used the preset system to play a film in the compartment of the private cinema, the film was disseminated through the LAN set up in the Defendant's business premises. The court found that the Defendant's such behavior and its business model infringed the Plaintiff's right to communicate works over information networks. The right to communicate works over information networks aims at enabling the copyright owner to prevent others from placing the work in the information network without authorization, making the work accessible to the public. To judge whether an act constitutes communication over information networks, the following conditions shall be met:

1. The actor places the work in the information network "by means of uploading them to the network server, setting up shared files or using file-sharing software";

2. The network in which the work is located must be open to the public, who can "download, browse or otherwise access" the work;

3. The public can access the work in the way mentioned above at "the time and place chosen by themselves. "

As the operator of the private cinema, the Defendant "provided works to the public in wired or wireless ways, so that the public can access the works at the time and place chosen by themselves," which met the condition of communication over information networks. Customers could decide the time and place of accessing the works independently, rather than passively receive the communication or broadcasting of the works. Such an "interactive" behavior is different from the one-way communication over networks such as via wireless (wired) radio. The one-way communication is related to the right to broadcast works. The emphasis placed on how a film was played at the private cinema: which occurred through the communication over the information network, rather than simply through projectors, slide projectors and other technical equipment, is to distinguish from the right to screen the works.

II. Scope of "Information Network": about the LAN

In this case, the Defendant placed the video files in the server; when customers used the preset system to play a movie in the compartment of the private cinema, the film was communicated through the LAN set up at the Defendant's business premises. Here comes the question: Is the LAN an information network? The definition of the right of communication over information networks does not specify the specific meaning and scope of "information networks," but it is specified under Article 2 of the *Provisions of the Supreme People's Court on Several Issues Concerning the Application of Law in Hearing Civil Disputes Involving Infringement of the Right of Communication over Information Networks*: "For the purposes of these Provisions, 'information networks' include the Internet, radio and television broadcasting networks, fixed communication networks and mobile communication networks, with computers, TV sets, fixed telephones, mobile phones and other electronic devices as receiving terminals, as well as local area networks open to the public." Obviously, the definition of information networks goes far beyond the scope of computer networks in our daily lives. In other words, any network systems that enable the public to access the required information remotely and autonomously (or interactively) are information networks provided under the Copyright Law. In this case, the Defendant adopted the mode of "films stored on host + operation of the system in the compartment + transmission via LAN." That mode is based on the LAN set up by the Defendant. The court held that there is no point in requiring the "information networks" over which works are communicated to be WAN or LAN. According to the law, the establishment of the right to communicate over information networks is to emphasize the way a work is communicated, which is "interactive on demand," rather than the scope of communication. The Defendant's customers are "non-specific users," and the reason that the LAN was adopted is only because the Defendant's business model limited the total number of people, the public can still access the works at any time.

Ⅲ. How to Understand"the Time and Place Chosen by Themselves"

In this case, the Defendant's business hours were from 10 a. m. to 10 p. m. every day. Consumers also needed to pay a certain price to enjoy the film and television works in the Defendant's business premises using the its on-demand system. Some people held that such provision of works in a limited time period and at a specific place did not meet the condition of "enabling the public to access the works at the time and place chosen by themselves." This view is a misunderstanding of the right of communication over information networks. The "right of communication over information networks" in China's Copyright Law originates from Article 8 of WCT, which is interpreted by the World Intellectual Property Organization (WIPO) as follows: "Interactive on-demand communication is the scope of this provision. The way to achieve this goal is to confirm that relevant communication activities include enabling members of the public to access works from different locations and at different times." It can be seen that the essence of this provision is to emphasize interactive communication to the public, rather than require any point on the spatial and temporal dimensions. As a result, in the limited time and geographical area specified by the disseminator, as long as the public can choose the time and place to "order and play the films" through the network, it is "interactive communication," which falls within the scope regulated by "the right of communication over information networks." Therefore, in this case, although the films involved could only be played at the Defendant's business premises during the business hours, it was still a violation of the right to communicate the works over the information networks.

(Writer: Ju Yiliang)

II

Civil Disputes Over
Trademark Rights

Contract Effectiveness and Ownership of Use Right in Case of Repeated Exclusive Trademark Licensing

—Dispute over Trademark License Contract (Shanghai Pafuluo Stationery Co. , Ltd. v. Shanghai Yixiang Stationery Co. , Ltd. and Picasso International Incorporated)

[**Abstract**]

If a trademark owner signs two exclusive license contracts with others, and there is an overlap in the license period, the later license contract won't necessarily be invalid even though the parties thereto know about the existence of the prior license contract. However, the parties to the later license contract can neither be deemed as bona fides third parties nor obtain the right to use the trademark in accordance with the later license contract.

[**Case Review**]

Plaintiff (Appellant) : Shanghai Pafuluo Stationery Co. , Ltd.

Defendant (Appellant) : Shanghai Yixiang Stationery Co. , Ltd.

Defendant (Appellee) : Picasso International Incorporated

Cause of Action : dispute over trademark license contract

First-Instance Case No. : Hu Yi Zhong Min Wu (Zhi) Chu Zi No. 250 (2012)

Second-Instance Case No. : Hu Gao Min San (Zhi) Zhong Zi No. 117 (2014)

The trademark involved was registered by Picasso International Incorporated ("Picasso") on May 21, 2003. On July 9, 2003, Picasso issued a Certificate of Authorization, authorizing Shanghai Pafuluo Stationery Co., Ltd. ("Pafuluo") to use the disputed trademark in the Chinese Mainland from July 9, 2003 to December 31, 2008. On September 8, 2008, it issued another Certificate of Authorization, authorizing Pafuluo to use the trademark involved on writing instruments commercially in the Chinese Mainland and conferring it the exclusive right to manufacture and sell in the Chinese Mainland for a period from September 10, 2008 to December 31, 2013. On March 12, 2009, the Trademark Office sent a Notice of Recordal of Trademark License Contract to Picasso, informing that its application for recordal submitted on June 30, 2008, which authorizes Pafuluo to use the trademark involved, has been approved. On February 11, 2010, Picasso and Pafuluo signed a License Agreement to extend the license period for ten years, commencing on January 1, 2014 and ending on December 31, 2003.

On January 1, 2012, Picasso and Pafuluo entered into an agreement for early termination of the recorded trademark license contract without prejudice to other provisions. On March 13, 2012, the Trademark Office published Issue 10 (2012) Trademark Gazette, terminating the recorded trademark license contract on January 1, 2012.

On February 16, 2012, Picasso and Shanghai Yixiang Stationery Co., Ltd. ("Yixiang") signed a Trademark License Contract in Shanghai, stipulating Article 2 Exclusive Use; Article 5 License Period: from January 15, 2012 to August 31, 2017; Special Provisions: Party A shall complete the recordal of the license contract within one year of signing this contract; except for delay due to the tardy examination procedure of the Trademark Office, Party B may terminate the contract if Party A fails to revoke Pafuluo's contract recorded by the State Trademark Office or fails record this contract at the State Trademark Office due to other reasons. On the same day, Picasso issued a letter of authorization, declaring that Yixiang is the sole and exclusive licensee in the Chinese Mainland.

Pafuluo argued that Picasso, the owner of No. 2001022 Trademark ("trademark involved"), authorized it in September 2008 to use the trademark exclusively in the Chinese Mainland for a period from September 2008 to December 2013. In February 2010, they agreed to extend the license period for 10 years. In February 2012, Picasso and Yixiang signed a Trademark License Contract, agreeing that Yixiang can use the trademark exclusively from January 2012 to August 2017 and authorizing Yixiang to crack down on counterfeits nationwide, resulting in the investigation over Pafuluo products by the local industry and commerce department. Picasso's act of signing Trademark License Contract with Yixiang without permission, complaining to the local industry and commerce department about Pafuluo's infringement and filing a lawsuit to the court for trademark infringement can be deemed as a malicious collusion that harms the legitimate interests of third parties and violates the mandatory provisions of laws and administrative regulations. It requested the court to rule the disputed contract invalid and order the two defendants to compensate for Pafuluo's economic losses totaling RMB 1,000,000.

The Defendant, Yixiang, argued that, (1) Pafuluo didn't obtain the exclusive license granted by Picasso to use the trademark involved. Pafuluo's exclusive license contract recorded by the Trademark Office was forged, so the licensing method recorded by the Trademark Office couldn't prove Pafuluo's exclusive license to use the trademark involved. There's no specific agreement on the nature of authorization in the Certificate of Authorization, so Pafuluo only obtained the sole right to use the trademark involved rather than the exclusive license stipulated by law. (2) According to the notice of the Trademark Office, the trademark licensing relationship between trademark owner Picasso and Pafuluo had been terminated early on January 1, 2012. Yixiang obtained the exclusive licensing right of the trademark involved on February 16, 2012 without infringing upon any right of Pafuluo nor maliciously colluding with Picasso. (3) As Pafuluo was still producing a large number of products bearing the trademark involved after Yixiang obtained the exclusive right to use the trademark involved, it's justified for Yixiang to complain to industrial and commercial administrative departments nationwide and filed infringement lawsuits. So, Pafuluo's losses weren't caused by bad faith. (4) Picasso's malicious collusion with Pafuluo and Shanghai Dazhe Industrial Co. , Ltd. , an outsider, by transferring the trademark involved to Dazhe company during the proceedings of this case infringed upon Yixiang's preemptive right and exclusively licensed right stipulated in the contract.

Picasso replied in writing that it didn't put the trademark license contract on records. When signing the contract with Yixiang, Yixiang had been informed of the license status of the trademark involved, including Pafuluo's act of forging the signature of Lin Daguang, person in charge of Picasso, to record the trademark license contract. Yixiang was fully aware that the prior license of the trademark hadn't yet been terminated, but only required Picasso to rescind Pafuluo's contract recorded by the Trademark Office as soon as possible and meanwhile agreed that neither party shall privately settle with Pafuluo. Therefore, it has fulfilled the obligation to disclose when licensing the trademark involved to Yixiang; all losses thus caused to Pafuluo shall be borne by Yixiang.

[Judgment]

Shanghai No. 1 Intermediate People's Court accepted the fact declared by Pafuluo about the license process of the trademark involved. It held that the contractual relationship by which Pafuluo obtained the right to use the trademark involved was true and valid, and Pafuluo enjoyed the exclusive right to use the trademark involved from September 10, 2008 to December 31, 2013. The purpose of signing the disputed contract by Yixiang is neither to harm the legitimate rights and interests of Pafuluo nor commit unfair competition in bad faith. During contract negotiations with Picasso, Yixiang learned of the fact that Pafuluo enjoyed the exclusive right to use the trademark involved, but had asked Picasso to rescind the recorded exclusive license contract signed with Pafuluo. So, Yixiang cannot be deemed to have bad faith in damaging Pafuluo's interests simply because it was aware of the above-mentioned fact. After signing the exclusive license contract with Picasso and paying the license fee, Yixiang's complaints to industrial and commercial administrative departments were not meant to damage the legitimate interests of Pafuluo, and similar complaints from Picasso and Yixiang also cannot prove that they're intended to harm the interests of Pafuluo. Only when the conclusion of contract violates the mandatory provisions of laws and administrative regulations can the autonomy of will of parties concerned be excluded. Article 3.1 of Judicial Interpretation of the Trademark Law alleged by Pafuluo defined three trademark licensing methods as stipulated in the Trademark Law, which is obviously not a mandatory provision. Therefore, the conclusion of the disputed contract didn't violate the mandatory provisions of laws and administrative regulations; there are no facts or laws to support Pafuluo's claim for invalidation of the disputed contract. Pafuluo's request for confirmation of invalidity of the disputed contract and corresponding letter of authorization, as well as the compensation thus claimed, were not supported by the court of first instance. To sum up, Shanghai No. 1 Intermediate People's Court rejected all the claims of Pafuluo.

Dissatisfied with the first-instance judgment, both Pafuluo and Yixiang filed an appeal.

After the trial, Shanghai High People's Court held that the facts were clearly ascertained and the law and regulations were properly applied in the first-instance judgment. It dismissed the appeal and affirm the original judgment.

[Case Study]

During the actual trademark operation, a trademark owner might grant exclusive license repeatedly for its own benefits. However, the rules for the change of intellectual property rights are not as clear as those for real right, resulting in intense conflicts of interests between various licensees. As this case was complicated, the court of second instance, based on the first-instance judgment, probed deeper into the legal significance of recordal of trademark license, conditions under which malicious collusion leads to invalidation of the contract, and application of the theory of differentiation between act of liability and act of disposition in the Trademark Law, etc. , and provided a clear answer as to who should enjoy the exclusive right to use the licensed trademark, laying a foundation for the thorough settlement of trademark infringement cases all over the country, further clarifying the legal rules for trademark licensing and helping to maintain a fair and good faith trademark usage order.

I. Conditions for determination of invalidity of the contract caused by malicious collusion

According to Article 52 of the Contract Law, "A contract shall be null and void if malicious collusion is conducted to damage the interests of a third party. " Malicious collusion is a declaration of intention to collude with each other for the purpose of harming the interests of others. The plaintiff has to prove the defendant's subjective intent to harm the interests of others and also its objective act of collusion. Malicious collusion leading to invalidity of contract is specially stipulated in the Contract Law of China and is rarely seen in the contract law of other countries. The core essence of contract is promise, transaction and execution. Contract is an intangible and abstract legal relationship, rather than its written or oral form. The core of a contract is transaction between the parties, and contract is an instrument to regulate their future acts. In judicial practice, courts are becoming less likely to adopt the system of contract invalidation because contract is an instrument for market transaction and its invalidation will lead to fracture of the transaction chain and pose an instrumental obstacle to the operation of the market, which is detrimental to the development of market economy. Malicious collusion referred to in Article 52 of the Contract Law is usually manifested as the transfer of property, escape of debts or collusion with the other party's agent to harm the interests of the other party by virtue of a contract. The essence of contract invalidation system is to stipulate that contracts in violation of mandatory provisions of laws and administrative regulations are invalid because the act itself is illegal.

In order to determine whether Yixiang had maliciously colluded with Picasso when they signed the later exclusive license contract, both subjective conditions and objective conditions shall be taken into account. In terms of subjective bad faith, Yixiang and Pafuluo produce and sell similar writing instruments and they are competitors in the same market; Picasso declared in its written statement of defense that Yixiang had been informed of its trademark license with Pafuluo; Yixiang and Picasso signed the disputed trademark license contract on February 16, 2012, prior to the cessation of recording announced by the Trademark Office on March 13, 2012; although the recording of trademark license contract was ceased on January 1, 2012, no evidences show that the contractual relationship between Pafuluo and Picasso for exclusive use of the trademark involved has been dissolved and it cannot be presumed dissolved based solely on the cessation of recording; Yixiang also said that it learned of the trademark license relationship between Pafuluo and Picasso. Therefore, it can be concluded that Yixiang had been aware of the exclusive license relationship between Pafuluo and Picasso concerning the trademark involved when it signed the disputed trademark license contract with Picasso, so it wasn't a bona fides third party. Despite this, it just means that Yixiang knew the above-mentioned exclusive license relationship but doesn't suggest that Yixiang maliciously colluded with Picasso to harm the interests of third parties. Yixiang signed the trademark license contract with Picasso for the purpose of using the trademark involved. Although it's improper for Yixiang to sign the disputed contract without asking Picasso to terminate the prior exclusive license contract signed with Pafuluo, resulting in an overlap of the license period, Yixiang had requested in the disputed contract that Picasso shall actively rescind the recorded license contract with Pafuluo, and no evidences show that Yixiang had subjective bad faith in harming the interests of Pafuluo.

In terms of the objective behavior, the plaintiff has to produce evidences to prove that the two defendants colluded with each other. The so-called collusion implies certain negative evaluation, meaning that two parties collude with each other for the purpose of harming others. In most circumstances, collusion can be inferred from behaviors on condition that they are conducted by contracting parties in bad faith. However, in this case, no direct evidence shows two parties colluded with each other. The reason why Yixiang and Picasso made complaints and whistle-blowing was that they believed Yixiang had obtained the exclusive right to use the trademark involved, Moreover, the administrative organ ruled that Pafuluo committed no violation. So, it's hard to say Yixiang and Picasso colluded with each other. The provision specially stipulated in the disputed contract that restricts the settlement of contracting parties with the third party is in line with Yixiang's desire to protect its contractual interests and is commonly seen in market competition, which can't be used to determine the malicious collusion between Yixiang and Picasso, either. Although Yixiang has apparent motivation to try to influence the exclusive license relationship between Picasso and Pafuluo concerning the trademark involved, it's justified for Yixiang to sign the exclusive license contract with Picasso, the trademark owner, and request Picasso not to license the trademark involved to third parties on the same kind of products since Yixiang and Pafuluo are business competitors. This case suggests that though a trademark owner might sign several trademark exclusive license contracts at the same time in bad faith, the standards for determination of invalidation of the contract caused by malicious collusion are very high, and the later contract itself is not necessarily invalid.

Ⅱ. Ownership of the right to use the trademark under repeated exclusive license

In this case, the trademark license contract between Yixiang and Picasso has been established and effective, but it doesn't mean the contract has been actually performed, which shall be subject to the actual performance of both parties. Both Yixiang and Picasso knew the exclusive license relationship between Pafuluo and Picasso in respect of trademark involved, and Yixiang wasn't a bona fides third party in this sense. The exclusive license contract between Picasso and Pafuluo was performed normally. Although its recording was ceased on January 1, 2012, no evidences show that the exclusive license contract between Pafuluo and Picasso has been terminated and it should be deemed to remain valid. According to Article19 of Interpretation of the Supreme People's Court on Certain Issues Concerning the Application of Law in the Trial of Civil Cases Involving Trademark Disputes, "A trademark license contract not recorded by the Trademark Office cannot be used against any bona fides third party." It can be contrarily interpreted that a trademark license contract can be used against mala fides third parties even if it's not recorded by the Trademark Office. As Yixiang wasn't a bona fides third party, the exclusive right to use the trademark involved obtained by Pafuluo based on its trademark license contract with Picasso can fight against the relationship between Yixiang and Picasso established through their trademark license contract. Although the trademark license contract between Picasso and Yixiang has been established and effective, Pafuluo's exclusive right to use the trademark involved continues to exist and Picasso can no longer dispose the right to use the trademark involved. Given that Picasso didn't actually fulfill its obligations under the trademark license contract with Yixiang, Yixiang couldn't obtain the right to use the trademark involved accordingly. In other words, the contract signed between Yixiang and Picasso can't deprive Pafuluo of its exclusive right to use the trademark involved. As a result, the status of trademark use that Pafuluo has realized according to the prior exclusive license contract shall not be deemed undermined by the later exclusive license contract.

Ⅲ. Disposition of the right to use a trademark

In the second judgment, the theory of differentiation between act of liability and act of disposition in civil law was applied to the change of trademark rights. The so-called act of liability refers to the act of setting certain obligations for the parties concerned without disposing the subject matter, which only produces the right of claim, whereas act of disposition refers to the act of directly exercising the right of dominion, resulting in the whole or partial restriction or elimination of the right. To enable the party concerned to obtain right through act of disposition, the actor must have the right of disposition, while act of liability aims to make the actor assume the performance obligation. Act of disposition comprises of act of real right and act of quasi-real right. The latter is an act of disposition with claim or intangible property as the subject matter. In this case, Picasso established two performance obligations under the Law of Obligations by signing trademark exclusive license contracts with Pafuluo and Yixiang respectively. Different from real right that follows the principle of "one thing, one right", several claims or liabilities may exist simultaneously because the main function of obligation system is to provide social trading tools. Categorization of claims is virtual in a sense, different from the substantial real right of tangible objects. Based on the co-existing obligatory relationships, Picasso has the performance obligation to Pafuluo and Yixiang respectively. However, this is only an obligation to be fulfilled according to the Contract Law and doesn't mean the completion of actual performance, which depends on Picasso's act of disposition. In this case, Pafuluo has obtained the exclusive right to use the trademark involved and Picasso received the license fee; the prior exclusive license contract had been performed by both parties without any disturbance until Picasso and Yixiang signed the contract. It should be noted that when disposing the exclusive right to use the trademark involved, Picasso disposed, in fact, the full and complete right to use the trademark involved. However, despite the fact that Picasso is the owner of the trademark involved, it does not have the right to dispose the use right of the trademark unless reclaiming the right by rescinding the contract with Pafuluo. Whether it is an exclusively licensed or otherwise licensed contract, the later contract between Picasso and Yixiang is an unauthorized disposition contract. However, this does not render it invalid. It can be performed after Picasso cancels the prior contract, and when it's difficult to perform the contract, the dispute over rights and obligations between the two parties can be settled through lawsuit. In a word, practical legal issues can be effectively solved by applying the theory of differentiation between act of liability and act of disposition in civil law to trademark license transactions.

Ⅳ. Other factors

In the final judgment, the concepts of trademark use value and use order were also considered and affirmed. In this case, Picasso, as a trademark owner, didn't use the trademark involved on its own, but licensed it to others instead; the actual user was Pafuluo. Trademark right, in a substantial sense, doesn't arise from registration. As a property right, it comes from the actual use of the trademark and the resulting goodwill. Neither common law system nor civil law system regards trademark registration as a way to obtain the property right. Trademark right originates from and accumulates in its actual use. If not actually used, it is simply a symbol or a mark that might not be protected by law. In this case, the licensed use of the trademark involved by Pafuluo for many years has undoubtedly established a certain market reputation, and consumers have established a specific connection between the trademark involved and Pafuluo, which is the essence of trademark right. The exclusive licensee should also get a fair share of the accumulated goodwill, which is justified by objective reality and substantial justice. This can be regarded as a "reflective benefit" that allows the exclusive licensee to bring tort actions on its own behalf. Underneath it is an order of trademark use, which, if not following legal procedure or disrupted by the collusion of the parties concerned, will also cause damage to relevant consumers who are not adequately informed. If the repeated licensing of Picasso, the "initiator" of this case, is legalized, it will undoubtedly violate the principle of fairness and good faith, disrupt the order of trademark use and ultimately harm the interests of relevant consumers. In view of this, the rights of the prior licensee will naturally prevail.

(Writer: Xu Zhuobin)

Determination of Nominative Use of Goods Trademark

—Dispute over trademark infringement and unfair competition
(Victoria's Secret Store Brand Management Company v.
Shanghai Mice Investment Management Co. , Ltd)

[Abstract]

A business operator legally obtaining the right to sell goods may use the goods trademark of the trademark owner indicatively to the extent of indicating the source of the goods. If the use of the trademark is beyond the scope of indicating the source of the goods, it will constitute an infringement upon the exclusive right to use relevant service trademark. Where the use of a trademark is likely to cause relevant public to mistakenly believe that the sales service is provided by the trademark owner or there exists association relationship such as trademark licensing between the business operator and the trademark owner, it shall be deemed that the use is beyond the scope of indicating the source of the goods being sold and has the function of indicating and identifying the source of service.

[Case Review]

Plaintiff (Appellee):Victoria's Secret Store Brand Management Company
Defendant (Appellant):Shanghai Mice Investment Management Co. , Ltd
Cause of Action:dispute over trademark infringement and unfair competition
First-Instance Case No. :Hu Yi Zhong Min Wu (Zhi) Chu Zi No. 33 (2014)
Second-Instance Case No. :Hu Gao Min San (Zhi) Zhong Zi No. 104 (2014)

The plaintiff enjoys the exclusive right to use four registered trademarks. On December 20, 2013, it applied to Shanghai Oriental Notary Public Office for evidence preservation. Two products were bought in the store "VICTORIA'S SECRET" at the entrance of 4F, Metro City, No. 1111 Zhaojiabang Road, Shanghai. In the product brochure and franchise manual obtained, "VICTORIA'S SECRET" and "维多利亚的秘密" are highlighted. Among them, the product brochure contains introductions to the brand "VICTORIA'S SECRET" and its products, and states that UniMice was founded in Vancouver, Canada in 1999 and the defendant is UniMice's headquarter in China. The last page shows that "VICTORIA'S SECRET" brand is operated by UniMice-Shanghai Mice Investment Management Co., Ltd, and contact information such as telephone, fax, website, address, etc., is provided. The franchise manual contains introductions to the sales system of "VICTORIA'S SECRET" brand, including decoration style, size and standards under the unified control of the defendant, consistent business philosophy, enterprise identification, management services and management system, and requirements on annual purchases, franchise fee, interest margin, etc. for regional distributors, provincial distributors, municipal distributors and single-unit franchisees respectively. The franchise fee ranges from RMB 60,000 to RMB 500,000. As of December 2013, there had been a total of 21 Victoria's Secret stores in Mainland China. The last page also provides contact information as the product brochure. The notarization process showed that "VICTORIA'S SECRET" mark was also highlighted at the 4F store signboard, in-store walls, containers, cashiers and employee badges; "VICTORIA'S SECRET" and "维多利亚的秘密" marks were used on products. An underwear fashion exhibition was being held at B1 floor of the building, and "VICTORIA'S SECRET" mark was highlighted on the background screen. On January 16, 2014, the plaintiff came to the 4F store at Metro City again and obtained a VIP membership card under notarization, on which "VICTORIA'S SECRET" was highlighted.

There is a column about VICTORIA'S SECRET atwww. nz86. com, which highlights "VICTORIA'S SECRET" and "维多利亚的秘密" at the top of the webpage and covers the publicity on "Join Investment". It's stated that the defendant is the head office of Victoria's Secret in China; Shanghai, Beijing, Guangzhou, Shenzhen, Chongqing and Tianjin general agents, China Headquarter of Victoria's Secret and Metro City Store are its direct-sale stores, flagship stores and concept stores; contact information such as telephone, company website and contact address are also provided as the same as franchise manual. In the columns about VICTORIA'S SECRET at www. china-ef. com and www. ne51. com, "VICTORIA'S SECRET" mark is highlighted as brand mark. Scan the QR code on the last page of the franchise manual to enter the WeChat account of Victoria's Secrets, it can be seen that "VICTORIA'S SECRET" mark is highlighted in the account name, and there are a lot of investment information about Victoria's Secret. It also states that the defendant is the operator of the brand.

On January 16, 2014, the plaintiff applied to Baiyun Notary Public Office of Guangzhou for evidence preservation, using the office telephone to dial 4000008115 to inquire about joining Victoria's Secret. Wei Yunxiao, who claimed to be the defendant's employee, answered the requirements for joining and sent specific brand information by email (showing that Wei Yunxiao is the director of the defendant's brand marketing department; fax, investment hotline, website and address are the same as those in the franchise manual) to introduce Victoria's Secret and franchising matters in details. In the email, "VICTORIA'S SECRET" and "维多利亚的秘密" are also highlighted, and it's mentioned that the defendant is the operator of this brand in China and regional distributor in Beijing, Shanghai, Guangzhou, Shenzhen, Chongqing and Tianjin who has set up flagship stores and franchised stores in China.

The court of first instance also found that the plaintiff is a wholly-owned subsidiary of Intimate Brands Holding, LLC, a company not involved in this case. Intimate Brands Holding, LLC is a wholly-owned subsidiary of the outsider Intimate Brands, Inc., whereas Intimate Brands, Inc. is a wholly-owned subsidiary of LBI. LBI has another wholly-owned subsidiary called Victoria's Secret Stores, LLC ("VSSLLC"). The plaintiff is in charge of the registration, use, management and protection of all "VICTORIA'S SECRET" (维多利亚的秘密) trademarks of LBI and is the owner of the above trademarks. LBI and other wholly-owned subsidiaries use "VICTORIA'S SECRET" (维多利亚的秘密) trademarks with the license of the plaintiff.

VSSLLC signed an Inventory Sale Agreement with American Fashion Brands, LLC ("AFB"), which took effect from January 1, 2007, authorizing AFB to sell certain inventories marked as "out of stock" in a number of regions including China. According to Article 5. 4 of the Agreement, a provision concerning intellectual property rights, "The buyer shall not and shall ensure that its purchasers and related parties and customers won't advertise its products by making use of or distributing goods that bear any name, trademark, trade name, icon or other intellectual property rights of the seller or any affiliated parties thereof in any way, and that the buyer and any such person shall have no right to use any product samples, product sample pictures, copies, the Internet or other media, or intellectual property rights of the seller or any affiliated parties thereof as a part of their signs, special stationery, business letters, labels or any other form of advertisements..."

In September 2007, Shanghai Jintian Apparel Co., Ltd ("Jintian") bought a batch of Victoria's Secret underwear worth about \$5.1 million from LBI.

On September 10, 2007, Dean Brocious, Brand Protection Director of LBI, issued a confirmation letter saying, "LBI is pleased to confirm that AFB has been selected to assist in cleaning up the excess quality inventories in Victoria's Secret exclusive store. LBI will continue to provide AFB with selected excess inventories in accordance with the terms and conditions of the Inventory Sale Agreement. AFB partners and buyers shall abide by the same rules and regulations...". On October 6, 2007, Mohamed A. Barry, Chief Executive Officer of AFB, issued an authorization saying, "AFB authorized Shanghai Jintian Apparel Co., Ltd to exclusively sell Victoria's Secret products in the People's Republic of China with the strong support of AFB and the approval of LBI as stated in LBI's letter on September 10, 2007."

Jintian signed a Strategic Cooperation Framework Agreement with the defendant in November 2011, agreeing that "Party A (Jintian) will entrust Party B (the defendant) with the full right to sell and the right to authorize distributors in respect of the genuine Victoria's Secret products purchased from LBI and authorized by AFB in the United States; Party B shall have all the rights enjoyed by Party A as authorized by AFB, and Party A won't develop any new distributors by itself except maintaining the existing ones..." On January 1, 2012, Jintian issued an exclusive distribution authorization, authorizing the defendant to be the sole distributor of VICTORIA'S SECRET products at the retail terminals in Beijing, Shanghai, Guangzhou, Shenzhen, Tianjin and Chongqing, and to be the seller of these products in China who has the right to sub-license the distribution right to provincial and municipal single-unit distributors in all parts of China for a period from January 1, 2012 to December 31, 2022.

On April 23, 2013, Shanghai No. 2 Intermediate People's Court made a judgment of first instance on the case filed by the plaintiff against Jintian for trademark infringement and unfair competition. It's decided that Jintian only purchased the inventory products from the plaintiff's parent company LBI Company and sold them in China, and that its act of declaring itself as the sole designated general distributor of Victoria's Secret, a top underwear brand in the United States, without providing conclusive evidence constitutes unfair competition due to false advertising.

The plaintiff claimed that its "VICTORIA'S SECRET" (Chinese name: 维多利亚的秘密) brand was founded in the 1970s and four trademarks including "VICTORIA'S SECRET" (Class 35 and Class 25) and "维多利亚的秘密" (Class 35 and Class 25) registered in China were to be protected in this case. The defendant was found to, without permission, use the plaintiff's trademark "VICTORIA'S SECRET" on its shop sign, employee badges, VP cards and fashion shows, etc., and use the plaintiff's trademarks "VICTORIA'S SECRET" and "维多利亚的秘密" in a large number of publicity and promotion activities. At the same time, it declared its store as the direct-sale store, exclusive store or flagship store of "VICTORIA'S SECRET" and "维多利亚的秘密", declared itself as the operation headquarter, brand operator in China, general marketing company in China, sole distributor in Beijing, Shanghai, Guangzhou, Shenzhen, Tianjin and Chongqing, public relations and marketing operator, China headquarter, etc. of "VICTORIA'S SECRET" and "维多利亚的秘密", and carried out franchising activities, all of which constituted trademark infringement and unfair competition. Therefore, the plaintiff sued to the court, requesting the defendant to stop trademark infringement and unfair competition immediately and compensate for its economic losses and reasonable expenses totaling RMB 5,100,000 yuan (same currency below).

The defendant, Mice, argued that (ⅰ) the Victoria products it sold were purchased from the plaintiff's parent company, Limited Brands, Inc. ("LBI"), and the plaintiff's trademarks were fairly used in the sales process of commodities, which didn't constitute trademark infringement and unfair competition; (ⅱ) the defendant has never made false advertising alleged by the plaintiff; and (ⅲ) the plaintiff's trademarks involved have never been commercially used in China. Therefore, the plaintiff's claim for compensation should be dismissed.

[Judgment]

Shanghai No. 1 Intermediate People's Court holds that the use of "VICTORIA'S SECRET" mark by the defendant on its signboard, in-store walls, containers, cashier's counters, employee badges, VIP cards and fashion shows, etc. has gone beyond the necessary scope of indicating the goods sold; when using the above mark, the defendant didn't attach other signs to distinguish the source of services, but declared that Metro City store was the direct-sale store of Victoria's Secret in Shanghai, and that it was the China headquarter, sole distributor in Beijing, Shanghai, Guangzhou, Shenzhen, Tianjin and Chongqing, and brand operator in China, etc. of Victoria's Secret, which is also beyond the necessary scope of indicating the goods sold, has the function of indicating the source of the service and is enough to make the relevant public mistakenly believe that the sales service is provided by the trademark owner (plaintiff) or there exists a trademark license relationship between the service provider and the trademark owner (plaintiff). Therefore, the defendant's use of "VICTORIA'S SECRET" mark already constitutes an infringement upon the plaintiff's service trademark "VICTORIA'S SECRET" (Class 35); its argument that the plaintiff's trademark was fairly used is not accepted. Since the defendant didn't use the Chinese mark "维多利亚的秘密" in the course of providing services, and the plaintiff's service trademark "维多利亚的秘密" (Class 35) was not commercially used in China, it's difficult to determine whether "VICTORIA'S SECRET" mark used by the defendant is similar to the plaintiff's service trademark "VICTORIA'S SECRET" (Class 35). Therefore, the defendant didn't infringe upon the plaintiff's service trademark "VICTORIA'S SECRET" (Class 35).

The information posted by the defendant atwww. nz86. com, www. china-ef. com and www. ne51. com mainly covered Victoria's Secret brand introduction, product introduction, store information and investment information and didn't involve the online sales of products. Taking into account the contents of the whole web page, the defendant used "VICTORIA'S SECRET" and "维多利亚的秘密" marks in its advertising to convey to the relevant public that it's the operator of Victoria's Secret and is in charge of the investment promotion business of this brand. In this sense, the marks were used as service marks for the service class same as that on which the plaintiff's trademarks "VICTORIA'S SECRET" (Class 35) and "维多利亚的秘密" (Class 35) are approved to be used; they can be deemed identical to the plaintiff's registered trademarks on the same service and therefore constitute trademark infringement.

To sum up, Shanghai No. 1 Intermediate People's Court ruled as follows: (ⅰ) Mice shall, from the date of entry into force of this judgment, stop infringing upon Victoria's exclusive right to use No. 9120211 registered trademark "VICTORIA'S SECRET" and No. 4481217 registered trademark "维多利亚的秘密" on Class 35 services; (ⅱ) Mice shall, within ten days from the date of the entry into force of this judgment, compensate for Victoria's economic losses and reasonable expenses incurred to stop the infringement totaling 500,000 yuan.

Dissatisfied with the first-instance judgment, Mice filed an appeal.

After the trial, Shanghai High People's Court ruled to dismiss the appeal and affirm the original judgement as there's no fact or law to support Mice's appeal.

[Case Study]

This case involves an internationally renowned brand "Victoria's Secret", which has a great social influence. Although the defendant didn't obtain the trademark license, no evidence shows that the goods it sold are counterfeit goods. So, it's difficult to determine the extent to which the defendant can use the trademark. The judge has correctly distinguished the nominative use and non-nominative use of trademarks, clearly defined the judicial criteria for determining the nominative use of goods trademark and the use of service trademark, that is, a business operator legally obtaining the right to sell goods may use the goods trademark of the trademark owner indicatively to the extent of indicating the source of the goods. If the use of the trademark is beyond the scope of indicating the source of the goods, it will constitute an infringement upon the exclusive rights to use relevant service trademark. Where the use of a trademark is likely to cause relevant public to mistakenly believe that the sales service is provided by the trademark owner or there exists association relationship such as trademark licensing between the business operator and the trademark owner, it shall be deemed that the use is beyond the scope of indicating the source of the goods being sold and has the function of indicating and identifying the source of service. This case is greatly exemplary for similar cases, and also helps to guide and standardize the use of trademarks by market operators in the process of goods circulation.

I. Whether Mice has obtained the license to use the goods trademark and service trademark of Victoria's Secret?

According to the Inventory Sale Agreement, inventory buyers shall not declare themselves as the seller's licensed or entrusted agents or affiliated parties; according to the confirmation letter issued by LBI, Jintian may sell the inventory products in China but shall abide by relevant terms and conditions of the Inventory Sale Agreement. Although Jintian has signed a Strategic Cooperation Framework Agreement with Mice and authorized Mice to be the sole distributor at the retail terminal, it only suggests that Mice has the right to exclusively sell the inventory products bearing the trademarks involved in China. Seen from the trading chain of inventories, the whole trading process doesn't involve the license of the trademarks involved. Whether or not Mice is aware of the Inventory Sale Agreement, it, as the buyer of inventory products, only obtains the ownership of these products according to the law, that is to say, it has the right to possess, use, profit from and dispose of these products. The transfer of real right does not mean that Mice automatically obtains the license to use the trademarks involved. Instead, it can only use the trademarks involved indicatively to the minimum extent necessary for the sale of the products. In this case, Victoria didn't allege that Mice's catalogue sales and Internet sales constitute infringement. So, even if Mice didn't engage in catalogue sales and Internet sales, it can't be used as a defense for its non-infringement. Victoria, as the owner of the trademarks involved, didn't authorize AFB, Jintian and Mice to use its trademarks "VICTORIA'S SECRET" and "维多利亚的秘密". AFB didn't obtain the license to use the trademarks involved, either, and it had no right to authorize others to use the trademarks involved. "Exclusive sale" in its authorization can't be interpreted as the license to use the goods trademarks and service trademarks involved. Therefore, there's no fact or law to support Mice's argument that it has been licensed to use the trademarks involved.

II. Whether Mice has infringed upon Victoria's exclusive right to use the service trademark involved

In this case, the goods sold by Mice are not counterfeit goods that bear

"VICTORIA'S SECRET" and "维多利亚的秘密" trademarks. Victoria didn't allege them as infringing products, either. The dispute lies in how to judge the use of "VICTORIA'S SECRET" and "维多利亚的秘密" marks by Mice in the sales activities. It should be noted that Victoria enjoys the exclusive right to use the registered trademarks "VICTORIA'S SECRET" and "维多利亚的秘密" on Class 35 services, meaning that no one may use "VICTORIA'S SECRET" and "维多利亚的秘密" on such services without permission. However, as the goods sold are not counterfeit goods, Mice shall have the right to attach "VICTORIA'S SECRET" and "维多利亚的秘密" marks to the goods, so that consumers can identify the source of these goods, and the trademark owner shall raise no objection provided that Mice has used the trademarks indicatively to the extent of indicating the source of the goods. Otherwise, it will constitute an infringement upon the exclusive rights to use relevant service trademark. If there is no restriction on the nominative use of goods trademarks in the course of sale, the existence value of relevant service trademark may be endangered. In view of the facts ascertained in this case, Mice's act of using "VICTORIA'S SECRET" mark on its signboard, in-store walls, containers, cashier's counters, employee badges, VIP cards, fashion shows, etc., declaring that Metro City store was the direct-sale store of Victoria's Secret in Shanghai, and that it was the China headquarter, sole distributor in Beijing, Shanghai, Guangzhou, Shenzhen, Tianjin and Chongqing, and brand operator of Victoria's Secret in China is likely to cause relevant public to mistakenly believe that the sales service is provided by the trademark owner or there exists a trademark license relationship between the service provider and the trademark owner, which has gone beyond the necessary scope of indicating the source of goods sold, has the function of indicating and identifying the source of the service and therefore constitutes an infringement upon the exclusive right to use the service trademark "VICTORIA'S SECRET". "VICTORIA'S SECRET" and "维多利亚的秘密" were used in online advertisements for the purpose of carrying out investment promotion activities related to the sales of products by taking advantage of the trademarks involved. In this sense, they can be deemed identical to the service trademarks involved used on the same kind of services. Therefore, the court of first instance has properly distinguished the goods trademarks from services trademarks involved and correctly ruled that Mice infringed upon Victoria's exclusive right to use the service trademarks involved.

Ⅲ. Determination of the amount of compensation

According to the law, the amount of compensation in unfair competition cases shall be determined based on the actual losses that the right owner has suffered as a result of the infringement; where the losses suffered by the right owner cannot be determined, the amount of compensation shall be determined based on the profits that the infringer has earned as a result of the infringement; where the losses suffered by the right owner, or the profits earned by the infringer, cannot be determined, the court shall determine the statutory amount of compensation based on the circumstances of the infringement, and the infringer shall bear reasonable expenses incurred by the infringed operator to investigate its act of unfair competition. In this case, it's difficult to calculate the actual losses suffered by Victoria and the profits earned by Mice as a result of the infringement, the statutory amount of compensation shall be determined based on the circumstances of the infringement. Given that Jintian continued false advertising after it's convicted of infringement and had major subject fault, the license fee charged by Mice from each franchised store amounted to 60,000 to 500,000 yuan, and Victoria has spent more than 200,000 yuan on safeguarding its right in this case, it's justified for the court of first instance to determine a compensation of 500,000 yuan (including reasonable expenses). The number of franchised stores opened by Mice is just one of the factors rather than the sole factor to be considered for determining the amount of compensation. Therefore, Mice's appeal opinion that the facts were wrongly ascertained by the court of first instance and the amount of compensation determined was too high was dismissed.

(Writer: Xu Zhuobin)

Cessation of Infringement and Application of Punitive Statutory Damages in Case of Conflict Between Trade Name and Trademark

—Dispute over trademark infringement and unfair competition (RT-Mart Investment Co. , Ltd v. Concord Investment (China) Co. , Ltd)

[Abstract]

This is a typical case of dispute over trademark infringement and unfair competition where the infringer intentionally attached itself to the goodwill of others and registered a trademark of others as the trade name in its enterprise name. In this case, the people's court focused on the civil liability of ceasing using the enterprise name and explored the application of punitive statutory damages.

[Case Review]

Appellant (Defendant-Appellant): RT-Mart Investment Co. , Ltd ("RT-Mart")
Appellee (Plaintiff-Appellee): Concord Investment (China) Co. , Ltd ("Concord")
Cause of Action: dispute over trademark infringement and unfair competition
First-instance Case No. : Hu Min Zhong No. 409 (2016)
Second-instance Case No. : Hu Zhi Min Chu Zi No. 731 (2015)
In November 2013, Concord, as an assignee, obtained the trademark "RT-Mart" ("大润发" in Chinese) approved to be used on Class 35 demonstration of goods and sales promotion (for others), and set up 318 large-scale "RT-Mart"

supermarkets in the Chinese Mainland, ranking top among foreign chain enterprises for many years. In January 2015, "RT-Mart" trademark was appraised by Shanghai Administration for Industry and Commerce as a famous trademark in Shanghai, classified into Class 35 and approved to be used on goods or services: sales promotion (for others).

In October 2014, RT-Mart Company was established, engaged in the sales of general merchandise. Meanwhile, Lilin and other branches were set up and a number of franchises were under preparation. In August 2015, RT-Mart signed a RT-Mart License Agreement with an outsider, authorizing it to use the trade name and service mark of RT-Mart. RT-Mart's website contains the words "RT-Mart Enterprise", which shows that the alleged infringing mark (a) " 大润发 " is directly above the picture of the mall. In "Company Profile" section, it says that it has opened branches in more than ten cities in Jiangxi Province, with a total business area of more than $400,000m^2$. In addition, the receipts and shopping bags from Lilin and other branches bear the characters "RT-Mart Investment Co. , Ltd" or use the alleged infringing mark (b) " 大润发 " or alleged infringing mark (a) " 大润发 " conspicuously. RT-Mart was once fined by Ganzhou Administration for Industry and Commerce and Market Supervision Administration of Guangzhou Development Zone for using the word "RT-Mart" conspicuously.

In 2015, Concord requested the court to order RT-Mart to stop the infringement and pay punitive damages of RMB 5,000,000 on the grounds that RT-Mart infringed upon its exclusive right to use registered trademarks and commit the act of unfair competition.

[Judgment]

Shanghai Intellectual Property Court, the court of first instance, holds that both RT-Mart and Concord are engaged in the services on which "RT-Mart" trademark is approved to be used; the two alleged infringing marks and enterprise name used conspicuously by RT-Mart contain characters that are identical with "RT-Mart" trademark, which is likely to mislead the relevant public. Besides, the court believes that "RT-Mart" trademark had been well known in the industry when RT-Mart was established after taking into account the registration time of "RT-Mart" trademark and the business scale, market ranking, etc. of Concord. Despite this, RT-Mart, as a competitor, still used the trade name identical to "RT-Mart" trademark, showing its apparent intent to attach itself to the reputation of "RT-Mart" trademark. Therefore, RT-Mart's act infringed upon the trademark right of Concord and constituted unfair competition; it shall stop the infringement immediately. With regard to the elimination of ill effects, RT-Mart was ordered to publish a statement in the newspaper given its wide range of the infringement. As to compensation, statutory damages will apply since no evidence can be used to infer the infringer's profits or calculate the trademark license fee directly. As for the claim for punitive damages, although RT-Mart's act meets the provision of Paragraph 1, Article 63 of the Trademark Law that "the infringement is committed in bad faith and the circumstance is serious", the basis for determining the amount of punitive damages does not exist and punitive damages shall not apply. However, the court of first instance holds that as the damage system in the Trademark Law is established to make up losses and punish infringers, the statutory damage system, as a miscellaneous provision on calculating the damage, shall also have the dual functions of compensation and punishment. Therefore, when determining the amount of statutory damages, RT-Mart's subjective bad faith can be taken into account. In view of the trademark popularity and its contribution to Concord, RT-Mart's subjective bad faith, circumstances and consequences of the infringement, etc., RT-Mart was ordered to compensate for Concord's economic losses and reasonable expenses totaling RMB 3, 000,000. Dissatisfied with the first instance judgment, RT-Mart filed an appeal.

Shanghai High People's Court, the court of second instance, holds that in addition to the reasons mentioned in the first instance judgment, the liability of stopping infringement shall be further clarified. Given that trade name is the core part of RT-Mart's enterprise name and is exactly the same as the registered trademark "RT-Mart" in writing, and that "RT-Mart" trademark enjoys high popularity and good reputation, such enterprise name, even though used in full name during daily activities, can still cause the relevant public to mistakenly believe there exists an relationship between RT-Mart and Concord. The continuation of such act will undoubtedly undermine the business ethics of good faith, fairness and order. Therefore, only by ordering RT-Mart to stop using the characters "RT-Mart" in its trade name can relevant public's misperception about the relationship between these two enterprises be completely eliminated. Given that the scale and scope of the infringement is large, the daily life of the general public is involved, the infringement consequence is serious and " RT-Mart" trade name is objectively attached to the good will of "RT-Mart" trademark, which cause the relevant public to misunderstand the relationship between RT-Mart and Concord, it is also necessary to eliminate the ill effects to make up for the damage to the goodwill. With regard to the amount of infringement damages, the court of second instance holds that the court of first instance has comprehensively considered the situation of the trademark involved and the circumstances of the infringement, especially the infringer's bad faith and consequences of the infringement; it's justified to determine the maximum statutory damages of RMB 3,000,000 (including reasonable expenses). To sum up, it's ruled to dismiss the appeal and affirm the original judgment.

[Case Study]

This case involves many aspects, but the focus lies in how the people's court applies the civil liability of stopping using the enterprise name and applies punitive statutory damages in case of conflict between the enterprise name and registered trademark.

Ⅰ. Civil liability of stopping the infringement in the use of enterprise name

Generally speaking, in case of conflicts between registered trademarks and enterprise names, the people's court will, following the principles of good faith, safeguarding fair competition and protecting prior rights, deal with them separately according to the circumstances, that is, in view of the claims of the parties, specific circumstances of the case and effects of the application of liability, determine whether the parties shall bear the civil liability of stopping or standardizing the use of the enterprise name①. It shall not, in every case, decide to

---

① According to Article 4 of Provisions of the Supreme People's Court on Issues Concerned in the Trial of Cases of Civil Disputes over the Conflict between Registered Trademark or Enterprise Name with Prior Right, " Where the enterprise name of the defendant infringes the right of the exclusive use of a trademark or constitutes unfair competition, the people's court may, in light of the litigation claims of the plaintiff and the specific situation of the case, order the defendant to stop or regularize the use of the enterprise name and assume corresponding civil liabilities. "

stop using or change the enterprise name simply on the ground that the conspicuous use of trade name in an enterprise name infringes upon the exclusive right to use a registered trademark.

To be specific, the people's court will, in practice, deal with the cases based on the registration order of the enterprise name and the trademark, legality of their registration, historical factors and current status of their usage combining with the claims of the parties. In the first case, if the registration and usage of the enterprise name is illegal, i. e. registering other's prior trademark with high popularity as a trade name in the enterprise name, and it's difficult to avoid market confusion whether it is used conspicuously or regularly, the people's court may treat it as an act of unfair competition and order to stop using or change the enterprise name in accordance with the claims of the plaintiff. In the second case, if the enterprise has no bad faith in registering the enterprise name, it is due to historical reasons that the enterprise name is registered earlier and it's known to the public to certain extent that the trade name is used conspicuously by such enterprise, which can be distinguished from the registered trademark and won't cause confusion among the relevant public, it won't be deemed to constitute trademark infringement. If that's the case, in order to protect the registered trademark and maintain a fair market competition order, the court will allow the enterprise to conspicuously use this trade name in a specific manner within a specific scope, i. e. it will restrict the way and scope of use of the enterprise name, so as to stop the defendant's infringement. [①] In the third case, if the enterprise name is not used by the enterprise in a standard way but the trade name is registered legally due to historical reasons, it can be treated as an infringement upon the exclusive right to use the registered trademark because using a trade name identical or similar to other's registered trademark on the same or similar goods conspicuously is likely to cause confusion among the relevant public and damage the registered trademark right of others. If so, the court may order to standardize or stop

---

① Zui Gao Fa Min Shen No. 1405 (2016), Zhejiang GBV Glasses Co., Ltd v. Hefei GBV Glasses Co., Ltd-dispute over trademark infringement. In this case, trademark infringement was not recognized. However, in order to protect the registered trademark and maintain a fair market competition order, Hefei GBV Glasses Co., Ltd was ordered to attach a region mark when using GBV trade name in the future, so as to distinguish the source of the goods.

the use of the enterprise name according to the claims of the parties. ①

To sum up, after determining the nature of the alleged infringing act according to the above rules, the court shall, in view of the nature and characteristics of such act, decide whether the civil liability of stopping infringement is applicable to the enterprise name and measure whether the concrete ways of bearing such civil liability can achieve the purpose and balance, in other words, whether the purpose of stopping infringement can be achieved after application. If there are a variety of means that can effectively achieve the purpose of stopping the infringement, the one that will have minimal adverse impact on the legitimate interests of the alleged infringer shall be adopted. ②

In the "RT-Mart" case, the court recognizes that two parties are competitors and RT-Mart also admitted it knew "RT-Mart" trademark when creating the enterprise name. Apparently, RT-Mart has the subjective intent of attaching itself to the goodwill of others. Its full use of the trade name identical to "RT-Mart" trademark during bushiness activities can easily lead to confusion among relevant consumers and hence constitutes unfair competition. Given that the "RT-Mart" trade name is the core part of RT-Mart's enterprise name and it has exactly the same words as the "RT-Mart" registered trademark, "RT-Mart" trademark enjoys high popularity and good reputation, the enterprise name, even if used in full in the business activities, can still cause the relevant consumers to mistakenly believe there's an association relationship between RT-Mart and Concord, and allowing such registration and continuous use thereof will undoubtedly undermine the business ethics of good faith, fairness and order, the court holds that only by ordering RT-Mart to stop using the characters "RT-Mart" in its trade name can relevant public's misperception about the relationship between these two enterprises be completely eliminated.

II. Compensation and punishment functions of statutory damages

Punitive damage system is formally prescribed in the Trademark Law amended

---

① P254 – 255, Guiding Intellectual Property Cases of the Supreme People's Court (3rd Series), China Legal Publishing House, First Edition, May 2011

② P263 – 264, Guiding Intellectual Property Cases of the Supreme People's Court (6rd Series), China Legal Publishing House, First Edition, July 2014 in 2013, but it's seldom applied in practice. In this case, the trademark owner requested the infringer to bear punitive damages of RMB 5,000,000, while the court expounded on the preconditions for applying punitive damages in trademark infringement cases and specific factors to be considered when applying punitive statutory damages.

1. Preconditions for applying punitive damages

Paragraph 2, Article 63 of the Trademark Law states that, "If the infringement is committed in bad faith and the circumstance is serious, the amount of damages may be more than one up to three times the aforesaid determined amount", which stipulates the precondition for the application of punitive damages. Firstly, there is "malicious" infringement. Compared to compensatory damages (including the right holder's losses, infringer's profits and multiple of license fee), punitive damages emphasize the punishment and containment of the infringement. Therefore, the subjective condition for applying punitive damages is stricter than that of compensatory damages, that is, "bad faith" is manifested in both the subjective intent of the infringer and evil subjective purpose. For example, RT-Mart has apparent bad faith in attaching itself to the trademark of others as it continued the infringement and constantly expanded the scope thereof to obtain more illegal profits despite receiving administrative punishment for many times. Secondly, though the objective consequence of "serious circumstance" is not specified by law, it can be judged according to the objective situations of trademark infringement cases, including the duration, frequency, scale, scope and way of infringement, the right holder's losses, the infringer's profits and the negative effects on society. For example, RT-Mart infringed upon Concord's trademark in a business area closely related to the daily life of the people, and the foodsafety of the public was under great threat, so it should be concluded that the circumstance is serious.

2. How to apply punitive statutory damages?

In addition to the above two preconditions, there's another basis for applying punitive damages, that is, "... the aforesaid determined amount" in Article 63 of the Trademark Law. That is to say, in order to apply punitive damages, the specific amount of punitive damages has to be determined by accurately calculating the specific amount of damages based on the right holder's losses, infringer's profits or the appropriate multiple of the amount of license fee. In RT-Mart case however, the specific amount of the above three compensatory damages cannot be calculated based on existing evidence, therefore there is no basis for applying punitive damages. However, RT-Mart's bad faith in infringing upon the trademark and act of unfair competition obviously comply with the above two preconditions, that is, the circumstance is serious and the infringer has apparent bad faith. In this case, it goes without saying that only using compensatory damages to make up for the losses suffered by Concord as a result of the infringement is not enough punishment and cannot curb the recurrence of such infringement.

For the above case where punitive damages should be applied but there is no applicable basis, the court came up with another way to achieve the punishment and containment functions of punitive damages, i.e. statutory damages. One view is that statutory damages stipulated by the Trademark Law is essentially an amount of compensation determined by the court on the basis of case facts when it's unable to ascertain the actual amount of damages, and should follow the principle of covering loss. However, the court held that statutory damages is not only meant to compensate for the right holder's losses, but also has punitive function. First of all, when determining statutory damages, the court actually takes into account the infringer's subjective state and the way of infringement, etc. , which must also be considered when determining punitive damages. So, the court will consider the degree of infringer's bad faith when applying statutory damages or punitive damages. Secondly, due to the difficulty in collecting evidences in practice, the court tends to apply statutory damages to determine the amount of compensation for trademark infringement. Should punishment on the infringer not be considered when applying the statutory damages, the punitive damage system will exist in name only. Lastly, the amendment of the Trademark Law aims to strengthen the protection of trademark rights and strives to accurately reflect the corresponding market value of the infringed trademark with due consideration to the infringer's subjective state. Therefore, statutory damages can realize the dual effects of compensation plus punishment, which also meet the legislative purpose of the newly amended Trademark Law. To sum up, when applying statutory damages, the court will consider the infringer's subjective bad faith and whether there are serious circumstances such as repeated infringement and trademark counterfeiting, and will determine a compensation amount appropriately higher than the market value, so that statutory damages can both compensate for the right holder's losses and meanwhile punish the infringer, which also meets the legislative purpose of the newly amended Trademark Law, that is, to further strengthen the compensation for infringement and curb the re0occurrence of trademark infringement.

In addition, it needs to be further clarified that, in accordance with Article 63 of the Trademark Law, the amount of punitive damages cannot be calculated on the basis of statutory damages, but shall be determined only based on the multiples of three kinds of compensatory damages, because the determination of both statutory damages and punitive damages at the court's discretion will result in remarkable difference in the amount of punitive damages. Therefore, punitive damages cannot be applied simultaneously with statutory damages.

To sum up, in accordance with the provisions of the law, the people's court has strengthened the protection of legitimate interests of the right holder in this trademark infringement and unfair competition. By ordering the infringer to completely stop using its enterprise name and applying punitive statutory damages, it helps to provide adequate judicial remedies to the right holder while make the infringer pay full price for the infringement, creating a legal atmosphere of strictly protecting intellectual property rights and resolutely curbing the infringing acts of infringers.

(Writer: Cao Wenjia)

Full Imitation and 3D Trademark Infringement Case

—Dispute over trademark infringement and unfair competition
（Bayerische Motoren Werke Aktiengesellschaft v. Shanghai
Chuangjia Garment Co., Ltd, Dema Group（int'l）
Holding Limited and Zhou Leqin）

[**Abstract**]

1. When there are more than one similar alleged infringing trademarks and one of them is registered before the prior registered trademark becomes well known, it cannot necessarily exempt the civil liability on the alleged infringing trademarks registered after the prior registered trademark becomes well known, but instead shall determine, according to the following three conditions, whether they are reproductions or imitations of the well-known registered trademark and their use shall be ceased: (i) whether the alleged infringer has apparent bad faith in committing the infringement; (ii) whether there exists inheritance of the goodwill of prior registered trademark when the alleged infringing trademarks later registered are used; and (iii) whether the alleged infringing trademarks later registered are identical or similar to the prior registered trademark, which is likely to mislead the public and may damage the interests of the prior trademark owner. 2. When the alleged infringing trademarks are registered and used by different entities/persons, the court shall determine whether they shall bear joint civil liability for infringement based on their common bad faith and obvious intention liaison. 3. In well-known trademark protection cases, the court shall, on a strict case-by-case basis and factual basis, decide to protect or not to protect the trademark as a well-known trademark or a general trademark according to different infringing acts and different trademarks respectively.

[Case Review]

Plaintiff: Bayerische Motoren Werke Aktiengesellschaft ("BMW")

Defendant: Shanghai Chuangjia Garments Co. Ltd ("Shanghai Chuangjia Garments Co. Ltd")

Defendant: Dema Group (int'l) Holding Limited ("Dema Company")

Defendant: Zhou Leqin

Cause of Action: dispute over trademark infringement and unfair competition

Case No. : Hu Zhi Min Chu Zi No. 58 (2015)

BMW is a world famous car manufacturer, with trademarks "●", "寶馬" and "BMW" registered on "motor vehicles" and other goods in Class 12, as well as trademarks "●", "●" and "BMW" on "leather and artificial leather" in Class 18 and clothing, shoes, hats and other goods in Class 25.

In July 2008, a natural person Zhou Leqin used "宝马" (Chinese version of BMW) and "BMW" as the trade name to establish the Dema Company with the former name of GERMAN BMW GROUP (INTL) HOLDING LIMITED. Subsequently, Dema Company obtained trademarks "*BMN*" and "⊕" in Class 25 through assignment, as well as "**BMN**" in Class 25 by registration. Zhou Leqin obtained trademark "⊗" in Class 25 through assignment as well as "⊗" in Class 25 and "⊗" in Class 18 by registration. Dema Company and Zhou Leqin set up BMN brand franchise system with Chuangjia Company since 2009 by licensing the above-mentioned trademarks to Chuangjia Company. Afterwards, during the process of operating the BMN brand franchise system, Dema Company and Chuangjia Company colored the trademarks "⊕" and "⊗" or used the trademark "⊗" in combination with the trademark "**BMN**", the logo "**BMN**" and such words as the Chinese version of the enterprise name of GERMAN BMW GROUP (INTL) HOLDING LIMITED, German BMW group, Germany BMW, BMW, etc., which were also widely used in the brand franchise manuals, business premises decoration, advertising promotion, etc. related to the BMN brand franchise system, as well as on clothing, shoes, bags and other goods that they produce and sell. So far, they have developed the franchise system in many provinces and cities across the country for sales.

BMW complained that since 2008, Dema Company, Zhou Leqin and Chuangjia Company have conspired to establish and operate the BMN brand franchise system by means of division of labor, and set up Dema Company using the plaintiff's well-known trademarks "宝马" and "BMW" as the trade name; they also registered and used the trademarks "" and "" in imitation of the plaintiff's well-known trademarks "**BMN**" and "BMW", and used infringing marks similar to the plaintiff's trademarks "BMW" (Class 18), "" and "" (Class 18, Class 25), and such words as the Chinese version of enterprise name of GERMAN BMW GROUP (INTL) HOLDING LIMITED, Dema Group (int'l) Holding Limited, Germany BMW, German BMW group, etc., all of which constituted trademark infringement and unfair competition. It's requested to order that (i) Chuangjia Company, Dema Company and Zhou Leqin immediately stop infringing upon the plaintiff's exclusive right to use the registered trademarks involved; (ii) Dema Company immediately stop using the Chinese version of the enterprise name of Dema Group (int'l) Holding Limited and GERMAN BMW GROUP (INTL) HOLDING LIMITED; (iii) Chuangjia Company, Dema Company and Zhou Leqin jointly compensate for BMW's economic losses totaling RMB 3,000,000 (including attorney's fees and reasonable expenses); and (iv) Chuangjia Company, Dema Company and Zhou Leqin publish a statement in a prominent position of China Industry & Commerce News to eliminate the adverse effects of the infringement.

[Judgment]

Shanghai Intellectual Property Court holds that, whereas (i) it's necessary to recognize the plaintiff's trademarks "", "BMW" and "寶馬" as well-know trademarks since Class 25 trademarks "" and "**BMN**" obtained through assignment and Class 25 trademark "" through registration by Dema Company, as well as Class 25 trademark "" through assignment and Class 25 trademark "", Class 18 trademark "" through registration by Zhou Leqin are reproductions or imitations thereof. Besides, the evidence provided by BMW in this case is sufficient to prove that its registered trademarks "", "BMW" and "寶馬"

have already been well-known trademarks at least since 2007 and continue to this day.

(ii) Knowing that "🔲", "BMW" and "寶馬" are the plaintiff's well-known trademarks, Chuangjia Company, Dema Company and Zhou Leqin still colluded maliciously and jointly established BMN brand franchise system, used the infringing marks in the production and sale of the allegedly infringing goods, BMN brand licensing, advertisements and other business activities, and committed the following act of trademark infringement and unfair competition: (1) established Dema Company using "宝马" and "BMW" as the trade name, and during the process of operating BMN brand franchise system, used the Chinese version of the enterprise name of GERMAN BMW GROUP (INTL) HOLDING LIMITED and authorized BMN licensed distributors to use it, constituting unfair competition. (2) used the Chinese version of Germany BMW and German BMW group, and authorized BMN licensed distributors to use the same on Class 25 and Class 18 goods, constituting infringement upon the plaintiff's well-known trademark "寶馬". (3) registered, used and authorized BMN licensed distributors to use the registered trademark " 🔲 " on Class 25 goods, constituting trademark infringement for imitating the plaintiff's well-known trademark " 🔲 ", misleading the public and probably damaging the interests of the plaintiff. (4) registered, used and authorized BMN licensed distributors to use the registered trademark " *BMN* " and " **BMN** " on Class 25 goods, which, as there's no evidence proving the actual use of " *BMN* " and hence no inheritance of the goodwill thereof during the registration and use of " **BMN** ", constituted trademark infringement for imitating the plaintiff's well-known trademark " **B M N** ", misleading the public and probably damaging the interests of the plaintiff. (5) used " 🔲 ", " ⊕ ", " ⊗ " and " 🔲 " logos on Class 18 and Class 25, infringing upon the plaintiff's exclusive right to use registered trademarks " 🔲 " and " 🔲 " (Class 18, Class 25). (6) used " 🔲 ", " **BMN** " and " **B M N** " logos on Class 18 goods, infringing upon the plaintiff's exclusive right to use registered trademarks " 🔲 ", " 🔲 " and " BMW ".

(iii) The following claims of BMW are not established in this case. (1) Given that " ⊕ " and " ⊗ " logos are not similar to the plaintiff's well-known trademark " 🔲 " and won't cause confusion among the relevant public, the registration and use of "⊕" and "⊗" logos don't constitute infringement on the plaintiff's well-known trademark "●". (2) As the Chinese version of Dema Company and Dema Group (int'l) Holding Limited are not identical nor similar to the Plaintiff's trademark "寶馬" and won't cause confusion among the relevant public, the use of the Chinese version of Dema Company and Dema Group (int'l) Holding Limited doesn't constitute unfair competition and trademark infringement. (3) As there is no evidence that the registered trademark "*BMN*" is used in this case, the plaintiff's opposition to Dema Company's registration of "*BMN*" trademark shall be dealt with by relevant administrative departments according to the law.

To sum up, Shanghai Intellectual Property Court made a judgment that (i) Chuangjia Company, Dema Company and Zhou Leqin immediately stop infringement on BMW's exclusive right to use the registered trademarks "●", "寶馬", "BMW", "●" and "●"; (ii) Dema Company immediately stop the act of unfair competition by stopping using the Chinese version of GERMAN BMW GROUP (INTL) HOLDING LIMITED; (iii) Chuangjia Company, Dema Company and Zhou Leqin publish a statement on China Industry & Commerce News to eliminate the impact on BMW caused by the infringement; (iv) Chuangjia Company, Dema Company and Zhou Leqin jointly compensate for BMW's economic losses and reasonable expenses totaling RMB 3,000,000; and (v) BMW's other claims are dismissed. After the judgment was made, no party file an appeal.

[Case Study]

This is a novel and typical case of trademark infringement and unfair competition dispute featured by system establishment, full imitation, and 3D mark infringement. There are many legal issues involved, for example, whether the registration and use of a trademark obtained by extended registration of another trademark that has been registered before the protected trademark becomes well-known is restricted by the well-known trademark, how to determine joint infringement when several infringers commit different but associated acts in trademark infringement cases, how to distinguish infringing acts and infringing marks correctly in cases involving protection of well-known trademarks, etc. This case presents the following obvious characteristics: (1) a franchise system was established to cover up illegal purposes. In such infringement cases, the alleged infringers often establish franchise system through trademark assignment, trademark registration, trade name registration, etc. to show the "legitimacy" of its use of the logo, thereby conceal the nature and purpose of their infringing acts. (2) Full imitation and diversified infringing acts were committed. In this kind of trademark infringement cases, the alleged infringers often mislead the public through full imitation of the right holder's logos, which not only include the infringement on all major trademarks of the right holder during the process of business operation, but also the unfair competition act of trade name infringement and even other infringing acts. (3) 3D mark infringement was committed jointly from registration to use. The alleged infringers completely imitated the right holder's logos by division of labor, assignment and registration of trademarks and trade names, and committed 3D infringement comprehensively by means of copying infringement through franchise system, etc. , which has brought about huge impact and caused serious damages.

(Writer: He Yuan)

Judicial Judgment on Conflict Between Registered Trademark Right and Enterprise Name Right

—Dispute over trademark infringement and unfair competition (Shanghai Guofu Longfeng Food Co., Ltd v. Ningbo Longfeng Food Co., Ltd and Shanghai Yiyang Food Co., Ltd)

[Abstract]

When there is a conflict of rights between an enterprise name used later and a trademark registered previously, the court shall consider the reputation of the prior registered trademark, way of using the enterprise name and subjective bad faith of the user, etc. If the conspicuous use of an enterprise name infringes upon the exclusive right to use a registered trademark, it shall be treated as trademark infringement according to the law. If the enterprise name is not used conspicuously, but its use is sufficient to cause market confusion, it shall be treated as unfair competition according to the law.

The judge may, through expounding the burden of proof and timely disclosing his/her moral conviction, push the parties concerned to produce evidence actively so as to ascertain their losses or profits. In goods counterfeiting case, he/she shall consider the contribution of the mark involved to the infringer's profits and other factors comprehensively, so as to determine a reasonable amount of compensation when giving strict protection.

[Case Review]

Plaintiff: Shanghai Guofu Longfeng Food Co., Ltd ("上海国福龙凤食品有限

公司" in Chinese）

Defendant: Ningbo Longfeng Food Co., Ltd（"宁波龙凤食品有限公司" in Chinese）

Defendant: Shanghai Yiyang Food Co., Ltd

Case No. of the Effective Judgment: Hu 0115 Min Chu No. 11825（2016）

The plaintiff, Shanghai Guofu Longfeng Food Co., Ltd（"Guofu Longfeng"）, was founded on August 20, 1992. In 1996, the plaintiff registered No. 887059 trademark "龍鳳"（the original complex form of simplified Chinese characters "龙凤", both translated as "Longfeng" in English）for Class 30 Tang Yuan and other goods, which remains valid till now after renewal of registration. Since 1994, Guofu Longfeng has set up branches in Beijing, Guangzhou, Hangzhou and other places successively, among which Ningbo Branch was established in 1997. Zhejiang Longfeng Food Co., Ltd, an affiliated company of Guofu Longfeng, was established on June 12, 2003. During the period from 2000 to 2016, Guofu Longfeng has carried out a large number of advertising via print media and electronic media. Both Guofu Longfeng and its affiliated companies have won many honors such as "Chinese Famous-brand Product", "Shanghai Famous Trademark" and "Shanghai Famous-brand Product".

The defendant, Ningbo Longfeng Food Co., Ltd（"Ningbo Longfeng"）was founded on February 1, 1999 in the name of Cixi Shiwei Food Co., Ltd. originally, which was changed to Ningbo Xinhuiyuan Food Co., Ltd in 2006 and to its current name in 2012. On October 21, 2014, Ningbo Longfeng registered No. 12695038 graphic trademark "NBo LongFeng" for Class 30 Tang Yuan and other goods. According to its tax filing account books（2013 ~ 2015）submitted, (ⅰ) the operating profit in 2013 is – 484,944. 30 yuan and total sales income excluding tax is 9,170, 477. 85 yuan, wherein the income of self-produced products is 518,237. 92 yuan; (ⅱ) the operating profit in 2014 is – 115,750. 16 yuan and total sales income excluding tax is 8,696,017. 96 yuan, wherein the income of self-produced products is 433,834. 78 yuan; (ⅲ) the operating profit in 2015 is – 25,757. 77 yuan and total sales income excluding tax is 9,458,788. 69 yuan, wherein the income of self-produced products is 506,171. 76 yuan. Ningbo Longfeng admitted that these tax filing account books were inconsistent with its actual incomes and expenditure as some of them were not recorded.

On Ningbo Longfeng's website and some product packaging, there are the characters "宁波龙凤食品有限公司", of which "宁波龙凤" is marked in a large font and more eye-catching color whereas "食品有限公司" is marked in a much smaller font. Some product names of Ningbo Longfeng contain the characters "龙凤", for example, 龙凤香糯小圆子(Longfeng Mini Glutinous Rice Ball), 龙凤云汤圆 (Longfeng Yun Tang Yuan), 龙凤金汤圆 (Longfeng Jin Tang Yuan), etc. Another defendant, Shanghai Yiyang Food Co., Ltd ("Shanghai Yiyang"), sells quick-frozen snacks of both Guofu Longfeng and Ningbo Longfeng.

Guofu Longfeng has been using golden packaging since 2014. The front of the packaging is printed with dragon and phoenix patterns on the left and right sides respectively. On the left side, there's a longitudinally rectangular red decorative strip marked with a white graphic mark "龍鳳 LONGFONG". The product name is printed on the front top. In the middle of front is a picture of ingredients of Tang Yuan stuffing and a tablespoon that contains a Tang Yuan from the opening of which you can see the stuffing. The packaging of Ningbo Longfeng's Jin Tang Yuan products take gold as the background color. On the left side of the front face, there is a longitudinally rectangular red decorative strip surrounded by a phoenix pattern and marked with a white graphic mark "NBo LongFeng 宁波龙凤". Below the Chinese characters "宁波龙凤", the characters "食品有限公司" are in a much smaller black font. At the upper right of front, there is the underscored product name "金汤圆" ("Jin Tang Yuan"). In the middle is a picture of a bowl with dragon pattern, a tablespoon and the ingredients of Tang Yuan stuffing; the bowl is full of Tang Yuan and inside the tablespoon is a Tang Yuan with its stuffing visible through a hole.

Guofu Longfeng complained that its "龍鳳" trademark registered for Tang Yuan and other goods has obtained a high reputation during actual use. Ningbo Longfeng, also a producer and seller of quick-frozen snacks, has committed unfair competition by using "龙凤" as its trade name, and its conspicuous use of the trade name "宁波龙凤" as well as use of product name that contains the characters "龙凤" on its website and product packaging infringed upon the plaintiff's exclusive right to use the registered trademark. The characters, patterns and combinations thereof used on the golden packaging of the plaintiff's Tang Yuan products belong to packaging and decoration unique to a well-known brand. Therefore, Ningbo Longfeng's act of using packaging and decoration similar to such packaging and decoration on its Jin Tang Yuan products constitutes unfair competition. Shanghai Yiyang, as one of the sellers of Ningbo Longfeng, has subjective fault and shall bear part of joint and several liability. The court is requested to order that, (ⅰ) the two defendants stop infringement on the plaintiff's trademark right; (ⅱ) the two defendants stop the act of unfair competition of using the packaging peculiar to the plaintiff well-known goods; (ⅲ) Ningbo Longfeng stop the act of unfair competition of using its enterprise name and change it to another name that doesn't contain the characters "龙凤" or similar characters; and (ⅳ) Ningbo Longfeng compensate for the plaintiff's economic losses and reasonable expenses totaling RMB 3,000,000, whereas Shanghai Yiyang shall be jointly and severally liable for RMB 300,000 therein.

Ningbo Longfeng argued that its enterprise name is registered in accordance with the law, and the use of abbreviation thereof doesn't constitute an infringement. The packaging and decoration of Ningbo Longfeng's products are different from those of the plaintiff and won't cause confusion among the consumers. The sales income of its self-produced products accounts for only a small part of its operating revenue, which mostly comes from the sales of foods of an outsider's brand.

Shanghai Yiyang argued that it actually sold 129 cases of the products involved, with a sales income of only RMB 10,000 yuan or so. The products were legally purchased and it had no intent to commit the infringement with Ningbo Longfeng jointly. So, it shall not be liable for compensation.

[**Judgment**]

After the trial, the People's Court of Pudong New Area, Shanghai held that this case involves a dispute over trademark infringement and unfair competition. Concerning trademark infringement, the plaintiff's "龍鳳" trademark registered and used on Tang Yuan and other goods has obtained a high reputation. Ningbo Longfeng conspicuous use of the characters "宁波龙凤" in its enterprise name on its website and product packaging is likely to cause confusion among the relevant public and infringes upon the plaintiff's exclusive right to use its registered trademark. Ningbo Longfeng's use of product name that contains the characters "龙凤" on Tang Yuan and other products misleads the public and also infringes upon the plaintiff's exclusive right to use its registered trademark.

Concerning unfair competition, Ningbo Longfeng began to use "龙凤" as its trade name in 2012 while the plaintiff's trade name and trademark have obtained a high reputation earlier. Therefore, the defendant can be deemed to have subjective intent to attach itself to this trademark by using "龙凤" as its trade name, which is likely to cause confusion among the relevant public about the source of goods. Such act has violated the principle of good faith and recognized business ethics, and constitutes unfair competition. With regard to unauthorized use of packaging and decoration peculiar to well-known goods, although Tang Yuan packaging of both the defendant and plaintiff adopts similar golden yellow color and some identical elements, they have great differences with each other that the relevant public won't confuse the defendant's goods with the plaintiff's goods by paying general attention. Therefore, it doesn't constitute unfair competition.

Ningbo Longfeng shall bear the civil liability of stopping infringement and compensating for the losses due to its trademark infringement and unfair competition, while Shanghai Yiyang, who knows the goods produced by Ningbo Longfeng are infringing goods but still sells them, has subjective fault and shall bear the corresponding liability for compensation due to joint infringement.

To sum up, the People's Court of Pudong New Area, Shanghai ruled that, (i) Ningbo Longfeng stop the infringement and change its enterprise name to another name that doesn't contain the characters "龙凤"; (ii) Shanghai Yiyang stop selling the infringing goods produced by Ningbo Longfeng; and (iii) Ningbo Longfeng compensate for the plaintiff's economic losses totaling RMB 1,000,000 and reasonable expenses incurred to stop the infringement totaling RMB 136,880; Shanghai Yiyang shall be jointly and severally liable for RMB 300,000 therein.

This judgment has come into effect since no party filed an appeal. The defendants have voluntarily fulfilled the obligation of changing enterprise name and paying compensation according to the judgment.

[Case Study]

I. Approaches to solve the conflict between registered trademark right and enterprise name right

According to Article 1 (1) of Interpretation of the Supreme People's Court on Certain Issues Concerning the Application of Law in the Trial of Civil Cases Involving Trademark Disputes (No. 32 [2002] Judicial Interpretation), "The conspicuous use of, as the trade name of an enterprise, words that are identical or similar to other's registered trademark on the same or similar goods, which is liable to cause misidentification among the relevant public, constitutes an act that causes any other prejudice to other's exclusive right to use the registered trademark. " Opinions of the Supreme People's Court on Several Issues Concerning Intellectual Property Trials Serving the Overall Objective under the Current Economic Situation further clarifies that, "we shall, under the principles of good faith, maintaining fair competition and protecting the prior rights, hear this kind of cases of right conflicts according to law. If an enterprise name infringes a prior exclusive right to use a registered trademark due to conspicuous use, it shall be handled as trademark infringement; or if the enterprise name is not used conspicuously but its use is sufficient to cause any market confusion and violation of fair competition, it shall be handled as unfair competition. If the trademark infringement is caused by the use of an enterprise name, the court may, as the case may be, rule to stop the use or limit the manners and scope of use of the enterprise name. If an enterprise name illegally uses another person's registered trademark with a high popularity, and it is difficult to avoid market confusion no matter whether it's used conspicuously or not, the court shall, at the request of the party concerned, rule to stop the use of or change the enterprise name. "

(1) Rules for determining trademark infringement caused by conspicuous use of trade name

The term "conspicuous use" refers to highlighting the trade name in an enterprise name, so that it has a relatively independent distinguishing function, which strengthens the role of trade name in distinguishing the source of goods. Usually, a trade name is made conspicuous by making the front, size or color stand out clearly. In the present case, Ningbo Longfeng displayed its enterprise name "宁波龙凤食品有限公司" on its website and product packaging, of which "宁波龙凤" is in a large font and more eye-catching color whereas "食品有限公司" is in a much smaller font. The font, font size and color of "宁波龙凤" are all different from those of "食品有限公司". In "宁波龙凤", "宁波" is a place name, while "龙凤" is the main part that has distinguishing function. Therefore, "龙凤" is used conspicuously by Ningbo Longfeng.

In this case, the plaintiff's "龍鳳" trademark registered and used on Class 30 Tang Yuan and other goods has obtained a high reputation. Ningbo Longfeng's conspicuous use of "宁波龙凤" mark similar to the plaintiff's registered trademark on Tang Yuan and other quick-frozen snacks is likely to cause the relevant public to misrecognize the source of the products or believe that there exist definite connections between the source of the products and the products under the registered trademark of the plaintiff.

(2) Factors to be considered when determining the use of an enterprise name constitutes unfair competition

According to Article 58 of the Trademark Law amended in 2013, "Where a party uses other's registered trademark or unregistered famous trademark as the trade name in its enterprise name and confuses the public, if it constitutes unfair competition, the infringer shall be handled in accordance with the Anti Unfair Competition Law of the People's Republic of China. When determining whether the use of an enterprise name constitutes unfair competition, the people's court shall review whether the defendant has the subjective intent to commit unfair competition and whether the public may be misled objectively. Concerning the subjective intent, it's usually difficult for the plaintiff to collect direct evidence, so the court may determine whether the defendant has the intent to commit unfair competition through indirect evidences, such as such as the popularity of the prior trademark, the defendant's legitimate reasons for registration of the enterprise name, way of using the enterprise name and existence of other counterfeiting acts, etc. As to the likelihood of causing confusion, the court mainly considers the distinctiveness and popularity of the prior trademark, and whether the enterprise name registered later has already become recognizable due to its use.

In this case, the plaintiff's trade name and trademark have obtained high popularity and commercial value through their long-term use and publicity, which can bring competitive advantage to the plaintiff. The plaintiff's commercial efforts to this end shall be respected and its legitimate competitive interests shall be protected in accordance with the law. Before the defendant used "龙凤" as its trade name, the plaintiff's "龙凤" brand has obtained a high reputation. The defendant has the subject intent to attach itself to the plaintiff's trademark by using "龙凤" as its trade name, which is likely to cause confusion among the relevant public objectively and violates the principle of good faith and recognized business ethics, therefore constituting unfair competition.

Ⅱ. Methods of hearing cases involving unauthorized use of packaging and decoration peculiar to well-known goods

The unique names, packaging and decoration of well-known goods are protected by the Anti-unfair Competition Law because they have the function of identifying the source of the goods and have become signs that can be used to distinguish the source of the goods. If they are not protected, it will not only be detrimental to the market achievements by users through fair competition but also will lead to market confusion and harm the interests of consumers. The name, packaging and decoration of well-known goods protected by the Anti-unfair Competition Law are in fact unregistered trademarks. When dealing with disputes over unauthorized use of the unique packaging and decoration of well-known goods, the court shall distinguish between counterfeiting and reasonable reference. As pointed out in the judgment for dispute over unfair competition-Ferrero International S. A. in Italy v. Montresor (Zhangjiagang) Food Co. , Ltd. and Zhengyuan Marketing Co. , Ltd. in Tianjin Economic-Technological Development Area (No. 47 Guiding Case), "For the design of goods packaging and decoration, different operators can learn from each other and carry out innovative design on this basis to form their own goods packaging and decoration which are obviously different from others. " This approach is required by market management and competition. However, the unique packaging and decoration of other's goods which have the function of identifying the source of such goods can't be imitated to the extent of causing market confusion and misidentification, otherwise it will constitute unfair competition.

In this case, although the plaintiff and defendant use similar golden color and same elements such as tablespoon and Tang Yuan on their Tang Yuan packaging, these two packaging differ from each other on the whole. Among the characters and patterns on Ningbo Longfeng's Jin Tang Yuan packaging, it is mainly the characters "宁波龙凤" in bold will cause confusion and constitute an infringement upon the plaintiff's trademark right. However, aside from this, the packaging and decoration will not mislead the general public to confuse the defendant's goods with the plaintiff's goods. So, Ningbo Longfeng's act doesn't constitute unfair competition.

III. Determination of civil liability in case of right conflicts

(1) Choice of stopping the use or regulating the use

According to Article 4 of Provisions of the Supreme People's Court on Issues Concerned in the Trial of Cases of Civil Disputes over the Conflict between Registered Trademark or Enterprise Name with Prior Right, "Where the enterprise name of the defendant infringes upon the right to the exclusive use of a trademark or constitutes unfair competition, the people's court may, in light of the litigation claims of the plaintiff and the specific situation of the case, order the defendant to stop or regularize the use of the enterprise name and assume corresponding civil liabilities." In Min Ti Zi No. 15 (2010) Case of dispute over trademark infringement-WangJiang Dumpling (Dalian) Catering Co., Ltd. v. Li Huiting, the Supreme People's Court held that if the registration and usage of the enterprise name is illegal, i. e. registering other's prior trademark with high popularity as a trade name in the enterprise name, and it's difficult to avoid market confusion regardless of conspicuous use thereof, the people's court may rule to stop using or change the enterprise name in accordance with the claims of the parties. If the registration and use of such enterprise name is not illegal but the conspicuous use of trade name therein infringes upon the plaintiff's exclusive right to use a registered trademark, it is sufficient to stop the infringement of the defendant by ordering it to regulate the use or stop the conspicuous use of the enterprise name. Under this circumstance, it's not advisable to order the defendant to stop using or change the enterprise name. In no way shall the court, in every case, decide to stop using or change the enterprise name simply on the ground that the conspicuous use of trade name in an enterprise name infringes upon the exclusive right to use a registered trademark.

In this case, it is illegal for Ningbo Longfeng to register and use the enterprise name, and it is difficult to avoid market confusion regardless of the conspicuous use thereof. Therefore, the defendant shall not only stop the conspicuous use of "宁波龙凤", but also change its enterprise name to a new name that won't contain the trade name "龙凤".

(2) Determination of the amount of compensation

As it's hard to find out the specific amount of the plaintiff's losses or the defendant's profits, the amount of compensation will be determined by the court at its discretion in most intellectual property infringement cases, and judges often apply excessive discretion, making them to determine a too low or too high amount. In recent years, the courts have stressed increasing compensation in judicial policies, but they shall be particularly cautious in determining the amount of compensation. On the one hand, high amount of compensation will strengthen the protection of intellectual property owners and intensify the prevention and suppression of infringement, reducing the occurrence of infringement and stimulating innovation and investment. On the other hand, if the infringer has to compensate for the infringee the profits earned through its own efforts other than as a result of the infringement, it will lead to excessive compensation.

In order to determine the amount of compensation as accurately as possible, the judges can, through expounding the burden of proof and timely disclosing their moral conviction, push the parties concerned to produce evidence actively. In this case, the plaintiff provided the defendant's annual reports obtained from the Administration of Industry and Commerce at first. According to these annual reports, the defendant has an annual operating income of nearly 10 million yuan, and the plaintiff requests to determine the amount of compensation based on such operating income. Later, the defendant submitted its tax filling account books to prove that its operating income mainly comes from the sales of frozen foods of an outsider's brand, and the annual sales income of the products involved is only a few hundred thousand yuan. However, after carefully examining the defendant's account books, the plaintiff found that some sales income wasn't recorded. Therefore, the profits earned as a result of the infringement can't be determined entirely according to the defendant's account books as the actual profits are higher than that specified in the account books. Finally, the court determined an amount of compensation totaling RMB 1,000,000 by taking into comprehensive consideration the reputation of the trademark involved, the nature of the infringing act, the defendant's income from the sale of infringing goods, and the contribution of the trademark involved to the defendant's profits, etc.

(Writers: Shao Xun, Yuan Tian)

Precondition for Determination of Trademark Infringement and Rules for Determination of Amount of Compensation

—Dispute over trademark infringement（Hengyuanxiang
（Group）Co. , Ltd v. PUMA China Limited, et al）

[Abstract]

After an ancient Chinese hieroglyphic is registered as a figurative trademark, whether the use of the logo on the same kind of goods by others is an act of "use as trademark" or "fair use" shall be judged based on the use status by the plaintiff and the defendant as well as the popularity of the trademark. When determining the amount of compensation based on the defendant's profits earned from the infringement, the profits can be calculated according to the sales profits of the infringing goods and the amount of compensation can be determined according to the proportion principle with comprehensive consideration to various factors.

[Case Review]

Plaintiff（Appellant）:Hengyuanxiang（Group）Co. , Ltd（"Hengyuanxiang"）
Defendant（Appellee）:PUMA China Limited（"PUMA"）
Defendant（Appellee）:Foshan Xinguang Knitting Co. , Ltd（"Xinguang"）
Cause of Action:dispute over trademark infringement
First-Instance Case No. :Huang Pu Min San（Zhi）Chu Zi No. 34（2015）
Second-Instance Case No. :Hu 73 Min Zhong No. 263（2016）

The plaintiff is the owner of No. 7823965 trademark " 𝛹 "（"trademark involved"), which is approved to be used on Class 25 jackets (clothing), shoes, knitwear and the like, valid from March 2014 to March 13,2024. From January to March 2015, the plaintiff bought, under notarization, Cabana racers and fleeces from Shanghai, Shenyang and PUMA Tmall flagship stores respectively. It's found that the shoe tongues and fleece trains are printed with the combination logo "PUMA" + " ", and " " logo can also be found outside the heels. Meanwhile, PUMA Tmall Store also used " " logo for product display and advertising. The defendant, Xinguang, is the commissioned manufacturer of fleeces. Through comparison, " " logo used by the two defendants are found to be exactly the same as the plaintiff's trademark involved in terms of constituent elements, with only a slight difference in the ratio of length to width. The hieroglyphic pattern " " on Page 615 of *Collections of Jin Inscriptions* (first edition) published by Central Bookstore in July 1985 and in "羊部" section of Dictionary of Bronze and Stone Inscriptions published by Taipei Weixin Book Co., Ltd in 1992 is exactly the same as the plaintiff's trademark involved in terms of constituent elements, with only a slight difference in the ratio of length to width.

On August 19, 2013, Beijing High People's Court issued Gao Xing Zhong Zi No. 559 (2012) Judgment that Hengyuanxiang's trademark "恒源祥" had become well-know before the date of application for registration of the disputed trademark, and unregistered "sheepshead" figurative mark, used together with "恒源祥" trademark on clothing, has been widely known to the industry and relevant public after long-term use and publicity. Therefore, it can be regarded as a well-known trademark.

Upon application by the plaintiff, the court preserved the evidences such as proof of purchase, sales vouchers and related invoices of the goods involved from November 2014 to May 2015. Of the six kinds of goods involved, PUMA purchased 38,771 pieces with a total purchase amount of RMB 3,660,000 +, total sales volume of 35,170 pieces and total sales income of RMB 9,640,000 +. Among them, the purchase amount of goods from Xinguang is RMB 1,700,000 + and corresponding sales income is RMB 3,790,000 +.

Hengyuanxiang alleged that trademark involved has been widely known to the industry and relevant public after a long period of use and publicity. The Two defendants' use of a trademark identical to its registered trademark on the same goods and PUMA's sale of the infringing goods have infringed upon the plaintiff's exclusive right to use its registered trademark and caused confusion and reverse confusion as to affiliation. Therefore, it sued to the court, requesting that (i) the two defendants immediately stop the production and sales of the infringing goods; (ii) PUMA compensate for the plaintiff's economic losses totaling RMB 12,000,000 (same currency below) and Xinguang shall be jointly and severally liable for compensation within the scope of losses caused by the goods it has produced, totaling RMB 4,710, 000 + ; (iii) the two defendants jointly compensate for the plaintiff's reasonable expenses incurred to stop the infringement, totaling RMB 120,000 + ; and (iv) PUMA shall, within 30 days from the date of entry into force of the judgment, publish a statement (for not less than seven days) on Liberation Daily and the front page of PUMA Tmall Flagship Store to eliminate the ill effects.

PUMA argued that ![logo] logo on the goods involved isn't used as a trademark, but instead is a representation of bronze inscription ![inscription] meant to indicate that the clothing and sneakers are new arrivals celebrating Chinese Lunar new year of the Goat. Therefore, it is fairly used which won't constitute an infringement on the trademark involved nor cause confusion among consumers. Even if it constitutes an infringement, the profit earned therefrom is only RMB 50,000 + and the plaintiff's claim for compensation totaling RMB 12,000,000 isn't supported by fact or law.

Xinguang argued that it's a designated manufacturer of PUMA who produces designated products according to PUMA's order and product design. Therefore, it has no subjective intent or attempt to infringe on the plaintiff's trademark right. ![logo] logo on the goods involved is meant to indicate Chinese New Year of the Goat rather than used as a trademark, which won't cause confusion among consumers nor constitute trademark infringement. Besides, the number of products produced is limited. So, it shall not be liable for the compensation as much as RMB 4,700,000 + .

[Judgment]

After the trial, Huangpu District People's Court of Shanghai held that the plaintiff is the owner of No. 7823965 trademark " ![mark] ", which, through long-term use and publicity by the plaintiff, has been widely known to the industry and relevant public, has obtained a high reputation and should be protected by law. The use of "⚌" logo by the two defendants has gone beyond the scope of explaining or objectively describing the characteristics of the goods, and objectively plays a role in distinguishing the source of the good, which, therefore, can be regarded as an act of "use as a trademark". Through comparison, "⚌" logo is only slightly different from the plaintiff's trademark involved in the ratio of length to width, and there is basically no visual difference between them with general attention of the relevant public. So, they can be regarded as the same logo. Fleeces and sneakers produced by the two defendants are exactly the goods on which the plaintiff's registered trademark is approved to be used. Their use of "⚌" logo on fleeces and sneakers and PUMA's use of "⚌" logo in product advertising of its Tmall flagship store is an act of using the same trademark as the plaintiff's registered trademark on the same kind of goods without the permission of the trademark registrant. PUMA is in fact selling goods that infringes upon the plaintiff's exclusive right to use its registered trademark. As a large-scale professional sportswear production and sales enterprise, PUMA shall and is able to fulfill the duty of trademark examination when carrying out product design, whereas Xinguang, entrusted by PUMA, failed to perform the duty of care regarding the ownership and license status of the plaintiff's trademark with high reputation at the time of production. Therefore, they can't be exempted from liability according to law. Given that their acts infringed upon the plaintiff's exclusive right to use its registered trademark, they shall bear the civil liability of stopping the infringement, eliminating the ill effects and compensating for the losses.

To sum up, in accordance with Article 48, Article 57 (1), Article 57 (3), Paragraph 1 and Paragraph 3 of Article 63 of the Trademark Law of the People's Republic of China, Article 8, Paragraph 1 (a), Paragraph (f) and Paragraph (h) of Article 15 of the Tort Law of the People's Republic of China, as well as Paragraph 1 and Paragraph 2 of Article 16, Article 17 of Interpretation of the Supreme People's Court Concerning the Application of Laws in the Trial of Cases of Civil Disputes Arising from Trademarks, Huangpu District People's Court of Shanghai decided as follows: (i) PUMA and Xinguang immediately stop infringing on the plaintiff's exclusive right to use its No. 7823965 trademark "⚌"; (ii) PUMA publish a statement on Liberation Daily and the front page of PUMA Tmall Flagship Store to eliminate the ill effects; (iii) PUMA compensate for the plaintiff's economic losses totaling RMB 2,900,000, while Xinguang is jointly liable for RMB 800,000 there; and (ⅵ) PUMA and Xinguang jointly compensate for the plaintiff's reasonable expenses totaling RMB 120,000 +.

Dissatisfied with the first-instance judgment, the plaintiff filed an appeal but failed to pay the appeal fee within the prescribed time limit, so it was deemed to be withdrawn by the appellant automatically. Both parties shall enforce the first-instance judgment.

[Case Study]

This case involves a dispute over trademark infringement caused by using ancient Chinese hieroglyphic as a logo. Whether such act can be deemed as fair use and how to delimit infringement boundaries in case of conflict with trademark right are controversial in practice. This judgment shows how the infringers' profits obtained from the infringement are determined and whether the principle of proportionality is applicable when determining the amount of compensation.

Ⅰ. "Use as a trademark" is the basis and precondition for infringement determination

Trademark use is the fundamental way to realize the function and manifest the value of the trademark, which is clearly defined in Article 48 of the newly amended Trademark Law of the P. R. C. In short, trademark use should include two prerequisites: (ⅰ) the trademark must be used in commercial activities; and (ⅱ) through its use, it can enable the relevant public to identify the source of the goods or services. In other words, trademark use is based on use in commercial activities; trademark is rooted in commercial activities, and trademark use cannot be separated from commercial environment. At the same time, this kind of use must bring the identification function of the trademark into play. In Pfizer's 3D trademark infringement case, the Supreme People's Court held that a mark which doesn't have the function of identifying the source of goods and producers cannot be deemed "used as a trademark". Other's use of this mark isn't an act of using identical or similar trademark and doesn't infringe upon the exclusive right to use a registered trademark. Therefore, "use as a trademark" shall refer to a kind of use that can identify the source of goods or services. In this case, it's without doubt that "⚎"

logo is used by the two defendants commercially. While there's no information on the producer of sneakers and fleeces, the prominent position of " ![logo] " logo on the products, the logo size and combined use with other words, as well as the way and position, etc. it's used in the advertisements for online sales, correspond to the way in which PUMA's own trademark is used, which obviously goes beyond the scope of illustrating or objectively describing the characteristics of the goods, and also objectively plays a role in distinguishing the source thereof. Besides, given the common practice of co-branding on cooperative goods in the industry, it will cause the relevant public to mistakenly believe that there exists commercial cooperation between the plaintiff and the two defendants. Therefore, regardless of the subjective cognizance of the two defendants, using " ![logo] " logo on the products in such way is an act of "use as a trademark."

Ⅱ. Accurate determination of fair use according to the Trademark Law

As to whether the two defendants have used ancient hieroglyphic logo fairly to describe and illustrate other characteristics of the goods, we believe that " ![glyph] " is the expression of "羊" in ancient Chinese bronze inscription, which, from a literal point of view, can be classified as a public domain resource. However, after thousands of years' evolution of Chinese characters, " ![glyph] " is no longer a word used by modern people in daily life, but becomes a figure instead. It's precisely because of its graphic feature that the plaintiff's application for registration of ![glyph] trademark was approved. Even though the plaintiff's " ![glyph] " trademark is the same as ancient Chinese bronze inscription " ![glyph] " in the public domain, it has, through long-term use and publicity by the plaintiff, become widely known to the industry and relevant public, and has obtained a high reputation. This logo has become distinctive to certain extent and can be regarded as a trademark that can distinguish the source of the goods. PUMA, as a well-known professional sportswear producer, shall and is able to fulfill the duty of trademark examination when carrying out product design. Moreover, " ![glyph] " is only among one of the many character fonts that can be used to express the Year of Goat; the two defendants can completely avoid the same design as the plaintiff's trademark involved. Therefore, their fair use defense isn't established.

Ⅲ. Whether sales profit or operating profit will be adopted when determining the defendant's illicit profit

During the trial, in order to prevent the loss of infringement evidence and facilitate the evidence collection in the future, the plaintiff made several evidence preservation requests. After examination, the court preserved such evidences as PUMA's account books and original vouchers relating to the goods involved, and invited the certified public accountants of relevant institutions to participate in the whole process. At last, with the joint efforts of all parties, the defendant provided the original purchase proof, sales vouchers and inventory records of the goods involved. This evidence preservation not only fixed the evidence on production and sales status of the alleged infringing goods, but also helped to ascertain the defendant's illicit profits more accurately. Based on the preserved evidences, it's calculated that the defendant, PUMA, achieved a sales profit (sales price-purchase price) of nearly RMB 6,000,000 from the goods involved. The plaintiff alleged such sales profit as PUMA's illicit profit, whereas PUMA considered that the illicit profit should be based on the gross sales amount and calculated as per 6% of the company's operating profits. The court held that firstly, the goods involved infringed upon the plaintiff's trademark right and the defendant's use of the plaintiff's trademark on such goods is illegal in itself. If the operation costs of these goods are deducted in the calculation of the defendant's illicit profit, the goods involved are undoubtedly treated as normal goods and the illegality of the defendant's act is ignored, which goes against the basic principles of fairness and justice in civil trials. Besides, the low cost of infringement will discourage the market players from doing business in good faith as well as respecting intellectual property. Secondly, the company's operating profit margin shall be calculated with consideration of various factors, including its labor costs, daily operation costs, advertising expenses and trademark license fee, etc. However, in view of the common practice and business model in the clothing industry, a considerable portion of the costs arise from its inventories, including the storage of the goods, logistics and reduction in the actual income caused by price-off promotions, etc. In this case, the accounting data preserved show that more than 90% of the goods involved have been sold, which won't bring other costs incurred by the unsalable inventory. Thirdly, the company's daily operating costs, labor costs and advertising expenses, etc. are not directly incurred by the infringing goods, and they shall not be deducted accordingly. To sum up, the defendant's illicit profit shall be determined as per the sales profits without deducting the operating costs of the infringing goods.

Ⅳ. Application of the principle of proportionality in determining the amount of compensation

The principle of proportionality is an important fundamental principle in many countries' administrative laws. It consists of three elements: suitability, necessity and proportionality, referring to that administrative authorities shall, when taking administrative actions, consider both the realization of administrative objectives and the protection of interests of relevant parties. If the realization of administrative objectives may have a negative impact on the rights and interests of the parties concerned, such negative impact shall be minimized as far as possible and there shall be an appropriate proportion between these two aspects. In July 2016, the Supreme People's Court explicitly put forward the policy for judicial protection of intellectual property rights, i. e. "judicial leadership, strict protection, categorized implementation of policies, and harmonious proportions", in which harmonious proportions means that the scope and intensity of protection of intellectual property rights shall be proportionate to the level of innovation and contribution thereof, and the cost of infringement must be proportionate to the infringer's subjective bad faith and harmful act, so as to realize the balanced development between the rights and interests of rights holders and the legitimate rights and interests of others as well as social & public interests and national interests. It can be said that intellectual property trial is a first mover in exploring and practicing the principle of proportionality. In this case, given that relevant consumers will not only be attracted by the plaintiff's trademark that enjoys a high reputation, but will also be affected by PUMA's own popular trademark and the fact that PUMA's products are of high quality when they choose to buy the clothing and sneakers involved, not all of PUMA's sales profits in this respect can be attributed to infringing the plaintiff's trademark. Therefore, the amount of compensation shall be determined with full consideration to the proportion of goods bearing " ▨ " logo among all goods, i. e. the contribution of " ▨ " logo to the profits of the goods. Accordingly, the above-mentioned judgement was given.

(Writers: Jin Minzhen, Hu Jiaqi, Qi Jimin)

Determination of Trademark Infringement After Natural Person's Name Is Registered as A Trademark

—Dispute over trademark infringement and unfair competition
(Ge Jun and TaoRenGe Company v.
Jinghua Artwork Auction Company)

[Abstract]

When a natural person chooses to register his name as a trademark, the trademark owner shall, in view of the personal symbol attribute of the name, refrain from taking actions when some other person who has the same name want to use such name. That's to say, the reasonable use of the name by others won't constitute infringement, provided that the name is used legitimately. If it is likely to cause confusion among the relevant public, the other person shall have the obligation of careful avoidance, otherwise it will constitute trademark infringement.

[Case Review]

Plaintiff:Ge Jun ("葛军" in Chinese)

Plaintiff: Shanghai TaoRenGe Pottery Co. , Ltd ("TaoRenGe")

Defendant:Shanghai Jinghua Artwork Auction Co. , Ltd ("Jinghua")

Cause of Action:dispute over trademark infringement and unfair competition

First-Instance Case No. :Pu Min San (Zhi) Chu Zi No. 298 (2015)

The plaintiff Ge Jun, who has a high influence in the field of Chinese ceramic art, is a master of arts and crafts in Jiangsu Province, master of ceramic art in

Jiangsu Province, master of Chinese ceramic arts and crafts and the director of Purple Sand Culture Research Center of Chinese Ceramic Culture Research Institute. He has registered such trademarks as "葛军" and "申壶坊", etc., and exclusively licensed all registered trademarks to another plaintiff, TaoRenGe. Later, Ge Jun received a "Dark-red Enameled Pottery & Aged Tea" auction brochure from the defendant, Jinghua, who also advertised the dark-red enameled potteries to be auctioned at www. arton. net and www. jinghuapaimai. com. The plaintiff found that nine of the dark-red enameled potteries were marked with "申壶葛军", attached with his above social reputations, which caused social misunderstanding and constituted false advertising. So, he contacted Jinghua and demanded that Jinghua stop auctioning the dark-red enameled potteries with "申壶葛军" marked at the bottom. However, Jinghua ignored this and continued the auction. Believing that Jinghua's act of proceeding with the auction despite knowing that the dark-red enameled potteries infringed upon the plaintiff's trademark right and constituted unfair competition not only impaired the plaintiff's goodwill, but also impaired his social reputation and affected the commercial value of dark-red enameled potteries designed and made by him, the plaintiff sued to court, requesting the defendant to stop selling the infringing dark-red enameled potteries, stop the unfair competition of false advertising, compensate for the plaintiff's economic losses and reasonable expenses, and make a public apology to eliminate the ill effects.

Jinghua argued that the alleged infringing mark "申壶葛军" was neither identical nor similar to the plaintiff's registered trademarks "申壶坊" and "葛军". It wouldn't cause confusion and therefore didn't constitute trademark infringement. Besides, "申壶葛军" was the name of another person. The auction brochure wasn't made by Jinghua, and Jinghua was entrusted to sell the goods, the source of which was to be guaranteed by the principal. As an auction house, it had fulfilled the duty of reasonable care and was unable to identify the source of the auction items. Even if the infringement was established, relevant information had been withdrawn at the auction site and the plaintiff had no evidence proving his losses and damage to his reputation. Therefore, the defendant refused to accept any of the claims of the plaintiff.

[Judgment]

Putuo District People's Court of Shanghai held that Ge Jun's registration of "葛军" trademark is essentially a way to use his name as a commercial mark, thereby commercialize his right of name, and his own popularity in related fields can also extend to the trademark to a certain extent. The defendant argued that "申壶葛军" used in the auction process was meant to indicate the goods maker (or potter) rather than "use the trademark", i. e. "申壶葛军" refers to the potter and "申壶葛军 + (某某刻) +壶款式名称" indicates that the pottery maker (or potter) is "申壶葛军", "某某" refers to the engraver of pottery sculpture, and "申壶葛军" seal also refers to the maker. The court held that, although the above cognition of the defendant was reasonable, considering the unity of practicability and artistry of the dark-red enameled pottery as a special commodity, both the commercial mark and signature of the copyright owner can be used to indicate the source of the goods. In particular, when these two are basically the same, there's no need and it's also impossible to strictly distinguish them from each other from the perspective of their function of distinguishing the source of the goods. "申壶葛军" has already acquired the benefits as a commercial mark and essentially plays the function of distinguishing the source of the goods. Therefore, the alleged infringing act of using "申壶葛军" is indeed an act of using it as a trademark according to the Trademark Law.

Comparing "申壶葛军" with the plaintiff's trademarks "申壶坊" and "葛军", it can be seen that "申壶葛军" is a combination of two characters "申壶" from "申壶坊" and other two characters "葛军". First of all, although "申壶坊" is a trademark with combined graphic and characters, seen from its black and white design resembling a seal, the characters "申壶坊" are core elements of the trademark. Considering the word-formation practice "attribute + subject" or "modifier + noun" in Chinese phrases, "申壶" is more distinctive in "申壶坊" in terms of its subordinate-principal semantics. "葛军" is a word mark and its core elements are prominent. Secondly, according to the plaintiff's proof, Ge Jun enjoys a high reputation in the dark-red enameled pottery filed; dark-red enameled potteries auctioned are often sold at a high price, and their art collection value is often greater than the practical value. Therefore, generally speaking, the market audiences are more targeted compared to the general public and are more likely to know the connection between "葛军" and

"申壶坊" trademarks, resulting in greater likelihood of causing confusion among the relevant public about "申壶葛军" and "申壶坊""葛军". The alleged infringing mark "申壶葛军" (including the form of seal) is used on the same kind of goods as the plaintiff's two registered trademarks. It can be deemed confusingly similar to the plaintiff's trademarks and constitute trademark infringement. In addition, the introduction of "申壶葛军" in the auction brochure is consistent with the evidences provided by the plaintiff, Ge Jun, regarding his honour and social status. It will mislead the consumers to believe that the goods are produced by the plaintiff, constituting unfair competition by false advertising.

As to the defendant's opinion that it's entrusted to sell the goods, has fulfilled the duty of reasonable care and shall not bear the liability for compensation, the court held that the seller can be exempted from liability only if he has acquired the goods legitimately and does not know that the goods sold are infringing goods. In this case, since the plaintiff has a high reputation in the field, the defendant, as a professional art auction organization, shall obviously bear a higher duty of care. However, it didn't make any warranty of defects of right to the public on the dark-red enameled potteries involved, and failed to deal with it in a prudent way after receiving the notice from the right holder. So, the defendant is aware of the possible infringement of the goods involved, and its opinion isn't adopted.

To sum up, according to Paragraph 1 (1), (6), (8) and Paragraph 2 of Article 15 of Tort Law of the People's Republic of China, Paragraph 1 of Article 3, Article 57 (3) and Paragraph 3 of Article 63 of Trademark Law of the People's Republic of China, Article 2, Article 9 and Article 20 of Anti-unfair Competition Law of the People's Republic of China, Article 3(2), Paragraph 2 of Article 4, Paragraph 2 of Article 9, Article 10, Paragraph 1 & 2 of Article 16, Article 17 and Paragraph 1 of Article 21 of Interpretation of the Supreme People's Court Concerning the Application of Laws in the Trial of Cases of Civil Disputes Arising from Trademarks, as well as Paragraph 1 (3) & Paragraph 3 of Article 8, Article 17 of Interpretation of the Supreme People's Court on Some Matters about the Application of Law in the Trial of Civil Cases Involving Unfair Competition, Putuo District People's Court of Shanghai ordered Jinghua to stop the trademark infringement and unfair competition, eliminate the ill effects and compensate the plaintiff's economic losses and reasonable expenses totaling RMB 30,000.

The first-instance judgment has entered into force as neither party file an appeal.

〔Case Study〕

This is a typical case involving determination of trademark infringement after a natural person's name is registered as a trademark.

Ⅰ.Boundary between fair use of the name and use as a trademark

Name is a specific symbol that distinguishes individual human beings through language, while trademark is a mark that identifies the source of goods or services mainly through visual elements such as words, letters, graphics and so on. Their commonness in semiotics makes it possible for the name to be used as a trademark. When the name of a natural person is registered and used as a trademark, the name and trademark overlap with each other in a sense and will inevitably lead to certain conflicts. In such circumstance, the natural person's name is no longer only a symbol to distinguish individual human beings, but also plays the function of distinguishing the source and carrying goodwill. However, given that the names of natural persons might be the same or similar, it is necessary to distinguish between the fair use of a name and use thereof as a trademark in commercial activities. When the defendant declares fair use of the name and denies using it as a trademark, the court shall consider whether such use can identify the source of goods or services. If it can identify the source of goods or services, it's used as a trademark. Otherwise, it's not used as a trademark.

In this case, even if, as the defendant declares, "申壶葛军" refers to the maker, dark-red enameled pottery is a special commodity featured by both practicability and artistry. Both of its commodity attribute and art work attribute are unified and its source can be indicated by either the trademark or signature of the copyright owner. Especially when these two are basically the same, there's no need and it's also impossible to strictly distinguish them from each other from the perspective of their function of distinguishing the source of the goods. "申壶葛军" has already acquired the benefits as a commercial mark and essentially plays the function of distinguishing the source of the goods. Therefore, it's used as a trademark according to the Trademark Law.

Ⅱ. Determination of infringement on natural person's name registered as a trademark

After a natural person's name is registered as a trademark, certain infringement shall be determined based on the likelihood of confusion and other general rules for determining trademark infringement as stipulated in the Trademark Law. According to relevant laws, similar trademark means the trademark against which infringement is alleged that, when compared with the registered trademark of the plaintiff, is similar in the shape of words, phonetics, meaning or the shape of the graphics and its color, or in the general formation resulting from the positions of the all the principal elements, or in the three-dimensional shape or the formation of colors, and is likely to cause misidentification among the general public as to the origin of the goods or misperception that the origin of the goods is specially connected to the goods represented by the registered trademark of the plaintiff. Besides, as the case may be, other factors shall also be considered in addition to the degree of similarity of constituent elements when determining trademark similarity, such as the extent of distinctiveness of the registered name trademark and the alleged infringing mark as a commercial sign, popularity of the name trademark, segmentation and definition of the relevant market and relevant public, judgement of intention to use, use status of the alleged infringing mark in commercial activities and other related market factors.

In this case, it's recognized by the court that "申壶葛军" is composed of the core elements of the plaintiff's registered trademarks "申壶坊" and "葛军", and is used on the same kinds of goods as these two trademarks. With full consideration to the plaintiff's popularity in the field and accurate market segmentation of dark-red enameled pottery, the court judged that the alleged infringing mark "申壶葛军" is likely to cause confusion among the relevant public and constitute confusing similarity.

Ⅲ. Circumstance under which the auction company is exempted from liability

Auction companies are entrusted by customers to auction items and they may differ from each other in the source of auctioned goods, auction mode, profit-making, etc. Therefore, the nature of auction company's auction behavior must be taken into full consideration. In this case, for example, the defendant makes profits through commission instead of the price differentials of goods, so it is not a direct seller. However, it assists in selling the goods by providing a trading platform for direct sellers.

As an indirect seller, the auction company can demand exemption from the liability for compensation on the grounds that the auctioned items are acquired legitimately, it does not know the existence of infringement and has fulfilled the duty of reasonable care. Such exemption must meet two conditions: the seller doesn't know the goods are infringing goods and it can prove the infringing goods sold have a legitimate source. Even if there is an entrustment agreement and the auctioned items are obtained legitimately, the auction company shall bear a higher duty of care in view of its professionalism and the popularity of the right holder. In this case, the auction company didn't make any warranty of defects of right to the public on the dark-red enameled potteries involved, nor taken any prudent measures such as further information verification, price range comparison, trademark retrieval, etc. after receiving the notice from the right holder, and it's not critical for a professional auction agency to take the above-mentioned fast, efficient and economic measures to deal with contemporary works of art. Therefore, the auction company is aware of the possible infringement of the goods involved and it doesn't meet the condition of being exempted from liability for compensation.

(Writers: Zhang Jialu, Lin Shuwei)

Examination of Plaintiff Qualification and Determination of Descriptive Use in Dispute Over Confirmation of Non-infringement of Trademark

—Dispute over confirmation of non-infringement of trademark (Columbia Sportswear Company v. Sino Textiles Corporation Limited)

[Abstract]

The biggest challenge of examining the qualification of plaintiff/defendant in a dispute over confirmation of non-infringement of trademark lies in how to identify interested parties. When the alleged infringing goods bear both the disputed mark and its own registered trademark, and the actual producer is indicated, whether the registered trademark owner is the actual producer doesn't affect the determination of the source of the goods because the primary function of the trademark is to distinguish the source of goods. The registered trademark owner may, on the ground that it has received infringement warning and both parties has a dispute over the source of the goods, bring an action as an interested party. "Descriptive fair use" means that the mark is used for the purpose of "describing" the goods and the act is "fair". Therefore, two requirements shall be met: (ⅰ) in terms of the subjective intent, the mark is used in good faith only for describing the goods as its connotation is consistent with the goods characteristics; (ⅱ) in terms of the objective effect, the disputed mark doesn't play the role of identifying the source of the goods and isn't used as a trademark.

[Case Review]

Plaintiff（Appellee）:Columbia Sportswear Company

Defendant（Appellant）: Sino Textiles Corporation Limited

Cause of Action:dispute over confirmation of non-infringement of trademark

First-Instance Case No. : Xu Min San（Zhi）Chu Zi No. 653（2013）

Second-Instance Case No. :Hu Yi Zhong Min Wu（Zhi）Zhong Zi No. 88（2014）

The plaintiff, Columbia Sportswear Company, registered No. 1236702 rhombic image trademark "❖", No. 5288005 trademark "❖Columbia Sportswear Company" and No. 5288009 trademark "Columbia" on Class 25 goods（clothing, shoes and hats）. At its official Chinese website, it declares that, "Columbia has designed unique and popular products, including its famous lining replacement system... Columbia's first three-in-one jacket, designed for hunting activities, is equipped with a waterproof outer layer and insulated lining that can be worn together or alone... "

From 2005 to 2012, magazines such as*Brand* and *China Garment* have made positive publicity on the plaintiff and its products. It was reported in Issue 4, 2009 *Chinese & Foreign Corporate Culture* that, "In 1982, Columbia became the first to propose 3-in-1 Interchange System, and developed a novel design that the liner of the jacket can be removed, which not only won recognition in the industry, but also caused quite a stir in the market. Now, many outdoor brands have adopted this practical design... "

The defendant was established on July 26, 2000, engaged in textile fiber technology, sales of knitwear and textile, textile raw materials（except cotton）and apparels, and apparels. On February 7, 2011, it was allowed to register No. 8022378 trademark "Base Layer" on Class 25 goods, valid until February 6, 2021.

Swire Resources is the plaintiff's general agent in China. On November 23, 2012, the defendant, Sinotextiles, commissioned a lawyer to send a letter to Swire Resources, saying the "Baselayer" mark on the outer packaging of two kinds of textiles sold by Swire Resources infringed upon its exclusive right to use its registered trademarks and Swire Resources shall stop the infringement and destroy the infringing mark. On December 6, 2016, the plaintiff, Columbia Sportswear, entrusted a lawyer to reply that it's the producer of the said products bearing "Baselayer" mark and the word "Baselayer" has been used fairly as the generic name of the goods. On December 14, 2012, Sinotextiles' lawyer replied that it didn't accept the plaintiff's claim that "Baselayer" constituted the generic name of the infringing goods. On December 19, 2012 and January 17, 2013, upon discovering that the above-mentioned textiles were sold by two stores authorized by the plaintiff, the defendant entrusted the lawyer again to send letters to store owners Shanghai Ganghui Real Estate Development Co., Ltd. and Shanghai No. 1 Yaohan Co., Ltd. respectively, claiming that their act of selling the above textiles also infringed upon its exclusive right to use its registered trademarks and they shall stop the infringement.

The alleged infringing goods are two kinds of products in this case. The outer packing is a cuboid plastic box, with the word "Baselyer" in the middle of the front, French word "Premiere couche" (translated as "基础层" in Chinese) next to it, "◆" and "Columbia" trademarks on the top of the front and product certificate label at the bottom of the back. The product certificate label indicates the following: Product Name: Casual Wear / Casual Pants (respectively); Trademark: ◆Columbia; Manufacturer: Far-Eastern Apparel Suzhou Co. Ltd; Distributor: Swire Resources (Shanghai) Trading Co. Ltd. The box cover is printed with rugged trademark "◆" while box bottom is marked with "◆" and "Columbia" trademarks. "Baselayer" font is larger than that of other words and trademarks. Of two products, the left chest, waist belt and lower part of jacket, as well as their collar label/pant label, wash care labels and tags are marked with "◆" and "Columbia" trademarks or "◆Columbia" trademark. The word of "Baselayer" is not used in either of the two products.

According to the evidence submitted by the plaintiff to prove that "Baselayer" is a generic name for outdoor sportswear:

If the keyword of "Baselyer" is entered on Wikipedia's search engine, it will automatically jump to the definition of the entry "Layered clothing", according to which layered clothing has at least three layers, i. e., the inner layer, the middle layer and the shell layer; inner layer provides comfort by keeping the skin dry, also called base layer or first layer.

When searching for "Baselayer" or "Baselayer" on the official websites of some outdoor sportswear brands around the world, such as ARC'TERYX, THE NORTH FACE, HENRI LLOYD, OZARK and DECATHLON, they are all categorized into inner layers of outdoor sportswear; men's jackets and vests bought at Shanghai Decathlon Mall also use "Baselayer" in the outer packaging.

Articles and reports related to the "base layer" published on *Outdoor Adventure*, *Design*, *ShangHai Times*, *Beijing Times* and other periodicals and newspapers, as well as www. sohu. com, http://sports. southcn. com and www. 8264. com show that "base layer" refers to the base layer of outdoor clothing.

Columbia complained that Sinotextiles had repeatedly sent lawyer's letters to its dealers, agents and related operators, declaring that "Baselayer" mark used on the inner layer of two self-produced outdoor sportswear infringed upon Sinotextiles' exclusive right to use its registered trademark and requiring them to stop the infringement. According to Columbia, "Baselayer" used on product packaging is only meant to illustrate and describe the type of the products, so that consumers may distinguish them correctly. Meanwhile, the clothing involved have been marked with the trade name and registered trademark in a prominent position, and are sold only in the plaintiff's stores, which won't lead to confusion. Given that Sinotextiles repeatedly sent letters but didn't sue to the court within a reasonable period of time, which has seriously damaged the plaintiff's good market reputation and put its product sales in trouble, the plaintiff filed a lawsuit to the court, requiring confirmation that its use of "Baselayer" mark on the inner layer of outdoor sportswear doesn't infringe on the defendant's exclusive right to use No. 8022378 registered trademark "Base Layer".

Sinotextiles argued that, (i) the plaintiff is not the manufacturer and distributor of the products involved; it has no direct interest in this case and is ineligible to act as the plaintiff herein; (ii) Sinotextiles' registered trademark "Base Layer" is distinctive on the approved products, which is neither a generic name of products nor directly indicates their functions; (iii) on the outer packaging of the products involved, "Baselayer" is obviously larger than the plaintiff's registered trademark, which constitutes conspicuous use and is not used fairly. To sum up, it's required to suspend the case or dismiss the plaintiff's claims.

[Judgment]

After the trial, Xuhui District People's Court of Shanghai held that there are two controversial issues in this case, i. e. whether the plaintiff has the right to file a lawsuit for confirmation of non-infringement and whether the plaintiff's use of "Baselayer" mark on the outer packaging of products infringes upon the defendant's exclusive right to use its registered trademark.

Concerning the first issue, both Columbia's general agent in China and the manager of the mall where its authorized stores are located have received the warning of trademark infringement, and all alleged infringing products bear Columbia's registered trademark. Columbia replied promptly and personally to Sinotextiles that "Baselayer" mark attached to the products are used fairly. Sinotextiles didn't accept this view but admitted that the plaintiff has an interest in the alleged infringing products before this case was brought. As Sinotextiles hasn't filed a lawsuit within a reasonable time limit, so it remains uncertain whether the relevant products authorized by the plaintiff to sell in Chinese market constitute infringement. Columbia, as a direct interested party, has the right to bring a lawsuit for confirmation of non-infringement in this case.

Regarding the second issue, since there is no substantial difference between the "Baselayer" mark used on the products involved and Sinotextiles' registered trademark "Base Layer", and they have the same class of goods to be used, the issue is actually a dispute over whether "Baselayer" mark is used descriptively and fairly, which shall be determined based on the meaning of "baselayer" in outdoor sportswear filed, and the purpose, manner and consequences of the plaintiff's use thereof. Firstly, existing evidences show that "baselayer" can refer to the base layer of outdoor sportswear and the plaintiff intended to use "Baselayer" to describe the characteristics of the products. Secondly, considering the way "Baselayer" is used and the effects resulting therefrom, "Baselayer" is only used on the outer packaging of the alleged infringing products with French version (both have the same Chinese meaning) at the same position, and the plaintiff's own well-know registered trademarks "◈", "Columbia" or "◈Columbia Sportswear Company" are marked on the outer packaging clearly and thoroughly. Therefore, the source of products is actually identified by the plaintiff's own well-known registered trademarks. "Baselayer", despite its larger font, is intended to indicate the function and uses of the products more clearly to the relevant public. It is not used as trademark and won't cause confusion about the source of the products.

To sum up, in accordance with Article 49 of Implementation Regulation of the Trademark Law of P. R. C. (2014 Revision) (currently Paragraph 1, Article 59 of the Trademark Law of the People's Republic of China (2013)), Xuhui District People's Court of Shanghai decided to confirm that Columbia Sportswear Company's use of "Baselayer" mark on the outer packaging of inner layer of outdoor sportswear doesn't infringe on the exclusive right of Sinotextiles Corporation Limited to use No. 8022378 registered trademark "Base Layer".

Dissatisfied with the first-instance judgment, Sinotextiles Corporation Limited filed an appeal.

After the trial, Shanghai No. 1 Intermediate People's Court held that the first-instance judgment is justified since facts have been clearly ascertained and laws have been correctly applied. Therefore, it's ruled to dismiss the appeal and affirm the original judgment.

[Case Study]

This case involves confirmation of non-infringement of trademark, which is unique in the intellectual property field. The judgment has clarified the examination standard of plaintiff's subject qualification and the determination method of descriptive use of trademark elements, which is of great typical significance in that it made positive exploration for the adjudication of similar cases.

I. Determination of plaintiff's subject qualification in cases involving confirmation of non-infringement of trademark

In Trademark Law, there's still no provision on examining the subject qualification of litigants. According to Article 119 of the Civil Procedure Law of the People's Republic of China (hereinafter referred to as the "Civil Procedure Law"), "The plaintiff is a citizen, legal person or any other organization with a direct interest in the case." According to Article 18 of Interpretation of the Supreme People's Court on Several Issues concerning the Application of Law in the Trial of Patent Infringement Dispute Cases, a basic consensus is reached in judicial practice on the conditions for filing a lawsuit for confirmation of non-infringement, that is, if the right holder gives a warning of infringement but fails to file a lawsuit within a reasonable period of time, it remains uncertain whether the relevant act of the person warned or the interested party has constituted infringement. During the examination, it's difficult to identify interested parties. We believe that the plaintiff's subject qualification shall be examined strictly based on "direct interest relationship" stipulated in the Civil Procedure Law, and the abstract interest relationship between market players doesn't equate to direct interest relationship because such abstract interest relationship is universal in view of the competitive relationship among market players and interest relations between the upstream and downstream segments of the industry. If two parties have no direct, clear and specific connection formed based on specific legal relationship in the intellectual property field, it's difficult to determine whether they have a direct interest relationship. Otherwise, the overly broad definition of interested party will not only lead to abusive litigation on confirmation of non-infringement, putting market players under unpredictable litigation risk, but also nullify the explicit provisions of the Civil Procedure Law.

In this case, the products involved bear two marks: the disputed mark "Baselayer" and Columbia Sportswear Company's ("Columbia") own registered trademark. The right holder gives trademark infringement warning on the products involved, but Colombia is not the actual manufacturer or seller thereof. So, is there an interest relationship between it and the right holder's failure to file a lawsuit after giving trademark infringement warnings? What kind of interest relationship?

The court started with the dispute as evidenced in the pre-lawsuit correspondences between two parties. After its dealer received the infringement warning, Colombia replied to the defendant promptly and personally that the alleged infringing mark was only used fairly. However, the defendant denied the fair use thereof but admitted before this case was brought that the plaintiff has an interest in the alleged infringing products. In other words, pre-litigation correspondences and behaviors can prove that both parties have a dispute provided in the Trademark Law.

In order to further clarify the specific and direct interest relationship in this case, the court carried out analysis based on the primary function of the trademark, i. e. distinguish the source of goods. According to the judgment, the products involved bear a registered trademark that Columbia has the exclusive right to use, so the products can be deemed to come from Columbia, and whether Columbia is the actual producer does not affect the identification of the source of these products. In this sense, Columbia has a direct interest in this case and has the right to bring this case. The deep logic behind this conclusion is that the primary goal of trademark law is to protect the identification function of trademarks, so as to ensure that consumers can identify the source of goods through trademarks. In this case, while the trademark right holder gave infringement warnings on the ground that the "Baselayer" word mark on the products involved would mislead consumers about the source of goods, Columbia, as the source indicated by the registered trademark on the products involved, has been directly involved in a dispute with the right holder according to the Trademark Law: who is the source of the products involved? Therefore, Columbia has a direct interest in this case; The definition of interested party is proper in this case, meeting the requirements on direct interests stipulated in the Civil Procedure Law.

Ⅱ. Determination of descriptive use of trademark

The primary function of trademark is to distinguish the source of goods. A mark that infringes on the exclusive right to use a registered trademark shall first be used as a trademark and has the function as a trademark. Therefore, in order to judge whether the use of "Baselayer" on the products involved constitutes trademark infringement, we should first examine whether "Baselayer" is used as a trademark or used descriptively and fairly as alleged by the plaintiff.

Descriptive fair use refers to an act of using words or graphics in other people's trademarks to describe its own goods, which stresses that the words or graphics are used to "describe" the goods in a "fair" way. In terms of subjective purpose, the words or graphics are only used to describe the goods in good faith as they are in line with the characteristics of the goods; in terms of the objective effects, the disputed mark doesn't play the role of identifying the source of goods and isn't used as a trademark.

(ⅰ) Subjective purpose: the meaning of a word is consistent with the characteristics of the goods and it's used in good faith to describe the goods

Whether a word is used to describe the characteristics of the goods shall be judged based on the objective connection between the meaning of the word mark and characteristics of the products involved. Consistency between the word meaning and product characteristics are the premise and basis for "descriptive use".

"Baselayer" consists of two English words: "base" and "layer", meaning "基础层" in Chinese. The court analyzed the correspondence between the meaning of "baselayer" in outdoor sportswear field and the characteristics of products involved. According to existing evidences, including media coverage on "three-layer" outdoor clothing, Wikipedia definition of "base layer", search results of "Base layer" on the official websites of some global outdoor sportswear brands, and "Base Layer" marked on the products sold in Decathlon mall, it can be determined that "baselayer" refers to the base layer of clothing in Chinese outdoor sportswear field. Therefore, the due meaning of "Baselayer" is consistent with the characteristics of the products involved. It truthfully describes the characteristics of the "base layer" of outdoor clothing and can be assumed to have been used in good faith for the purpose of describing the products.

(ⅱ) Objective effects: it doesn't play the role of identifying the source of goods and isn't used as a trademark

In practice, the use of words, graphics and other elements is very complex, and a subtle difference in the way they are used may result in completely different effects. The court should analyze the overall perception of the relevant public about the use behavior and the effects resulting therefrom. Words or graphics can be deemed to be used fairly only if they don't have the function of identifying the source of goods.

The plaintiff used "Baselayer" as follows: (1) it's only used on the outer packaging of products rather than the products themselves; (2) French version, which also means "基础层" in Chinese, is provided at the same position; (3) the plaintiff's own well-know registered trademarks "♦", "Columbia" or "♦Columbia Sportswear Company" are marked on the front top of the outer package, box cover, box bottom and back product certificate clearly and thoroughly; and (4) "Baselayer" is in a larger font compared with other words and marks.

A typical issue reflected is that when the products involved bear both the disputed mark and its own registered trademark, and the disputed mark is larger than its own registered trademark, whether the disputed mark is undoubtedly used conspicuously as a trademark. There is no definite answer to this question, and it is up to the impression left on the consumers by the products. In previous infringement cases of "attaching to famous brands", some merchants often highlight the disputed marks with higher reputation and tone down their own registered trademarks. As far as the relevant public concerned, such disputed marks actually play the role of trademarks. In this case, the court carefully compared the identification function of "Baselayer" and "Columbia" trademarks, and analyzed which one plays the identification function based on the way they're used.

On one hand, the word mark "Baselayer" itself has weak identification function. "Baselayer" contains the words "base" and "layer", which aren't made up by the defendant. Sinotextiles, engaged in textile business, also admits that the trademark was registered based on the "base layer" meaning of the word, and its intrinsic distinctiveness is weak. Besides, Sinotextiles didn't submit evidence that it has launched products with the registered trademark "Base Layer" on the market, so it hasn't yet established a second meaning on the word "Baselayer" and its registered trademark hasn't become distinctive through actual use. Therefore, "Baselayer" fails to guide consumers to distinguish the source of goods.

On the other hand, the series of trademarks of "Columbia" are well known and have strong identification functions. The plaintiff's "Columbia" brand is a world-famous outdoor clothing brand, which also enjoys high popularity in Chinese outdoor sportswear field.

With regard to the way the disputed mark is used, "Baselayer" is only used on the outer packaging of products with French version, which also has the meaning of "基础层" in Chinese, next to it. The plaintiff's own trademarks are also marked thoroughly and clearly. When the relevant public see the products involved, they will only associate the well-known "Columbia" series trademarks with the plaintiff, rather than associate "Baselayer" with the defendant. Though "Baselayer" is larger, it's meant to show the public more clearly that the product is a basic layer of outdoor sportswear. It's apparent that the plaintiff doesn't dilute its own trademark while highlight other's marks. Instead, it offers obvious visual cues to consumers by marking its well-known trademark in all directions, which is completely different from previous infringing acts of "attaching to famous brands". Therefore, it's the plaintiff's own trademarks rather than "Baselayer" that actually play the role of identifying the source of goods. Though "Baselayer" is larger, it's not conspicuously used as a trademark.

In light of the above analysis of subjective purpose and objective effects, the disputed mark has been used in good faith to describe the characteristics of the products and doesn't play the role of indicating their source in fact. It's used in good faith within a reasonable scope. Therefore, it constitutes descriptive fair use.

In this case involving confirmation of non-infringement of trademark, it's difficult to examine the plaintiff's subject qualification and determine descriptive use of the dispute mark. The court has accurately grasped the purport of the litigation system and legislative purpose of the Trademark Law when making the judgment, clarifying the adjudication rules for the trial of similar cases. Meanwhile, the case is also a positive example that well-known enterprise takes the initiative to safeguard its rights by filing a lawsuit for confirmation of non-infringement. Columbia, as one of the most famous enterprises in global sportswear field, has taken the initiative to stop the damage when competitor's improper exercise of intellectual property rights damages its reputation, which is of great practical significance to enterprises safeguarding their rights through litigation.

(Writers: Li Xiaoping, Zhang Min)

Determination of Boundary
Between Fair Use and Infringing Use of
Geographic Indication Certification Marks

—Dispute over trademark infringement (Hangzhou Xihu Longjing Tea Industry Association v. Shanghai Yuqianchun Tea Co. , Ltd.)

[Abstract]

Certification mark is one of the trademarks explicitly protected by Trademark Law of P. R. C. Its function is to enable the relevant public to identify the source of specific goods or services through the mark, infringement upon which will make it impossible for the relevant public to identify the unique characteristics of goods or services, thereby damage the goodwill of the trademark and reputation of goods or services. In this case, the court considers whether the defendant's act is an infringing use or fair use of the geographical indication certification mark, which has certain reference significance for hearing relevant cases in judicial practice.

[Case Review]

Plaintiff: Hangzhou Xihu Longjing Tea Industry Association
Defendant: Shanghai Yuqianchun Tea Co. , Ltd
Cause of Action: dispute over trademark infringement
First-Instance Case No. : Yang Min San (Zhi) Chu Zi No. 422 (2014)
In July 2011, Hangzhou Municipal People's Government approved that " in order to strengthen the protection and development of West Lake Longjing tea, Hangzhou Xihu Longjing Tea Industry Association will be the main body to be

responsible for the registration and follow-up supervision of geographic indication certification mark '西湖龙井' ("West Lake Longjing")..." On June 28, 2011, the plaintiff registered No. 9129815 geographic indication certification mark "西湖龙井" for tea in Class 30 with the approval of the Trademark Office, which is valid until June 27, 2021. In May 2012, Zhejiang Provincial Administration for Industry & Commerce issued a well-known trademark certificate to the plaintiff, which states that "西湖龙井 was recognized as a well-known trademark by the State Administration for Industry and Commerce."

Article 2 of Regulations on the Protection of Hangzhou West Lake Longjing Tea Base stipulates that, "the term 'West Lake Longjing Tea Base' as mentioned in these regulations refers to the tea fields delimited by Hangzhou Municipal People's Government for protection within the scope of Hu Pao and Maojiabu to the east, Yangfumiao, Longmenkan and Hejiacun to the west, Shejing and Fusan to the south, and Laodongyue and Jinyujiing to the north in Xihu District, Hangzhou City." Article 5 of Rules on the Administration of Geographic Indication Certification Mark "西湖龙井" formulated by the plaintiff requires that "Products bearing the geographic indication certification mark '西湖龙井' shall be produced by West Lake Longjing Tea Base delimited by Hangzhou Municipal People's Government...", Article 6 thereof stipulates the quality of products using "西湖龙井" trademark, and Article 7 stipulates the requirements for picking and processing of products using "西湖龙井" trademark.

On July 30, 2014, Yao Weiyu, notary of Shanghai Xuhui Notary Public Office, Lu Wen, staff of Shanghai Xuhui Notary Public Office, and Song Lijun, entrusted by Watson & Band Law Offices, came to the store at No. 472 Neijiang Road, Shanghai. Song Lijun bought a gift box of tea as an ordinary consumer, and obtained a business card printed with the words "Shanghai Yuqianchun Tea Co., Ltd" and an invoice affixed with the seal of "Shanghai Yuqianchun Tea Co., Ltd".

After comparison in court, the alleged infringing goods is tea in gift box, with a paper packaging bag outside and four metal tea cans of the same size inside the gift box. The paper bag, gift box and tea cans are printed with the word "西湖龍井" ("West Lake Longjing" in traditional Chinese) vertically, while the back of the business card is printed with such words as 虎牌西湖龙井 ("Tiger Brand West Lake Longjing"), National Gift Base in Hangzhou Xihu District, Huangshan Xie Yu Da Tea Co., Ltd, Caoxi, Huangshan Maofeng, Suzhou Wujun Biluochun Tea Co.,

Ltd, Wujun Tea, Yunnan Pu'er Simao Xingyang Tea Co. , Ltd, Xingyang Tea, and Shanghai Franchised Dealer".

Shanghai Yuqianchun Tea Co. , Ltd, the defendant, was founded on January 18, 2007 with a registered capital of 500,000 yuan. It's engaged in the wholesale and retail of prepackaged food (excluding cooked food, stewed meat and frozen and refrigerated food), the sale of general merchandise, arts and crafts, auto parts, building materials, decoration materials, wine (limited to retail), hardware and electrical equipment, as well as indoor and outdoor decoration. During the trial, Yuqianchun declared that it sells mid-and-low end loose-leaf tea including Longjing, pan-fired tea and Yunwu tea, etc. , mainly the green tea. In this case, it sold loose leaf "Tiger Brand" Longjing with Yuqianchun's packaging instead of special "Tiger Brand" packaging.

Hangzhou Xihu Longjing Tea Industry Association complained that "West Lake Longjing" tea has a long history and is known as the king of tea in China. With the strong support of Hangzhou Municipal People's Government, it applied to the State Trademark Office for registration of geographic indication certification mark "西湖龙井" on February 18, 2011 and got the approval on June 28, 2011 (registration No. 9129815), which was approved to be used on tea in Class 30. The mark specially proves the place of origin and certain quality of "西湖龙井" products and has acquired a high goodwill. On April 27, 2012, it's recognized by the Trademark Office as a well-known trademark in China. On July 30,2014, the plaintiff bought some tea from the defendant's store located at No. 472 Neijiang Road, Yangpu District, Shanghai, and obtained a business card and invoice from the defendant. It's found that "西湖龙井" mark was conspicuously used on the tea packaging and the business card. On September 16, 2014, the plaintiff sent a lawyer's letter to Yuqianchun, asking it to immediately stop the infringement and contact the plaintiff to negotiate the compensation, which, however, was ignored. Believing that Yuqianchun's unauthorized use of the geographic indication certification mark on its self-produced and self-sold tea infringed upon the plaintiff's exclusive right to use this registered geographic indication certification mark, the plaintiff sued to court, requesting that (i) Yuqianchun stop infringing on the plaintiff's exclusive right to use the registered trademark "西湖龙井"; (ii) Yuqianchun compensate for the plaintiff's economic losses totaling 100,000 yuan (including reasonable expenses incurred to stop the infringement, same currency below); and (iii) Yuqianchun publish a statement in Liberation Daily and Xinmin Evening News to eliminate the ill effects.

Yuqianchun argued that it's mainly engaged in the sales of tea, and has free bags and a few tea boxes in the store to facilitate customers to keep and carry the tea. The gift box involved is a sample bought a few years ago; in this case, it's deliberately induced by the customer to use the tea box marked with West Lake Longjing Tea. The product sold is loose leaf tea instead of gift tea; the notarization process is illegal as the notary didn't present his identity document when notarizing the purchase process.

[Judgment]

After the trial, Yangpu District People's Court of Shanghai held that the plaintiff, as the owner of "西湖龙井" trademark, shall permit the use of the certification mark if the products of natural persons, legal persons or other organizations meet the requirements on origin, craftsmanship and quality. However, it has the right to prohibit the use thereof on products that don't meet the requirements on origin, craftsmanship and quality, and hold relevant persons or organizations liable for infringement according to law.

Packaging bags, gift boxes and tea cans that bear the words "西湖龍井" are used on the defendant's tea products. "西湖龍井" is prominently located in the middle of the packaging, which can be deemed to have been used as a trademark. Compared with the trademark involved, their mere difference in character pattern (Simplified Chinese/Traditional Chinese), font and alignment are likely to cause the relevant public to mistakenly believe that the defendant's products come from a specific place of origin with certain qualities. The word "Tiger Brand" is neither on the alleged infringing products or their outer packaging, and the defendant fails to provide evidence that its products originate from the designated production area of "西湖龙井" and that they meet the quality requirements of "西湖龙井" products. Therefore, the conspicuous use of "西湖龍井" on the products involved can't be deemed as fair use, but instead an act that infringes upon the plaintiff's exclusive right to use registered trademark. Besides, "虎牌西湖龙井" ("Tiger Brand West Lake Longjing" in Chinese) printed by the defendant on its business card, which misleads the relevant public about the source of its tea products, is similar to the plaintiff's trademark involved and also infringes upon the plaintiff's exclusive right to use the registered trademark.

Failing to provide evidence that its products meet the product origin and quality requirements demanded by the certification mark involved, the defendant's use of a mark similar to the trademark involved on its products and in its advertisements has infringed upon the plaintiff's exclusive right to use the registered trademark involved. Therefore, it shall bear the civil liability of stopping the infringement and compensating for the losses, etc.

Accordingly, pursuant to Paragraph 1 & 3 of Article 3, Paragraph 2 of Article 16, Article 48, Article 57 (2), Paragraph 1 & 3 of the Trademark Law of the People's Republic of China, Paragraph 2 of Article 4 of Regulation on the Implementation of the Trademark Law of the People's Republic of China, Paragraph 2 of Article 9, Article 10, Paragraph 1 & 2 of Article 16, Paragraph 1 of Article 17, and Paragraph 1 of Article 21 of Interpretation of the Supreme People's Court Concerning the Application of Laws in the Trial of Cases of Civil Disputes Arising from Trademarks, the court ruled as follows: (i) Shanghai Yuqianchun Tea Co., Ltd shall, from the date of entry into force of this judgment, immediately stop infringing upon the exclusive right of Hangzhou Xihu Longjing Tea Industry Association to use No. 9129815 registered trademark "西湖龙井"; (ii) Shanghai Yuqianchun Tea Co., Ltd shall, within ten days from the date of entry into force of this judgment, compensate for the economic losses of Hangzhou Xihu Longjing Tea Industry Association totaling 30,000 yuan (including reasonable expenses of 1,720 yuan); and (iii) other claims of Hangzhou Xihu Longjing Tea Industry Association are rejected.

As neither party filed an appeal, the first-instance judgment has already taken effect.

[Case Study]

Compared with ordinary trademarks, certification mark is used to ensure the quality of certain products, which helps enterprises to sell their products and consumers to choose the products. It guarantees the quality of these products and hence laws and regulations provide additional restrictions on its registration and transfer, etc. Infringing a certification mark will undermine the ability of the public to identify the special quality of goods or services through the mark, which not only has a negative impact on the trademark registrant, but also adversely affect the goodwill of the mark and the reputation of goods or services using the certification mark. In this case, the dispute lies in whether the defendant's use of the geographic indication certification mark is infringing use or fair use. The court took the following factors into consideration during the trial.

Ⅰ. Definition and content of geographic indication certification mark

According to Article 3 of the Trademark Law of P. R. C, " A registered trademark means a trademark, inclusive of a goods trademark, a service mark, a collective mark or a certification mark, that has been approved and registered by the Trademark Office; the trademark registrant shall enjoy an exclusive right to use the trademark, which shall be protected by law. Certification mark, as a special registered trademark, is a mark which is owned by an organization that exercises supervision over a particular product or service and which is used to indicate that third-party goods or services meet certain standards pertaining to place of origin, raw materials, manufacturing method, quality, or other characteristics. "

Geographic indication certification mark indicates that a product comes from a certain region, and its quality, reputation or other characteristics depend on its geographical origin and are determined by the natural or human factors of that region. Applying for registration of a geographic indication certification mark is beneficial to the protection of local specialties and the promotion of regional commodity market. Its external value lies in its popularity while intrinsic value is the natural and human factors in the place of production and processing. Firstly, this geographical origin is not only indicating the origin of a product, but also indicating its quality, reputation and other characteristics, reminding people of its unique qualities. Secondly, natural factors mainly include water quality, soil, topography, climate, etc. ; the same variety of products will have quite different qualities if they are not in the same geographical and climatic environment. Human factors include materials, formulations, techniques, historical traditions, etc. Lastly, geographic indication certification mark is composed of words, letters, patterns or combinations thereof, with " place name + product name" at its core. It will show the words " Chinese geographic indication certification mark " or " Chinese geographic indication" etc. , so that consumers may have a trust in the quality, reputation or other characteristics of the products. Among them, the place name can be either a name or nominatum that indicating the particular geographical origin of goods or services or a word, phrase or symbol that can represent a certain geographical area through its consistent use for a long period of time. It doesn't need to be consistent with an administrative division or a village that has the same name, nor consistent with the current official name of the geographical area.

According to the provisions of the Trademark Law, Regulation on the Implementation of the Trademark Law and Measures for the Registration and Administration of Collective Marks and Certification Marks, certification mark registrant shall be an enterprise, a public institution or a social organization or the like with legal personality that has the ability to inspect and supervise the goods or services. Any party applying for the registration of a certification mark shall furnish documents certifying the qualification of the subject, usage rules of the mark well as detailed information of the professionals and special testing equipment of its own or of any other organization authorized by it to show its capability of supervising the particular quality of the goods. Any party applying for the registration of a geographic indication as a certification mark shall also furnish the approval documents issued by the government, which has jurisdiction there over, or the competent authority of the industry. The registrant can't use the certification mark by itself, but can license the mark to others.

"西湖龙井" is a geographic indication certification mark approved and registered by the State Administration for Industry and Commerce after going through certain procedure. It's approved to be used on tea in Class 33, and its usage rules have been disclosed to the public by SAIC at the time of registration according to relevant procedures. The users shall abide by these rules when using the certification mark.

Ⅱ. Fair use of geographic indication certification mark

According to Paragraph 2, Article 16 of the Trademark Law, "Geographical indication refers to a mark that indicating the place of origin of a product, whose quality, reputation or other characteristics are mainly determined by the natural or human factors in that place." According to Paragraph 2, Article 6 of Regulation on the Implementation of the Trademark Law, "Where a geographic indication is registered as a certification mark, the natural person, legal person or other organization whose commodities meet the conditions for using the geographic indication may request for using the certification mark, and the organization that controls the certification mark shall consent. Where a geographic indication is registered as a collective mark, the natural person, legal person or other organization whose commodities meet the conditions for using the geographic indication may request for becoming a member of the body, society or other organization that has registered the geographic indication as a collective mark, and the body, society or other organization shall accept him or it to be a member according to the constitutions thereof. Anyone who does not request for becoming a member of the body, society or other organization that has registered the geographic indication as a collective mark, he or it may use the geographic indication fairly, and the body, society or other organization shall not interdict. "

According to the above provisions, geographic indication certification mark is distinct from general trademarks in that it's used to indicate the place of origin, raw materials, manufacturing method, quality or other characteristics of a product, including geographical origin of the product or service. The registrant is responsible for certifying the quality of this product or service, and shall allow natural persons, legal persons or other organizations whose products meet the conditions for using the geographic indication to use the certification mark fairly. It shall not deprive natural persons, legal persons or other organizations whose products, despite no request is made for using the certification mark, are produced in the indicated place of origin, meet the conditions for using the geographic indication, or are manufactured using raw materials or manufacturing method certified by the certification mark, of their rights to fairly use the certification mark. However, the registrant may prohibit natural persons, legal persons or other organizations, whose products are not produced in the indicated place of origin, don't meet the conditions for using the geographic indication, or are manufactured without using raw materials or manufacturing method certified by the certification mark, from using the certification mark on these products and hold them liable for infringing upon its trademark right.

The unique qualities of West Lake Longjing Tea, as a traditional famous tea in China, are mainly determined by natural factors, picking conditions and production process in the tea production area. The plaintiff, as the owner of "西湖龙井" (West Lake Longjing) trademark, shall consent to the request of natural persons, legal persons or other organizations for using the certification mark when their products meet the requirements on origin, process and quality. However, it may prohibit natural persons, legal persons or other organizations from using the certification mark on products that don't meet the requirements on origin, process and quality, and hold them liable for infringement according to law.

At the same time, as geographic indication certification mark is a trademark shared by qualified people, its registrant shall formulate unified administration rules and disclose them to the public, so that all sectors of society can jointly exercise supervision to protect the certain qualities of products and protect the interests of consumers. Article 5 of Rules on the Administration of Geographic Indication Certification Mark "西湖龙井" formulated by the plaintiff requires that "Products bearing the geographic indication certification mark '西湖龙井' shall be produced by West Lake Longjing Tea Base delimited by Hangzhou Municipal People's Government..., "Article 6 thereof stipulates the qualities of products using "西湖龙井" trademark, and Article 7 stipulates the requirements for picking and processing of products using "西湖龙井" trademark. The plaintiff shall have the ability and obligation to test and supervise the certification mark involved. When a party submits materials proving that its goods or services have met the above standards, it shall be allowed to use the certification mark after going through certain procedures. However, the plaintiff may prohibit the party from using this certification mark on products that don't meet the above standards and hold it liable for infringement.

Ⅲ. Determination of infringement on geographic indication certification mark

Since geographic indication certification mark infringement is caused by using the mark on products that don't meet the requirements on place of origin, raw materials, manufacturing methods and certain qualities, judging whether the products are produced in the required place of origin or with the required raw materials, manufacturing methods and qualities becomes an important fact to determine certification mark infringement, and this fact shall be ascertained based on the evidence submitted by the parties. In cases of certification mark infringement, the assignment of burden of proof pertaining to the place of origin, raw materials, manufacturing methods and certain qualities of the alleged infringing products becomes another essential issue.

According to the above burden of proof and the basic principle of its assignment, in cases of geographic indication certification mark infringement, certification mark registrant, as the party claiming the existence of its right, needs to provide factual evidence required by law to prove its acquisition of the right, while the party accused of infringement who claims that the right of trademark registrant shall be restricted, when defending itself on the ground that its products are produced in the required place of origin and the certification mark has been used fairly, should provide factual evidence required by law to support its defense, i. e. provide evidence that its products bearing the certification mark originate from the place of origin indicated by the certification mark.

Ⅳ. Whether the defendant's use of a trademark similar to the trademark involved on its products and business card constitutes infringement

The defendant argued that the packaging box involved was a sample bought a few years ago. During the notarization process, the customer deliberately induced it to use the tea box marked with "West Lake Longjing Tea", and the actual product it sold was "Tiger Brand" tea. The court held that according to Article 57 of the Trademark Law, "A person infringes the exclusive right to use a registered trademark if he uses a trademark that is similar to a registered trademark in relation to identical goods, or uses a trademark that is identical with or similar to a registered trademark in relation to similar goods, without the consent of the owner of the registered trademark, and liable to create confusion. " The plaintiff's certification mark is approved to be used on tea in Class 30. The defendant's use of the words "西湖龍井" in the middle of packaging bags, gift boxes and tea cans of its tea products constitutes "use as a trademark". Compared with the trademark involved, their mere difference in character pattern (Simplified Chinese/Traditional Chinese), font and alignment are likely to cause the relevant public to mistakenly believe that the defendant's products come from certain place of origin with certain qualities. Therefore, "西湖龍井" can be deemed similar to the trademark involved. Besides, the word "Tiger Brand" is neither on the alleged infringing products nor on their outer packaging, and the defendant fails to provide evidence to prove that its products originate from the designated production area of "西湖龙井" and that they meet the quality requirements of "西湖龙井" products. Therefore, the defendant's use of a trademark similar to the trademark involved on its products constitutes infringement.

According to Article 48 of the Trademark Law, "The use of a trademark means the use of the trademark on goods, packages or containers of the goods or in trading documents, or the use of the trademark in advertising, exhibition or any other business activities so as to distinguish the origin of goods." The plaintiff accused the defendant of infringing its trademark right by printing "虎牌西湖龙井" ("Tiger Brand West Lake Longjing") on its business card. In this regard, the court believes that business card is used to introduce a party itself in commercial activities, which provides a way to promote itself to others and can be regarded as "advertising" stipulated in Article 48 of the Trademark Law. The defendant printed "虎牌西湖龙井" on its business card with the aim to make the relevant public to identify the source of its tea products. According to the defendant's statement in court, it sells mid-and-low-end loose-leaf tea including Longjing, pan-fired tea, Yunwu tea and other green teas. However, it failed to provide evidence proving that the tea sold in its store is "Tiger Brand" West Lake Longjing Tea. To say the least, even if there's "Tiger Brand" West Lake Longjing Tea in its store, the defendant still needs to further prove that the tea comes from the designated production area of "西湖龙井" (West Lake Longjing Tea) and that they meet the quality requirements of "西湖龙井" products. "虎牌西湖龙井" (Tiger Brand West Lake Longjing) used on the defendant's business card is similar to the plaintiff's trademark involved and infringed upon the plaintiff's exclusive right to use the registered trademark.

(Writer: Shen Jingjie)

Civil Disputes
over Patent

Objective Comparison and Judgment Method of Design

—Shanghai M&G Stationery Inc. v. Deli Group et al. on design patent infringement dispute

[**Abstract**]

More often than not, whether two designs are identical or similar depends on, to a great extent, subjective factors, which affects judicial justice or consistency of judging standards. To apply the "overall observation and integrated conclusion" principle in specific cases more objectively, both the similarities and differences between the alleged infringing design and the patented design in a design infringement case should be taken into account. We should respectively carry out objective analysis on the impacts of identical and differentiated design features of the alleged infringing design and the patented design on their overall visual effect, so as not to be susceptible to subjective factors. Anyone who, without contributing creative labor, exploits a design patent by simply changing or adding non-substantially different design elements, patterns and colors based on a patented design, shall be deemed to have infringed upon the design patent.

[**Case Review**]

Plaintiff: Shanghai M&G Stationery Inc.
Defendant: Deli Group
Defendant: Jinan Kunsen Trading Co. , Ltd.
Cause of Action: Design patent infringement dispute
First-Instance Case No. : (2016) H 73 MC No. 113

The Plaintiff Shanghai M&G Stationery Inc. (hereinafter referred to as M&G) is the owner of the design patent (Patent No.: ZL200930231150.3) of the pen (AGP67101), for which application was filed on November 26, 2009 and authorization was proclaimed on July 21, 2010. It remains valid now. The authorized design (as shown in the figure attached) involves a pen holder and a pen cap with clip on it. The pen holder is an evenly elongated rounded cylinder having a square frustum with central hole protruded on top; it's slightly smaller inside near the conical nib and four surfaces around are gibbous at the center. The pen cap is an evenly rounded cylinder about 1/4 long of the former, with a square frustum protruded on top. The clip is flat and rectangular with undulated ridges inside, whose head is connected archwise to the top frustum of pen cap and bottom is cambered. The clip is slightly longer than the cap by 1/10 of the entire clip. According to the brief description of the patent, the pen features the overall shape as the key design element, which is best reflected in the top view. On August 14, 2015, the State Intellectual Property Office of the P.R.C ("SIPO") issued an evaluation report on the patent involved at the Plaintiff's request, making a preliminary conclusion that the whole design is free of defects specified in the conditions for the grant of patent rights. In response to the Defendant Deli Group (hereinafter referred to as Deli)'s request for patent invalidation, the former Patent Reexamination Board of SIPO made a decision that the authorized design is not identical to the control design substantially and the patent involved should remain valid on August 8, 2016.

On November 30, 2015, the entry of Deli A32160 in the "item" search box of Taobao led to the search result of "7 items in total," priced from RMB 1.0/Piece to RMB 26.90/Box (12 pieces). The entrusted agents of Shanghai Office of King & Wood Mallesons bought 4 boxes of Deli Pop Star Fashion A32160 gel pens at a price of RMB 26.90/Box from deliks. tmall. com (each hereinafter referred to as "Alleged Infringing Product"), which was notarized by Shanghai Huangpu Public Notary Office. The operator of above-mentioned deliks. tmall. com, the Defendant Jinan Kunsen Trading Co., Ltd. (hereinafter referred to as Kunsen), acknowledged that it made and sold the Alleged Infringing Product.

The Alleged Infringing Product (as shown in the figure attached) consists of a pen holder and a pen cap with clip on it. The pen holder is an evenly rounded cylinder with an annular concave line at approximately 1/3 away from the nib; a square frustum with central hole is protruded on top; the pen holder is slightly smaller inside near the conical nib, and four surfaces around are gibbous at the center. The pen cap is an evenly rounded cylinder about 1/4 long of the former, with a square frustum protruded on top. The clip is rectangular with rectangular frustum protruded outside and smooth surface inside. Its head is connected archwise to the top frustum of pen cap and bottom is straight. The clip is slightly longer than the cap by 1/10 of the entire clip.

The Plaintiff M&G claimed: it is the owner of the design patent involved; the Alleged Infringing Product is identical to its patented product and similar to such product in design; and therefore, the two Defendants commit the infringement upon the Plaintiff's design patent. The Plaintiff M&G requested the court to rule that: 1. the two Defendants stop the infringement; 2. the two Defendants destroy all the infringing products in stock and special equipment and molds used to make those products; and 3. the Plaintiff Deli compensates for the Plaintiff's economic losses totaling RMB 1,800,000 and pay reasonable expenses of RMB 200,000 incurred by the Plaintiff for stopping the infringement.

The Defendant Deli argued that the Alleged Infringing Product is neither identical nor similar to the Plaintiff's patented product in design, and therefore it should not be deemed to have infringed upon the Plaintiff's patent; Even if there is an infringement, the compensation and reasonable expenses claimed by the Plaintiff are too high.

The Defendant Kunsen did not make any defense.

[Judgment]

After trial, Shanghai Intellectual Property Court held that the Alleged Infringing Product and the patented product involved are of the same kind of product. The main issue in dispute of this case was whether the alleged infringing design is similar to the patented design. To determine this, the court respectively investigated the impacts of identical and differentiated design features of the alleged infringing design and the patented design on their overall visual effect by applying the "overall observation and integrated conclusion" principle.

As for the identical design features, the style of the patented design is determined by such design features as the shapes of pen holder body and top, pen cap body and top, length of pen cap against pen holder, connection between pen clip and pen cap and their relative length, etc., which are also found in the alleged infringing design. Therefore, it can be concluded that the designs are similar with respect to the overall design style and main design features.

Regarding the differentiated design features, there are four differentiated design features between the alleged infringing design and the patented design and they are not significant enough to make a substantial difference to the overall visual effect: the part inside the clips is hardly noticeable to consumers; the cambers on the lower part of clips are different slightly and locally from the perspective of whole pen and even clip; although the rectangular frustum protrudes outside the clip occupied a large area on the clip, its impact on the overall visual effect of whole pen is limited if such elements as the pen clip's overall shape, size, connection with pen cap and length against pen cap, which largely affect the overall visual effect of the pen, are the same; concave line on the pen holder is a local design feature that had limited impact on the overall visual effect, as it is just intertwined around the pen holder in small area.

As for the impact of color and pattern on the determination of similarity, since color protection isn't explicitly stated in the summary of the patented design, color should not be factored in when determining its scope of protection and infringement thereupon. The alleged infringing design is similar to the patented design in shape but adds some colors and patterns of its own. However, these are additional design elements that have no substantial impact on the judgment of infringement.

The Plaintiff and the Defendant Deli are both leading stationery manufacturers in China, who should put more effort into independent research and development of new products and be aware of the legal risks involved therein. The Defendant Deli infringed upon the Plaintiff's design patent as it, without contributing creative labor, exploited such patent by simply changing or adding non-substantially different design elements and patterns and colors based on the Plaintiff's patented design.

In conclusion, pursuant to Article 118 of the *General Principles of the Civil Law of the People's Republic of China*, and Paragraph 2, Article 11 and Article 65 of the *Patent Law of the People's Republic of China*, Shanghai Intellectual Property Court rendered a judgment that the Defendant Deli Group should immediately stop manufacturing or selling the product that infringed upon the Plaintiff's design patent; the Defendant Kunsen should immediately stop offering to sell or selling the product that infringed upon the Plaintiff's design patent; and the Defendant Deli should compensate for the Plaintiff's economic losses totaling RMB 50, 000 and pay reasonable expenses of RMB 50,000 incurred for stopping the infringement.

No party appealed against the first-instance judgment, and the judgment came into effect.

[Case Study]

As the products involved in this case are pens, which are common in daily life and are alike, except slight differences, in design, the infringement judgment in this case are prone to subjective factors.

Design patent is a special kind of patent right, and is greatly distinguished from invention patent or utility patent when it comes to the objects under protection. Both invention patent and utility patent are designed to protect technical solutions that are used to produce functional effects, while design patent is designed to protect a product design that is used to produce visual effects. Thus, designs are usually protected globally under two models, i. e. under copyright laws and under patent laws. Even in a country where designs are protected under patent laws, there may be different standards on design patent grant and infringement judgment. In China, the standards for granting design patents and judging infringement set out in *Guidelines for Patent Examination* and used in juridical practices are constantly changing. In most circumstances, design patent infringement cases are more complicate and prone to subjective factors compare with invention and utility patent cases. Different judges may sometimes draw completely opposite conclusions on similarity due to the differences in personal experience and cognition.

According to the provisions of Articles 10 and 11 of the *Interpretation of the Supreme People's Court on Several Issues Concerning the Application of Law in the Trial of Patent Infringement Dispute Cases*, a comprehensive judgment should be carried out based on the regular consumers' knowledge and cognitive ability while taking into account the design features of the patented design and the alleged infringing design, as well as the overall visual effect of the designs. This way of determining design similarity is usually referred to as the " overall observation and integrated conclusion" principle. However, this is only a guiding principle. How to apply it to specific cases? How to minimize the influence of subjective factors on judges so as to reach a relatively objective conclusion? A detailed description of the explorations on these questions in this case is presented below:

Firstly, the identical design features and the differentiated design features of the alleged infringing product and the patented design product should be identified respectively.

This process should be completed during court investigation. The parties to a specific case should be guided to make their respective statements as to both the identical design features and the differentiated design features when the two products are compared. If attention is focused on the differentiated design features when judging whether there are any differences between the overall visual effects of the alleged infringing product and the patented design product, the judges tend to magnify the differentiated design features subjectively and jump into the conclusion that the alleged infringing product and the patented design product are not similar.

Secondly, the respective impacts of identical and differentiated design features on overall visual effect should be analyzed based on regular consumers' knowledge and cognitive ability. We should do as follows:

I. In analyzing the impact of the identical design features on overall visual effect, we should first exclude any and all elements which are deemed as usual due to the limitation of function or for any other reason. For example, the round shape of a tire is exclusively determined by the function of tires, so its impact on overall visual effect should be excluded. In this case, the long cylinder shape of the pen which has also been a usual design should be excluded when its impact on the overall visual effect is analyzed. It should be noted that a usual design is different from a prior design. A prior design means a design that has been known by the public domestically and globally prior to the application date. Among prior designs, only the one which has been well known to regular consumers and to which regular consumers can directly associate a product name can be called a usual design. For example, the mention of packing boxes will evoke images of cuboid and cube shapes.

II. We should not exclude the impact of a design element on overall visual effect only because the design element has appeared in a prior design, unless and except it has become a usual design due to the limitation of function or for any other reason or the identical design features of the alleged infringing product and the patented design product have appeared in a single prior design. In China, brand new designs which are developed independently with no reference to prior designs are rare among the granted design patents for the time being. Most design patents adopt elements of prior designs by combination or mixing to form new designs. As for the category of pens involved in this case, pens are usually alike, except slight differences, in design, but the overall shapes, partial shapes and sizes are actually different and unique. Many design elements of pen holder, pen cap and pen clip are identical or similar to those in prior designs. The stability of a granted patent should not be denied just because any of its elements has appeared in a prior design, nor should it be excluded indiscriminately from the factors that have impact on overall visual effect. However, the following are exceptions: I. An element has become a usual design due to the limitation of function or for any other reason (as above); II. The main identical design features of the alleged infringing product and the patented design product have appeared in a single prior design. Thus, the prior design defense is established. In this case, among the identical design features of the alleged infringing product and the patented design product, the main shapes of pen holder and pen cap (evenly elongated rounded cylinder) and the pen cap to pen holder length ratio (The pen cap was about 1/4 long of the pen holder) are already present in a prior design, and the prior design was referred to by Deli as a control design for invalidation application. After the trial, the former Patent Reexamination Board of SIPO held that the patented design substantially differentiates from the control design as it is not identical to the control design substantially and thus made a decision that the granted patent should remain valid. The patented design has passed SIPO's evaluation on compliance with conditions for granting patent rights, patent invalidation examination and other procedures. As the Defendant had no reason to deny its validity, the court could not deny its validity just because a design feature or several design features have appeared in a prior design, nor should it be excluded indiscriminately from the factors having impact on overall visual effect. In this case, the main shapes of pen holder and pen cap of the patented design and the prior design are evenly elongated rounded cylinder, and the pen cap is about 1/4 long of the pen holder. The above main shapes and length ratio indeed substantially have an influence on the overall visual effect, but the pen holder and the pen cap of the prior design have several up to down ridges which have substantial impact on the overall visual effect. In addition, between the alleged infringing product and the patented design product, in addition to their main shapes of pen holder and pen cap and pen cap to pen holder length ratio, there are identical features in top shapes of pen holder and pen cap, the way to connect pen clip and pen cap and the length of pen clip longer than pen cap. All these have significant impact on the overall visual effect, and all these are not seen in a prior design. Therefore, in this case, when considering the impact of identical design features on the overall visual effect, the court did not exclude the main shapes of pen holder and pen cap or the pen cap to pen holder length ratio. After analyzing respective impacts of identical design features and differentiated design features on the overall visual effect, the court held that the alleged infringing product and the patented design product are similar in overall design style and main design features.

III. In the prior design defense, the comparison shall be made with one single prior design, other than several prior designs. If the SIPO confirms that a patented design has met the conditions for grant of a patent or declares in the invalidation declaration proceedings that the patented design is valid, in the infringement case, it is not necessary to question the validity of the patented design, otherwise the granted patent will be put in an unsteady status. If the alleged infringing product is different from a prior design but has some similarities with the prior design, when deciding whether they are substantially identical, the court shall consider the following issues: 1. whether the difference between the alleged infringing product and the prior design is slight and non-substantial; 2. whether the alleged infringing product is derived from a prior design, and the specific derivative method is inspired by a prior design in the identical or a similar category; 3. whether the alleged infringing product is derived from a combination of prior designs or prior design features, and the combination method is inspired by a prior design in the identical or a similar category. In any of the above circumstances, the Defendant's prior design defenses shall be accepted.

IV. The directly visible parts of a product in normal use have more impact on the overall visual effect than other parts of a product. The partial and slight changes that are less easy to be observed have no substantial impact on the overall visual effect. For example, it is less easy for regular consumers to observe the design inside a pen clip as it is located between the pen clip and the pen cap, so it can be concluded that it has no substantial impact on the overall visual effect, and such is the case with the differentiated design feature of the undulated ridges inside the pen clip of the alleged infringing product.

V. The proportion of a differentiated design feature in all design features is a factor in determining its impact on the overall visual effect. In this case, the bottom pen clip of the alleged infringing product is straight, but that of the patented design is cambered; the pen holder of the alleged infringing product has an annular concave line at approximately 1/3 away from the nib, but the patented design does not have the concave design. The court held that the bottom pen clip which is only a slight and partial part in the design of the pen has very limited impact on the overall visual effect; the concave design on the pen holder is at approximately 1/3 away from the nib and is a local design feature that has limited impact on the overall visual effect, as it is just intertwined around the pen holder in small area. It should be noted that the proportion of a differentiated design feature in all design features is only a referential factor, other than a decisive factor, in determining their impact on the general visual effect. A differentiated design feature can't be deemed to have a significant impact on the overall visual effect just because it covers a big area, and other factors should also be taken into consideration. In this case, the pen clip of the alleged infringing design is covered by rectangular frustum protrusions outside, while that of the patented design isn't. The rectangular frustum protrusions outside occupy a large area on the pen clip, but the impact of the pen clip on the overall visual effect mainly depend on its overall shape, size, the method to connect to the pen cap and the length relative to the pen cap. As all these factors are the same, the court held that, the rectangular frustum protrusions covering the pen clip have limited impact on the overall visual effect of the pen, and thus do not constitute substantial difference.

VI. If the color and pattern of a design are not protected, the impact of the color and pattern of the alleged infringing design on its overall visual effect should not be taken into account. Only the design features shown or reflected in the picture or photo below fall in the protection scope of a design patent. Shape, pattern and color were three basic design elements of a product design. If anyone applies for protecting the color of a design, he or she should specify it in a brief description. If he or she does not apply for protecting the color of a design in the brief description, the impact of the color should not be considered when determining the protection scope of a patent and judging an infringement case.

(Writer: Xu Fei)

Attachments:

The Plaintiff's patent

Front View

Top View

Part 1's Left View

The Defendant's product

Judicial Determination of
Priority Right Defense

—Shengji (Shanghai) Household Articles Co. , Ltd. v.
President Starbucks Coffee (Shanghai) Company
Limited et al. on dispute over design patent infringement

[**Abstract**]

Before the date of filing of the application for patent, any person who has already made the identical product and continues to make or use it within the original scope only shall enjoy priority right. The priority right holder shall not be deemed to commit infringement if the priority right holder continues to manufacture the identical product within the original scope, and the follow-up selling of the same identical product shall also not constitute infringement.

[**Case Review**]

Plaintiff: Shengji (Shanghai) Household Articles Co. , Ltd.
Defendant: President Starbucks Coffee (Shanghai) Company Limited
Defendant: Zengcheng Zenghao Stainless Steel Co. , Ltd.
Cause of Action: Dispute over design patent infringement
First-Instance Case No. : (2015) HZMCZ No. 504

Shengji (Shanghai) Household Articles Co. , Ltd. (hereinafter referred to as Shengji Company) is the patentee of the design of "drinking cup (0506 – 2)," the patent application date of which is May 26, 2014, and the date of authorization proclamation fell on October 1, 2014. On June 29, 2015, Shengji Company purchased by notarization one 12oz orange stainless steel tumbler. As shown on the product label, the distributor is President Starbucks Coffee (Shanghai) Company Limited (hereinafter referred to as Starbucks) and the manufacturer is Zengcheng Zenghao Stainless Steel Co., Ltd. (hereinafter referred to as Zenghao Company); item number: 435180. Through comparison, its design is similar to the involved patent.

E-mail correspondences among STRABUCKS COFFEE COMPANY, WOODMAX and Zenghao Company from November 2013 to February 2014 involve the design, mould unloading, problems in delivered samples of a Starbucks cup, etc., and the designd rawing of the cup attached to the emails was almost identical to the design of the allegedly infringing product purchased by notarization.

On February 24, 2014, Starbucks Coffee placed an order with WOODMAX by email for purchasing 10,680 12oz green DIAMAND PHINNY tumblers and 10,008 12oz red DIAMAND PHINNY tumblers. On February 25, 2014, WOODMAX placed an order (with the order number, article number, color, etc. same as the order mentioned above) with Zenghao Company by email, in which the picture of cup is almost identical to the design of the allegedly infringing product, and the only difference is color. Zenghao Company completed packing and customs clearance of the ordered product on June 14, 2014.

On February 2, 2015, Starbucks ordered 1,248 12oz orange stainless steel tumblers from Dongguan Walmax. On February 7, 2015, Dongguan Walmax ordered 1,248 orange stainless steel tumblers from Zenghao Company, and the picture of the cup attached to the order was almost identical to the design of the allegedly infringing product. The order was delivered on April 9, 2015. On June 9, 2015, it was stated on the VAT invoice issued by Dongguan Walmax to Starbucks that a total of 1,260 "435180 12oz orange stainless steel tumblers" were ordered in two batches.

The Plaintiff Shengji Company claimed that it is the patentee of the involved design patent and the product sold by the Defendant Starbucks and produced by the Defendant Zenghao Company fell in the protection scope of the design patent. Thus, it sued Starbucks and Zenghao Company to the court and requested that the defendants stop any infringing behavior and compensate it for economic losses and reasonable expenses totaling RMB 212,200.

The Defendant Starbucks defended that: the alleged infringing product is neither identical to nor similar with the involved patent and does not fall in the protection scope of the involved patent; the alleged infringing product uses a prior design and thus does not constitute infringement; the alleged infringing product had been manufactured before the patent application date, and constitutes prior use, and does not infringe upon the patent right; the alleged infringing product has legitimate source, and should not incur any liability for damage even if there is any infringement.

The Defendant Zenghao Company defended that: the alleged infringing product is neither identical to nor similar with the involved patent and does not fall in the protection scope of the involved patent; the alleged infringing product uses a prior design and thus does not constitute infringement; the alleged infringing product had been manufactured before the patent application date, and constitutes prior use, and does not infringe upon the patent right; the alleged infringing product has legitimate source, and should not incur any liability for damage even if there is any infringement.

[**Judgment**]

After the trial, Shanghai Intellectual Property Court concluded that the Plaintiff is the patentee of the design patent of the involved "drinking cup (0506 – 2)"; and without permission of the patentee, any entity or individual shall not manufacture, offer to sell, sell or import the patented product for the purpose of production and operation. There is no substantial difference in the impact on the overall visual effect between the alleged infringing design and the patented design; the two designs are similar designs; and the alleged infringing product falls in the protection scope of the Plaintiff's involved design patent. However, according to the submitted evidence, the ordered product had been designed and manufactured through the coordination and cooperation of Starbucks, WOODMAX and Zenghao Company before the patent application date. Zenghao Company accepted the order on February 25, 2014, and finished the manufacture, packing and customs declaration of the first batch of ordered product on June 14, 2014. In other words, Zenghao Company got prepared for producing the ordered product before the patent application date, i. e. May 26, 2014, and completed the production. The alleged infringing product was almost (only different in color) identical to the first batch of ordered product that Zenghao Company began to manufacture before the patent application date. Color is not within the protection scope of the involved patent and should not be considered in determining whether the design features of the two products are identical, so the alleged infringing product is identical to the product that Zenghao Company manufactured before the patent application date. No evidence proves that the production by Zenghao Company according to new orders is beyond the original scope. Zenghao Company had already manufactured the same product before the application date of the involved patent, and only continued to manufacture the product within the original scope. Therefore, it enjoys the priority right and the priority right defense made by Zenghao Company should be established. The priority right holder shall not be deemed to conduct infringement if the priority right holder continues to manufacture the same product within the original scope, and the follow-up selling of the same product manufactured shall also not constitute infringement. Starbucks is the distributor of the alleged infringing product, and provides evidence proving that the product sold by it is purchased from Zenghao Company which enjoys the priority right. Thus, the sale of the product manufactured by Zenghao Company shall not constitute infringement.

In conclusion, in accordance with provisions of Article 59(2) and Article 69 (2) of the *Patent law of the People's Republic of China* and Articles 8 and 15(3) of the *Interpretation by the Supreme People's Court on Some Issues Concerning the Application of Laws to the Trial of Patent Infringement Disputes*, Shanghai Intellectual Property Court decided to reject the claims of the Plaintiff Shengji Company.

After the first instance judgment was issued, the parties did not lodge an appeal and the first instance judgment had come into force.

[Case Study]

Article 69 (2) of the Patent Law provides for priority right. Before the application date of a patent, any person who has already manufactured the identical product, used identical method or has made necessary preparations for the manufacture or use of the identical product and continues to manufacture the identical product or use the method within the original scope shall not be deemed to have infringed upon the patent right. There have been a lot of disagreements in judicial practice as to the interpretation and application of the provision. The issue in dispute of this case is whether the priority right defense made by Starbucks and Zenghao Company can be established.

Ⅰ. Nature of Priority Right

The priority right system is closely related to the prior patent application system. The person who first applies for and is granted a patent is not necessarily the first person to make or implement an invention. However, due to the monopoly nature of a patent, after the patent right is granted, no entity or individual may exploit the patent without authorization of the patentee. In this case, in order to make up for the deficiency of the doctrine of patent application priority and reasonably balance the interest relationship between the priority right holder and the patentee, the Patent Law stipulates the priority right system which restricts the exercise of patent right to some extent.

As to the nature of the priority right, first, the priority right exists in relation to a particular patent right, and only after the patent is granted does the related priority right matter come into being; secondly, the holder of the priority right is not specific, and there may be more than one priority right holders; thirdly, for right exercise, a priority right holder may continue to manufacture and use within the original scope but may not request any other person to take or not to take any action; finally, for right exercise effect, there is no such thing as infringement upon a priority right or subsequent remedies, and the priority right holder may only use it to defend against any infringement claim. In conclusion, a priority right is a self-exercise right in nature and only has the function of defending. There is no remedy for this right in law and it is more like a defending right.

Ⅱ. Priority Right and Prior Art (Design)

Priority right defense and prior design defense are both common non-infringement defenses against accusations of patent infringements. They are likely to overlap in fact finding. In practice, if the production of the identical product or the use of the identical method by a prior user before the patent application date is not made public, such user shall only claim for priority right defense; if the identical product or method has been made public before the patent application date due to use or sale, such product or method shall constitute a prior art, thus, the priority right defense and prior art (design) defense can be claimed simultaneously.

As they are different defenses, different trial courses shall apply in juridical practices. The priority right defense is the cause of statutory restriction for right exercise and also the exception when the infringement accusation is not true; and the prior art defense is one of reasonable use situation where the alleged infringing activity is essentially a non-infringing activity, rather than exceptional provision of infringement. They are subject to different conditions for accepting a defense. There are four conditions for accepting a priority right defense: whether or not the prior user has produced relevant products (used relevant methods) or made necessary preparations for such production (use) before the patent application date; whether or not relevant products are the same products; whether or not the prior art is obtained legally; and whether or not the production is subject to the original scope. There are two conditions for accepting a prior art defense: whether or not the comparison art forms the prior art; and whether alleged infringing product applies the prior art. The rules for comparison are different. Establishment of infringement is the prerequisite for application of priority right defense. Therefore, in case of priority right defense, there should be two technical comparisons: the technical solution adopted for the alleged infringing product and the patent claim should be first compared, and the second technical comparison, namely whether the alleged infringing product and the prior product made before the patent application date are identical, is necessary only if they are the same or identical. However, prior art defense is not necessarily based on the establishment of infringement. Prior art defense can be established by direct comparison of the alleged infringing product and the prior art, and it is not necessary to compare the technical solution adopted for the alleged infringing product and the patented technical solution. The consequences of two defense establishments are different. After the establishment of priority right defense, the production by the prior user beyond the original scope is still likely to constitute an infringement; after the establishment of prior art defense, the allegation of the patentee that the production behavior of the same defendant constitutes an infringement is not legally established.

III. Elements to be Considered in Determining Priority Right Defense

1. Determination of the original scope. The original intent of the priority right system is to make up for the deficiency of application priority principle. If the original scope is too extensive, it will affect the patent application system to some

extent. Thus, the juridical explanation tends to restrict the original scope by defining it as production scale, which is more a quantitative restriction of the original scope. In addition, the explanation of the original scope has limits on exercising entities. If a prior user assigns its technology to or grants a license to any other party after the application date, and the alleged infringing party claims that the exercise by the other party falls in the original scope, such claim shall be denied, except that the such technology or design is assigned or succeeded together with the whole original company. To distribute the burden of proof as to the original scope, for priority right defense, a prior user shall provide valid evidence to prove the existence of the priority right against the infringement allegation by the patentee, and the defender shall bear the burden of proof.

In this case, Zenghao Company and Starbucks does not provide evidence to prove the accurate production scale of Zenghao Company before the patent application date, but the evidences provided by them can prove that, Zenghao Company delivered 20,688 products in June 2014 according to the order dated February 2014 which was issued before the patent application date. The alleged infringing product was purchased on June 29, 2015, and the VAT invoice dated June 9, 2015 indicated that Zenghao Company only delivered 1,260 products to Starbucks. From the perspective of quantity, 1,260 fell into the scope of 20,688, and the real manufacturer is Zenghao Company without change in the subject of implementation, so the court determined that the evidence is inadequate to prove that the production of Zenghao Company exceeds the original scope.

2. Determination of identical product. If the interpretation of identical product is too broad or too narrow, the original purpose of the priority right system and its implementation effect will be impaired, so the interpretation of identical product shall take into account the original intent of the patent system. A patent right is an exclusive enforcement right to a technical solution, and the protection of a prior user is based on the protection of the prior technical solution. Thus, the determination identical product shall involve the technical solution itself, and product name, product model or other designations are not related. Identical product refers to the circumstance where the alleged infringing product is the same as the relevant product manufactured before the patent application date. The two products can either be identical products, or be materially identical with the relevant part of the involved patent. In this regard, first, identical product refers to the comparison between the

alleged infringing product and the product made before the patent application date; second, the standard for such comparison is whether their design features are identical or have no substantial difference. There are two circumstances: two products are identical and all the design features are the same; notwithstanding the fact that they are not identical, they have the same design features corresponding to the patent involved.

In this case, after comparison, the alleged infringing product is almost identical with the design drawing attached to the emails sent between November 2013 and February 2014, and the design shown in the pictures of cup attached to the order placed on February 25, 2014. That is to say, the alleged infringing product is basically identical with the design of the ordered product produced by Zenghao Company before the patent application date. The color of the product is not within the protection scope of the involved patent, and does not affect the determination whether the two products and the relevant design part of the involved patent are identical. Therefore, the alleged infringing product is identical with the relevant product produced by Zenghao Company prior to the patent application date.

3. The product is produced before the patent application date and the prior art is legally acquired. A prior user shall have produced the identical product, used the identical method, or have made necessary preparations for such production and use before the patent application date. The product produced and the method used are easily defined. Production records and sale orders can serve as evidence. The explanation of "have made necessary preparations for such production and use" shall include technical preparation and production preparation. In addition, technical source shall be legal. The defense shall not be claimed based on technologies or designs illegally obtained.

In this case, by taking into account all the existing evidences, it can be determined that Starbucks, WOODMAX and Zenghao Company worked together to design and produce the ordered products. Zenghao Company accepted the order on February 25, 2014 and completed the production, packing and customs clearance of all the ordered products on June 14, 2014. Therefore, it can be determined that Zenghao Company had made preparations for producing relevant products and produced relevant products before the patent application date May 26, 2014, and the technical source is legal.

4. Defending entities of priority right. A prior user may propose the priority

right defense. The prior user generally refers to the manufacturer, and the activities he defends include production of the identical product and use of the identical method, as well as subsequent sale and offer for sale. Furthermore, in an infringing case, the distributor may also propose the priority right defense. In this case, Zenghao Company had already manufactured the same products before the involved patent application date, only continues to manufacture the products within the original scope and enjoys the priority right. Thus, the priority right defense made by Zenghao Company should be established. The priority right holder shall not be deemed to conduct infringement if the priority right holder continues to manufacture the identical product within the original scope, and the follow-up selling of the identical product manufactured shall also not constitute infringement. Starbucks is the retailer of the alleged infringing product, and provides evidence to prove that the product sold by it was from Zenghao Company which enjoys the priority right. A claim may also be made that the sale of products manufactured by Zenghao Company which enjoys the priority right shall not constitute infringement.

(Writer: Chen Yaoyao)

Conditions for A Court to Accept Unilateral Authentication Conclusion as Evidence

—Sandvik Intellectual Property AB v. Zhejiang MP Mining Equipment Corp. , Ltd. on dispute over invention patent infringement

[Abstract]

During the trial of a patent infringement dispute case, due to the inaccessibility of sales channels of the alleged infringing product or the patentee's limited capability in collecting evidence, the patentee is sometimes unable to obtain the real object of the alleged infringing product, and can only submit evidence by means of photo and video. If that is the case, how to analyze by comparing with these photos and videos to make comparative infringement judgment (or inference) is a major problem to be solved in trial practice. Although there is no real object of the alleged infringing product in this case, according to the photos and videos provided by the patentee and in combination with the expertise of technical staff, all the technical solutions of the alleged infringing product are confirmed. Finally, the plaintiff's claims are supported. This case shows that the court goes to great lengths indeed to protect intellectual property rights.

[Case Review]

Plaintiff: Sandvik Intellectual Property AB
Defendant: Zhejiang MP Mining Equipment Corp. , Ltd.
Cause of Action: Dispute over invention patent infringement
First-Instance Case No. : (2015) HZMCZ No. 748
The Plaintiff Sandvik Intellectual Property AB filed to the court the following

claims: 1. the Defendant should immediately stop its activities that have infringed upon the invention patent right owned by the Plaintiff in No. ZL03820653. 6 "a crusher and a method to crush raw materials," including manufacturing, sales and offering for sales of the alleged infringing products; 2. the Defendant should compensate the Plaintiff for its economic losses totaling RMB 1 million; and 3. the Defendant should pay the Plaintiff for its reasonable expenses totaling RMB 364, 580. Facts and Causes: The Plaintiff made an application to National Intellectual Property Administration, PRC for an invention patent titled "a crusher and a method to crush raw materials" on August 27, 2003, and the patent was granted on October 10, 2007. It remains valid now. During a market survey made on November 26, 2014 by the Plaintiff at Bauma China 2014 held at Shanghai New International Expo Center, it discovered that the GS300 vertical impact crusher displayed by the Defendant (hereinafter referred to as the alleged infringing product) infringed upon the above-said invention patent right of the Plaintiff. At the same time, the Plaintiff found that the "MP Products" catalog listed on the Defendant's website (www. mpcrusher. com) also included the GS300 vertical impact crusher. After analyzing the alleged infringing product, the Plaintiff believed that the alleged infringing product completely falls into the protection scope of the Plaintiff's patent. SSIPEX Judicial Authentication Center also issued the "Judicial Authentication Opinion" stating that the technical features of the alleged infringing product are identical with all the technical features of the Plaintiff's Patent Claims 1 – 7. The Plaintiff held that, the Defendant, without permission, used the invention patent of the Plaintiff to manufacture, sell, offer to sell or use the alleged infringing product and infringed upon the invention patent right enjoyed by the Plaintiff, so it shall bear the civil liability for stopping the infringement and making compensation for losses.

The Defendant, Zhejiang MP Mining Equipment Corp. , Ltd. , argued that the technical features of the alleged infringing product are not completely identical with the technical features of the Plaintiff's patent as the rotor of the alleged infringing product is four-channel and the "L-shaped baffle" angle of the alleged infringing product is 100° instead of 90° as stated in the Plaintiff's patent. The Defendant requested to reject all the claims made by the Plaintiff.

On November 26, 2014, at the request of the Plaintiff, a public notary from Shanghai Changning Notary Office and the Plaintiff's lawyer came to the site of "Bauma China 2014" held at Shanghai New International Expo Center. The

Plaintiff's lawyer got two brochures and one name card at a booth named "Quzhou MP Mining Equipment Co. , Ltd. ," and took photos and shot videos of the booth and the displayed objects with a camera of the Notary Office. Shanghai Changning Notary Office witnessed the aforesaid process and issued (2014) HCZZ No. 8107 Notarial Certificate. According to the Notarial Certificate, the Plaintiff's lawyer took photos and shot videos of the appearance and internal structure of the alleged infringing product of this case. The Defendant acknowledged that the alleged infringing product was produced by it.

On September 9, 2015, Huiye Law Firm appointed SSIPEX Judicial Authentication Center to authenticate and conclude whether the GS300 vertical impact crusher manufactured by Quzhou MP Mining Equipment Co. , Ltd. has all the identical or equivalent technical features stated in Patent Claims 1 – 7 of the invention patent with Announcement No. "CN100341627C" granted to Sandvik Intellectual Property AB. The reviewed documents included: 1. one CN100341627C patent certificate in paper; and 2. one (2014) HCZZ No. 8107 Notarial Certificate (including one disk of site booth videos and photos). On October 29, 2015, SSIPEX Judicial Authentication Center issued the HGS [2015] JZ No. 011 Judicial Authentication Opinion on Infringement stating that the technical features of the GS300 vertical impact crusher are identical with all the technical features set out the Patent Claims 1 – 7 of the CN100341627C invention patent. When appearing in court for questioning, an appraiser, Ye Zhichan, expressly stated that even though the reviewed materials in the process of judicial authentication are only photos and videos, it can be seen that the alleged infringing product has an L-shaped guide rod; although it is uncertain if it is a 90°angle, it can be inferred that the technical effect of the L-shaped guide rod has the same technical effect as the corresponding technical feature stated in the involved patent.

[Judgment]

Shanghai Intellectual Property Court held that, on the basis of Claims 1, 2 and 3, Claim 4 added a technical feature that the horizontal leg of the L-shaped guide rod is toward the rotating direction of the rotor, so that any dust generated by the rotor will be obstructed by the vertical leg of the guide rod in the direction having an upward component and a tangential component about the rotor. Through comparison, the alleged infringing product has an L-shaped guide bar, and its horizontal leg is located between the hexagonal internal and external hoppers, tangential to the rotor, so it is in the rotating direction of the rotor. Its vertical leg and the upper form a relatively sealed structure, so it can prevent the dust generated by the rotor. The court held that: firstly, the Defendant had no evidence to prove that the L-shaped guide rod angle of the alleged infringing product is 100° instead of 90°, and the photo and video materials of the alleged infringing product as provided by the Plaintiff show no prominent difference in angle; secondly, even if the L-shaped guide rod angle of the alleged infringing product is 100°, compared with 90°, it is an equivalent feature that basically realizes the same function and achieves the same effect by basically the same means, namely that both of them can realize the functions of "accumulating raw materials to form a slope body" and "blocking dust generated by the rotor," and the Defendant did not have evidence to prove that the use of a 100° guide rod is capable of other significantly different functions and effects; finally, according to the last paragraph of the patent specification, "however, it is possible to form a prefabricated slope body, such as steel plate, ceramic tile or similar plate, which will have an expected tangential inclination of rotor immediately after the crusher is activated," and the L-shaped guide rod angle is not limited to 90°. Thus, Shanghai Intellectual Property Court held that the alleged infringing product has the added technical feature of Claim 4. In addition, the court did not support the prior art defense proposed by the Defendant. For the purpose of determining the amount of compensation, the court applied the statutory compensation rules, taking into account the contract price of the alleged infringing product exported to Vietnam.

Shanghai Intellectual Property Court issued (2015) HZMCC No. 748 Civil Judgment on November 4, 2016, requesting that the Defendant Zhejiang MP Mining Equipment Co., Ltd. immediately stop its infringement upon the invention patent titled "a crusher and a method to crush raw materials" (Patent No. ZL03820653.6) owned by the Plaintiff Sandvik Intellectual Property AB and compensate the Plaintiff for its economic losses in the amount of RMB 500,000 and its reasonable expenses in the amount of RMB 120,000. After the judgment was issued, neither of the Parties made an appeal, and the judgment became legally effective.

[Case Study]

This case mainly involves two issues: I. when will the court accept unilateral authentication (particularly non-physical materials) as evidence; and II. how to determine whether the technical features not visible in photo and video materials fall into the protection scope of a patent.

I. Conditions for the acceptance of unilateral authentication (particularly non-physical materials) as evidence

Generally, in the trial of a patent infringement case, the plaintiff applies to the court for fact finding of technical problems; the court commits to a qualified expert institution agreed by the parties or designated by the court the authentication task; the authentication proceeds under the guidance of the court, including identification of the scope and contents of reviewed materials, appraisers, convening of site authentication meeting and implementation of time schedule; and finally, the expert institution issues to the court the authentication opinion, and the court makes a judgment on authentication conclusion after the authentication opinion is questioned by the parties. In recent years, with the increasing specialization of patent cases, many parties choose to appoint professional intellectual property judicial authentication institutions to conduct qualitative infringement authentication in the stage of investigation and evidence collection. On one hand, it can be used to predict the possibility of winning the lawsuits. On the other hand, it can be used as important evidence to support their arguments. In fact, the courts' attitude towards unilateral authentication has also changed stage by stage. At the very beginning, almost all unilateral authentication conclusions were rejected. Later, parts of authentication conclusions were accepted. Nowadays, technical support is resorted to and a unilateral authentication can be accepted after the opinions of both the plaintiff and defendant are fully considered as evidence. In the field of patent trial, such systems as technical investigators, technical consulting experts and expert jurors have brought confidence to judges in ascertaining technical facts, and it has also reduced unnecessary authentication costs and lightened the load on the parties concerned.

Undoubtedly, the acceptance of unilateral authentication is not without conditions. It is possible that the conclusions of some unilateral authentications are denied because there is something wrong with the materials entrusted for authentication, logic reasoning etc. According to relevant provisions of the Civil Procedure Law and the Rules of Evidence in Civil Proceedings, authentication opinion is one of the legal types of evidence, and the court will decide after examination whether it can become a basis for the final decision. When examining the authentication opinion issued by an appraiser, the judge shall check if it contains the following items: (1) the entrusting party's name and the entrusted authentication scope; (2) materials entrusted for authentication; (3) the basis for authentication and the scientific and technological means used; (4) a description of the authentication process; (5) a definite authentication conclusion; (6) a statement of the appraiser's qualification; (7) signature and seal of the appraiser and the authentication institution. Where a party has evidence sufficient to refute the authentication conclusion made by an institution engaged by the other party unilaterally and applies for a new authentication, the people's court shall approve the application. In this case, the unilateral authentication report submitted by the Plaintiff to the court complies with the aforesaid (1), (4), (5), (6) and (7) items, but fails to comply with the aforesaid (2) and (3) items due to the lack of physical materials. The court, after consulting related technical experts, made further interpretation. 1. In general, an invention or utility model patent infringement dispute case is different from a design patent infringement dispute case, and product pictures can't reflect the technical features of the alleged infringing product. That means an actual product shall be submitted for examination and comparison, and such actual product shall be the alleged infringing product recognized by both the plaintiff and the defendant. In this case, because of some objective reasons, the Plaintiff could not obtain the real product, but presented the notarized videos and photos which were taken at the expo showing the internal and external structures of the alleged infringing product. The court held that the notarized videos and photos are objective; their contents reflect most of the technical features of the real product, supported by relevant product data as shown on the Defendant's official website. The court could confirm their authenticity, and deem them a substitute for the actual product. 2. Although the contents of videos and pictures cannot fully present some technical features, the appraiser compared the technical features and made a logical inference based on the technical parameters shown on the Defendant's official website, assembly relationships between product parts and mechanical principles.

3. As for the unilateral authentication report submitted by the Plaintiff, the Defendant neither produce any powerful arguments when questioned by experts in court nor apply for a new authentication. To sum up, the court believed that the basis, technical means and logical reasoning of the unilateral authentication are persuasive, and the final authentication conclusion is convincing.

Thus, it can be seen that, in addition to the general requirements of applicable laws, the conditions for a court to accept a unilateral authentication include: 1. the authenticity and relevance of reviewed materials shall be subject to strict examination. The preferred practice is notarization or the counter-parties' admission, and generally speaking a real object of the alleged infringing product is required. If there is reasonable ground for the failure to provide the real object, any video or photo that clearly shows the technical features is acceptable. 2. The appraiser is required to accept technical examination so as to prevent the authentication institution from making an unconvincing conclusion by simply stating comparative results in order to cater to the needs of the entrustor. Specifically, the court sets higher requirements on the reasoning process, requiring the appraiser to elaborate on and list the evidences, participate in the technical identification procedures organized by the court, and respond to questions (orally or in writing) from technical investigators and consulting experts hired by the court (not limited to trial). 3. The counter-party does not produce any powerful arguments against the unilateral authentication. In many cases, most of the defendants have a negative attitude towards the prosecution, neither presenting a strong rebuttal nor actively participating in the new authentication procedure. Under such circumstances, it is quite important to adopt the unilateral authentications for the trial of such cases.

II. Infringement inference for undetectable technical features

The infringement inference in a case without physical evidence includes two circumstances:

1. Technical features detectable from video and photo materials. The appearance of the technical features is visible in the video materials, but the specific parameters can't be measured. In this case, as for the technical feature of the L-shaped guide rod, the appraiser expressly, when appearing in court for questioning, stated that even though the reviewed materials in the process of judicial authentication are photos and videos, it could be seen clearly that the alleged infringing product has an L-

shaped guide rod; notwithstanding that he could not see if it is a 90° angle, he could infer that the technical effect of the L-shaped guide rod has the same technical effect as the corresponding technical feature stated in the involved patent. In this aspect, after consulting with experts and carefully reading the patent description, the court supported the appraiser's opinion. The court held that the L-shaped guide rod angle of the alleged infringing product is not a vertical 90° angle, but it was an equivalent feature that basically realizes the same function and achieves the same effect by basically the same means.

2. Technical features undetectable from video and photo materials. In this case, a technical feature is stated in Claim 1 of the patent concerned-"the first feeder (56, 90 and 96) is to feed the first stream of raw materials vertically to the rotor." According to the patent description, 56 refers to an internal hopper, 90 refers to a sliding throttle valve, and 96 refers to an internal hopper inlet. However, no sliding throttle valve is shown in the video and photo materials. In this aspect, it was suggested that "the first feeder" is a functional technical feature whose structure is expressly stated in the claims, so the alleged infringing product does not have this technical feature corresponding to "the first feeder." In this aspect, after consulting with the technical investigator, the court held that, even if the sliding throttle valve does not appear in the video materials, according to applicable laws and regulations as well as the words on the patent description, it can be inferred that the alleged infringing product has such technical feature due to the following reasons: (1) according to the provisions of Article 19(4) of the *Rules for Implementation of the Patent Law of People's Republic of China*, any technical feature set out in claims can be referred to by the reference sign in the appended drawing, and such sign shall follow the technical feature and be bracketed to facilitate the understanding of the claim. No reference sign may be deemed as a limitation on the understanding of the claims. Thus, the sliding throttle valve (90) is inserted only for reference to the part on the appended drawing. It is a preferential technical option instead of a necessary feature. In other words, to realize the process of "feeding the first stream of raw materials to the rotor," in addition to an internal hopper (56) and an internal hopper inlet (96), the first feeder may have (but not be obligated to) the sliding throttle valve; (2) whether " the first feeder" is a functional feature. According to the provisions of Article 8 of the *Interpretation II by the Supreme People's Court on Some Issues Concerning the Application of Laws to the Trial of Patent Infringement*

Disputes, functional features refer to the technical features which define the structures, components, procedures, conditions or the mutual relationship thereof, among others, through their functions or effects in invention and creation, except when the ordinary workers in the field can directly and explicitly determine the specific exploitation mode for achieving the aforesaid functions or effects only by reading the claims. After reading the technical background and invention content of the patent description, the court held that the invention point of the involved patent is the second feeder, and the first feeder is a prior art in the field, so it should not be deemed as a functional technical feature. The video materials show an internal hopper (56) and an internal hopper inlet (96). The appraiser also said that he could see the first feeder, and the court confirmed the appraiser's remark.

On conclusion, the court held that, in a patent infringement case without physical evidence, even if video materials can't demonstrate certain technical features, the court can, with the aid of authentication opinion, technical support including technical investigation and interpretation of the patent claims, infer the existence of patent infringement and make a fair judgment.

（Writer：Hu Mi）

IV

Civil Dispute Cases
of Unfair Competition

Affirmation of Unfair Competition in Online Live Broadcast of E-Sports Games

—Shanghai Yaoyu Culture Media Co. , Ltd. v. Guangzhou Douyu Network Technology Co. , Ltd. on copyright infringement and unfair competition dispute

[Abstract]

With the development of e-sports games industry, unfair competition disputes involving the industry are increasing, and lags, limitations and other problems existing in the *Anti-Unfair Competition Law* about specific unfair competition behaviors are becoming more and more prominent. As the principle provisions of Article 2 of the *Anti-Unfair Competition Law* were applied in this case, any person who, without express authorization or permission, broadcasted on live e-sports games and enjoyed business results from e-sports games invested in, sponsored and operated by others for its own business benefits and competition advantages shall be deemed to have a hitchhike, violating the good faith principle stipulated in the *Anti-Unfair Competition Law*, betraying generally recognized business ethics, damaging lawful rights and interests of the games operators, thus constituting an unfair competition.

[Case Review]

Plaintiff (Appellee) : Shanghai Yaoyu Culture Media Co. , Ltd. (Yaoyu)

Defendant (Appellant) : Guangzhou Douyu Network Technology Co. , Ltd. (Douyu)

Cause of Action : Copyright infringement and unfair competition dispute

First-Instance Case No.：（2015）PMS（Z）CZ No. 191

Second-Instance Case No.：（2015）HZMZZ No. 641

DOTA2, a world-famous e-sports game developed by Valve Corporation, was operated by Beijing Perfect World Network Technology Co., Ltd in Chinese Mainland. In 2014, the Appellee (the Plaintiff in the first instance) Shanghai Yaoyu Culture Media Co., Ltd. (Yaoyu) and the aforesaid operator entered into a strategic cooperation contract under which the two parties would jointly operate 2015 DOTA2 Asia Championships. Through the contract, Yaoyu was granted an exclusive license to broadcast the event in Mainland China and was responsible for the whole implementation and management of the event (including players management, event promotion, venue leasing, venue setting-up, equipment leasing and purchase, host employment, event presentation, logistic support, as well as program filming, production, Live Broadcasting, NVOD and VOD). The parties also agreed on a total price for the event, i.e. RMB 11,700,704, of which RMB 8,200,704 would be paid by Yaoyu.

Yaoyu hosted the event from January to February 2015, which included qualifiers and finals. 120 qualifiers were held in January 2015 and all the teams contested on Internet with computers in this phase. The top teams in these qualifiers and other invited teams contested in offline finals during February 5 – 9, 2015 at the venue provided by Yaoyu in Shanghai. During the aforesaid period, Yaoyu broadcasted in real time the event on live through"huomao TV". In addition, Yaoyu exclusively granted Huya (except for huomao TV) a license to broadcast the event, both Live Broadcasting and Re-broadcasting, for total royalties of RMB 6 million.

However, Douyu broadcasted the event by intercepting match screens on the client end from the onlooker view and broadcasting in real time them with host reviews on its website on live without authorization. Yaoyu alleged that Douyu broadcasted 80 qualifiers of the event, but Douyu argued that it only broadcasted 8 qualifiers on live, during January 6 – 28, 2015. On January 15, 2015, when Yaoyu applied for notarization of evidence preservation, Douyu broadcasted on live two sessions, i.e. DK v. TongFu and HGT v. Inv, in about 1 hour, and also announced in advance the live broadcasting of another 4 sessions on the same day.

Yaoyu held that Douyu, without authorization, intercepted event screens and broadcasted, in real time and on live, the event, and thus infringed upon legal interests of Yaoyu. Therefore, Yaoyu filed a lawsuit before Shanghai Pudong New

Area People's Court to require Douyu to: 1. stop its infringement; 2. compensate for its economic losses in the amount of RMB 8 million and reasonable expenses in the amount of RMB 211,000 (including RMB 200,000 attorney fees and RMB 11,000 notary fees); 3. publish a statement on*Xinmin Evening News* to eliminate the effects.

Douyu argued that the client end of the involved game had the onlooker view function that could provide 10 different views of the same session for onlookers and did not limit the outflow of event screens. The footage in live broadcast of Douyu came from one of the onlooker views and differentiated from the live broadcast of Yaoyu due to different views. Douyu did not have any infringement or unfair competition, so Douyu requested the court to reject all claims of Yaoyu.

[Judgment]

Pudong New Area People's Court of Shanghai held that Douyu, with the knowledge that Yaoyu invested a lot in and operated the event and without express authorization or permission, broadcasted on live some sessions of the event for its users, directly damaging lawful rights and interests of Yaoyu, disturbing normal operation order of the e-sports games industry, violating the good faith principle and generally recognized business ethics, thus constituting an unfair competition against Yaoyu. Thus, according to the provisions of Article 2(1), Article 9(1) and Article 20 of the *Anti-Unfair Competition Law of the People's Republic of China*, and Article 15(1)(ⅵ) and (ⅷ) and Article 15(2) of the *Tort Law of the People's Republic of China*, the court decided: 1. The Defendant shall compensate the Plaintiff for its economic losses in the amount of RMB 1 million and its reasonable right protection expenses in the amount of RMB 100,000, i.e. RMB 1.1 million in total; 2. The Defendant shall publish at a prominent place of Douyu Website (www. douyutv. com) a statement to eliminate adverse impact from its unfair competition; 3. All other claims of the Plaintiff shall be rejected.

Douyu appealed to Shanghai Intellectual Property Court and asserted that at present, the domestic games broadcasting websites mostly applied such method that the pictures of events were cut out through the client and then broadcasted to the players with the comments and incidental music of its own platform, while the game makers never had any objection to that; the Game Client involved in this case didn't have any tip that the broadcast through cutting out pictures was prohibited; according to the civil principle that no action was guilty without explicit provision in the law, the behavior that Douyu broadcasted the screens obtained through the client with creative comments made as an onlooker was substantially a report about the event involved, and such behavior was not beyond the reasonable use range of onlooker function of Game Client. The application of Article 2 of the *Anti-Unfair Competition Law* in the first instance was wrong.

Yaoyu defended that any sponsorship or live broadcasting or rebroadcasting of an e-sports game on any games broadcasting website required the license from the operator or the licensor and the payment of royalties and this was common practice and business practice internationally and domestically. The function of watching the event through the client was provided for personal purpose only, other than for business purpose. The unfair competition behavior of Douyu affected the Appellee's ability to sign contracts with advertisers and licensors, diverted the attentions and traffics of the Appellee's website, and damaged the economic interests of the Appellee.

The second instance court held that, in this case, through the agreement between Yaoyu and Chengdu Perfect, the Appellee was granted an exclusive license to broadcast the event in Chinese mainland and was responsible for the whole implementation and management of the event (including players management, event promotion, venue leasing, venue setting-up, equipment leasing and purchase, host employment, event presentation, logistic support, as well as program filming, production, Live Broadcasting, NVOD and VOD). The Appellee assumed all the implementation expenses. Yaoyu had the right to receive a return as it contributed series of labor, material and financial investment, and increased website traffic and advertising revenue, enhanced the popularity, and strengthened the stickiness of network users through video broadcasting, and also increased the economic value of the live broadcasting platform. Thus, it is a long-standing usual practice in e-sports games industry that the broadcasting of an e-sports game requires the license of the game operator. It follows the general business principle "one who invests will gain". It protects the legitimate interests of game operators. It conforms to the good faith principle in market competition. Douyu failed to make any investment to the organization and operation of the event involved and failed to obtain the video broadcasting right, while it enjoyed free of charge the commercial achievements arising from the event organized and operated by Yaoyu by investing lots of manpower, material resources and financial resources for the purpose of seeking commercial benefits and competitive advantages, which was a behavior of "hitchhike" in fact, captured the number of audiences which originally belonged to Yaoyu, caused the serious bypass of Yaoyu's website traffic, affected the advertising revenue capacity of Yaoyu, damaged Yaoyu's commercial opportunities and competitive advantages and weakened the value-added force of Yaoyu's online live platform. For these reasons, the behavior of Douyu breached the principle of good faith in the Anti-Unfair Competition Law, violated the recognized business ethics, damaged the legal interests and rights of Yaoyu and destroyed the market competition orders, and was obviously illegitimate. Accordingly, the appeal was rejected and the original judgment was upheld.

[Case Study]

This case is the first case of online broadcast dispute of e-sports game event in China. However, the e-sports games industry has been developing rapidly in China in recent years, so the limits of competition freedom among competitors in this industry and how to protect intellectual property rights are hot issues attracting people's attention.

Ⅰ. Freedom and regulation of market competition

The competition in the e-sports games industry is the same as the general market competition. We should not only encourage free competition among competitors in the industry to promote vigorous development of the industry, but also prevent laissez-faire competition, so as not to disturb and destroy the whole market order. Free competition, simply speaking, refers to the market competition conducted by all market participants without external intervention. Generally, free competition can make market participants follow the survival of the fittest principle, and make the allocation of resources further optimized. The more intense the competition, the more optimized the allocation of resources, the more prosperous the market economy will be. But encouraging free competition in the market does not mean allowing disorderly and vicious unfair competition.

The freedom of competition must be based on the principle of fairness, which is an ethical norm of free competition and an appropriate regulation and correction of the freedom of competition. According to Article 2 (1) of the Anti-Unfair Competition Law, in carrying on transactions in the market, operators shall follow the principle of voluntariness, equality, fairness, good faith, and observe generally recognized business ethics. These are basic requirements of fair competition for market participants. And the generally recognized business ethics refer to generally recognized and accepted behavior standards in a particular business field. They are public and general.① The principles of fairness and good faith constitute the fundamental competition principles, and generally accepted business ethics are specific business practice formed on the basis of these principles. The essence of these principles set forth in Article 2(1) of the Anti-Unfair Competition Law is that market participants should respect a fair competition order in market competition.

II. Ascertainment of unfair competition in this case

The *Annual Report on Intellectual Property Rights Cases of the Supreme People's Court* (2010) issued by the Supreme People's Court in 2011, which analyzed and commented Shandong Food Import and Export Co. , Ltd. et al. v. Ma Daqing et al. on unfair competition dispute case, provided guidelines for handling similar cases. The Supreme People's Court held that when determining unfair competition according to Articles 2(1) and (2) of the *Anti-Unfair Competition Law*, the following conditions should be satisfied: 1. the law doesn't make special provisions for such competition behavior; 2. the legitimate rights and interests of other operators have been actually damaged due to such competition behavior; and 3. such competition behavior is illegitimate or accountable as it violates the principle of good faith and generally accepted business ethics. In the case study, the Supreme People's Court also stated that business opportunities which can be reasonably expected under normal circumstances can become the legal interests protected by the law, especially by the Anti-Unfair Competition Law; however, only when the competitors don't follow the principle of good faith and violate accepted business ethics to seize through improper means the business opportunities others can expect can the act be prohibited by the Anti-Unfair Competition Law. Thus it can be seen

---

① See the *Annual Report on Intellectual Property Rights Cases of the Supreme People's Court* (2010) ,Item 25.

that, as for the illegitimate nature of a competition behavior, it is key in juridical practice to determine whether anyone improperly uses or damages any other's competitive edge; "the legitimate rights and interests of other operators have been actually damaged ..." is provided to reflect the infringement nature of the unfair competition; with respect to the elements of the unfair competition, "damage" shall include the loss in reasonably expected profits or reasonably expected business opportunities.

E-sports games are newly emerging, so the organizers need to put a lot of efforts in investment, planning, operation, promotion, advertising, management, etc. In this case, through an agreement, Yaoyu was granted an exclusive license to broadcast the event in Chinese mainland and was responsible for the whole implementation and management of the event. It contributed a lot of labor, property and financial resources to the event, so it should have the right to get returns by broadcasting the event to increase website traffic and improve economic value of video broadcasting platforms. As mentioned above, e-sports game live broadcasting platforms attract online users by organizing, operating and broadcasting game competitions, improve the traffic of online users, increase the stickiness of online users and attract relevant advertisers to place advertisements. For live broadcasting platforms, the right to broadcast e-sports games is one of business opportunities to get commercial profits, increase website traffic and improve website popularity. Yaoyu's such right to seek for commercial profits should be protected by law, and no one may improperly damage such right.

It is a long-standing usual practice in e-sports games industry that the broadcasting of an e-sports game requires the license of the game operator. It follows the general business principle "one who invests will gain". It protects the legitimate interests of game operators. It conforms to the good faith principle in market competition. In this case, both parties were professional operators of e-sports games broadcasting websites, and they had a direct competition relationship. Douyu knew that the involved event was organized by Yaoyu, that Yaoyu had the exclusive license to broadcast the event, and that Yaoyu contributed a lot in the event, and should have known that it was the usual practice that the broadcasting of an e-sports game required the license of the game operator. Douyu did not contribute in the organization or operation of the event and was not licensed to broadcast the event, but enjoyed the business results from the event in which Yaoyu contributed a lot of financial, labor and property resources and a lot of efforts, for its own business profits and competition edge. This was a "hitchhike" actually, seizing the audiences of Yaoyu, diverting the traffic of Yaoyu's website, damaging Yaoyu's profitability in advertising and Yaoyu's competition advantage, and also weakening the added value of Yaoyu's broadcasting website. The behavior of Douyu violated the good faith principle set out in the Anti-Unfair Competition Law and generally-accepted business ethics, damaged the legitimate rights and interests of Yaoyu, and distributed thegenerally-accepted market competition order formed in the industry. Thus, it was illegitimate and should be prohibited by the Anti-Unfair Competition Law.

(Writers: Lu Fengyu and Zhu Yonghua)

Whether the Use of Others' Trademarks for Indicating the Change of a Product's Seller Shall be Determined as Trademark Infringement and False Advertising

—Dispute over False Advertising between K. D. F. Distribution (Shanghai) Co. , Ltd. on the One Hand and Aquatherm Pipe System (Shanghai) Co. , Ltd. and Shanghai Ousu Trade Co. , Ltd. on the Other Hand

[Abstract]

Where an operator uses others' trademarks to a reasonable extent on the principle of good faith for the purpose of indicating the change of a product's seller, such use shall be a proper use of trademarks and shall not constitute a trademark infringement; where an operator informs the customers of the change of a product's distributor or brand truthfully and in detail, its use of others' trademarks will not confuse the relevant public and shall not constitute false advertising.

[Case Review]

Plaintiff (Appellant) : K. D. F. Distribution (Shanghai) Co. , Ltd.
Defendant (Appellee) : Aquatherm Pipe System (Shanghai) Co. , Ltd.
Defendant (Appellee) : Shanghai Ousu Trade Co. , Ltd.
Cause of Action : dispute over false advertising
First-Instance Case No. : (2013) XMS (Z) CZ No. 1017
Second-Instance Case No. : (2015) HZMZZ No. 161

The Plaintiff K. D. F. Distribution (Shanghai) Co., Ltd. (hereinafter referred to as "K. D. F.") is the owner of the word trademark "洁水" approved to be registered in 2002 on products under Category 17 such as plastic pipe. On April 6, 2006, K. D. F. and the third party Aquatherm GmbH signed an exclusive distribution agreement, whereby K. D. F. was granted the exclusive right to distribute Aquatherm GmbH's water pipe products in China. Aquatherm GmbH registered the two trademarks "" and "aquatherm" on sewer devices under Category 19 in China. On June 30, 2013, K. D. F. and Aquatherm GmbH terminated the cooperation agreement between them and K. D. F. ceased to distribute the products of Aquatherm GmbH. On July 1, 2013, the Defendant Aquatherm Pipe System (Shanghai) Co., Ltd. (hereinafter referred to as "Aquatherm") became a new distributor of Aquatherm GmbH in China. Before July 1, 2013, the trademark "洁水" registered by the Plaintiff K. D. F. was only used for promoting and selling the products of Aquatherm GmbH. After July 1, 2013, K. D. F. continued to hold the trademark "洁水" and used the same for promoting the water pipe products of other producers. After obtaining the rights to distribute the products of Aquatherm GmbH, Aquatherm authorized the Defendant Shanghai Ousu Trade Co., Ltd. (hereinafter referred to as "Ousu") to exclusively distribute the products of Aquatherm GmbH in Shanghai. The two Defendants used words "德国阔盛", formerly known as "AQUA-SCIE (德国洁水 in Chinese)", "德国阔盛" (formerly known as "AQUA-SCIE (德国洁水 in Chinese)")—continuing to provide quality products, " aquatherm (formerly known as "AQUA-SCIE (德国洁水 in Chinese)") 德国阔盛" in their promotional articles and brochures; and when they used such words, they also used expressions such as "the former distributor used the word mark "洁水" to promote the products, but from July 1, Aquatherm GmbH officially started to use the Chinese mark "阔盛" to promote its products in China", "Aquatherm Gmbh officially started to use the Chinese mark "阔盛" to promote its products in China from July 1, 2013. The Chinese mark "洁水" used in China is owned by the former distributor and now has nothing to do with Aquatherm Gmbh and its products, and so on.

The Plaintiff K. D. F. held that, the words used by the Defendants Aquatherm and Ousu, such as "德国阔盛", formerly known as "AQUA-SCIE (德国洁水 in Chinese)" and "德国阔盛" (formerly known as "AQUA-SCIE (德国洁水 in

Chinese)")—continuing to provide quality products, included the trademark "洁水", so such use shall constitute an infringement upon the Plaintiff's trademark and as such use may confuse the consumers, it shall constitute false advertising. Therefore, the Plaintiff brought the case to the Court, requesting the Court to order the two Defendants to stop their acts of trademark infringement and false advertising and to compensate the Plaintiff RMB5 million for its economic loss and reasonable expenses.

[**Judgment**]

Shanghai Xuhui District People's Court held that, the use of the trademark "洁水" by Aquatherm and Ousu in their promotional materials claimed by K. D. F. was a proper use and would not confuse the relevant public. As the two Defendants' expressions mentioned above were consistent with facts and were not false, and as the relevant public would not get confused about the promotional words accused when they read the contents mentioned above with general attention, and would not misunderstand the relationship between the trademark "洁水" and the products promoted by the two Defendants, such use shall not constitute false advertising. All the claims of the Plaintiff were rejected in the first instance judgment.

The Plaintiff refused to accept the first instance judgment and filed an appeal to Shanghai Intellectual Property Court.

Shanghai Intellectual Property Court held that, as there had been a stable relationship between the trademark "洁水" and the products of Aquatherm GmbH, Aquatherm and Ousu were obliged to inform the consumers that the products corresponding to the trademark "洁水" changed; such use of the trademark "洁水" was based on the principle of good faith and within the reasonable scope and would not result in consumers' confusion about the origin of relevant products. The words used by Aquatherm and Ousu such as "AQUA-SCIE（德国洁水 in Chinese）"—continuing to provide quality products and "德国阔盛", formerly known as "AQUA-SCIE（德国洁水 in Chinese）" were not accurate to some extent, but after reading the whole promotional content, the consumers would not get confused about whether the trademark "洁水" itself changed or not and about the origin of the products sold by Aquatherm. In other words, such use did not confuse the consumers. Therefore, the appeal was rejected and the original judgment was affirmed.

[Case Study]

What was special about this case was that, the Plaintiff, as a distributor, registered the trademark "洁水", but only used the same for promoting the products of Aquatherm GmbH. To determine whether the use of the trademark "洁水" by the Defendants in publicity based on the change of brand agency relationship shall constitute an act of trademark infringement and false advertising, further analysis was required.

Ⅰ. Determination of proper use of trademarks

Article 59 of the *Trademark Law* of China specifies that, the holder of the exclusive right to use a registered trademark shall not be entitled to prohibit others from properly using the generic name, graphics or models of a commodity, or information directly indicating the quality, main raw materials, functions, purposes, weight, quantity or other features of the commodity, or the names of geographical locations as contained in the registered trademark. This Article is a legal provision of China regarding the proper descriptive use of trademarks. The so-called proper use of trademarks refers to the unauthorized use of others' registered trademarks by an operator for describing its products or services to enable the consumers to identify the same. Allowing the proper use of trademark is the result of balancing the interests of the trademark owners and public interests. The basic function of a trademark is to identify the origin of products or services. A trademark owner is only entitled to use its registered trademark on approved products or services and to prohibit others from using trademarks that are identical or similar to its registered trademark on such approved products or services. A trademark owner is not entitled to monopolize its registered trademarks. Therefore, to determine whether the use of others' trademarks by an operator in business activities shall constitute trademark infringement, it is required to consider whether such use impairs the association of the trademarks with relevant products or services, namely, whether such use will result in the relevant public's confusion about the origin of relevant products or services. Where the use of others' trademarks in business activities is only aimed at describing or explaining certain objective circumstances and will not result in relevant public's confusion about the origin of relevant products or services, such use shall not be the use of trademarks within the meaning specified by the Trademark Law but a proper use of trademarks, and shall not be prohibited by trademark owners.

According to the provisions regarding the proper use of trademarks in the Trademark Law of China, the proper use of trademarks shall be based on the principle of good faith and within a reasonable scope. To determine whether the use of trademarks shall constitute proper use, it is required to consider whether the use of others' trademarks is based on the principle of good faith, whether such use is reasonable and will result in consumers' confusion, etc. First, whether the use of trademarks is based on the principle of good faith. To determine that, it is required to consider whether such use is necessary. Generally speaking, if an operator can describe the characteristics of its products or services clearly without using others' trademark, its use of others' trademark is unnecessary. Especially, the use of well-known trademarks usually is not based on the principle of good faith. In this case, before July 1, 2013, the Plaintiff used its registered trademark "洁水" only for promoting the products of Aquatherm GmbH. After long-term use, there had been a stable and unique relationship between the trademark and the products of Aquatherm GmbH, and to the knowledge of relevant consumers, the trademark "洁水" was corresponding to the products of Aquatherm GmbH. After July 1, 2013, the distributor of the products of Aquatherm GmbH in China was changed from the Plaintiff to the Defendant Aquatherm and the Plaintiff continued to hold the brand "洁水" and used the same in its cooperation with other suppliers. As there had been a stable relationship between the trademark and the products of Aquatherm GmbH, the two Defendants were required to inform the consumers in promotional activities that the products corresponding to the trademark "洁水" changed and that the products currently promoted by Aquatherm were the products previously corresponding to the trademark "洁水". Therefore, the two Appellees' use of the trademark "洁水" in their promotional materials was not aimed at taking advantage of the Appellant's goodwill but aimed at describing the objective facts. Second, whether the use of trademarks is reasonable and will result in consumers' confusion. The use of others' trademarks by an operator for describing the characteristics of its products or services shall be reasonable. If such use exceeds the reasonable scope, resulting in consumers' confusion or about the origin of products, it shall not constitute proper use of trademarks. In this case, as the trademark "洁水" only corresponded to the products of Aquatherm GmbH, which was known to the consumers, and the use of expressions such as "德国阔盛", formerly known as "AQUA-SCIE（德国洁水 in Chinese）" by the two Defendants was within the reasonable scope. Meanwhile, while using the promotional words accused of infringing trademarks, the two Defendants also stated the change of distributor and brand of relevant products. The consumers, when reading such promotional words used by the two Appellees, would usually understand that Aquatherm was selling the products previously corresponding to the trademark "洁水", namely the products of Aquatherm GmbH and would not get confused about the origin of products.

Ⅱ. Determination of acts of false advertising

Pursuant to Article 9 of the *Anti-Unfair Competition Law*, the operators shall not conduct misleading false advertising of commodities' quality, ingredients, performance, applications, manufacturer, term of validity and place of origin etc. by advertising or other ways. The false advertising specified in the *Anti-Unfair Competition Law* is limited to "misleading" false advertising. In other words, only misleading advertising content can impair the market order of fair competition and the lawful rights and interests of consumers, and false advertising content that is not misleading may not be blamed substantially under the *Anti-Unfair Competition Law*.

The determination of "misleading" in dispute over false advertising is not exactly the same as that of "confusion" in dispute over trademark infringement. Confusion within the meaning specified in the Trademark Law usually refers to confusion about the origin of products or services, namely, the consumers misunderstand that two different products are of the same origin or that there is a certain relationship between operators of certain products. "Misleading" in case of false advertising has a broader meaning, and all factors that may mislead the consumers are misleading. In this case, as the Plaintiff is still the owner of the trademark "洁水" and the trademark itself does not change at all. The promotional words such as "德国阔盛", formerly known as "AQUA-SCIE（德国洁水 in

Chinese)" used by the two Appellees are not accurate, but the determination of "misleading" false advertising shall be based on factors such as daily experiences, general attention of the relevant public, misleading facts and information about the products promoted.

First, the promotional words used by the two Appellees shall be interpreted as a whole. As the consumers usually accept commercial promotion as a whole, to determine whether certain promotional content is misleading, it is necessary to determine whether the promotional content as a whole can mislead the relevant public. It is immaterial that some words or sentences of the promotional content are misleading. Even if some parts of the promotional content are misleading when they are interpreted separately, the promotional content interpreted as a whole may not be misleading to the consumers, and in such case, it will not mislead the consumers. As mentioned above, when the two Defendants used the promotional words accused of infringing others' rights, they also introduced the background such as change of distributor and brand of relevant products. Therefore, to determine whether the above promotional words claimed by the Plaintiff shall constitute false advertising requires interpreting such words in a reasonable manner in the context of the whole promotional content rather than separately. Second, the determination shall be based on general attention of the relevant public, existing experience and information about the products promoted. Whether the promotional content is misleading has a close relationship with the knowledge and experience of the relevant public. In this case, when the two Defendants used the promotional words accused of infringing others' rights, they also introduced the background such as change of distributor and brand of relevant products, and consumers had certain knowledge of relevant brands and products, so the relevant public shall understand the real meaning of the promotional content with general attention and would not get confused about whether the trademark "洁水" itself changed and about the origin of the products sold by Aquatherm.

What needs to be emphasized is that, if the two Defendants used promotional words such as "德国阔盛", formerly known as "AQUA-SCIE (德国洁水 in Chinese)" separately, as the Plaintiff still uses the trademark "洁水" in selling others' products, such promotional words may cause confusion, and consumers who do not know about the change of relevant brands and new consumers may interpret the same as that the trademark "洁水" is changed to the trademark "阔盛" and the former ceases to be used; in such case, the use of such promotional words shall constitute acts of false advertising. However, when the two Defendants used the above promotional words, they also introduced the change of brands truthfully. In such case, the promotional words would not mislead consumers and the use of such promotional words shall constitute acts of false advertising within the meaning given under the *Anti-Unfair Competition Law*.

（Written by：Fan Jingbo）

Blocking Ads Embedded at the Beginning of Video Programs While Displaying Videos Streamed from Others Shall Constitute Acts of Unfair Competition

—Dispute over Unfair Competition between Shenzhen Juwangshi Technology Co. , Ltd. and Beijing IQIYI Science & Technology Co. , Ltd.

[Abstract]

With the development of internet technology, the lagging and limitations of provisions of the *Anti-Unfair Competition Law* regarding acts of unfair competition become increasingly obvious. In this case, by application of Article 2 of the *Anti-Unfair Competition Law*, it is made clear that the video aggregation software called "VST" developed and run by Juwangshi can enable users to watch online videos of IQIYI Company without watching any embedded ads, which violates the principle of good faith and damages the lawful rights of IQIYI Company to obtain commercial profits relying on its legal business model and shall therefore constitute acts of unfair competition. As the first dispute case over unfair competition in connection with video aggregation in China, this case can be used for reference in the trial of similar cases.

[Case Review]

Plaintiff (Appellee): Beijing IQIYI Science & Technology Co. , Ltd.
Defendant (Appellant): Shenzhen Juwangshi Technology Co. , Ltd.

Cause of Action: dispute over unfair competition

First-Instance Case No. : (2015) YMS (Z) CZ No. 1

Second-Instance Case No. : (2015) HZMZZ No. 728

Beijing IQIYI Science & Technology Co. , Ltd. (hereinafter referred to as "IQIYI Company") is the operator of IQIYI, one of China's main online video sites, which streams video programs for free but has ads embedded at the beginning of the programs (namely users have to watch some ads before watching the programs provided by IQIYI Company for free). For a fee, users can subscribe for IQIYI membership, which allows them to skip the ads. IQIYI Company earns income by charging advertising fees of the ads embedded at the beginning of programs and membership fees to pay video copyright, bandwidth, promoting and other expenses and to make profits. The video aggregation software called "VST" developed and run by Shenzhen Juwangshi Technology Co. , Ltd. (hereinafter referred to as "Juwangshi") decrypts the verification algorithm of IQIYI Company to obtain valid access to the videos streamed on IQIYI while blocking the embedded ads. IQIYI Company holds that, the VST software aggregates videos from various large, well-known video sites including IQIYI without paying any copyright, bandwidth and other operating expenses, which results in the drop in both IQIYI's popularity among users and views of ads embedded in programs streamed on IQIYI, and thus has damaged the interests of IQIYI Company. Therefore, in accordance with Article 2 of the *Anti-Unfair Competition Law*, IQIYI claimed that the above acts of Juwangshi shall constitute acts of unfair competition and demanded compensation for economic loss and reasonable expenses from Juwangshi.

[Judgment]

Shanghai Yangpu District People's Court held upon trial that, as there was a competitive relationship between IQIYI Company and Juwangshi and IQIYI Company adopted encryption measures for its videos and as the VST software of Juwangshi enabled users to watch videos from IQIYI without watching any embedded ads, the acts of Juwangshi shall constitute acts of unfair competition. Juwangshi decrypted the verification algorithm of IQIYI Company to obtain valid KEY value and generate the SC value requesting to display the videos, thus blocking the embedded ads of IQIYI Company and enabling users to watch videos without watching any embedded ads.

Juwangshi did not directly delete the embedded ads but objectively enabled users to watch videos without any embedded ads. Such behaviors of Juwangshi directly intervened in and seriously damaged the operation of IQIYI Company. Juwangshi, by doing so, attracted network users who were unwilling to watch the embedded ads on IQIYI and to pay the membership fee charged by IQIYI Company to use Juwangshi's software without paying any copyright fee and bandwidth costs, which reduced the market share of IQIYI Company. Juwangshi achieved competitive advantage in an improper manner, directly resulting in the drop in IQIYI Company's ad revenue and membership incomes from membership fees. Such behaviors of Juwangshi violated the principle of good faith and recognized business ethics and shall be governed by Article 2 of the *Anti-Unfair Competition Law*. Therefore, it was determined that the behaviors of Juwangshi of displaying videos from IQIYI while blocking the embedded ads by technical means shall constitute acts of unfair competition, and Juwangshi was ordered to compensate IQIYI Company RMB 36,000 for its economic loss and reasonable expenses.

The Defendant Juwangshi refused to accept the first-instance judgment and filed an appeal.

Upon trial, Shanghai Intellectual Property Court held that, IQIYI Company's behaviors of streaming video programs for free but having ads embedded at the beginning of the programs and charging membership fees to obtain commercial profits shall be protected by laws. Juwangshi directly displayed the videos from IQIYI while blocking ads by technical means, enabling users to watch videos from IQIYI without paying any time and expense costs, which would attract users of IQIYI Company to be users of Juwangshi and reduce the page views of ads of IQIYI Company. When Juwangshi enabled its users to watch videos from IQIYI, it did not pay any copyright and other operating costs, and relevant costs were borne by IQIYI Company. IQIYI paid such costs and also suffered the loss of commercial profits caused by the drop in both users and page views of ads. Juwangshi shall know that its use of relevant technologies would damage others' interests while bringing benefits to it and still used such technology, which violated the principle of good faith and recognized business ethics and affected the legal operating activities of IQIYI Company. The judgment of the court of the first trial that the behaviors of Juwangshi of displaying videos from IQIYI while blocking embedded ads by technical means shall constitute acts of unfair competition was affirmed.

[Case Study]

In this case, in accordance with provisions of Article 2 of the *Anti-Unfair Competition Law*, IQIYI Company claimed that Juwangshi's behaviors of providing videos from IQIYI Company while blocking embedded ads shall constitute acts of unfair competition. To determine whether such behaviors shall constitute acts of unfair competition, the following factors shall be considered:

I . Whether such behaviors are specified in other laws and regulations

The application of Article 2 of the *Anti-Unfair Competition Law* requires that such behaviors are not specified in both the *Anti-Unfair Competition Law* and other laws and regulations. Some hold that, Article 48 of the *Copyright Law* specifies that, without the permission from the copyright owner or obligee related to the copyright, intentionally avoiding or destroying the technical measures taken by the obligee on his works, sound recordings or video recordings, etc. to protect the copyright or the rights related to the copyright shall be acts of infringement. As Juwangshi provided videos from IQIYI to its users while blocking embedded ads by destroying the technical measures taken by IQIYI Company on its videos, IQIYI Company may safeguard its lawful rights and interests in accordance with the above provisions of the *Copyright Law* and Article 2 of the *Anti-Unfair Competition Law* shall not be applied. Technical measures for protecting copyrights refer to effective technologies, devices or components used to prevent and restrict others from providing works, performances, sound recordings and video recordings to the public through information network without the consent of the obligees. In this case, Juwangshi decrypted the verification algorithm of IQIYI Company to obtain the valid KEY value and generate the SC value requesting to display videos, thus blocking embedded ads of IQIYI Company and enabling users to watch videos without watching any ads, which destroyed the technical protection measures taken by IQIYI Company on its videos. If IQIYI Company brought an infringement action against the behavior of destroying technical measures, it may obtain relieves in accordance with the existing *Copyright Law* and the *Regulations on the Protection of the Right of Communication through Information Network*.

However, in this case, IQIYI Company did not exercise its right of action against the behavior of destroying technical measures. In this case, IQIYI claimed its operating activities of obtaining commercial profits by providing videos for free but having ads embedded at the beginning of videos or charging membership fees. Destroying technical measures was just the way in which Juwangshi affected the business activities of IQIYI Company and the result was that Juwangshi enabled its users to watch videos from IQIYI Company without ads, as a result of which, the commercial interests of IQIYI generated by such business activities including advertising revenue and membership fee revenue were damaged. The rights protected by the technical protective measures under the *Copyright Law* are proprietary rights specifically granted to copyright owners by the *Copyright Law*, such as right of reproduction, the right of communication through information network, etc. Accordingly, the relieves in connection with destroying technical measures only cover the copyrights and proprietary rights and can not be extended to cover commercial interests generated by business model. For this reason, IQIYI Company claimed that the behaviors of Juwangshi of providing videos from IQIYI Company while blocking embedded ads were not acts specified by the *Copyright Law*. Therefore, this case met the requirements for application of Article 2 of the *Anti-Unfair Competition Law*.

Ⅱ. Whether the behavior of directly displaying videos while blocking ads by decrypting technical measures shall constitute acts of unfair competition

IQIYI Company provided videos to general users and had ads embedded at the beginning of the videos and charging membership fee for allowing members to skip ads, which did not violate the basic principles and prohibitive provisions of the *Anti-Unfair Competition Law*, and the operating activities of seeking commercial profits by adopting such business model shall be protected by the *Anti-Unfair Competition Law*. Juwangshi decrypted the encryption technologies of IQIYI Company by using crawler technology, to obtain the secret key of IQIYI Company and obtain the real address of videos of IQIYI Company and then directly display such videos. Although Juwangshi did not actively carry out any ads blocking activities, it still enabled its users to skip the ads of IQIYI Company. Juwangshi, as the developer and operator of the involved software, knew that such technology would enable its users to skip IQIYI Company's ads and still actively pursued such results, aiming at attracting

IQIYI Company's users to be Juwangshi's users without paying any copyright, bandwidth and other necessary costs by taking advantages of the unwillingness of network users to pay time and expense costs. Juwangshi achieved competitive advantage at the expense of reducing the advertising revenue and membership fee revenue of IQIYI Company. Therefore, the behaviors of Juwangshi violated the principle of good faith and recognized business ethics and damaged the lawful interests and rights of IQIYI Company, and shall constitute acts of unfair competition regulated by Article 2 of the *Anti-Unfair Competition Law*.

(Writer: Yang Wei)

Judicial Protection for
English Name of Enterprise

—Dispute over Unauthorized Use of Name of Other Enterprises between Jiangsu Tianrong Group Co. , Ltd. and Hunan Haohua Chemical Co. , Ltd.

[**Abstract**]

English names of Chinese enterprises actually used in foreign trade, corresponding to their Chinese names and having the function of identifying the enterprises may be deemed as the enterprise names specified in Article 5(3) of the *Anti-Unfair Competition Law of the People's Republic of China*. In case one uses the English name of another enterprise on its export commodities, causing damage to the enterprise, such use shall constitute an act of unfair competition.

The amount of liquidated damages for unfair competition may be determined based on the loss suffered by the obligee due to infringement during the period of infringement. The actual loss suffered by the obligee due to infringement can be the sales volume of the infringing commodities multiplied by the unit profit of such commodities. During determination of the annual interval distribution of the sales volume of the infringing commodities, the actual loss of the obligee may be the annual sales volume of the infringing commodities multiplied by the annual unit profit of the obligee's commodities. Generally, the profit of the obligee's commodities should be subject to the operating profit while any and all selling expenses, administration expenses, financial costs, business taxes and surcharges shall be deducted from the sales profit.

[Case Review]

Plaintiff: Jiangsu Tianrong Group Co. , Ltd.

Defendant: Hunan Haohua Chemical Co. , Ltd.

Valid Case No. : (2015) PMS (Z) CZ No. 1887

The Plaintiff Jiangsu Tianrong Group Co. , Ltd. (hereinafter referred to as "Tianrong Company") was established on September 29, 1998. Tianrong Company, originally named Liyang Lihua Chemical Co. , Ltd. , changed its name to Jiangsu Lihua Chemical Co. , Ltd. on March 4, 2003 and was renamed Jiangsu Tianrong Group Limited on August 16, 2006 and then changed its name to Jiangsu Tianrong Group Co. , Ltd. on August 25, 2006.

As listed in the Registration Form for Foreign Trade Operator, the English company name of Tianrong Company is "JIANGSU TIANRONG GROUP CO. , LTD". As listed in the document issued by the Central Insecticides Board & Registration Committee (CIBRC) of the Directorate of Plant Protection, Quarantine and Storage of the Ministry Of Agriculture & Farmers Welfare, Government of India (Department of Agriculture, Cooperation & Farmers Welfare) on October 9, 2015, the padan active compound manufactured by Tianrong Company (minimum available content: 98%) have been registered with the Government of India, and the English name of Tianrong Company is "JIANGSU TIANRONG GROUP CO. , LTD".

On May 6, 2014, Pudong New Area Market Supervision and Administration Bureau checked and detained 16,000 kilos of padan active compounds manufactured by Hunan Haohua Chemical Co. , Ltd. (hereinafter referred to as "Haohua Company") and to be exported to India. The outer packing of these padan active compounds was marked with words "Manufacturer: M/s. Liyang Chemical Factory, China (Jiangsu Tianrong Group Company, Ltd. , China)" and no other trademark or company name was found on the packing bags.

Zhang, the Deputy General Manager of Haohua Company, replied to the inquiry of Pudong New Area Market Supervision and Administration Bureau on June 19, 2014, claiming that, as introduced by others, Haohua Company entered into a contract with Tropical Agrosystem (India) Pvt. Limited on March 10, 2014. According to that contract, Haohua Company would sell 16,000 kilos of padan active compounds to Tropical Agrosystem (India) Pvt. Limited. Haohua Company did not register with Indian governmental authority while Tianrong Company had completed its registration. Therefore, to enable the padan active compounds manufactured by Haohua Company to pass the customs inspection in India, the English name of Tianrong Company was labeled on the external package of the commodity according to the requirements of the Indian client. Haohua Company had been exporting pesticides to Indian market for about six or seven years through Sundat(s) PTE Ltd. which had gone through registration formalities in India. Therefore, the name of Sundat(s) PTE Ltd. was marked on the packages of the pesticides of Haohua Company.

Pudong New Area Market Supervision and Administration Bureau issued PSJACZ [2014] No. 150201402201 Written Decision of Administrative Penalty on July 5, 2014, stating that: Haohua Company used the English name of Tianrong Company, which violated the regulations of Articles 30 and 37 of the *Product Quality Law of the People's Republic of China* and constituted illegal use of other companies' name. Haohua Company was ordered to make corrections and received the following punishment: 16,000 kilos of padan active compounds (640 bags) shall be confiscated and a penalty of RMB 300,000 shall be fined.

In this case, according to the application made by Tianrong Company, the court acquired the customs clearance materials of Haohua Company concerning the export of padan active compounds. According to the customs clearance materials of Haohua Company from June 2012 to January 2014 provided by Shanghai Customs, the name of manufacturer marked at the shipping mark column of certain commercial invoices and packing lists of Haohua Company was the English name of Tianrong Company or "SUNDAT (S) PTE. LTD., SINGAPORE". The Plaintiff and the Defendant confirmed that the total price of the padan active compounds whose manufacturer's name marked on the commercial invoices and packing lists was the English name of Tianrong Company was USD 3,971,920, and agreed to convert the USD into RMB at the rate of 6.1565.

According to the audit reports of Tianrong Company from 2012 to 2014, the main products of Tianrong Company included two series of pesticides, series of padan, series of fenothiocarb and other series of herbicides. The operating receipt, operating costs and other data of padan were separately listed in the audit reports. The operating receipt, operating costs and other data were listed in the audit reports of Haohua Company from 2012 to 2014. However, the operating receipt and operating costs of padan had not been separately listed in such audit reports.

The Plaintiff Tianrong Company alleged that padan active compounds were a mildly toxic pesticide which may be exported to Indian market after being registered with Indian government authority according to Indian laws. Tianrong Company had gone through registration formalities with Indian governmental authority for the padan active compounds while Haohua Company had not handled such registration formalities with Indian governmental authority. For the purpose of exporting padan active compounds to India, Haohua Company used the English name of Tianrong Company without permission. Haohua Company exported padan active compounds with the value of RMB 24,453,125.48 to India by illegally using the English name of Tianrong Company from June 2012 to January 2014. The estimated gross profit rate of padan active compounds of Tianrong Company in 2014 was 42.62%, based on which the profit of Haohua Company by exporting the commodities involved was RMB 10,421,922.08. In addition, Tianrong Company paid attorney fee of RMB 500,000 for this case. Haohua Company used the company name of Tianrong Company without permission, causing loss to Tianrong Company. Such use shall constitute acts of unfair competition and Haohua Company shall bear liabilities for damages. Therefore, Tianrong Company requested the court to order Haohua Company to compensate Tianrong Company for its economic loss of RMB 10,421,922.08 and the attorney fee of RMB 500,000.

The Defendant Haohua Company argued that it previously exported padan to India through SUNDAT (S) PTE. LTD., SINGAPORE. According to the requirements of Indian client, it marked the English name of Tianrong Company on its packages, but that batch of commodities had been detained by Pudong New Area Market Supervision and Administration Bureau. Haohua Company had never marked the English name of Tianrong Company on the packaging bags of the padan exported to India before, and the English name of Tianrong Company was only marked on the commercial invoices and packing lists of certain batches of commodities. Haohua Company used the English name of Tianrong Company for the purpose of export only, which did not result in the Client's misunderstanding that the commodities involved were manufactured by Tianrong Company, did not influence the export of Tianrong Company's commodities and did not cause any economic loss to Tianrong Company. The English name of Tianrong Company had not been registered with the competent enterprise registration authority according to the laws and was not one of these company names protected by the *Anti-Unfair Competition Law*.

[Judgment]

After the hearing, Shanghai Pudong New Area People's Court concluded that, the English name of Tianrong Company had correspondence with its Chinese name, was actually used by Tianrong Company during its operation and had the function of identifying Tianrong Company, so the English name shall be one of these company names within the meaning given in Article 5(3) of the *Anti-Unfair Competition Law* and shall be protected by the *Anti-Unfair Competition Law*. Haohua Company used the English name of Tianrong Company to export padan to India. Subjectively, such use was intentional, and objectively, such use misled the relevant public to erroneously identify the commodities involved as manufactured by Tianrong Company. As a result, the export market share of Tianrong Company was reduced and damage was caused to Tianrong Company. Haohua Company's behavior damaged the lawful interests of Tianrong Company, disturbed normal foreign trade market order, and therefore shall constitute the unauthorized use of other companies' name within the meaning given in Article 5(3) of the *Anti-Unfair Competition Law*.

The amount of damages for unfair competition may be calculated based on the loss suffered by the obligee due to infringement during the period of infringement (i. e. sales volume of the infringing commodity multiplied by the unit profit of the same commodity of the obligee). The operating profit ratio of the padan product of Tianrong Company could be calculated according to the annual audit report of Tianrong Company. Based on the operating profit ratio of the padan product of Tianrong Company as well as the export volume of padan product of Haohua Company, the economic loss of Tianrong Company calculated by the court was RMB 3,125,069.20.

Therefore, Shanghai Pudong New Area People's Court made a judgment, ordering Haohua Company to compensate Tianrong Company for its economic loss of RMB 3,125,069.20 and the reasonable expenses of RMB 200,000. After the judgment, neither Party lodged an appeal and Haohua Company voluntarily paid the compensation fixed in the judgment.

[Case Study]

I. Conditions for the English name used by enterprise in foreign trade to be protected by the *Anti-Unfair Competition Law*

Chinese enterprises usually use their Chinese names in domestic operating activities, and usually need to use their English names in foreign trade operating activities. Article 10 of the *Regulation of the People's Republic of China on Administration of the Registration of Enterprise Legal Persons* specifies that "a business entity may use one name only. The name applied to be registered by a business entity shall be examined by the registration authorities and, after such name is approved and registered, the business entity shall enjoy the exclusive right to use such name within the specified scope". At present, the application for approval and registration of the English names of Chinese enterprises is not accepted by competent business entity registration authorities. Article 9 of the *Foreign Trade Law* specifies that: "a foreign trade operator engaged in import and export of goods or technologies shall register with the department in charge of foreign trade under the State Council or institutions authorized by such department; however, those exempt from registration under laws, administrative regulations and rules of the department in charge of foreign trade under the State Council shall be excluded. The detailed rules on the registration shall be formulated by the department in charge of foreign trade under the State Council. Customs shall not handle the declaration and clearance procedure for goods imported or exported by a foreign trade operator who fails to go through the registration formalities in accordance with the rules. At the time of registration, a foreign trade operator shall submit the *Registration Form for Foreign Trade Operators*, in which a column "English name of the operator" is included." A foreign trade operator may determine its English name on its own and such English name will not be subject to the substantive examination by the competent authority at the time of registration.

The main focus of dispute in this case was whether the English name used by Chinese enterprises in foreign trade belonged to the company names specified in Article 5(3) of the *Anti-Unfair Competition Law*. Article 6(1) of the *Interpretation of the Supreme People's Court on Some Issues Concerning the Application of Laws in the Trial of Civil Cases Involving Unfair Competition* specifies that, the name of any enterprise legally registered with the competent enterprise registration authority and the name of any foreign enterprise used within the territory of China for commercial purpose shall be ascertained as an "enterprise name" stipulated in Article 5(3) of the *Anti-Unfair Competition Law*. The shop name in an enterprise name that has certain market popularity and is well-known to the relevant public may be ascertained as an enterprise name stipulated in Article 5 (3) of the *Anti-Unfair Competition Law*. According to the Interpretation, the following three types of enterprise names will be protected by the *Anti-Unfair Competition Law*: I. an enterprise name registered with the competent enterprise registration authority; II. a name of any foreign enterprise used within the territory of China for commercial purpose; III. the shop name in any enterprise name that has certain market popularity and is well-known to the relevant public.

There are two opposite views concerning the question of whether the enterprise names protected by the *Anti-Unfair Competition Law* are limited to the three types listed above. From one point of view, unless explicitly specified by laws or judicial interpretations, other names used to identify enterprises shall not be determined as enterprise names. From another point of view, the above Judicial Interpretation lists types of names that may be determined as enterprise names but does not exclude other names that may be determined as enterprise names. We think that the second point of view is obviously more reasonable. An enterprise name is the name of a market entity and serves as an important operating identification of an enterprise. Customers or other operators may identify the business entities through different business identifications. The purpose of the protection granted to enterprise names by the *Anti-Unfair Competition Law* is to prevent acts of unfair competition which may cause confusion. The enterprise name (whether Chinese name or name in foreign language) properly used by an enterprise during its operation which can identify the business entity shall be protected by laws.

In judicial practice, the range of various types of enterprise names referred to in the *Anti-Unfair Competition Law* tends to be expanded. The *Interpretation of the Supreme People's Court on Some Issues Concerning the Application of Laws in the Trial of Civil Cases Involving Unfair Competition* issued by the Supreme People's Court in 2006 specifies the conditions for a shop name to be protected by the *Anti-Unfair Competition Law*, but the abbreviations of enterprise names are not included in the scope of protection. The *Opinions of the Supreme People's Court on Several Issues Concerning the Overall Situation of Trial Services for Intellectual Properties Under Current Economic Conditions* issued by the Supreme People's Court in 2009 stipulates that, "the shop name in an enterprise name or the abbreviation of an enterprise or an enterprise name that has certain market popularity, is well-known to the relevant public or actually serves as an trade name shall be deemed as an enterprise name and protected by the *Anti-Unfair Competition Law*". In the (2008) MSZ No. 758 Case of dispute over infringement of enterprise name right between Shandong Crane Factory Co., Ltd. and Shandong Shanqi Heavy Industry Co., Ltd. and the dispute case over unauthorized use of other enterprises' names between Tianjin China Youth Travel Agency (plaintiff) and Tianjin Guoqing International Travel Service (No. 29 instructive case), the Supreme People's Court stipulated that, the abbreviation of an enterprise name that has certain market popularity, is well-known to the relevant public or actually serves as an trade name may be deemed as an enterprise name. Therefore, the enterprise names specified in Article 5(3) of the *Anti-Unfair Competition Law* are not limited to such enterprise names registered with the competent enterprise registration authority according to the law. Also, the *Anti-Unfair Competition Law* and the judicial interpretation do not explicitly specify that English names can be protected by the *Anti-Unfair Competition Law*, it cannot be concluded that English names cannot be protected by the *Anti-Unfair Competition Law*.

Foreign trade is an important part of China's economy, and the enterprise names used by Chinese enterprises in foreign trade gradually become an important business mark bearing the goodwill of enterprises. Tianrong Company used the English company name "JIANGSU TIANRONG GROUP CO., LTD." at the time of registration as a foreign trade operator. Tianrong Company also used such English name to carry out the registration of the padan pesticide manufactured by it with relevant Indian authority. "天容" was the Plaintiff's shop name whose Chinese pinyin was "TIANRONG". "JIANGSU TIANRONG GROUP CO., LTD." had correspondence with its Chinese name. Such English name was used by Tianrong Company during its operation, and possessed the function of identifying market operating entity, and therefore shall belong to the company names specified in Article 5(3) of the *Anti-Unfair Competition Law* and shall be protected by the *Anti-Unfair Competition Law*. Tianrong Company and Haohua Company were both engaged in the manufacturing and export of padan active compounds. Because the padan active compounds manufactured by Haohua Company had not been registered with the relevant authority of agriculture of India, Haohua Company was unable to export the padan active compounds to India in its own name. Haohua Company used the English name of Tianrong Company to export commodities to India. Subjectively, such use was intentional, and objectively, such use misled the relevant public to erroneously identify the commodities involved as manufactured by Tianrong Company. As a result, the export market share of Tianrong Company was reduced and damage was caused to Tianrong Company. Haohua Company's behavior damaged the lawful interests of Tianrong Company, disturbed normal foreign trade market order, and therefore shall constitute the unauthorized use of other companies' names within the meaning given in Article 5(3) of the *Anti-Unfair Competition Law*.

Ⅱ. Determination of compensation amount

Article 14 of the *Interpretations of Supreme People's Court on Several Issues Concerning Application of Laws in the Triat of Civil Trademark Dispute Cases* stipulates that, the benefit acquired due to infringement specified in Article 56(1) of the *Trademark Law* can be calculated as the sales volume of the infringing commodities multiplied by the unit profit of such commodities; where the unit profit can. not be ascertained, the unit profit of the commodity bearing relevant registered trademark shall apply. Article 15 stipulates that, the loss suffered due to infringement specified in Article 56(1) of the *Trademark Law* can be the decreased amount of the sales volume of the obligee due to infringement (or the sales volume of the infringing commodities) multiplied by the unit profit of such commodities bearing the relevant registered trademark. According to the regulations above, in this case, the compensation amount can be the product of the sales volume of the infringing commodities multiplied by the unit profit of the commodities. In this case, the sales volume of the infringing commodities was determined by both Parties, but the unit profit of the commodities was in dispute.

Profit can be divided into operating profit and selling profit. The *Trademark Law* and the *Anti-Unfair Competition Law* have not explicitly specified whether the compensation for profit refers to compensation for operating profit or selling profit. Article 20(3) of the *Regulations of the Supreme People's Court on Certain Issues Concerning the Application of Laws in the Trial of Patent Disputes* effective as of

July 1, 2001 stipulates that, the profit gained by the infringer due to infringement can be the product of the total sales volume of the infringing products in the market multiplied by the reasonable profit of each infringing product. The profit of the infringer from the infringement is generally calculated according to the operating profit of the infringer. As for the infringer whose income mainly comes from infringement, its profit from infringement may be calculated according to its selling profit. This regulation is adopted by the judicial interpretation regarding patent disputes amended hereafter. From our point of view, in disputes over trademark infringement and counterfeiting, the regulations above may also be followed, i. e. the profit gained by the infringer due to infringement is generally calculated based on the infringer's operating profit; as for the infringer whose income mainly comes from infringement, its profit may be calculated according to its selling profit. Generally, financial expense and administration expense have a considerable proportion in enterprise expenditure. Normally, such expenses belong to the actual expenditure of the Defendant. Therefore, such expenses shall be deducted from the profit of the Defendant from infringement, i. e. in case of general infringement act, the profit from infringement shall be calculated based on the operating profit, which is fair to the Parties involved and complies with the actual situation of profit making of the infringer. In addition to the infringing product, the Defendant also carried out other normal business, and the value of the commodities involved only accounted for a small part of its operating receipt. The Defendant's income did not mainly come from infringement. Therefore, it would be more reasonable to calculate the compensation amount according to the operating profit.

The calculation of compensation amount according to the profit margin of the Defendant's products or based on the profit margin of the Plaintiff's products may be determined according to the Plaintiff's claim and the proofs provided by the Parties. The profit gained by the Defendant due to infringement could be the product of the sales volume of infringing products multiplied by the unit profit of the products sold by the Defendant. The loss suffered by the Plaintiff could be the product of the sales volume of infringing products multiplied by the unit profit of the product sold by the Plaintiff. As for such calculation method, it is presumed that every time an infringing product is sold by the Defendant, the market share of a product of the Plaintiff will be seized, in which case the sales volume of the Plaintiff will be decreased by one. In this case, the Plaintiff and the Defendant had submitted their annual audit reports.

The annual audit report of Haohua Company only included its income statement while the operating receipt and operating costs of padan products had not been separately listed. According to its annual audit report, the profit margin of padan products could not be calculated. The annual audit report of Tianrong Company included its income statement, and the operating receipt and operating costs of padan products had been separately listed in the report, based on which the profit margin of padan products of Tianrong Company could be calculated. The unit profit of padan products of Haohua Company could not be determined, and the compensation amount could be determined according to the unit profit of the padan products of Tianrong Company.

(Writers: Shao Xun, Yuan Tian)

Determination of Whether the Acts of Unfair Competition Concerning Collusion in Submission of Bids Could be Deduced from Defects in Invitation and Submission of Bids

—Dispute over Unfair Competition Concerning Collusion in Submission of Bids between Tianjin Zhongli Shendun Electronic Technology Co. , Ltd. on the One hand and Shanghai Eurotect Trading Co. , Ltd. , etc. on the Other Hand

[Abstract]

Where there are some defects in the bid documents and the bidding procedure, it shall not be directly concluded that there is any collusion between the winning bidder and the bid inviting party. To determine whether such defects could result in the invalidity of the bidding result, it is necessary to make judgment based on the institutional value of the bidding procedure and on whether such defects may result in the frustration of the purpose of the bidding procedure. In this case, the defects in the invitation and submission of bids would not result in the invalidity of the bidding result, and just from the defects, it could not be deduced that there was collusion between the winning bidder and the bid inviting party. Therefore, there was no act of unfair competition concerning collusion in submission of bids.

[Case Review]

Plaintiff (Appellant): Tianjin Zhongli Shendun Electronic Technology Co. , Ltd.

Defendant (Appellee):Shanghai Eurotect Trading Co. , Ltd.

Defendant (Appellee):Shanghai Construction Group Co. , Ltd.

Defendant (Appellee):Shanghai Installation Engineering Group Co. , Ltd.

Defendant (Appellee): Shanghai Tower Construction and Development Co. , Ltd.

Defendant (Appellee):China National Technical Import and Export Corporation

Cause of Action: dispute over unfair competition concerning collusion in submission of bids

First-Instance Case No. :(2014) PMS (Z) CZ No. 216

Second-Instance Case No. : (2015) HZMZZ No. 182

The Plaintiff Tianjin Zhongli Shendun Electronic Technology Co. , Ltd. (hereinafter referred to as "Zhongli Shendun") and the Defendant Shanghai Eurotect Trading Co. , Ltd. (hereinafter referred to as "Eurotect Company") were bidders for the Involved Project named "professional supply of surge protective devices and intelligent monitoring systems for the sub-contracted electromechanical system engineering of Shanghai Tower". Shanghai Construction Group Co. , Ltd. (hereinafter referred to as "Construction Group"), Shanghai Installation Engineering Group Co. , Ltd. (hereinafter referred to as "Installation Engineering Company"), Shanghai Tower Construction and Development Co. , Ltd. (hereinafter referred to as "Shanghai Tower Company") and China National Technical Import and Export Corporation (hereinafter referred to as "Technical Import and Export Company") were the bid inviting agencies of the Involved Project.

According to the notice of invitation for bids and the bid invitation document of the Involved Project, the requirements for bidders included the following: the manufacturers participating in the bid shall have the paid-in capital or contractual capacity of no less than RMB 2 million and shall have completed more than three similar projects in China over the past five years; a bidder shall, at the time of submission of its bid, provide a letter of undertaking issued by a local (municipal) bank stating that it was willing to issue a performance guarantee equal to 10% of the amount of the contract awarded and an advance payment guarantee equal to 15% of the amount of the contract awarded for the bidder (the guarantees shall be issued after the bidder wins the bid). The "Power Supply" section specified the voltage of electrical equipment, and the frequency was fixed as 50Hz; the distance between cables of the upper-level switch-type SPDs (namely surge protective devices or lightning arresters) and the secondary voltage-limiting type SPDs shall exceed 10m; the technical parameters for the four-level SPDs were specified, including that: the Ucs of SPDs at the first three levels shall be 420V; the Ins of such SPDs shall equal or exceed 80KA, 40KA and 20KA respectively; the Ups of such SPDs shall be equal to or lower than 3.0KV, 2.4KV and 1.7KV respectively; the waveform shall be 8/20μs and the fuse and combination SPDs shall be used. The bids shall be opened at 9:00 a. m. of August 6, 2012; the deadline of written inquiry shall be 12:00 a. m. of July 10, 2012; and if necessary, a meeting for answering questions about the bid would be held; and the written question-answering documents would be issued 15 days prior to the deadline for submission of bids. The bids for the Involved Project would be evaluated by adopting the comprehensive evaluation method.

On July 10, 2012, the Defendant Eurotect Company and another bidder asked the Defendant Technical Import and Export Company questions about relevant contents of bid invitation document. On August 2 of the same year, Technical Import and Export Company delivered the supplementary bid invitation document to bidder including the Plaintiff Zhongli Shendun and Eurotect Company, changing the bid opening time to 1:00 p. m. of August 21, 2012 and stating that the requirements of "A-level lightning protection" and "Class A qualification for lightning protection engineering design and construction" in technical bid invitation document were not applicable to the bidders.

The bid documents of Eurotect Company included the inspection reports of offered products, its financial statements of the recent three years, introductions to similar projects completed by Eurotect Company during the past 5 years, etc. The Ucs of the first-level products offered by Eurotect Company were 385V DC. The test level of the second-level products offered by Eurotect Company was Level I, and Ucs and the Ins of such products were 385V and 12.5KA respectively. The Ucs and Ups of the third-level products offered by Eurotect Company were 385V and 1.75KV respectively and all such products were protected by fuse protectors.

On August 21, 2012, the bid evaluation committee of the Involved Project, upon preliminary examination and detailed examination, recommended Eurotect Company (first place) and Zhongli Shendun (second place) as the bid-winning candidates. Later, the bid inviting party announced that Eurotect Company was determined as the first bid-winning candidate, but did not announce the second bid-winning candidate.

Zhongli Shendun refused to accept the bid evaluation result and raised an objection with the bid inviting party and also lodged a complaint with the Shanghai Leading Group Office for Invitation and Submission of Bids for Electromechanical Equipment. Upon discussion, the bid evaluation committee issued the meeting minutes, deciding to "affirm the original bid evaluation result" and replying to the objections raised by Zhongli Shendun, including questions raised by the Plaintiff in this case about the registered capital, performance capacity, guarantees and technical parameters of third-level products of Eurotect Company. On July 11, 2013, the Leading Group Office issued an opinion on the treatment of the complaint lodged by Zhongli Shendun which stated that: 1. the bidding process of the project of professional supply of surge protective devices and intelligent monitoring systems for the sub-contracted electromechanical system engineering of Shanghai Tower complied with the legal procedure; 2. some expressions in the bid invitation document were not precise but would not affect the bid evaluation decision of the bid evaluation committee. Zhongli Shendun filed an administrative lawsuit against the opinion but then withdrew the same.

On July 1, 2013, the Defendants Construction Group, Installation Engineering Company and Shanghai Tower Company issued a letter of acceptance to Eurotect Company and issued a bid-losing notice to Zhongli Shendun.

The Plaintiff Zhongli Shendun claimed that, it was a famous company in China specializing in the production of lightning protection equipment and was one of the editors in chief of national standards for lightning protection and all the products offered by it in this bidding process met the requirements of the bid invitation document. Upon investigation, it found that, the Defendant Eurotect Company's registered capital and performance capacity, projects completed by Eurotect Company in recent 5 years, the time when the first-level products of Eurotect Company obtained the type test reports, and failure of Eurotect Company to provide an undertaking in connection with performance guarantee and advance payment guarantee and to provide the mandatory registration form of products did not comply with the requirements of bid invitation document; meanwhile, the bid documents submitted by Eurotect Company did not comply with the requirements of bid invitation document and the products offered by Eurotect Company did not meet the technical requirements of bid invitation document, including that: the first-level products offered by Eurotect Company were direct current equipment not the alternating current equipment required by the bid invitation document; the second-level products offered by Eurotect Company were switch-type not voltage-limiting required by bid invitation document; the Ucs of all the third-level products offered by Eurotect Company did not meet relevant requirements; the second-level products offered by Eurotect Company were Level I test products not Level II test products required by bid invitation document and their nominal discharge currents did not meet relevant requirements; the voltage protection parameters of the third-level products offered by Eurotect Company did not meet relevant requirements; products offered by Eurotect Company were not fuse and combination SPDs (namely surge protective devices) required by bid invitation document; and the lightning protection engineering qualification did not meet relevant requirements. In addition, at the time of submission of its bid, Defendant I's registered capital was far below the Plaintiff's registered capital and the amount of this Project; its lightning protection qualification was also lower than that of the Plaintiff; and it did not have any achievement in connection with its first-level products. As a result, the scores of Defendant I on such items should have been lower than that of the Plaintiff, but its scores were higher than that of the Plaintiff. Therefore, it could be concluded that the scores were unreasonable. The other four Defendants did not conduct prequalification and only announced one bid-winning candidate, which violated relevant laws and regulations. They also postponed the bid opening to enable Eurotect Company to obtain product test reports and handle formalities for mandatory registration. Based on the above, it could be concluded that the five Defendants colluded with each other in submission of bids, which shall constitute an act of unfair competition. Therefore, the Plaintiff requested the Court to order that the bidding result of the project of professional supply of surge protective devices and intelligent monitoring systems for the sub-contracted electromechanical system engineering of Shanghai Tower shall be invalid.

The Defendant Eurotect Company argued that: 1. It had the qualification to submit a bid. (1) Although its registered capital was RMB 1 million, it provided its financial statements for recent three years and introductions to the projects completed by it in recent 5 years in its bid documents and such materials showed that it met the requirements for the performance capacity of RMB 2 million and the projects completed in recent 5 years. (2) All products offered by it had obtained the type test reports and had been registered with the Meteorological Administration, and the bid invitation document did not require providing mandatory registration forms. The parameters of the first-level products in bid invitation document were referring to the old national standards but the first-level products offered by Defendant I were referring to the mew national standards, so Defendant I, after receiving the bid invitation document, carried out product tests in accordance with old national standards and obtained the type test reports on August 17, 2012 and then handled formalities for mandatory registration on August 21 of the same year, both before the deadline for submission of bids. (3) The requirements of providing an undertaking in connection with performance guarantee and advance payment guarantee appeared in the notice of invitation for bids and did not appear in the bid invitation document which only specified that the guarantees needed to be issued after winning the bid. 2. The products offered by it met the technical requirements of bid invitation document. (1) The "alternating current equipment" in Section 5 of the bid invitation document referred to electrical environment and relevant content did not require providing alternating current products. Direct current surge protective device could also provide protection for alternating current system. To summarize, the Plaintiff's claim was based on its misunderstanding. (2) According to Article 2.2.1 of the bid invitation document, the first-level products may be switch-type. (3) The bid invitation document specified that the Ucs of the first-level, second-level and third-level products shall be 420V, but products with higher Ucs were not necessarily better. Where the lightning proof products met the requirements of national standards, the lightning proof products with lower Ucs could provide better protection to the equipment protected but could suffer a greater loss; otherwise, the lightning proof products with higher Ucs could suffer a smaller loss but the equipment protected could suffer a greater loss. The products offered by Eurotect Company are the best choices that met requirements of national standards and were recognized by the bid evaluation committee. (4) The parameters of the second-level products in the bid invitation document were referred to Level II test, but the products offered by it were Level I test products; according to table 5.4.1 - 2 of national standard GB50343 - 2004 and table 5.4.3 - 3 of national standard GB50343 - 2012, the nominal discharge current of 12.5KA in Level I test was equal to the nominal discharge current of 50KA in Level II test; therefore, the products offered by it met the requirements of "exceeding or equal to 40KA". (5) According to table 6.4.4 of national standard GB 50057 - 2010 and table 5.4.3 - 1 of national standard GB

50343 – 2012, the impact resistance voltage of electric equipment was 2.5KV, so where the surplus capacity of 20% was reserved, the third-level SPDs with the Ups lower than 2KV met the requirements of national standard. Ups of the products offered by it were 1.75 KV and met the requirements of national standard. Although the requirement of "lower or equal to 1.7KV" was not met, such products were recognized by the bid evaluation committee. Meanwhile, GB 18802.1 – 2002 specified preferred values, of which 1.8KV was the closest to the requirement of the bid invitation document, so in theory, Ups of corresponding products shall be 1.8KV rather than 1.7KV or 1.75KV. (6) There was no fuse and combination products so called by the Plaintiff in textbooks, the industry and standards, and Eurotect Company connected the fuse protector with lightning protector by using a wire following the normal practice and such practice complied with requirements of the bid invitation document. (7) The bid inviting party made it clear in the supplementary document that the requirements for lightning protection engineering qualification applied to designs and construction but not to products or bidders. In this case, the bid evaluation was a comprehensive one and did not just focus on parameters. The Plaintiff's claim that the Defendants colluded with each other in the bidding process lacked factual basis and was just a conjecture.

The Defendants Construction Group, Installation Engineering Company and Shanghai Tower Company jointly argued that: 1. The bid evaluation committee had re-examined the objections raised by the Plaintiff but still affirmed the original bid evaluation result, which was recognized by the administrative department. 2. According to provisions of laws, after answering questions raised by bidders, the bid inviting party must postpone the bid opening. Therefore, the Plaintiff's claim that the bid inviting party postponed the bid opening for the benefit of Eurotect Company lacked factual basis. 3. The Plaintiff did not provide any evidence to prove that there was any communication between the winning bidder and the bid inviting party in connection with collusion. The bidding project involved in this case adopted the comprehensive bid evaluation method, so the winner bidder would be the company which satisfied all the requirements to the maximum extent not the company which completely complied with the requirements of the bid invitation document. Of course, Eurotect Company met all the requirements for winning the bid. 4. As the requirement of lightning protection engineering qualification was not applicable to the bidders, the experts did not consider it when they evaluated it. 5. The involved bidding project adopted the post-qualification not the prequalification claimed by the Plaintiff. If the first bid-winning candidate did not meet the bid-winning requirements for any reason, the bid inviting party would invite bids again and would not determine the second bid-winning candidate as the winning bidder. So, whether the second bid-winning candidate was announced or not had nothing to do with this case.

The Defendant Technical Import and Export Company argued that: 1. Laws did not require that the qualification examination shall adopt prequalification, and the involved bidding project adopted post-qualification. 2. The reason why it only announced the first bid-winning candidate was that it was not required to announce all candidates. 3. The postponement of bid opening was caused by the fact that the deadline for submission of bids was less than 15 days after the bid inviting party sent clarification documents with respect to the questions raised by bidders, so according to laws, the bid opening must be postponed.

[Judgment]

Upon trial, Shanghai Pudong New Area People's Court held that, the Plaintiff of this case did not provide evidence to prove the collusion between the Defendants but only concluded that the Defendants colluded in the submission of bids on the grounds that the Defendant Eurotect Company was not qualified to submit bids, that products offered by Eurotect Company did not meet the requirements of the bid invitation document, that the other four Defendants knew such situations but still allowed Eurotect Company to participate in the bid, postponed the bid opening for the benefit of Eurotect Company and determined Eurotect Company as the winning bidder and that the bidding process did not comply with provisions of laws.

Therefore, the focus of this case would be on whether the circumstances claimed by the Plaintiff were true; if they were true, whether it could be concluded that the Defendants colluded with each other in submission of bids as specified in the *Regulations on Implementation of the Law on Bid Invitation and Submission* (hereinafter referred to as "Implementation Regulations").

First, it is about the postponement of bid opening. Within the scope specified in the bid invitation document, the bid inviting party issued clarification documents to the bidders with respect to the questions raised by them. According to the *Law on Bid Invitation and Submission* and the *Implementation Regulations*, it complied with laws and was reasonable to postpone the bid opening when the time between the issue of clarification documents and the deadline for submission of bids was less than 15 days. Second, it is about the bid process. According to Articles 15(2) and 20 of the *Implementation Regulations*, the bid inviting party may adopt one of the two methods to examine bidders' qualification, namely prequalification or post-qualification; such Articles did not specify that the prequalification was a must as claimed by the Plaintiff. In this case, the bid invitation document also specified the requirements for qualification of potential bidders, and after bid opening, the bid evaluation committee examined the qualification of the bidders, so obviously the bid evaluation committee adopted the post-qualification. The bid evaluation committee recommended that Eurotect Company and the Plaintiff shall be the first and second bid-winning candidates respectively but the bid inviting party only announced the first bid-winning candidate, which violated the provisions of the *Implementation Regulations* but was not one of the circumstances specified by the Law on Bid Invitation and Submission which may result in the invalidity of the bidding result, and from which the collusion between the Defendants could not be concluded. Third, it is about the Plaintiff's claim that Eurotect Company was not qualified to submit a bid. Upon examination, the bid documents of Eurotect Company included relevant qualification documents, and such documents were recognized by the bid evaluation committee during the re-evaluation, so the Plaintiff's claim that Eurotect Company was not qualified to submit a bid lacked factual basis. Last, it is about the Plaintiff's claim that products offered by Eurotect Company did not meet the technical requirements of the bid invitation document. National standards specified relevant technical parameters of the involved products, and technical parameters of products offered by Eurotect Company met all of the requirements of national standards. Although some parameters of products offered by Eurotect Company were not exactly the same as the requirements of the bid invitation document, members of the bid evaluation committee, according to the bid evaluation rules and based on their professional knowledge, concluded that Eurotect Company was qualified to submit a bid and ranked first in terms of comprehensive scores after examining and grading multiple indicators such as the surge protective device and intelligent monitoring systems offered by the bidder. After the Plaintiff raised an objection, the bid evaluation committee, upon re-evaluation, recognized the technical performance of the products offered by Eurotect Company and affirmed the original bid evaluation result. The Plaintiff held that

Eurotect Company shall not be the winning bidder because parameters of products offered by it were not consistent with the bid invitation document. Such opinion was inconsistent with the purpose of the comprehensive bid evaluation method. The Plaintiff's conclusion that the bid inviting party colluded with the winning bidder lacked both factual and legal basis. In conclusion, the Plaintiff did not have any evidence to prove that the Defendants colluded with each other, and all circumstances claimed by the Plaintiff were insufficient to prove that the Defendants colluded with each other. Therefore, the claims of the Plaintiff lacked factual bases.

To sum up, in accordance with Article 15 of the *Anti-Unfair Competition Law of the People's Republic of China* and Article 64(1) of the *Civil Procedure Law of the People's Republic of China*, Shanghai Pudong New Area People's Court ruled that all claims of the Plaintiff Zhongli Shendun shall be rejected.

The Defendant Zhongli Shendun refused to accept the first-instance judgment and filed an appeal.

After trial, Shanghai Intellectual Property Court believed that the facts affirmed in the first instance were clear, the application of laws was correct, and the judgment made was correct, therefore, the appeal shall be refused and the original judgment shall be affirmed.

[Case Study]

There were some defects in the involved bidding process. The focus of dispute in this case was whether it could be concluded that the bid inviting party colluded with the winning bidder just from such defects, thus resulting in the invalidity of the bidding result.

I. Defective bidding process is not equal to collusive tendering

During invitation and submission of bids, both the bid inviting party and the bidders shall comply with the *Law on Bid Invitation and Submission* and the *Implementation Regulations*. Meanwhile, as the invitation and submission of bids are civil acts, according to the principle of autonomy, for both the bid inviting party and the bidders, the bid invitation document published shall be the "constitution" that they shall strictly abide by during invitation and submission of bids. Where the bid documents of the winning bidder do not comply with the requirements of the bid invitation document in some respects (hereinafter referred to as defective bidding process) but there is no collusion specified in the *Regulations on Implementation of the Law on Bid Invitation and Submission*, should it be concluded based on such defects that the bid inviting party colludes with the winning bidder?

The author holds that, the *Law on Bid Invitation and Submission* and the *Implementation Regulations* specify the collusions, the legal consequence of which is the invalidity of the bidding result. Where there are defects in invitation and submission of bids but there is no collusion specified by the laws, not all defects in invitation and submission of bids will necessarily cause invalidity of the bidding result. The collusion in submission of bids are objectively collusion and subjectively intentional while the defects in invitation and submission of bids are objective facts, so it cannot be concluded just based on defects that the bid inviting party and the winning bidder intentionally collude with each other. Therefore, even when there are defects in invitation and submission of bids, to determine the collusion between the bid inviting party and the winning bidder, it is necessary to consider the effects of the defects on the purpose of the bidding process. It is improper to determine small defects as acts of unfair competition and to tolerate corresponding speculation and violation and render the *Anti-Unfair Competition Law* not binding. For example, in the collusive tendering case brought against the defendant Xu, etc. ,[1] the notice of invitation for bids specifies that when a bidder is an agency, it must obtain the certificate of exclusive agency issued by its manufacturer; the defendant counterfeits an agency certificate and colludes with the other two bidders to submit bids together, causing lack of competition between the bidders and damaging the value of the bidding process; such behavior shall be collusive tendering. In the collusive tendering case between the plaintiff Beijing Heer Info Tech Co. , Ltd. and the Defendants Jiangsu Wisedu System Co. , Ltd. , etc. ,[2] the copyright of the computer software offered by Wiscom System Co. , Ltd. belongs to the affiliate of Wiscom System Co. , Ltd. and Wiscom System Co. , Ltd. only has the right to use such software, and Wiscom System Co. , Ltd. also fails to submit the license agreement in its bid documents. The court holds that, such behavior is defective but the key to influence the contractor's development capacity is to obtain the right to use the

---

[1] Shanghai Chongming People's Court (2012) CXCZ No. 91 Paper of Criminal Judgment
[2] Beijing Shijingshan District People's Court (2012) SMCZ No. 609 Paper of Civil Judgment

relevant computer software and the ownership of such software is immaterial in this case, and therefore determines that such defects are not sufficient to result in the invalidity of the bidding result and that there is no collusion.

Ⅱ. The judgment shall be based on whether relevant defects would result in frustration of the bidding purpose

The purpose of invitation and submission of bids is to require the bidders to compete with each other under the same conditions on the principles of openness, fairness, justness and good faith so as to achieve the optimal allocation of manpower, financial resources and material resources. The invitation and submission of bids, as a system, has the basic value of introducing the competitive contracting mechanism to give equal opportunities to bidders and enable the best and most suitable bidder to win the bid and thus enable the bid inviting party to acquire optimal goods or services at a relatively low price. The collusive tendering directly violates such basic value and frustrates the purpose of bid invitation. However, not all defects in bid invitation and submission will necessarily frustrate the purpose of bid invitation. So in light of the institutional value of bid invitation and submission, defects in bid invitation and submission do not necessarily mean that the bid winner colludes with the bid inviting party. The key to determine collusion is whether such defects could result in frustration of the purpose of bid invitation, which is also the focus of examination in collusive tendering cases.

In this case, the subject of the bidding project is surge protective devices and intelligent monitoring systems, mainly including surge protective devices and their intelligent monitoring systems. So the purpose of bid invitation is to select the optimal lightning proof products and corresponding intelligent monitoring systems. Lightning protection plan is a systematic project, and the factors deciding the lightning protection result include technical parameters, installation locations and design of monitoring systems of SPDs at different levels. The Plaintiff claimed Defendant I's incompliance with the requirements of the bid invitation document and the violations of laws by the bidding process. The circumstances that were defective included that: Defendant I failed to submit the undertaking in connection with guarantees, the Ucs and voltage protection parameters of the third-level products did not meet the requirements of the bid invitation document and the bid inviting party only announced one bid-winning candidate. Other circumstances claimed by the

Plaintiff, upon investigation, were caused by the Plaintiff's misunderstanding of the bid invitation document or laws. As the purpose of the bid invitation was to select optimal lightning proof products and monitoring systems, the facts that Defendant I failed to submit the undertaking in connection with guarantees and the bid inviting party only announced one bid-winning candidate were not closely related to the purpose of the bid invitation and belonged to minor defects and were insufficient to prove that there was collusive tendering. The incompliance of the two technical parameters mentioned above was closely related to the purpose of the bid invitation, but to determine whether the incompliance was sufficient to prove that there war collusive tendering, the effect of the incompliance on the purpose of the bid invitation shall also be considered. National standards specified technical parameters of the involved products and where the national standards were met, the key to influence the lightning protection result was the combination between parameters. The Plaintiff's claim that the incompliance of parameters with the bid invitation document shall disqualify Defendant I from winning the bid was not consistent with the meaning of the comprehensive bid evaluation method, and the conclusion on the lightning protection result based on several parameters did not conform to the truth. As the technical performance of the products offered by Defendant I fully met the requirements of the national standards, upon examining and comprehensively grading the surge protective devices and monitoring systems offered by the bidders and other indicators, members of the bid evaluation committee, based on the bid evaluation rules and their professional knowledge, held that, although some parameters of the products offered by Defendant I were not exactly consistent with the requirements of the bid invitation document, such products met the requirements of the involved project and Defendant I ranked first in terms of comprehensive performance. After the Plaintiff raised an objection, the bid evaluation committee, upon re-evaluation, recognized the technical performance of the products offered by Defendant I. Therefore, the court determined that the Plaintiff's conclusion based on the above circumstances that the bid inviting party colluded with the winning bidder lacked both factual and legal basis.

(Writer: Ye Jufen)

Affirmation of Legal Nature of Blocking Video Advertisement by Tools Software

—Beijing IQIYI Science & Technology Co. , Ltd. vs Shanghai Damo Network Technology Co. , Ltd. Unfair Competition Dispute Case

[Abstract]

The benefits agreed between the website operator and the users which are generated by the video sharing website by the business model of "advertising + free video" shall be protected by laws. The operator of third-party tools software shall not harm by any technical means the legal or agreed interests generated by others through proper business model. In case any tools software blocks the video advertisement at the video sharing network by some technical means and obtains its own competitive advantages in violation of commercial ethics and principle of honesty and credibility which disturbs the normal operation of the video sharing website, causes damage to the legal interests of the website operator and constitutes unfair competition, the relevant person shall bear the civil liability.

[Case Review]

Plaintiff (Appellee): Beijing IQIYI Science & Technology Co. , Ltd.

Defendant (Appellant): Shanghai Damo Network Technology Co. , Ltd.

Cause of Action: dispute over unfair competitions

First-Instance Case No. : (2015) MMS (Z) CZ No. 271

Second-Instance Case No. : (2016) H73MZ No. 33

The Plaintiff Beijing IQIYI Science & Technology Co. , Ltd. (hereinafter referred to as IQIYI) is founded in 2007 and is mainly engaged in internet information services. The website operated by IQIYI (www. iqiyi. com) provides network users with video display service and achieves good performance and obtains high awareness in the industry. The business model of the website is as follows: spend a large amount of funds to buy the copyrights of authorized editions of video programs and pay for the expenses of bandwidth, promotion and publicity. The Plaintiff maintains the normal operation of the website by means of the following two income sources: 1. advertising revenue in a mode of "advertising + free video" (play commercial advertisement before video to collect advertising expenses, and users may watch the video for free by watching the advertisement); 2. income of membership fee in a mode of "paid membership + free video" (users pay the membership fees and directly watch video programs without advertisement during the validity of their membership). As for the 1st first source of income, generally, the Plaintiff will charge the advertising expenses by cpm according to the network advertising contract between the Plaintiff and the client (i. e. based on the person-time watching the advertisement before the video).

The Defendant Shanghai Damo Network Technology Co. , Ltd. (hereinafter referred to as Damo) is founded in 2012 and mainly engaged in the design and development of computer software and hardware. At the website operated by it (www. ad-safe. com), the Defendant provides the users with a piece of software called "ADSafe" (hereinafter referred to as Software Involved) for free. The Software Involved is developed by the Defendant which is a piece of comprehensive intelligent advertisement block software with a tagline of "cleaning is so good". The copyright of the software is owned by the Defendant. According to the software introduction at the website homepage, one of the main functions of the Software Involved is "no wait for watching video" which "can skip advertisement for 30, 60 or 90 seconds and avoid all interference". This function may be used by users at their own discretion.

The Plaintiff obtained pieces of evidence on September 19, 2014 and April 24, 2015, evidencing that if the users installed and used the function of "no wait for watching video" of the Software Involved, they may skip a 60-second advertisement displayed before the video and directly watch the video at the computer terminal and Android terminal of "IQIYI" website.

During the court trial, the Plaintiff stated the display mechanism of the videos and advertisements in its website when the user clicks the video display page, a main player will be loaded at the page. The main player is comprised of advertisement player and video player. After the user clicks and plays the video, the advertisement player will be loaded first and a request for advertisement data will be sent to the server based on which the advertisement will be displayed; after the advertisement, a specific signal will be sent to the main player, the video player will be loaded and the video program will be played. The Plaintiff also explained the operating principle of the "no wait for watching video" function of the Software Involved: after the user clicks the video, a network data processing layer will be generated. If the user installs the Software Involved and uses the "no wait for watching video" function, the advertisement data request in the video player will be blocked, and only the request for playing the video program will be answered. As a result, the user may skip advertisement and directly play the video program.

The Plaintiff alleged that Damo advertised the Software Involved and induced users to download the Software Involved and use the "no wait for watching video" function. As are sult, users may skip the advertisement and directly watch video programs at the website of IQIYI which caused damages to the legal interests obtained by IQIYI by displaying advertisement and constituted unfair competition. Therefore, the Plaintiff requested the court to order the Defendant to stop its infringement act, eliminate effects and indemnify the Plaintiff for its economic loss of RMB 2 million (in RMB, similarly hereinafter) and a reasonable expense of RMB 83,500.

The Defendant Damo argued that, first of all, the Software Involved developed and operated by the Defendant was not against the Plaintiff and did not mean to damage other's rights and interests or seek improper commercial interests. The purpose of the Software Involved was to better satisfy consumer demands and help consumers select neutral technical tools. Users can decide whether to install or how to use the Software Involved at their own discretion, and the Defendant only provided them with the Software Involved and did not commit the behavior of skipping the advertisement. Secondly, the legal interests obtained by the Plaintiff in the business model of "advertisement + free video" were not protected by laws. Even if the incomes of the Plaintiff decreased duo to the application of the Software Involved by users, it was all due to market development and the choice made by users themselves. Therefore, the provision of the Software Involved to users by the Defendant did not constitute unfair competition. What's more, even if the Defendant constituted unfair competition, the Defendant did not damage the Plaintiff's goodwill, personal rights or other rights, and the Plaintiff failed to provide any evidence to prove its loss and the profit made by the Defendant. Therefore, the Defendant refused to accept the civil liability for eliminating effects and making compensation.

[Judgment]

After the trial, Shanghai Minghang District People's Court held that the focus of dispute in the case was: 1. Whether the business mode of "advertisement + free video" was proper and should be protected; 2. Whether the Software Involved with the function of "no wait for watching video" operated by the Defendant belonged to a neutral technical tool developed by the Defendant for public interest and (if not) whether the Software Involved constituted infringement. As for the first dispute focus, the court held that the business mode of "advertisement + free video" was not owned by the Plaintiff alone and should not be protected by laws. However, such business mode could be deemed as an agreement between the users and the Plaintiff concerning the watching of video program. If the Plaintiff sends an offer of "advertisement + free video" to the users, and the users click the video, a commitment should be deemed to constitute, and the parties will reach an agreement in which case the business mode will be binding upon the parties. It was found through investigation that the commercial advertising in the agreement was not malicious or illegal advertising. Therefore, the interests agreed between the Plaintiff and the users according to the agreement were protected by laws and should not be damaged by any other person. As for the second dispute focus, the court held that the Software Involved developed and operated by the Defendant was a profit-making one. The different services provided by the Plaintiff and the Defendant were related to each other and constituted competitive relation. The object argued by the Plaintiff in this case was the "no wait for watching video" function of the Software Involved. The Defendant knew perfectly or should have known that the main objects blocked by this function were the commercial advertisements normally played at the video sharing website and seduced users to download the Software Involved by means of advertising, free download and addition of rule source by users themselves because the Defendant knew that many users were unwilling to pay time cost and money. As a result, the Defendant increased downloads of the Software Involved, gained the popularity of the Software Involved, increased its awareness and obtained competitive edge. The behavior of the Defendant directly damaged the interests agreed between the Plaintiff and the users and caused commercial loss to the Plaintiff in the short run. In the long run, if the incomes of the video sharing website is seriously affected, and the website operator is unable to pay the copyright fee of authorized edition of video programs, no one is willing to operate the unprofitable video sharing website which will finally damage the interests of consumers. Therefore, the "no wait for watching video" function of the Software Involved developed and operated by the Defendant was not for protecting consumers and other public interests, was not necessary and proper for protecting public interests, violated business ethics and principle of honesty and credibility, damaged the legal interests of the Plaintiff, obtained a benefit and constituted unfair competition.

To sum up, according to Articles 2 and 20 of the *Anti-Unfair Competition Law of the People's Republic of China*, and Articles 9(1) and 15(1) and 15(6) of the *Tort Liability Law of the People's Republic of China*, Shanghai Minhang District People's Court made the following judgment: the Defendant Damo shall immediately stop its infringement act and indemnify the Plaintiff for its economic loss of RMB 2 million and reasonable expense of RMB 33,500.

The Defendant Damo refused to accept the first-instance judgment and filed an appeal.

After trial, Shanghai Intellectual Property Court believed that the facts affirmed in the first instance were clear, the application of laws was correct, trial procedures were legal and the judgment made was correct, and therefore, the appeal shall be refused and the original judgment shall be affirmed.

[Case Study]

This case is a new type of unfair competition dispute case caused by blocking the advertisement at other's website by using tools software and through technical means. The alleged behavior is not a kind of unfair competition act listed in the *Anti-Unfair Competition Law of the People's Republic of China*. Therefore, it is difficult during the trial to apply the principle terms set out in Article 2 of the *Anti-Unfair Competition Law of the People's Republic of China* to regulate and adjust the new competitive behavior in the internet environment. In this case, the business mode is not protected by law, but the legal or agreed interests generated by it shall be protected by law; meanwhile, whether the alleged act in the internet environment constitutes unfair competition is determined based on the key components of traditional tort and according to behavior subject, nature of illegality of behavior and consequence of damage which accurately seizes the legislative spirit and application conditions of the *Anti-Unfair Competition Law of the People's Republic of China* and can be used for reference.

Ⅰ. Whether there is a competitive relation between the behavior subjects

According to the judicial policies enacted by the Supreme People's Court with respect to the trial of unfair competition case, competitive relation is a kind of social relation formed in the process of competition by equal and qualified market players. Existence of competitive relation is one of the important factors to be considered for affirmation of unfair competition.

First of all, both the Plaintiff and the Defendant are operators conducting their business activities in the market. The biggest feature of business activities in the market is "for profit". Making profit does not mean achieving earnings. There are many types of profit making, including immediate interests and long-term interests. For example, in the internet industry, the software developers input manpower and material resources to research and develop software, and invest capitals to provide users with their software for free at the early stage so as to attract users to download their software, improve their popularity and website awareness for the purpose of increasing website value which possesses the nature of rentability.

Secondly, horizontal competition in the same business scope may exist between the Plaintiff and the Defendant, and certain competitive circumstance such as harming others to benefit oneself or taking advantages of others may occur. For example, in this case, although the Plaintiff and the Defendant provided users with different network services, the target object of the "no wait for watching video" function of the Software Involved is those video sharing websites meeting the operating principle of the Software Involved. Without such video sharing websites, the "no wait for watching video" function will have no operation basis and value. Therefore, although the Plaintiff and the Defendant provided users with different services, they were related to each other (i. e. the services provided by the Plaintiff were used by the Defendant) and a competitive relation adjusted by the *Anti-Unfair Competition Law of the People's Republic of China* exists between the parties.

What's more, a specific competitive relation exists between the Plaintiff and the Defendant. In practice, the alleged competitive behavior may aim at specific operators or optional operators. In the later case, in the event that the infringer, the infringement act and the consequence of damage are specific, and a causal relationship of infringement exists between the infringer and the infringed, in principle, any optional operator damaged by the infringer may become an eligible subject making a claim.

Ⅱ. Whether the alleged behavior constitutes unfair competition

Market economy requires fair, legitimate and ordered competition, and the sound development of internet economy requires an ordered market circumstance and explicit market competition rules. To determine whether the alleged behavior constitutes unfair competition, we may consider the following two factors: 1. whether the alleged behavior is a kind of market competition; 2. whether the alleged behavior violates the principle of honesty and credibility or recognized commercial ethics.

On the one hand, in the internet environment, the nature of market competition doesn't change and still aims to obtain transaction opportunity and improve competitive advantage. For example, in this case, the Defendant obtained the opportunity to deal with the users of video sharing website by advertising the "no wait for watching video" function of the software operated by it so as to enlarge the number of users of the Software Involved and improve its own competitive edge. Therefore, the alleged behavior can be considered as a market competition behavior.

On the other hand, technology updating is faster and competitive modes and means are more complicated in the internet environment. The inappropriateness of competitive behavior is mainly reflected in whether the application of certain technology violates the principle of honesty and credibility or recognized commercial ethics and does not mean the evaluation of the technology. Specifically, technical innovation should be worth being encouraged, but any kind of technology which can be used for legal and undisputed purpose may also be applied for illegal purpose or infringing other's interests. Therefore, only when there is a relevant piece of evidence proving that the technology developer deliberately seduces or incites others to or helps others implement infringement act during the business activities for its own interests can the developer undertake the liability for tort. In this case, the Defendant developed the "no wait for watching video" function of the Software Involved, knew that many users were unwilling to pay time cost and money, and seduces them to download and use the Software Involved for the purpose of increasing its market transaction opportunity and obtaining competitive edge in the market relying on the user group of the Plaintiff. In essence, the behavior of the Defendant improperly took advantage of other's market achievement to seek competitive edge for itself, and violated the principle of honesty and credibility and recognized commercial ethics and was improper.

III. Whether the alleged behavior caused consequence of damage

With the booming development of internet technology, there are numerous business models and the competition is stiff. As for any behavior which has not been explicitly prohibited in the *Anti-Unfair Competition Law of the People's Republic of China*, the application of principle terms shall be subject to the principle of prudence. In other words, only when the legal interests of other operators are damaged and the fair competition order can't be maintained if the unfair competition is not stopped can the principle terms be applied.

On the one hand, the source of legal interests of the operator protected by law must be legal and proper. In internet environment, most of the sources of rights and interests in market competition are based on the business model. However, the business model is not protected by law. If the business model does not violate the basic spirit and prohibitive rules in the *Anti-Unfair Competition Law of the People's Republic of China*, the legal and agreed commercial interests obtained by the operator based on the business model can be protected by law and others can't damage such interests in any wrongful way. For example, the business model of "advertisement + free video" offered to users by the Plaintiff was an effective and convenient way for service provision and consumption between the Plaintiff and the consumers which was gradually formed for the purpose of adapting to the network environment. This operation model was not protected by any explicitly legal provisions, was not exclusively owned by the Plaintiff and had no legal interests. However, in this business model, when the users chose to watch videos by means of "advertisement +

free video", they should be deemed to have entered into a video watching agreement with the Plaintiff and both of them should be bound by the agreement. The interests agreed between the users and the Plaintiff in that mode were legitimate and proper and should not be damaged by any other person.

On the other hand, consumer's interests and public interests are protected by laws which shall not be damaged by the alleged competitive behavior. For example, the "no wait for watching video" function of the Software Involved seems to be beneficial to the users who can directly watch ad-free video programs free of charge. However, in the long run, the interests of the video sharing website will be severely damaged, as a result of which the video sharing website can't afford the expenses for purchasing the copyrights of video programs and has no profit to make. Finally, no one is willing to operate the video sharing website, and the interests of video consumers will be damaged. Therefore, when determining whether consumer's interests or public interests are damaged, we should make consideration from the perspective of the long-term development of market competition so as to give a play to the leading role of judiciary in intellectual property protection and further construct a stable and fair market competition order and good business environment.

(Writers: Gu Yaan, Chen Yiyu)

Affirmation of Legal Nature of the Act of Disclosing the Judgment Document of the Competitor without Permission

—Yangzhou Longjuanfeng Catering Enterprise Management Co. , Ltd. vs Shanghai Shengmin Food and Beverage Management Co. , Ltd. Unfair Competition Dispute Case

[**Abstract**]

Before the effectiveness of the judgment document, the facts involved and legislative confirmation belong to pending judicial issue. In the event that the operator discloses the ineffective judgment document of its competitor to the public through the internet and other channels and exaggerates, misinterprets or makes a deliberate misinterpretation of the relevant fact, the relevant public will misunderstand the competitor whose goodwill will be damaged and normal operation will be destroyed, and the operator will constitute business discrediting. In the event that, upon the effectiveness of the judgment document, the content of the judgment document disclosed to the public by the operator fails to truthfully reflect such facts ascertained and conclusion affirmed in the effective judgment document and makes the public misunderstand the operator's competitor whose goodwill is damaged by the false statement fabricated and distributed by the operator, the operator shall be deemed to constitute business discrediting.

[**Case Review**]

Plaintiff（Appellee）: Yangzhou Longjuanfeng Catering Enterprise Management

Co. , Ltd.

Defendant (Appellant): Shanghai Shengmin Food and Beverage Management Co. , Ltd.

Cause of Action: dispute over unfair competitions

First-Instance Case No. : (2015) MMS (Z) CZ No. 1291

Second-Instance Case No. : (2016) H73MZ No. 132

Both of the Plaintiff Yangzhou Longjuanfeng Catering Enterprise Management Co. , Ltd. (hereinafter referred to as Longjuanfeng) and the Defendant Shanghai Shengmin Food and Beverage Management Co. , Ltd. (hereinafter referred to as Shengmin) were engaged in the franchised business in catering industry (including storm potato snack) and storm potato products were sold at the stores of both parties.

The Defendant was founded in July 2, 2013 and is engaged in catering enterprise management and sale of edible agricultural products (excluding swine products). Kafu System Co. , Ltd. not involved in the case granted the exclusive usage license of the male version and female version of "storm potato" in China to the Defendant. According to the works registration certificate, the works were created on August 27, 2009 and published for the first time on October 23, 2009. Li Fengjiu, Piao Zhonghao and Liu Junmo who were not involved in the case granted the usage license of the design patent of skewered potato chips to the Defendant on June 17, 2013.

The Plaintiff Longjuanfeng was founded on February 24, 2014 with its legal representative being Li Caizhang and its business scope being the retail of prepackaged food and bulk food and catering enterprise management. On the establishment date of the Plaintiff, Li Caizhang issued a letter of authorization to grant a license to the Plaintiff to use the No. 8867370 "Longjuanfeng" trademark whose exclusive usage license was obtained by Li Caizhang from Su Baofu who was not involved in the case on August 21, 2012. The trademark was approved to be used for class 29 goods with the validity from August 21, 2012 to August 20, 2022. On October 11, 2014, Li Caizhang registered the copyright of the pattern identification created by him whose creation time and first publishing time indicated in the registration certificate were respectively October 8, 2013 and January 22, 2014. Li Caizhang obtained the design patents of skewered ham sausage (Longjuanfeng), skewered sweet potato (Longjuanfeng) and skewered potato (Longjuanfeng) from January 2015 to April 2015 and obtained the design patent of a spiral-potato-chips-making machine (large).

On February 13, 2015, the Plaintiff applied to Jiangsu Yangzhou Notary Office for notarization of evidence preservation. According to the contents in the light disk attached to the notarization, the website operated and managed by the Defendant contained the following information: the words "fake brand" were shown on the webpage, below which there were some patterns and identification including the corporate image identification of the Plaintiff (i. e. the pattern created by Li Caizhang + the words of "STORM POTATO").

On March 13, 2015, the Plaintiff applied to Jiangsu Yangzhou Notary Office for notarization of evidence preservation again. According to the contents in the light disk attached to the notarization, when one clicked the words "fake brand" under the column of "storm potato" on the webpage operated and managed by the Defendant and entered the relevant page, he can see the following information: the words "case of cracking down on counterfeit goods: safeguard consumers' rights" were shown at the upward side of the webpage, and the relevant information of the Defendant was indicated below these words; the information of the Plaintiff (i. e. the pattern identification created by Li Caizhang with words of "STORM POTATO" "fake brand") was listed below the information of the Defendant; meanwhile, four lines of words ("Defendant's brand &enterprise:" "Brand: STORM POTATO" "Enterprise: Yangzhou Longjuanfeng Catering Enterprise Management Co., Ltd." "Defendant: Li Caizhang") were shown at the right side of the identification; below the information of the Plaintiff was the (2014) YGZMCZ No. 70 Civil Judgment.

On February 11, 2015, Jiangsu Yangzhou Guangling District People's Court made (2014) YGZMCZ No. 70 Civil Judgment with respect to the case of unfair competition dispute among Shengmin, Longjuanfeng and Li Caizhang. As stated in the judgment, Li Caizhang used to cooperate with Shengmin and entered into a contract with it, and knew the decoration, image design and other details of the franchised outlet of Shengmin. Then Li Caizhang established Longjuanfeng and operated commodities of the same classification and developed alliance business in the name of Longjuanfeng. The overall decoration and image design of the stores operated or authorized by Longjuanfeng were similar to the style and image of the franchised outlet of Shengmin while some details were exactly the same or highly similar which would make the consumers mistake the commodities operated by Longjuanfeng for something originated from or closely related to Shengmin.

Longjuanfeng took advantage of the popularity of commodities of Shengmin by making the similar decoration, constituted unfair competition and should immediately stop its infringement act. After the first instance judgment, Longjuanfeng and Li Caizhang refused to accept the judgment and filed an appeal. After the trial, Yangzhou Intermediate People's Court made a judgment on September 1, 2015 to reject the appeal and affirm the original judgment.

The Plaintiff alleged that since July 2014, the Defendant published an ineffective judgment at its company website and highlighted the enterprise name, legal representative and trademark of the Plaintiff at the column of "fake brand" on the website to fabricate information that the Plaintiff counterfeited the Defendant's brand and received judgment from the court. However, during the second trial of the unfair competition dispute between the Plaintiff and the Defendant, the Defendant published the ineffective judgment on the website to confuse the public and make them think that the brand of the product of the Plaintiff were forged and fake ones. Although the Defendant then provided the effective judgment of second instance, the court held in the judgment that the unfair competition by the Plaintiff against the Defendant was not limited to the Plaintiff's store decoration which was similar with that of the Defendant, which was largely different from the relevance and legal consequence of "fake brand created by the Plaintiff" announced by the Defendant on the website. The Plaintiff held that the Defendant made false and misleading publicity about its product and fabricated information to slander the Plaintiff which constituted vicious competition and caused serious damage to the business reputation and commodity goodwill of the Plaintiff. Therefore, the Plaintiff requested the court to order the Defendant to stop its infringement act, eliminate effects and indemnify the Plaintiff for its economic loss of RMB 80,000, notarial fee of RMB 2,040 and attorney fee of RMB 6000.

The Defendant argued that the result of protecting rights and cracking down on fake goods published on its official website was to protect its own brand and the reference of legal instruments was proper and reasonable. Based on the written judgment of first instance, the Defendant held that counterfeit brand was a common expression of infringement of trade mark and unfair competition. The Defendant held that what is behind a brand was more than the brand itself and should include patent and store decoration, etc. The decoration and design represented the core value of its brand. Therefore, the Plaintiff should be deemed to infringe its brand because it infringed the decoration of its famous commodity. As a result, the Defendant published the ineffective written judgment above on the website for the purpose of explaining the progress of case to its clients, and the publishing of effective written judgment on the website and the statement of "counterfeit brand" were not malicious slander again the Plaintiff but belonged to proper and legal acts for the purpose of protecting its own brand. Therefore, the Defendant requested the court to reject all claims made by the Plaintiff.

[Judgment]

After trial, Shanghai Minhang District People's Court held that, on the one hand, the facts and legislative confirmation involved in the ineffective judgment document belonged to pending judicial issues. In this case, before the effectiveness of the judgment document of first instance, Shengmin published the ineffective judgment on its website with a title of "counterfeit brand, case of cracking down on counterfeit goods" which would confuse the relevant public who would think that Longjuanfeng destroyed the normal operation of its competitor and would cause damage to Longjuanfeng's goodwill and constitute business discrediting. On the other hand, the judgment document involved in this case ordered Longjuanfeng to immediately stop applying decoration similar to that of the licensed franchised outlet of Shengmin and did not affirm whether the brand of Longjuanfeng was "counterfeit brand". Upon the effectiveness of judgment, the statement made by Shengmin on its official website failed to reflect such facts ascertained and contents affirmed in the effective judgment and exceeded the scope of infringement affirmed in the judgment document which lacked factual basis and fabricated information. In this case, although Shengmin published the judgment document at the lower part of the webpage, the public who visited the website did not necessarily see the entire content of the judgment; on the contrary, the public would consider the behavior of Shengmin as the extraction and summary of the judgment and wrongly though that the brand of Longjuanfeng was a "counterfeit brand". What's more, Shengmin published those contents on its official website. Based on the connectivity of internet, any network user may see the aforesaid contents. Therefore, Shengmin's acts above reduced the evaluation and trust of Longjuanfeng among the public, damaged its goodwill and constituted business discrediting.

To sum up, according to Articles 14 and 20 of the *Anti-Unfair Competition Law of the People's Republic of China*, Items 1, 6 and 8 of Article 15 (1) and Article 15 (2) of the *Tort Liability Law of the People's Republic of China*, and Article 17(1) of the *Interpretation of the Supreme People's Court on Some Issues Concerning the Application of Laws in the Trial of Civil Cases Involving Unfair Competition*, Shanghai Minhang District People's Court ordered as follows: Shengmin shall immediately stop its infringement act, eliminate effects and indemnify Longjuanfeng for its economic loss of RMB 30,000, notarial fee of RMB 2,040 and attorney fee of RMB 5,000 (in total: RMB 37,040).

The Defendant refused to accept the first-instance judgment and filed an appeal.

After trial, Shanghai Intellectual Property Court believed that the facts affirmed in the first instance were clear, the application of laws was correct, trial procedures were legal and the judgment made was correct, therefore, the appeal shall be refused and the original judgment shall be affirmed.

[Case Study]

It is a new judicial issue in practice in unfair competition dispute whether the publishment by an operator of the content of judgment against its competitor (especially ineffective judgment) constitutes business discrediting. Article 14 of the *Anti-Unfair Competition Law* stipulates that an operator shall not utter or disseminate falsehoods to damage the goodwill of a competitor or the reputation of it or its goods. Therefore, to determine whether publishing the competitor's ineffective or effective judgment constitutes business discrediting, the court may consider the following circumstances:

I. Whether a competitive relation exists between the two parties

The competitive relation may be identified based on the scope of business set out in the business license and the actual operation condition. In this case, both the Plaintiff and the Defendant were catering enterprise management companies engaged in the catering brand franchising business in China, and "storm potato" products were operated by the licensed franchised outlets of both parties. Therefore, a horizontal competition relation exists between the parties and the requirements set out in the *Anti-Unfair Competition Law* with respect to the affirmation of behavior agent of business discrediting are met.

II. Whether the behavior of "fabricating and spreading false statement" exists

Two conditions precedent shall be satisfied before the publishment of the judgment document: 1. The judgment has come into force. Before the effectiveness of the judgment, the fact in question belongs to pending judicial issue and the dispute focus is undecided. 2. The contents of judgment published must be fair, proper and objective without any deliberate misinterpretation out of context, exaggeration or distort which is against the judicial concept of fairness and justice. In the event that any person publishes any ineffective judgment in an inappropriate manner or the contents of an effective judgment published by any person fail to truthfully reflect such facts ascertained and conclusions made in the judgment, such person shall be deemed to fabricate and spread false information. In this case, before and after the effectiveness of the judgment, the Plaintiff's brand was alleged to be "counterfeit brand" on the webpage of the Defendant, and the judgment published on the website was called "case of cracking down on counterfeit goods". However, a brand is a composite concept containing external and internal meanings. The external meaning refers to the external, concrete and tangible identification of the brand which may directly have strong sensuous impact on the public, including name, trademark, packaging and decoration. Internal meaning refers to the mental feelings of the public and belongs to after-use impression, experience and evaluation of the public. Therefore, decoration infringement is a kind of infringement against brand but can't be deemed as a counterfeit brand. They are not equal to each other. Although the Defendant published the (2014) YGZMCZ No. 70 Civil Judgment at the lower part of the webpage, the public who visited the website did not necessarily see the entire content of the judgment; on the contrary, the public would consider the statement of the Defendant as the extraction and summary of the judgment and wrongly though that the brand of the Plaintiff was a "counterfeit brand" which belonged to the fact ascertained and conclusion made in the judgment. "Case of cracking down on counterfeit goods" has extensive meanings which can't make the public visiting the webpage accurately know that the Plaintiff actually infringed the decoration of the licensed franchised outlet of the Defendant. Therefore, the words of "counterfeit brand" and "case of cracking down on counterfeit goods" were exaggeration or misinterpretation of those facts ascertained and conclusions made in the judgment and constituted fabrication and spreading of false information.

Ⅲ. Whether the goodwill of the competitor is damaged

The legislative purpose of prohibiting business discrediting is to prevent the operator from damaging other's goodwill by means of improper evaluation. In market transactions, operators shall follow the principle of fair competition, honesty and good faith and give objective and fair evaluation to other operators based on facts. In this case, although the Plaintiff was affirmed to infringe the decoration of the Defendant, the brand of the Plaintiff was not identified as a counterfeit one in the judgment and the Plaintiff also could conduct franchising business with its own brand. The Defendant alleged on its website that the brand of the Plaintiff was a "counterfeit brand" which would mislead the existing and potential franchisees and clients of the Plaintiff who would suspect and distrust the Plaintiff's brand and would influence the options of joining or consumption of the public. Brand is the lifeline of an enterprise. A counterfeit brand will cause worse evaluation and more negative effect than decoration infringement. Therefore, the behaviors of the Defendant will make the public form excessive bad impressions on the enterprise image and product quality of the Plaintiff whose social evaluation will be reduced and business reputation and commodity goodwill will be wrongly damaged.

To sum up, the critical point of the trial of such kind of case lies in the determination of whether the relevant behavior will mislead the others and make the public have improper evaluation on the competitor whose goodwill will be damaged as a result. Based on the legislative purpose, in this case, essential elements of business discrediting in unfair competition are analyzed so as to draw a judgment conclusion which possesses certain typical significance.

(Writers: Mou Peng, Chen Yiyu)

Criminal Cases on Intellectual Property

V

Confirmation of Criminal Liability of Provider of Business Premises for Providing Place for Counterfeit Registered Trademark

—Case of selling commodities with counterfeit registered trademark by Li Ruguo et al

[Abstract]

If the provider of premises is fully aware of the criminal act of any commercial tenant who is suspected of selling commodities with counterfeit registered trademark and still leases the premises to the tenant, indulges the tenant to hide the fake commodities in the premises, offer information in advance for the purpose of escaping inspection and investigation or permits the tenant to sell counterfeit commodities, the provider of premises shall be deemed as an accomplice for the crime of selling commodities with counterfeit registered trademark and receive punishment.

[Case Review]

Public prosecution organ: Shanghai Jingan District People's Procuratorate

Defendants: Li Ruguo, Wan Jianping

Cause of action: crime of selling commodities with counterfeit registered trademark

First-Instance Case No.: (2015) PX (Z) CZ No. 50 Paper of Sentence

Second-Instance Case No.: (2016) H03XZ No. 46

Shanghai Hancheng Enterprise Management Co., Ltd. (hereinafter referred to as Hancheng Company) was founded in 2003 and is responsible for the leasing and daily property management of Nan Zheng Building located in No. 580, Nanjing West Road (also known as "Taobao City"). From November 2010 to May 2013, there were 33 cases where the tenants of "Taobao City" were convicted of the crime of selling commodities with counterfeit registered trademark, and the money involved in those cases amounted to more than RMB 300 million. As the actual controller of Hancheng Company, the Defendant Li Ruguo was fully aware that the tenants in "Taobao City" sold counterfeit commodities and had been investigated by administrative and judicial authorities for many times. However, Hancheng Company and its management still leased the premises to tenants and permitted them to sell counterfeit commodities in the premises to obtain illegal gains. During the aforesaid period, the Defendant Li Ruguo made profits by collecting monthly extensive operating fees from the tenants in cash which was not included in the accounting book which amounted to RMB 937,500 in two years. To attract tourists, the Defendant Li Ruguo suggested to collect rack rent for float in the lobby from the scalpers to allow scalpers to solicit customers to shop in the premises. The Defendant Wan Jianping was fully aware that many stores in Taobao City sold counterfeit commodities. To avoid inspection and according to the requirements of stores, Wan Jianping decorated many stores selling counterfeit commodities and installed concealed compartments, electronic remote control doors and other facilities in the stores to hide and furtively sell commodities with counterfeit registered trademarks. It was found through investigation that there were 3,827 commodities with counterfeit registered trademarks which were sold by those stores with a value of RMB 27,463,290.

Meanwhile, the Defendant Li Ruguo had the stores decorated by others, and appointed shop assistants to sell counterfeit commodities. The value of counterfeit commodities with registered trademarks of "PRADA" and "CHANEL" etc. seized and detained was RMB 606,930.

The public prosecution organ alleged that the Defendant Li Ruguo sold commodities with counterfeit registered trademarks which he was full aware of with huge sales volume. Meanwhile, Li Ruguo knew perfectly well that the tenants infringed others' intellectual properties but still leased the premises to them and the sales volume was huge. Therefore, the Defendant Li Ruguo should be convicted of a crime of selling commodities with counterfeit registered trademark and undertake the relevant criminal liability. The Defendant Wan Jianping was fully aware that the tenants sold commodities with counterfeit registered trademarks and still decorated their stores, and thus should be convicted of a crime of selling commodities with counterfeit registered trademark and undertake the relevant criminal liability.

The Defendants Li Ruguo and Wan Jianping and their defenders raised no objection to their particulars of offense and accusation alleged in the indictment but alleged that, although Li Ruguo was the actual controller of Hancheng Company, he was unrelated to the criminal case of Taobao City. What's more, there was no direct evidence proving that Li Ruguo knew the acts of tenants and the extensive operating fees collected were not directly utilized by Li Ruguo. Therefore, Li Ruguo only played a secondary role in the circumstance specified in this section. A reduced punishment could be given to Li Ruguo.

The defender of the Defendant Wan Jianping held that Wan Jianping did not introduce the commodities to consumers and did not obtain any benefit from the selling of counterfeit commodities by the stores because the decoration price of store remained unchanged whether concealed compartments were installed or not. A reduced punishment could be given to Wan Jianping.

[Judgment]

After the trial, Shanghai Putuo District People's Court held that, as the shareholder and actual controller of Hancheng Company, the Defendant Li Ruguo played a decisive role in the illegal financial management and bookkeeping of Hancheng Company as well as the store leasing, property management and market operation management mode of Taobao City and was fully aware of the large amount of counterfeit commodities sold in Taobao City in the past few years. Taking advantage of his controlling power and by means of decision making, incitement and acquiescence, the Defendant Li Ruguo leased the premises to tenants through Hancheng Company and its management, permitted the stores to sell counterfeit commodities, indulges them to build concealed compartments to hide counterfeit commodities, and informed the stores in advance to avoid investigation. The Defendant Li Ruguo shall be directly responsible for frequent counterfeit commodity selling, decoration and hiding, solicitation by scalpers and tour guide in Taobao City. The Defendant Li Ruguo was fully aware of the crime of selling commodities with counterfeit registered trademarks committed by others with huge sales volume, provided the criminals with site for business operation, convenience and assistance, should be deemed as an accomplice and undertake criminal liability for joint crime of selling counterfeit commodities committed by the stores in Taobao City indicated in the criminal judgment. Based on his role in the joint crime, the Defendant Li Ruguo can be deemed as an accessory offender. Meanwhile, the Defendant Li Ruguo was fully aware of a large amount of counterfeit commodities sold by the bags and suitcases stores and decided to collect extensive operating fees from stores to directly make profits from the selling of counterfeit commodities in disguised form. Therefore, the illegal incomes of the Defendant Li Ruguo shall be recovered. The Defendant Li Ruguo operated stores to sell commodities which he knew perfectly well bore counterfeit registered trademarks with huge sales volume and thus constituted the crime of selling commodities with counterfeit registered trademarks. According to the relevant judicial interpretation, any person selling commodities with counterfeit registered trademark with huge sales volume shall be sentenced to fixed-term imprisonment of no less than three years but not more than seven years and a fine according to the law. Considering that the commodities seized were to be sold and hadn't been sold due to some reasons beyond the will of the operators, based on the affirmation of attempted crime, the offender may be given a lesser punishment compared with the punishment given to a consummated offender. During the trial, the Defendant Li Ruguo truthfully confessed his crime and may be given a lesser punishment according to the law. The Defendant Li Ruguo voluntarily prepay RMB 100,000 as the fine through his family which shall be considered by the court at the time of sentencing.

The Defendant Wan Jianping assisted the tenants in decorating the stores for hiding counterfeit commodities and avoiding investigation while he was fully aware that the tenants were selling commodities with counterfeit registered trademark. The Defendant Wan Jianping had committed the crime of selling commodities with counterfeit registered trademarks and shall be punished as an accomplice committing the crime of selling commodities with counterfeit registered trademarks. As the Defendant Wan Jianping assisted the tenants in decorating the stores, he may be deemed to play a secondary role in the joint offence and be an accessory offender whom may be given a lesser punishment according to the law. Considering the huge sales volume of the commodities seized in the stores to be sold and because those commodities hadn't been sold due to some reasons beyond the will of the operators, based on the affirmation of attempted crime, the offender may be given a lesser punishment compared with the punishment given to a consummated offender. During the trial, the Defendant Wan Jianping truthfully confessed his crime and may be given a lesser punishment according to the law.

To sum up, according to Articles 214, 23, 25(1), 27, 67(3), 53, 64, 72(1) and (3), 73(2) and (3) of the *Criminal Law of the People's Republic of China* and Articles 2(2), 12(1) and 16 of the *Interpretation of the Supreme People's Court and the Supreme People's Procuratorate Concerning Some Issues on the Specific Application of Law for Handling Criminal Cases of Infringement upon Intellectual Property Rights*, the court makes the following judgment: Ⅰ. The Defendant Li Ruguo committed the crime of selling commodities with counterfeit registered trademarks and shall be sentenced to fixed-term imprisonment of three years and six months and a fine of RMB 1 million. Ⅱ. The illegal gains of the Defendant Li Ruguo shall be recovered according to the law. Ⅲ. The Defendant Wan Jianping committed the crime of selling commodities with counterfeit registered trademarks and shall be sentenced to fixed-term imprisonment of one year and eleven months with one year and eleven months reprieve and a fine of RMB 20,000.

Upon the first instance judgment, the Defendant Li Ruguo filed an appeal.

After the trial, Shanghai No. 3 Intermediate People's Court rejected the appeal and affirmed the original judgment.

[Case Study]

Ⅰ. The provider of business premises who commits a crime of allowing others to sell commodities with counterfeit registered trademark in the premises shall be regulated according to the criminal law

In this case, the behavior of the Defendant Li Ruguo shall be analyzed from two aspects: on the one hand, Li Ruguo operated stores to sell commodities which he knew were with counterfeit registered trademarks with huge sales volume. According to the relevant judicial interpretation, Li Ruguo constituted the crime of selling commodities with counterfeit registered trademarks; on the other hand, as the actual controller of Hancheng Company and by means of decision making, incitement and acquiescence, the Defendant Li Ruguo leased the premises to tenants through Hancheng Company and its management, permitted the stores to sell counterfeit commodities and assisted them in avoiding the industrial and commercial inspection. There is no direct laws and regulations with respect to and many disputes exist in practice concerning whether the later behavior constitutes criminal offence and shall be adjusted by the criminal law.

Some hold that, as the provider and manager of the business premises, the Defendant Li Ruguo leased the premises to tenant while he was fully aware that some tenants were selling commodities with counterfeit registered trademarks and thus shall be deemed as indirectly infringing trademark. In this case, based on the modest and restrained principle of criminal law, it's not suggested to bring it into the scope of criminal punishment. After investigation, the court held that, according to the regulations of existing criminal law, there is no accusation against and no direct legal provisions concerning the provider of premises for assisting others in selling counterfeit commodities. However, it doesn't mean that such kind of act can be downgraded to civil tort and be punished accordingly. First of all, as for the purpose of behavior, the provider of business premises knew perfectly well that some tenants were selling counterfeit commodities. However, the provider did not prevent them from selling counterfeit commodities and allowed them to continue to sell counterfeit commodities in the premises so as to obtain illegal gains. Subjectively, the behavior of the provider was equivalent to the guilty intent of "direct marketing". In this case, during the period when the Defendant Li Ruguo leased the premises to tenants, he collected expenses for selling bags and suitcases (i. e. extensive operating fee) of more than RMB 930,000 from some tenants in Taobao City for the purpose of protecting the illegal acts of tenants rather than maintaining normal market dealing order. Secondly, as for the behavior object, the sale of counterfeit commodities by tenant is not a common civil tort. Meanwhile, the number, amount and scope of sale of counterfeit commodities have reached the standard for criminal offence. In this case, there were 33 cases where the tenants involved were sentenced to be guilty for committing the crime of selling commodities with counterfeit registered trademarks with amount involved in the case being more than RMB 300 million, and it was not a common trademark infringement. The Defendant Li Euguo allowed the tenants to build concealed compartments in their stores to hide counterfeit commodities and receive information in advance to avoid supervision and constituted "technical assistance" by an accomplice committing the crime of selling commodities with counterfeit registered trademarks. Finally, as for the consequence, although the provider of premises did not directly sell counterfeit commodities, he was slack to prevent the criminal act and objectively caused the occurrence of the crime endlessly which failed to be restrained in a long term. To sum up, such kind of behavior is obviously different from indirect trademark infringement and shall be regulated by criminal penalty.

Ⅱ. Path choice for punishment against the provider of premises for allowing others to sell counterfeit commodities in the premises

According to the provisions of Article 15 of the *Supreme People's Court, the Supreme People's Procuratorate and the Ministry of Public Security on Issuing the Opinions on Several Issues concerning the Application of Law in Handling Intellectual Property Right Infringement Criminal Cases*, whoever, well aware of other person's criminal acts of infringing intellectual property right, provides him with such services as Internet access, server hosting, network storage space, communication channel, generation charge, expense settlement, etc, the offender shall be punished as an accomplice of infringing intellectual property right. However, in practice, the crime committed by the accomplice for infringing intellectual property is not limited to the aforesaid acts and generally includes production, leasing, transport, life caring, provision of funds and other auxiliary acts. As for the crime of infringing intellectual property, on the one hand, a directly criminal act must be done, on the other hand, the accomplice shall have conducted other auxiliary acts which objectively facilitate the act of perpetrating and contribute to the reinforcement of the joint offender's criminal intent. In this case, there were 33 cases where the tenants involved were convicted of the crime of selling commodities with counterfeit registered trademark. As the actual controller of the business premises involved in the case, the Defendant Li Ruguo leased the premises to those tenant for a long term and indulged and allowed them to sell counterfeit commodities in the premises so as to make a profit, and shall be treated as an abettor committing the crime of selling commodities with counterfeit registered trademarks.

For the purpose of determining the act of assistance, whether the relevant person has caused a "danger" which damages legal interests, whether there is a violation of duty of care and other factors shall be comprehensively considered. In this case, the Defendant Li Ruguo allowed the tenants to build concealed compartments to hide counterfeit commodities, and informed the stores in advance to avoid investigation, shall be directly responsible for frequent counterfeit commodity selling, decoration and hiding, solicitation by scalpers and tour guide in Taobao City, and was an abettor of the crime of selling commodities with counterfeit registered trademarks.

Ⅲ. Material difference between individual crime and unit crime

In this case, the Defendant Li Ruguo argued that although he was the actual controller of Hancheng Company, the relevant criminal case was not handled by him and thus shall constitute unit crime. According to the basic interpretation of unit crime in the *Criminal Law*, unit crime refers to any act conducted by a company, enterprise, public institution, organ or organization for the purpose of seeking illegal interests for the unit or any act conducted according to the decision made by the entire unit and in the name of the unit. To affirm a unit crime, one must consider the integrity of the unit's will and the group of the unit's interests. According to Article 3 of the *Interpretation by the Supreme People's Court on Some Issues Concerning the Application of Laws to the Trial of Unit Crime*, any person who commits a crime in the name of his/her unit and secretly owns the illegal gains shall be convicted and punished according to the provisions of the Criminal Law concerning the crime committed by natural person. In this case, the Defendant Li Ruguo was one of the shareholders of Hancheng Company, and Hancheng Company had never convened any shareholders' meeting or meeting of the board of directors to deliberate any resolution. According to the existing pieces of evidence available, the financial, personnel and store leasing affairs of Hancheng Company were all controlled and management by the Defendant Li Ruguo who had absolute power of control against the operation and management of Taobao City. During the operation, it was the will of Li Ruguo rather than the whole unit to collect extensive operation fees and not to sign the leasing agreements with the operators of stores. According to the flow of funds, Li Riguo actually collected payments in the name of Hancheng Company and those payments were all paid into the individual account of Li Ruguo. Therefore, the illegal gains were all obtained by Li Ruguo. Therefore, from the perspective of integrity of unit's will or the group of unit's interests, there were no sufficient pieces of evidence in this case to prove unit crime, and the crime shall be deemed to be committed by Li Ruguo himself.

(Writers: Hua Bifang, Wang Meng)

Recognition of the Nature of Counterfeiting Registered Trademark by Separating the Commodities from the Logos

—From the perspective of the case of Li and Xu counterfeiting the registered trademark

[Abstract]

This case is a criminal case on foreign infringement over intellectual property, and correctly determines the nature of the behavior of separating the commodities from the logos, which is controversial in judicial practice. In terms of the exclusive right of the trademark owner to use the trademark, as the exclusive right to use the trademark is counterfeited and infringed before the overseas personnel separated the commodities from the logos, it should be recognized that such overseas personnel were the perpetrator of the registered trademark counterfeiting crime and should be deemed as committing the crime of counterfeiting the registered trademark.

[Case Review]

Public prosecution organ: Shanghai Minhang District People's Procuratorate
Defendants: Li and Xu
Cause of action: crime of counterfeiting the registered trademark
First-instance case No.: (2014) MX (Z) CZ No. 72
From May 2010, the defendant Li, together with Xu et al, for the purpose of seeking illegal benefits, purchased such commodities as snow boot, rain shoes and glasses under the counterfeited registered trademarks including UGG, HUNTER and

Ray · Ban, in which case, the defendant Li was in charge of contacting customers and arranging the orders, the defendant Xu assisted Li in following up the orders, handling the payment and accounting matters, etc. , and they delivered such commodities to UK through such logistics companies as EMS and DHL by misrepresenting the commodity name and separating commodities from the logos. In January 2013, as required by the customers in UK, the defendants Li and Xu, through consignment sales where the commodities and trademarks are separated, sold and delivered to UK the sun glasses under the counterfeited registered trademarks of Ray · Ban and CHANEL, and received over RMB 120,000 (all the amounts hereafter are denominated in RMB) as the payment for goods by transfer through Western Union and cash. In February 2013, when inspecting the packages above-said, Shanghai Customs discovered 12,357 logos of the registered trademark Ray · Ban, 2,000 logos of the registered trademark CHANEL, and 800 pieces of CHANEL glasses cloth. Upon verification of the trademark owner, the logs and commodities above were counterfeited. On November 19, 2013 and March 26, 2014, the Defendants Li and Xu, after being respectively notified by the public security organ through telephone, gave themselves up to the police and truthfully confessed the criminal facts. It was ascertained that, from May 4, 2010 to February 1, 2013, the sales amount in relevant accounts of Li and Xu was equivalent to over RMB 4.25 million.

The public prosecution organ charged that, as the behavior of the Defendants Li and Xu constituted the crime of selling commodities under counterfeited registered trademarks, and a joint offense, the same was submitted to this court for judgment in accordance with the provisions of Article 214 of the *Criminal Law of the People's Republic of China*.

The Defendants Li and Xu did not raise any objection to the facts above in the court hearing.

The defender of the defendant Li alleged that: in the illegal operating revenue of RMB 4.25 million, some commodities did not have the logos of the registered trademarks, instead, the logos for direct purchase of UK customers; the defendant Li, as required by the UK customers, sold the commodities bearing the counterfeited registered trademarks to the two designated UK customers, not directly to non-specific persons; the behavior of the defendant Li should be considered as the provision of intermediary services, which played an auxiliary role in the whole crime, and did not cause physical damages to the market economy of the PRC, with less hazard to society.

The defender of the defendant Xu alleged that: as the defendant Xu gave himself/herself to the police, and only got his/her salaries, without additional payments, he/she only played an auxiliary role in the crime and should be considered as the accessory offender; the defendant Xu participated in the crime after 2011, so, he/she should only be liable for the legal responsibilities of the crime he/she participated in.

[Judgment]

After taking overall consideration of the pieces of evidence in the trial, Shanghai Minhang District People's Court found that: from January 2010 to January 2013, the defendant Li purchased and sold counterfeited commodities under the registered trademarks including UGG, HUGO BOSS, Ray · Ban, POLO, ARMANI JEANS, GUCCI, BOSS, DIOR, MARC JACOBS and CHANEL (including logos), at the amount of RMB 992,029. 40, USD 26,611. 20. Specifically, there are 13 facts, which are evidenced by corresponding e-mails (including the contract orders), electronic ledgers of the company, details of bank accounts, trademark registration materials of relevant trademark owner, etc. According to the electronic accounts of the defendant Li's company, details of the individual bank account opened by the defendant Li in the Bank of China, and the judicial authentication opinions issued by Shanghai Cai Rui Certified Public Accountants Co. , Ltd. , the public prosecution organ charged that the amount received by the defendant Li from selling the commodities under counterfeited registered trademarks reached over RMB 4. 25 million in total, which was basically recognized by the defendant Li; however, this court held that, except for the 13 identified criminal facts of over RMB 1. 173 million in total, there were no contract orders corresponding to the remaining amount, or there were no trademark registration materials corresponding to the commodities for such remaining amount or no registered trademark was used for such commodities, which meant a complete chain of pieces of evidence could not be formed, therefore, this court could not verify or recognize such amount. After March 2011, the defendant Xu helped the defendant Li to follow up the orders, handle the payments and keep record of accounts. The amount of crime the defendant Xu participated in was over RMB 949,964.40.

The Defendant Li received orders from specific foreign customers, purchased commodities under counterfeited registered trademarks, made clear of the style of the required commodities under counterfeited registered trademarks through the contract orders in collusion with the defendant Xu, and sold the commodities to overseas customers by separating the commodities from the logos. This court held that, according to the division of labor, the defendant Li and the defendant Xu respectively ordered the commodities and counterfeited the logos of the registered trademarks in the PRC. The essence of their behaviors was to instigate others to manufacture and produce commodities or logos under the counterfeited registered trademarks. And as they were aware of the illegality of their behaviors, in order to avoid the customs supervision, they delivered the commodities abroad by separating the commodities from the logos. Then, the commodities and logos would be combined by the overseas personnel into the commodities bearing the counterfeited registered trademarks for sale. That is to say, the defendants, without the permit or authorization of the owners of the registered trademarks, sought illegal benefits by using the trademarks same with the registered trademarks of the trademark owners for the same commodities, instead of directly purchasing and selling the finished commodities bearing the counterfeited registered trademarks. The criminal behaviors of the Defendants Li and Xu occurred in the PRC, constituting the crime of counterfeiting registered trademarks. The amount received by the defendant Li from illegal operation should be calculated according to the actual selling price of the infringing products manufactured, stored, transported and sold by him/her, i.e. RMB 1,173,733.30 in total; and the amount of illegal operation the defendant Xu participated in was RMB 949,964.40.

In conclusion, this court concluded that, the Defendants Li and Xu violated the trademark regulations of the People's Republic of China, and, for the purpose of seeking illegal benefits, used the trademarks same with those of the registered trademark owners on the same commodities without the permit of the registered trademark owners. The case was particularly serious. Their behaviors constituted the crime of counterfeiting registered trademarks as well as a joint offense, so, the same should be punished according to law. The defendant Li played a leading role in the joint offense, i.e. the principal criminal; and the defendant Xu played a secondary and auxiliary role in the joint offense, i.e. the accessory criminal, deserving a lesser punishment. The Defendants Li and Xu gave themselves up to police and truthfully confessed the criminal facts, constituting a voluntary surrender, so, a lighter punishment might be imposed. This court corrected the accusations made by the public prosecution organ, which were incorrect.

Accordingly, it was hereby judged in accordance with relevant provisions of the *Criminal Law of the People's Republic of China* that: i. as the defendant Li committed the crime of counterfeiting registered trademarks, and was sentenced to a fixed-term imprisonment of one year and six months, penalized with RMB 500,000 and expelled from the PRC; ii. the defendant Xu committed the crime of counterfeiting registered trademarks, and was sentenced to a fixed-term imprisonment of one year, granted with a one-year probation period, and penalized with RMB 20,000; iii. the seized commodities and logos under the counterfeited registered trademarks should be confiscated; iv. the illegal incomes should be recovered.

[Case Study]

In this case, the defendants ordered and purchased the commodities and counterfeited the logos of registered trademarks through different channels, and delivered the same abroad by separating the commodities from the logos, which were combined together for sale by overseas personnel. It was clearly stated in the results of judgment that the behaviors of the defendants fell into the act of counterfeiting registered trademarks. Due to lack of evidences related to part of the amount charged in this case, a complete chain of pieces of evidence could not be formed, so, the people's court did not recognize such amount, which had great model significance.

The disputed focus of this case was to determine the nature of the behavior of selling fake goods by separating commodities from the logos. During the trial, there were two different opinions for the issues above: one held that, according to the division of labor, the Defendants Li and Xu respectively ordered the commodities and counterfeited the logos of the registered trademarks in the PRC. And as they were aware of the illegality of their behaviors, in order to avoid the customs supervision, they delivered the commodities abroad by separating the commodities from the logos. Then, the commodities and logos would be combined by the overseas personnel into the commodities bearing the counterfeited registered trademarks for sale. The criminal behaviors of the Defendants Li and Xu occurred in the PRC, constituting the crime of counterfeiting registered trademarks. The other one held that, subjectively, the Defendants Li and Xu sought benefits through circulation of commodities, constituting the crime of selling commodities under counterfeited registered trademarks.

It is specified in Article 213 of the *Criminal Law of the People's Republic of China* concerning the crime of counterfeiting registered trademarks that "whoever, without permission from the owner of a registered trademark, uses a trademark which is identical with the registered trademark on the same kind of commodities shall, if the circumstances are serious..."; in Article 214, the crime of selling commodities under counterfeited registered trademarks is specified as "whoever, knowingly sells commodities bearing counterfeited registered trademarks shall, if the amount of sales is relatively large..."; as specified in Article 8 (Ⅱ) of the *Interpretation of the Supreme People's Court and the Supreme People's Procuratorate Concerning Some Issues on the Specific Application of Law for Handling Criminal Cases of Infringement upon Intellectual Property Rights*: "the word 'uses' in Article 213 of the *Criminal Law* means the use of a registered trademark or counterfeited registered trademark on the commodity and packing or container of the commodity, as well as the product specifications and transaction documents, or the use of a registered trademark or counterfeited registered trademark for advertising, exhibition and other commercial activities", and the provisions in the Criminal Law concerning the crime of selling commodities bearing counterfeited registered trademarks are focused on the regulations of circulation links, i. e. the doer does not produce or otherwise purchase the illegally made logo of a registered trademark, and only sells the complete commodities bearing the counterfeited registered trademark.

According to the facts of this case, the Defendants Li and Xu, according to the division of labor, respectively ordered the complete commodities and counterfeited the logos of the registered trademarks in the PRC. Each commodity has a corresponding logo of the counterfeited registered trademark. And the Defendants Li and Xu were aware of the illegality of their behaviors, but, in order to avoid the customs supervision, they delivered the commodities abroad by separating the commodities from the logos. Then, the commodities and logos would be combined by the overseas personnel into the commodities bearing the counterfeited registered trademarks for sale. In other words, before delivering the commodities by separating the commodities from the logos, the Defendants Li and Xu implemented the behavior of ordering the commodities and logos of the counterfeited registered trademarks, and matched the quantities and models of the commodities and logos according to the orders. From the perspective of the trademark owner, it was then confirmed that the exclusive right of the trademark owner to use the trademark was counterfeited and infringed, which constituted the "use" behaviors specified by law. And the overseas personnel, for the purpose of completing the sale of the commodities bearing counterfeited registered trademarks, would be sure to paste the illegally-made logos of the registered trademarks on relevant commodities. As a result, in this case, the Defendants Li and Xu were the perpetrators of the behavior of counterfeiting registered trademarks. The behaviors of Li and Xu were to seek illegal benefits by using the trademarks same with the registered trademarks of the owners on the same commodities without permission or authorization of the owners of the registered trademarks, instead of directly purchasing and selling the finished commodities bearing the counterfeited registered trademarks, and therefore, such behaviors constituted the crime of counterfeiting registered trademarks.

(Writers: Tian Lifeng Ji Qiuling)

Understanding and Recognition of "Substantial Similarity" in the Identification of Computer Software Copyright Infringement

—Case of Copyright Infringement by the Defendant Wang Jie el al

[Abstract]

The substantial similarity of computer software shall be identified by comparing the server program and client program of the software in accordance with the industry practices and software characteristics and with the exclusion of public documents and third party documents. If, after comparison, the two pieces of software are highly similar and have identical personalized information, and there is no other explanation but copy, the two pieces of software shall be determined as substantially similar.

[Case Review]

Public prosecution organ: Shanghai Xuhui District People's Procuratorate

Defendant (Appellant): Wang Jie

Defendant (Appellant): Wan Zhen

Defendant (Appellant): Sun Guolong

Defendant (Appellant): Lou Bo

Defendant: Jin Wenbing

Defendant: Shen Liangjun

Defendant: Huang Wenfeng

Defendant: An Minghao

Cause of action: crime of infringement on copyright

First-instance case No.: (2013) XXX (Z) CZ No. 20

Second-instance case No. ：(2014) HYZX（Z）ZZ No. 7

In September 2006, Shanghai Wulong Network Technology Development Co.，Ltd.（hereinafter referred to as Wulong）was incorporated, and its main business was the operation of English learning software through internet. In October 2008, Wulong registered the computer software copyright of its online English learning software *Wulong Academy* 1.0（which was wholly owned by Wulong）in the National Copyright Administration. From 2009, Wulong changed its equities and increased its capitals and shares. The defendant Wang Jie was the legal representative of the company. Until 2011, Wulong successively developed and operated the English learning software of *Wulong Academy* 2.0 and *Wulong Academy* 3.0, for which the software copyright registration was not remade.

In February 2012, Shanghai Jiayixing Information Technology Co.，Ltd.（hereinafter referred to as Jiayixing）was incorporated, with Xu Can and Lou Bo as the shareholders under industrial and commercial registration, Xu Can as its legal representative, Wang Jie and Wan Zhen as its actual controller and the person in charge of operation, and Wan Zhen as its general manager. Before and after the establishment of the company, the defendants Wang Jie and Wan Zhen recruited several former staffs of Wulong into Jiayixing. The defendant Wang Jie arranged the defendants Jin Wenbing, Sun Guolong, Shen Liangjun, Huang Wenfeng and An Minghao to copy lots of the documents under the server and client programs of *Wulong Academy* 3.0, and make them into *Jiayuxing* software. Wang Jie directly planned and instructed the production of *Jiayuxing* software. Wan Zhen was in charge of the daily administration of the company, and then operated *Jiayuxing* software through internet in the name of Jiayixing, gaining profits by soliciting agent and selling the time card of such software to the agent. In the activities above, Jin Wenbing, Shen Liangjun and Huang Wenfeng mainly engaged in the operation of the web page of *Jiayuxing* software and its maintenance, Sun Guolong mainly engaged in the setup and maintenance of the server, An Minghao participated in the early-stage work for establishment of Jiayixing, the testing of the software afore-said, as well as the promotional and marketing activities of subsequent software, and the defendant Lou Bo, except for contributing part of the capitals for establishment of Jiayixing, also participated in the early-stage planning and subsequent marketing of *Jiayuxing* software.

According to the authentication opinions given by Shanghai Stars Digital

Forensic Center, *Wulong Academy* 3.0 and *Jiayuxing* software were substantially similar in both server program and client program; according to the judicial audit, from May 2012 to December 2012, the defendants Wang Jie, Wan Zhen, Jin Wenbing, Sun Guolong, Shen Liangjun, Huang Wenfeng, Lou Bo and An Minghao obtained RMB 1,060,273 of the amount of illegal operation by operating *Jiayuxing* software.

The public prosecution organ held that, the defendants Wang Jie, Wan Zhen, Jin Wenbing, Sun Guolong, Shen Liangjun, Huang Wenfeng, Lou Bo and An Minghao, with a view to seek profits, reproduced and released the computer software of the copyright owner without permission of the copyright owner, and the amount of illegal operation reached over RMB1.06 million, which could be considered as a serious circumstance, and their behaviors violated the provisions of Articles 217(ⅰ) and 25(Ⅰ) of the *Criminal Law of the People's Republic of China*, as a result, they should be investigated for the criminal responsibilities for a joint crime by virtue of copyright infringement.

[**Judgment**]

After the trial, Shanghai Xuhui District People's Court concluded that: the copyright owner had the right to amend the software and enjoyed the copyright to the amended copyright. The software of *Wulong Academy* 3.0 was an amended update of *Wulong Academy* 1.0 and *Wulong Academy* 2.0 to which Wulong had the copyright, and Wulong would continue to enjoy the copyright to *Wulong Academy* 3.0. According to the actual contribution and daily operation & management conditions of Jiayixing, it could be ascertained that the defendants Wang Jie and Wan Zhen were the actual controller and owner of Jiayixing. They asked the defendants Lou Bo, Jin Wenbing, Sun Guolong, Shen Liangjun, Huang Wenfeng and An Minghao, former employees or agents of Wulong, to copy the documents related to *Wulong Academy* 3.0, to which Wulong had the copyright, make them into *Jiayuxing* software, and put the software into operation. After comparison, the two pieces of software were not identical, but substantially similar in the main structure and functions, constituting substantial similarity and such illegal acts of reproduction as specified by the criminal law, therefore, relevant defendants should be declared guilty of and punished for copyright infringement. Among them, the defendants Wang Jie and Wan Zhen played a leading role in the joint offense, i. e. the principal criminals; and the defendants Lou Bo, Jin Wenbing, Sun Guolong, Shen Liangjun, Huang Wenfeng and An Minghao played a secondary and auxiliary role in the joint offense, i. e. the accessory criminals, and their criminal circumstances were less serious or minor, deserving a lesser punishment or an exemption. Although, during the trial, the defendants Wang Jie, Wan Zhen, Jin Wenbing, Shen Liangjun, Huang Wenfeng and An Minghao argued for the nature of their behaviors, it could be ascertained that they made the confession truthfully, so they deserved a lighter punishment according to law; the defendants Lou Bo and Sun Guolong gave themselves up to police, deserving a lighter punishment according to law.

In accordance with provisions of Articles 217(i), 25(I), 26(I), 27, 53, 64, 67(I) & (III), 72(I) & (III) and 73(II) & (III) of the *Criminal Law of the People's Republic of China*, as well as Article 5(II) of the *Interpretation of the Supreme People's Court and the Supreme People's Procuratorate Concerning Some Issues on the Specific Application of Law for Handling Criminal Cases of Infringement upon Intellectual Property Rights*, it was judged that: the defendant Wang Jie committed the crime of copyright infringement, and should be sentenced to a fixed-term imprisonment of three years and penalized with RMB 100,000; the defendant Wan Zhen committed the crime of copyright infringement, and should be sentenced to a fixed-term imprisonment of three years, granted with a three-year probation period, and penalized with RMB 50,000; the defendant Lou Bo committed the crime of copyright infringement, and should be sentenced to a fixed-term imprisonment of six months, granted with an one-year probation period, and penalized with RMB 10,000; the defendants Jin Wenbing, Sun Guolong, Shen Liangjun, Huang Wenfeng and An Minghao committed the crime of copyright infringement, but should be exempted from criminal punishment; all the computers, hard disks, *Jiayuxing* software learning cards and other items related to the crime of this case seized from the defendants should be confiscated.

After the first-instance judgment, the defendants Wang Jie, Wan Zhen, Sun Guolong and Lou Bo refused to accept it and appealed to Shanghai No. 1 Intermediate People's Court.

After the trial, Shanghai No. 1 Intermediate People's Court concluded that, the facts judged in the first instance were clear, with reliable and adequate evidence, the conviction was accurate and the judicial procedures were legal, therefore, the appeal was rejected and the original judgment was upheld.

[Case Study]

This case is a typical case of new types of crime where the employees, for the purpose of seeking personal gains, organize a new company to steal, reproduce and release the computer software of the company where they previously served, thus, infringing the copyright of the owner to the computer software. As specified in the criminal law of our country, reproduction and release are the objective manifestation patterns of the copyright infringement crime. Unlike the mechanical reproduction of general works, usually, the reproduction of computer software is somewhat professional and concealed, with a high degree of technology, so, the court needs to recognize the identity of the software from both legal and technological aspects, to determine whether or not the copyright is infringed. The countries have not yet agreed on the unified standards for the determination of computer software infringement, still continuing the exploration through practice. At current stage, the principle of "substantial similarity + getting in touch + excluding reasonable explanations" is one of the popular judgment standards used in the judicial practices of our country, i. e. if the alleged software is identical or substantially similar to the copyrighted software, there are pieces of evidence proving that the alleged infringer (or defendant) gets in touch with the copyrighted software, and no reasonable explanation is made to the substantial similarity between the two pieces of software, the same can be determined as an infringement or the crime can be founded. In this case, all the defendants are former employees of Wulong, and they admit that Jiayuxing software is made by copying part of the software "Wulong Academy", so, it is not hard to recognize the two elements of "getting in touch" and "excluding reasonable explanations". The key of this case lies on whether or not the "reproducing" behavior of the defendants makes the two pieces of software "identical" or "substantially similar", leading to the infringement over the copyright of Wulong Academy software. In this regard, the judgment made by the court is clear. The substantial similarity of computer software shall be identified by comparing the server and client program documents of the software in accordance with the industry practices and software characteristics and with the exclusion of public documents and third party documents. If, after comparison, the two pieces of software are highly similar and have identical personalized information, and there is no other explanation but copy, the two pieces of software shall be determined as substantially similar, thus, constituting the reproduction defined by the criminal law.

I. Thoughts and expressions shall be separated in case of recognition of substantial similarity

The computer software works also need to follow the protection principle of "separating thoughts from expressions" in the copyright law. After separating the thoughts from the expressions, the recognition of substantial similarity is actually the comprehensive judgment made after comparing the expression forms of the two pieces of software works. Whereas, computer software has its own particularity it is technical plan and thinking result as well, with the double attributes of "practical functions" and "literary works", the thoughts and expressions of computer software are often interpenetrating, and hard to be clearly separated. In the case filed by Computer Associates International Inc against Altai, Inc, the United States Court of Appeals for the Second Circuit establishes the three-step method of abstraction, filtering and comparison, trying to separate the thoughts and expressions. Abstraction means dissociating the thoughts not protected by the copyright law from the two pieces of software; filtering means filtering out the similar but public contents of the two pieces of software; at last, comparing the contents remained after abstraction and filtering, to determine whether or not the two pieces of software are substantially similar. This method is further used by many courts, and of great referential significance to the judicial practices in our country. In this case, prior to making the substantial similarity comparison of the two pieces of software, the court determines that, it shall analyze the two pieces of software first, then delete the public documents and third-party documents, and make comparison. This practice can be considered as a practical application of the method of abstraction, filtering and comparison. In this way, the scope of protection for the computer software is determined, and the substantial similarity comparison can be made on a targeted and accurate basis.

Ⅱ. The objects of substantial similarity comparison shall be determined according to the industry practices and software characteristics

Whether or not two pieces of software are substantially similar cannot be determined only on basis of the user interface and functions, but in accordance with the characteristics of such software and the industry practices, so as to scientifically determine the objects of the substantial similarity comparison. According to the provisions in the *Regulations on Computer Software Protection*, the scope of protection for computer software is divided into computer program and its related files, and therefore, the substantial similarity of computer software is also divided into two categories: i. substantial similarity of files; ii. substantial similarity of program. And, as the files are similar to literary works, which are specific and visible, it can be determined whether or not they are identical or similar without professional identification. Besides, according to the facts of this case, it is clearly stated in the application form for copyright registration of the software involved that the whole set of software is comprised of client program and server program, which means, from the characteristics of the software involved, the objects of the substantial similarity comparison of the two pieces of computer software are the client program and server program. In addition, according to the industry practices, the method of comparing the client program is more often applied to compare similar computer software. So, the court, in combination of the characteristics of the software involved and the industry practices, determines that the client programs and server programs of the two pieces of software shall be the comparison objects. It will reflect the core and full image of the two pieces of software, and it is scientific and reasonable. In this case, the contents (such as voice package) which are argued by the defendants to be not included in the comparison objects are part of the software, but have no substantial influence on the judgment of the substantial similarity between the two pieces of software, therefore, there is no need to compare them.

Ⅲ. The substantial similarity shall be comprehensively recognized by combining the proportion of similarity and personalized characteristics

After confirming that the client and server programs of the two pieces of software are the objects of substantial similarity objects, an overall comparison shall be made respectively on the documents under the client program and server program as well as the document catalog. The higher the similarity ratio between the documents and document catalogs is, the greater the probability that the two pieces of software are substantially similar will be. In this case, after comparison, the documents and document catalogs, whether under the client program or the server program, the similarity ratio reaches over 70%, which is far beyond the similarity range of normal software. The probability of copying is quite high. However, as for the similarity ratio of documents and document catalogs which will lead two software programs to be recognized as substantially similar, there is no unified standard. So, two pieces of software cannot be recognized as substantially similar only on basis of the similarity ratio of program documents. The substantial similarity of computer software shall be comprehensively determined on a quantitative basis and in combination of other factors. In practice, such as writing programs, in most cases, the developer will add some individual or development related information in the software program, such as the name and email address of the developer and the signing information of the company. Generally, such information is unique, with a particular meaning. In case of identical personalized information when comparing two pieces of software, by excluding reasonable explanations, it can be proved that there is probability of reproduction between the two pieces of software. In this case, considering that *Jiayuxing* software contains such unique personalized information of *Wulong Academy* software as "Wulong Academy", "Wang Jie" and the website containing the name of Wulong, and in consideration of the high ratio of similarity between the two pieces of software, the court finally recognize the substantial similarity of the two pieces of software, and then determines that the defendants commit the crime of copyright infringement.

(Writers: Wang Limin Liu Qiuyu)

Judicial Recognition and Reflection on the "Amount of Illegal Operation" in the Crime of Counterfeiting Registered Trademarks

—Crime of counterfeiting registered trademarks by the defendant unit Shanghai Xiangyun Luggages & Bags Co. , Ltd. et al

[Abstract]

Where existing evidence cannot prove the marked price or selling price of the commodities bearing counterfeited registered trademarks, the middle market price of the infringed products shall be not taken as the standards for identifying the amount of illegal operation. Instead, the big price difference between the fake products and authentic products shall be fully considered, to reasonably determine the selling price of the infringed product under the principle of compatibility of crime, responsibility and punishment, so as to correctly determine the crime of and punishment to the defendant.

[Case Review]

Public prosecution organ: Shanghai Songjiang District People's Procuratorate

Defendant (Appellant): Huang Yunhuo

Defendant unit: Shanghai Xiangyun Luggages & Bags Co. , Ltd.

Defendant: Zhu Haiyong

Defendant: Yao Tianguan

First-instance case No. : (2014) XX (Z) CZ No. 35

Second-instance case No. : (2015) HSZXZZ No. 4

From May 2011 to December 2011, without consent and authorization of the trademark right owner Zhejiang Weixing New Building Materials Co., Ltd., the defendant Zhu Haiyong, when operating Shanghai Weisu New Building Materials Co., Ltd. (hereinafter referred to as Weisu), commissioned the defendant unit Shanghai Xiangyun Luggages & Bags Co., Ltd. (hereinafter referred to as Xiangyun), operated by the defendant Huang Yunhuo and with the defendant Yao Tianguan as the production manager, to produce PP-R plastic fittings bearing the counterfeited registered trademark of "VASEN" by way of providing moulds and processing materials supplied by customers. The defendant unit Xiangyun and the defendants Huang Yunhuo and Yao Tianguan manufactured over 390,000 plastic fittings for the defendant Zhu Haiyong. After deduction of the plastics fittings marked with Pegasus, over 210,000 PP-R plastic fittings were recognized as counterfeiting the registered trademark of VASEN. And the middle market price of the authentic products reached over three million yuan. On August 17, 2012, the public security organ discovered 5,400 meters of PP-R plastic pipes and 12,710 plastic fittings which were verified to be bearing the counterfeited registered trademark of VASEN, as well as 1 box qualifications and 1 set portable machine marked with "Weixing Pipe" in the factory of the defendant Zhu Haiyong.

After further investigation, the defendant Zhu Haiyong was criminally detained by Linhai Public Security Bureau on June 6, 2012 due to production and sale of plastic pipes and fittings bearing the counterfeited registered trademark VASEN at the beginning of 2011, and was arrested on July 13 of the same year. On April 26, 2013, Zhu Haiyong was sentenced by Zhejiang Linhai People's Court to a fixed-term imprisonment of one year and two months and penalized with RMB 140,000 for the crime of counterfeiting the registered trademark. On August 5, 2013 when Zhu Haiyong was released after serving the full term of the sentence, Zhu Haiyong was criminally detained by Songjiang Branch of Shanghai Municipal Public Security Bureau for this case, and the enforcement measure was changed into a guarantor pending trial on September 11, 2013. On February 24, 2014, the defendant Yao Tianguan appeared for this case upon notification by the public security organ. On February 27, 2014, the defendant Huang Yunhuo appeared for this case upon notification by the public security organ.

The public prosecution organ affirmed that, the defendant Zhu Haiyong, in collusion with the defendant Huang Yunhuo (the person in charge of the defendant unit Xiangyun) as well as the defendant Yao Tianguan (other direct responsible person), without permission from the owner of a registered trademark, used a trademark which is identical with the registered trademark on the same kind of commodities. The circumstance was quite serious. There behaviors violated Articles 213, 220 and 25(Ⅰ) of the *Criminal Law of the People's Republic of China*. The criminal facts were clear, with reliable and adequate evidences. Therefore, they should be investigated for criminal liabilities for the crime of counterfeiting registered trademarks.

The defendant Zhu Haiyong and the defender argued that, there was no sufficient evidence for such quantity of infringing products as alleged by the public prosecution organ, and the production statistics of the defendant unit Xiangyun could not prove that the production quantity was more than 200,000; as for the value of the infringing products, the public prosecution organ calculated it at 36% of the value of authentic products, which was short of evidence, so, it was more reasonable to calculate the value at 22% of the real-time selling price of the defendant.

The defendant Huang Yunhuo and defender argued that, they had objection to the total quantity of the infringing products, as some of the products in the statistics of the defendant unit were not VASEN, and even if it was stated in the statistics that they were VASEN products, it could not be identified whether or not the physical products were marked with "VASEN"; besides, they had objection to the amount of crime affirmed in the prosecution, the value of the infringing products shall be calculated at 22% of the value of authentic products at the time of sale.

[Judgment]

After the trial, Shanghai Xuhui District People's Court concluded that: none of the parties in this case had objection to the fact that the defendant Zhu Haiyong commissioned the defendant unit Xiangyun to process VASEN plastic pipes, and the dispute focuses lied on the specific quantity and the amount of illegal operation. As recorded in the sales statistics of Xiangyun, the defendant unit processed a total of 392,992 plastic pipes for the defendant Zhu Haiyong. After deduction of the quantity of plastic pipes which were expressly stated in the sales statistics to be marked with other brands, 217,577 plastic pipes should be recognized as the products counterfeiting VASEN. The defendant Zhu Haiyong argued that, such total quantity included the plastic pipes without counterfeiting VASEN, for which there was no sufficient evidence, and the counterfeited plastic pipes found by the public security organ in Zhu Haiyong's factory were all marked with VASEN, so, the court did not adopt this argument. As for the amount of illegal operation, as the defendant did not provide the actual selling price, at the time of prosecution, the public prosecution organ recognized the amount of illegal operation by multiplying the market price of the infringed products by the trade discount of 36%. However, in consideration that, in reality, the selling price of the infringing products, by wholesale or retail, was usually lower than that of the authentic products, and the defendant Zhu Haiyong was then involved in another case where Zhu Haiyong was criminally penalized by Zhejiang Linhai People's Court for producing the plastic pipes and fittings bearing counterfeiting the registered trademark-VASEN, and the infringing products were sold at 22% of the price of authentic VASEN products, from the perspective favorable to the defendant, in this case, the amount of illegal operation was calculated at 22% of the market price of the infringed products, i. e. more than RMB 670,000. In conclusion, the defendant Zhu Haiyong, in collusion with the defendant Huang Yunhuo (the person in charge of the defendant unit Xiangyun) as well as the defendant Yao Tianguan (other direct responsible person), without permission from the owner of a registered trademark, used a trademark which is identical with the registered trademark on the same kind of commodities, with the quantity of infringing products reaching over 210,000 and the amount of illegal operation reaching over RMB 670,000. The circumstances were quiteserious, and their behaviors constituted the crime of counterfeiting a registered trademark, which should be penalized. Therefore, the accusations of the public prosecution organ were founded. The defendants and the defendant unit committed a joint offense. The defendant Zhu Haiyong was the principal criminal. The defendant unit Xiangyun and the defendants Huang Yunhuo and Yao Tianguan were the accessory criminals, deserving a lighter punishment according to law. After declaration of the judgment and prior to completion of the criminal penalty, it was found that there were other pending crimes committed by the defendant Zhu Haiyong prior to declaration of the judgment, i. e. omitted crimes, for which a combined punishment should be imposed according to law. The defendant unit Xiangyun and the defendants Huang Yunhuo and Yao Tianguan gave themselves up to police, deserving a lighter punishment according to law.

In accordance with provisions of Articles 213, 220, 25(Ⅰ), 26(Ⅰ) & (Ⅳ), 27, 53, 64, 67(Ⅰ), 69, 70, 72(Ⅰ) & (Ⅲ) and 73(Ⅱ) & (Ⅲ) of the *Criminal Law of the People's Republic of China* as well as Article 1 of the *Interpretation of the Supreme People's Court and the Supreme People's Procuratorate Concerning Some Issues on the Specific Application of Law for Handling Criminal Cases of Infringement upon Intellectual Property Rights*, it was judged that: the defendant unit Shanghai Xiangyun Luggages & Bags Co., Ltd. committed the crime of counterfeiting a registered trademark, and was penalized with RMB 20,000; the defendant Zhu Haiyong committed the crime of counterfeiting a registered trademark, and was sentenced to a fixed-term imprisonment of three years and six months, imposed with a penalty of RMB 100,000. Together with fixed-term imprisonment of one year and two months and the penalty of RMB 140,000 sentenced for previous crimes, the court decided a fixed-term imprisonment of four years and the penalty of RMB 240,000; the defendant Huang Yunhuo committed the crime of counterfeiting a registered trademark, and was sentenced to a fixed-term imprisonment of one year, with one-year probation period, and penalized with RMB 10,000; the defendant Yao Tianguan committed the crime of counterfeiting a registered trademark, and was sentenced to a fixed-term imprisonment of nine months, with one-year probation period, and penalized with RMB 5,000; illegal profits gained by the defendant unit Shanghai Xiangyun Luggages & Bags Co., Ltd. and the defendants Zhu Haiyong, Huang Yunhuo and Yao Tianguan were recovered according to law; the seized commodities bearing the counterfeited registered trademark, trademarks, tools for criminal purpose and other articles related to the crime of this case were confiscated.

After the first-instance judgment, the defendant Huang Yunhuo refused to accept the judgment and filed an appeal, which was withdrawn during the trial of Shanghai No. 3 Intermediate People's Court, and the first-instance judgment came into force.

[Case Study]

In the judicial practices related to the crime of counterfeiting a registered trademark, there are different methods for and theoretical disputes on the recognition of the amount of illegal operation. The *Interpretation of the Supreme People's Court and the Supreme People's Procuratorate Concerning Some Issues on the Specific Application of Law for Handling Criminal Cases of Infringement upon Intellectual*

Property Rights (hereinafter referred to as *IPR Interpretation*) clearly defines " the amount of illegal operation", and specifies that the value of sold infringing products shall be calculated at the actual selling price. The value of the infringing products that have been produced, stored and transported but have not been sold shall be calculated at the marked price or the identified average selling price of the infringing products. Where the infringing products have no marked price or the actual selling price is not identified, the value shall be calculated at the middle market price of the infringed products. As specified above, "the amount of illegal operation" shall be recognized by the following order of priority: (1) the marked price or the identified average selling price of the infringing products; (2) the middle market price of the infringed products. The above methods for identification are not optional, but progressive. Only when the value cannot be identified by the first method can the latter one be applied. However, in practice, most of the time, the defendant does not have a complete and standard financial account book, and the marked price of the commodity involved cannot be identified, in which case, "the middle market price of the infringed products" will be applied in many cases, thus, arising many disputes on such practice.

I . Comments on the method of "middle market price"

There is not doubt that, calculating the amount of illegal operation at " the middle market price of the infringed products" helps to save the investigation and judicial costs as well as prevent ineffective combat, having strong deterrent effects on the criminals. However, without making all efforts to affirm the actual selling price of the infringing products, it is inadvisable to take "the middle market price of the infringed products" as the standard for calculating the amount of illegal operation. Main reasons are as follows:

First, such practice goes against the spirit of "restraining criminal law". Where the infringing products are sold at a price clearly lower than the market price of the authentic products ("sell fake products as fake") , if "the middle market price of the infringed products" is taken as the standard for calculating the value of counterfeited products, the expected sales amount is actually calculated at a selling price which was impossible to be applied by the defendant. In practice, without careful consideration, even in civil cases, the benefits obtained by the infringer from infringement will not be calculated at the price of the authentic products. More often, the amount of tort compensation is determined on basis of such factors as the status of the right owner's rights as well as the malicious degree, consequences and influence of the infringement. Therefore, in criminal cases where more emphases are laid on the proving ability of evidences and standard of proofs, we should be more cautious. Sometimes, it is unscientific and unfair to impose a criminal punishment only on basis of the quantity of seized infringing products and the price of authentic products. It is also goes against the spirit of "restraining criminal law".

Second, such practice goes against the principle of "equal measurement of penalty". "Equal application of law" was one of the basic principles established in the Criminal Law of China. It contains the three requirements of "equal conviction", "equal measurement of penalty" and "equal execution of punishment". Under the circumstance where the defendants "sell fake products as fake" and the consumers "buy fake products on purpose ", if merely in accordance with provisions of the judicial interpretation, the actual selling price can be identified, the amount of illegal operation shall be calculated at the lower selling price, and if the actual selling price or marked price can be identified, the amount of illegal operation shall be calculated at the "the middle market price of the infringed products", which has big difference from the actual selling price, in which case, if the number of counterfeited products sold by different defendants are the same, different defendant will be imposed with different criminal penalty on basis of whether or not the court identifies the actual selling price. Obviously, this goes against the requirement of "equal measurement of penalty".

II. Suggestions on application of "middle market price"

In terms of the actual requirement for criminal protection of intellectual property rights, the existence of "middle market price" is necessary and reasonable, but it shall only be applied in accordance with strict conditions, and under the principle of subjective and objective consistency. In case the defendant "passes off the false as genuine" in the crime of counterfeiting a registered trademark, there is little difference between the actual selling price of the counterfeited commodities and the market price of the infringed products. If there is no marked price or identified selling price of the infringing products, the middle market price of the infringed products shall be applied, but of course, the defendant shall be proved to have indeed "passed off the false as genuine". By obtaining evidences from the sales place, sales mode and sales channel of the defendant, it shall be proved that the defendant indeed sells the infringing products as genuine products, to achieve the illegal purpose of confusing the consumers. Under the circumstance of "selling fake products as fake", there is big difference between the actual selling price of the counterfeited commodities and the market price of the infringed products. And it is seldom that the crime of counterfeiting a registered trademark is not accomplished, so, it is impossible to make adjustment on basis of attempted crime when the amount is inconsistent with the actual value. Therefore, the actual selling price shall be the preferred standard for calculating the value of the infringing products. Where there is no actual selling price, the marked selling price of the infringing products shall be applied. If there is no marked price and purchase or sales record for the infringing products, the actual selling price of the defendant can be affirmed through mutual verification, i. e. inquiring the defendant of the previous selling price, obtaining the sales conditions by combining the witness testimony, and obtaining the middle market price of the infringing products through market investigation and entrusted assessment, so as to impose the punishment in accordance with the crime. In this case, the court determines the selling price of the infringing products involved on basis of the selling price of previous commodities confessed by the defendants and by investigating the price of similar products sold at the same time in other cases, and then, makes correct decisions on the conviction and measurement of penalty concerning the defendants, reflecting the principles of "benefiting the defendants" and "equal measurement of penalty" which the court has always been followed in judicial judgment.

(Writers: Wang Limin Liu Qiuyu)

VI

Administrative Cases on Intellectual Property

Burden of Proof for Trade Secrets of Computer Software Constituting Legal Elements

—Shanghai Mougan Advertising Co. , Ltd. v. Shanghai Jing'an District Market Supervision Administration, Shanghai ShopEx Network Technology Co. , Ltd. and Kumei (Shanghai) Information Technology Co. , Ltd. Case on Appeal of Administrative Penalty

[**Summary**]

The Case is the first administrative case accepted by the Intellectual Property Tribunal of Shanghai High People's Court, which involves the legal protection on trade secrets of computer software. The legal protection on the computer software can be sought from the different paths of copyright or trade secrets, but the legal constitutive requirements of such two rights are completely different. In the administrative cases, if the third party asserts that its software constitutes the trade secret and the administrative authority also confirms that such software constitutes the trade secret and when conducting investigation, the administrative authority shall provide proofs that the software is in consistence with the conditions in Article 10 (Ⅲ) of the *Anti-Unfair Competition Law*. If the administrative authority provides no evidence to prove that it has investigated that the computer software meets the requirement for "being unknown to the public"; though such software meets other constitutive requirements of trade secrets, the corresponding administrative penalty made by it is short of factual and legal basis. The people's court repealed the wrong part of the administrative penalty according to law, which fully reflected the principle of "judicature leading" of intellectual property rights protection in China.

[Case Review]

Appellant (Defendant in the first instance): Shanghai Jing'an District Market Supervision Administration (hereinafter referred to as "Jing'an Market Supervision Administration").

Appellant (Third Party in the first instance): Shanghai ShopEx Network Technology Co., Ltd. (hereinafter referred to as "ShopEx").

Appellant (Third Party in the first instance): Kumei (Shanghai) Information Technology Co., Ltd. (hereinafter referred to as "Kumei").

Appellee (Plaintiff in the first instance): Shanghai Mougan Advertising Co., Ltd. (hereinafter referred to as "Mougan").

Cause of Action: dispute over decision of administrative penalty

First-Instance Case No. : (2016) H73XC No. 1

Second-Instance Case No. : (2016) HXZ No. 738

The Plaintiff Mougan is named from the change of Shanghai GuanYi Software Technology Co., Ltd. (hereinafter referred to as "GuanYi"). ShopEx and Kumei held that GuanYi made false advertising on its website and at the same time, maliciously employed their employees with fat salary to obtain their source code of software and documents thereof, which constituted the false advertising and infringement upon trade secrets, thus they reported the same to Zhabei Branch of Shanghai Administration for Industry and Commerce (hereinafter referred to as "Zhabei Branch for Industry and Commerce"). Upon receiving the report, Zhabei Branch for Industry and Commerce acquired evidences from the computer data and relevant webpage of GuanYi, and entrusted Shangxin Judicial Expertise Office to compare the forensics data with the CD data provided by the ShopEx. Afterwards, the Office issued a judicial appraisal opinion, stating that the "identifiable part" of documents in the computer from GuanYi is identical to the code of relevant software provided by the ShopEx, which may be deemed as coming from the same source; there were the same relevant documents. Shanghai Zhabei District Market Supervision Administration (which is established by Zhabei Branch of the Administration for Industry and Commerce and relevant departments through integration of functions, hereinafter referred to as "Zhabei Market Supervision Administration") made decision of administrative penalty against GuanYi as follows: I. the behavior of

GuanYi releasing false information on its website constituted a false advertising and it is ordered to stop its illegal behavior, eliminate effects therefrom and impose penalty on it with the fine of RMB 10,000 only. II. ShopEx and Kumei jointly researched and developed the software involved. GuanYi employed the relevant former employees of ShopEx and Kumei who participated in the research and development of the software and signed the non-disclosure agreement and there was the software involved and documents obtained from ShopEx in the computer for work of the said personnel. Based on the judicial appraisal opinion, GuanYi can be affirmed that it infringed upon the trade secrets, and the penalty that it was ordered to stop such illegal behaviors with a fine of RMB 20,000 only shall be imposed upon GuanYi. To sum up, the penalty in combination shall be implemented: I. it is ordered to stop the act of false advertising; II. it is ordered to stop the act of infringement on trade secrets; III. it is fined with an amount of RMB 30,000 (THIRTY THOUSAND ONLY).

Mougan refused such penalty decision and filed an administrative lawsuit to Shanghai Intellectual Property Court.

[**Judgment**]

After trial, Shanghai Intellectual Property Court held that the decision of administrative penalty made by Zhabei Market Supervision Administration with respect to the false advertising of Mougan is correct and shall be affirmed. However, as ShopEx and Kumei failed to indicate the range of confidential point of involved information, the software program and documents were mistakenly regarded as the objects of protection for trade secrets. And Zhabei Market Supervision Administration also fails to determine the scope of technical information, and it is impossible to judge whether such information has reached the level of trade secrets "not widely known and easily accessible to relevant personnel of such field." Therefore, the determination of infringement of trade secrets by GuanYi made by Zhabei Market Supervision Administration shall be repealed. It is hereby judged: I. in the decision of administrative penalty, the decision of administrative penalty made due to GuanYi infringing upon trade secrets shall be repealed, namely, "it is ordered to stop illegal behaviors," "it is fined with an amount of RMB 20,000 (TWENTY THOUSAND ONLY)"; II. The remaining claims made by the Plaintiff shall be rejected.

After judgment in the first instance, Jing'an Market Supervision Administration (as Zhabei District and Jing'an District of Shanghai has been combined, Jing'an Market Supervision Administration proceeds with the original responsibilities of Zhabei Market Supervision Administration), ShopEx and Kumei rejected such judgment and respectively filed lawsuits.

After trial, Shanghai High People's Court held that as regard whether the involved information constitute trade secrets, it is necessary to review whether such information meets four legal requirements of trade secrets. In the administrative proceedings, the administrative authority which affirms there are infringement acts of trade secrets and makes administrative penalty thereon shall assume the burden of proof of claimants in the civil actions, namely, it is his burden of proof to prove that the trade secrets determined by it meet legal requirements. In this case, Jing'an Market Supervision Administration shall first prove that the involved information is under the state of "not being known to the public," namely, the same is not directly accessible from the public channel on an objective basis, while it cannot presume that the relevant information is inevitably not widely known and easily accessible to relevant personnel of such field only by virtue of the holder having taken the confidential measures. Only when the involved information meets the elements of confidentiality, the administrative authority may further determine whether such information has value and practicability and whether the holder has taken the necessary confidential measures and other elements, so as to determine whether there are trade secrets in this case. It was meaningless for Jing'an Market Supervision Administration to make determination on whether it had value and practicability and whether the holder had taken the necessary confidential measures and compare the involved information and the software accused of infringement under the condition of failure to prove that the involved information was "not known to the public"; in addition, it also failed to prove that in the judicial appraisal opinion, the comparison had been completely made on both. Thus, the decision of administrative penalty made by Zhabei Market Supervision Administration due to GuanYi infringing trade secrets of others shall be repealed due to lack of factual and legal basis. To sum up, the court in the second instance judges according to law that the appeal shall be rejected and the original judgment shall be affirmed.

[Case Study]

The main legal issue involved in this case is whether the duplication and use of software inevitably constitutes an act of infringing upon trade secrets of the software?

In this case, the administrative authority found out that in the computer of the company of the penalized person, there were files that had copied third-person source programs and documents, and if such third-person source programs and documents constitute works, the act of copying and using the said software by the penalized person without permission was suspected of constituting infringement upon copyright of others' works. However, the competition of liabilities for infringement upon copyright and trade secrets will be incurred due to such improper reproduction and use of the software only when the software simultaneously constitutes the works and the trade secrets. In other words, if the software constitutes the works but does not constitute the trade secrets, it will not constitute an infringement of trade secret even if the actor infringes its copyright.

Ⅰ. Definition of the term "trade secrets"

The computer software constitutes works when it conforms to original, tangible and reproducible intellectual achievements. And according to the provisions of Article 10 (Ⅲ) of *Anti-Unfair Competition Law* in China, trade secrets mean the technical and operation information which is unknown to the public, able to bring economic benefits to the owners, has practical value and is protected by the owners with security measures. Namely, the trade secrets refer to the information of technology and management with confidentiality, value and practicability, for which the owners have adopted security measures. If the holder of the software intends to seek the legal remedy by virtue of trade secrets, it must simultaneously have the above-said four legal requirements which are integral.

The computer software shall first have confidentiality if it conforms to the legal requirements of trade secrets. As specified in Article 9 (Ⅰ) of the *Interpretation of the Supreme People's Court Concerning the Application of Law in the Trial of Civil Cases Involving Unfair Competition*, the relevant information which is unknown or easily accessible to the relevant personnel of such field shall be regarded as those "not being known to the public" as stated in Article 10 (Ⅲ) of the *Anti-unfair*

Competition Law, thus, the confidentiality requirement of the trade secrets shall mean that the such information is widely unknown to the such industry and is objectively unable to be directly accessible from the public channel.

Ⅱ. The burden of proof for the software constituting the trade secret

As specified in Article 14 of the *Interpretation of the Supreme People's Court Concerning the Application of Law in the Trial of Civil Cases Involving Unfair Competition*, the party involved who accuses others of infringing upon its trade secrets shall be liable for the burden of proof over the facts that its own trade secrets conform to the legal requirements, the information from the opposite party involved is identical or substantially identical to its trade secrets and the opposite party involved takes improper measures. The evidences that the trade secrets conform to the legal requirements include the carrier of trade secrets, specific content of trade secrets, commercial value of trade secrets and specific security measures to be taken on such trade secrets etc.

Ⅲ. The administrative authority shall bear the burden of proof for the involved information constituting a trade secret in administrative cases

As stated above, in the civil cases involving the infringement of trade secrets of software, the plaintiff shall bear the burden of proof to prove that its software meets the legal requirements of trade secrets. And in the administrative cases of trade secrets, the administrative authority that makes decision on specific administrative penalty shall testify the legality of its penalty decision, that is, it shall bear the burden of proof that its identified trade secrets meet the requirements of confidentiality, value and practicality as required by law and protected by the holder with security measures.

In this case, the administrative authority shall present evidences to prove that the software in the whole is under the state of "being unknown to the public," namely, such software is not widely known and easily accessible to the relevant personnel of such field, and it cannot be assumed that the information is necessarily not widely known and easily accessible to the relevant personnel of such field only because the claimant has taken measures to keep the software confidential. In this case, the "matters entrusted for appraisal" in the *Judicial Appraisal Opinion* issued by the appraisal institution only refer to the content identity comparison of the relevant documents of the fixed evidence and the appraisal object and the authenticity appraisal of the documents, and the specific appraisal process does not involve in the determination of the factual state whether the involved source program and files are "not known to the public." The presumption made by the administrative authority that the information is necessarily not widely known and easily accessible to the relevant personnel of such field only because the third party has taken measures to keep the software confidential, is short of factual and legal basis. Therefore, in this case, the administrative authority does not provide evidences to prove that the source code and files involved in this case meet the requirement of confidentiality of trade secrets.

Although the administrative authority proved that the source code and files involved meet the legal requirements of value, practicability and confidentiality measures being taken for trade secrets, it failed to prove that they meet the requirement of confidentiality, and there are some flaws in the information identity comparison, thus the penalty decision that the infringement of its identified trade secrets is established is short of factual basis and shall be repealed.

Ⅳ. The relation between administrative cases and infringement actions

In the case on appeal that involves the administrative action due to the refusal of the administrative penalty, the scope of trial conducted by the court in the second instance shall be only limited to the review of the judgment made in the first instance and the relevant administrative penalty imposed by the administrative authority, without involving in the determination of the civil liability concerning whether the penalized person infringes upon copyright of others' software and works. Therefore, if the third party held that the reproduction and use of its software by the penalized person otherwise involved in infringement of copyright, it may file a separate lawsuit on tort, and the result of this administrative case neither affects the exercise of civil rights of relevant right holder, nor affects the determination of civil copyright infringement cases.

(Writer: Wang Jing)

VII

Cases on Judicial Proceedings of Intellectual Property

The Discontinuation Effect of Civil Statute of Limitations on Criminal Proceedings Where the Right Holder Fails to Report a Case

—BURBERRY LIMITED v. Chen Kai and Lu Qiumin
(case of dispute over the trademark infringement)

[Summary]

The criminal proceedings in which the right holder fails to report the case does not certainly have the legal consequences of limitation of action; however, the right holder shall cooperate with the public security organ in investigating relevant facts of the case, which has two legal consequences on the right holder: first, the legal consequence on the commencement of limitation of action, as he/she has known the existence of tort; second, the legal consequence on the discontinuance of limitation of action, as he/she has good reasons to believe that his/her own rights has been protected by public power at the same time as he/she cooperates with the public security organ in investigation, and the specific facts of infringement and the extent of protection over rights are subject to the outcome of criminal proceedings. Therefore, the above-said causes shall belong to the "other matters with the same effect of interruption for limitation of action as filing of lawsuit."

[Case Review]

Plaintiff (the Appellee): BURBERRY LIMITED
Defendant (the Appellant): Lu Qiumin
Defendant: Chen Kai

Cause of Action: Dispute over infringement of trademark right

First-instance Case No.: (2014) YMS (Z) CZ No. 381

Second-instance Case No.: (2015) HZMZZ No. 6

BURBERRY LIMITED is the holder of No. 75130 and No. G733385 registered trademarks "BURBERRY." Since October 2009, Chen Kai, in collusion with Lu Qiumin, registered the Taobao shop in the name of others, through which it sold the clothing with counterfeit registered trademark of "BURBERRY" at a low price; the department concerned found such infringement in the process of administrative enforcement of law and filed a criminal prosecution against them and afterwards, they were sentenced by the court on the ground of selling the counterfeit registered trademark goods on August 24, 2012. On March 21, 2012, BURBERRY LIMITED was informed of the infringement by Chen Kai and Lu Qiumin and the report of placing a case on file when it was requested by the public security organ to confirm whether the seized goods was the counterfeit registered trademark goods or not and issue a price certificate. On August 15, 2014, BURBERRY LIMITED filed a first-instance civil action in this case, requesting to order that Chen Kai and Lu Qiumin shall stop infringement and they shall jointly and severally compensate the Plaintiff for the economic losses and reasonable expenses at an amount of RMB 1 million.

The Appellant Lu Qiumin refused the judgment of first instance and filed an appeal, arguing that BURBERRY LIMITED shall file a lawsuit at latest by March 30, 2014, thus, as regard to the lawsuit filed by it on August 15, 2014, the statute of limitations had passed and the court in the first instance did not correctly apply the law. As the court in the first instance has identified that Lu Qiumin and Chen Kai stopped the infringements as of March 20, 2012, according to Article 18 of the *Interpretations of Supreme People's Court on Several Issues concerning Application of Laws in Trying Civil Trademark Dispute Cases* (hereinafter referred to as the *Interpretations for Applicable Law of Trademark Cases*), the amount of damages for infringement shall be calculated based on the profits earned preceding two years from the date when BURBERRY LIMITED filed a lawsuit to the people's court. And no infringements and profits from infringements existed during such two years before the day when the lawsuit on this case was filed, and thus there was no need to compensate for losses. Therefore, Lu Qiumin requested the court to revoke the original judgment and make a new judgment according to law.

The Appellee BURBERRY LIMITED argued that the lawsuit in the first instance was made within the limitation of action. After it learned of the infringements on March 21, 2012 and provided the relevant materials to the public security organ, based on the reliance on the criminal justice and common practice of criminal procedure prior to civil procedure in practice, it did not file a civil lawsuit at that time. But at that time, the criminal procedure has been existed; therefore, the limitation of action shall be interrupted and recounted after the criminal procedure was concluded. The effective date of the involved criminal judgment was September 3, 2012, therefore, the lawsuit made on August 15, 2014 did not exceed the limitation of action.

The Defendant Chen Kai in the first instance stated that he had no objection to the original judgment.

[Judgment]

Shanghai Yangpu District People's Court believed upon trial that although, on March 21, 2012, BURBERRY LIMITED learned of that the public security organ had placed a case on file against and investigated Chen Kai and Lu Qiumin, whether these two persons can be confirmed as the infringement subjects and relevant evidences for infringements are required to be determined after the criminal judgment takes effect. The period of limitation of action in this case shall be counted from the effective date of the criminal judgment; therefore, the lawsuit made by BURBERRY LIMITED did not exceed such limitation of action, and Chen Kai and Lu Qiumin shall undertake civil liabilities for their infringements upon others' registered trademark rights. Shanghai Yangpu District People's Court, according to Article 8 of *the Tort Liability Law of the People's Republic of China*, Articles 52 (Ⅰ) and (Ⅱ) and Article 56 (1) of *the Trademark Law of the People's Republic of China* (as amended in 2001), and Articles 9(Ⅰ), 10, 17, 18 and 21 (1) of the *Interpretations of Supreme People's Court on Several Issues concerning Application of Laws in Trying Civil Trademark Dispute Cases*, made the following judgment: Chen Kai and Lu Qiumin shall jointly and severally compensate BURBERRY LIMITED for economic losses of RMB 150,000 and reasonable expenses of RMB 15,000 and The remaining claims of BURBERRY LIMITED shall be rejected.

After the first-instance judgment, the Defendant Lu Qiumin refused to accept this judgment and filed an appeal.

Shanghai Intellectual Property Court held upon trial that the criminal proceeding involved did not certainly have the legal effect of limitation of action, as the trademark right holder failed to report the case on a criminal basis. However, the period of limitation of action shall start from the day when the Appellee was requested by the public security organ to issue a price certificate and identify the genuine and fake goods. And at the same time, it had good reasons to believe that its rights may be protected by the ongoing criminal investigation. And the specific behavior, scale, consequence of infringement by the Defendant in the first instance will be necessarily determined based on the final affirmation of the criminal judgment. Therefore, such situation belongs to the "other matters with the same effect of interruption for limitation of action as filing of lawsuit" and the period of limitation of action shall be interrupted accordingly. Thus, the lawsuit made by the Appellee did not exceed the limitation of action, and the infringers shall undertake civil liabilities. The provision that the loss shall be calculated based on the profits from infringement during the period preceding two years from the date of filing a lawsuit is applicable to the situation that the infringement lasts and the right holder files a lawsuit more than two years after learning of the infringement, and this case does to apply to such provision. Thus, the grounds of appeal proposed by the Appellant shall not be established. The facts affirmed by the original court are clear; the trial procedure is legal and the result of judgment is proper, therefore the original judgment shall be affirmed, while the applicable law shall be corrected due to incompleteness.

[Case Study]

This case is a civil dispute over infringement of trademark right that is incurred by the criminal offence on the ground of sale of counterfeit registered trademark goods and the parties involved in this case have no objections to the criminal behaviors affirmed in the criminal judgment and the infringements affirmed by the court in the first instance; the disagreement between the parties involved is about that whether the lawsuit filed by the Appellee to the court in the first instance has exceeded the prescribed period of litigation and the amount of damages shall be calculated based on the provision in the *Interpretations for Applicable Law of Trademark Cases* that it shall be calculated on the basis of the profits from infringement preceding two years from the date of lawsuit.

Ⅰ. This case is an issue about the starting of limitation of action or the suspension of limitation of action

The limitation of action refers to a system that the fact that right holder does not exercise the rights lasts the legal period and the effectiveness of impairment immediately occurs to its rights. Namely, the right holder loses the right to request the court to conduct protection due to the expiration of the limitation of action when the obligor exercises the right of defense on the limitation of action. According to Article 135 of the *General Rule of Civil Law* and Article 18 of the *Interpretations for Applicable Law of Trademark Cases* in China, the limitation of action that the right holder whose trademark rights are infringed applies to the people's court to take protection is two years, starting from the date when the trademark registrant or the interested person knows or should know the infringements.

The limitation of action is a system to limit the time of right holder exercising his/her own rights, and the purpose of establishing such system is to supervise and urge the right holder to exercise rights and safeguard the stability of transaction relationship, not to exempt the debtor from his/her obligations and not to protect the improper interests of the debtor. Thus, the *Regulations on Limitation of Action* as established by the Supreme Court specifies that when the parties involved make no defense on limitation of action, the court shall not actively interpret and make judgment by application of regulations on limitation of action; such regulations also limit the time and stage of making defense on limitation of action. Upon the expiration of the period of limitation of action, the right holder loses its right to get the enforcement protection of the court and does not loss its substantive rights.

Besides, to balance the interests of the parties involved, a barrier system on the limitation of action is also established by law, namely, the suspension or interruption of the limitation of action is the barrier system on the limitation of action. The dispute in this case seems to be the problem concerning the determination of starting point of period of limitation of action with respect to the trademark infringement action, but in essence, is the problem that whether the criminal prosecution procedure against the Appellant and the Defendant in the first instance constitutes the reason for suspension of the limitation of action, as the laws in China specify that the period of limitation of action shall be counted from the date when the right holder knows or should know the infringement upon his/her rights. It can be seen that the provision on starting point of limitation of action is clear, without ambiguity and argument. The dispute between the parties involved is actually the problem that whether the limitation of action shall be restarted or not, and it is possible to recount the period of the limitation of action only when the situation of interruption occurs; thus, the dispute in this case in essence is whether the reasons for interruption of limitation of action occur.

Article 140 of the *General Principles of the Civil Law* in China stipulates that: "the prescribed period of litigation is interrupted due to the filing of lawsuit, requirements proposed by either party involved or the consent of performing the obligation, and from the date of interruption, the period of limitation of action shall be recounted. " There are specific circumstances as specified from Article 11 to Article 19 of the *Regulations on Limitation of Action* as established by the Supreme Court. This case is about the problem of interruption of limitation of action for crossed cases of civil law and criminal law, which is specified in Article 15 of the *Regulations on Limitation of Action*. It is worth noting that this Article indicates the application of the situation that "the right holder reports a case or accuses to ..." and the criminal behavior that the Defendant in the first instance infringes the exclusive right to use registered trademark in this case was not found by the right holder and "reported or sued," but the public security organ initiated the criminal investigation after finding illegal acts, thus, such provision cannot be directly applied to this case. Article 13 of the *Regulations on Limitation of Action* specifies the matters that can be identified as the same effect of interruption for the limitation of action as that of filing an action, but with respect to 8 causes as listed therein, they are different from this case. Then, whether the provisions in subparagraph (9) of this Article that "other matters with the same effect of suspension of limitation of action as that of filing an action" can be applied?

In this case, the Appellee, as the right holder, did not know its rights were infringed and knew such situation only when it was requested to issue a price certificate and identify genuine and fake goods, at the same time, it also learned that the Appellant and the Defendant in the first instance were under criminal investigation. This case itself can be interpreted in this way: 1. as the right holder, it knows that its own rights are infringed, and the period of limitation of action shall be counted according to law; 2. as the right holder of trademark, it actively cooperates with the public security organ in making relevant identification, which indicates the positive attitude toward the protection of rights; 3. under the premise that the infringement acts have been included in the criminal procedure, the right holder shall have good reasons to believe that its civil rights can be protected; 4. objectively, the specific behavior, scale, consequence of infringement by the Appellant and the Defendant in the first instance will be necessarily determined based on the final affirmation of the criminal judgment. The extent of protection on civil rights of the Appellee is also closely related to the outcome of the criminal proceedings. Thus, although such criminal procedure was not initiated by the right holder through reporting a case or suing, the existence and duration of such criminal procedure shall have the effect of interruption for limitation of action, which belongs to the matters that have the same effect of interruption for the limitation of action as that of filing an action. The Appellee had known the infringement of rights when receiving the requirement of the public security organ to issue the price certificate and identify the genuine and false goods, and then the period for limitation of action shall be counted, but at the same time, it was aware of that the criminal investigation procedure was made against the behavior of the two infringers; based on the above-said reasons analyzed, the period for limitation of action shall be interrupted accordingly. With the end of the criminal procedure, the cause for the interruption of the limitation of action shall be excluded and the period for limitation of action shall be recounted; therefore, the lawsuit was filed by the Appellee within the limitation of action and the infringers shall assume the civil liabilities with respect to their infringements according to law.

As a result, this case shall be applicable to the provision in relation to the interruption of the limitation of action, instead of the provision in relation to the starting of the limitation of action.

Ⅱ. Whether the provision that the loss shall be calculated based on the profits from infringement during the period preceding two years from the date of filing a lawsuit is applicable to this case

The another reason why the Appellant refused the judgment in the first instance is that the compensation for loss shall be calculated based on the profits from infringement during the period preceding two years from the date of filing the lawsuit, according to Article 18 of the *Interpretations for Applicable Law of Trademark Cases* as established by the Supreme Court. During such period, the two Defendants in the first instance had stopped the acts of selling goods bearing the counterfeit registered trademark. Since there is no infringement, there is no profit from infringement and no liability for compensation shall be assumed. In short, even though the lawsuit was filed by the Plaintiff in the first instance within the limitation of action, if the provision in this Article is applicable, no compensation shall be required to be made. That's because preceding two years from the date of filing the lawsuit, two Defendants had stopped infringement for a long time, and there was no profit from infringement? Then the calculation of compensation is made without any basis.

The provision quoted by the Appellant is a part of Article 18 of the *Interpretations for Applicable Law of Trademark Cases*, i. e. "…the registrant or the interested party files a lawsuit beyond two years, and if the infringements still last during such period of filing a lawsuit, within the effective period of exclusive right of the registered trademark, the people's court shall judge that the Defendant should cease to infringe and the amount of damages for infringement shall be calculated preceding two years from the date when the right holder files a lawsuit to the people's court." It can be seen that such provision is applicable to the situation that the infringement lasts and if the right holder files a lawsuit more than two years after learning of the infringement, the amount of compensation shall be calculated based on profits from infringements preceding two years from the date of filing a lawsuit. This provision applies only to situation that the lawsuit is brought more than two years after being aware of a continuing infringement, without involving in any circumstance of interruption of limitation of action. And this case does not apply to the provided situation due to the discontinuance of limitation of action and the right holder filing a lawsuit within two years upon the discontinuance of limitation of action.

To sum up, the application of provisions by the court of second instance is affirmed as set forth in Article 140 of the *General Rule of Civil Law* and Article 13 (9) of the *Regulations of Limitation of Action*, that the criminal procedure in this case belongs to the "other matters with the same effect of interruption for limitation of action as filing of lawsuit," which has the effect of interruption for limitation of action, and the lawsuit was filed by the Appellee within the limitation of action; thus, its claims shall be protected by the court. The first-instance judgment has been affirmed and the reasons for judgment and legal basis have been supplemented on a detailed basis, for which the application of legal provisions and judicial interpretation is correct and complete.

(Writer: Chen Huizhen)

Behavior Preservation for Cases of Infringement upon Joint Copyright

—Actoz Soft Co. , Ltd. v. Wemade Entertainment Co. , Ltd. and Shanghai Kingnet Technology Co. Ltd（case of dispute over pre-litigation cessation of infringement upon copyright）

[Summary]

The owner, who enjoys the joint copyright to the computer software that cannot be separated for use, when authorizing and licensing others to use the copyright, shall reach a consensus with other co-owners through consultation. If the authorization is granted to others without negotiation, the signed contract is suspected of infringing upon the joint copyright and other co-owners apply to the court for prohibiting the performance of such contract, which complies with the legal requirements of emergency and timely stop-loss.

[Case Review]

Applicant（Respondent in the reconsideration）: Actoz Soft Co. , Ltd.

Respondent（Applicant in the reconsideration）: Wemade Entertainment Co. , Ltd.

Respondent（Applicant in the reconsideration）: Shanghai Kingnet Technology Co. Ltd.

Cause of Action: dispute over infringement of copyright of computer software

Case No. : (2016) H73XB No. 1

Case No. of the reconsideration: (2016) H73XBF No. 1

Both the Applicant Actoz Soft Co. , Ltd. (hereinafter referred to "Actoz") and the Respondent Wemade Entertainment Co. , Ltd. (hereinafter referred to "Wemade") are South Korean companies, and jointly own the copyright of the game software named as the Legend of Mir 2, which has been normally operated in China for 15 years. On June 28, 2016, Wemade and the Respondent Shanghai Kingnet Technology Co. Ltd. (hereinafter referred to as "Kingnet") signed the licensing contract with respect to the mobile game and web game of the involved software with the contract price of 300 million won. The affiliated company of Kingnet made an online announcement in relation to such contract, and Wemade sent a written notice to Actoz after signing the contract.

Actoz alleged in the application: Wemade arbitrarily exercised the indivisible joint copyright without consultation with it, which is in violation of provisions in Article 13 of the *Copyright Law of the People's Republic of China* and Article 9 of the *Regulations for the Implementation of the Copyright Law of the People's Republic of China.* In order to prevent the act of authorization from causing irreparable losses to and having material adverse effects on the legal rights and interests of the Applicant and the current operating order of the game, the court is requested to prohibit two Respondents from actually performing the contract signed by them without consultation with the Applicant and RMB 50 million in cash shall be provided as a guarantee.

[**Judgment**]

Shanghai Intellectual Property Court held that the Applicant and the Respondent Wemade jointly owned the copyright of the game software involved and if Wemade signed an external licensing contract without reaching consensus with the Applicant through negotiation, it was suspected of infringing the right of the Applicant as the joint copyright owner. Seeing that two Respondents may put into commercial operation after signing a contract, if such behavior was not promptly stopped, the irreparable damages will be caused to the rights of the joint copyright owner; thus, it was ordered that two Respondents immediately ceased to perform the contract involved.

After ruling in the case, two Respondents refused the ruling and made application for reconsideration. They alleged in reconsideration that this case did not meet the conditions of pre-litigation act preservation that should be met, namely, it was emergent and the losses arising therefrom cannot be made up without preservation. As Actoz and Wemade once made "conciliation minute," both parties may individually sign a licensing agreement with overseas third party; the consensus to be reached by the joint copyright owners through negotiation is not a legal prerequisite for exercising copyright; Wemade had given a notice in good faith and Actoz failed to make objections or provide good reasons to object to the license within the reasonable time limit; when Wemade undertook to share the permitted earnings, Actoz was unlikely to suffer irreparable damages. Kingnet had begun to perform the contract involved and had made announcement with respect to the contract to the public through its parent company (listed company), and the cessation of performing the licensing contract would affect the normal operation and share price and do harm to the public interests.

Shanghai Intellectual Property Court held through reconsideration that the conciliation minute provided by the Applicant in reconsideration did not specify that Wemade had the right to separately license to others with respect to the software involved. The performance of the contract involved necessarily caused actual damages to the joint copyright owner; to timely prevent the performance of a contract that may infringe upon the rights of others also helps the parties to the contract to stop losses in time; to maintain the performance and image of the company should not be based on the possibility of infringing the rights of others and it is hardly legitimate for the opinion that the ruling of act preservation must affect the share price so as to damage the public interests. Thus, it is ordered that the reconsideration request made by two Respondents in reconsideration shall be rejected.

[Case Study]

The joint copyright owners shall reach consensus through consultation when exercising the copyright of computer software that cannot be separated for use, which is not only the pre-procedure stipulated by relevant laws, but also the basic requirement of the principle of equality, honesty and good faith that civil subjects should follow. The condition that "either party may exercise its rights other than the assignment" is satisfied only if no agreement is reached through consultation and there is no reasonable reason for such agreement. In case of unauthorized external license without consultation, the signed contract may be invalid due to infringement of right in common. Prohibiting the performance of invalid contracts can prevent the actual occurrence of copyright infringement or further expansion of losses, which meets the conditions of emergency and prevention of irreparable damage as required by relevant provisions on act preservation of stopping infringement before litigation. Thus, the request made by the joint right owner shall be supported. This case has reference value to the handling of the act preservation case for infringement of joint copyright rights.

(Writer: Chen Huizhen)

Pre-litigation Evidence Preservation for Cases of Infringement upon Copyright of Computer Software

—the Applicants Autodesk and Adobe v. the Respondent Shanghai Fengyuzhu Exhibition Co. , Ltd. (case of pre-litigation evidence preservation)

[Summary]

After the court took the preservative measures according to law, the Applicant filed a lawsuit to the court. During the trial of the case, the court basically ascertained the facts of the case, based on the result of evidence preservation, with the claims made by the parties as the point of penetration, gradually narrowing the gap between the parties and promoting reconciliation between the two sides. The parties involved eventually made settlement by way of "compensation + software legalization" and had completed the performance of settlement agreement.

[Case Review]

Applicant: Autodesk

Applicant: Adobe

Respondent: Shanghai Fengyuzhu Exhibition Co. , Ltd.

Cause of Action: dispute over infringement of copyright of computer software

Case No. : (2015) HZMBZ No. 1 and No. 2

Autodesk and Adobe, the two U. S. companies, provided the infringement clue that Shanghai Fengyuzhu Exhibition Co. , Ltd. had applied the series of computer software including AutoCAD, Photoshop and Acrobat from such two companies on a commercial basis. In consideration of that they objectively could not obtain relevant evidences, and such evidences were easily concealed or destroyed, thus the Applicants requested Shanghai Intellectual Property Court to conduct pre-litigation evidence preservation.

[Judgment]

Shanghai Intellectual Property Court held after investigation that as the Applicant had provided the preliminary clue to the Respondent's infringement, the evidences applied for preservation conformed to the conditions that evidences might be destroyed or might be hard to recover later as prescribed by law. Moreover, as the Applicant could not collect the above-said evidences on its own for objective reasons, such application met the conditions of pre-litigation evidence preservation; then the Court ruled that the preservation of evidence should be done to the relevant information with regard to the above series of software on the computers and other facilities within the business premises of the Respondent and worked closely with Shanghai No. 3 Intermediate People's Court to give full play to the institutional advantage of "joint work" so as to timely and efficiently complete the evidence preservation of about 400 computers and successfully complete the implementation of preservation rulings.

[Case Study]

To strengthen the judicial protection of the intellectual property right should not only be reflected in the construction and implementation of substantive legal system, but also in the implementation of procedural systems such as temporary injunction and evidence preservation. This pre-litigation evidence preservation measures were applied according to law, which not only fixed the relevant evidence in time, but also fully demonstrated the strength of intellectual property rights judicial protection.

(Writer: Wu Yingzhe)

Judicial Review of Pre-litigation Act Preservation for Unfair Network Competition

—Zhejiang Taobao Network Co. , Ltd. v. Shanghai Zaihe Network Technology Co. , Ltd. (case of dispute over application for pre-trial cessation of intellectual property infringement)

[Summary]

This case is the one that the courts across the country have made the first pre-litigation act preservation ruling on unfair competition in the field of e-commerce after the act preservation system is specified in the new civil procedure law. The court, based on the provisions in the civil procedure law and relevant substantial law on intellectual property right, by reference to TRIPs Agreement and extraterritorial judicial practice, summarizes the application conditions of pre-litigation act preservation: (1) the Applicant has the possibility of winning a lawsuit; (2) the irreparable damages might be caused to the Applicant due to failure to take preservation measures; (3) taking preservation measures does not damage the public interests. As a temporary measure of judicial protection, the pre-litigation act preservation of this case has improved the timeliness and effectiveness of judicial remedy.

[Case Review]

Applicant: Zhejiang Taobao Network Co. , Ltd.
Respondent: Shanghai Zaihe Network Technology Co. , Ltd.
Respondent: Zaixin Software (Shanghai) Co. , Ltd.
Cause of Action: dispute on application for stopping infringement upon

intellectual property rights before litigation.

Case No. : (2015) PJZ No. 1

The Applicant Zhejiang Taobao Network Co. , Ltd. (hereinafter referred to as "Taobao") made an application for pre-litigation act preservation on October 23, 2015, alleged that it is the owner and actual operator of "www. taobao. com," and the Respondent Shanghai Zaihe Network Technology Co. , Ltd. (hereinafter referred to as "Zaihe") is the owner and operator of the "B5M" website (www. b5m. com); both of them are the online trade platform and directly compete with each other. Zaihe provided the "B5M" webpage plug-ins on the official website of "B5M" for download, which was developed and provided with technical support by Zaixin Software (Shanghai) Co. , Ltd. (hereinafter referred to as Zaixin). After a user installs such plug-in, when it does shopping on "www. taobao. com" by using the major browsers such as IE, Baidu and Sogou, the advertising column and search box of "B5M" website will be appeared on the page of "www. taobao. com," and the links such as "being immediately reduced in cash" or "being immediately reduced by RMB 1 yuan through B5M Scanning QR Code" appear prominently near the original price on the page of product details; the user will skip to the page of "B5M" website by clicking such links, and complete the order, payment and other transaction procedures in such website.

The Applicant held that the act of the Respondent Zaihe sought improper interests by virtue of the popularity and reputation of the brand "www. taobao. com," and such behavior not only robbed the commercial benefits that should have been enjoyed by the Applicant, but also brought great negative evaluation to the market image of "www. taobao. com", which has constituted an act of unfair competition. The Respondent Zaixin, as the developer and technical service supporter of "B5T," without performing the duty of care, provided assistance in the unfair competition of Zaihe and shall undertake joint and several liabilities. In order to prevent two Respondents from continuing to carry out unfair competition practices, the Applicant once conducted security upgrade, but such technical measures were cracked by two Respondents. Later, the Applicant reported to Pudong New Area Market Supervision Administration of Shanghai and requested the administrative authorities to dispose of the unfair competition practices conducted by the Respondents, and a case had been registered. But the Respondents still carried out the unfair competition in a crazy manner. Statistics show that during the period from

July to August 2015, the Respondents had independent access to "www. taobao. com" for more than 53. 06 million times by way of embedding the "B5T" into "www. taobao. com. " and the users mistakenly clicked the links embedded with "B5M" for more than 78. 59 million times on the page of "www. taobao. com," by which the huge sum of commercial interests that should be earned by the Applicant was robbed, resulting in the expected loss of revenue of "www. taobao. com" up to hundreds of millions of yuan. In view of the hearing cycle of cases on unfair competition and the processing period of administrative reporting cases, as well as the commercial promotion activities planned by the Plaintiff during the period of "Double Eleventh Day," if the unfair competition practices conducted by two Respondents could not be prevented timely, the irreparable damages therefrom would be caused to the Applicant. For this purpose, the Applicant made an application to the court to order that two Respondents shall stop continuing unfair competition practices to the Applicant by way of "B5T" webpage plug-in.

The Applicant had submitted the notarization of preservation of evidences in connection with "B5T" website and its records, Respondents' alleged infringements, complaints of the Applicant's users, netizen's discussions on Taobao Forum and other third party website, and the number of clicks on its website marked by the Applicant through monitoring "B5M," as well as the evidence materials including the materials concerning the Applicant reporting to Pudong New Area Market Supervision Administration of Shanghai and the written reply to report given by the Administration, and provided the guarantee for this purpose.

[Judgment]

After the trial, Pudong New Area People's Court of Shanghai held that the pre-litigation act preservation shall meet the following conditions: (1) the Applicant has the possibility of winning a lawsuit; (2) the irreparable damages might be caused to the Applicant due to failure to take preservation measures; (3) taking preservation measures does not damage the public interests. In this case, according to the evidence materials provided by the Applicant, they could preliminarily prove that the publisher of "B5T" plug-in is the Respondent Zaixin, and the Respondent Zaihe made the shopping page of "www. taobao. com" appearing the signs such as "being immediately reduced in cash" by way of embedding "B5T" into the shopping page of "www. taobao. com" so as to lead to that the users who originally wanted to conduct transactions on "www. taobao. com" were directed to the "B5M" website and conducted transactions with the defendant Zaihe. After analysis based on the said conditions, firstly, both "www. taobao. com" and "B5M" website are the shopping websites, with the directly competitive relation. The said behavior of Zaihe made it obtain users and opportunities of transaction with the help of the Applicant's platform without paying corresponding advertising and promotional expenses, which is suspected of improper taking use of the popularity and user base of "www. taobao. com." Therefore, the behaviors of two Respondents may constitute unfair competition. Secondly, the volume of business on "www. taobao. com" is huge, and the "Double Eleventh Day" called by the shopping carnival was coming; if the accused infringements above were not stopped in time, irreparable damage might be incurred to the competitive advantage and market shares of the Applicant. Finally, taking preservation measures could not damage the public interests and the Applicant had provided effective guarantees. To sum up, this case conformed to the conditions of pre-litigation act preservation. Therefore, Pudong New Area People's Court of Shanghai made a ruling according to Articles 101, 154 (Ⅰ) (4) of the *Civil Procedure Law of the People's Republic of China* and Article 171 of the *Interpretation of the Supreme People's Court concerning the Application of the Civil Procedure Law of the People's Republic of China*, that Zaihe and Zaixin shall immediately stop inserting "B5T" into Taobao webpage.

Two Respondents refused the ruling and filed reconsideration with the major ground as follows: 1. no commodities was sold on "B5M" website operated by Zaihe, while the registered members would be provided with the freight and discount subsidies after shopping on the website including "www. taobao. com" and "Tmall" which did not constitute competitive relation with "www. taobao. com." 2. "B5T" plug-in was developed by Zaixin, and "B5M" website provided the registered members who voluntarily installed such plug-in with purchasing agency service, and the purchasing behavior of the members were actually the transactions conducted by them with the shopping website including "www. taobao. com"; therefore, such behavior not only did not affect the interests of merchants, but also promoted the deal increase of "www. taobao. com" because of its subsidy to registered members. 3. The Internet, as the emerging industry, encourages the small, medium and micro businesses to operate legally, subject to no substantive trial of the case, the injunction was made, which did not conform to the public interests.

As regard to the reasons of reconsideration provided by the Respondents, Pudong New Area People's Court of Shanghai held that based on existing evidences, "B5M" website also provided purchasing service with respect to commodities appeared on such website in addition to the provision of search service of commodity information, which can be seen that such website belongs to the shopping website. Whether such commodities were directly supplied by the website operator or provided through the so-called purchasing agency service, did not affect the identification of nature of such website. Therefore, the parties to this case had competitive relation. The person applying for reconsideration inserted "B5T" webpage plug-in into the webpage of "www. taobao. com" easily led those users mistake the relationship of "B5M" and "www. taobao. com." which might constitute unfair competition. Therefore, the reasons of reconsideration above shall not be supported. Pudong New Area People's Court hereby decided that the application for reconsideration made by Zaihe and Zaixin shall be rejected and the original ruling shall be affirmed.

[Case Study]

The act preservation is also known as the temporary injunction. The word "Injunction" is originated from the laws of Britain and America and refers to an order made by a court requiring a party to do or not to do a particular act. The Temporary Injunction refers to a system made by the court to order the parties concerned to do or restrain from doing a particular act before making final judgment on the dispute of case. The Temporary Injunction is called as "Provisional Measures" in Article 50 of TRIPs Agreement. In order to meet the requirements of joining in the World Trade Organization and complying with the TRIPs Agreement, the Patent Law revised in 2000 and the Trademark Law revised in 2001 and the Copyright Law in China specify the system of stopp inginfringements prior to litigation, and the Supreme Court later has issued the relevant judicial interpretation; but no such provisions on unfair competition has been specified. Until the amendment to the Civil Procedure Law was made in 2012, the act preservation system was specified on a unified basis, and the scope of application extended to the whole field of civil proceedings; such act preservation was divided into pre-litigation act preservation and in-litigation act preservation based on the different stages of application. For this case, the courts have made the first pre-litigation act preservation ruling on unfair competition in the field of e-commerce after the act preservation system is specified in the new civil procedure law.

When the parties concerned applied for the pre-litigation act preservation, no conclusive conclusion has been made on whether this case was involved in infringement. In case of no permission or delay in release, the reduction in the market shares of the right holder might be caused; in case of improper release, the loss might be incurred by the accused infringer. In the intellectual property cases in the field of Internet, in view of that the alleged infringement can often cause great damage in a short time and continue to expand the scope of the damage, whether or not to make an act preservation ruling has a more significant impact on the interests of the parties concerned. On the other hand, in practice, the accused infringers often put off the lawsuit progress by way of objection to jurisdiction and appeal, resulting in the longer relief cycles, which might cause the embarrassing situation that the intellectual property owner "wins the case but loses the market." For some right holders, it is more important to timely prevent the in-progress torts than to obtain the economic compensation after going through the prolonged lawsuit; therefore, the act preservation becomes the more important relief means. But at the same time, the act preservation system is also a double-edged sword, and it can enhance the strength of protection on intellectual property by proper application; otherwise, it will hinder the development of science and technology culture; thus, it is crucial to grasp the application conditions of pre-lawsuit behavior preservation.

The *Civil Procedure Law* stipulates that the conditions of pre-lawsuit preservation are that the situation is emergent and the irreparable damage will be caused to its legal rights and interests without immediate application, without involving in the judgment on whether the accused behavior infringes upon rights or not. The laws including the *Copyright Law* provide that the pre-lawsuit behavior preservation shall meet the following two conditions: "there are evidences to prove that a tort is being or is about to be committed" and "the irreparable damage will be caused to the legal rights and interests of the right holder without prevention in time." The author held that if the court makes no judgment on the substantive tort possibility to the accused infringer, namely, to take the behavior preservation based on the unilateral application of the right holder, then this violates the principle of fairness in civil litigation. Therefore, the "possibility of winning a lawsuit" for the right holder in substance shall be taken as the condition of pre-lawsuit behavior preservation. At the same time, TRIPs Agreement also requires the judicial authority of the member state to give consideration to the interests of the Respondents and the public when protecting the legal interests and rights of the right holder. Therefore, during the investigation of this case, the pre-litigation behavior preservation shall meet the following conditions: (1) the Applicant has the possibility of winning a lawsuit; (2) the irreparable damages might be caused to the Applicant due to failure to take preservation measures; (3) taking preservation measures does not damage the public interests.

Ⅰ. About "the Possibility of Winning a Lawsuit"

As the term suggests, "the Possibility of Winning a Lawsuit" involves in the judgment of probability. Although the Applicant is not required to prove the inevitability of winning a lawsuit, it shall still prove the possibility of torts. However, it is always controversial that the court will not support the application of preservation until what standard of proof should the evidence provided by the applicant meet and to what extent is the likelihood of winning a lawsuit. If the standards are not strict enough, it is likely that the rights will be abused, which makes the act preservation system become a tool to attack the competitors; on the contrary, if the standards are strict enough, the scope of application for act preservation system will be unduly limited, and the functions of such system will not be exerted, which goes against the timeliness and effectiveness of judicial remedy.

From the perspective of comparative law, English Court implements the substantial dispute standard on such conditions, as long as the vexatious actions and the situation that the action is obviously unlikely to win are able to be eliminated; in America, the preponderance of evidence is required for the establishment of tort, but as regard to the problems such as the effectiveness and enforceability of rights, the attitude of presumptive establishment is applied; in German, Japan and Taiwan of China, the Applicant is only required to explain the right of claim and simultaneously is allowed to make up the shortcoming of explanatory content by way of guarantee.

By using the extraterritorial experience above for reference, when reviewing the "possibility of winning a lawsuit" by the right holder, the following two points are mainly reviewed: first, the applicant is required to submit relevant evidences of ownership to prove that it is the right holder of the intellectual property claimed by it and has those protected rights or interests; second, as regard to the possibility that the act of the Respondent constitutes infringement, it is required to submit the evidences that the Respondent is carrying out or is about to carry out the torts. After excluding the situation that there is obviously no possibility of winning a lawsuit, a relatively flexible standard shall be applied for the judgment of the "possibility of winning a lawsuit," and a balance shall be sought between the protection of right holder and the avoidance of wrong preservation, and the overall judgment shall be made based on the comprehensive consideration of other factors such as whether the irreparable damage is caused or not, the balance between the two parties' interests and the public interests, and whether the applicant provides the effective guarantees or not.

In this case, the interests requested by the Applicant to be protected are the competitive advantage for the internet shopping platforms. The base of survival for the internet shopping platforms is user traffic and the Applicant has made its internet shopping platform "www. taobao. com" obtain a tremendous user traffics and high popularity and reputation through operation, population and promotion for many years, becoming a leader in the industry. The user traffic and the platform credibility have great commercial value with respect to the internet shopping platform, which belongs to the commercial interests that can be protected by the competition law. According to evidences submitted by the Applicant, the court affirmed based on the following points that it is possible for the act of the Respondents to constitute the unfair competition: first, the website of the Respondents also directly provides the network shopping function in addition to the search function of commodities, which has the competitive relation with the Applicant; second, after network users install the plug-in of the Respondents in the computer, when they log in the page of "www. taobao. com." the banner ads and the search box of the Respondents will appear and even a discount purchase button with the similar style is inserted under the price tag and purchase button of "www. taobao. com." and after users click them, the page will skip to the website of the Respondents for the purpose of concluding transactions, which makes users mistakenly believe that the Respondents have an association with "www. taobao. com." Based on the said situation, although it is hard to identify that the act of the Respondents inevitably constitutes the unfair competition, it embedded the plug-in in the Applicant's web page through technical means and guided users to make deals with them, which easily makes users confused, and such act has the surface feature of unfair competition, and is likely to constitute act of unfair competition. Therefore, the court affirmed that the Applicant to this case had the "possibility of winning a lawsuit."

Ⅱ. About "irreparable damage"

As regard to how to determine the "irreparable damage," some views consider that if the Applicant can prove its possibility of winning a lawsuit, the court may presume that it will suffer the irreparable damages[①]. But the author holds that only if the irreparable damage exists with the afterwards compensation, it is necessary to allow the parties to apply to the court to order the other party to do or not to do a certain act before the court makes the final judgment; otherwise, they can wait for the court's final decision. In this sense, the condition of "irreparable damage" has independent significance and is the legitimate basis of the preservation system. The "possibility of winning a lawsuit" is only the sufficient condition of pre-litigation act preservation, and the "irreparable damage" is the necessary condition of pre-litigation act preservation, both of which are indispensable.

In general, it can be determined that the irreparable damage is incurred under the following circumstances: (1) the infringements involve in the content of the copyright-related personal rights or goodwill; (2) the occurrence of torts would proceed with seriously seizing the applicant's market shares and affecting the major interests of the applicant; (3) if such torts are not stopped timely, they will seriously expand the scope and damage consequence of torts; (4) the Respondent has no adequate solvency[②]. In the cases of anti-unfair competition, "irreparable damage" refers to the damage to the applicant's competitive advantage and market shares due to the Respondent's accused unfair competition behavior that is difficult to be recovered. For example, in the case of application for act preservation between the applicant Eli Lilly and the Respondent Huang Mengwei[③], the Respondent admitted

---

① Written by Zhang Guangliang: the *Civil Remedy for Infringement of Intellectual Property Right*, Law Press, Version 1, Page 49 in June 2003.

② Edited by the Intellectual Property Tribunal of Beijing High People's Court: the *Research on Intellectual Property Litigation Practice*, Intellectual Property Publishing House, Version in January 2008, Page 409.

③ (2013) HYZMW (Z) CZ No. 119 Civil Ruling of Shanghai No. 1 Intermediate People' Court of the People's Republic of China.

of downloading the confidential documents that belonged to the applicant and promised that the specified person of the applicant is allowed to inspect and delete the said documents, but it refused to perform such obligations. The Respondent's refusal made the applicant's trade secrets in danger of being disclosed, and once being disclosed, the competitive advantage enjoyed by the applicant on the basis of trade secrets would be lost, so there is an irreparable damage here.

In this case, the competitive advantage claimed by the Applicant mainly reflected in the user traffic of the network shopping platform "www. taobao. com. " The act of the Respondents is suspected of making use of the popularity and user base of "www. taobao. com. " and easily makes users confused. There is tremendous volume of transactions on "www. taobao. com. " and the shopping carnival "Double Eleventh Day" was just arriving when the Applicant made application, if the alleged infringement could not be stopped effectively, any change in the competitive advantage and market shares of the Applicant might happen. Once the Respondents seized the market shares of the Applicant through the accused infringements, even though subsequently the court held that the Respondent's conduct constituted unfair competition, and made judgment that it shall stop such act of unfair competition, it was hard for the competitive advantage and market shares of the Applicant to be recovered in a short time. Based on such facts, the court affirmed that this case met the condition of "irreparable damage. "

Ⅲ. About "no damage to the public interests"

The so-called public interests refer to the interests consistent with the interests of the non-specific majority under a certain social condition or within specific scope. The intellectual property has dual attributes of private goods and public goods, and how to reasonably determine its scope of protection, not only concerns the interests of the rights holder, but also concerns the public interests. For this purpose, while vesting in intellectual property owners with the exclusive right to use, the legislation of intellectual property ensures the reasonable use of intellectual property by the public through appropriate restrictions, such as rational use system in the field of copyright, mandatory licensing system in the field of patent rights, etc. Therefore, the public interest should also be weighed as considering whether to adopt the measure of pre-litigation act preservation which directly affects the interests of a party. In the cases of unfair competition, the public interest usually refers to the interests of numerous consumers. In this case, the act of the Respondents is likely to confuse the consumers and are contrary to the public interests; and the pre-litigation act preservation applicable to this case does not damage the interests of consumers or other public interests.

In consideration of that the pre-litigation act preservation sacrificed the interests of procedural protection and freedom of movement of the Respondents to some extent after all, to ensure the Respondents could obtain the relief under the situation of wrong preservation, the court requested the Applicant to provide a certain guarantee to balance the interests of two sides. In the determination of guarantee amount, the court comprehensively considered the likelihood of the Applicant winning the lawsuit and losses that might be incurred by the Respondents due to stopping relevant conducts and other factors.

To sum up, the court made the ruling of pre-litigation act preservation as regard to this case. After the Respondents refused to accept the ruling and filed a request for reconsideration, the court held a hearing to fully hear the views of both sides, and taking the above-said conditions as the main points of review, the court dismissed the reconsideration filed by the Respondents and affirmed the decisions in original ruling.

（Writer：Ye Jufen）